History of Ethics

virtue.

obligation.

BLACKWELL READINGS IN THE HISTORY OF PHILOSOPHY

Series Editors: Fritz Allhoff and Anand Jayprakash Vaidya

The volumes in this series provide concise and representative selections of key texts from the history of philosophy. Expertly edited and introduced by established scholars, each volume represents a particular philosophical era, replete with important selections of the most influential work in metaphysics, epistemology, moral and political philosophy, and the philosophy of science and religion.

1   *Ancient Philosophy: Essential Readings with Commentary*
    Edited by Nicholas Smith with Fritz Allhoff and Anand Jayprakash Vaidya
2   *Medieval Philosophy: Essential Readings with Commentary*
    Edited by Gyula Klima with Fritz Allhoff and Anand Jayprakash Vaidya
3   *Early Modern Philosophy: Essential Readings with Commentary*
    Edited by A. P. Martinich with Fritz Allhoff and Anand Jayprakash Vaidya
4   *Late Modern Philosophy: Essential Readings with Commentary*
    Edited by Elizabeth S. Radcliffe and Richard McCarty with Fritz Allhoff and Anand Jayprakash Vaidya

    Forthcoming
5   *The Philosophy of Science: An Historical Anthology*
    Fritz Allhoff, Marc Alspector-Kelly, and Timothy McGrew

History of Ethics

Essential Readings with Commentary

Edited by

Daniel Star

Boston University, United States

and

Roger Crisp

University of Oxford, United Kingdom

WILEY Blackwell

Registered Offices
John Wiley & Sons, Inc., 111 River Street, Hoboken, NJ 07030, USA
John Wiley & Sons Ltd, The Atrium, Southern Gate, Chichester, West Sussex, PO19 8SQ, UK

Editorial Office
9600 Garsington Road, Oxford, OX4 2DQ, UK

For details of our global editorial offices, customer services, and more information about Wiley products visit us at www.wiley.com.

Wiley also publishes its books in a variety of electronic formats and by print-on-demand. Some content that appears in standard print versions of this book may not be available in other formats.

Library of Congress Cataloging-in-Publication Data
Names: Star, Daniel, 1971– editor. | Crisp, Roger, 1961– editor.
Title: History of ethics : essential readings with commentary / edited by Daniel Star and Roger Crisp.
Description: Hoboken, NJ : John Wiley & Sons, 2019. | Series: Blackwell readings in the history of philosophy |
    Includes bibliographical references and index. |
Identifiers: LCCN 2018054705 (print) | LCCN 2019002467 (ebook) | ISBN 9781119235934 (AdobePDF) |
    ISBN 9781119235873 (ePub) | ISBN 9781405193887 (hardcover)
Subjects: LCSH: Ethics–History.
Classification: LCC BJ71 (ebook) | LCC BJ71 .H55 2019 (print) | DDC 170.9–dc23
LC record available at https://lccn.loc.gov/2018054705

Cover Design: Wiley
Cover Image: © Daniel Star

Set in 9.5/11.5pt Bembo by SPi Global, Pondicherry, India

10 9 8 7 6 5 4 3 2 1

Contents

Acknowledgements   vii
List of Sources   ix
Introduction   xi

Part I   Ancient and Medieval Ethics   1

1   *Gorgias* and *Republic*: The Authority of Morality   3
    Plato

2   *Republic* (Continued): Justice and Virtue   25
    Plato

3   *Republic* (Continued): The Good   41
    Plato

4   *Nicomachean Ethics*: The Good Life   53
    Aristotle

5   *Nicomachean Ethics* (Continued): The Nature of Virtue   67
    Aristotle

6   *Nicomachean Ethics* (Continued): Responsibility and Practical Wisdom   77
    Aristotle

7   *Epicurus to Menoeceus* and *Principal Doctrines*   91
    Epicurus

8   *The Discourses of Epictetus* and *The Manual, or Enchiridion*   99
    Epictetus

9   *The Enchiridion*   113
    Saint Augustine

10 *Summa Contra Gentiles* and *Summa Theologica*   121
    Saint Thomas Aquinas

Part II   Modern Ethics   137

1   *Leviathan*   139
    Thomas Hobbes

2   *Fifteen Sermons Preached at the Rolls Chapel* and *Dissertation II*: On the Nature of Virtue   147
    Joseph Butler

3   *A Treatise of Human Nature* and *An Enquiry Concerning the Principles of Morals*:
    Reason and the Passions   165
    David Hume

4   *An Enquiry Concerning the Principles of Morals*: Virtue and Utility   183
    David Hume

5   *The Theory of Moral Sentiments*   201
    Adam Smith

6   *Groundwork of the Metaphysics of Morals* and *The Metaphysics of Morals*:
    Reason and the Good Will   219
    Immanuel Kant

7   *Groundwork of the Metaphysics of Morals* (Continued): The Categorical Imperative 231
    Immanuel Kant

8   *An Introduction to the Principles of Morals and Legislation*   247
    Jeremy Bentham

9   *Utilitarianism* and *The Subjection of Women*   255
    John Stuart Mill

10 *On the Genealogy of Morality*   281
    Friedrich Nietzsche

11 *The Methods of Ethics*   299
    Henry Sidgwick

Part III   Foundations of Contemporary Ethics   **331**

1   *Principia Ethica*   333
    G. E. Moore

2   *The Right and the Good*   343
    W. D. Ross

3   *Language, Truth and Logic*   359
    Alfred Jules Ayer

4   *The Naturalistic Fallacy*   367
    W. K. Frankena

5   *Modern Moral Philosophy*   377
    G. E. M. Anscombe

6   *The Problem of Abortion and the Doctrine of the Double Effect*   389
    Philippa Foot

7   *Ethics*: Inventing Right and Wrong   397
    J. L. Mackie

8   *A Theory of Justice*   411
    John Rawls

9   *Ethical Theory and Utilitarianism*   431
    R. M. Hare

Index   443

Acknowledgements

The editors would like to thank Samantha Brennan, David Brink, Desmond Clarke, Daniel Dahlstrom, Aaron Garrett, Charles Griswold, Terence Irwin, Paul Katsafanas, Brian Leiter, David Roochnik, and Susanne Sreedhar for all of their helpful suggestions and feedback regarding the texts and commentaries. We would also like to express our gratitude to Fritz Allhoff and Jeff Dean for their support in the early stages of the project, as well as express our gratitude to our final editors at Wiley, Marissa Koors and Liz Wingett. Finally, we wish to thank Joseph Cregan for his invaluable assistance in indexing and final preparation of the volume for publication, and the Faculty of Philosophy at the University of Oxford for providing funding to support this assistance.

List of Sources

The editor and the publisher gratefully acknowledge the permission granted to reproduce the copyright material in this book:

1   Plato, "Gorgias" from *The Dialogues of Plato*, trans. B. Jowett, pp. 71-78. New York: Charles Scribner's Sons, 1911 and Plato, "Republic" from *The Republic of Plato*, Vol. 1 trans. B. Jowett, pp. 335-354, 356-362, 365-369. Oxford: Clarendon Press, 1908.

2   Plato, "Republic" from *The Republic of Plato*, Vol. 1, trans. B. Jowett pp. 412-413, 427-445. Oxford: Clarendon Press, 1908.

3   Plato, "Republic" from *The Republic of Plato*, Vol. 2, trans. B. Jowett, pp. 502-511, 514-521. Oxford: Clarendon Press, 1908.

4   Aristotle, from *Nicomachean Ethics*, ed. & trans. Roger Crisp, pp. 3-19, pp. 193-199. Cambridge: Cambridge University Press, 2000. Reproduced with permission from Cambridge University Press.

5   Aristotle, from *Nicomachean Ethics*, ed. & trans. Roger Crisp, pp. 20-36. Cambridge: Cambridge University Press, 2000. Reproduced with permission from Cambridge University Press.

6   Aristotle, from *Nicomachean Ethics*, ed. & trans. Roger Crisp, pp. 37-48, 103, 107-118. Cambridge: Cambridge University Press, 2000. Reproduced with permission from Cambridge University Press.

7   Epicurus, "The Extant Remains" trans. Cyril Bailey. 1926, pp. 83, 85, 87, 89, 91, 93, 95, 97, 99, 101, 103. New York: Georg Olms, 1970. Reproduced with permission from Oxford University Press.

8   Epictetus, from *The Discourses of Epictetus*, trans. P. E. Matheson, pp. 5-7, 32-33, 48-49, 81-82, 90-91, 93-95, 146, 148, 267, 268, 269. New York: The Heritage Press, 1968. © The George Macy Companies, Inc., 1968. Reproduced with permission from Oxford University Press.

9   St Augustine, from *Basic Writings of St Augustine*, Vols. 1 & 2, ed. Whitney J. Oates, pp. 662-669, 671-672, 504. New York: Random House, 1948.

10   St Thomas Aquinas, from *Basic Writings of Saint Thomas Aquinas*, ed. Anton C. Pegis, pp. 5-9, 43-53, 56-60. Indianapolis: Hackett Publishing Company, 1997. Reproduced with permission from Hackett Publishing Company.

11   St Thomas Aquinas, from *Basic Writings of Saint Thomas Aquinas*, ed. Anton C. Pegis, pp. 748-750, 466-470. Indianapolis: Hackett Publishing Company, 1997. Reproduced with permission from Hackett Publishing Company.

12   St Thomas Aquinas, "Injustice" from *Summa Theologiae*, Vol. 38, ed. Marcus Lefébure, 2A2AE, pp. 63-79. London, Blackfriars, 1975. © The Dominican Council as Trustee for the English Province of the Order of Preachers, 1975. Reproduced with permission from Cambridge University Press.

13   Thomas Hobbes, from *The English Works of Thomas Hobbes*, Vol. III, ed. Sir William Molesworth, pp. 110-122, 124-127, 130-135. London: John Bohn, 1839.

14   Joseph Butler, from *Sermons: Charges, Fragments and Correspondence*, pp. 5-13, 16-20, 137-152. London: Macmillan & Co., 1900.

15   Joseph Butler, *The Analogy of Religion*, pp. 286-295. London: Macmillan & Co., 1900.

16   David Hume, "A Treatise of Human Nature" from *Philosophical Works*, Vol. 2, pp. 164-170, 216-223, 224-239, 285-288, 353-366 and Vol. 4, pp. 362-363. Boston, MA: Little, Brown & Company, 1854.

17   David Hume, "An Enquiry Concerning the Principles of Morals" from *Philosophical Works*, Vol. 4, pp. 244-251, 252-267, 275-296, 346. Boston, MA: Little, Brown & Company, 1854.

18   Smith, Adam, *The Theory of Moral Sentiments*, pp. 3-9, 14-25, 132-157. London: Henry G. Bohn, 1853.

19   Immanuel Kant, "Groundwork of the Metaphysics of Moral and The Metaphysics of Morals (Reason and the Good Will)" from *Practical Philosophy*, ed. Mary J. Gregor, pp. 49-60, 373, 374, 375, 516-519, 524-527, 536-537. Cambridge: Cambridge University Press, 1996. Reproduced with permission from Cambridge University Press.

20   Immanuel Kant, "Groundwork of the Metaphysics of Moral and The Metaphysics of Morals (The Categorical Imperative)" *Practical Philosophy*, ed. Mary J. Gregor. Cambridge: Cambridge University Press, 1996. pp. 61-89. Reproduced with permission from Cambridge University Press.

21   Jeremy Bentham, "An Introduction to the Principles of Morals and Legislation" from *Utilitarianism and On Liberty*, 2e, ed. Mary Warnock, pp. 17-22, 27-29, 35-36, 41-43. Oxford: Blackwell Publishing Ltd, 2003.

22   John Stuart Mill, "On Liberty" from *Utilitarianism and On Liberty*, 2e, ed. Mary Warnock, pp. 185-202, 210-214, 216-227, 230-235. Oxford: Blackwell Publishing Ltd, 2003.

23   John Stuart Mill, The Subjection of Women, pp. 1, 8-13, 31-35, 45-50, 79-80, 107-109. New York: Frederick A. Stokes Company, 1911.

24   Friedrich Nietzsche, from *On the Genealogy of Morality: A Polemic*, tr. Maudemarie Clark and Alan J. Swensen, pp. 2-5, 9-12, 16-26, 30-31, 36-37, 39-40, 45-48, 56-65. Indianapolis: Hackett Publishing Company Inc., 1998. Reproduced with permission from Hackett Publishing Company.

25   Henry Sidgwick, from *The Methods of Ethics*, 7e, pp. vii-viii, xi-xiii, xvi-xxiii, 1, 2-14, 23-25, 27, 33, 96, 99-103, 109, 170-175, 210, 308-3011, 338-343, 373-384, 386-389, 391-395, 402-407, 411-414, 418-422, 425-426, 467-469, 473, 476, 485-492, 496-509. Indianapolis: Hackett, 1981. © Macmillan & Co. 1907.

26   G.E. Moore, from *Principia Ethica*, 2e. ed. Thomas Baldwin, pp. 51-73. Cambridge: Cambridge University Press, 1993. Reproduced with permission from Cambridge University Press

27   W. D. Ross, *The Right and the Good*, ed. Philip Stratton-Lake, pp. 16-47. Oxford: Oxford University Press, 2002, reproduced with permission from Oxford University Press.

28   Alfred Jules Ayer, *Language, Truth and Logic*, pp. 102-113. New York: Dover Publications, Inc., 1952. Reproduced with permission from Dover Publications.

29   W. K. Frankena, "The Naturalistic Fallacy" from *Mind*, New Series, 48(192), pp. 464-477. Oxford: Oxford University Press, 1939. Reproduced with permission from Oxford University Press.

30   G. E. M. Anscombe, "Modern Moral Philosophy" from *Philosophy*, Vol. 33, No. 124, pp. 1-19. Cambridge: Cambridge University Press, 1958. Reproduced with permission from Cambridge University Press.

31   Philippa Foot, "The Problem of Abortion and the Doctrine of Double Effect" *Oxford Review*, No. 5, 1967, pp. 5-15 from *Virtues and Vices and Other Essays in Moral Philosophy*, Philippa Foot, Oxford University Press, 2002, pp. 19-32.

32   J. L. Mackie, "Ethics: Inventing Right and Wrong" from *Ethics: Inventing Right and Wrong*, pp. 15-49. Harmondsworth: Penguin Books, 1990. Reproduced with permission from Penguin Books Ltd.

33   J. Rawls "A Theory of Justice" from *A Theory of Justice*: Revised Edition, pp. 10-24, 52-23, 53-55, 55-56, 118-120, 120-122, 130-131, 132, 132-134, 134-135, 221-227. Cambridge, MA: Harvard University Press, 1999. Copyright © 1971, 1999 by the President and Fellows of Harvard College. The Belknap Press of Harvard University Press, 1999. Reproduced with permission from President and Fellows of Harvard College.

34   R.M. Hare, "Ethical Theory and Utilitarianism", from *Contemporary British Philosophy: Personal Statements*, ed. H.D. Lewis, pp. 113-131. London: George Allen & Unwin, 1976. © R. M. Hare 1976. Reproduced with permission from Pr J. Hare.

Introduction

This is a book of selections from the history of Western moral philosophy ('ethics' for short), accompanied by introductory commentaries that are intended to be helpful for students new to the topic. The history of ethics in the Western world is extremely rich and varied. It is not possible to capture its complexity in a tidy narrative or a short series of commentaries. Nonetheless, when one is new to a large subject like this, it can be very helpful to be provided with stories that highlight many of the main elements of the subject. With such stories in hand, one can find it easier to interpret what one is reading, even if further study would lead one to outgrow the stories that were of help at the beginning. Despite the necessary limitations of stories like those we provide herein, one would make very slow progress without them. All this is to say that the commentary in this book is intended to be modest but useful. It is not meant to be a substitute for the readings themselves, or for the large secondary literature.

The needs of both students and professors guided us in the selection of source materials, but the primary aim was to provide a well-rounded, thorough, yet not overly long selection of texts that students might reasonably hope to complete reading in a semester. This made for some difficult decisions about what to include and what to omit. It was decided that some texts, or parts of texts, that are often omitted in other collections should be included (e.g. Aquinas on self-defense, Kant on virtue, and a wide range of excerpts from Sidgwick's *Methods*). At the same time, we were aware that many worthy philosophical works could not be included. When it came to twentieth century philosophy, we had to be particularly choosy, stopping in the 1970s and concentrating on (i) the rise of contemporary metaethics; and (ii) philosophers whose work counts as original, but whose ideas students might find it particularly fruitful to compare to the ideas of earlier philosophers in this volume.

Several themes weave through the history of Western moral philosophy. Here we will discuss four. Unless otherwise noted, the philosophers mentioned are all represented by selections from their writings in this volume, and when we refer to them by name we have these selections in mind.

1. The need to justify adherence to morality, especially in the light of the egoist challenge

One of the most important features of Ancient Greek ethics was a concern to answer skeptical challenges to the putative authority of morality, especially the concern that self-interest and morality might come apart from each other, and that, if they do, it might be rational to pursue one's own self-interest, rather than act morally. The selections here start with Plato addressing skeptical challenges to morality. One goal of the *Republic* is to establish that it is actually in the best interest of individual citizens for them to be just – that is, virtuous. The egoist challenge is not the only skeptical challenge to morality that we see Plato address, but he appears to think it is the most serious. Aristotle's *Ethics*, on the other hand, does not explicitly address egoists. Nonetheless, it is concerned with showing that individual flourishing or happiness consists in living a life of virtuous activity.

If one way to attempt to reconcile morality and self-interest involves seeking to demonstrate that a life of virtue is the best life to lead, a second, modern approach involves starting with an amoral account of self-interest, and attempting to demonstrate that morality itself has its foundations in self-interest (so understood). Hobbes's social contract theory is the most well-known approach of the second kind.

Hobbes's account of morality as an institution with its foundations in appeals to self-interest was a significant intellectual achievement, but it did not put an end to the continuing concern with the issue of how best to reconcile morality and self-interest. Butler's approach to this issue exhibits more continuity with the views of Plato and Aristotle than Hobbes's, but it demonstrates a heightened recognition that the motive of self-interest is distinct from moral motivation, even though the two can, in his view, work in harmony. According to Kant, the truly rational person will always act morally (or, when pursuing his own happiness, which Kant thinks it is often permissible to do, will always respect the limits on doing so imposed on us by our moral duties). At the same time as he argues for this ideal, Kant expresses pessimism about our ability to live up to it, and about our tendency to deceive ourselves as to our true motives: we often take ourselves to be acting morally when we are really acting out of self-interest. Nietzsche's account of morality is very different than Hobbes's, but he too views it as an institution with a history. Nietzsche has much less time for a priori reasoning than Hobbes and much more skepticism about the value of morality; for Nietzsche, morality has its origins in a complex series of events by which the weak came to exercise control over the strong, and its present status is tainted by history, as it continues to hold worthy people back from genuinely flourishing. Finally, Sidgwick, inspired by Butler but also by the utilitarianism of Bentham and Mill, finds himself unable to locate rational arguments that will allow him to conclude either that morality can be reconciled with self-interest, or that morality always trumps self-interest. As a result, Sidgwick somewhat reluctantly concludes that there is a basic 'dualism of practical reason', such that, so far as reason is concerned, there is no criterion for deciding between rational egoism and impartial benevolence (utilitarianism).

Whether or not one believes the skeptical challenge to morality that comes from rational egoist quarters is worth all the attention it has received, it should be said that it has encouraged a long history of reflection concerning the exact nature of human wellbeing. We are all interested in this topic, which can be considered in isolation from the skeptical challenge. Or we should be, anyway: do we not each want to know how to make our own life go well? This is a popular topic in contemporary ethics, where the comparative strengths and weaknesses of a range of sophisticated accounts of wellbeing have received much discussion. In the present volume, Epicurus and Epictetus might be considered examples of philosophers who take it to be their very first order of business to determine what the good life consists in. When we consider Epicurus, in particular, we find a philosopher for whom defending an account of wellbeing, i.e. hedonism (the view that wellbeing consists in the experience of pleasure), was, arguably, his primary aim. The utilitarian philosophers of the modern era (Bentham, Mill, and Sidgwick) are also interested in determining what happiness consists in, due to the fact that they take it that the fundamental moral truth is that we should each act so as to produce the most happiness it is possible for us to produce.

Some challenges to morality are not motivated by either thought of the egoist alternative or the 'might makes right' amoralism of Callicles and Thrasymachus (see the first selections from Plato). There is no reason to think that modern moral sceptics, like Ayer and Mackie, are at all motivated by either amoral or immoral attitudes (Nietzsche is a more difficult case to classify here). Rather, they are led to endorse various forms of anti-realism due to more philosophical concerns. We return to these thinkers later.

2. Understanding virtue and moral psychology

Ancient philosophers, generally speaking, took a longer view in ethics than modern philosophers. They were concerned to answer the question 'How should one live?' which includes not only the question so central to modern ethics ('How should one act?'), but also the question of what kind of person one should be – what kind of character one should have. This distinction should not be exaggerated, as it might be claimed to be in Anscombe's famous article 'Modern Moral Philosophy', which was one of the driving forces behind the development of modern 'virtue ethics', discussed further in section 4. Plato and Aristotle are indeed concerned about how one should act, but to a greater extent than many moderns they recognize the influence of character on action and hence the importance of moral education.

According to Plato, the virtuous life (which is the same as the happy life) consists of possessing the virtue of justice, broadly understood. This includes the more specific virtues of wisdom, courage, and moderation. Aristotle's list of virtues was significantly longer, including for example generosity and even wit; but like Plato, he insists on the centrality of wisdom or knowledge to each virtue. It is instructive to compare these lists of virtues with the cardinal virtues of Aquinas (prudence, justice, temperance, and wisdom) and to ponder the significance of the lack of attention paid by recent virtue ethicists to developing lists of their own. This may be because ancient philosophers tended to be thinking and writing not primarily for fellow academics, but for people in general, with a view to changing their lives – though again this is a contrast that should not be overdrawn.

The philosopher most influential on modern thought about the virtues is, without doubt, Aristotle, although Plato, Hume, Nietzsche, and others have provided important inspiration. But we can discern a break from the ancient tradition in the unwillingness of most moderns to argue for the equivalence of virtue and happiness. This may well be partly the result of the work on the relation of virtue and happiness by Butler and Sidgwick, and Kant's attempt to provide morality with an autonomous foundation of its own.

Another contrast between modern and earlier thinkers lies in the role of knowledge in virtue. For Plato, the truly virtuous person is the one who has knowledge of the 'Forms', and the acquisition of such knowledge requires a long and arduous intellectual process over many decades. Both Augustine and Aquinas see belief in and understanding of God to be essential to virtue. But more recent secular or less centrally theological accounts of virtue, such as those of Hume and Smith, have tended to emphasize to a great extent the important of sympathy and compassion.

A further difference between ancient and later thinkers lies in the importance of success. For Aristotle, happiness lies in the noble or virtuous life, and this requires successfully performing various virtuous actions. A genuine intention to act virtuously that fails is not sufficient. After Aristotle, and with the development of Christianity, we see developing a view that could be called volitionalism, according to which moral value lies only in one's intentions, not in the actions or outcomes to which they lead. Kant was a volitionalist, and what matters for him is the good will, which is of unconditional value even if for whatever reason its aims are not accomplished. The clash between on the one hand our continuing inclination to reward success and on the other hand our recognition of the attractions of volitionalism lead to the problem of moral luck, outlined so clearly by Smith.

Another central question in moral psychology concerns the nature of moral motivation. The Aristotelian virtuous person is never conflicted. They are brought up well to find pleasure in virtuous actions, and will even die on the battlefield without any urge to run, knowing that to do so would be to damage their own chances of true happiness (since fleeing would be vicious, it would make them unhappy). For Kant, however, moral motivation is a matter not so much of 'sainthood', but of 'heroism'. For Kant, moral worth lies in the victory of reason over the passions, and there can be no such victory if the passions are on the same side. One important question for Kantian ethicists is how this view of moral worth can sit alongside Kant's view that moral virtue plays a significant role in ethics and is to be encouraged.

3. Understanding the nature of moral thought and language

In twentieth century philosophy, a useful (some have thought problematic) distinction arose between 'metaethics' and 'normative ethics'. The first is the part of ethics that is concerned with the nature of moral truths (or lack of them, for anti-realists), moral language and thought, and moral knowledge. The second concerns itself with the articulation and defense of moral principles. A complete account of ethics would include both metaethics and normative ethics. When we look at earlier philosophers like Hume and Kant, we can see both domains of philosophical reflection, although this distinction is not explicitly drawn (interestingly, metaethics and normative ethics are more distinct and separable in the work of some philosophers, e.g. Hume, than in the work of others, e.g. Kant).

To start with metaethics, three related issues became particularly important in the modern era: (i) the place of ethical facts in the universe as revealed to us by modern science; (ii) the autonomy of moral reasoning, with respect to reasoning about the natural world; and (iii) the philosophical consequences of a special motivating role that many philosophers believe moral judgements play in our psychology. We'll briefly discuss each in turn.

The idea that there are important differences between ethics, as a subject, and scientific study of the world was recognized by the ancients. Aristotle suggested, for instance, that we should not expect the same degree of precision in ethics as we are able to achieve in science. Nonetheless, it was only with the arrival of modern science (an extremely long and complex event, stretching from the sixteenth to the eighteenth century) that a picture of the natural world arose that seemed to some to threaten the idea that there can be objective moral facts or truths. According to Aristotelian science and the Christian orthodoxy that incorporated it (Aquinas's efforts here were especially significant), everything in nature has a *telos*, or purpose. Modern science gradually overturned this idea, leaving human goals and the principles by which we might think they are morally constrained or promoted, looking somewhat unmoored in the natural world: what, in the world, could a moral fact *be*, given that we don't find any need to posit moral facts in the natural sciences? One response, which we saw earlier when discussing Hobbes, was to view such facts as constructed out of self-interest. Another, found in Smith and Hume, was to view them as determined by the point of view of an idealized, emotionally sophisticated human observer. There is also the possibility of accepting that moral principles are not known through empirical reflection, but as a priori, self-evident truths (Kant, Sidgwick, Moore, and Ross are all important thinkers in this tradition). One might think such truths exist in a Platonic realm separate from the natural world, or in our rational capacities, or can be derived from our moral concepts (the first view is the hardest to square with secular naturalism). More skeptical responses are also available, as we see when we come to Ayer and Mackie.

A closely related, but independent, concern can be found in Hume. This is the idea that it is never possible to deduce an 'ought' from an 'is'. When we engage in moral reasoning, Hume contends, there is never any room for reasoning that moves from claims about the way the world is to claims about the way we should act. Strictly speaking, this could be true even if we have a naturally given purpose in the universe, since we might still ask, 'Why should I do what my natural purpose would have me do?' (perhaps this wouldn't make sense if we were not able to make free choices, but philosophers in the Aristotelian and Christian traditions that we have in mind generally take it that we are able to act freely). This thought that reasoning concerning morality is *autonomous* is widely accepted in modern philosophy: Kant, Sidgwick, Moore, Ayer, and others disagree about many things, but not about this. Mill, however, is an exception. Although he was, like Hume, a naturalist, and an empiricist in his general methodology, his 'proof of utilitarianism', difficult as it is to interpret, appears to violate Hume's stricture that we cannot deduce an 'ought' from an 'is' (and consequently, few philosophers have been moved by it).

Closely related to Hume's principle is Moore's 'naturalistic fallacy', a term that Moore uses to refer to attempts to provide naturalistic definitions of moral terms, all of which are committing a significant error, he thinks. Moore, like Ross and Sidgwick, adopts a metaphysics known as 'non-naturalism' and an accompanying epistemology generally referred to as 'intuitionism' (Sidgwick explicitly distinguished between good and bad forms of intuitionism).

Hume also famously claimed that 'reason is and ought only to be the slave of the passions', rejecting the ancient claim (also subsequently defended by Kant) that it is the faculty of reason's job to exercise control over our individual psychologies, and that it is only by reason doing this job properly that we are able to act in a morally proper fashion. In the present context, the relevance of Hume's approach to understanding our psychology is that he draws attention to the problem of explaining how it is that mere beliefs, absent corresponding desires, might motivate us to act (he claims that mere belief, or the mere use of reason, in the absence of relevant desires, cannot motivate us). Ethics is first and foremost a practical enterprise, and if someone claims that he or she ought to do a certain act, it seems highly peculiar for them not to be motivated to do it. Unlike the first two issues in metaethics, not all moral philosophers since Hume have thought there is really a problem here: non-naturalist intuitionists like Sidgwick, Moore, and Ross do not seem moved by this issue. However, other philosophers, including especially Ayer, as well as many subsequent metaethicists, take this to be a key reason for being suspicious of non-naturalist intuitionism, since its defenders standardly do not attempt to explain how it is that our desires are able to take their leave from self-evidently true propositions.

Although Ayer has no time for Moore's non-naturalist intuitionism, both philosophers share an appreciation of the 'is'/'ought' gap, as well as an interest in understanding moral language. The turn to the study of language that occurred in 'analytic' philosophy in the twentieth century is on display in the excerpts from Ayer and Moore. Frankena's response to Moore (also included here) is instructive partly because it shows up some limitations in Moore's approach of basing philosophical arguments on certain features of our language. Philosophy of language continues to be an important part of contemporary philosophy, but the relationship between language and metaphysics is now generally thought to be considerably more complex than it was in Moore's time.

4. Formulating and defending particular principles of morality

Although the goal of formulating and defending particular principles of morality is not wholly modern (early examples might be thought to include Plato's account of what justice consists in, and Aquinas's account of the doctrine of double effect), it is of explicit interest to modern philosophers: especially, with respect to the present volume, Kant, Bentham, Mill, Sidgwick, Ross, Foot, Rawls, and Hare.

Two types of moral principle are worth contrasting here. Principles can be restricted in domain, or they can be maximally general. Examples of the first kind are defended herein by Aquinas, Foot, and Rawls. Aquinas and Foot are each concerned to defend their own versions of the doctrine of double effect (in Foot's case, one might more accurately say she ends up defending a descendant of that doctrine). In the relevant excerpt from Aquinas, we see the principle cast in terms of self-defense, but it is also mentioned that it will have application to cases involving soldiers fighting in a war (this is one domain in which reasoning that involves this doctrine continues to be popular). Foot more carefully investigates various ways in which one might understand the relevant principle (although Aquinas comes at the beginning, and Foot at the end, of a long Catholic tradition of discussion of this principle or doctrine, Foot's discussion is novel and not constrained by tradition). In neither case does the philosopher in question ask us to take the principle at issue to be the single fundamental principle of ethics, as its domain of application is restricted (it doesn't have anything to tell us about acts of charity, for instance). Similarly, in defending an account of political justice, with respect to social institutions, Rawls is clear about the fact that he is not providing a complete moral theory, let alone very general, fundamental moral principles. We can contrast these examples with Kant's search for a 'supreme principle of morality'. Each of his formulations of this principle is meant to tell us something about the permissibility of acts in general: that is, acts of any and every kind. Similarly, the utilitarian principle defended by Bentham, Mill, Sidgwick, and Hare (each in their own way) is all encompassing with respect to human actions.

Two negative reactions to this interest amongst philosophers in locating correct moral principles are also worth highlighting. First, an interest in the first half of the twentieth century in focusing, first and foremost, on investigating the nature of *language* led philosophers like Ayer to view normative ethics as something that does not really belong to philosophy proper. For a time, 'analytic philosophy' was almost synonymous with 'philosophy of language', and normative ethics began to decline in popularity. More importantly in the long term, a return to an interest in virtue, initiated by Anscombe (in the paper republished here), was driven initially by the thought that the modern interest in articulating and defending moral principles of right and wrong action represented a mistaken turn in the history of ethics.

A large part of Anscombe's motivation for this skepticism regarding the enterprise of discussing moral principles rested on a view about the difference between religious and secular ethics: if the notion of obligation only makes sense within a religious framework, then it makes more sense, she argued, for secular philosophers to focus on understanding virtue. This latter enterprise, she suggested, is more compatible with a naturalistic conception of the world. The somewhat popular return to virtue initiated by Anscombe has led some subsequent 'virtue ethicists' to continue to be skeptical about the importance of moral principles, while others have defended the idea that principles of right action might themselves be formulated in terms of virtue (on this view, right acts might be those acts virtuous people would do, roughly speaking). Furthermore, some 'particularists' have claimed that moral obligations, or truths about what we ought to do, while talk of them is legitimate and appropriate (few philosophers follow Anscombe in thinking that only the religious are entitled to speak of moral obligations), cannot be captured by or codified in general moral principles.

Part I

Ancient and Medieval Ethics

1

Gorgias and *Republic*: The Authority of Morality

Plato

In the excerpts from *Gorgias* and the *Republic* provided here, Plato presents us with three attempts to call morality or justice into question. The relevant Greek word, *dikaiosunê*, is usually translated as 'justice', but it is very general in scope as Plato uses it, so it might also be translated as 'morality'. The first two attempts, presented by the sophists Callicles and Thrasymachus, are responded to immediately by Socrates – Plato's mouthpiece throughout – who is not prepared to let them represent genuine philosophical options. He takes them to be based on a failure to genuinely appreciate the nature of the subject at hand, a failure that springs from the sophist motivation in using arguments – a sophist's primary aim is to benefit personally by winning arguments, rather than to use arguments to get closer to the truth (in the present day, it can help to think of the differences between debating classes and philosophy classes). We should bear this in mind if at times we feel that Thrasymachus is giving in too easily to some of Socrates's arguments. We may wonder whether Plato has been completely fair to his opponents; but, more positively, we might take it that Plato means to suggest that the other side is not even particularly good at *rationally* defending their own positions – they are accustomed to believing that insults and intellectual bullying will help them achieve their ends just as well, and will simply lose interest in rational argumentation when winning no longer looks likely.

Callicles and Thrasymachus put forward popular and politically potent forms of skepticism that stand in opposition to philosophy. Their approaches are different, and the responses that are required are thus also different: Callicles distinguishes between morality as an artifice designed to protect the weak, and natural justice, which, he takes it, directs the strong to dominate the weak (comparisons with Nietzsche are sometimes made by contemporary scholars), whereas Thrasymachus argues that it is *good* for the strong to dominate the weak. The first position is countered with arguments that challenge the claims about what is natural and what is conventional, whereas the second position is seen to be in need of a response that takes off from noting how strange it is to suppose that justice is bad and injustice good. The short excerpt from *Gorgias* is provided for the sake of contrast (and only the first part of Socrates's response is provided), but the student may particularly benefit from focusing on three of the arguments that Socrates uses against Thrasymachus: (i) from '…I cannot hear without amazement that you class injustice with wisdom and virtue, and justice with the opposite' (348 E) onwards; (ii) from 'You would not deny that a state may be unjust and may be unjustly trying to enslave other states…?' (351 B) onwards; and (iii) from '…whether the just have a better and happier life than the unjust is a further question which we also proposed to consider' (352 D) onwards.

The third of our three challenges is not responded to in as direct or immediate a manner, but Plato sets it out extremely well. It is presented by Glaucon, who, unlike Callicles and Thrasymachus, is genuinely respectful of Socrates. Glaucon is not so much committed to a form of skepticism as seriously worried by

History of Ethics – Essential Readings with Commentary, First Edition. Edited by Daniel Star and Roger Crisp.
© 2020 John Wiley & Sons Ltd. Published 2020 by John Wiley & Sons Ltd.

what he takes to be the strongest form of moral skepticism he can think of, and he hopes that Socrates can free him of his concerns. Glaucon provides us with some wonderful thought experiments that seem to suggest self-interest and morality can irretrievably come apart – there is the story of the Ring of Gyges (which is likely to remind the contemporary reader of Tolkien's *Lord of the Rings*). But perhaps even more important are the thought experiments that follow it, where we are asked to imagine a moral person whose every action is misinterpreted by others as immoral and who therefore will only ever meet with punishment and derision when acting morally; and an immoral person whose every immoral act is met with rewards and praise.

Glaucon is asking us to fix our minds on the question, do I always have overwhelming reasons to be moral? The challenge provided by Glaucon's thought experiments is simply one that asks how morality could be such that we each have reasons to follow it even when it appears to conflict with self-interest. Plato recognizes that *this* challenge is a serious one, and one can read the remainder of the *Republic* as an attempt to answer it.

In order to answer Glaucon's challenge, Plato's Socrates first says that it will be necessary to provide a detailed account of morality or justice in individual persons (in other words, an account of the moral or just individual). Plato recognizes that there may be different routes to understanding the nature of morality (in the third excerpt in this book, we will see Plato mentioning a 'longer and more circuitous' route); but the one that he thinks it is best to follow in the *Republic* involves our first looking to ascertain what morality or justice consists of on the level of the ideal community, since this may be easier to ascertain than it would be if we began by first looking at the individual. After we have done this, we can return to morality on the level of the individual with a clearer sense of what we are looking for.

Gorgias

[…]

CALLICLES. The truth is, Socrates, that you, who pretend to be engaged in the pursuit of truth, are appealing now to the popular and vulgar notions of right, which are not natural, but only conventional. Custom and nature *483* are generally at variance with one another: and hence, if a person is too modest to say what he thinks, he is compelled to contradict himself; and you, ingeniously seeing the advantage which may be won from this, dishonestly contrive that when a person speaks according to this rule of custom, you slyly ask him a question, which is to be referred to the rule of nature; and if he is talking of the rule of nature, you slip away to custom: as in this very discussion about doing and suffering injustice, when Polus was speaking of the conventionally dishonorable, you pursued his notion of convention from the point of view of nature; for by the rule of nature, that only is the more disgraceful which is the greater evil – as, for example, to suffer injustice; but by the rule of custom, to do evil is the more disgraceful. For this suffering of injustice is not the part of a man, but of a slave, who indeed had better die than live; for when he is wronged and trampled upon, he is unable to help himself, or any other about whom he cares. The reason, as I conceive, is that the makers of laws are the many weak; and they make laws and distribute praises and censures with a view to themselves and to their own interests; and they terrify the mightier sort of men, and those who are able to get the better of them, in order that they may not get the better of them; and they say, that dishonesty is shameful and unjust; meaning, when they speak of injustice, the desire to have more than their neighbors, for knowing their own inferiority they are only too glad of equality. And therefore this seeking to have more than the many, is conventionally said to be shameful and unjust, and is called injustice, whereas nature herself intimates that it is just for the better to have more than the worse, the more powerful than the weaker; and in many ways she shows, among men as well as among animals, and indeed among whole cities and races, that justice consists in the superior ruling over and having more than the inferior. For on what principle of justice did Xerxes invade Hellas, or his father the Scythians (not to speak of numberless other examples)? They, I conceive, act according to nature; yes, and according to the law of nature: not, perhaps, according to that artificial law, which *484* we frame and fashion, taking the best and strongest of us from their youth upwards, and taming them like young lions, and charming them with the sound of the voice, saying to them, that with equality they must be content, and that this is the honorable and the just. But if there were a man who had sufficient force, he would shake off and break through, and escape from all this he would trample under foot all our formulas and spells and charms, and all our laws, sinning against nature: the slave would rise in rebellion and be lord over us, and the light of natural justice would shine forth. And this I take to be the lesson of Pindar, in the poem in which he says that –

'Law is the king of all, mortals as well as immortals;'

this, as he says,

'Makes might to be right, and does violence with exalted hand; as I infer from the deeds of Heracles, for without buying them', –

I do not remember the exact words, but the meaning is that, he carried off the oxen of Geryon without buying them, and without their being given to him by Geryon, according to the law of natural right, and that the oxen and other possessions of the weaker and inferior properly belong to the stronger and superior. And this is true, as you may ascertain, if you will leave philosophy and go on to higher things: for philosophy, Socrates, if pursued in moderation and at the proper age, is an elegant accomplishment, but too much philosophy is the ruin of human life. Even if a man has good parts, still, if he carries philosophy into later life, he is necessarily ignorant of all those things which a gentleman and a person of honor ought to know; for he is ignorant of the laws of the State, and of the language which ought to be used in the dealings of man with man, whether private or public, and altogether ignorant of the pleasures and desires of mankind and of human character in general. And people of this sort, when they betake themselves to politics or business, are as ridiculous as I imagine the politicians to be, when they make their appearance in the arena of philosophy. For, as Euripides says, –

'Every man shines in that and pursues that, and devotes the greatest portion of the day to that in which he most excels;'

485 and if he is inferior in anything, he avoids and depreciates that, and praises the other from partiality to himself, and because he thinks that he will thus praise himself. But the right way is to have both: philosophy, as a part of education, is an excellent thing, and there is no disgrace to a man while he is young in pursuing such a study; when, Socrates, he becomes an older man, then the thing is ridiculous, and I feel towards philosophers as I do towards those who lisp and imitate children. For when I see a little child, who is not of an age to speak plainly, lisping at his play, that pleases me; there is an appearance of grace and freedom in his utterance, which is natural to his childish years. But when I hear some small creature carefully articulating his words, that offends me; the sound is disagreeable, and has to my ears the twang of slavery. And when I see a man lisping as if he were a child, that appears to me ridiculous and unmanly and worthy of stripes. Now, I have the same feeling about students of philosophy; when I see one of your young men studying philosophy, that I consider to be quite in character, and becoming a man of a liberal education, and him who neglects philosophy I regard as an inferior man, who will never aspire to anything great or noble. But if I see him continuing to study philosophy in later life, and not leaving off, I think that he ought to be beaten, Socrates; for, as I was saying, such an one, even though he have good natural parts, becomes effeminate. He flies from the busy centre and the market-place, in which, as the poet says, men become distinguished: he creeps into a corner for the rest of his life, and talks in a whisper with three or four admiring youths, but never speaks out like a freeman in a satisfactory manner. Now I, Socrates, am very well inclined towards you, and my feeling may be compared with that of Zethus towards Amphion, in the play of Euripides, of *486* which I was just now speaking: for I am disposed to say to you much what Zethus said to his brother, that you, Socrates, are careless when you ought to be careful; and having a soul so noble, are chiefly remarkable for a puerile exterior; neither in a court of justice could you state a case, or give any probability or proof, nor offer valiant counsel on another's behalf: and you must not be offended, my dear Socrates, for I am speaking out of good-will towards you, if I ask whether you are not ashamed at being in this case? which, indeed, I affirm to be that of all those who will carry the study of philosophy too far. For suppose that some one were to take you, or any one of your sort, off to prison, declaring that you had done wrong when you had done no wrong, you must allow that you would not know what to do: there you would stand giddy and gaping, and not having a word to say; and when you went up before the court, even if the accuser were a poor creature and not good for much, you would die if he were disposed to claim the penalty of death. And yet, Socrates, what is the value of an art which converts a man of sense into a fool, who is helpless, powerless, when the danger is greatest, to save either himself or others; while he is being despoiled by his enemies of all his goods, and deprived of his rights of citizenship? being a man, if I may use the expression, who may be boxed on the ears with impunity. Then, my good friend, take my advice, and refute no more; learn 'the arts of business, and acquire the reputation of wisdom', leaving to others these niceties; whether they are better described as follies or absurdities, they will only give you poverty for the inmate of your dwelling.

Cease, then, emulating these paltry splitters of words, and emulate only the man of substance and honor, who is well to do.

SOCRATES. If my soul, Callicles, were made of gold, should I not rejoice to discover one of those stones with which they test gold, and one of the best sort too which I might apply? and if the application showed that my soul had been well cultivated, then I should know that I was in a satisfactory state, and that no other test was needed by me.

CAL. What makes you say that, Socrates?

SOC. I will tell you; I think that in you I have found the desired touchstone.

CAL. Why?

SOC. Because I am sure that if you agree with me in any of the opinions which my soul forms, I have at *487* last found the truth indeed. For I consider that if a man is to make a complete trial of the good or evil of the soul, he ought to have three qualities – knowledge, good-will, frankness, which are all possessed by you. Many whom I have known were unable to make the examination, because they were not wise as you are; others are wise, but they will not tell me the truth, because they have not the interest in me which you have; and these two strangers, Gorgias and Polus, are undoubtedly wise men and my very good friends, but they are not frank enough, and they are too modest. Why, their modesty is so great that they are driven to contradict themselves, first one and then the other of them, in the face of a large company, on matters of the highest moment. But you have all the qualities in which these others are deficient, having received an excellent education; to this many Athenians can testify. And I am sure that you are my friend. How do I prove that? I will tell you: I know that you, Callicles, and Tisander of Aphidnae, and Andron the son of Androtion, and Nausicydes of the deme of Cholarges, studied philosophy together: there were four of you, and I once heard you advising with one another as to the extent to which the pursuit should be carried, and the opinion, as I know, which found favor among you was, that the study should not be pushed too much into detail. You were cautioning one another not to be over wise, lest, without your knowing, this should be the ruin of you. And now when I hear you giving the same advice to me which you then gave to your most intimate friends, I have in that a sufficient evidence of your real good-will to me. And of the frankness of your nature and freedom from modesty I am assured by yourself, and the assurance is confirmed by your last speech. Well then, the inference clearly is, that if you and I agree in an argument on any point, that point will have been sufficiently tested by you and me, and will not require to be referred to any further test. For you cannot have been led to agree with me, either from lack of knowledge or from superfluity of modesty, nor from a desire to deceive me, for you are my friend, as you tell me yourself. And therefore when you and I are agreed, the result will be the attainment of the perfect truth. Now there can be no nobler inquiry, Callicles, than that for which you reprove me, – What ought the character of a *488* man to be, and what his pursuits, and how far he is to go, both in maturer years and in youth? For be assured of this, that if I err in my own conduct I do not err intentionally, but from my own ignorance. Do not then desist from advising me, now that you have begun, until I have learned clearly what this is which I am to practice, and how I may acquire it. And if you find me assenting to your words, and hereafter not doing that to which I assented, call me 'dolt', and 'good-for-nothing', and deem me unworthy of receiving further instruction. Once more, then, tell me what you and Pindar mean by natural justice: do you not mean that the superior should take the property of the inferior by force; that the better should rule the worse, the noble have more than the mean? Am I not right in my recollection?

CAL. Yes; that is what I was saying, and what I still maintain.

SOC. And do you mean by the better the same as the superior? for I could not make out what you were saying at the time – whether you meant by the superior the stronger, and that the weaker must obey the stronger, as you seemed to imply when you said that great cities attack small ones In accordance with natural right, because they are superior and stronger, as though the superior and stronger and better were the same; or whether the better may be also the inferior and weaker, and the superior the worse, or whether better is to be defined in the same way as superior: this is the point which I want to have clearly explained. Are the superior and better and stronger the same or different?

CAL. Well; I tell you plainly that they are the same.

SOC. Then the many are by nature superior to the one, against whom, as you were saying, they make the laws?

CAL. Certainly.

SOC. Then the laws of the many are the laws of the superior?

CAL. Very true.

SOC. Then they are the laws of the better; for the superior are far better, as you were saying?

CAL. Yes.

SOC. Then the laws which are made by them are by nature noble, as they are the superior?

CAL. Yes.

SOC. And are not the many of opinion, as you were lately saying, that justice is equality, and that to do *489* is more disgraceful than to suffer injustice? and that equality and not excess is justice? – is that so or no? Answer, Callicles, and let no modesty be found to come in the way: I must beg of you to answer, in order that if you agree with me I may be fortified in my judgment by the assent of so competent an authority.

CAL. Yes; that is the opinion of the many.

SOC. Then not only custom but nature also affirms that to do is more disgraceful than to suffer injustice, and that justice is equality, so that you seem to have been wrong in your former assertion, and accusation of me, when you said that nature and custom are opposed, and that I, knowing this, was

artfully playing between them, appealing to custom when the argument is about nature, and to
nature when the argument is about custom?

CAL.   This man always will be talking nonsense. At your age, Socrates, are you not ashamed to be word-
catching, and when a man trips in a word, thinking that to be a piece of luck? do you not see, – have
I not told you already, that by superior I mean better? do you imagine me to say, that if a rabble of
slaves and nondescripts, who are of no use except perhaps for their physical strength, gets together,
their ipsissima verba are laws?

SOC.   Ho! my philosopher, is that your line?

CAL.   Certainly.

SOC.   I was thinking, Callicles, that something of the kind must have been in your mind, and that is why
I repeated the question, what is the superior, because I wanted to know clearly what you meant;
for you surely do not think that two men are better than one, or that your slaves are better than
you because they are stronger? Then please to begin again, and tell me who the better are, if they
are not the stronger; and I will ask you to be a little milder in your instructions, or I shall have to
run away from you.

CAL.   You are ironical.

SOC.   No, by the hero Zethus, Callicles, in whose person you were just now saying many ironical things
against me, I am not: tell me, then, whom you mean by the better?

CAL.   I mean the more excellent.

SOC.   Do you not see that you are yourself repeating words and explaining nothing? – will you tell me
whether you mean by the better and superior the wiser, or if not, whom?

CAL.   Most assuredly, I do mean the wiser.

489 SOC.   Then according to you, one wise man may often be superior to ten thousand fools, and he ought
to rule them, and they ought to be his subjects, and he ought to have more than they should. That
is what I believe that you mean (and you must not suppose that I am catching words), if you allow
that the one is superior to the ten thousand?

CAL.   Yes; that is what I mean, and that is what I conceive to be natural justice, – that the better and wiser
should rule and have more than the inferior.

Republic

Book I

[…]

Several times in the course of the discussion Thrasymachus had made an attempt to get the argument into his own hands, and had been put down by the rest of the company, who wanted to hear the end. But when *336 B* Polemarchus and I had done speaking and there was a pause, he could no longer hold his peace; and, gathering himself up, he came at us like a wild beast, seeking to devour us. We were quite panic-stricken at the sight of him.

He roared out to the whole company: What folly, Socrates, has taken possession of you all? And why, sillybillies, *C* do you knock under to one another? I say that if you want really to know what justice is, you should not only ask but answer, and you should not seek honour to yourself from the refutation of an opponent, but have your own answer; for there is many a one who can ask and cannot answer. And now I will not have you say that justice is *D* duty or advantage or profit or gain or interest, for this sort of nonsense will not do for me; I must have clearness and accuracy.

I was panic-stricken at his words, and could not look at him without trembling. Indeed I believe that if I had not fixed my eye upon him, I should have been struck dumb; but when I saw his fury rising, I looked at him first, and was therefore able to reply to him. *E*

Thrasymachus, I said, with a quiver, don't be hard upon us. Polemarchus and I may have been guilty of a little mistake in the argument, but I can assure you that the error was not intentional. If we were seeking for a piece of gold, you would not imagine that we were 'knocking under to one another', and so losing our chance of finding it. And why, when we are seeking for justice, a thing more precious than many pieces of gold, do you say that we are weakly yielding to one another and not doing our utmost to get at the truth? Nay, my good friend, we are most willing and anxious to do so, but the fact is that we cannot. And if so, you people who know all things should pity us and not be angry with us.

How characteristic of Socrates! he replied, with a bitter laugh; – that's your ironical style! Did I not foresee – *337* have I not already told you, that whatever he was asked he would refuse to answer, and try irony or any other shuffle, in order that he might avoid answering?

You are a philosopher, Thrasymachus, I replied, and well know that if you ask a person what numbers make up twelve, taking care to prohibit him whom you ask from answering twice six, or three times four, or six times two, *B* or four times three, 'for this sort of nonsense will not do for me,' – then obviously, if that is your way of putting the question, no one can answer you. But suppose that he were to retort, 'Thrasymachus, what do you mean? If one of these numbers which you interdict be the true answer to the question, am I falsely to say some other number which is not the right one? – is that your meaning?' – How would you answer him? *C*

Just as if the two cases were at all alike! he said.

Why should they not be? I replied; and even if they are not, but only appear to be so to the person who is asked, ought he not to say what he thinks, whether you and I forbid him or not?

I presume then that you are going to make one of the interdicted answers?

I dare say that I may, notwithstanding the danger, if upon reflection I approve of any of them.

But what if I give you an answer about justice other and better, he said, than any of these? What do you deserve *D* to have done to you?

Done to me! – as becomes the ignorant, I must learn from the wise – that is what I deserve to have done to me.

What, and no payment! a pleasant notion!

I will pay when I have the money, I replied.

But you have, Socrates, said Glaucon: and you, Thrasymachus, need be under no anxiety about money, for we will all make a contribution for Socrates.

Yes, he replied, and then Socrates will do as he always does – refuse to answer himself, but take and pull to *E* pieces the answer of some one else.

Why, my good friend, I said, how can any one answer who knows, and says that he knows, just nothing; and who, even if he has some faint notions of his own, is told by a man of authority not to utter them? The natural thing is, that the speaker should be some one like yourself who professes to know and can tell what he knows. *338* Will you then kindly answer, for the edification of the company and of myself?

Glaucon and the rest of the company joined in my request, and Thrasymachus, as any one might see, was in reality eager to speak; for he thought that he had an excellent answer, and would distinguish himself. But at first

B   he affected to insist on my answering; at length he consented to begin. Behold, he said, the wisdom of Socrates; he refuses to teach himself, and goes about learning of others, to whom he never even says Thank you.

That I learn of others, I replied, is quite true; but that I am ungrateful I wholly deny. Money I have none, and therefore I pay in praise, which is all I have; and how ready I am to praise any one who appears to me to speak well you will very soon find out when you answer; for I expect that you will answer well.

C   Listen, then, he said; I proclaim that justice is nothing else than the interest of the stronger. And now why do you not praise me? But of course you won't.

Let me first understand you, I replied. Justice, as you say, is the interest of the stronger. What, Thrasymachus, is the meaning of this? You cannot mean to say that because Polydamas, the pancratiast, is stronger than we are, and finds the eating of beef conducive to his bodily strength, that to eat beef is therefore equally for our good who are

D   weaker than he is, and right and just for us?

That's abominable of you, Socrates; you take the words in the sense which is most damaging to the argument.

Not at all, my good sir, I said; I am trying to understand them; and I wish that you would be a little clearer.

Well, he said, have you never heard that forms of government differ; there are tyrannies, and there are democracies, and there are aristocracies?

Yes, I know.

And the government is the ruling power in each state?

Certainly.

E   And the different forms of government make laws democratical, aristocratical, tyrannical, with a view to their several interests, and these laws, which are made by them for their own interests, are the justice which they deliver to their subjects, and him who transgresses them they punish as a breaker of the law, and unjust. And that is what I mean when I say that in all states there is the same principle of justice, which is the interest of the government;

339   and as the government must be supposed to have power, the only reasonable conclusion is, that everywhere there is one principle of justice, which is the interest of the stronger.

Now I understand you, I said; and whether you are right or not I will try to discover. But let me remark, that in defining justice you have yourself used the word 'interest' which you forbade me to use. It is true, however, that in your definition the words 'of the stronger' are added.

B   A small addition, you must allow, he said.

Great or small, never mind about that: we must first inquire whether what you are saying is the truth. Now we are both agreed that justice is interest of some sort, but you go on to say 'of the stronger'; about this addition I am not so sure, and must therefore consider further.

Proceed.

I will; and first tell me, Do you admit that it is just for subjects to obey their rulers?

I do.

C   But are the rulers of states absolutely infallible, or are they sometimes liable to err?

To be sure, he replied, they are liable to err.

Then in making their laws they may sometimes make them rightly, and sometimes not?

True.

When they make them rightly, they make them agreeably to their interest; when they are mistaken, contrary to their interest; you admit that?

Yes.

And the laws which they make must be obeyed by their subjects, – and that is what you call justice?

Doubtless.

D   Then justice, according to your argument, is not only obedience to the interest of the stronger but the reverse?

What is that you are saying? he asked.

I am only repeating what you are saying, I believe. But let us consider: Have we not admitted that the rulers may be mistaken about their own interest in what they command, and also that to obey them is justice? Has not that been admitted?

Yes.

E   Then you must also have acknowledged justice not to be for the interest of the stronger, when the rulers unintentionally command things to be done which are to their own injury. For if, as you say, justice is the obedience which the subject renders to their commands, in that case, O wisest of men, is there any escape from the conclusion that the weaker are commanded to do, not what is for the interest, but what is for the injury of the stronger?

Nothing can be clearer, Socrates, said Polemarchus.

Yes, said Cleitophon, interposing, if you are allowed to be his witness.   *340*

But there is no need of any witness, said Polemarchus, for Thrasymachus himself acknowledges that rulers may sometimes command what is not for their own interest, and that for subjects to obey them is justice.

Yes, Polemarchus, – Thrasymachus said that for subjects to do what was commanded by their rulers is just.

Yes, Cleitophon, but he also said that justice is the interest of the stronger, and, while admitting both these *B* propositions, he further acknowledged that the stronger may command the weaker who are his subjects to do what is not for his own interest; whence follows that justice is the injury quite as much as the interest of the stronger.

But, said Cleitophon, he meant by the interest of the stronger what the stronger thought to be his interest, – this was what the weaker had to do; and this was affirmed by him to be justice.

Those were not his words, rejoined Polemarchus.

Never mind, I replied, if he now says that they are, let us accept his statement. Tell me, Thrasymachus, I said, *C* did you mean by justice what the stronger thought to be his interest, whether really so or not?

Certainly not, he said. Do you suppose that I call him who is mistaken the stronger at the time when he is mistaken?

Yes, I said, my impression was that you did so, when you admitted that the ruler was not infallible but might be sometimes mistaken.

You argue like an informer, Socrates. Do you mean, for example, that he who is mistaken about the sick is a *D* physician in that he is mistaken? or that he who errs in arithmetic or grammar is an arithmetician or grammarian at the time when he is making the mistake, in respect of the mistake? True, we say that the physician or arithmetician or grammarian has made a mistake, but this is only a way of speaking; for the fact is that neither the grammarian nor any other person of skill ever makes a mistake in so far as he is what his name implies; they none of them err unless their skill fails them, and then they cease to be skilled artists. No artist or sage or ruler errs at the time when he is what his name implies; though he is commonly said to err, and I adopted the common *E* mode of speaking. But to be perfectly accurate, since you are such a lover of accuracy, we should say that the ruler, in so far as he is a ruler, is unerring, and, being unerring, always commands that which is for his own interest; and *341* the subject is required to execute his commands; and therefore, as I said at first and now repeat, justice is the interest of the stronger.

Indeed, Thrasymachus, and do I really appear to you to argue like an informer?

Certainly, he replied.

And do you suppose that I ask these questions with any design of injuring you in the argument?

Nay, he replied, 'suppose' is not the word – I know it; but you will be found out, and by sheer force of *B* argument you will never prevail.

I shall not make the attempt, my dear man; but to avoid any misunderstanding occurring between us in future, let me ask, in what sense do you speak of a ruler or stronger whose interest, as you were saying, he being the superior, it is just that the inferior should execute – is he a ruler in the popular or in the strict sense of the term?

In the strictest of all senses, he said. And now cheat and play the informer if you can; I ask no quarter at your hands. But you never will be able, never.

And do you imagine, I said, that I am such a madman as to try and cheat Thrasymachus? I might as well shave *C* a lion.

Why, he said, you made the attempt a minute ago, and you failed.

Enough, I said, of these civilities. It will be better that I should ask you a question: Is the physician, taken in that strict sense of which you are speaking, a healer of the sick or a maker of money? And remember that I am now speaking of the true physician.

A healer of the sick, he replied.

And the pilot – that is to say, the true pilot – is he a captain of sailors or a mere sailor?

A captain of sailors.

The circumstance that he sails in the ship is not to be taken into account; neither is he to be called a sailor; the *D* name 'pilot' by which he is distinguished has nothing to do with sailing, but is significant of his skill and of his authority over the sailors.

Very true, he said.

Now, I said, every art has an interest?

Certainly.

For which the art has to consider and provide?

Yes, that is the aim of art.

And the interest of any art is the perfection of it – this and nothing else?

E   What do you mean?

I mean what I may illustrate negatively by the example of the body. Suppose you were to ask me whether the body is self-sufficing or has wants, I should reply: Certainly the body has wants; for the body may be ill and require to be cured, and has therefore interests to which the art of medicine ministers; and this is the origin and intention of medicine, as you will acknowledge. Am I not right?

342   Quite right, he replied.

But is the art of medicine or any other art faulty or deficient in any quality in the same way that the eye may be deficient in sight or the ear fail of hearing, and therefore requires another art to provide for the interests of seeing and hearing – has art in itself, I say, any similar liability to fault or defect, and does every art require another supplementary art to provide for its interests, and that another and another without end? Or have the arts to look

B   only after their own interests? Or have they no need either of themselves or of another? – having no faults or defects, they have no need to correct them, either by the exercise of their own art or of any other; they have only to consider the interest of their subject-matter. For every art remains pure and faultless while remaining true – that is to say, while perfect and unimpaired. Take the words in your precise sense, and tell me whether I am not right.

Yes, clearly.

C   Then medicine does not consider the interest of medicine, but the interest of the body?

True, he said.

Nor does the art of horsemanship consider the interests of the art of horsemanship, but the interests of the horse; neither do any other arts care for themselves, for they have no needs; they care only for that which is the subject of their art?

True, he said.

But surely, Thrasymachus, the arts are the superiors and rulers of their own subjects?

To this he assented with a good deal of reluctance.

Then, I said, no science or art considers or enjoins the interest of the stronger or superior, but only the interest

D   of the subject and weaker?

He made an attempt to contest this proposition also, but finally acquiesced.

Then, I continued, no physician, in so far as he is a physician, considers his own good in what he prescribes, but the good of his patient; for the true physician is also a ruler having the human body as a subject, and is not a mere moneymaker; that has been admitted?

Yes.

And the pilot likewise, in the strict sense of the term, is a ruler of sailors and not a mere sailor?

E   That has been admitted.

And such a pilot and ruler will provide and prescribe for the interest of the sailor who is under him, and not for his own or the ruler's interest?

He gave a reluctant 'Yes'.

Then, I said, Thrasymachus, there is no one in any rule who, in so far as he is a ruler, considers or enjoins what is for his own interest, but always what is for the interest of his subject or suitable to his art; to that he looks, and that alone he considers in everything which he says and does

343   When we had got to this point in the argument, and every one saw that the definition of justice had been com- pletely upset, Thrasymachus, instead of replying to me, said: Tell me, Socrates, have you got a nurse?

Why do you ask such a question, I said, when you ought rather to be answering?

Because she leaves you to snivel, and never wipes your nose: she has not even taught you to know the shepherd from the sheep.

What makes you say that? I replied.

B   Because you fancy that the shepherd or neatherd fattens or tends the sheep or oxen with a view to their own good and not to the good of himself or his master; and you further imagine that the rulers of states, if they are true rulers, never think of their subjects as sheep, and that they are not studying their own advantage day and

C night. Oh, no; and so entirely astray are you in your ideas about the just and unjust as not even to know that justice and the just are in reality another's good; that is to say, the interest of the ruler and stronger, and the loss of the subject and servant; and injustice the opposite; for the unjust is lord over the truly simple and just: he is the stronger, and his subjects do what is for his interest, and minister to his happiness, which is very far from being their own. Consider further, most foolish Socrates, that the just is always a loser in comparison with the unjust. *D* First of all, in private contracts: wherever the unjust is the partner of the just you will find that, when the partnership is dissolved, the unjust man has always more and the just less. Secondly, in their dealings with the State: when there is an income-tax, the just man will pay more and the unjust less on the same amount of income; and when there is anything to be received the one gains nothing and the other much. Observe also what happens when they *E* take an office; there is the just man neglecting his affairs and perhaps suffering other losses, and getting nothing out of the public, because he is just; moreover he is hated by his friends and acquaintance for refusing to serve them in unlawful ways. But all this is reversed in the case of the unjust man. I am speaking, as before, of injustice on a large scale in which the advantage of the unjust is most apparent; and my meaning will be most clearly seen *344* if we turn to that highest form of injustice in which the criminal is the happiest of men, and the sufferers or those who refuse to do injustice are the most miserable – that is to say tyranny, which by fraud and force takes away the property of others, not little by little but wholesale; comprehending in one, things sacred as well as profane, private and public; for which acts of wrong, if he were detected perpetrating any one of them singly, he would *B* be punished and incur great disgrace – they who do such wrong in particular cases are called robbers of temples, and man-stealers and burglars and swindlers and thieves. But when a man besides taking away the money of the citizens has made slaves of them, then, instead of these names of reproach, he is termed happy and blessed, not *C* only by the citizens but by all who hear of his having achieved the consummation of injustice. For mankind censure injustice, fearing that they may be the victims of it and not because they shrink from committing it. And thus, as I have shown, Socrates, injustice, when on a sufficient scale, has more strength and freedom and mastery than justice; and, as I said at first, justice is the interest of the stronger, whereas injustice is a man's own profit and interest.

Thrasymachus, when he had thus spoken, having, like a bath-man, deluged our ears with his words, had a mind *D* to go away. But the company would not let him; they insisted that he should remain and defend his position; and I myself added my own humble request that he would not leave us. Thrasymachus, I said to him, excellent man, how suggestive are your remarks! And are you going to run away before you have fairly taught or learned whether they are true or not? Is the attempt to determine the way of man's life so small a matter in your eyes – to determine *E* how life may be passed by each one of us to the greatest advantage?

And do I differ from you, he said, as to the importance of the inquiry?

You appear rather, I replied, to have no care or thought about us, Thrasymachus – whether we live better or worse from not knowing what you say you know, is to you a matter of indifference. Prithee, friend, do not keep *345* your knowledge to yourself; we are a large party; and any benefit which you confer upon us will be amply rewarded. For my own part I openly declare that I am not convinced, and that I do not believe injustice to be more gainful than justice, even if uncontrolled and allowed to have free play. For, granting that there may be an unjust man who is able to commit injustice either by fraud or force, still this does not convince me of the superior advantage of injustice, and there may be others who are in the same predicament with myself. Perhaps we may be wrong; if so, you in your wisdom should convince us that we are mistaken in preferring justice to injustice. *B*

And how am I to convince you, he said, if you are not already convinced by what I have just said; what more can I do for you? Would you have me put the proof bodily into your souls?

Heaven forbid! I said; I would only ask you to be consistent; or, if you change, change openly and let there be no deception. For I must remark, Thrasymachus, if you will recall what was previously said, that although you *C* began by defining the true physician in an exact sense, you did not observe a like exactness when speaking of the shepherd; you thought that the shepherd as a shepherd tends the sheep not with a view to their own good, but like a mere diner or banqueter with a view to the pleasures of the table; or, again, as a trader for sale in the market, and not as a shepherd. Yet surely the art of the shepherd is concerned only with the good of his subjects; he has only *D* to provide the best for them, since the perfection of the art is already ensured whenever all the requirements of it are satisfied. And that was what I was saying just now about the ruler. I conceived that the art of the ruler, considered as ruler, whether in a state or in private life, could only regard the good of his flock or subjects; whereas you *E* seem to think that the rulers in states, that is to say, the true rulers, like being in authority.

Think! Nay, I am sure of it.

Then why in the case of lesser offices do men never take them willingly without payment, unless under the idea
346 that they govern for the advantage not of themselves but of others? Let me ask you a question: Are not the several
arts different, by reason of their each having a separate function? And, my dear illustrious friend, do say what you
think, that we may make a little progress.

Yes, that is the difference, he replied.

And each art gives us a particular good and not merely a general one – medicine, for example, gives us health;
navigation, safety at sea, and so on?

Yes, he said,

B And the art of payment has the special function of giving pay: but we do not confuse this with other arts, any
more than the art of the pilot is to be confused with the art of medicine, because the health of the pilot may be
improved by a sea voyage. You would not be inclined to say, would you, that navigation is the art of medicine, at
least if we are to adopt your exact use of language?

Certainly not.

Or because a man is in good health when he receives pay you would not say that the art of payment is
medicine?

I should not.

Nor would you say that medicine is the art of receiving pay because a man takes fees when he is engaged in
healing?

C Certainly not.

And we have admitted, I said, that the good of each art is specially confined to the art?

Yes.

Then, if there be any good which all artists have in common, that is to be attributed to something of which they
all have the common use?

True, he replied.

And when the artist is benefited by receiving pay the advantage is gained by an additional use of the art of pay,
which is not the art professed by him?

He gave a reluctant assent to this.

D Then the pay is not derived by the several artists from their respective arts. But the truth is, that while the art of
medicine gives health, and the art of the builder builds a house, another art attends them which is the art of pay.
The various arts may be doing their own business and benefiting that over which they preside, but would the artist
receive any benefit from his art unless he were paid as well?

I suppose not.

E But does he therefore confer no benefit when he works for nothing?

Certainly, he confers a benefit.

Then now, Thrasymachus, there is no longer any doubt that neither arts nor governments provide for their own
interests; but, as we were before saying, they rule and provide for the interests of their subjects who are the weaker
and not the stronger – to their good they attend and not to the good of the superior. And this is the reason, my
dear Thrasymachus, why, as I was just now saying, no one is willing to govern; because no one likes to take in
347 hand the reformation of evils which are not his concern without remuneration. For, in the execution of his work,
and in giving his orders to another, the true artist does not regard his own interest, but always that of his subjects;
and therefore in order that rulers may be willing to rule, they must be paid in one of three modes of payment,
money, or honour, or a penalty for refusing.

What do you mean, Socrates? said Glaucon. The first two modes of payment are intelligible enough, but what
the penalty is I do not understand, or how a penalty can be a payment.

B You mean that you do not understand the nature of this payment which to the best men is the great inducement
to rule? Of course you know that ambition and avarice are held to be, as indeed they are, a disgrace?

Very true.

And for this reason, I said, money and honour have no attraction for them; good men do not wish to be openly
demanding payment for governing and so to get the name of hirelings, nor by secretly helping themselves out of
the public revenues to get the name of thieves. And not being ambitious they do not care about honour.

C Wherefore necessity must be laid upon them, and they must be induced to serve from the fear of punishment.
And this, as I imagine, is the reason why the forwardness to take office, instead of waiting to be compelled, has
been deemed dishonourable. Now the worst part of the punishment is that he who refuses to rule is liable to be

ruled by one who is worse than himself. And the fear of this, as I conceive, induces the good to take office, *D*
not because they would, but because they cannot help – not under the idea that they are going to have any
benefit or enjoyment themselves, but as a necessity, and because they are not able to commit the task of ruling
to any one who is better than themselves, or indeed as good. For there is reason to think that if a city were
composed entirely of good men, then to avoid office would be as much an object of contention as to obtain
office is at present; then we should have plain proof that the true ruler is not meant by nature to regard his own
interest, but that of his subjects; and every one who knew this would choose rather to receive a benefit from
another than to have the trouble of conferring one. So far am I from agreeing with Thrasymachus that justice *E*
is the interest of the stronger. This latter question need not be further discussed at present; but when
Thrasymachus says that the life of the unjust is more advantageous than that of the just, his new statement
appears to me to be of a far more serious character. Which of us has spoken truly? And which sort of life,
Glaucon, do you prefer?

I for my part deem the life of the just to be the more advantageous, he answered.

Did you hear all the advantages of the unjust which Thrasymachus was rehearsing?   *348*

Yes, I heard him, he replied, but he has not convinced me.

Then shall we try to find some way of convincing him, if we can, that he is saying what is not true?

Most certainly, he replied.

If, I said, he makes a set speech and we make another recounting all the advantages of being just, and he answers
and we rejoin, there must be a numbering and measuring of the goods which are claimed on either side, and in *B*
the end we shall want judges to decide; but if we proceed in our inquiry as we lately did, by making admissions to
one another, we shall unite the offices of judge and advocate in our own persons.

Very good, he said.

And which method do I understand you to prefer? I said. That which you propose.

Well, then, Thrasymachus, I said, suppose you begin at the beginning and answer me. You say that perfect
injustice is more gainful than perfect justice?

Yes, that is what I say, and I have given you my reasons.   *C*

And what is your view about them? Would you call one of them virtue and the other vice?

Certainly.

I suppose that you would call justice virtue and injustice vice?

What a charming notion! So likely too, seeing that I affirm injustice to be profitable and justice not.

What else then would you say?

The opposite, he replied.

And would you call justice vice?

No, I would rather say sublime simplicity.

Then would you call injustice malignity?   *D*

No; I would rather say discretion.

And do the unjust appear to you to be wise and good?

Yes, he said; at any rate those of them who are able to be perfectly unjust, and who have the power of subduing
states and nations; but perhaps you imagine me to be talking of cutpurses. Even this profession if undetected has
advantages, though they are not to be compared with those of which I was just now speaking.

I do not think that I misapprehend your meaning, Thrasymachus, I replied; but still I cannot hear without *E*
amazement that you class injustice with wisdom and virtue, and justice with the opposite.

Certainly, I do so class them.

Now, I said, you are on more substantial and almost unanswerable ground; for if the injustice which you were
maintaining to be profitable had been admitted by you as by others to be vice and deformity, an answer might have
been given to you on received principles; but now I perceive that you will call injustice honourable and strong,
and to the unjust you will attribute all the qualities which were attributed by us before to the just, seeing that you *349*
do not hesitate to rank injustice with wisdom and virtue.

You have guessed most infallibly, he replied.

Then I certainly ought not to shrink from going through with the argument so long as I have reason to think
that you, Thrasymachus, are speaking your real mind; for I do believe that you are now in earnest and are not
amusing yourself at our expense.

I may be in earnest or not, but what is that to you? – to refute the argument is your business.

B   Very true, I said; that is what I have to do: But will you be so good as answer yet one more question? Does the just man try to gain any advantage over the just?

Far otherwise; if he did he would not be the simple musing creature which he is.

And would he try to go beyond just action?

He would not.

And how would he regard the attempt to gain an advantage over the unjust; would that be considered by him as just or unjust?

He would think it just, and would try to gain the advantage; but he would not be able.

C   Whether he would or would not be able, I said, is not to the point. My question is only whether the just man, while refusing to have more than another just man, would wish and claim to have more than the unjust?

Yes, he would.

And what of the unjust – does he claim to have more than the just man and to do more than is just?

Of course, he said, for he claims to have more than all men.

And the unjust man will strive and struggle to obtain more than the unjust man or action, in order that he may have more than all?

True.

We may put the matter thus, I said – the just does not desire more than his like but more than his unlike, whereas the unjust desires more than both his like and his unlike?

D   Nothing, he said, can be better than that statement.

And the unjust is good and wise, and the just is neither?

Good again, he said.

And is not the unjust like the wise and good and the just unlike them?

Of course, he said, he who is of a certain nature, is like those who are of a certain nature; he who is not, not.

Each of them, I said, is such as his like is?

Certainly, he replied.

Very good, Thrasymachus, I said; and now to take the case of the arts: you would admit that one man is a

E musician and another not a musician?

Yes.

And which is wise and which is foolish?

Clearly the musician is wise, and he who is not a musician is foolish.

And he is good in as far as he is wise, and bad in as far as he is foolish?

Yes.

And you would say the same sort of thing of the physician?

Yes.

And do you think, my excellent friend, that a musician when he adjusts the lyre would desire or claim to exceed or go beyond a musician in the tightening and loosening the strings?

I do not think that he would.

But he would claim to exceed the non-musician?

Of course.

350   And what would you say of the physician? In prescribing meats and drinks would he wish to go beyond another physician or beyond the practice of medicine?

He would not.

But he would wish to go beyond the non-physician?

Yes.

And about knowledge and ignorance in general; see whether you think that any man who has knowledge ever would wish to have the choice of saying or doing more than another man who has knowledge. Would he not rather say or do the same as his like in the same case?

That, I suppose, can hardly be denied.

B   And what of the ignorant? would he not desire to have more than either the knowing or the ignorant?

I dare say.

And the knowing is wise?

Yes.

And the wise is good?

True.

Then the wise and good will not desire to gain more than his like, but more than his unlike and opposite?

I suppose so.

Whereas the bad and ignorant will desire to gain more than both?

Yes.

But did we not say, Thrasymachus, that the unjust goes beyond both his like and unlike? Were not these your words?

They were.

And you also said that the just will not go beyond his like but his unlike? C

Yes.

Then the just is like the wise and good, and the unjust like the evil and ignorant?

That is the inference.

And each of them is such as his like is?

That was admitted.

Then the just has turned out to be wise and good and the unjust evil and ignorant.

Thrasymachus made all these admissions, not fluently, as I repeat them, but with extreme reluctance; it was a D hot summer's day, and the perspiration poured from him in torrents; and then I saw what I had never seen before, Thrasymachus blushing. As we were now agreed that justice was virtue and wisdom, and injustice vice and ignorance, I proceeded to another point:

Well, I said, Thrasymachus, that matter is now settled; but were we not also saying that injustice had strength; do you remember?

Yes, I remember, he said, but do not suppose that I approve of what you are saying or have no answer; if however I were to answer, you would be quite certain to accuse me of haranguing; therefore either permit me E to have my say out, or if you would rather ask, do so, and I will answer 'Very good', as they say to story-telling old women, and will nod 'Yes' and 'No'.

Certainly not, I said, if contrary to your real opinion.

Yes, he said, I will, to please you, since you will not let me speak. What else would you have?

Nothing in the world, I said; and if you are so disposed I will ask and you shall answer.

Proceed.

Then I will repeat the question which I asked before, in order that our examination of the relative nature of 351 justice and injustice may be carried on regularly. A statement was made that injustice is stronger and more power- ful than justice, but now justice, having been identified with wisdom and virtue, is easily shown to be stronger than injustice, if injustice is ignorance; this can no longer be questioned by any one. But I want to view the matter, Thrasymachus, in a different way: You would not deny that a state may be unjust and may be unjustly B attempting to enslave other states, or may have already enslaved them, and may be holding many of them in subjection?

True, he replied; and I will add that the best and most perfectly unjust state will be most likely to do so.

I know, I said, that such was your position; but what I would further consider is, whether this power which is possessed by the superior state can exist or be exercised without justice or only with justice.

If you are right in your view, and justice is wisdom, then only with justice; but if I am right, then without C justice.

I am delighted, Thrasymachus, to see you not only nodding assent and dissent, but making answers which are quite excellent.

That is out of civility to you, he replied.

You are very kind, I said; and would you have the goodness also to inform me, whether you think that a state, or an army, or a band of robbers and thieves, or any other gang of evil-doers could act at all if they injured one another?

No indeed, he said, they could not. D

But if they abstained from injuring one another, then they might act together better?

Yes.

And this is because injustice creates divisions and hatreds and fighting, and justice imparts harmony and friendship; is not that true, Thrasymachus?

I agree, he said, because I do not wish to quarrel with you.

How good of you, I said; but I should like to know also whether injustice, having this tendency to arouse hatred, wherever existing, among slaves or among freemen, will not make them hate one another and set them at variance and render them incapable of common action?

Certainly.

E   And even if injustice be found in two only, will they not quarrel and fight, and become enemies to one another and to the just?

They will.

And suppose injustice abiding in a single person, would your wisdom say that she loses or that she retains her natural power?

Let us assume that she retains her power.

Yet is not the power which injustice exercises of such a nature that wherever she takes up her abode, whether
352 in a city, in an army, in a family, or in any other body, that body is, to begin with, rendered incapable of united action by reason of sedition and distraction; and does it not become its own enemy and at variance with all that opposes it, and with the just? Is not this the case?

Yes, certainly.

And is not injustice equally fatal when existing in a single person; in the first place rendering him incapable of action because he is not at unity with himself, and in the second place making him an enemy to himself and the just? Is not that true, Thrasymachus?

Yes.

And O my friend, I said, surely the gods are just?

Granted that they are.

B   But if so, the unjust will be the enemy of the gods, and the just will be their friend?

Feast away in triumph, and take your fill of the argument; I will not oppose you, lest I should displease the company.

Well then, proceed with your answers, and let me have the remainder of my repast. For we have already shown that the just are clearly wiser and better and abler than the unjust, and that the unjust are incapable of common
C action; nay more, that to speak as we did of men who are evil acting at any time vigorously together, is not strictly true, for if they had been perfectly evil, they would have laid hands upon one another; but it is evident that there must have been some remnant of justice in them, which enabled them to combine; if there had not been they would have injured one another as well as their victims; they were but half-villains in their enterprises; for had they
D been whole villains, and utterly unjust, they would have been utterly incapable of action. That, as I believe, is the truth of the matter, and not what you said at first. But whether the just have a better and happier life than the unjust is a further question which we also proposed to consider. I think that they have, and for the reasons which I have given; but still I should like to examine further, for no light matter is at stake, nothing less than the rule of human life.

Proceed.

I will proceed by asking a question: Would you not say that a horse has some end?

E   I should.

And the end or use of a horse or of anything would be that which could not be accomplished, or not so well accomplished, by any other thing?

I do not understand, he said.

Let me explain: Can you see, except with the eye?

Certainly not.

Or hear, except with the ear?

No.

These then may be truly said to be the ends of these organs?

They may.

353 But you can cut off a vine-branch with a dagger or with a chisel, and in many other ways?

Of course.

And yet not so well as with a pruning-hook made for the purpose?

True.

May we not say that this is the end of a pruning-hook?

We may.

Then now I think you will have no difficulty in understanding my meaning when I asked the question whether the end of anything would be that which could not be accomplished, or not so well accomplished, by any other thing?

I understand your meaning, he said, and assent.   *B*

And that to which an end is appointed has also an excellence? Need I ask again whether the eye has an end?

It has.

And has not the eye an excellence?

Yes.

And the ear has an end and an excellence also?

True.

And the same is true of all other things; they have each of them an end and a special excellence?

That is so.

Well, and can the eyes fulfil their end if they are wanting in their own proper excellence and have a defect instead? *C*

How can they, he said, if they are blind and cannot see?

You mean to say, if they have lost their proper excellence, which is sight; but I have not arrived at that point yet. I would rather ask the question more generally, and only inquire whether the things which fulfil their ends fulfil them by their own proper excellence, and fail of fulfilling them by their own defect?

Certainly, he replied.

I might say the same of the ears; when deprived of their own proper excellence they cannot fulfil their end?

True.

And the same observation will apply to all other things?   *D*

I agree.

Well; and has not the soul an end which nothing else can fulfil? for example, to superintend and command and deliberate and the like. Are not these functions proper to the soul, and can they rightly be assigned to any other?

To no other.

And is not life to be reckoned among the ends of the soul?

Assuredly, he said.

And has not the soul an excellence also?

Yes.

And can she or can she not fulfil her own ends when deprived of that excellence?   *E*

She cannot.

Then an evil soul must necessarily be an evil ruler and superintendent, and the good soul a good ruler?

Yes, necessarily.

And we have admitted that justice is the excellence of the soul, and injustice the defect of the soul?

That has been admitted.

Then the just soul and the just man will live well, and the unjust man will live ill?

That is what your argument proves.

And he who lives well is blessed and happy, and he who lives ill the reverse of happy?   *354*

Certainly.

Then the just is happy, and the unjust miserable?

So be it.

But happiness and not misery is profitable.

Of course.

Then, my blessed Thrasymachus, injustice can never be more profitable than justice.

Let this, Socrates, he said, be your entertainment at the Bendidea.

For which I am indebted to you, I said, now that you have grown gentle towards me, and have left off scolding. Nevertheless, I have not been well entertained; but that was my own fault and not yours. As an epicure snatches a *B* taste of every dish which is successively brought to table, he not having allowed himself time to enjoy the one before, so have I gone from one subject to another without having discovered what I sought at first, the nature of justice. I left that inquiry and turned away to consider whether justice is virtue and wisdom or evil and folly; and when there arose a further question about the comparative advantages of justice and injustice, I could not refrain from passing on to that. And the result of the whole discussion has been that I know nothing at all. For I know not what justice is, and therefore I am not likely to know whether it is or is not a virtue, nor can I say whether the just man is happy or unhappy.

BOOK II

357 WITH these words I was thinking that I had made an end of the discussion; but the end, in truth, proved to be only a beginning. For Glaucon, who is always the most pugnacious of men, was dissatisfied at Thrasymachus' retirement; he wanted to have the battle out. So he said to me: Socrates, do you wish really to persuade us, or only to
B seem to have persuaded us, that to be just is always better than to be unjust?

I should wish really to persuade you, I replied, if I could.

Then you certainly have not succeeded. Let me ask you now : – How would you arrange goods – are there not some which we welcome for their own sakes, and independently of their consequences, as, for example, harmless pleasures and enjoyments, which delight us at the time, although nothing follows from them?

I agree in thinking that there is such a class, I replied.

C Is there not also a second class of goods, such as knowledge, sight, health, which are desirable not only in themselves, but also for their results?

Certainly, I said.

And would you not recognize a third class, such as gymnastic, and the care of the sick, and the physician's art; also the various ways of money-making – these do us good but we regard them as disagreeable; and no one would
D choose them for their own sakes, but only for the sake of some reward or result which flows from them?

There is, I said, this third class also. But why do you ask?

Because I want to know in which of the three classes you would place justice?

358 In the highest class, I replied, – among those goods which he who would be happy desires both for their own sake and for the sake of their results.

Then the many are of another mind; they think that justice is to be reckoned in the troublesome class, among goods which are to be pursued for the sake of rewards and of reputation, but in themselves are disagreeable and rather to be avoided.

I know, I said, that this is their manner of thinking, and that this was the thesis which Thrasymachus was maintaining just now, when he censured justice and praised injustice. But I am too stupid to be convinced by him.

B I wish, he said, that you would hear me as well as him, and then I shall see whether you and I agree. For Thrasymachus seems to me, like a snake, to have been charmed by your voice sooner than he ought to have been; but to my mind the nature of justice and injustice have not yet been made clear. Setting aside their rewards and results, I want to know what they are in themselves, and how they inwardly work in the soul. If you please, then,
C I will revive the argument of Thrasymachus. And first I will speak of the nature and origin of justice according to the common view of them. Secondly, I will show that all men who practise justice do so against their will, of necessity, but not as a good. And thirdly, I will argue that there is reason in this view, for the life of the unjust is after all better far than the life of the just – if what they say is true, Socrates, since I myself am not of their opinion. But still I acknowledge that I am perplexed when I hear the voices of Thrasymachus and myriads of others dinning
D in my ears; and, on the other hand, I have never yet heard the superiority of justice to injustice maintained by any one in a satisfactory way. I want to hear justice praised in respect of itself; then I shall be satisfied, and you are the person from whom I think that I am most likely to hear this; and therefore I will praise the unjust life to the utmost of my power, and my manner of speaking will indicate the manner in which I desire to hear you too praising justice and censuring injustice. Will you say whether you approve of my proposal?

Indeed I do; nor can I imagine any theme about which a man of sense would oftener wish to converse.

E I am delighted, he replied, to hear you say so, and shall begin by speaking, as I proposed, of the nature and origin of justice.

They say that to do injustice is, by nature, good; to suffer injustice, evil; but that the evil is greater than the good.
359 And so when men have both done and suffered injustice and have had experience of both, not being able to avoid the one and obtain the other, they think that they had better agree among themselves to have neither; hence there arise laws and mutual covenants; and that which is ordained by law is termed by them lawful and just. This they affirm to be the origin and nature of justice; – it is a mean or compromise, between the best of all, which is to do injustice and not be punished, and the worst of all, which is to suffer injustice without the power of retaliation; and justice, being at a middle point between the two, is tolerated not as a good, but as the lesser evil, and honoured
B by reason of the inability of men to do injustice. For no man who is worthy to be called a man would ever submit to such an agreement if he were able to resist; he would be mad if he did. Such is the received account, Socrates, of the nature and origin of justice.

Now that those who practise justice do so involuntarily and because they have not the power to be unjust will best appear if we imagine something of this kind: having given both to the just and the unjust power to do what they will, let us watch and see whither desire will lead them; then we shall discover in the very act the just and unjust man to be proceeding along the same road, following their interest, which all natures deem to be their good, and are only diverted into the path of justice by the force of law. The liberty which we are supposing may be most completely given to them in the form of such a power as is said to have been possessed by Gyges, the ancestor of Croesus the Lydian.[1] According to the tradition, Gyges was a shepherd in the service of the king of Lydia; there was a great storm, and an earthquake made an opening in the earth at the place where he was feeding his flock. Amazed at the sight, he descended into the opening, where, among other marvels, he beheld a hollow brazen horse, having doors, at which he stooping and looking in saw a dead body of stature, as appeared to him, more than human, and having nothing on but a gold ring; this he took from the finger of the dead and reascended. Now the shepherds met together, according to custom, that they might send their monthly report about the flocks to the king; into their assembly he came having the ring on his finger, and as he was sitting among them he chanced to turn the collet of the ring inside his hand, when instantly he became invisible to the rest of the company and they began to speak of him as if he were no longer present. He was astonished at this, and again touching the ring he turned the collet outwards and reappeared; he made several trials of the ring, and always with the same result – when he turned the collet inwards he became invisible, when outwards he reappeared. Whereupon he contrived to be chosen one of the messengers who were sent to the court; where as soon as he arrived he seduced the queen, and with her help conspired against the king and slew him, and took the kingdom. Suppose now that there were two such magic rings, and the just put on one of them and the unjust the other; no man can be imagined to be of such an iron nature that he would stand fast in justice. No man would keep his hands off what was not his own when he could safely take what he liked out of the market, or go into houses and lie with any one at his pleasure, or kill or release from prison whom he would, and in all respects be like a god among men. Then the actions of the just would be as the actions of the unjust; they would both come at last to the same point. And this we may truly affirm to be a great proof that a man is just, not willingly or because he thinks that justice is any good to him individually, but of necessity, for wherever any one thinks that he can safely be unjust, there he is unjust. For all men believe in their hearts that injustice is far more profitable to the individual than justice, and he who argues as I have been supposing, will say that they are right. If you could imagine any one obtaining this power of becoming invisible, and never doing any wrong or touching what was another's, he would be thought by the lookers-on to be a most wretched idiot, although they would praise him to one another's faces, and keep up appearances with one another from a fear that they too might suffer injustice. Enough of this.

Now, if we are to form a real judgement of the life of the just and unjust, we must isolate them; there is no other way; and how is the isolation to be effected? I answer: Let the unjust man be entirely unjust, and the just man entirely just; nothing is to be taken away from either of them, and both are to be perfectly furnished for the work of their respective lives. First, let the unjust be like other distinguished masters of craft; like the skilful pilot or physician, who knows intuitively his own powers and keeps within their limits, and who, if he fails at any point, is able to recover himself. So let the unjust make his unjust attempts in the right way, and lie hidden if he means to be great in his injustice: (he who is found out is nobody:) for the highest reach of injustice is, to be deemed just when you are not. Therefore I say that in the perfectly unjust man we must assume the most perfect injustice; there is to be no deduction, but we must allow him, while doing the most unjust acts, to have acquired the greatest reputation for justice. If he have taken a false step he must be able to recover himself; he must be one who can speak with effect, if any of his deeds come to light, and who can force his way where force is required by his courage and strength, and command of money and friends. And at his side let us place the just man in his nobleness and simplicity, wishing, as Aeschylus says, to be and not to seem good. There must be no seeming, for if he seem to be just he will be honoured and rewarded, and then we shall not know whether he is just for the sake of justice or for the sake of honours and rewards; therefore, let him be clothed in justice only, and have no other covering; and he must be imagined in a state of life the opposite to the former. Let him be the best of men, and let him be thought the worst; then he will have been put to the proof; and we shall see whether he will be affected by the fear of infamy and its consequences. And let him continue thus to the hour of death; being just and seeming to be unjust. When both have reached the uttermost extreme, the one of justice and the other of injustice, let judgement be given which of them is the happier of the two.

---

[1] Reading Γύγῃ τῷ Κροίσου τοῦ Λυδοῦ προγόνῳ.

Heavens! my dear Glaucon, I said, how energetically you polish them up for the decision, first one and then the other, as if they were two statues.

I do my best, he said. And now that we know what they are like there is no difficulty in tracing out the sort of
E life which awaits either of them. This I will proceed to describe; but as you may think the description a little too coarse, I ask you to suppose, Socrates, that the words which follow are not mine. – Let me put them into the mouths of the eulogists of injustice: They will tell you that the just man who is thought unjust will be scourged, racked, bound – will have his eyes burnt out; and, at last, after suffering every kind of evil, he will be impaled:
362 Then he will understand that he ought to seem only, and not to be, just; the words of Aeschylus may be more truly spoken of the unjust than of the just. For the unjust is pursuing a reality; he does not live with a view to appearances – he wants to be really unjust and not to seem only: –

His mind has a soil deep and fertile,

B   Out of which spring his prudent counsels.[1]

In the first place, he is thought just, and therefore bears rule in the city; he can marry whom he will, and give in marriage to whom he will; also he can trade and deal where he likes, and always to his own advantage, because he has no misgivings about injustice; and at every contest, whether in public or private, he gets the better of his antagonists, and gains at their expense, and is rich, and out of his gains he can benefit his friends, and harm his
C enemies; moreover, he can offer sacrifices, and dedicate gifts to the gods abundantly and magnificently, and can honour the gods or any man whom he wants to honour in a far better style than the just, and therefore he is likely to be dearer than they are to the gods. And thus, Socrates, gods and men are said to unite in making the life of the unjust better than the life of the just.

[…]

On what principle, then, shall we any longer choose justice rather than the worst injustice? when, if we only unite the latter with a deceitful regard to appearances, we shall fare to our mind both with gods and men, in life
366 C and after death, as the most numerous and the highest authorities tell us. Knowing all this, Socrates, how can a man who has any superiority of mind or person or rank or wealth, be willing to honour justice; or indeed to refrain from laughing when he hears justice praised? And even if there should be some one who is able to disprove the truth of my words, and who is satisfied that justice is best, still he is not angry with the unjust, but is very ready to
D forgive them, because he also knows that men are not just of their own free will; unless, peradventure, there be some one whom the divinity within him may have inspired with a hatred of injustice, or who has attained knowledge of the truth – but no other man. He only blames injustice who, owing to cowardice or age or some weakness, has not the power of being unjust. And this is proved by the fact that when he obtains the power, he immediately becomes unjust as far as he can be.

The cause of all this, Socrates, was indicated by us at the beginning of the argument, when my brother and I
E told you how astonished we were to find that of all the professing panegyrists of justice – beginning with the ancient heroes of whom any memorial has been preserved to us, and ending with the men of our own time – no one has ever blamed injustice or praised justice except with a view to the glories, honours, and benefits which flow from them. No one has ever adequately described either in verse or prose the true essential nature of either of them abiding in the soul, and invisible to any human or divine eye; or shown that of all the things of a man's soul which
367 he has within him, justice is the greatest good, and injustice the greatest evil. Had this been the universal strain, had you sought to persuade us of this from our youth upwards, we should not have been on the watch to keep one another from doing wrong, but every one would have been his own watchman, because afraid, if he did wrong, of harbouring in himself the greatest of evils. I dare say that Thrasymachus and others would seriously hold the language which I have been merely repeating, and words even stronger than these about justice and injustice, grossly, as I conceive, perverting their true nature. But I speak in this vehement manner, as I must frankly confess
B to you, because I want to hear from you the opposite side; and I would ask you to show not only the superiority which justice has over injustice, but what effect they have on the possessor of them which makes the one to be a good and the other an evil to him. And please, as Glaucon requested of you, to exclude reputations; for unless you

---

[1] Seven against Thebes, 574.

take away from each of them his true reputation and add on the false, we shall say that you do not praise justice, but the appearance of it; we shall think that you are only exhorting us to keep injustice dark, and that you really C agree with Thrasymachus in thinking that justice is another's good and the interest of the stronger, and that injustice is a man's own profit and interest, though injurious to the weaker. Now as you have admitted that justice is one of that highest class of goods which are desired indeed for their results, but in a far greater degree for their own sakes – like sight or hearing or knowledge or health, or any other real and natural and not merely conventional D good – I would ask you in your praise of justice to regard one point only: I mean the essential good and evil which justice and injustice work in the possessors of them. Let others praise justice and censure injustice, magnifying the rewards and honours of the one and abusing the other; that is a manner of arguing which, coming from them, I am ready to tolerate, but from you who have spent your whole life in the consideration of this question, unless I hear the contrary from your own lips, I expect something better. And therefore, I say, not only prove to us that E justice is better than injustice, but show what they either of them do to the possessor of them, which makes the one to be a good and the other an evil, whether seen or unseen by gods and men.

I had always admired the genius of Glaucon and Adeimantus, but on hearing these words I was quite delighted, and said: Sons of an illustrious father, that was not a bad beginning of the Elegiac verses which the admirer of *368* Glaucon made in honour of you after you had distinguished yourselves at the battle of Megara: –

'Sons of Ariston,' he sang, 'divine offspring of an illustrious hero.'

The epithet is very appropriate, for there is something truly divine in being able to argue as you have done for the superiority of injustice, and remaining unconvinced by your own arguments. And I do believe that you are not convinced – this I infer from your general character, for had I judged only from your speeches I should have B mistrusted you. But now, the greater my confidence in you, the greater is my difficulty in knowing what to say. For I am in a strait between two; on the one hand I feel that I am unequal to the task; and my inability is brought home to me by the fact that you were not satisfied with the answer which I made to Thrasymachus, proving, as I thought, the superiority which justice has over injustice. And yet I cannot refuse to help, while breath and speech remain to me; I am afraid that there would be an impiety in being present when justice is evil spoken of and not lifting up a hand in her defence. And therefore I had best give such help as I can.   C

Glaucon and the rest entreated me by all means not to let the question drop, but to proceed in the investigation. They wanted to arrive at the truth, first, about the nature of justice and injustice, and secondly, about their relative advantages, I told them, what I really thought, that the inquiry would be of a serious nature, and would require very good eyes. Seeing then, I said, that we are no great wits, I think that we had better adopt a method which I D may illustrate thus; suppose that a short-sighted person had been asked by some one to read small letters from a distance; and it occurred to some one else that they might be found in another place which was larger and in which the letters were larger – if they were the same and he could read the larger letters first, and then proceed to the lesser – this would have been thought a rare piece of good fortune.

Very true, said Adeimantus; but how does the illustration apply to our inquiry?   E

I will tell you, I replied; justice, which is the subject of our inquiry, is, as you know, sometimes spoken of as the virtue of an individual, and sometimes as the virtue of a State.

True, he replied.

And is not a State larger than an individual?

It is.

Then in the larger the quantity of justice is likely to be larger and more easily discernible. I propose therefore that we inquire into the nature of justice and injustice, first as they appear in the State, and secondly in the *369* individual, proceeding from the greater to the lesser and comparing them.

That, he said, is an excellent proposal.

And if we imagine the State in process of creation, we shall see the justice and injustice of the State in process of creation also.

I dare say.

When the State is completed there may be a hope that the object of our search will be more easily discovered.

Yes, far more easily.   B

But ought we to attempt to construct one? I said; for to do so, as I am inclined to think, will be a very serious task. Reflect therefore.

I have reflected, said Adeimantus, and am anxious that you should proceed.

A State, I said, arises, as I conceive, out of the needs of mankind; no one is self-sufficing, but all of us have many wants. Can any other origin of a State be imagined?

There can be no other.

C   Then, as we have many wants, and many persons are needed to supply them, one takes a helper for one purpose and another for another; and when these partners and helpers are gathered together in one habitation the body of inhabitants is termed a State.

True, he said.

And they exchange with one another, and one gives, and another receives, under the idea that the exchange will be for their good.

Very true.

Then, I said, let us begin and create in idea a State; and yet the true creator is necessity, who is the mother of our invention.

2

Republic (Continued): Justice and Virtue

Plato

The political vision of the *Republic* is striking in many of its details. We are told that the community of the ideal state is ruled by a class of *guardians*, that these guardians are to be drawn meritocratically from across the community, and that there is no reason why women should not join their ranks (this would have been unacceptable to many contemporaries of Plato). At the same time, we are told that it will be necessary for everyone to show allegiance to a myth or 'noble lie', according to which people can be categorized, without any chance of one's natural status changing, into people who contain gold, people who contain silver, and people who contain copper or iron (this is consistent with a somewhat fluid meritocracy, as Plato indicates that people of each kind can give birth to people of a different kind).

This ideal political state, Plato tells us, is divided into three parts, each corresponding to one of the types of metal mentioned in the guiding myth: the guardians proper, the auxiliaries, and workers (sometimes Plato includes the auxiliaries in the class of guardians). The guardians and auxiliaries are much smaller in number than the workers, and they alone are to receive a rigorous, tightly controlled education. To rule well, guardians must be philosophers. The auxiliary class constitutes a militia that works closely with the ruling guardians to protect the community from both internal and external threats.

Plato asks us to consider four important ethical properties or virtues of the good community. *Wisdom* is a property that communities can have only in virtue of the knowledge of guardians concerning how to best rule the community. *Courage* belongs, in the first instance, to the auxiliary arm, and it requires the militia to be trained to always retain a 'saving power of true opinion in conformity with law about real and false dangers' (explicitly a definition of courage, 430 B). Temperance, or self-control, is based in a uniform commitment, throughout the community, to having the best part (i.e. the guardians) rule the whole community. Finally, in a *just* state, the guardians are the only rulers, auxiliaries always follow the orders of the guardians, and the workers never attempt to go beyond the boundaries of their jobs. Plato offers a definition of justice as 'doing [only] one's own business', as befits one's nature (433 A–B).

After justice has been located in the community, Plato moves on to discuss the three parts of the soul, each of which is said to correspond to a part of the community. Reason corresponds to the guardians proper, spirit to the auxiliaries, and desire to the workers. Reason pursues knowledge and learning (more is said about this function of reason in the next selection of text from the *Republic*), but it also rules over the whole of a person's mind and is the only part that can do so from a vantage point where what is actually good for the whole can be ascertained. Desires, like the workers, have a wide range of different roles and interests. The desire for food is essential, but it is quite different from more cultivated desires that follow reason; in the virtuous person, particular desires, like workers, will never try to extend their influence beyond their proper roles.

Spirit is the most difficult of the three parts of the soul for us to understand. We are told that children and animals have spirit, yet spirit is also meant to be very much capable of listening to reason – in fact,

History of Ethics – Essential Readings with Commentary, First Edition. Edited by Daniel Star and Roger Crisp.
© 2020 John Wiley & Sons Ltd. Published 2020 by John Wiley & Sons Ltd.

Plato contends that it is a closer companion to reason than it is to desire (reflecting the way in which it is the role of the auxiliaries to directly assist the guardians proper). To understand spirit from our contemporary perspective, it can be helpful to focus on emotions like anger and fear, and the way we often do distinguish between irrational instances of such emotions (such as when another has not really threatened or hurt you, or when you are unable to be in the same room as spiders that you know to be harmless). Such emotions seem to be neither purely cognitive states (like a belief that Paris is the capital of France), nor pure feelings or desires. And while we might think infants and other animals can experience such emotions, we don't think they experience them in the particularly complex ways that rational human adults do. Plato illustrates how spirit is distinct from desire by considering the example of Leontius, who is angry at his own desires for propelling him forward to look at corpses (440 A).

The four virtues first considered in the community are supposed to have direct parallels in the individual. In the first instance, wisdom belongs to reason, courage to spirit (which learns when fear is and is not appropriate), and temperance to every part of the good soul (desires can be reasonable when they recognize they are to be ruled by reason). And just as morality in the community involves each part doing its job properly, according to its role, and not seeking to usurp the role of any other part, so morality in the individual must involve the parts of the mind working together in harmony, each properly doing its own job. Here, in fact, is the key to answering Glaucon's original challenge to Socrates to demonstrate that it is genuinely in a person's self-interest to lead a moral life: the psychic harmony that only the moral or just person can achieve is the true basis for a good life, and psychic disharmony, like political disharmony in the state, must always involve suffering.

Book III

[...]

Such, then, are our principles of nurture and education: Where would be the use of going into further details 412 B about the dances of our citizens, or about their hunting and coursing, their gymnastic and equestrian contests? For these all follow the general principle, and having found that, we shall have no difficulty in discovering them.

I dare say that there will be no difficulty.

Very good, I said; then what is the next question? Must we not ask who are to be rulers and who subjects?

Certainly.   C

There can be no doubt that the elder must rule the younger.

Clearly.

And that the best of these must rule.

That is also clear.

Now, are not the best husbandmen those who are most devoted to husbandry?

Yes.

And as we are to have the best of guardians for our city, must they not be those who have most the character of guardians?

Yes.

And to this end they ought to be wise and efficient, and to have a special care of the State?

True.   D

And a man will be most likely to care about that which he loves?

To be sure.

And he will be most likely to love that which he regards as having the same interests with himself, and that of which the good or evil fortune is supposed by him at any time most to affect his own?

Very true, he replied.

Then there must be a selection. Let us note among the guardians those who in their whole life show the greatest eagerness to do what is for the good of their country, and the greatest repugnance to do what is against her E interests.

Those are the right men.

And they will have to be watched at every age, in order that we may see whether they preserve their resolution, and never, under the influence either of force or enchantment, forget or cast off their sense of duty to the State.

How cast off? he said.

I will explain to you, I replied. A resolution may go out of a man's mind either with his will or against his will; with his will when he gets rid of a falsehood and learns better, against his will whenever he is deprived of a truth. 413

I understand, he said, the willing loss of a resolution; the meaning of the unwilling I have yet to learn.

Why, I said, do you not see that men are unwillingly deprived of good, and willingly of evil? Is not to have lost the truth an evil, and to possess the truth a good? and you would agree that to conceive things as they are is to possess the truth?

Yes, he replied; I agree with you in thinking that mankind are deprived of truth against their will.

And is not this involuntary deprivation caused either by theft, or force, or enchantment?   B

Still, he replied, I do not understand you.

I fear that I must have been talking darkly, like the tragedians. I only mean that some men are changed by persuasion and that others forget; argument steals away the hearts of one class, and time of the other; and this I call theft. Now you understand me?

Yes.

Those again who are forced, are those whom the violence of some pain or grief compels to change their opinion.

I understand, he said, and you are quite right.

And you would also acknowledge that the enchanted are those who change their minds either under the softer C influence of pleasure, or the sterner influence of fear?

Yes, he said; everything that deceives may be said to enchant.

Therefore, as I was just now saying, we must inquire who are the best guardians of their own conviction that what they think the interest of the State is to be the rule of their lives. We must watch them from their youth

D upwards, and make them perform actions in which they are most likely to forget or to be deceived, and he who
remembers and is not deceived is to be selected, and he who fails in the trial is to be rejected. That will be the way?
     Yes.

And there should also be toils and pains and conflicts prescribed for them, in which they will be made to give
further proof of the same qualities.
     Very right, he replied.

And then, I said, we must try them with enchantments – that is the third sort of test – and see what will be their
behaviour: like those who take colts amid noise and tumult to see if they are of a timid nature, so must we take
E our youth amid terrors of some kind, and again pass them into pleasures, and próve them more thoroughly than
gold is proved in the furnace, that we may discover whether they are armed against all enchantments, and of a
noble bearing always, good guardians of themselves and of the music which they have learned, and retaining under
all circumstances a rhythmical and harmonious nature, such as will be most serviceable to the individual and to the
State. And he who at every age, as boy and youth and in mature life, has come out of the trial victorious and pure,
414 shall be appointed a ruler and guardian of the State; he shall be honoured in life and death, and shall receive sep-
ulture and other memorials of honour, the greatest that we have to give. But him who fails, we must reject. I am
inclined to think that this is the sort of way in which our rulers and guardians should be chosen and appointed. I
speak generally, and not with any pretension to exactness.
     And, speaking generally, I agree with you, he said.
B   And perhaps the word 'guardian' in the fullest sense ought to be applied to this higher class only who preserve
us against foreign enemies and maintain peace among our citizens at home, that the one may not have the will, or
the others the power, to harm us. The young men whom we before called guardians may be more properly designated auxiliaries and supporters of the principles of the rulers.
     I agree with you, he said.

How then may we devise one of those needful falsehoods of which we lately spoke – just one royal lie which
C may deceive the rulers, if that be possible, and at any rate the rest of the city?
     What sort of lie? he said.

Nothing new, I replied; only an old Phoenician tale[1] of what has often occurred before now in other places, (as
the poets say, and have made the world believe,) though not in our time, and I do not know whether such an
event could ever happen again, or could now even be made probable, if it did.
     How your words seem to hesitate on your lips!
     You will not wonder, I replied, at my hesitation when you have heard.
     Speak, he said, and fear not.
D   Well then, I will speak, although I really know not how to look you in the face, or in what words to utter the
audacious fiction, which I propose to communicate gradually, first to the rulers, then to the soldiers, and lastly to
the people. They are to be told that their youth was a dream, and the education and training which they received
from us, an appearance only; in reality during all that time they were being formed and fed in the womb of the
E earth, where they themselves and their arms and appurtenances were manufactured; when they were completed,
the earth, their mother, sent them up; and so, their country being their mother and also their nurse, they are bound
to advise for her good, and to defend her against attacks, and her citizens they are to regard as children of the earth
and their own brothers.
     You had good reason, he said, to be ashamed of the lie which you were going to tell.
415   True, I replied, but there is more coming; I have only told you half. Citizens, we shall say to them in our tale,
you are brothers, yet God has framed you differently. Some of you have the power of command, and in the composition of these he has mingled gold, wherefore also they have the greatest honour; others he has made of silver,
to be auxiliaries; others again who are to be husbandmen and craftsmen he has composed of brass and iron; and the
species will generally be preserved in the children. But as all are of the same original stock, a golden parent will
B sometimes have a silver son, or a silver parent a golden son. And God proclaims as a first principle to the rulers,
and above all else, that there is nothing which they should so anxiously guard, or of which they are to be such good
guardians, as of the purity of the race. They should observe what elements mingle in their offspring; for if the son
C of a golden or silver parent has an admixture of brass and iron, then nature orders a transposition of ranks, and the
eye of the ruler must not be pitiful towards the child because he has to descend in the scale and become a husbandman

---

[1] Cp. Laws, 663 E.

or artisan, just as there may be sons of artisans who having an admixture of gold or silver in them are raised to honour, and become guardians or auxiliaries. For an oracle says that when a man of brass or iron guards the State, it will be destroyed. Such is the tale; is there any possibility of making our citizens believe in it?

Not in the present generation, he replied; there is no way of accomplishing this; but their sons may be made to D believe in the tale, and their sons' sons, and posterity after them.

I see the difficulty, I replied; yet the fostering of such a belief will make them care more for the city and for one another.

[...]

But where, amid all this, is justice? son of Ariston, tell me where. Now that our city has been made habitable, 427 D light a candle and search, and get your brother and Polemarchus and the rest of our friends to help, and let us see where in it we can discover justice and where injustice, and in what they differ from one another, and which of them the man who would be happy should have for his portion, whether seen or unseen by gods and men.

Nonsense, said Glaucon: did you not promise to search yourself, saying that for you not to help justice in her E need would be an impiety?

I do not deny that I said so; and as you remind me, I will be as good as my word; but you must join.

We will, he replied.

Well, then, I hope to make the discovery in this way: I mean to begin with the assumption that our State, if rightly ordered, is perfect.

That is most certain.

And being perfect, is therefore wise and valiant and temperate and just.

That is likewise clear.

And whichever of these qualities we find in the State, the one which is not found will be the residue?

Very good.   428

If there were four things, and we were searching for one of them, wherever it might be, the one sought for might be known to us from the first, and there would be no further trouble; or we might know the other three first, and then the fourth would clearly be the one left.

Very true, he said.

And is not a similar method to be pursued about the virtues, which are also four in number?

Clearly.

First among the virtues found in the State, wisdom comes into view, and in this I detect a certain peculiarity.   B

What is that?

The State which we have been describing is said to be wise as being good in counsel?

Very true.

And good counsel is clearly a kind of knowledge, for not by ignorance, but by knowledge, do men counsel well?

Clearly.

And the kinds of knowledge in a State are many and diverse?

Of course.

There is the knowledge of the carpenter; but is that the sort of knowledge which gives a city the title of wise and good in counsel?

Certainly not; that would only give a city the reputation of skill in carpentering.   C

Then a city is not to be called wise because possessing a knowledge which counsels for the best about wooden implements?

Certainly not.

Nor by reason of a knowledge which advises about brazen pots, he said, nor as possessing any other similar knowledge?

Not by reason of any of them, he said.

Nor yet by reason of a knowledge which cultivates the earth; that would give the city the name of agricultural?

Yes.

Well, I said, and is there any knowledge in our recently-founded State among any of the citizens which advises, D not about any particular thing in the State, but about the whole, and considers how a State can best deal with itself and with other States?

There certainly is.

And what is this knowledge, and among whom is it found? I asked.

It is the knowledge of the guardians, he replied, and is found among those whom we were just now describing as perfect guardians.

And what is the name which the city derives from the possession of this sort of knowledge?

The name of good in counsel and truly wise.

E   And will there be in our city more of these true guardians or more smiths?

The smiths, he replied, will be far more numerous.

Will not the guardians be the smallest of all the classes who receive a name from the profession of some kind of knowledge?

Much the smallest.

And so by reason of the smallest part or class, and of the knowledge which resides in this presiding and ruling
429 part of itself, the whole State, being thus constituted according to nature, will be wise; and this, which has the only knowledge worthy to be called wisdom, has been ordained by nature to be of all classes the least.

Most true.

Thus, then, I said, the nature and place in the State of one of the four virtues has somehow or other been discovered.

And, in my humble opinion, very satisfactorily discovered, he replied.

Again, I said, there is no difficulty in seeing the nature of courage, and in what part that quality resides which gives the name of courageous to the State.

How do you mean?

B   Why, I said, every one who calls any State courageous or cowardly, will be thinking of the part which fights and goes out to war on the State's behalf.

No one, he replied, would ever think of any other.

The rest of the citizens may be courageous or may be cowardly, but their courage or cowardice will not, as I conceive, have the effect of making the city either the one or the other.

Certainly not.

The city will be courageous in virtue of a portion of herself which preserves under all circumstances that opinion
C about the nature of things to be feared and not to be feared in which our legislator educated them; and this is what you term courage.

I should like to hear what you are saying once more, for I do not think that I perfectly understand you.

I mean that courage is a kind of salvation.

Salvation of what?

Of the opinion respecting things to be feared, what they are and of what nature, which the law implants through
D education; and I mean by the words 'under all circumstances' to intimate that in pleasure or in pain, or under the influence of desire or fear, a man preserves, and does not lose this opinion. Shall I give you an illustration?

If you please.

You know, I said, that dyers, when they want to dye wool for making the true sea-purple, begin by selecting their white colour first; this they prepare and dress with much care and pains, in order that the white ground may
E take the purple hue in full perfection. The dyeing then proceeds; and whatever is dyed in this manner becomes a fast colour, and no washing either with lyes or without them can take away the bloom. But, when the ground has not been duly prepared, you will have noticed how poor is the look either of purple or of any other colour.

Yes, he said; I know that they have a washed-out and ridiculous appearance.

430   Then now, I said, you will understand what our object was in selecting our soldiers, and educating them in music and gymnastic; we were contriving influences which would prepare them to take the dye of the laws in perfection, and the colour of their opinion about dangers and of every other opinion was to be indelibly fixed by their nurture and training, not to be washed away by such potent lyes as pleasure – mightier agent far in washing
B the soul than any soda or lye; or by sorrow, fear, and desire, the mightiest of all other solvents. And this sort of universal saving power of true opinion in conformity with law about real and false dangers I call and maintain to be courage, unless you disagree.

But I agree, he replied; for I suppose that you mean to exclude mere uninstructed courage, such as that of a wild beast or of a slave – this, in your opinion, is not the courage which the law ordains, and ought to have another name.

C   Most certainly.

Then I may infer courage to be such as you describe?

Why, yes, said I, you may, and if you add the words 'of a citizen', you will not be far wrong; – hereafter, if you like, we will carry the examination further, but at present we are seeking not for courage but justice; and for the purpose of our inquiry we have said enough.

You are right, he replied.

Two virtues remain to be discovered in the State – first, temperance, and then justice which is the end of our search.

D

Very true.

Now, can we find justice without troubling ourselves about temperance?

I do not know how that can be accomplished, he said, nor do I desire that justice should be brought to light and temperance lost sight of; and therefore I wish that you would do me the favour of considering temperance first.

Certainly, I replied, I should not be justified in refusing your request.

E

Then consider, he said.

Yes, I replied; I will; and as far as I can at present see, the virtue of temperance has more of the nature of harmony and symphony than the preceding.

How so? he asked.

Temperance, I replied, is the ordering or controlling of certain pleasures and desires; this is curiously enough implied in the saying of 'a man being his own master'; and other traces of the same notion may be found in language.

No doubt, he said.

There is something ridiculous in the expression 'master of himself'; for the master is also the servant and the servant the master; and in all these modes of speaking the same person is denoted.

431

Certainly.

The meaning is, I believe, that in the human soul there is a better and also a worse principle; and when the better has the worse under control, then a man is said to be master of himself; and this is a term of praise: but when, owing to evil education or association, the better principle, which is also the smaller, is overwhelmed by the greater mass of the worse – in this case he is blamed and is called the slave of self and unprincipled.

B

Yes, there is reason in that.

And now, I said, look at our newly-created State, and there you will find one of these two conditions realized; for the State, as you will acknowledge, may be justly called master of itself, if the words 'temperance' and 'self-mastery' truly express the rule of the better part over the worse.

Yes, he said, I see that what you say is true.

Let me further note that the manifold and complex pleasures and desires and pains are generally found in children and women and servants, and in the freemen so called who are of the lowest and more numerous class.

C

Certainly, he said.

Whereas the simple and moderate desires which follow reason, and are under the guidance of mind and true opinion, are to be found only in a few, and those the best born and best educated.

Very true.

These two, as you may perceive, have a place in our State; and the meaner desires of the many are held down by the virtuous desires and wisdom of the few.

D

That I perceive, he said.

Then if there be any city which may be described as master of its own pleasures and desires, and master of itself, ours may claim such a designation?

Certainly, he replied.

It may also be called temperate, and for the same reasons?

Yes.

And if there be any State in which rulers and subjects will be agreed as to the question who are to rule, that again will be our State?

E

Undoubtedly.

And the citizens being thus agreed among themselves, in which class will temperance be found – in the rulers or in the subjects?

In both, as I should imagine, he replied.

Do you observe that we were not far wrong in our guess that temperance was a sort of harmony?

Why so?

Why, because temperance is unlike courage and wisdom, each of which resides in a part only, the one making
432 the State wise and the other valiant; not so temperance, which extends to the whole, and runs through all the notes
of the scale, and produces a harmony of the weaker and the stronger and the middle class, whether you suppose
them to be stronger or weaker in wisdom or power or numbers or wealth, or anything else. Most truly then may
we deem temperance to be the agreement of the naturally superior and inferior, as to the right to rule of either,
both in states and individuals.

B   I entirely agree with you.

And so, I said, we may consider three out of the four virtues to have been discovered in our State. The last of
those qualities which make a state virtuous must be justice, if we only knew what that was.

The inference is obvious.

The time then has arrived, Glaucon, when, like huntsmen, we should surround the cover, and look sharp that
C justice does not steal away, and pass out of sight and escape us; for beyond a doubt she is somewhere in this country: watch therefore and strive to catch a sight of her, and if you see her first, let me know.

Would that I could! but you should regard me rather as a follower who has just eyes enough to see what you
show him – that is about as much as I am good for.

Offer up a prayer with me and follow.

I will, but you must show me the way.

Here is no path, I said, and the wood is dark and perplexing; still we must push on.

D   Let us push on.

Here I saw something: Halloo! I said, I begin to perceive a track, and I believe that the quarry will not escape.
Good news, he said.

Truly, I said, we are stupid fellows.

Why so?

Why, my good sir, at the beginning of our inquiry, ages ago, there was justice tumbling out at our feet, and we
never saw her; nothing could be more ridiculous. Like people who go about looking for what they have in their
E hands – that was the way with us – we looked not at what we were seeking, but at what was far off in the distance;
and therefore, I suppose, we missed her.

What do you mean?

I mean to say that in reality for a long time past we have been talking of justice, and have failed to recognize
her.

I grow impatient at the length of your exordium.

433   Well then, tell me, I said, whether I am right or not: You remember the original principle which we were
always laying down at the foundation of the State, that one man should practise one thing only, the thing to which
his nature was best adapted; – now justice is this principle or a part of it.

Yes, we often said that one man should do one thing only.

Further, we affirmed that justice was doing one's own business, and not being a busybody; we said so again and
B again, and many others have said the same to us.

Yes, we said so.

Then to do one's own business in a certain way may be assumed to be justice. Can you tell me whence I derive
this inference?

I cannot, but I should like to be told.

Because I think that this is the only virtue which remains in the State when the other virtues of temperance and
courage and wisdom are abstracted; and, that this is the ultimate cause and condition of the existence of all of them,
C and while remaining in them is also their preservative; and we were saying that if the three were discovered by us,
justice would be the fourth or remaining one.

That follows of necessity.

If we are asked to determine which of these four qualities by its presence contributes most to the excellence of
the State, whether the agreement of rulers and subjects, or the preservation in the soldiers of the opinion which
D the law ordains about the true nature of dangers, or wisdom and watchfulness in the rulers, or whether this other
which I am mentioning, and which is found in children and women, slave and freeman, artisan, ruler, subject, – the quality, I mean, of every one doing his own work, and not being a busybody, would claim the
palm – the question is not so easily answered.

Certainly, he replied, there would be a difficulty in saying which.

Then the power of each individual in the State to do his own work appears to compete with the other political virtues, wisdom, temperance, courage.

Yes, he said.

And the virtue which enters into this competition is justice?   *E*

Exactly.

Let us look at the question from another point of view: Are not the rulers in a State those to whom you would entrust the office of determining suits at law?

Certainly.

And are suits decided on any other ground but that a man may neither take what is another's, nor be deprived of what is his own?

Yes; that is their principle.

Which is a just principle?

Yes.

Then on this view also justice will be admitted to be the having and doing what is a man's own, and belongs to him?

Very true.   *434*

Think, now, and say whether you agree with me or not. Suppose a carpenter to be doing the business of a cobbler, or a cobbler of a carpenter; and suppose them to exchange their implements or their duties, or the same person to be doing the work of both, or whatever be the change; do you think that any great harm would result to the State?

Not much.

But when the cobbler or any other man whom nature designed to be a trader, having his heart lifted up by wealth *B* or strength or the number of his followers, or any like advantage, attempts to force his way into the class of warriors, or a warrior into that of legislators and guardians, for which he is unfitted, and either to take the implements or the duties of the other; or when one man is trader, legislator, and warrior all in one, then I think you will agree with me in saying that this interchange and this meddling of one with another is the ruin of the State.

Most true.

Seeing then, I said, that there are three distinct classes, any meddling of one with another, or the change of one into another, is the greatest harm to the State, and may be most justly termed evil-doing?   *C*

Precisely.

And the greatest degree of evil-doing to one's own city would be termed by you injustice?

Certainly.

This then is injustice; and on the other hand when the trader, the auxiliary, and the guardian each do their own business, that is justice, and will make the city just.

I agree with you.   *D*

We will not, I said, be over-positive as yet; but if, on trial, this conception of justice be verified in the individual as well as in the State, there will be no longer any room for doubt; if it be not verified, we must have a fresh inquiry. First let us complete the old investigation, which we began, as you remember, under the impression that, if we could previously examine justice on the larger scale, there would be less difficulty in discerning her in the individual. That larger example appeared to be the State, and accordingly we constructed as good a one as we *E* could, knowing well that in the good State justice would be found. Let the discovery which we made be now applied to the individual – if they agree, we shall be satisfied; or, if there be a difference in the individual, we will come back to the State and have another trial of the theory. The friction of the two when rubbed together may *435* possibly strike a light in which justice will shine forth, and the vision which is then revealed we will fix in our souls.

That will be in regular course; let us do as you say.

I proceeded to ask: When two things, a greater and less, are called by the same name, are they like or unlike in so far as they are called the same?

Like, he replied.

The just man then, if we regard the idea of justice only, will be like the just State?   *B*

He will.

And a State was thought by us to be just when the three classes in the State severally did their own business; and also thought to be temperate and valiant and wise by reason of certain other affections and qualities of these same classes?

True, he said.

C   And so of the individual; we may assume that he has the same three principles in his own soul which are found
     in the State; and he may be rightly described in the same terms, because he is affected in the same manner?
        Certainly, he said.
        Once more then, O my friend, we have alighted upon an easy question – whether the soul has these three
     principles or not?
        An easy question! Nay, rather, Socrates, the proverb holds that hard is the good.
D   Very true, I said; and I do not think that the method which we are employing is at all adequate to the accurate
     solution of this question; the true method is another and a longer one. Still we may arrive at a solution not below
     the level of the previous inquiry.
        May we not be satisfied with that? he said; – under the circumstances, I am quite content.
        I too, I replied, shall be extremely well satisfied.
        Then faint not in pursuing the speculation, he said.
E   Must we not acknowledge, I said, that in each of us there are the same principles and habits which there are in
     the State; and that from the individual they pass into the State? – how else can they come there? Take the quality
     of passion or spirit; – it would be ridiculous to imagine that this quality, when found in States, is not derived from
     the individuals who are supposed to possess it, e.g. the Thracians, Scythians, and in general the northern nations;
     and the same may be said of the love of knowledge, which is the special characteristic of our part of the world, or
436 of the love of money, which may, with equal truth, be attributed to the Phoenicians and Egyptians.
        Exactly so, he said.
        There is no difficulty in understanding this.
        None whatever.
        But the question is not quite so easy when we proceed to ask whether these principles are three or one; whether,
     that is to say, we learn with one part of our nature, are angry with another, and with a third part desire the satisfac-
B   tion of our natural appetites; or whether the whole soul comes into play in each sort of action – to determine that
     is the difficulty.
        Yes, he said; there lies the difficulty.
C   Then let us now try and determine whether they are the same or different.
        How can we? he asked.
        I replied as follows: The same thing clearly cannot act or be acted upon in the same part or in relation to the
     same thing at the same time, in contrary ways; and therefore whenever this contradiction occurs in things appar-
     ently the same, we know that they are really not the same, but different.
        Good.
        For example, I said, can the same thing be at rest and in motion at the same time in the same part?
        Impossible.
        Still, I said, let us have a more precise statement of terms, lest we should hereafter fall out by the way. Imagine
     the case of a man who is standing and also moving his hands and his head, and suppose a person to say that one
     and the same person is in motion and at rest at the same moment – to such a mode of speech we should object,
D   and should rather say that one part of him is in motion while another is at rest.
        Very true.
        And suppose the objector to refine still further, and to draw the nice distinction that not only parts of tops, but
     whole tops, when they spin round with their pegs fixed on the spot, are at rest and in motion at the same time (and
     he may say the same of anything which revolves in the same spot), his objection would not be admitted by us,
E   because in such cases things are not at rest and in motion in the same parts of themselves; we should rather say that
     they have both an axis and a circumference; and that the axis stands still, for there is no deviation from the perpen-
     dicular; and that the circumference goes round. But if, while revolving, the axis inclines either to the right or left,
     forwards or backwards, then in no point of view can they be at rest.
        That is the correct mode of describing them, he replied.
        Then none of these objections will confuse us, or incline us to believe that the same thing at the same time, in
437 the same part or in relation to the same thing, can act or be acted upon in contrary ways.
        Certainly not, according to my way of thinking.
        Yet, I said, that we may not be compelled to examine all such objections, and prove at length that they are
     untrue, let us assume their absurdity, and go forward on the understanding that hereafter, if this assumption turn
     out to be untrue, all the consequences which follow shall be withdrawn.

Yes, he said, that will be the best way.

Well, I said, would you not allow that assent and dissent, desire and aversion, attraction and repulsion, are all of B them opposites, whether they are regarded as active or passive (for that makes no difference in the fact of their opposition)?

Yes, he said, they are opposites.

Well, I said, and hunger and thirst, and the desires in general, and again willing and wishing, – all these you would refer to the classes already mentioned. You would say – would you not? – that the soul of him who desires C is seeking after the object of his desire; or that he is drawing to himself the thing which he wishes to possess: or again, when a person wants anything to be given him, his mind, longing for the realization of his desire, intimates his wish to have it by a nod of assent, as if he had been asked a question?

Very true.

And what would you say of unwillingness and dislike and the absence of desire; should not these be referred to the opposite class of repulsion and rejection?

Certainly.

Admitting this to be true of desire generally, let us suppose a particular class of desires, and out of these we will select hunger and thirst, as they are termed, which are the most obvious of them?

Let us take that class, he said.

The object of one is food, and of the other drink?

Yes.

And here comes the point: is not thirst the desire which the soul has of drink, and of drink only; not of drink qualified by anything else; for example, warm or cold, or much or little, or, in a word, drink of any particular sort: but if the thirst be accompanied by heat, then the desire is of cold drink; or, if accompanied by cold, then of warm E drink; or, if the thirst be excessive, then the drink which is desired will be excessive; or, if not great, the quantity of drink will also be small: but thirst pure and simple will desire drink pure and simple, which is the natural satisfaction of thirst, as food is of hunger?

Yes, he said; the simple desire is, as you say, in every case of the simple object, and the qualified desire of the qualified object.

But here a confusion may arise; and I should wish to guard against an opponent starting up and saying that no 438 man desires drink only, but good drink, or food only, but good food; for good is the universal object of desire, and thirst, being a desire, will necessarily be thirst after good drink; and the same is true of every other desire.

Yes, he replied, the opponent might have something to say.

Nevertheless I should still maintain, that of relatives some have a quality attached to either term of the relation; B others are simple and have their correlatives simple.

I do not know what you mean.

Well, you know of course that the greater is relative to the less?

Certainly.

And the much greater to the much less?

Yes.

And the sometime greater to the sometime less, and the greater that is to be to the less that is to be?

Certainly, he said.

And so of more and less, and of other correlative terms, such as the double and the half, or again, the heavier C and the lighter, the swifter and the slower; and of hot and cold, and of any other relatives; – is not this true of all of them?

Yes.

And does not the same principle hold in the sciences? The object of science is knowledge (assuming that to be the true definition), but the object of a particular science is a particular kind of knowledge; I mean, for example, D that the science of house-building is a kind of knowledge which is defined and distinguished from other kinds and is therefore termed architecture.

Certainly.

Because it has a particular quality which no other has?

Yes.

And it has this particular quality because it has an object of a particular kind; and this is true of the other arts and sciences?

Yes.

Now, then, if I have made myself clear, you will understand my original meaning in what I said about relatives. My meaning was, that if one term of a relation is taken alone, the other is taken alone; if one term is qualified, the

E other is also qualified. I do not mean to say that relatives may not be disparate, or that the science of health is healthy, or of disease necessarily diseased, or that the sciences of good and evil are therefore good and evil; but only that, when the term science is no longer used absolutely, but has a qualified object which in this case is the nature of health and disease, it becomes defined, and is hence called not merely science, but the science of medicine.

I quite understand, and I think as you do.

439 Would you not say that thirst is one of these essentially relative terms, having clearly a relation –

Yes, thirst is relative to drink.

And a certain kind of thirst is relative to a certain kind of drink; but thirst taken alone is neither of much nor little, nor of good nor bad, nor of any particular kind of drink, but of drink only?

Certainly.

B Then the soul of the thirsty one, in so far as he is thirsty, desires only drink; for this he yearns and tries to obtain it?

That is plain.

And if you suppose something which pulls a thirsty soul away from drink, that must be different from the thirsty principle which draws him like a beast to drink; for, as we were saying, the same thing cannot at the same time with the same part of itself act in contrary ways about the same.

Impossible.

No more than you can say that the hands of the archer push and pull the bow at the same time, but what you say is that one hand pushes and the other pulls.

C Exactly so, he replied.

And might a man be thirsty, and yet unwilling to drink?

Yes, he said, it constantly happens.

And in such a case what is one to say? Would you not say that there was something in the soul bidding a man to drink, and something else forbidding him, which is other and stronger than the principle which bids him?

I should say so.

D And the forbidding principle is derived from reason, and that which bids and attracts proceeds from passion and disease?

Clearly.

Then we may fairly assume that they are two, and that they differ from one another; the one with which a man reasons, we may call the rational principle of the soul, the other, with which he loves and hungers and thirsts and feels the flutterings of any other desire, may be termed the irrational or appetitive, the ally of sundry pleasures and satisfactions?

E Yes, he said, we may fairly assume them to be different.

Then let us finally determine that there are two principles existing in the soul. And what of passion, or spirit? Is it a third, or akin to one of the preceding?

I should be inclined to say – akin to desire.

Well, I said, there is a story which I remember to have heard, and in which I put faith. The story is, that Leontius, the son of Aglaion, coming up one day from the Piraeus, under the north wall on the outside, observed some dead bodies lying on the ground at the place of execution. He felt a desire to see them, and also a dread and

440 abhorrence of them; for a time he struggled and covered his eyes, but at length the desire got the better of him; and forcing them open, he ran up to the dead bodies, saying, Look, ye wretches, take your fill of the fair sight.

I have heard the story myself, he said.

The moral of the tale is, that anger at times goes to war with desire, as though they were two distinct things.

Yes; that is the meaning, he said.

B And are there not many other cases in which we observe that when a man's desires violently prevail over his reason, he reviles himself, and is angry at the violence within him, and that in this struggle, which is like the struggle of factions in a State, his spirit is on the side of his reason; – but for the passionate or spirited element to take part with the desires when reason decides that she should not be opposed,[1] is a sort of thing which I believe that you never observed occurring in yourself, nor, as I should imagine, in any one else?

[1] Reading μὴ δεῖν ἀντιπράττειν, without a comma after δεῖν.

Certainly not.

Suppose that a man thinks he has done a wrong to another, the nobler he is the less able is he to feel indignant C at any suffering, such as hunger, or cold, or any other pain which the injured person may inflict upon him – these he deems to be just, and, as I say, his anger refuses to be excited by them.

True, he said.

But when he thinks that he is the sufferer of the wrong, then he boils and chafes, and is on the side of what he believes to be justice; and because he suffers hunger or cold or other pain he is only the more determined to persevere D and conquer. His noble spirit will not be quelled until he either slays or is slain; or until he hears the voice of the shepherd, that is, reason, bidding his dog bark no more.

The illustration is perfect, he replied; and in our State, as we were saying, the auxiliaries were to be dogs, and to hear the voice of the rulers, who are their shepherds.

I perceive, I said, that you quite understand me; there is, however, a further point which I wish you to consider.

What point? E

You remember that passion or spirit appeared at first sight to be a kind of desire, but now we should say quite the contrary; for in the conflict of the soul spirit is arrayed on the side of the rational principle.

Most assuredly.

But a further question arises: Is passion different from reason also, or only a kind of reason; in which latter case, instead of three principles in the soul, there will only be two, the rational and the concupiscent; or rather, as the State 441 was composed of three classes, traders, auxiliaries, counsellors, so may there not be in the individual soul a third element which is passion or spirit, and when not corrupted by bad education is the natural auxiliary of reason?

Yes, he said, there must be a third.

Yes, I replied, if passion, which has already been shown to be different from desire, turn out also to be different from reason.

But that is easily proved: – We may observe even in young children that they are full of spirit almost as soon as they are born, whereas some of them never seem to attain to the use of reason, and most of them late enough. B

Excellent, I said, and you may see passion equally in brute animals, which is a further proof of the truth of what you are saying. And we may once more appeal to the words of Homer, which have been already quoted by us,

He smote his breast, and thus rebuked his soul[1]; for in this verse Homer has clearly supposed the power which C reasons about the better and worse to be different from the unreasoning anger which is rebuked by it.

Very true, he said.

And so, after much tossing, we have reached land, and are fairly agreed that the same principles which exist in the State exist also in the individual, and that they are three in number.

Exactly.

Must we not then infer that the individual is wise in the same way, and in virtue of the same quality which makes the State wise?

Certainly.

Also that the same quality which constitutes courage in the State constitutes courage in the individual, and that D both the State and the individual bear the same relation to all the other virtues?

Assuredly.

And the individual will be acknowledged by us to be just in the same way in which the State is just?

That follows of course.

We cannot but remember that the justice of the State consisted in each of the three classes doing the work of its E own class?

We are not very likely to have forgotten, he said.

We must recollect that the individual in whom the several qualities of his nature do their own work will be just, and will do his own work?

Yes, he said, we must remember that too.

And ought not the rational principle, which is wise, and has the care of the whole soul, to rule, and the passionate or spirited principle to be the subject and ally?

Certainly.

[1] Od. xx. 17, quoted supra, III. 390 D.

And, as we were saying, the united influence of music and gymnastic will bring them into accord, nerving and sustaining the reason with noble words and lessons, and moderating and soothing and civilizing the wildness of
442 passion by harmony and rhythm?

Quite true, he said.

And these two, thus nurtured and educated, and having learned truly to know their own functions, will rule[1] over the concupiscent, which in each of us is the largest part of the soul and by nature most insatiable of gain; over this they will keep guard, lest, waxing great and strong with the fullness of bodily pleasures, as they are termed, the
B concupiscent soul, no longer confined to her own sphere, should attempt to enslave and rule those who are not her natural-born subjects, and overturn the whole life of man?

Very true, he said.

Both together will they not be the best defenders of the whole soul and the whole body against attacks from without; the one counselling, and the other fighting under his leader, and courageously executing his commands and counsels?

True.

C And he is to be deemed courageous whose spirit retains in pleasure and in pain the commands of reason about what he ought or ought not to fear?

Right, he replied.

And him we call wise who has in him that little part which rules, and which proclaims these commands; that part too being supposed to have a knowledge of what is for the interest of each of the three parts and of the whole?

Assuredly.

And would you not say that he is temperate who has these same elements in friendly harmony, in whom the
D one ruling principle of reason, and the two subject ones of spirit and desire are equally agreed that reason ought to rule, and do not rebel?

Certainly, he said, that is the true account of temperance whether in the State or individual.

And surely, I said, we have explained again and again how and by virtue of what quality a man will be just.

That is very certain.

And is justice dimmer in the individual, and is her form different, or is she the same which we found her to be in the State?

There is no difference in my opinion, he said.

E Because, if any doubt is still lingering in our minds, a few commonplace instances will satisfy us of the truth of what I am saying.

What sort of instances do you mean?

443 If the case is put to us, must we not admit that the just State, or the man who is trained in the principles of such a State, will be less likely than the unjust to make away with a deposit of gold or silver? Would any one deny this?

No one, he replied.

Will the just man or citizen ever be guilty of sacrilege or theft, or treachery either to his friends or to his country?

Never.

Neither will he ever break faith where there have been oaths or agreements?

Impossible.

No one will be less likely to commit adultery, or to dishonour his father and mother, or to fail in his religious duties?

No one.

B And the reason is that each part of him is doing its own business, whether in ruling or being ruled?

Exactly so.

Are you satisfied then that the quality which makes such men and such states is justice, or do you hope to discover some other?

Not I, indeed.

---

[1] Reading προστατήσετον with Bekker; or, if the reading προστήσετον, which is found in the MSS., be adopted, then the nominative must be supplied from the previous sentence: 'Music and gymnastic will place in authority over ...' This is very awkward, and the awkwardness is increased by the necessity of changing the subject at τηρήσετον.

Then our dream has been realized; and the suspicion which we entertained at the beginning of our work of construction, that some divine power must have conducted us to a primary form of justice, has now been verified?   *C*

Yes, certainly.

And the division of labour which required the carpenter and the shoemaker and the rest of the citizens to be doing each his own business, and not another's, was a shadow of justice, and for that reason it was of use?

Clearly.

But in reality justice was such as we were describing, being concerned however, not with the outward man, but with the inward, which is the true self and concernment of man: for the just man does not permit the several ele- *D* ments within him to interfere with one another, or any of them to do the work of others, – he sets in order his own inner life, and is his own master and his own law, and at peace with himself; and when he has bound together the three principles within him, which may be compared to the higher, lower, and middle notes of the scale, and the intermediate intervals – when he has bound all these together, and is no longer many, but has become one *E* entirely temperate and perfectly adjusted nature, then he proceeds to act, if he has to act, whether in a matter of property, or in the treatment of the body, or in some affair of politics or private business; always thinking and calling that which preserves and cooperates with this harmonious condition, just and good action, and the knowledge which presides over it, wisdom, and that which at any time impairs this condition, he will call unjust action, and *444* the opinion which presides over it ignorance.

You have said the exact truth, Socrates.

Very good; and if we were to affirm that we had discovered the just man and the just State, and the nature of justice in each of them, we should not be telling a falsehood?

Most certainly not.

May we say so, then?

Let us say so.

And now, I said, injustice has to be considered.

Clearly.

Must not injustice be a strife which arises among the three principles – a meddlesomeness, and interference, and *B* rising up of a part of the soul against the whole, an assertion of unlawful authority, which is made by a rebellious subject against a true prince, of whom he is the natural vassal, – what is all this confusion and delusion but injustice, and intemperance and cowardice and ignorance, and every form of vice?

Exactly so.

And if the nature of justice and injustice be known, then the meaning of acting unjustly and being unjust, or, *C* again, of acting justly, will also be perfectly clear?

What do you mean? he said.

Why, I said, they are like disease and health; being in the soul just what disease and health are in the body.

How so? he said.

Why, I said, that which is healthy causes health, and that which is unhealthy causes disease.

Yes.

And just actions cause justice, and unjust actions cause injustice?   *D*

That is certain.

And the creation of health is the institution of a natural order and government of one by another in the parts of the body; and the creation of disease is the production of a state of things at variance with this natural order?

True.

And is not the creation of justice the institution of a natural order and government of one by another in the parts of the soul, and the creation of injustice the production of a state of things at variance with the natural order?

Exactly so, he said.

Then virtue is the health and beauty and well-being of the soul, and vice the disease and weakness and deformity *E* of the same?

True.

And do not good practices lead to virtue, and evil practices to vice?

Assuredly.

Still our old question of the comparative advantage of justice and injustice has not been answered: Which is the *445* more profitable, to be just and act justly and practise virtue, whether seen or unseen of gods and men, or to be unjust and act unjustly, if only unpunished and unreformed?

In my judgement, Socrates, the question has now become ridiculous. We know that, when the bodily constitution is gone, life is no longer endurable, though pampered with all kinds of meats and drinks, and having all wealth and all power; and shall we be told that when the very essence of the vital principle is undermined and corrupted,

B life is still worth having to a man, if only he be allowed to do whatever he likes with the single exception that he is not to acquire justice and virtue, or to escape from injustice and vice; assuming them both to be such as we have described?

Yes, I said, the question is, as you say, ridiculous. Still, as we are near the spot at which we may see the truth in the clearest manner with our own eyes, let us not faint by the way.

Certainly not, he replied.

C   Come up hither, I said, and behold the various forms of vice, those of them, I mean, which are worth looking at.

I am following you, he replied: proceed.

I said, The argument seems to have reached a height from which, as from some tower of speculation, a man may look down and see that virtue is one, but that the forms of vice are innumerable; there being four special ones which are deserving of note.

What do you mean? he said.

I mean, I replied, that there appear to be as many forms of the soul as there are distinct forms of the State.

How many?

D   There are five of the State, and five of the soul, I said.

What are they?

The first, I said, is that which we have been describing, and which may be said to have two names, monarchy and aristocracy, accordingly as rule is exercised by one distinguished man or by many.

True, he replied.

E   But I regard the two names as describing one form only; for whether the government is in the hands of one or many, if the governors have been trained in the manner which we have supposed, the fundamental laws of the State will be maintained.

That is true, he replied.

3

Republic (Continued): The Good

Plato

This is probably the most widely read section of text in Plato's entire corpus. It makes for enjoyable reading and is the place where commentators most often begin when they wish to discuss the famous and historically influential 'Theory of the Forms' (this is not a term that Plato himself uses, but we see such a theory ascribed to Plato in Aristotle's *Metaphysics*). Within the context of the *Republic,* this is really less a fully fledged theory than an important component of the third of three similes. It is presented as part of the story of the Cave, which itself follows discussion of the Sun, and the Line.

The Sun is a simile for the Good. Just as the Sun enables us to visually perceive objects in the world, so the Good enables us to come to possess knowledge in the intelligible realm. Furthermore, just as the Sun nourishes objects in the visible realm, so the Good confers existence on the objects of knowledge. If this last claim seems obscure, think about how hard it is to explain what it is for something to be a flower, for instance, without fixing your mind on what a *good*, healthy flower is like. We will see that Aristotle also thinks that individual things aim to be good; but, unlike Plato, he does not think this general fact licenses any move to focus on some purely good, merely ideal form that we might term *the* Good.

The Line, divided into four parts, is a difficult device to understand. It can be approached in two different ways. We can either focus on the proportions and relations between different parts of the Line, or on the ascending hierarchy in cognitive states up to the ideal state of knowledge, represented by the fourth of the four sections of the Line. We are first asked to imagine a Line divided into two parts of unequal lengths, a smaller part representing the visible realm and a larger part representing the intelligible realm, and to then imagine each of these two parts similarly divided again. Shadows and reflections, in the smallest of the four parts, are said to stand in a similar relation to concrete physical objects (in the second part) as the imperfect shapes that we entertain when doing geometry (in the third part) stand in to mathematical first principles (in the fourth part). We are told that a hierarchy of epistemic states correspond to the four sections of the Line: conjecture, confidence, thought, and knowledge. Seeing a shadow, we might *conjecture* that a physical object of a certain shape casts this shadow; turning to face the object, we might *confidently believe* that a particular object confronts us; *thinking* about this object, we might construe it as being of a certain type (or form); and, finally, focusing on the type the object instantiates, we might come to *know* the type (or form) itself. A crucial part of the picture presented here is that genuine knowledge makes no use of anything perceptible (511 C).

In some important respects, the story of the Cave repeats ideas encountered when we were introduced to the Sun and the Line. There is a recasting here of the hierarchy of epistemic states through which it is possible for the mind to ascend, and the idea that light (the Good) is the ground of both knowledge and existence recurs (517 B–C). But it is only when we get to this story that we find a dramatic narrative that provides us with a picture of the human predicament. Two aspects of this predicament are particularly noteworthy. First, the story indicates that people typically are slaves of convention, confusing shadows with

History of Ethics – Essential Readings with Commentary, First Edition. Edited by Daniel Star and Roger Crisp.
© 2020 John Wiley & Sons Ltd. Published 2020 by John Wiley & Sons Ltd.

reality. Even when they manage to see the light, they find themselves strongly attracted back to the world of conventional beliefs. More positively, we are told, second, that knowledge of the Good – which it seems possible, with great difficulty, to achieve – is a necessary condition for proper moral conduct, both private and political.

One of the most difficult and interesting problems that suggests itself to us when we read the *Republic* is that of deciding how three things are meant to fit together: (i) the partial rejection and partial acceptance of conventional morality (while the story of the Cave seems to suggest that convention is to be left behind, there are other places in the text where Plato makes it clear that the moral individual will not steal, will not murder, etc.; that is, will act in ways that conventional morality is right to say he should); (ii) the highly abstract metaphysical picture of ascent to knowledge of the Good provided in the story of the Cave; and (iii) the psychological story of the moral individual that we saw in the previous extract. Why should we think the individual whose soul is in a harmonious state will act morally (by standards that we can accept)? Are we meant to conclude that people act immorally because of insatiable desires (when their souls are out of harmony), or because of lack of knowledge of the Good? How is achieving psychic harmony meant to be related to the ascent to knowledge of the Good in itself?

These questions remain good ones to bear in mind when reading more of the text of the *Republic* than has been provided here, but most commentators have not found that further reading has allowed them to answer them to their own complete satisfaction. One may suspect that this is because Plato's apparent solution to Glaucon's challenge, while heroically constructed, manages to be an apparent solution only by at once attempting to radically internalize morality in one direction (making it about harmony within the individual) and radically externalize it in another (making it otherworldly and ineffable).

Book VI

And so with pain and toil we have reached the end of one subject, but more remains to be discussed; – how and by what studies and pursuits will the saviours of the constitution be created, and at what ages are they to apply themselves to their several studies?

Certainly.

I omitted the troublesome business of the possession of women, and the procreation of children, and the appoint- 502 D ment of the rulers, because I knew that the perfect State would be eyed with jealousy and was difficult of attainment; but that piece of cleverness was not of much service to me, for I had to discuss them all the same. The women and E children are now disposed of, but the other question of the rulers must be investigated from the very beginning. We were saying, as you will remember, that they were to be lovers of their country, tried by the test of pleasures and 503 pains, and neither in hardships, nor in dangers, nor at any other critical moment were to lose their patriotism – he was to be rejected who failed, but he who always came forth pure, like gold tried in the refiner's fire, was to be made a ruler, and to receive honours and rewards in life and after death. This was the sort of thing which was being said, and then the argument turned aside and veiled her face; not liking to stir the question which has now arisen. B

I perfectly remember, he said.

Yes, my friend, I said, and I then shrank from hazarding the bold word; but now let me dare to say – that the perfect guardian must be a philosopher.

Yes, he said, let that be affirmed.

And do not suppose that there will be many of them; for the gifts which were deemed by us to be essential rarely grow together; they are mostly found in shreds and patches.

What do you mean? he said. C

You are aware, I replied, that quick intelligence, memory, sagacity, cleverness, and similar qualities, do not often grow together, and that persons who possess them and are at the same time high-spirited and magnanimous are not so constituted by nature as to live orderly and in a peaceful and settled manner; they are driven any way by their impulses, and all solid principle goes out of them.

Very true, he said.

On the other hand, those steadfast natures which can better be depended upon, which in a battle are impregna- D ble to fear and immovable, are equally immovable when there is anything to be learned; they are always in a torpid state, and are apt to yawn and go to sleep over any intellectual toil.

Quite true.

And yet we were saying that both qualities were necessary in those to whom the higher education is to be imparted, and who are to share in any office or command.

Certainly, he said.

And will they be a class which is rarely found?

Yes, indeed.

Then the aspirant must not only be tested in those labours and dangers and pleasures which we mentioned E before, but here is another kind of probation which we did not mention – he must be exercised also in many kinds of knowledge, to see whether the soul will be able to endure the highest of all, or will faint under them, as in any 504 other studies and exercises.

Yes, he said, you are quite right in testing him. But what do you mean by the highest of all knowledge?

You may remember, I said, that we divided the soul into three parts; and distinguished the several natures of justice, temperance, courage, and wisdom?

Indeed, he said, if I had forgotten, I should not deserve to hear more.

And do you remember the word of caution which preceded the discussion of them?[1]

To what do you refer?

We were saying, if I am not mistaken, that he who wanted to see them in their perfect beauty must take a longer B and more circuitous way, at the end of which they would appear; but that we could add on a popular exposition of them on a level with the discussion which had preceded. And you replied that such an exposition would be enough for you, and so the inquiry was continued in what to me seemed to be a very inaccurate manner; whether you were satisfied or not, it is for you to say.

---

[1] Cp. IV. 435 D.

Yes, he said, I thought and the others thought that you gave us a fair measure of truth.

C But, my friend, I said, a measure of such things which in any degree falls short of the whole truth is not fair measure; for nothing imperfect is the measure of anything, although persons are too apt to be contented and think that they need search no further.

Not an uncommon case when people are indolent.

Yes, I said; and there cannot be any worse fault in a guardian of the State and of the laws.

True.

D The guardian, then, I said, must be required to take the longer circuit, and toil at learning as well as at gymnastics, or he will never reach the highest knowledge of all which, as we were just now saying, is his proper calling.

What, he said, is there a knowledge still higher than this – higher than justice and the other virtues?

Yes, I said, there is. And of the virtues too we must behold not the outline merely, as at present – nothing short

E of the most finished picture should satisfy us. When little things are elaborated with an infinity of pains, in order that they may appear in their full beauty and utmost clearness, how ridiculous that we should not think the highest truths worthy of attaining the highest accuracy!

A right noble thought[2]; but do you suppose that we shall refrain from asking you what is this highest knowledge?

Nay, I said, ask if you will; but I am certain that you have heard the answer many times, and now you either do

505 not understand me or, as I rather think, you are disposed to be troublesome; for you have often been told that the idea of good is the highest knowledge, and that all other things become useful and advantageous only by their use of this. You can hardly be ignorant that of this I was about to speak, concerning which, as you have often heard

B me say, we know so little; and, without which, any other knowledge or possession of any kind will profit us nothing. Do you think that the possession of all other things is of any value if we do not possess the good? or the knowledge of all other things if we have no knowledge of beauty and goodness?

Assuredly not.

You are further aware that most people affirm pleasure to be the good, but the finer sort of wits say it is knowledge?

Yes.

And you are aware too that the latter cannot explain what they mean by knowledge, but are obliged after all to say knowledge of the good?

How ridiculous!

C Yes, I said, that they should begin by reproaching us with our ignorance of the good, and then presume our knowledge of it – for the good they define to be knowledge of the good, just as if we understood them when they use the term 'good' – this is of course ridiculous.

Most true, he said.

And those who make pleasure their good are in equal perplexity; for they are compelled to admit that there are bad pleasures as well as good.

Certainly.

And therefore to acknowledge that bad and good are the same?

D True.

There can be no doubt about the numerous difficulties in which this question is involved.

There can be none.

Further, do we not see that many are willing to do or to have or to seem to be what is just and honourable without the reality; but no one is satisfied with the appearance of good – the reality is what they seek; in the case of the good, appearance is despised by every one.

Very true, he said.

506 Of this, then, which every soul of man pursues and makes the end of all his actions, having a presentiment that there is such an end, and yet hesitating because neither knowing the nature nor having the same assurance of this as of other things, and therefore losing whatever good there is in other things, – of a principle such and so great as this ought the best men in our State, to whom everything is entrusted, to be in the darkness of ignorance?

Certainly not, he said.

---

[2] Or, separating καὶ μάλα from ἄξιον, 'True, he said, and a noble thought': or ἄξιον τὸ διανόημα may be a gloss.

I am sure, I said, that he who does not know how the beautiful and the just are likewise good will be but a sorry guardian of them; and I suspect that no one who is ignorant of the good will have a true knowledge of them.

That, he said, is a shrewd suspicion of yours.

And if we only have a guardian who has this knowledge our State will be perfectly ordered? B

Of course, he replied; but I wish that you would tell me whether you conceive this supreme principle of the good to be knowledge or pleasure, or different from either?

Aye, I said, I knew all along that a fastidious gentleman[3] like you would not be contented with the thoughts of other people about these matters.

True, Socrates; but I must say that one who like you has passed a lifetime in the study of philosophy should not be always repeating the opinions of others, and never telling his own. C

Well, but has any one a right to say positively what he does not know?

Not, he said, with the assurance of positive certainty; he has no right to do that: but he may say what he thinks, as a matter of opinion.

And do you not know, I said, that all mere opinions are bad, and the best of them blind? You would not deny that those who have any true notion without intelligence are only like blind men who feel their way along the road?

Very true.

And do you wish to behold what is blind and crooked and base, when others will tell you of brightness and D beauty?

Still, I must implore you, Socrates, said Glaucon, not to turn away just as you are reaching the goal; if you will only give such an explanation of the good as you have already given of justice and temperance and the other virtues, we shall be satisfied.

Yes, my friend, and I shall be at least equally satisfied, but I cannot help fearing that I shall fail, and that my indiscreet zeal will bring ridicule upon me. No, sweet sirs, let us not at present ask what is the actual nature of the E good, for to reach what is now in my thoughts would be an effort too great for me. But of the child of the good who is likest him, I would fain speak, if I could be sure that you wished to hear – otherwise, not.

By all means, he said, tell us about the child, and you shall remain in our debt for the account of the parent.

I do indeed wish, I replied, that I could pay, and you receive, the account of the parent, and not, as now, of the 507 offspring only; take, however, this latter by way of interest,[4] and at the same time have a care that I do not render a false account, although I have no intention of deceiving you.

Yes, we will take all the care that we can: proceed.

Yes, I said, but I must first come to an understanding with you, and remind you of what I have mentioned in the course of this discussion, and at many other times.

What? B

The old story, that there is a many beautiful and a many good, and so of other things which we describe and define; to all of them the term 'many' is applied.

True, he said.

And there is an absolute beauty and an absolute good, and of other things to which the term 'many' is applied there is an absolute; for they may be brought under a single idea, which is called the essence of each.

Very true.

The many, as we say, are seen but not known, and the ideas are known but not seen.

Exactly.

And what is the organ with which we see the visible things? C

The sight, he said.

And with the hearing, I said, we hear, and with the other senses perceive the other objects of sense?

True.

But have you remarked that sight is by far the most costly and complex piece of workmanship which the artificer of the senses ever contrived?

No, I never have, he said.

---

[3] Reading ἀνὴρ καλός: or reading ἀνὴρ καλῶς, 'I quite well knew from the very first, that you,' &c.

[4] A play upon τόκος, which means both 'offspring' and 'interest'.

D   Then reflect: has the ear or voice need of any third or additional nature in order that the one may be able to hear and the other to be heard?

Nothing of the sort.

No, indeed, I replied; and the same is true of most, if not all, the other senses – you would not say that any of them requires such an addition?

Certainly not.

But you see that without the addition of some other nature there is no seeing or being seen?

How do you mean?

Sight being, as I conceive, in the eyes, and he who has eyes wanting to see; colour being also present in them, *E* still unless there be a third nature specially adapted to the purpose, the owner of the eyes will see nothing and the colours will be invisible.

Of what nature are you speaking?

Of that which you term light, I replied.

True, he said.

508   Noble, then, is the bond which links together sight and visibility, and great beyond other bonds by no small difference of nature; for light is their bond, and light is no ignoble thing?

Nay, he said, the reverse of ignoble.

And which, I said, of the gods in heaven would you say was the lord of this element? Whose is that light which makes the eye to see perfectly and the visible to appear?

You mean the sun, as you and all mankind say.

May not the relation of sight to this deity be described as follows?

How?

B   Neither sight nor the eye in which sight resides is the sun?

No.

Yet of all the organs of sense the eye is the most like the sun?

By far the most like.

And the power which the eye possesses is a sort of effluence which is dispensed from the sun?

Exactly.

Then the sun is not sight, but the author of sight who is recognized by sight?

True, he said.

And this is he whom I call the child of the good, whom the good begat in his own likeness, to be in the visible *C* world, in relation to sight and the things of sight, what the good is in the intellectual world in relation to mind and the things of mind:

Will you be a little more explicit? he said.

Why, you know, I said, that the eyes, when a person directs them towards objects on which the light of day is no longer shining, but the moon and stars only, see dimly, and are nearly blind; they seem to have no clearness of vision in them?

Very true.

D   But when they are directed towards objects on which the sun shines, they see clearly and there is sight in them?

Certainly.

And the soul is like the eye: when resting upon that on which truth and being shine, the soul perceives and understands, and is radiant with intelligence; but when turned towards the twilight of becoming and perishing, then she has opinion only, and goes blinking about, and is first of one opinion and then of another, and seems to have no intelligence?

Just so.

E   Now, that which imparts truth to the known and the power of knowing to the knower is what I would have you term the idea of good, and this you will deem to be the cause of science,[5] and of truth in so far as the latter becomes the subject of knowledge; beautiful too, as are both truth and knowledge, you will be right in esteeming *509* this other nature as more beautiful than either; and, as in the previous instance, light and sight may be truly said to

---

[5] Reading διανοοῦ.

be like the sun, and yet not to be the sun, so in this other sphere, science and truth may be deemed to be like the good, but not the good; the good has a place of honour yet higher.

What a wonder of beauty that must be, he said, which is the author of science and truth, and yet surpasses them in beauty; for you surely cannot mean to say that pleasure is the good?

God forbid, I replied; but may I ask you to consider the image in another point of view?

In what point of view?   B

You would say, would you not, that the sun is not only the author of visibility in all visible things, but of generation and nourishment and growth, though he himself is not generation?

Certainly.

In like manner the good may be said to be not only the author of knowledge to all things known, but of their being and essence, and yet the good is not essence, but far exceeds essence in dignity and power.

Glaucon said, with a ludicrous earnestness: By the light of heaven, how amazing!   C

Yes, I said, and the exaggeration may be set down to you; for you made me utter my fancies.

And pray continue to utter them; at any rate let us hear if there is anything more to be said about the similitude of the sun.

Yes, I said, there is a great deal more.

Then omit nothing, however slight.

I will do my best, I said; but I should think that a great deal will have to be omitted.

I hope not, he said.

You have to imagine, then, that there are two ruling powers, and that one of them is set over the intellectual D world, the other over the visible. I do not say heaven, lest you should fancy that I am playing upon the name (οὐρανός, ὁρατός). May I suppose that you have this distinction of the visible and intelligible fixed in your mind?

I have.

Now take a line which has been cut into two unequal[6] parts, and divide each of them again in the same proportion, and suppose the two main divisions to answer, one to the visible and the other to the intelligible, and then compare the subdivisions in respect of their clearness and want of clearness, and you will find that the first section E in the sphere of the visible consists of images. And by images I mean, in the first place, shadows, and in the second 510 place, reflections in water and in solid, smooth, and polished bodies and the like: Do you understand?

Yes, I understand.

Imagine, now, the other section, of which this is only the resemblance, to include the animals which we see, and everything that grows or is made.

Very good.

Would you not admit that both the sections of this division have different degrees of truth, and that the copy is to the original as the sphere of opinion is to the sphere of knowledge?

Most undoubtedly.   B

Next proceed to consider the manner in which the sphere of the intellectual is to be divided.

In what manner?

Thus: – There are two subdivisions, in the lower of which the soul uses the figures given by the former division as images; the inquiry can only be hypothetical, and instead of going upwards to a principle descends to the other end; in the higher of the two, the soul passes out of hypotheses, and goes up to a principle which is above hypotheses, making no use of images[7] as in the former case, but proceeding only in and through the ideas themselves.

I do not quite understand your meaning, he said.

Then I will try again; you will understand me better when I have made some preliminary remarks. You are C aware that students of geometry, arithmetic, and the kindred sciences assume the odd and the even and the figures and three kinds of angles and the like in their several branches of science; these are their hypotheses, which they and everybody are supposed to know, and therefore they do not deign to give any account of them either to themselves or others; but they begin with them, and go on until they arrive at last, and in a consistent manner, at D their conclusion?

Yes, he said, I know.

---

[6] Reading ἄνισα.

[7] Reading ὥπερ ἐκεῖνο εἰκόνων.

And do you not know also that although they make use of the visible forms and reason about them, they are thinking not of these, but of the ideals which they resemble; not of the figures which they draw, but of the absolute
E square and the absolute diameter, and so on – the forms which they draw or make, and which have shadows and reflections in water of their own, are converted by them into images, but they are really seeking to behold the things themselves, which can only be seen with the eye of the mind?

511   That is true.

And of this kind I spoke as the intelligible, although in the search after it the soul is compelled to use hypotheses; not ascending to a first principle, because she is unable to rise above the region of hypothesis, but employing the objects of which the shadows below are resemblances in their turn as images, they having in relation to the shadows and reflections of them a greater distinctness, and therefore a higher value.

B   I understand, he said, that you are speaking of the province of geometry and the sister arts.

And when I speak of the other division of the intelligible, you will understand me to speak of that other sort of knowledge which reason herself attains by the power of dialectic, using the hypotheses not as first principles, but only as hypotheses – that is to say, as steps and points of departure into a world which is above hypotheses, in order that she may soar beyond them to the first principle of the whole; and clinging to this and then to that which
C depends on this, by successive steps she descends again without the aid of any sensible object, from ideas, through ideas, and in ideas she ends.

I understand you, he replied; not perfectly, for you seem to me to be describing a task which is really tremendous; but, at any rate, I understand you to say that knowledge and being, which the science of dialectic contemplates, are clearer than the notions of the arts, as they are termed, which proceed from hypotheses only: these are
D also contemplated by the understanding, and not by the senses: yet, because they start from hypotheses and do not ascend to a principle, those who contemplate them appear to you not to exercise the higher reason upon them, although when a first principle is added to them they are cognizable by the higher reason. And the habit which is concerned with geometry and the cognate sciences I suppose that you would term understanding and not reason, as being intermediate between opinion and reason.

You have quite conceived my meaning, I said; and now, corresponding to these four divisions, let there be four
E faculties in the soul – reason answering to the highest, understanding to the second, faith (or conviction) to the third, and perception of shadows to the last – and let there be a scale of them, and let us suppose that the several faculties have clearness in the same degree that their objects have truth.

I understand, he replied, and give my assent, and accept your arrangement.

Book VII

514 AND now, I said, let me show in a figure how far our nature is enlightened or unenlightened: – Behold! human beings living in an underground den, which has a mouth open towards the light and reaching all along the den; here they have been from their childhood, and have their legs and necks chained so that they cannot move, and can only see before
B them, being prevented by the chains from turning round their heads. Above and behind them a fire is blazing at a distance, and between the fire and the prisoners there is a raised way; and you will see, if you look, a low wall built along the way, like the screen which marionette players have in front of them, over which they show the puppets.

I see.

C   And do you see, I said, men passing along the wall carrying all sorts of vessels, and statues and figures of animals
515 made of wood and stone and various materials, which appear over the wall? Some of them are talking, others silent.

You have shown me a strange image, and they are strange prisoners.

Like ourselves, I replied; and they see only their own shadows, or the shadows of one another, which the fire throws on the opposite wall of the cave?

B   True, he said; how could they see anything but the shadows if they were never allowed to move their heads?

And of the objects which are being carried in like manner they would only see the shadows?

Yes, he said.

And if they were able to converse with one another, would they not suppose that they were naming what was actually before them?[8]

---

[8] Reading παρόντα.

Very true.

And suppose further that the prison had an echo which came from the other side, would they not be sure to fancy when one of the passers-by spoke that the voice which they heard came from the passing shadow?

No question, he replied.

To them, I said, the truth would be literally nothing but the shadows of the images.   C

That is certain.

And now look again, and see what will naturally follow if the prisoners are released and disabused of their error. At first, when any of them is liberated and compelled suddenly to stand up and turn his neck round and walk and look towards the light, he will suffer sharp pains; the glare will distress him, and he will be unable to see the realities of which in his former state he had seen the shadows; and then conceive some one saying to him, that what he saw D before was an illusion, but that now, when he is approaching nearer to being and his eye is turned towards more real existence, he has a clearer vision, – what will be his reply? And you may further imagine that his instructor is pointing to the objects as they pass and requiring him to name them, – will he not be perplexed? Will he not fancy that the shadows which he formerly saw are truer than the objects which are now shown to him?

Far truer.

And if he is compelled to look straight at the light, will he not have a pain in his eyes which will make him turn E away to take refuge in the objects of vision which he can see, and which he will conceive to be in reality clearer than the things which are now being shown to him?

True, he said.

And suppose once more, that he is reluctantly dragged up a steep and rugged ascent, and held fast until he is 516 forced into the presence of the sun himself, is he not likely to be pained and irritated? When he approaches the light his eyes will be dazzled, and he will not be able to see anything at all of what are now called realities.

Not all in a moment, he said.

He will require to grow accustomed to the sight of the upper world. And first he will see the shadows best, next the reflections of men and other objects in the water, and then the objects themselves; then he will gaze upon the light of the moon and the stars and the spangled heaven; and he will see the sky and the stars by night better than B the sun or the light of the sun by day?

Certainly.

Last of all he will be able to see the sun, and not mere reflections of him in the water, but he will see him in his own proper place, and not in another; and he will contemplate him as he is.

Certainly.

He will then proceed to argue that this is he who gives the season and the years, and is the guardian of all that is in the visible world, and in a certain way the cause of all things which he and his fellows have been accustomed C to behold?

Clearly, he said, he would first see the sun and then reason about him.

And when he remembered his old habitation, and the wisdom of the den and his fellow-prisoners, do you not suppose that he would felicitate himself on the change, and pity them?

Certainly, he would.

And if they were in the habit of conferring honours among themselves on those who were quickest to observe the passing shadows and to remark which of them went before, and which followed after, and which were together; and who were therefore best able to draw conclusions as to the future, do you think that he would care D for such honours and glories, or envy the possessors of them? Would he not say with Homer,

Better to be the poor servant of a poor master, and to endure anything, rather than think as they do and live after their manner?

Yes, he said, I think that he would rather suffer anything than entertain these false notions and live in this miser- E able manner.

Imagine once more, I said, such a one coming suddenly out of the sun to be replaced in his old situation; would he not be certain to have his eyes full of darkness?

To be sure, he said.

And if there were a contest, and he had to compete in measuring the shadows with the prisoners who had never moved out of the den, while his sight was still weak, and before his eyes had become steady (and the time which 517 would be needed to acquire this new habit of sight might be very considerable), would he not be ridiculous? Men would say of him that up he went and down he came without his eyes; and that it was better not even to think of ascending; and if any one tried to loose another and lead him up to the light, let them only catch the offender, and they would put him to death.

No question, he said.

B   This entire allegory, I said, you may now append, dear Glaucon, to the previous argument; the prison-house is the world of sight, the light of the fire is the sun, and you will not misapprehend me if you interpret the journey upwards to be the ascent of the soul into the intellectual world according to my poor belief, which, at your desire, I have expressed – whether rightly or wrongly God knows. But, whether true or false, my opinion is that in the

C   world of knowledge the idea of good appears last of all, and is seen only with an effort; and, when seen, is also inferred to be the universal author of all things beautiful and right, parent of light and of the lord of light in this visible world, and the immediate source of reason and truth in the intellectual; and that this is the power upon which he who would act rationally either in public or private life must have his eye fixed.

I agree, he said, as far as I am able to understand you.

Moreover, I said, you must not wonder that those who attain to this beatific vision are unwilling to descend to

D   human affairs; for their souls are ever hastening into the upper world where they desire to dwell; which desire of theirs is very natural, if our allegory may be trusted.

Yes, very natural.

And is there anything surprising in one who passes from divine contemplations to the evil state of man, misbehaving himself in a ridiculous manner; if, while his eyes are blinking and before he has become accustomed to the surrounding darkness, he is compelled to fight in courts of law, or in other places, about the images or the shadows

E   of images of justice, and is endeavouring to meet the conceptions of those who have never yet seen absolute justice?

Anything but surprising, he replied.

518   Any one who has common sense will remember that the bewilderments of the eyes are of two kinds, and arise from two causes, either from coming out of the light or from going into the light, which is true of the mind's eye, quite as much as of the bodily eye; and he who remembers this when he sees any one whose vision is perplexed and weak, will not be too ready to laugh; he will first ask whether that soul of man has come out of the brighter life, and is unable to see because unaccustomed to the dark, or having turned from darkness to the day is dazzled

B   by excess of light. And he will count the one happy in his condition and state of being, and he will pity the other; or, if he have a mind to laugh at the soul which comes from below into the light, there will be more reason in this than in the laugh which greets him who returns from above out of the light into the den.

That, he said, is a very just distinction.

But then, if I am right, certain professors of education must be wrong when they say that they can put a knowl-

C   edge into the soul which was not there before, like sight into blind eyes.

They undoubtedly say this, he replied.

Whereas, our argument shows that the power and capacity of learning exists in the soul already; and that just as the eye was unable to turn from darkness to light without the whole body, so too the instrument of knowledge can only by the movement of the whole soul be turned from the world of becoming into that of being, and learn

D   by degrees to endure the sight of being, and of the brightest and best of being, or in other words, of the good.

Very true.

And must there not be some art which will effect conversion in the easiest and quickest manner; not implanting the faculty of sight, for that exists already, but has been turned in the wrong direction, and is looking away from the truth?

Yes, he said, such an art may be presumed.

And whereas the other so-called virtues of the soul seem to be akin to bodily qualities, for even when they

E   are not originally innate they can be implanted later by habit and exercise, the virtue of wisdom more than anything else contains a divine element which always remains, and by this conversion is rendered useful and

519   profitable; or, on the other hand, hurtful and useless. Did you never observe the narrow intelligence flashing from the keen eye of a clever rogue – how eager he is, how clearly his paltry soul sees the way to his end; he is the reverse of blind, but his keen eyesight is forced into the service of evil, and he is mischievous in proportion to his cleverness?

Very true, he said.

But what if there had been a circumcision of such natures in the days of their youth; and they had been severed

B   from those sensual pleasures, such as eating and drinking, which, like leaden weights, were attached to them at their birth, and which drag them down and turn the vision of their souls upon the things that are below – if, I say, they had been released from these impediments and turned in the opposite direction, the very same faculty in them would have seen the truth as keenly as they see what their eyes are turned to now.

Very likely.

Yes, I said; and there is another thing which is likely, or rather a necessary inference from what has preceded, that neither the uneducated and uninformed of the truth, nor yet those who never make an end of their education, will be able ministers of State; not the former, because they have no single aim of duty which is the rule of all their   C
actions, private as well as public; nor the latter, because they will not act at all except upon compulsion, fancying that they are already dwelling apart in the islands of the blest.

Very true, he replied.

Then, I said, the business of us who are the founders of the State will be to compel the best minds to attain that knowledge which we have already shown to be the greatest of all – they must continue to ascend until they arrive at the good; but when they have ascended and seen enough we must not allow them to do as they do now.   D

What do you mean?

I mean that they remain in the upper world: but this must not be allowed; they must be made to descend again among the prisoners in the den, and partake of their labours and honours, whether they are worth having or not.

But is not this unjust? he said; ought we to give them a worse life, when they might have a better?

You have again forgotten, my friend, I said, the intention of the legislator, who did not aim at making any one   E
class in the State happy above the rest; the happiness was to be in the whole State, and he held the citizens together by persuasion and necessity, making them benefactors of the State, and therefore benefactors of one another; to   520
this end he created them, not to please themselves, but to be his instruments in binding up the State.

True, he said, I had forgotten.

Observe, Glaucon, that there will be no injustice in compelling our philosophers to have a care and providence of others; we shall explain to them that in other States, men of their class are not obliged to share in the toils of   B
politics: and this is reasonable, for they grow up at their own sweet will, and the government would rather not have them. Being self-taught, they cannot be expected to show any gratitude for a culture which they have never received. But we have brought you into the world to be rulers of the hive, kings of yourselves and of the other citizens, and have educated you far better and more perfectly than they have been educated, and you are better able to share in the double duty. Wherefore each of you, when his turn comes, must go down to the general under-   C
ground abode, and get the habit of seeing in the dark. When you have acquired the habit, you will see ten thousand times better than the inhabitants of the den, and you will know what the several images are, and what they represent, because you have seen the beautiful and just and good in their truth. And thus our State, which is also yours, will be a reality, and not a dream only, and will be administered in a spirit unlike that of other States, in which men fight with one another about shadows only and are distracted in the struggle for power, which in their   D
eyes is a great good. Whereas the truth is that the State in which the rulers are most reluctant to govern is always the best and most quietly governed, and the State in which they are most eager, the worst.

Quite true, he replied.

And will our pupils, when they hear this, refuse to take their turn at the toils of State, when they are allowed to spend the greater part of their time with one another in the heavenly light?

Impossible, he answered; for they are just men, and the commands which we impose upon them are just; there   E
can be no doubt that every one of them will take office as a stern necessity, and not after the fashion of our present rulers of State.

Yes, my friend, I said; and there lies the point. You must contrive for your future rulers another and a better life than that of a ruler, and then you may have a well-ordered State; for only in the State which offers this, will   521
they rule who are truly rich, not in silver and gold, but in virtue and wisdom, which are the true blessings of life. Whereas if they go to the administration of public affairs, poor and hungering after their own private advantage, thinking that hence they are to snatch the chief good, order there can never be; for they will be fighting about office, and the civil and domestic broils which thus arise will be the ruin of the rulers themselves and of the whole State.

Most true, he replied.

And the only life which looks down upon the life of political ambition is that of true philosophy. Do you know   B
of any other?

Indeed, I do not, he said.

And those who govern ought not to be lovers of the task? For, if they are, there will be rival lovers, and they will fight.

No question.

Who then are those whom we shall compel to be guardians? Surely they will be the men who are wisest about affairs of State, and by whom the State is best administered, and who at the same time have other honours and another and a better life than that of politics?

They are the men, and I will choose them, he replied.

.

4

Nicomachean Ethics: The Good Life

Aristotle

In his discussion with the sophist, Thrasymachus, Socrates rightly points out (352D) that the question they are discussing is highly significant: how should one live? That question was central for both Plato and Aristotle. Both Socrates and Plato had seen important connections between the good life and the happy life, between the happy life and the virtuous life, and between the virtuous life and the life of knowledge or understanding. We see Aristotle making those very same connections in the passage to follow.

If I know how I should live, then I understand 'the good'. But what is that? In the first sentence of the *Nicomachean Ethics* (*NE* for short), Aristotle tells us that it is 'that at which everything aims'. Our activities, then, have aims; but, as he goes on to point out, activities, and hence their ends or goods, can be ranked. Bridlemaking is purely instrumental – its aim is bridles, and they are what matter. And bridlemaking is inferior to horsemanship in general. The highest good, then, will be what we want purely for its own sake and not for the sake of anything else. That will be our aim in ethics; and if we are doing politics, he tells us in I.2, our aim will be even higher: the good of a whole city, not just an individual.

Aristotle took the views of others seriously. When we start thinking about some philosophical issue, he thought, we should set down what has been said about it by other philosophers and by 'the many', and try to make these views consistent. This has the upshot that, if one comes up with an argument for some philosophical conclusion, one should 'test' that conclusion against standard philosophical views and the views of common sense. That is exactly what we see Aristotle doing in *NE* I.8, when he claims that his view that happiness is the exercise of virtue fits well with the philosophical view that happiness is a good of the soul. And this discussion takes him into questions people often ask about happiness. How do we get it (I.9)? What is the role of luck in happiness, and can what happens after one's life affect how good one's own life has been (I.10–11)?

Another important aspect of Aristotle's method is his position on precision. In I.3, he suggests that ethics is more like carpentry than mathematics: it is a practical matter. And practice comes into learning about philosophical ethics itself. To gain from thinking about ethics requires that one has been brought up well and has reached a certain level of maturity. This is partly because one starts reflecting on ethics using the beliefs one already has (I.5).

Aristotle's respect for the views of others does not prevent his criticizing them. In I.4 and I.5, he launches a broadside into several of those views. The life of pleasure is fit only for cattle, while even the honour sought by those living the political life cannot be the ultimate good, since one seeks to be honoured *for* something. Perhaps virtue, then, is the good? Even that is insufficient, since a virtuous person might have an accident and end up in a coma for the whole of their life, and no one could call such a life happy. Nor can happiness consist in wealth – that is merely a means to some other end.

Plato saw the ultimate good as a 'form' – a real universal property – and in I.6 we find Aristotle using some complicated arguments in an attempt to bring goodness down to earth again. He then, in I.7,

History of Ethics – Essential Readings with Commentary, First Edition. Edited by Daniel Star and Roger Crisp.
© 2020 John Wiley & Sons Ltd. Published 2020 by John Wiley & Sons Ltd.

considers the very *concept* of happiness, insisting that happiness is 'complete' and 'self-sufficient'. What Aristotle means by these claims has been highly contested by modern scholars. On one side, so-called 'inclusivists' argue that Aristotle is insisting that happiness must, in some sense, contain all goods; in one plausible version of this position, his thought is that any theory of happiness must list all the ultimate goods there are. On the other side, 'dominant' theorists insist that in Aristotle's view happiness is superior to other goods. These writers tend to stress the conclusion of Aristotle's famous 'function' argument in I.7, according to which happiness is 'activity of the soul in accordance with virtue, and if there are several virtues, *in accordance with the best and most complete*' (and here it is worth noting that the Greek word translated 'complete' here can also be translated as 'most final' or 'perfect'). What is the 'best virtue'? By 'virtue', Aristotle essentially means 'excellence', and the highest virtue is understanding. Exercising that is 'contemplation', and – the dominant theorists argue – it is the superiority of that activity to ordinary human political and moral activity for which Aristotle is arguing in X.6–8.

Whichever interpretation of Aristotle is right, we can be sure that his respect for the views of others does not result in conservatism in his position. The ancient philosophers saw as one of their main challenges the question of how morality or virtue can be justified. On the whole, rational egoism seems to have been thought plausible by both philosophers and the many, so the most effective way to justify morality would be to show how it always advances the agent's own happiness to live and act virtuously. And if we read his position as 'dominant', then it is equally radical: that happiness consists only in intellectual activity.

A lot rests, then, on the function argument. It is worth bearing in mind that the Greek word translated here as 'function' is really a technical philosophical term for 'characteristic activity'. So Aristotle's idea is that if we can identify the characteristic activity of human beings, then we can equate that with their happiness. This argument is short; but if we understand it to be claiming that happiness consists in moral virtue, then we can see much of the rest of the *NE*, with its portraits of the virtuous life, as providing further support for this claim.

Book I

Chapter 1   *everything aims at good.*

Every skill and every inquiry, and similarly every action and rational choice, is thought to aim at some good; and so   *1094a*
the good has been aptly described as that at which everything aims. But it is clear that there is some difference
between ends: some ends are activities, while others are products which are additional to the activities. In cases
where there are ends additional to the actions, the products are by their nature better than the activities.

Since there are many actions, skills, and sciences, it happens that there are many ends as well: the end of medicine
is health, that of shipbuilding, a ship, that of military science, victory, and that of domestic economy, wealth. But
when any of these actions, skills, or sciences comes under some single faculty – as bridlemaking and other sciences
concerned with equine equipment come under the science of horsemanship, and horsemanship itself and every
action in warfare come under military science, and others similarly come under others – then in all these cases the
end of the master science is more worthy of choice than the ends of the subordinate sciences, since these latter ends
are pursued also for the sake of the former. And it makes no difference whether the ends of the actions are the
activities themselves, or something else additional to them, as in the sciences just mentioned.

Chapter 2   *政治學的地位 – human good / ends / chief good.*

So if what is done has some end that we want for its own sake, and everything else we want is for the sake of this
end; and if we do not choose everything for the sake of something else (because this would lead to an infinite progression, making our desire fruitless and vain), then clearly this will be the good, indeed the chief good. Surely then,
knowledge of the good must be very important for our lives? And if, like archers, we have a target, are we not more
likely to hit the right mark? If so, we must try at least roughly to comprehend what it is and which science or faculty
is concerned with it.

Knowledge of the good would seem to be the concern of the most authoritative science, the highest master science. And this is obviously the science of politics, because it lays down which of the sciences there should be in   *1094b*
cities, and which each class of person should learn and up to what level. And we see that even the most honourable
of faculties, such as military science, domestic economy, and rhetoric, come under it. Since political science employs
the other sciences, and also lays down laws about what we should do and refrain from, its end will include the ends
of the others, and will therefore be the human good. For even if the good is the same for an individual as for a city,
that of the city is obviously a greater and more complete thing to obtain and preserve. For while the good of an
individual is a desirable thing, what is good for a people or for cities is a nobler and more godlike thing. Our
enquiry, then, is a kind of political science, since these are the ends it is aiming at.

Chapter 3

Our account will be adequate if its clarity is in line with the subject-matter, because the same degree of precision
is not to be sought in all discussions, any more than in works of craftsmanship. The spheres of what is noble and
what is just, which political science examines, admit of a good deal of diversity and variation, so that they seem to
exist only by convention and not by nature. Goods vary in this way as well, since it happens that, for many, good
things have harmful consequences: some people have been ruined by wealth, and others by courage. So we should
be content, since we are discussing things like these in such a way, to demonstrate the truth sketchily and in outline,
and, because we are making generalizations on the basis of generalizations, to draw conclusions along the same lines.
Indeed, the details of our claims, then, should be looked at in the same way, since it is a mark of an educated person
to look in each area for only that degree of accuracy that the nature of the subject permits. Accepting from a mathematician claims that are mere probabilities seems rather like demanding logical proofs from a rhetorician.

Each person judges well what he knows, and is a good judge of this. So, in any subject, the person educated in it   *1095a*
is a good judge of that subject, and the person educated in all subjects is a good judge without qualification. This is
why a young person is not fitted to hear lectures on political science, since our discussions begin from and concern
the actions of life, and of these he has no experience. Again, because of his tendency to follow his feelings, his studies
will be useless and to no purpose, since the end of the study is not knowledge but action. It makes no difference
whether he is young in years or juvenile in character, since the deficiency is not related to age, but occurs because
of his living and engaging in each of his pursuits according to his feelings. For knowledge is a waste of time for

people like this, just as it is for those without self-restraint. But knowledge of the matters that concern political science will prove very beneficial to those who follow reason both in shaping their desires and in acting.

Let these comments – about the student, how our statements are to be taken, and the task we have set ourselves – serve as our preamble.

Chapter 4

Let us continue with the argument, and, since all knowledge and rational choice seek some good, let us say what we claim to be the aim of political science – that is, of all the good things to be done, what is the highest. Most people, I should think, agree about what it is called, since both the masses and sophisticated people call it happiness, understanding being happy as equivalent to living well and acting well. They disagree about substantive conceptions of happiness, the masses giving an account which differs from that of the philosophers. For the masses think it is something straightforward and obvious, like pleasure, wealth, or honour, some thinking it to be one thing, others another. Often the same person can give different accounts: when he is ill, it is health; when he is poor, it is wealth. And when people are aware of their ignorance, they marvel at those who say it is some grand thing quite beyond them. Certain thinkers used to believe that beyond these many good things there is something else good in itself, which makes all these good things good. Examining all the views offered would presumably be rather a waste of time, and it is enough to look at the most prevalent ones or those that seem to have something to be said for them.

Let us not forget, however, that there is a difference between arguments from first principles and arguments to *1095b* first principles. For Plato rightly used to wonder about this, raising the question whether the way to go is from first principles or to first principles, as in the racecourse whether it is from the judges to the post or back again as well. For while we should begin from things known, they are known in two senses: known by us, and known without qualification. Presumably we have to begin from things known by us. This is why anyone who is going to be a competent student in the spheres of what is noble and what is just – in a word, politics – must be brought up well in his habits. For the first principle is the belief *that* something is the case, and if this is sufficiently clear, he will not need the reason *why* as well. Such a person is in possession of the first principles, or could easily grasp them. Anyone with neither of these possibilities open to him should listen to Hesiod:

> This person who understands everything for himself is the best of all,
> And noble is that one who heeds good advice.
> But he who neither understands it for himself nor takes to heart
> What he hears from another is a worthless man.[1]

Chapter 5

But let us begin from where we digressed. For people seem, not unreasonably, to base their conception of the good – happiness, that is – on their own lives. The masses, the coarsest people, see it as pleasure, and so they like the life of enjoyment. There are three especially prominent types of life: that just mentioned, the life of politics, and thirdly the life of contemplation. The masses appear quite slavish by rationally choosing a life fit only for cattle; but they are worthy of consideration because many of those in power feel the same as Sardanapallus.[2]

Sophisticated people, men of action, see happiness as honour, since honour is pretty much the end of the political life. Honour, however, seems too shallow to be an object of our inquiry, since honour appears to depend more on those who honour than on the person honoured, whereas we surmise the good to be something of one's own that cannot easily be taken away. Again, they seem to pursue honour in order to convince themselves of their goodness; at least, they seek to be honoured by people with practical wisdom, among those who are familiar with them, and for their virtue. So it is clear that, to these people at least, virtue is superior.

One might, perhaps, suppose virtue rather than honour to be the end of the political life. But even virtue seems, in itself, to be lacking something, since apparently one can possess virtue even when one is asleep, or inactive *1096a* throughout one's life, and also when one is suffering terribly or experiencing the greatest misfortunes; and no one would call a person living this kind of life happy, unless he were closely defending a thesis. But enough of this, because these issues have been sufficiently dealt with in our everyday discussions.

---

[1] Hesiod, *Works and Days*, 293, 295–7.
[2] A mythical king of Assyria.

The third kind of life is that of contemplation, which we shall examine in what follows.

The life of making money is a life people are, as it were, forced into, and wealth is clearly not the good we are seeking, since it is merely useful, for getting something else. One would be better off seeing as ends the things mentioned before, because they are valued for themselves. But they do not appear to be ends either, and many arguments have been offered against them. So let us put them to one side.

Chapter 6

It would perhaps be quite a good idea to examine the notion of the universal and go through any problems there are in the way it is employed, despite the fact that such an inquiry turns out to be difficult going because those who introduced the Forms[3] are friends. It will presumably be thought better, indeed one's duty, to do away with even what is close to one's heart in order to preserve the truth, especially when one is a philosopher. For one might love both, but it is nevertheless a sacred duty to prefer the truth to one's friends.

Those who introduced this idea did not set up Forms for series in which they spoke of priority and posteriority, and this is why they did not postulate a Form of numbers. But the good is spoken of in the categories of substance, of quality and of relation; and that which exists in itself, namely, substance, is naturally prior to what is relative (since this seems like an offshoot and attribute of what is). So there could not be some common Form over and above these goods.

Again, good is spoken of in as many senses as is being: it is used in the category of substance, as for instance god and intellect, in that of quality – the virtues, in that of quantity – the right amount, in that of relation – the useful, in that of time – the right moment, and in that of place – the right locality, and so on. So it is clear that there could not be one common universal, because it would be spoken of not in all the categories, but in only one.

Again, since there is a single science for the things answering to each individual Form, there should have been some single science for all the goods. But as it happens there are many sciences, even of the things in one category. For example, the right moment: in war, it is military science, in illness, medicine; or the right amount: in diet, it is medicine, in exercise, gymnastics.

One might also be puzzled about what on earth they mean by speaking of a 'thing-in-itself', since the definition *1096b* of humanity is one and the same in humanity-in-itself and human being. Inasmuch as they are human, they will not differ. And if this is so, the same will be true of good.

Nor will a thing be any the more good by being eternal, since a long-lasting white thing is no whiter than a short-lived one.

The Pythagoreans[4] seem to give a more plausible account of the good, when they place the one in their column of goods; and Speusippus[5] seems to have followed them in this. But let this be the topic of another discussion.

An objection to what we have said might be that they did not speak about every good, and that things which are pursued and valued for their own sake are called good by reference to a single Form, while those that tend to be instrumental to these things or in some way to preserve them or prevent their contraries are called good for the sake of these – in a different way, in other words. Clearly, then, things should be called good in two senses: things good in themselves, and things good for the sake of things good in themselves. So let us distinguish things good in themselves from those that are means to them and see whether the former are called good with reference to a single Form. What sort of things should one put in the class of things good in themselves? Those that are sought even on their own, such as understanding, sight, certain types of pleasure, and honours? For even if we do seek these for the sake of something else, one would nevertheless put them in the class of things good in themselves. Perhaps nothing but the Form? Then the Form would be useless. But if those other things are in the class of things good in themselves, the same definition of the good will have to be exemplified in all of them, as is that of whiteness in snow and white lead. But the definitions of honour, practical wisdom and pleasure are distinct, and differ with respect to their being good. There is therefore no common good answering to a single Form.

But how, then, are things called good? For they do not seem like items that have the same name by chance. Is it through their all deriving from one good, or their all contributing to one good, or is it rather by analogy? For as sight is good in the body, so intellect is in the soul, and so on in other cases. But perhaps we should put these

---

[3] I.e., Plato and his followers.
[4] Followers in Southern Italy of Pythagoras of Samos, who flourished around 530 BCE.
[5] Nephew of Plato, and head of Plato's Academy from 407–339 BCE.

questions aside for the time being, since seeking precision in these matters would be more appropriate to another area of philosophy.

But the same is true of the Form. For even if there is some one good predicated across categories, or a good that is separate, itself in itself, clearly it could not be an object of action nor something attainable by a human being, which is the sort of thing we are looking for.

1097a   Perhaps someone might think that it would be better to understand it with an eye to those goods that are attainable and objects of action. For with this as a sort of paradigm we shall know better the goods that are goods for us, and if we know them, we shall attain them. This argument has some plausibility, but seems to be inconsistent with the sciences: they all aim at some good and seek to remedy any lack of the good, but they leave to one side understanding the universal good. And if there were such an important aid available, it is surely not reasonable to think that all practitioners of skills would be ignorant of it and fail even to look for it.

There is also a difficulty in seeing how a weaver or carpenter will be helped in practising his skill by knowing this good-in-itself, or how someone who has contemplated the Form itself will be a better doctor or general. For apparently it is not just health that the doctor attends to, but human health, or perhaps rather the health of a particular person, given that he treats each person individually.

That is enough on these issues.

Chapter 7

But let us return again to the good we are looking for, to see what it might be, since it appears to vary between different actions and skills: it is one thing in medicine, another in military science, and so on in all other cases. What then is the good in each case? Surely it is that for the sake of which other things are done? In medicine it is health, in military science, victory, in housebuilding, a house, and in other cases something else; in every action and rational choice the end is the good, since it is for the sake of the end that everyone does everything else. So if everything that is done has some end, this will be the good among things done, and if there are several ends, these will be the goods.

Our argument, then, has arrived at the same point by a different route, but we should try to make it still clearer. Since there appear to be several ends, and some of these, such as wealth, flutes, and implements generally, we choose as means to other ends, it is clear that not all ends are complete. But the chief good manifestly is something complete. So if there is only one end that is complete, this will be what we are looking for, and if there are several of them, the most complete. We speak of that which is worth pursuing for its own sake as more complete than that which is worth pursuing only for the sake of something else, and that which is never worth choosing for the sake of something else as more complete than things that are worth choosing both in themselves and for the sake of this end. And so that which is always worth choosing in itself and never for the sake of something else we call complete without qualification.

1097b   Happiness in particular is believed to be complete without qualification, since we always choose it for itself and never for the sake of anything else. Honour, pleasure, intellect, and every virtue we do indeed choose for themselves (since we would choose each of them even if they had no good effects), but we choose them also for the sake of happiness, on the assumption that through them we shall live a life of happiness; whereas happiness no one chooses for the sake of any of these nor indeed for the sake of anything else.

The same conclusion seems to follow from considering self-sufficiency, since the complete good is thought to be self-sufficient. We are applying the term 'self-sufficient' not to a person on his own, living a solitary life, but to a person living alongside his parents, children, wife, and friends and fellow-citizens generally, since a human being is by nature a social being. We must, however, set some limit on these, since if we stretch things so far as to include ancestors and descendants and friends of friends we shall end up with an infinite series. But we must think about this later. For now, we take what is self-sufficient to be that which on its own makes life worthy of choice and lacking in nothing. We think happiness to be such, and indeed the thing most of all worth choosing, not counted as just one thing among others. Counted as just one thing among others it would clearly be more worthy of choice with even the least good added to it. For the good added would cause an increase in goodness, and the greater good is always more worthy of choice. Happiness, then, is obviously something complete and self-sufficient, in that it is the end of what is done.

But perhaps saying that happiness is the chief good sounds rather platitudinous, and one might want its nature to be specified still more clearly. It is possible that we might achieve that if we grasp the characteristic activity of a human being. For just as the good – the doing well – of a flute-player, a sculptor or any practitioner of a skill, or generally whatever has some characteristic activity or action, is thought to lie in its characteristic activity, so the same would seem to be true of a human being, if indeed he has a characteristic activity.

Well, do the carpenter and the tanner have characteristic activities and actions, and a human being none? Has nature left him without a characteristic activity to perform? Or, as there seem to be characteristic activities of the eye, the hand, the foot, and generally of each part of the body, should one assume that a human being has some characteristic activity over and above all these? What sort of thing might it be, then? For living is obviously shared   *1098a* even by plants, while what we are looking for is something special to a human being. We should therefore rule out the life of nourishment and growth. Next would be some sort of sentient life, but this again is clearly shared by the horse, the ox, indeed by every animal. What remains is a life, concerned in some way with action, of the element that possesses reason. (Of this element, one part has reason in being obedient to reason, the other in possessing it and engaging in thought.) As this kind of life can be spoken of in two ways, let us assume that we are talking about the life concerned with action in the sense of activity, because this seems to be the more proper use of the phrase.

If the characteristic activity of a human being is an activity of the soul in accordance with reason or at least not entirely lacking it; and if we say that the characteristic activity of anything is the same in kind as that of a good thing of the same type, as in the case of a lyre-player and a good lyre-player, and so on, without qualification, in the same way in every case, the superiority of the good one in virtue being an addition to the characteristic activity (for the characteristic activity of the lyre-player is to play the lyre, that of the good lyre-player to play it well); then if this is so, and we take the characteristic activity of a human being to be a certain kind of life; and if we take this kind of life to be activity of the soul and actions in accordance with reason, and the characteristic activity of the good person to be to carry this out well and nobly, and a characteristic activity to be accomplished well when it is accomplished in accordance with the appropriate virtue; then if this is so, the human good turns out to be activity of the soul in accordance with virtue, and if there are several virtues, in accordance with the best and most complete. Again, this must be over a complete life. For one swallow does not make a summer, nor one day. Neither does one day or a short time make someone blessed and happy.

So let this serve as an outline of the good, since perhaps we have first to make a rough sketch, and then fill it in later. One would think that anyone with a good outline can carry on and complete the details, and that in this task time will bring much to light or else offer useful assistance. This is how skills have come to advance, because anyone can fill in the gaps. But we must bear in mind what we said above, and not look for the same precision in everything, but in each case whatever is in line with the subject-matter, and the degree appropriate to the inquiry. A carpenter and a geometrician approach the right-angle in different ways: the carpenter in so far as it is useful for his work, while the geometrician seeks to know what it is, or what sort of thing it is, in that he aims to contemplate the truth. We should therefore do the same in every other case, so that side-issues do not dominate the tasks in hand. Nor should we demand an explanation in the same way in all cases. A sound proof that something *is* the case will suffice   *1098b* in some instances, as with first principles, where the fact itself is a starting-point, that is, a first principle. Some first principles we see by induction, some by perception, some by a kind of habituation, and others in other ways. We must try to investigate each type in the way appropriate to its nature, and take pains to define each of them well, because they are very important in what follows. The first principle seems to be more than half the whole thing, and to clarify many of the issues we are inquiring into.

Chapter 8

But we must consider the first principle in the light not only of our conclusion and premises, but of the things that people say about it. For all the data harmonize with the truth, but soon clash with falsity.

Goods have been classified into three groups: those called external goods, goods of the soul, and goods of the body. Goods of the soul are the ones we call most strictly and most especially good, and the actions and activities of the soul we may attribute to the soul. Our conception of happiness, then, is plausible in so far as it accords with this view, a venerable one that has been accepted by philosophers.

Our account is right also in that we are claiming that the end consists in certain actions and activities. For the end thus turns out to be a good of the soul and not an external good.

Another belief that harmonizes with our account is that the happy person lives well and acts well, for we have claimed that happiness is pretty much a kind of living well and acting well.

Again, all the things that people look for in happiness appear to have been included in our account. Some think that happiness is virtue, some practical wisdom, others a kind of wisdom; while others think it is a combination of these or one of these along with more or less pleasure. Yet others include external prosperity as well. Some of these views are popular and of long standing, while others are those of a few distinguished men. It is not likely that either group is utterly mistaken, but rather that at least one component of their view is on the right track, perhaps even most of them.

Our account of happiness is in harmony with those who say that happiness is virtue or some particular virtue, since activity in accordance with virtue is characteristic of virtue. Presumably though, it makes a great difference *1099a* whether we conceive of the chief good as consisting in possession or in use, that is to say, in a state or in an activity. For while a state can exist without producing any good consequences, as it does in the case of a person sleeping or lying idle for some other reason, this is impossible for an activity: it will necessarily engage in action, and do so well. As in the Olympic Games it is not the most attractive and the strongest who are crowned, but those who compete (since it is from this group that winners come), so in life it is those who act rightly who will attain what is noble and good.

It is also the case that the life of these people is pleasurable in itself. For experiencing pleasure is an aspect of the soul, and each person finds pleasure in that of which he is said to be fond, as a horse-lover finds it in a horse, and someone who likes wonderful sights finds it in a wonderful sight. In the same way, a lover of justice finds it in the sphere of justice and in general a person with virtue finds pleasure in what accords with virtue. The pleasures of the masses, because they are not pleasant by nature, conflict with one another, but the pleasures of those who are fond of noble things are pleasant by nature. Actions in accordance with virtue are like this, so that they are pleasant to these people as well as in themselves. Their life therefore has no need of pleasure as some kind of lucky ornament, but contains its pleasure in itself, because, in addition to what we have already said, the person who does not enjoy noble actions is not good. For no one would call a person just if he did not enjoy acting justly, or generous if he did not enjoy generous actions; and the same goes for the other virtues. If this is so, it follows that actions in accordance with virtue are pleasant in themselves. But they are also good and noble as well as pleasant; indeed, since the good person is a good judge of goodness and nobility, actions in accordance with virtue have them to a degree greater than anything else; and here he judges in accordance with our views.

Happiness, then, is the best, the noblest and the pleasantest thing, and these qualities are not separate as in the inscription at Delos:

> Noblest is that which is the most just, and best is being healthy.
> But most pleasant is obtaining what one longs for.

This is because the best activities have all of these qualities. And we say that happiness consists in them, or one of them – the best.

Nevertheless, as we suggested, happiness obviously needs the presence of external goods as well, since it is impos- *1099b* sible, or at least no easy matter, to perform noble actions without resources. For in many actions, we employ, as if they were instruments at our disposal, friends, wealth, and political power. Again, being deprived of some things – such as high birth, noble children, beauty – spoils our blessedness. For the person who is terribly ugly, of low birth, or solitary and childless is not really the sort to be happy, still less perhaps if he has children or friends who are thoroughly bad, or good but dead. As we have said, then, there seems to be an additional need for some sort of prosperity like this. For this reason, some identify happiness with good fortune, while others identify it with virtue.

Chapter 9

Hence the problem also arises of whether happiness is to be acquired by learning, habituation, or some other training, or whether it comes by virtue of some divine dispensation or even by chance.

If there is anything that the gods give to men, it is reasonable that happiness should be god-given, especially since it is so much the best thing in the human world. But this question would perhaps be more suited to another inquiry. Even if it is not sent by the gods, however, but arises through virtue and some sort of learning or training, it is evidently one of the most divine things. For that which is the prize and end of virtue is clearly the chief good, something both divine and blessed.

It would also be something widely shared, since everyone who was not incapacitated with regard to virtue could attain it through some kind of learning and personal effort. And if it is better to be happy in this way than by chance, it is reasonable that happiness should be attained like this. For what is in accordance with nature is by nature as noble as it can be, and so is what is in accordance with skill and every other cause, especially that in accordance with the best cause. To entrust what is greatest and most noble to chance would be quite inappropriate.

The answer to our question is also manifest from our account of happiness, since we said that it was a certain kind of activity of the soul in accordance with virtue; and of the other goods, some are necessary conditions of happiness, and others are naturally helpful and serve as useful means to it.

And this agrees with what we said at the beginning. We took the end of political science to be the chief good, and political science is concerned most of all with producing citizens of a certain kind, namely, those who are both good and the sort to perform noble actions.

It is with good reason, then, that we do not call an ox, a horse or any other animal happy, because none of them *1100a* can share in such activity. And for this same reason, a child is not happy either, since his age makes him incapable of doing such actions. If he is called blessed, he is being described as such on account of the potential he has, since, as we have said, happiness requires complete virtue and a complete life. For there are many vicissitudes in life, all sorts of chance things happen, and even the most successful can meet with great misfortunes in old age, as the story goes of Priam[6] in Trojan times. No one calls someone happy who meets with misfortunes like these and comes to a wretched end.

Chapter 10

Should we then call no one happy while they are alive, but rather, as Solon advises, wait to see the end?[7] Even if we must assume this to be right, is it really the case that he is happy when he is dead? Or is this not quite ridiculous, especially for us, claiming as we do that happiness is some kind of activity?

But if it is not that we call the dead person happy, and Solon meant not this, but that we can at that stage safely call a person blessed in so far as he is now beyond the reach of evils and misfortunes, even this claim is open to dispute. For both good and evil are thought to happen to a dead person, since they can happen to a person who is alive but not aware of them. Take, for example, honours and dishonours, and the good and bad fortunes of his children or his descendants generally. But this view also gives rise to a problem. Though a person may have lived a blessed life into his old age and died accordingly, many reverses may happen in connection with his descendants. Some of them may be good and meet with the life they deserve, others the contrary; and clearly the relation to their ancestors can vary to any degree. It would indeed be odd if the dead person also were to share in these vicissitudes, and be sometimes happy, sometimes wretched. But it would also be odd if the fortunes of descendants had no effect on their ancestors for any time at all.

But we should return to the original question, since considering it might shed light on the one now under discussion. If we must wait to see the end and only then call a person blessed, not as such but as having been so before, surely it is odd that – because we do not wish to call the living happy on account of possible changes in their for- *1100b* tunes, and because happiness is understood as something permanent and not at all liable to change, while the living experience many turns of the wheel – when he is happy, he will not be truly described as such? For clearly, if we were to follow his fortunes, we should often call the same person happy and then wretched, representing the happy person as a kind of chameleon, or as having an unsound foundation. Or is following a person's fortunes the wrong thing to do? For they are not what doing well or badly depend on, though, as we said, they are required as complementary to a fully human life. What really matter for happiness are activities in accordance with virtue, and for the contrary of happiness the contrary kind of activities.

The question we have been discussing is further confirmation of our account, since nothing in the sphere of human achievement has more permanence than activities in accordance with virtue. They are thought to be more lasting even than the sciences, and the most honourable to be the more lasting, because the blessed spend their lives engaged, quite continually, in them above all (which seems to be why there is no forgetting in connection with these activities).

[6] King of Troy at the time of its destruction by Agamemnon.
[7] See Herodotus, *Histories* 1.30–2. Solon was an Athenian lawgiver in the early sixth century, thought to be the founder of democracy.

The quality in question, then, will belong to the happy person, and he will be happy throughout his life. For he will spend all, or most, of his time engaged in action and contemplation in accordance with virtue. And he will bear changes in fortune in a particularly noble way and altogether gracefully, as one who is 'genuinely good' and 'four-square without a flaw'.[8]

Many things, however, both large and small, happen by chance. Small pieces of good fortune or its contrary clearly do not affect the balance of life. But many great events, if they are good, will make a life more blessed, since they will themselves naturally embellish it, and the way a person deals with them can be noble and good. But if they turn out the other way, they will oppress and spoil what is blessed, since they bring distress with them and hinder many activities. Nevertheless, even in their midst what is noble shines through, when a person calmly bears many great misfortunes, not through insensibility, but by being well bred and great-souled.

If activities are, as we have said, what really matter in life, no one blessed could become wretched, since he will
1101a never do hateful and petty actions. For the truly good and wise person, we believe, bears all the fortunes of life with dignity and always does the noblest thing in the circumstances, as a good general does the most strategically appropriate thing with the army at his disposal, and a shoemaker makes the noblest shoe out of the leather he is given, and so on with other practitioners of skills. If this is so, the happy person could never become wretched, though he will not be blessed if he meets with luck like that of Priam. Nor indeed will he be unstable and changeable. He will not be shifted easily from happiness, and not by ordinary misfortunes, but by many grave ones. He would not recover from these to become happy again in a short space of time. If he does recover, it will be after a long and complete period of great and noble accomplishments.

What is to prevent us, then, from concluding that the happy person is the one who, adequately furnished with external goods, engages in activities in accordance with complete virtue, not for just any period of time but over a complete life? Or should we add that he will live like this in the future and die accordingly? The future is obscure to us, and we say that happiness is an end and altogether quite complete. This being so, we shall call blessed those of the living who have and will continue to have the things mentioned, but blessed only in human terms.

So much for the distinctions we draw in these areas.

Chapter 11

Nevertheless, the idea that the fortunes of a person's descendants and all his friends have no effect on him seems excessively heartless and contrary to what people think. But, given that the things that happen are many and various, some affecting us more and others less, it looks as if it would be a long – even interminable – job to distinguish them in detail. It will be enough, perhaps, to give a general outline.

If, then, as some of a person's misfortunes have a certain weight and influence on his life, while others seem lighter, so too there are similar differences between the fortunes of all his friends; and if it makes a difference whether each of these misfortunes happens to people when they are alive or when they are dead (a greater difference even than whether the dreadful crimes in tragedies happened before the play or are perpetrated on the stage); then this difference must be taken into account in our reasoning, or rather, perhaps, the fact that there is a puzzle
1101b about whether the dead can partake of any good or evil. For it does seem, from what we have said, that if anything good or bad does actually affect them, it will be pretty unimportant and insignificant, either in itself or in relation to them; or if not, it must at least be of such an extent and kind as not to make happy those who are not happy already nor to deprive those who are happy of their being blessed. So when friends do well, and likewise when they do badly, it does seem to have some effect on the dead. But it is of such a nature and degree as neither to make not happy those who are happy, nor anything like that.

[...]

Book X

Chapter 6

Now that we have discussed the virtues, friendships and pleasures, it remains for us to offer an outline account of happiness, since we assume it to be the end in human affairs. Our argument will be more concise if we first sum up what has been said already.

---

[8] Simonides; see Plato, *Protagoras* 339b. Simonides (*c.* 556–468) was a Greek poet from Ceos.

We said, then, that it is not a state, since if it were it might be possessed by someone asleep all his life, living a vegetable existence, or someone suffering the greatest misfortunes. So if this is implausible, we should put it rather *1176b* in the class of activities, as we said above. And some activities are necessary, that is, worth choosing for the sake of something else, while others are worthy of choice in themselves; clearly, happiness must be classed as one of those worthy of choice in themselves and not as one of those worth choosing for the sake of something else. For happiness lacks nothing, but is self-sufficient; and an activity is worthy of choice in itself when nothing is sought from it beyond the activity. Actions in accordance with virtue seem like this, since doing noble and good actions is worthy of choice in itself.

But pleasurable amusements also seem to be in this class; for people do not choose them for the sake of other things, since they are more harmed than benefited by them, through failing to take care of their bodies and their property. And most of those called happy have recourse to pastimes like this, which is why those who are adroit in them are highly esteemed at the courts of tyrants; they offer themselves as pleasant purveyors of what the tyrants are after, and the tyrants want people like this. And so these amusements seem to be connected with happiness, because those in positions of power spend their leisure time on them.

But presumably people like this prove nothing, since virtue and intellect, from which come good activities, do not depend on positions of power. And if these people, never having tasted pure and gracious pleasure, have recourse to bodily pleasures, that is no reason to believe these pleasures to be more worthy of choice, since children also believe that what they give honour to is best. So it is to be expected that, just as different things appear honourable to children and adults, so it will be with good people and bad.

As we have often said, then, what is honourable and pleasant is what is so for the good person. And for each person the activity that accords with his own proper state is the most worthy of choice, and therefore for the good person it is that which accords with virtue.

Happiness, then, does not consist in amusement, because it would be absurd if our end were amusement, and we laboured and suffered all of our lives for the sake of amusing ourselves. For we choose virtually everything for the sake of something else, except happiness, since it is the end; but serious work and exertion for the sake of amusement is manifestly foolish and extremely childish. Rather, as Anacharsis[9] puts it, what seems correct is amusing ourselves so that we can engage in some serious work, since amusement is like relaxation, and we need relaxation because we cannot continuously exert ourselves. Relaxation, then, is not an end, since it occurs for the sake of activity.   *1177a*

And the happy life seems to be one in accordance with virtue, and this implies a level of seriousness, and is not spent in amusement. And we say that serious things are better than funny or amusing ones, and that in every case the activity of the better person, or the better part of a person, is more serious, more virtuous; and the activity of what is better is superior, and for this very reason more conducive to happiness. And absolutely anyone, a slave no less than the best of people, can enjoy the bodily pleasures; but no one attributes a share in happiness to a slave, unless he also attributes to him a share in the life we live. For happiness does not consist in occupations like this, but in activities in accordance with virtue, as we have also said before.

Chapter 7

If happiness is activity in accordance with virtue, it is reasonable to expect that it is in accordance with the highest virtue, and this will be the virtue of the best element. Whether this best element is intellect or something else we think naturally rules and guides us and has insight into matters noble and divine, and whether it is divine or just the most divine element within us, its activity, in accordance with its own proper virtue, will be complete happiness.

That this activity is that of contemplation we have already said. This would seem to agree both with our earlier discussion and with the truth. For this is the highest activity, intellect being the highest element in us, and its objects are the highest objects of knowledge. And it is also the most continuous, since we can contemplate more continuously than we can do anything. And we think that happiness must have pleasure mixed in with it; and the most pleasant of activities in accordance with virtue is agreed to be that in accordance with wisdom. At any rate, philosophy seems to involve pleasures remarkable for their purity and stability, and it is reasonable to expect that those who have knowledge will pass their time more pleasantly than those who are still in search of it. And the self-sufficiency that is spoken of will belong to the activity of contemplation most of all. For though a wise person, a just person, and anyone with any other virtue, all require the necessities of life, nevertheless, when they are adequately provided

---

[9] Primarily legendary Scythian prince, said to have travelled in Greece in the sixth century and become famous for his wisdom.

with such things, the just person will need people as associates in and objects of his just actions, and the same is true of the temperate person, the courageous person and each of the others; but the wise person can contemplate even when he is by himself, the more so the wiser he is. Maybe he can do it better with collaborators, but he is neverthe-
1177b less the most self-sufficient.

Again, contemplation alone seems to be liked for its own sake, since nothing results from it apart from the fact that one has contemplated, whereas from the practical virtues, to a greater or lesser extent, we gain something beyond the action. Again, happiness seems to depend on leisure, because we work to have leisure, and wage war to live in peace. The activity of the practical virtues occurs in politics or war, and actions in these spheres seem to involve exertion. This seems entirely so as regards those in war, since no one chooses to make war, or even starts a war, for the sake of making war; for if someone turned his friends into enemies to bring about battles and killings he would seem utterly murderous. But the activity of a politician also involves exertion, and, apart from the business of politics itself, it is designed to secure power and honours, or at least happiness for himself and the citizens, which is different from politics and which we clearly pursue as something different.

So, among actions performed in accordance with virtue, those in politics and war are distinguished by their nobil-ity and extent, but they involve exertion, aim at some end, and are not worthy of choice for their own sake. The activity of intellect, on the other hand, in so far as it involves contemplation, seems superior in its seriousness, to aim at no end beyond itself, and to have its own proper pleasure, which augments the activity; it seems also to possess self-sufficiency, time for leisure, and freedom from fatigue, as far as these are humanly possible. And clearly this activity also involves whatever else is attributed to the blessed person. Thus it will be complete happiness for a human being – if it consumes a complete span of life, because there is nothing incomplete in matters of happiness.

Such a life is superior to one that is simply human, because someone lives thus, not in so far as he is a human being, but in so far as there is some divine element within him. And the activity of this divine element is as much superior to that in accordance with the other kind of virtue as the element is superior to the compound. If the intellect, then, is something divine compared with the human being, the life in accordance with it will also be divine compared with human life. But we ought not to listen to those who exhort us, because we are human, to think of human things, or because we are mortal, think of mortal things. We ought rather to take on immortality as much as possible, and do all that we can to live in accordance with the highest element within us; for even if its bulk
1178a is small, in its power and value it far exceeds everything.

It would seem, too, to constitute each person, since it is his authoritative and better element; it would be odd, then, if he were to choose not his own life, but something else's.

And what we said above will apply here as well: what is proper to each thing is by nature best and pleasantest for it; for a human being, therefore, the life in accordance with intellect is best and pleasantest, since this, more than anything else, constitutes humanity. So this life will also be the happiest.

Chapter 8

The life in accordance with the other kind of virtue is happy in a secondary way, since the activities in accordance with it are human. For we do just actions, courageous actions, and the other actions in accordance with the virtues, in relation to each other, observing what is proper to each in contracts, services and actions of all kinds, and in feel-ings as well; and all of these are manifestly human. Some feelings seem in fact to have their origin in the body and virtue of character in many ways to be closely bound up with the feelings.

Practical wisdom, too, is tied up with virtue of character, and this with practical wisdom, since the first principles of practical wisdom are in accordance with the virtues of character, and correctness in the virtues of character is in accordance with practical wisdom. And since they are also united with the feelings, the virtues of character must be concerned with the compound. Because the virtues of the compound are human, so are the life and happiness in accordance with them. The virtue of intellect, however, is separate. Let us leave it at that, since a detailed account would be beyond the scope of our project.

It would seem also to require external means to a small extent, or to a smaller extent than virtue of character. Let us accept that they both require the necessities of life, and to an equal extent, since even though the politician expends more effort on matters of the body and suchlike, any difference here would be a small one; nevertheless, in what they need for their activities, there will be a big difference. For the generous person will need money for doing generous actions; and the just person will need it for repaying debts, since wishes are uncertain, and even those who are not just pretend that they wish to act justly. And the courageous person will need power, and the temperate person opportunity, if they are to accomplish any of the actions that accord with their virtue. For how else will he, or any of the others, make manifest what he is?

It is debated as well whether it is the rational choice or the actions that are more really characteristic of virtue, on *1178b* the assumption that it depends on both. Its being complete would clearly involve both, but for actions many things are needed, and the greater and nobler the actions, the greater the number of things needed. But a person who is contemplating needs none of these, for that activity at any rate; indeed, one might say that they are even obstacles, to contemplation at least. But in so far as he is a human being and lives together with a number of others, he chooses to do actions in accordance with virtue; he will therefore need such things for the living of a human life.

That complete happiness consists in some contemplative activity is also apparent from the following. We assume the gods to be supremely blessed and happy; but what sorts of actions should we attribute to them? Just actions? But will they not obviously be ridiculous if they make contracts, return deposits and so on? Courageous acts, then, enduring what is fearful and facing dangers because it is noble to do so? Or generous acts? To whom will they give? And it will be absurd if they have money or anything like it. And what would their temperate acts consist in? Is such praise not cheap, since they have no bad appetites? If we were to run through them all, anything to do with actions would appear petty and unworthy of the gods.

Nevertheless, everyone assumes that they are at least alive and therefore engage in activity, since we do not take them to sleep like Endymion.[10] So if we remove from a living being the possibility of action, and furthermore the very possibility of producing anything, what is left apart from contemplation? So the god's activity, which is superior in blessedness, will be contemplative; and therefore the human activity most akin to this is the most conducive to happiness.

There is an indication of this in the fact that the other animals have no share in happiness, being completely deprived of the activity in question. For while the life of the gods is entirely blessed, and that of human beings is so to the extent that it contains something like this sort of activity, none of the other animals is happy, because they have no share at all in contemplation. Happiness, then, extends as far as contemplation, and the more contemplation there is in one's life, the happier one is, not incidentally, but in virtue of the contemplation, since this is honourable in itself. Happiness, therefore, will be some form of contemplation.

But because the happy person is human, he will also need external prosperity; for human nature is not self-sufficient for contemplation, but the body must be healthy and provided with food and other care. Nevertheless, we *1179a* should not think that someone who is going to be happy will need many substantial things, just because one cannot be blessed without external goods. For neither self-sufficiency nor action depends on excess, and we can do noble actions without ruling over land and sea, because we can act in accordance with virtue even from modest resources. This can be seen quite clearly, since private individuals seem to do good actions no less – indeed more – than those in positions of power. And it is enough to have moderate resources, since the life of a person whose activity conforms with virtue will be happy. Solon, too, was presumably right in his portrayal of happy people, when he said that they had been modestly furnished with external goods, but had done what he regarded as the noblest actions and had lived temperately. For people can do what they ought even when their possessions are modest. Anaxagoras also seems to have assumed the happy person to be neither rich nor powerful, since he said that he would not be surprised if the happy person appeared an absurd sort of person to the masses;[11] for since they perceive only externals, it is by these that they judge. The beliefs of the wise, then, seem to harmonize with our arguments.

But while such things do carry some conviction, the truth in practical issues is judged from the facts of our life, these being what really matter. We must therefore examine what has been said in the light of the facts of our life, and if it agrees with the facts, then we should accept it, while if it conflicts, we must assume it to be no more than theory.

The person whose activity is in accordance with intellect and who cultivates it seems to be in the best condition and dearest to the gods. For if the gods feel any concern for human affairs, as they seem to, it would be reasonable for them to find enjoyment in what is best and most closely related to them – namely, intellect – and to reward those who like and honour this most, on the assumption that these people care for what is loved by the gods, and act rightly and nobly. And it is quite clear that all of these qualities belong most of all to the wise person; he, therefore, is dearest to the gods. And it is likely that this same person is also the happiest; so in this way too the wise person will be more happy than anyone else.

---

[10] Loved by Selene, goddess of the moon, Endymion was made immortal, and sleeps in a cave on Mt Latmus in Caria.

[11] Anaxagoras 59 A 30 DK.

Nicomachean Ethics (Continued): The Nature of Virtue

Aristotle

Aristotle ends the first book of *NE* with a discussion of the soul. His conception of the soul is broad, including, for example, the capacity of a plant to take in nutrition. For him, the soul is closely related to life itself. Human souls can be seen as bipartite, with a rational and a nonrational part. Each part has its own virtues or excellences. The rational part is the site of the intellectual virtues, the most important in connection with ethics being practical wisdom (involved with virtue of character) and understanding (purely intellectual). The nonrational part can itself be subdivided, one of its subparts having more in common with reason than the other and being capable of obeying it. The virtues here are the virtues of character: generosity, courage, and so on.

Intellectual virtue comes mainly from teaching, while the virtues of character, Aristotle tells us in II.1, arise through habituation. Such virtue is not like, say, a mathematical ability, which could be found in a child prodigy. Rather it is more like learning a skill, such as carpentry, and takes time. And an important aspect of habituation concerns pleasures and pains. Moral education is in large part training in finding one's pleasures and pains in the right places. Note that Aristotle is a 'realist' or 'objectivist' about ethics. The right way to live and act is not a matter of taste or an agent's own desires.

But if learning to be just requires doing just actions, isn't there a problem? If I perform just actions, must I not already be just? Aristotle solves this difficulty in II.4. Imagine that I have borrowed a book, and I return it on the instructions of my mother. I have done a just action; but I have not done it as a virtuous person would. This, Aristotle claims, is because acting as a virtuous person would requires the meeting of three conditions: I have to know what I am doing, rationally choose the action for its own sake (and not, say, to avoid punishment), and act on the basis of a firm character. Moral education, in other words, is a journey from doing virtuous actions to acting virtuously.

Firm character is a matter of possessing a set of dispositions or 'states' (II.5). Further, properly to understand what virtue is requires understanding the idea of 'the mean' (II.2; II.6). It is very important to note that Aristotle's 'doctrine of the mean' is not a simple doctrine of moderation. Consider a feeling such as anger. This is something all human beings are subject to, and so the virtuous person has to feel anger in the virtuous or right way. There are two ways to go wrong: one can feel anger too much or too little. How this works on a single occasion is easy enough to understand: if someone carelessly bumps into me on the street, both incandescent rage and total insensitivity would be inappropriate. But the doctrine is not just about amount. It also concerns, for example, the right time, and it would be absurd to claim that – if I am bumped into at, say, 3:00 p.m., this is in a mean between 2:00 p.m. and 4:00 p.m.

The doctrine, then, has to be understood diachronically. The virtuous person will get angry to the right extent, at the right times, with the right people, and so on. The irascible person will get angry to an excessive extent, at the wrong times, with the wrong people, and so on; while the person with the 'deficient' vice will *fail* to get angry to a sufficient extent, at the right times, and so on. Unfortunately, as Aristotle later

History of Ethics – Essential Readings with Commentary, First Edition. Edited by Daniel Star and Roger Crisp.
© 2020 John Wiley & Sons Ltd. Published 2020 by John Wiley & Sons Ltd.

explains in his account of generosity, this means you can have *both* vices: you can get angry when you shouldn't, for example, and fail to get angry when you should. This analysis also explains how the doctrine applies to actions, such as the giving away of money (which again must be done to the right extent, at the right times, and so on).

Aristotle says that the mean at which we should aim is 'relative to us'. This might suggest some kind of subjectivism, such that, if I am extremely irascible, for example, the right degree of anger for me in some situation might still be considerably greater than that we might think appropriate for a virtuous person. One way to understand Aristotle is as claiming that our personal circumstances are relevant to what is virtuous for us. If I am poor, then a gift of a few dollars may be generous even though it would be mean of a richer person to offer such a present.

To make the doctrine work theoretically requires a feeling or action that can be neutrally described. For that reason, Aristotle has serious problems later with justice, where it is quite hard to see which feeling or action could play the relevant role. He also sometimes seems himself not to understand the key point that virtues must involve a single action or feeling. Consider what he says about envy and spite, for example, in his list of virtues and vices in II.7: they are given a single mean (appropriate indignation), when in fact they concern quite different things – respectively, pain at the good fortune of others and pleasure in their misfortune. Nevertheless, the structure at the heart of the doctrine has great explanatory power and brings out how human life involves various spheres, and how the virtuous person must positively act and feel appropriately in those spheres. Ethics is not just a list of prohibitions.

Some have thought the doctrine empty, saying little more than that one should do what is right. Aristotle's practical advice in II.9 brings out its usefulness. As long as one has some basic grasp of what might be, say, generous, one can assess one's own character and, if necessary, attempt to steer it in the right direction by acting appropriately in the future.

Book I

Chapter 13

Since happiness is a certain kind of activity of the soul in accordance with complete virtue, we ought to look at virtue. For perhaps then we might be in a better position to consider happiness.

Besides, the true politician is thought to have taken special pains over this, since he wants to make citizens good and obedient to the laws. As an example, we have the lawgivers of the Cretans and the Spartans, and any others of that ilk. If this inquiry is a part of political science, pursuing it will clearly accord with our original purpose.

Clearly, it is human virtue we must consider, since we were looking for human good and human happiness. By human virtue, we mean that of the soul, not that of the body; and happiness we speak of as an activity of the soul. If this is right, the politician clearly must have some understanding of the sphere of the soul, as the person who is to attend to eyes must have some understanding of the whole body; more so, indeed, in that political science is superior to medicine, and held in higher esteem, and even among doctors, the sophisticated ones go to a great deal of effort to understand the body. The politician, then, must consider the soul, and consider it with a view to understanding virtue, just to the extent that is required by the inquiry, because attaining a higher degree of precision is perhaps too much trouble for his current purpose.

Some aspects of the soul have been dealt with competently in our popular works as well, and we should make use of these. It is said, for example, that one element of the soul has reason, while another lacks it. It does not matter for the moment whether these elements are separate like the parts of the body or anything else that can be physically divided, or whether they are naturally inseparable but differentiated in thought, like the convex and concave aspects of a curved surface.

Of the element without reason, one part seems to be common: the vegetative, the cause of nutrition and growth. For one should assume such a capacity of the soul to exist in everything that takes in nutrition, even embryos, and *1102b* to be the same in fully grown beings, since this is more reasonable than assuming that they have a different capacity.

The virtue of this element is clearly something shared and not specific to human beings. For this part and its capacity are thought more than others to be active during sleep, and the good and bad person to be hardest to distinguish when they are asleep (hence the saying that the happy are no different from the wretched for half of their lives – which makes sense, since sleep is a time when the soul is not engaged in the things that lead to its being called good or bad), except that in some way certain movements on a small scale reach the soul, and make the dreams of good people better than those of ordinary people. But enough of this. Let us leave the nutritive capacity aside, since by nature it plays no role in human virtue.

But there does seem to be another natural element in the soul, lacking reason, but nevertheless, as it were, partaking in it. For we praise the reason of the self-controlled and of the incontinent, that is, the part of their soul with reason, because it urges them in the right direction, towards what is best; but clearly there is within them another natural element besides reason, which conflicts with and resists it. For just as paralysed limbs, when one rationally chooses to move them to the right, are carried off in the opposite direction to the left, so also in the soul: the impulses of incontinent people carry them off in the opposite direction. In the body we do indeed see the lack of control, while in the soul we do not see it; but I think that we should nevertheless hold that there is some element in the soul besides reason, opposing and running counter to it. In what way it is distinct from the other elements does not matter. But it does seem to partake in reason, as we said. The element in the soul of the self-controlled person, at least, obeys reason and presumably in the temperate and the brave person it is still more ready to listen, since in their case it is in total harmony with reason.

So the element without reason seems itself to have two parts. For the vegetative part has no share at all in reason, while the part consisting in appetite and desire in general does share in it in a way, in so far as it listens to and obeys it. So it has reason in the sense that a person who listens to the reason of his father and his friends is said to have reason, not reason in the mathematical sense. That the element without reason is in some way persuaded by reason is indicated as well by the offering of advice, and all kinds of criticism and encouragement. And if we must say that *1103a* this element possesses reason, then the element with reason will also have two parts, one, in the strict sense, possessing it in itself, the other ready to listen to reason as one is ready to listen to the reason of one's father.

Virtue is distinguished along the same lines. Some virtues we say are intellectual, such as wisdom, judgement and practical wisdom, while others are virtues of character, such as generosity and temperance. For when we are talking about a person's character, we do not say that he is wise or has judgement, but that he is even-tempered or temperate. Yet we do praise the wise person for his state, and the states worthy of praise we call virtues.

Book II

Chapter 1

Virtue, then, is of two kinds: that of the intellect and that of character. Intellectual virtue owes its origin and development mainly to teaching, for which reason its attainment requires experience and time; virtue of character (*ēthos*) is a result of habituation (*ethos*), for which reason it has acquired its name through a small variation on '*ethos*'. From this it is clear that none of the virtues of character arises in us by nature. For nothing natural can be made to behave differently by habituation. For example, a stone that naturally falls downwards could not be made by habituation to rise upwards, not even if one tried to habituate it by throwing it up ten thousand times; nor can fire be habituated to burn downwards, nor anything else that naturally behaves in one way be habituated to behave differently. So virtues arise in us neither by nature nor contrary to nature, but nature gives us the capacity to acquire them, and completion comes through habituation.

Again, in all the cases where something arises in us by nature, we first acquire the capacities and later exhibit the activities. This is clear in the case of the senses, since we did not acquire them by seeing often or hearing often; we had them before we used them, and did not acquire them by using them. Virtues, however, we acquire by first exercising them. The same is true with skills, since what we need to learn before doing, we learn by doing; for *1103b* example, we become builders by building, and lyre-players by playing the lyre. So too we become just by doing just actions, temperate by temperate actions, and courageous by courageous actions. What happens in cities bears this out as well, because legislators make the citizens good by habituating them, and this is what every legislator intends. Those who do not do it well miss their target; and it is in this respect that a good political system differs from a bad one.

Again, as in the case of a skill, the origin and means of the development of each virtue are the same as those of its corruption: it is from playing the lyre that people become good and bad lyre-players. And it is analogous in the case of builders and all the rest, since from building well, people will be good builders, from building badly, bad builders. If this were not so, there would have been no need of a person to teach them, but they would all have been born good or bad at their skill.

It is the same, then, with the virtues. For by acting as we do in our dealings with other men, some of us become just, others unjust; and by acting as we do in the face of danger, and by becoming habituated to feeling fear or confidence, some of us become courageous, others cowardly. The same goes for cases of appetites and anger; by conducting themselves in one way or the other in such circumstances, some become temperate and even-tempered, others intemperate and bad-tempered. In a word, then, like states arise from like activities. This is why we must give a certain character to our activities, since it is on the differences between them that the resulting states depend. So it is not unimportant how we are habituated from our early days; indeed it makes a huge difference – or rather all the difference.

Chapter 2

The branch of philosophy we are dealing with at present is not purely theoretical like the others, because it is not in order to acquire knowledge that we are considering what virtue is, but to become good people – otherwise there would be no point in it. So we must consider the matter of our actions, and in particular how they should be performed, since, as we have said, they are responsible for our states developing in one way or another.

The idea of acting in accordance with right reason is a generally accepted one. Let us here take it for granted – we shall discuss it later, both what right reason is and how it is related to the other virtues. But this we must agree on *1104a* before we begin: that the whole account of what is to be done ought to be given roughly and in outline. As we said at the start, the accounts we demand should be appropriate to their subject-matter; and the spheres of actions and of what is good for us, like those of health, have nothing fixed about them.

Since the general account lacks precision, the account at the level of particulars is even less precise. For they do not come under any skill or set of rules: agents must always look at what is appropriate in each case as it happens, as do doctors and navigators. But, though our present account is like this, we should still try to offer some help.

First, then, let us consider this – the fact that states like this are naturally corrupted by deficiency and excess, as we see in the cases of strength and health (we must use clear examples to illustrate the unclear); for both too much exercise and too little ruin one's strength, and likewise too much food and drink and too little ruin one's health, while the right amount produces, increases and preserves it. The same goes, then, for temperance, courage and the other virtues: the person who avoids and fears everything, never standing his ground, becomes cowardly, while he who fears nothing, but confronts every danger, becomes rash. In the same way, the person who enjoys every pleasure and never restrains himself becomes intemperate, while he who avoids all pleasure – as boors do – becomes, as it were, insensible. Temperance and courage, then, are ruined by excess and deficiency, and preserved by the mean.

Not only are virtues produced and developed from the same origins and by the same means as those from which and by which they are corrupted, but the activities that flow from them will consist in the same things. For this is also true in other more obvious cases, like that of strength. It is produced by eating a great deal and going through a great deal of strenuous exercise, and it is the strong person who will be most able to do these very things. The same applies to virtues. By abstaining from pleasures we become temperate, and having become so we are most able to abstain from them. Similarly with courage: by becoming habituated to make light of what is fearful and to face up *1104b* to it, we become courageous; and when we are, we shall be most able to face up to it.

Chapter 3

We must take as an indication of a person's states the pleasure or pain consequent on what he does, because the person who abstains from bodily pleasures and finds his enjoyment in doing just this is temperate, while the person who finds doing it oppressive is intemperate; and the person who enjoys facing up to danger, or at least does not find it painful to do so, is courageous, while he who does find it painful is a coward. For virtue of character is concerned with pleasures and pains: it is because of pleasure that we do bad actions, and pain that we abstain from noble ones. It is for this reason that we need to have been brought up in a particular way from our early days, as Plato says,[1] so we might find enjoyment or pain in the right things; for the right education is just this.

Again, if the virtues are to do with actions and situations of being-affected, and pleasure and pain follow from every action and situation of being affected, then this is another reason why virtue will be concerned with pleasures and pains.

The fact that punishment is based on pleasure and pain is further evidence of their relevance; for punishment is a kind of cure, and cures by their nature are effected by contraries.

Again, as we said recently, every state of the soul is naturally related to, and concerned with, the kind of things by which it is naturally made better or worse. It is because of pleasures and pains that people become bad – through pursuing or avoiding the wrong ones, or at the wrong time, or in the wrong manner, or in any other of the various ways distinguished by reason. This is why some have classified virtues as forms of insensibility or states of rest; but this is wrong, because they speak without qualification, without saying 'in the right way' and 'in the wrong way', 'at the right time' and 'at the wrong time', and the other things one can add.

We assume, then, that virtue will be the sort of state to do the best actions in connection with pleasures and pains, and vice the contrary. The following considerations should also make it plain to us that virtue and vice are concerned with the same things.

There are three objects of choice – the noble, the useful, and the pleasant – and three of avoidance – their contraries, the shameful, the harmful, and the painful. In respect of all of these, especially pleasure, the good person tends to go right, and the bad person to go wrong. For pleasure is shared with animals, and accompanies all objects of *1105a* choice, because what is noble and what is useful appear pleasant as well.

Again, pleasure has grown up with all of us since infancy and is consequently a feeling difficult to eradicate, ingrained as it is in our lives. And, to a greater or lesser extent, we regulate our actions by pleasure and pain. Our whole inquiry, then, must be concerned with them, because whether we feel enjoyment and pain in a good or bad way has great influence on our actions.

Again, as Heraclitus says, it is harder to fight against pleasure than against spirit.[2] But both skill and virtue are always concerned with what is harder, because success in what is harder is superior. So this is another reason why the whole concern of virtue and political science is pleasures and pains: the person who manages them well will be good, while he who does so badly will be bad.

Let it be taken as established, then, that virtue is to do with pleasures and pains; that the actions which produce it also increase it, or, if they assume a different character, corrupt it; and that the sphere of its activity is the actions that themselves gave rise to it.

---

[1] Plato, *Republic* 401e–402a; *Laws* 653a–c.
[2] Heraclitus, 22 B 85 DK. *fl. c.* 500 BCE. Important Ionian philosopher.

Chapter 4

Someone might, however, wonder what we mean by saying that becoming just requires doing just actions first, and becoming temperate, temperate actions. For if we do just and temperate actions, we are already just and temperate; similarly, if we do what is literate or musical, we must be literate or musical.

But surely this is not true even of the skills? For one can produce something literate by chance or under instruction from another. Someone will be literate, then, only when he produces something literate and does so in a literate way, that is, in accordance with his own literacy.

Again, the case of the skills is anyway not the same as that of the virtues. For the products of the skills have their worth within themselves, so it is enough for them to be turned out with a certain quality. But actions done in accordance with virtues are done in a just or temperate way not merely by having some quality of their own, but rather if the agent acts in a certain state, namely, first, with knowledge, secondly, from rational choice, and rational
1105b choice of the actions for their own sake, and, thirdly, from a firm and unshakeable character. The second and third of these are not counted as conditions for the other skills, only the knowledge. With regard to virtues, knowledge has little or no weight, while the other two conditions are not just slightly, but all-important. And these are the ones that result from often doing just and temperate actions. Actions, then, are called just and temperate when they are such as the just and the temperate person would do. But the just and temperate person is not the one who does them merely, but the one who does them as just and temperate people do. So it is correct to say that it is by doing just actions that one becomes just, and by doing temperate actions temperate; without doing them, no one would have even a chance of becoming good.

But the masses do not do them. They take refuge in argument, thinking that they are being philosophers and that this is the way to be good. They are rather like patients who listen carefully to their doctors, but do not do what they are told. Just as such treatment will not make the patients healthy in body, so being this kind of philosopher will not make the masses healthy in soul.

Chapter 5

Next we must consider what virtue is. There are three things to be found in the soul – feelings, capacities, and states.– so virtue should be one of these. By feelings, I mean appetite, anger, fear, confidence, envy, joy, love, hate, longing, emulation, pity, and in general things accompanied by pleasure or pain. By capacities, I mean the things on the basis of which we are described as being capable of experiencing these feelings – on the basis of which, for example, we are described as capable of feeling anger, fear or pity. And by states I mean those things in respect of which we are well or badly disposed in relation to feelings. If, for example, in relation to anger, we feel it too much or too little, we are badly disposed; but if we are between the two, then well disposed. And the same goes for the other cases.

Neither the virtues nor the vices are feelings, because we are called good or bad on the basis not of our feelings, but of our virtues and vices; and also because we are neither praised nor blamed on the basis of our feelings
1106a (the person who is afraid or angry is not praised, and the person who is angry without qualification is not blamed but rather the person who is angry in a certain way), but we are praised and blamed on the basis of our virtues and vices. Again, we become angry or afraid without rational choice, while the virtues are rational choices or at any rate involve rational choice. Again, in respect of our feelings, we are said to be moved, while in respect of our virtues and vices we are said not to be moved but to be in a certain state.

For these reasons they are not capacities either. For we are not called either good or bad, nor are we praised or blamed, through being capable of experiencing things, without qualification. Again, while we have this capacity by nature, we do not become good or bad by nature; we spoke about this earlier.

So if the virtues are neither feelings nor capacities, it remains that they are states. We have thus described what virtue is generically.

Chapter 6

But we must say not just that virtue is a state, but what kind of state. We should mention, then, that every virtue causes that of which it is a virtue to be in a good state, and to perform its characteristic activity well. The virtue of the eye, for example, makes it and its characteristic activity good, because it is through the virtue of the eye that we see well. Likewise, the virtue of the horse makes a horse good – good at running, at carrying its rider and at facing the enemy. If this is so in all cases, then the virtue of a human being too will be the state that makes a human being good and makes him perform his characteristic activity well.

We have already said how this will happen, and it will be clear also from what follows, if we consider what the nature of virtue is like.

In everything continuous and divisible, one can take more, less, or an equal amount, and each either in respect of the thing itself or relative to us; and the equal is a sort of mean between excess and deficiency. By the mean in respect of the thing itself I mean that which is equidistant from each of the extremes, this being one single thing and the same for everyone, and by the mean relative to us I mean that which is neither excessive nor deficient – and this is not one single thing, nor is it the same for all. If, for example, ten are many and two are few, six is the mean if one takes it in respect of the thing, because it is by the same amount that it exceeds the one number and is exceeded by the other. This is the mean according to arithmetic progression. The mean relative to us, however, is not to be obtained in this *1106b* way. For if ten pounds of food is a lot for someone to eat, and two pounds a little, the trainer will not necessarily prescribe six; for this may be a lot or a little for the person about to eat it – for Milo,[3] a little, for a beginner at gymnastics, a lot. The same goes for running and wrestling. In this way every expert in a science avoids excess and deficiency, and aims for the mean and chooses it – the mean, that is, not in the thing itself but relative to us.

If, then, every science does its job well in this way, with its eye on the mean and judging its products by this criterion (which explains both why people are inclined to say of successful products that nothing can be added or taken away from them, implying that excess and deficiency ruin what is good in them, while the mean preserves it, and why those who are good at the skills have their eye on this, as we say, in turning out their product), and if virtue, like nature, is more precise and superior to any skill, it will also be the sort of thing that is able to hit the mean.

I am talking here about virtue of character, since it is this that is concerned with feelings and actions, and it is in these that we find excess, deficiency and the mean. For example, fear, confidence, appetite, anger, pity, and in general pleasure and pain can be experienced too much or too little, and in both ways not well. But to have them at the right time, about the right things, towards the right people, for the right end, and in the right way, is the mean and best; and this is the business of virtue. Similarly, there is an excess, a deficiency and a mean in actions. Virtue is concerned with feelings and actions, in which excess and deficiency constitute misses of the mark, while the mean is praised and on target, both of which are characteristics of virtue. Virtue, then, is a kind of mean, at least in the sense that it is the sort of thing that is able to hit a mean.

Again, one can miss the mark in many ways (since the bad belongs to the unlimited, as the Pythagoreans portrayed it, and the good to the limited), but one can get things right in only one (for which reason one is easy and the other difficult – missing the target easy, hitting it difficult). For these reasons as well, then, excess and deficiency are characteristics of vice, the mean characteristic of virtue:

For good people are just good, while bad people are bad in all sorts of ways.[4]

Virtue, then, is a state involving rational choice, consisting in a mean relative to us and determined by reason – the *1107a* reason, that is, by reference to which the practically wise person would determine it. It is a mean between two vices, one of excess, the other of deficiency. It is a mean also in that some vices fall short of what is right in feelings and actions, and others exceed it, while virtue both attains and chooses the mean. So, in respect of its essence and the definition of its substance, virtue is a mean, while with regard to what is best and good it is an extreme.

But not every action or feeling admits of a mean. For some have names immediately connected with depravity, such as spite, shamelessness, envy, and, among actions, adultery, theft, homicide. All these, and others like them, are so called because they themselves, and not their excesses or deficiencies, are bad. In their case, then, one can never hit the mark, but always misses. Nor is there a good or bad way to go about such things – committing adultery, say, with the right woman, at the right time, or in the right way. Rather, doing one of them, without qualification, is to miss the mark.

It would be equally wrong, therefore, to expect there to be a mean, an excess and a deficiency in committing injustice, being a coward, and being intemperate, since then there would be a mean of excess and a mean of deficiency, an excess of excess and a deficiency of deficiency. Rather, just as there is no excess and deficiency of temperance and courage, because the mean is, in a sense, an extreme, so too there is no mean, excess or deficiency in the cases above.

---

[3] Famous athlete from Croton of the later sixth century.
[4] Unknown.

However they are done, one misses the mark, because, generally speaking, there is neither a mean of excess or deficiency, nor an excess or deficiency of a mean.

Chapter 7

But this general account on its own is not enough. We must also apply it to particular cases, because though more general discussions of actions are of wider application, particular ones are more genuine. This is because actions are to do with particulars, and what we say should accord with particulars. We may take them from our diagram.

1107b   In fear and confidence, courage is the mean. Of those who exceed it, the person who exceeds in fearlessness has no name (many cases lack names), while the one who exceeds in confidence is rash. He who exceeds in being afraid and is deficient in confidence is a coward.

With respect to pleasures and pains – not all of them, and less so with pains – the mean is temperance, the excess intemperance. People deficient with regard to pleasures are not very common, and so do not even have a name; let us call them insensible.

In giving and taking money, the mean is generosity, while the excess and deficiency are wastefulness and stinginess. People with these qualities are excessive and deficient in contrary ways to one another. The wasteful person exceeds in giving away and falls short in taking, while the stingy person exceeds in taking and falls short in giving away. (At present, we can be content with giving a rough and summary account of these things; a more detailed classification will come later.)

There are other dispositions connected with money. One mean is magnificence, for the magnificent person, in so far as he deals with large amounts, differs from the generous one, who deals with small. The excess is tastelessness and vulgarity, the deficiency niggardliness, and they differ from the states opposed to generosity; how they differ will be stated below.

In honour and dishonour, the mean is greatness of soul, while the excess is referred to as a kind of vanity, the deficiency smallness of soul. And just as we said generosity is related to magnificence, differing from it by being concerned with small amounts, so there is a virtue having to do with small honours that corresponds in the same way to greatness of soul, which is to do with great ones. For one can desire small honours in the right way, and in excessive and deficient ways as well. The person who exceeds in his desires is described as a lover of honour, the person who is deficient as not caring about it, while the one in between has no name. Their dispositions are nameless as well, except that of the lover of honour, which is called love of honour. This is why those at the extremes lay claim to the middle ground. We ourselves sometimes refer to the person in the middle as a lover of honour, sometimes as one who does not care about

1108a   it; and sometimes we praise the person who loves honour, sometimes the one who does not care about it. The reason for our doing this will be stated below. For now, let us discuss the remaining virtues and vices in the way laid down.

In anger too there is an excess, a deficiency, and a mean. They are virtually nameless, but since we call the person in between the extremes even-tempered, let us call the mean even temper. Of those at the extremes, let the one who is excessive be quick-tempered, and the vice quick temper, while he who is deficient is, as it were, slow-tempered, and his deficiency slow temper.

There are three other means, having something in common, but also different. For they are all to do with our association with one another in words and actions, but differ in that one is concerned with the truth to be found in them, while the other two are respectively concerned with what is pleasant in amusement and in life as a whole. We should talk about these things as well, then, so that we can better see that in all things the mean is praiseworthy, while the extremes are neither praiseworthy nor correct, but blameworthy. Most of them again have no names, but, for the sake of clarity and intelligibility, we must try, as in the other cases, to produce names ourselves.

With respect to truth, then, let us call the intermediate person truthful and the mean truthfulness; pretence that exaggerates is boastfulness and the person who has this characteristic is a boaster, while that which understates is self-depreciation and the person who has this is self-depreciating. In connection with what is pleasant in amusement, let us call the intermediate person witty, and the disposition wit; the excess clownishness, and the person with that characteristic a clown; and the person who falls short a sort of boor and his state boorishness. With respect to the remaining kind of pleasantness, that found in life in general, let us call the person who is pleasant in the right way friendly and the mean friendliness, while he who goes to excess will be obsequious if there is no reason for it, and a flatterer if he is out for his own ends; someone who falls short and is unpleasant all the time will be a quarrelsome and peevish sort of person.

There are also means in the feelings and in connection with the feelings. Shame, for example, is not a virtue, but praise is also bestowed on the person inclined to feel it. Even in these cases one person is said to be intermediate, and another – the shy person who feels shame at everything – excessive; he who is deficient or is ashamed of nothing at all is called shameless, while the person in the middle is properly disposed to feel shame.

Appropriate indignation is a mean between envy and spite; these three are concerned with pain and pleasure felt *1108b*
at the fortunes of those around us. The sort of person to experience appropriate indignation is pained by those who
do well undeservedly; the envious person goes beyond him and is pained by anybody's doing well; while the spiteful
person, far from being pained at the misfortunes of others, actually feels enjoyment.

There will also be an opportunity elsewhere to discuss means like these.

As for justice, since it is a term used in more than one way we shall distinguish its two varieties after discussing
the other virtues, and say how each variety is a mean.

Chapter 8

Of these three dispositions, then, two are vices – one of excess, the other of deficiency – and the third, the mean, is
virtue. Each is in a way opposed to each of the others, because the extremes are contrary to the mean and to one
another, and the mean to the extremes. For as the equal is greater in relation to the less, but less in relation to the
greater, so the mean states are excessive in relation to the deficiencies, but deficient in relation to the excesses; this
is so in both feelings and actions. For the courageous person seems rash in relation to the coward, and a coward in
relation to the rash person. Similarly, the temperate seems intemperate in relation to the insensible, but insensible in
relation to the intemperate, and the generous person wasteful in relation to the stingy person, but stingy in relation
to the wasteful. This is why those at one extreme push away the intermediate person to the other, the coward calling
the courageous person rash, the rash person calling him a coward, and analogously in other cases.

Since they are set against one another in this way, the greatest opposition is that of the extremes to one another,
rather than to the mean. For they are further from each other than from the mean, as the great is further from the
small and the small further from the great than either is from the equal. Again, some of the extremes seem rather like
the mean, as rashness seems like courage, and wastefulness like generosity. The greatest dissimilarity is that between
extremes; and the things that are furthest from each other are defined as contraries, so that the further things are apart,
the more contrary they will be. In some cases, the deficiency is more opposed to the mean than is the excess, in others *1109a*
the excess is more opposed than the deficiency; for example, it is not rashness, the excess, which is more opposed to
courage, but cowardice, the deficiency; while it is not insensibility, the deficiency, but intemperance, the excess, which
is more opposed to temperance. There are two reasons for this.

One derives from the nature of the thing itself. Because one extreme is nearer and more like the mean, we set in
opposition to the mean not this but rather its contrary; for example, since rashness is thought to be more like courage and nearer to it, and cowardice less like it, it is cowardice rather than rashness that we set in opposition, because
things that are further from the mean are thought more contrary to it. This, then, is one reason, deriving from the
nature of the thing itself.

The other derives from our nature. It is the things to which we ourselves are naturally more inclined that appear
more contrary to the mean; for example, we are naturally more inclined to pleasures, and are therefore more prone
to intemperance than self-discipline. We describe as more contrary to the mean, then, those extremes in the direction
of which we tend to go; this is why intemperance, an excess, is more contrary to temperance.

Chapter 9

Enough has been said, then, to show that virtue of character is a mean, and in what sense it is so; that it is a mean
between two vices, one of excess and one of deficiency; and that it is such because it is the sort of thing able to hit
the mean in feelings and actions. This is why it is hard to be good, because in each case it is hard to find the middle
point; for instance, not everyone can find the centre of a circle, but only the person with knowledge. So too anyone
can get angry, or give and spend money – these are easy; but doing them in relation to the right person, in the right
amount, at the right time, with the right aim in view, and in the right way – that is not something anyone can do,
nor is it easy. This is why excellence in these things is rare, praise-worthy and noble.

So the person who is aiming at the mean must first steer away from the extreme that is in greater opposition to
it, as Calypso advised:

Beyond this spray and swell keep your ship.[5]

---

[5] Homer, *Odyssey* xii.219 f.

For one of the extremes is a greater missing of the mark, the other less so; and since hitting the mean is extremely hard, we must take the next best course, as they say, and choose the lesser of two evils. This will be done best in the *110* way we are suggesting.

But we must also consider the things towards which we as individuals are particularly prone. For we each have different natural tendencies, and we can find out what they are by the pain and pleasure that occur in us. And we should drag ourselves in the opposite direction, because we shall arrive at the mean by holding far off from where we would miss the mark, just as people do when straightening warped pieces of wood. In everything, we should be on our guard especially against the pleasant – pleasure, that is – because we are not impartial judges of it. So we should adopt the same attitude to it as the elders did towards Helen, and utter their words in everything we do;[6] for by dismissing pleasure in this way, we shall miss the mark to a lesser degree.

To sum up, then, it is by doing these things that we shall best be able to hit the mean. Admittedly, however, hitting it is difficult, especially in particular cases, since it is not easy to determine how one should be angry, with whom, for what reasons, and for how long; indeed we sometimes praise those who fall short and call them even-tempered, and sometimes those who flare up, describing them as manly. But the person who is blamed is not the one who deviates a little, either in excess or deficiency, from the right degree, but the one who deviates rather more, because he does not escape our notice. But how far and to what extent someone must deviate before becoming blameworthy it is not easy to determine by reason, because nothing perceived by our senses is easily determined; such things are particulars, and judgement about them lies in perception.

This much, then, is clear – that the mean state is in every case to be praised, but that sometimes we must incline towards the excess, sometimes towards the deficiency, because in this way we shall most easily hit the mean, namely, what is good.

---

[6] Homer, *Iliad* iii. 156–60.

6

Nicomachean Ethics (Continued): Responsibility and Practical Wisdom

Aristotle

Right at the start of book III of the *NE*, Aristotle notes the close link between virtue and vice on the one hand, and praise and blame on the other. We praise and blame only what is voluntary, so it is vital to be clear about what counts as voluntary and what doesn't.

Aristotle's account is influenced by the legislation in force at Athens in his day, and he begins by identifying two 'excusing conditions' – force and ignorance – that remain central in philosophical and everyday understandings of the voluntary. In the case of force, the 'first principle' or origin of the action is external to the agent. If I go to Kos, but only because the wind has blown me, my going isn't voluntary. One obvious question at this point is whether there could not be 'inner' compulsion. Partly as a result of reflecting on this question, Aristotle moves on to discuss 'mixed actions', such as a captain's offloading cargo in a storm to save his ship. The origin of his action is internal, so it must count as voluntary; but Aristotle allows that it can be called involuntary 'without qualification', and he probably means that it is the kind of thing no one would choose to do as an end in itself. Nevertheless, there is a limit to the voluntariness of what is inner. In cases of severe torture, for example, pardon rather than blame is called for.

Aristotle adds a third category in addition to the voluntary and the involuntary: the non-voluntary. Imagine that I drop something on you from my window, not knowing you were passing. This sounds involuntary: I didn't know you were there. But if I don't regret what I've done, Aristotle suggests, my action is not involuntary but non-voluntary. It is as if he doesn't want to let me off the hook, as if when I'm not sorry there may be a case for blaming me.

As far as ignorance is concerned, Aristotle draws an important distinction between acting in ignorance and acting through ignorance. A drunk acts only in ignorance, and can be blamed – he is responsible for getting himself into that state. Nor can I plead ignorance of morality itself: the only ignorance that counts is of the particular facts of the case.

Aristotle perhaps says too little about the fact that actions can be described in different ways. If I am rude to the woman in the blue suit, that may well be voluntary. No one made me, and I knew what I was doing. But what if the woman was also my new boss? Was I voluntarily rude to my new boss? Hardly – I didn't know it was her.

Aristotle's focus on virtue also lies behind his argument in the following chapters of book III. Rational choice, deliberation, and wish are discussed because the virtuous person is the person who deliberates, rationally chooses, and wishes correctly. Rational choice indeed involves deliberation, and we rationally choose to do what we have judged right after deliberation. So rational choice is deliberative desire and is the point at which virtuous thought emerges in the world through the agent's actions.

In III.5, Aristotle faces the objection that a vicious person should not be blamed, because their character makes them act, and that character is not up to them. Aristotle's response is robust: it is up to them, in that

History of Ethics – Essential Readings with Commentary, First Edition. Edited by Daniel Star and Roger Crisp.
© 2020 John Wiley & Sons Ltd. Published 2020 by John Wiley & Sons Ltd.

they could have acted differently in their youth. Is this reasonable if, say, the vicious person has been brought up in extremely difficult circumstances by other vicious people?

Book VI of the *NE* continues the discussion of intellectual activity in the context of virtue. The book begins with what appears to be a criticism of the doctrine of the mean: that telling someone to hit the mean is as unhelpful as telling a sick person to adopt the treatment a doctor would recommend. But Aristotle himself has shown in II.9 how the doctrine can be of use if one already has some basic understanding of morality, such as the kind of thing that would count as generous or stingy. Rather, he is here stressing the significance of the intellectual virtues, as well as the habituated virtues of character that lead us in the direction of what is right. In his definition of virtue in II.6, he said that the virtuous mean is determined by the reason (the *logos*) by reference to which the practically wise person would determine it. Is this some kind of moral rule or set of rules? No: practical wisdom, as we learn in VI.8, has an important quasi-perceptual aspect. The virtuous person is able – perhaps after deliberation – to *see* what is right in the circumstances they are in. And seeing that is grasping practical truth (VI.5). There is a right way to act in any situation, and it requires practical wisdom to be able to discern that in all cases. But practical wisdom is not the only intellectual virtue, and book VI includes explanation and discussion of scientific knowledge, wisdom, and other excellences.

Towards the end of the book, in VI.12, Aristotle considers the objection that practical wisdom is unnecessary, since virtue of character should be enough for acting well. His response is that, although virtue makes our aim right, practical wisdom enables us to grasp 'the things towards it'. It has sometimes been thought that Aristotle is here giving reason, in the form of practical wisdom, something of a back seat, whose job is just to find the means to our ends. But it seems clear that it does more than this, since Aristotle has a name for the capacity for means-end reasoning: cleverness. Rather, perhaps, although our virtue disposes us to be, say, generous, practical wisdom, on the basis of an understanding of virtue, enables us see what generosity would actually consist of in this case.

Further, since any virtue of character requires practical wisdom, and being practically wise requires possessing all the virtues, one possesses either all virtues or none. This idea, often referred to as the *doctrine of the reciprocity of the virtues*, may seem extreme and implausible, but as he often does, Aristotle is speaking about an ideal for ordinary people to emulate: the perfectly virtuous person.

Book III

Chapter 1

Since virtue is to do with feelings and actions, and since voluntary feelings and actions are praised and blamed, while the involuntary ones are pardoned and occasionally even pitied, presumably anyone considering virtue must determine the limits of the voluntary and the involuntary. It will be useful as well for legislators, in connection with honours and punishments.

Things that happen by force or through ignorance are thought to be involuntary. What is forced is what has an *1110a* external first principle, such that the agent or the person acted upon contributes nothing to it – if a wind, for example, or people with power over him carry him somewhere.

As for things done through fear of greater evils or for the sake of something noble – if a tyrant, for example, had one's parents and children in his power and ordered one to do something shameful, on the condition that one's doing it would save them, while one's not doing it would result in their death – there is some dispute about whether they are involuntary or voluntary. The same sort of thing happens also in the case of people throwing cargo over-board in storms at sea. Without qualification, no one jettisons cargo voluntarily; but for his own safety and that of others any sensible person will do it.

Such actions, then, are mixed, though they seem more like voluntary ones, because at the time they are done they are worthy of choice, and the end of an action depends on the circumstances. So both voluntariness and involun-tariness are to be ascribed at the time of the action. In fact, the person acts voluntarily, because in actions like this the first principle of moving the limbs that serve as instruments lies in him; and where the first principle lies in a person, it is in his power to act or not to act. Such actions are therefore voluntary, but, without qualification, they are presumably involuntary, since no one would choose any of them in itself.

People are sometimes praised for actions like this, when they endure some disgrace or pain in return for great and noble objects; and if they do the contrary, they are blamed, since it is characteristic of a bad person to endure the greatest disgraces for no noble end or for something unimportant.

In some cases, not praise but pardon is given, when a person does wrong because of things that strain human nature to breaking-point and no one would endure. But some things perhaps we cannot be compelled to do, and rather than do them we ought to die after the most terrible suffering; for the things that compelled Euripides' Alcmaeon to kill his mother seem absurd.[1] It is nevertheless hard sometimes to determine what should be chosen at what cost, and what should be endured for what gain; and harder still to stand by our decisions, because the expected consequences are generally painful, and what one is compelled to do is shameful. This is why those who *1110b* have been compelled or not are praised and blamed.

What sort of actions, then, should we describe as forced? If we speak without qualification, is it not whenever the cause is in the external circumstances and the agent contributes nothing? On the other hand, actions that in themselves are involuntary, but worth choosing at a certain time and for certain benefits, and have their first prin-ciple in the agent, are in themselves involuntary, but at that time and for those benefits voluntary. But they are more like voluntary actions, because actions are in the sphere of particulars, and here the particulars are voluntary. It is not easy, however, to explain what sort of things ought to be chosen in return for what, since there are many dif-ferences in particulars.

If someone were to claim that sweet and noble things are forcible (in that they compel us from an external posi-tion), he would be committed to all actions' being forced, since it is with those ends in view that everyone does everything. And people who are forced to act and do so involuntarily find it painful, while those who act because of what is pleasant or noble do so with pleasure. It is ridiculous to blame external circumstances and not oneself for being an easy prey to such things, and to take responsibility for noble actions oneself, but to make pleasant things responsible for shameful ones. What is forced, then, seems to be what has an external first principle, where the person forced contributes nothing.

Everything done through ignorance is non-voluntary, but what is involuntary also causes pain and regret; for the person who acted through ignorance, and is not upset in the slightest by what he has done, has not acted voluntarily, in that he did not know what he was doing, nor again involuntarily, in that he is not pained. Of those who act

---

[1] The play is now lost. Alcmaeon's father, Amphiaraus of Argos, had been persuaded by his wife to join an expedition against Thebes. Amphiaraus foresaw his own death, and charged his sons to avenge him, by killing his wife.

through ignorance, then, the one who regrets what he did seems to be an involuntary agent, while the one who shows no regret, since he is a different case, can be thought of as a non-voluntary agent; since he is a separate case, it is better that he should have a name of his own.

Acting through ignorance seems to be different from acting in ignorance, because the drunk or the person in a rage is not thought to act through ignorance, but through drunkenness or anger; he does so, however, not knowingly but in ignorance. In fact, every wicked person is ignorant of what he should do and refrain from doing, and missing the mark in this way makes people unjust and generally bad. An action is not properly called involuntary, however, if the agent is ignorant of what is beneficial, because it is not ignorance in rational choice that causes the involuntariness (that rather causes wickedness), nor ignorance of the universal (since people are blamed for that), but ignorance of particulars – the circumstances of the action and what it is concerned with. For it is on these that pity and pardon depend, since someone who is ignorant of any of them is acting involuntarily.

1111a

Perhaps it would be no bad thing, therefore, to delineate their nature and number. A person may be ignorant of who he is, of what he is doing, of the sphere in which or to what he is doing it, and sometimes also of what it is that he is doing it with (e.g., a tool), of what it is for (e.g., safety), and of the way in which he is doing it (e.g., gently or roughly). No one could be ignorant of all of these unless he were mad, and clearly not of the person doing the action; for how could he be ignorant of himself? But someone could be ignorant of what he is doing: people, for example, who say they are 'flustered while speaking', or 'did not know that it was a secret', as Aeschylus said of the Mysteries, or 'let it off when they wanted to show how it worked', as the person said of the catapult. Again, someone might think his son an enemy, as did Merope,[2] or that a pointed spear had a button on it, or that a stone was a piece of pumice. Or one might kill someone with a drink intended to save him. Or when wanting only to seize a person's hand, as in sparring, one might hurt him. There may be ignorance, then, concerning all of these aspects of the action, and the person who is ignorant of any of them seems to have acted involuntarily, especially in the case of the most important – these seem to be to what the action is being done and what it is for. It is, then, an action called involuntary on the basis of this particular kind of ignorance that must also give rise to pain and regret.

So, since what is involuntary is what is done by force or because of ignorance, what is voluntary would seem to be what has its first principle in the person himself when he knows the particular circumstances of the action.

It is probably a mistake to describe actions done through spirit or appetite as involuntary. For, first, none of the other animals, or children, will act voluntarily; and, secondly, is it meant that none of the actions we do through appetite and spirit is done involuntarily, or that we do the noble ones voluntarily, the disgraceful ones involuntarily? Would this not be absurd, since there is only one cause in play? And it would presumably also be odd to describe as involuntary things that we ought to desire; and there are indeed some things at which we ought to feel angry, and others, like health and learning, that we ought to want. Also, what is involuntary is thought to be painful, but what is in accordance with appetite pleasant. Again, what is the difference, as far as their being involuntary is concerned, between actions that miss the mark on the basis of calculation and those that miss it on the basis of spirit? For both are to be avoided, and the non-rational feelings are thought to be no less part of human nature, so that actions arising from spirit and appetite are also characteristic of a human being. It would be odd, then, to class them as involuntary.

1111b

Chapter 2

Now that we have delineated what is voluntary and what involuntary, we should next discuss rational choice; for it is thought to be very closely tied to virtue, and a better guide to men's characters than their actions.

Rational choice is obviously a voluntary thing, but it is not the same as what is voluntary, which is a broader notion: children and the other animals share in what is voluntary, but not in rational choice, and we describe actions done spontaneously as voluntary, but not as done in accordance with rational choice.

People who claim it is appetite or spirit or wish or some kind of belief do not seem to be right, since rational choice is not shared by beings who lack reason, while appetite and spirit are shared. Again, the incontinent person acts from appetite, but not from rational choice; while the self-controlled person does the contrary, and acts from rational choice, but not from appetite. Also, appetite can be in opposition to rational choice, but not to appetite. Again, appetite is concerned with what is pleasant and what is painful, rational choice with neither. Still less is it spirit, since actions done from spirit are least of all thought to be in accordance with rational choice.

---

[2] In Euripides' *Cresphontes* (lost). Merope was wife of Cresphontes, king of Messenia.

But, though it does seem closely connected with wish, it is not this either. For there is no rational choice of what is impossible, and someone claiming that he was rationally choosing this would be thought a fool. But there may be wish even for things that are impossible, such as immortality. And wish can also be for things one could never bring about by one's own efforts, such as that some actor or athlete win in a competition. No one, however, rationally chooses things like this, but only things that he thinks might come about through his own efforts. Again, wish is more to do with the end, rational choice with what is conducive to the end; for example, we wish to be healthy, but we rationally choose things that will make us healthy; and we wish to be happy, and say that we do, but to claim that we rationally choose to be so does not sound right. For in general rational choice seems to be concerned with things that are in our power.

Neither could it be belief, because belief seems to be concerned with everything – no less with what is eternal and what is impossible than with what is in our power. Besides, distinctions are made here on grounds of truth and falsity, not badness and goodness, as happens with rational choice.

Now perhaps no one does claim that it is the same as belief in general. But it is not even the same as any *1112a* particular species of belief, since our characters arise from our rationally choosing what is good and bad, not from having certain beliefs. And what we rationally choose is to obtain or avoid something good or bad, while we hold beliefs about what that is, whom it benefits, or in what way; we never really believe to obtain or avoid things. And rational choice is praised for its being of what is right rather than for its being correct, while belief is praised for being true. And we rationally choose what we best know to be good, while we hold beliefs about what we do not know at all to be good. And it appears as well that it is not the same people who are best at rationally choosing and at believing: some seem quite good at believing, but through vice choose what they should not. Whether belief is prior to rational choice or accompanies it makes no difference, because it is not this we are considering, but whether it is the same as some species of belief.

Given that it is none of the things we have mentioned, what is it, then, or what sort of thing is it? It is obviously something voluntary, but not everything that is voluntary is an object of rational choice. Well, is it what has been decided by prior deliberation? For rational choice does involve reason and thought, and its name (*prohairesis*) too seems to signify something that is chosen (*haireton*) before (*pro*) other things.

Chapter 3

Do people deliberate about everything, and is everything an object of deliberation, or is there no deliberation about some things? Presumably, we ought to describe as an object of deliberation what a sane person would deliberate about, not some fool or lunatic.

No one deliberates about eternal things, such as the universe, or the fact that the diagonal is incommensurable with the side; nor things that involve movement but always happen in the same way, either from necessity or by nature or through some other cause, such as the solstices or the rising of the stars; nor things that happen now in one way, now in another, such as droughts and rains; nor what happens by chance, such as the finding of treasure. We do not deliberate even about all human affairs; no Spartan, for example, would deliberate about the best form of government for the Scythians. The reason is that we could not bring about any of these things.

Rather, we deliberate about what is in our power, that is, what we can do; this is what remains. For nature, necessity and chance do seem to be causes, but so also do intellect and everything that occurs through human agency. Each group of people deliberates about what they themselves can do.

There is no deliberation about precise and self-sufficient sciences – letters, for example, because we are in no *1112b* doubt about how they should be written. Rather, what we deliberate about are things that we bring about, and not always in the same way – questions of medicine and of finance, for example, and of navigation more than of gymnastics, in that navigation has not been developed to such a level of exactness. We deliberate about other fields in the same way, and more about the skills than about the sciences, since we are less certain about the skills.

Deliberation is concerned with what usually happens in a certain way, where the consequences are unclear, and where things are not definite. On important issues, we do not trust our own ability to decide and call in others to help us deliberate.

We deliberate not about ends, but about things that are conducive to ends. For a doctor does not deliberate about whether to cure, nor an orator whether to persuade, nor a politician whether to produce good order; nor does anyone else deliberate about his end. Rather they establish an end and then go on to think about how and by what means it is to be achieved. If it appears that there are several means available, they consider by which it will be achieved in the easiest and most noble way; while if it can be attained by only one means, they consider how this will bring it about, and by what further means this means is itself to be brought about, until they arrive at the first cause, the last thing to be found. For the person who deliberates seems to inquire and analyse in the way described as though he were dealing with a geometrical figure (it seems that not all inquiry is deliberation – mathematics, for example – but that all deliberation is inquiry), and the last step in the analysis seems to be the first that comes to be.

If people meet with an impossibility, they give up: take, for example, the case where they need money, but there is none available. But if it seems possible they will try to do it. What is possible is what can be accomplished by our own efforts; what can be brought about through our friends is in a sense accomplished by our own efforts, in that the first principle is in us. The question is sometimes what tools to use, sometimes what use to make of them. The same goes for other cases: sometimes the question is the means, sometimes how they are to be used or the means to that use.

It seems, then, as we have said, that a human being is a first principle of actions. Deliberation is about what he can do himself, and actions are done for the sake of other things, because it is not the end but what is con-
1113a ducive to an end that is the object of deliberation. Nor are particulars the object, such as whether this is bread or has been baked as it should; these are matters of perception, and if we are always deliberating, it will never come to an end.

The objects of deliberation and of rational choice are the same, except that the object of rational choice has already been determined, since it is what has been decided upon as the result of deliberation that is the object of rational choice. For each person stops inquiring how he is to act as soon as he has traced the first principle back to himself, that is, to the part of him that gives commands, because it is this that rationally chooses. There is a good illustration of this in the ancient constitutions depicted by Homer: the kings proclaimed to the people what they had rationally chosen.

Since the object of rational choice is one of the things in our power that is desired after deliberation, rational choice will be deliberative desire for things in our power; for, when we have decided on the basis of deliberation, we desire in accordance with our deliberation.

Let this serve as an outline of rational choice, the nature of its objects, and the fact that it is concerned with what is conducive to ends.

Chapter 4

Wish, we have said, is for the end; but some think that the end here is the good, others the apparent good. Those who claim that the object of wish is the good are committed to the view that what a person wishes if he is choosing incorrectly is not an object of wish (if it were an object of wish, it would also be a good, but it was, perhaps, bad). On the other hand, those who claim the apparent good to be the object of wish must say that nothing is an object of wish by nature, but only what seems so to each person; and different people have different, and perhaps opposing, views.

If these consequences are unsatisfactory, then, should we say that, without qualification and in truth, the object of wish is the good, but for the individual it is the apparent good? Then for the good person the object of wish is that which is truly an object of wish, but for the bad person it is any chance thing. This is like the case of bodies, where things that are truly healthy are healthy for bodies that are in good condition, while for those that are diseased other things are healthy; and the same goes for things that are bitter, sweet, hot, heavy, and so on. The good person judges each case rightly, and in each case the truth is manifest to him. For each state has its own conception of what is noble and pleasant, and one might say that the good person stands out a long way by seeing the truth in each case, being a sort of standard and measure of what is noble and pleasant. In the case of the masses, however,
1113b pleasure seems to deceive them, because it looks like a good when it is not; people therefore choose what is pleasant thinking it to be a good, and avoid pain thinking it to be an evil.

Chapter 5

Since, then, the object of wish is the end, and the object of wish and of rational choice is what conduces to the end, actions concerning what conduces to the end will be in accordance with rational choice and voluntary. The activities of the virtues are concerned with what conduces to the end; virtue, then, is in our power, and so is vice. Where it is in our power to act, it is also in our power not to act, and where saying 'No' is in our power, so is saying 'Yes'; so that if it is in our power to act when it would be noble, it will also be in our power not to act when it would be shameful, and if it is in our power not to act when it would be noble, it will also be in our power to act when it would be shameful. Now if it is in our power to do noble and shameful actions, and the same goes for not doing them, and if, as we saw, being good and bad consists in this, then it is in our power to be good or bad.

The saying, 'No one is voluntarily wicked, nor involuntarily blessed', seems partly false, and partly true. For no one is involuntarily blessed, but wickedness is voluntary; otherwise we shall have to disagree with what we have just said, and deny that a human being is a first principle or the begetter of his actions as he is of his children. But if it is clear that he is, and we cannot refer back to any other first principles beyond those within us, the actions whose first principles are within us will themselves also be in our power and voluntary.

This view seems to be backed up not only by each of us as private individuals, but also by legislators themselves. For they punish and penalize anyone who does wicked things, unless he acts by force or through ignorance for which he is not himself culpable, and they reward anyone who does noble things, as if encouraging the one while deterring the other. But no one is urged to do what is neither in our power nor voluntary; people assume it to be a waste of time to persuade us not to be hot or in pain or hungry or anything else like that, because we shall experience them anyway.

Indeed, legislators punish an offender for ignorance itself, if he is thought to be responsible for the ignorance. For example, there are double penalties for a drunken offender; the first principle lies in him, in that he had the power not to get drunk, and his getting drunk was the cause of his ignorance. And they punish those who are ignorant of *1114a* any uncomplicated point of law that they ought to have known. The same sort of thing happens in other cases where people are thought to be ignorant through negligence, on the ground that it was in their power not to be ignorant, because it was up to them whether they took care.

Well, perhaps he is the sort of person not to take care. Nevertheless, people are themselves responsible for turning out like this, through the slackness of their lives – responsible for being unjust by doing wrong, or intemperate by spending their time in drinking and the like; in each sphere people's activities give them the corresponding character. This is clear from the case of people training for any competition or action, since they practise the relevant activity continually. A person would have to be utterly senseless not to know that states in each sphere arise from their corresponding activities.

Again, it is unreasonable to think that someone who does unjust actions does not wish to be unjust, or that someone who does intemperate actions does not wish to be intemperate. If a person does what he knows will make him unjust, he will be unjust voluntarily. It does not follow, however, that, if he wishes, he will stop being unjust and be just. For neither does the ill person become well like this; but he is ill voluntarily, by living incontinently and ignoring his doctors, if that was what happened. At that time, it was open to him not to be ill, but it is no longer so once he has thrown away his chance; similarly, one can no longer recover a stone once one has thrown it, though it was in one's power to throw it, because the first principle lay within one. So too from the start it was open to the unjust person and the intemperate person not to become such, so that they are what they are voluntarily; but now that they have become what they are, it is no longer possible for them to be otherwise.

But it is not only the vices of the soul that are voluntary; those of the body are too for some people, whom we go on to blame. For nobody blames someone unattractive by nature, but we do if he is so through not exercising and looking after himself. The same goes for weakness and disability; nobody would criticize a person blind by nature, or as the result of a disease or an injury, but rather pity him; everyone, however, would blame a person who was blind from drinking or some other intemperance. So bodily vices in our power are blamed, while those not in our power are not. And if so, then in other cases the vices that are blamed will be those in our power.

But suppose somebody argues: 'Everyone aims at what appears good to him, but over this appearance we have *1114b* no control; rather, how the end appears to each person depends on what sort of person he is. So, if each person is in some way responsible for his own state, he will also be in some way responsible for how it appears. If he is not, however, then no one will be responsible for his own wrongdoing, but he will do these things through ignorance of the end, thinking that they will result in what is best for him. His aiming at the end is not up to him, but he must be born with a kind of vision, to enable him to judge nobly and to choose what is truly good. And a person is naturally good if he has this naturally noble capacity, since it is the greatest and noblest thing, and one cannot acquire or learn it from another; rather, his state will result from its natural character, and when it is naturally good and noble, this will be complete and true natural excellence.'

If this is true, how will virtue be any more voluntary than vice? For how the end appears and is determined – by nature or whatever – is the same for both the good and the bad person, and it is by referring everything else to this that they do whatever they do.

So whether it is not by nature that the end appears to each person in whatever way it does appear, but the person plays some role as well, or whether the end is fixed by nature, but virtue is voluntary because the good person does the remaining actions voluntarily, vice will be no less voluntary than virtue. For the part played by the person himself is found to the same extent in the actions of the bad person, even if not in the end.

If, then, as we suggested, virtues are voluntary (because we are in some way partly responsible for our states of character, and it is by our being the kind of people that we are that we assume such and such as our end), vices also will be voluntary; they are on the same footing.

With regard to virtues in general, then, we have given an outline account of their genus: they are means, they are states, they lead to actions that are in accordance with virtues and such as those from which they developed, they are in our power and voluntary, and they are as correct reason prescribes.

Actions and states, however, are not voluntary in the same way. For, being aware of the particulars we are in control of actions from the first principle to the end, but, though we control the first principle, the progress through the particular stages of states is not noticeable, as happens with illnesses; but, because it was in our power to behave in this way or that, states are voluntary.

1115a

Let us now resume consideration of the virtues, and one by one say what each is, what sort of things it is concerned with, and in what way; at the same time, it will be clear how many there are.

[…]

Book VI

Chapter 1

Since we have already stated that one should rationally choose the mean, not the excess or the deficiency, and that the mean is as correct reason prescribes, let us now analyse this prescription.

In all the states of character we have mentioned, and in the others as well, there is a sort of target, and it is with his eye on this that the person with reason tightens or loosens his string. There is also a sort of standard for the mean states, which, as we say, lie between excess and deficiency and are in accordance with correct reason.

But to say this, though true, is not at all clear. For in all other practices of which there is a science it is true to say that one should exert oneself and relax neither too much nor too little, but to the extent of the mean that is prescribed by correct reason. But having grasped only this, someone would be none the wiser; for example, you would not know what sort of treatments to use on your body if someone were to say that you should employ those that medicine requires, and in the way that a medical practitioner employs them. With states of the soul as well, then, we must not only offer this truism, but also determine what correct reason is and what its standard is.

1139a

When we had classified the virtues of the soul, we said that some are virtues of character, others of thought. We have discussed the virtues of character; so let us now speak as follows of those that remain.

[…]

Chapter 5

We may grasp what practical wisdom is by considering the sort of people we describe as practically wise. It seems to be characteristic of the practically wise person to be able to deliberate nobly about what is good and beneficial for himself, not in particular respects, such as what conduces to health or strength, but about what conduces to living well as a whole.

An indication of this is the fact that we call people practically wise in some particular respect whenever they calculate well to promote some good end that lies outside the ambit of a skill; so, where living well as a whole is concerned, the person capable of deliberation will also be practically wise.

No one deliberates about what cannot be otherwise, or about things he cannot do. So, if scientific knowledge involves demonstration, but there is no demonstration of anything whose first principles can be otherwise (since every such thing might be otherwise), and if one cannot deliberate about what is necessary, then practical wisdom

1140b

cannot be scientific knowledge. Nor can it be skill. It is not scientific knowledge because what is done can be otherwise; and it is not skill because action and production are generically different.

It remains therefore that it is a true and practical state involving reason, concerned with what is good and bad for a human being. For while production has an end distinct from itself, this could not be so with action, since the end here is acting well itself. This is why we think Pericles and people like him are practically wise, because they can see what is good for themselves and what is good for people in general; and we consider household managers and politicians to be like this.

This is also how temperance (*sōphrosunē*) got its name, because it preserves (*sōzein*) practical wisdom (*phronēsis*). It preserves the kind of supposition we have described; it is not every supposition that is ruined and distorted by what is pleasant or painful – not, for example, the supposition that a triangle does or does not have not two right angles – but rather those about what is done. For the first principle of what is done consists in the goal it seeks. But if a person has been ruined by pleasure or pain, it follows that this first principle will not be evident to him, nor the fact that this ought to be the goal and cause of everything he chooses and does; for vice tends to destroy the first principle.

Practical wisdom, then, must be a true state involving reason, concerned with action in relation to human goods. Moreover, while there is a virtue in skill, there is none in practical wisdom. In skill the person who misses the mark voluntarily is preferable, but with practical wisdom, as with the virtues, the reverse is true. Clearly, then, practical wisdom is a virtue and not a skill. And since there are two parts of the soul that possess reason, it will be the virtue of one of them, namely, that which forms beliefs, both belief and practical wisdom being concerned with what can be otherwise. Moreover it is not merely a state involving reason; an indication of this is the fact that such a state can be forgotten, but practical wisdom cannot.

[...]

Chapter 8

Political science and practical wisdom are the same state, but their being is different.

There are two sides to practical wisdom as concerned with the city; that which co-ordinates is legislative science, while that concerned with particulars has the name 'political science', which properly belongs to both. That concerned with particulars is practical and deliberative, since a decree is to be acted on, as the last thing reached in deliberation. This is why it is only people exhibiting this kind of practical wisdom who are said to participate in politics: they are the only ones who practise politics in the way that craftsmen practise.

Practical wisdom is also thought of especially in terms of that form of it that is concerned with oneself, the individual; it has the name 'practical wisdom', which properly is common to the various kinds, namely, household management, legislative science, and political science, the latter being subdivided into deliberative and judicial science.

One species of practical wisdom will indeed be knowledge of what is in one's own interests, but there is much disagreement about it.

The person who knows his own interests and makes these his concern seems to be a practically wise person, *1142a* while politicians are seen as busybodies. So Euripides says:

> How can I be a practically wise person, when I might have lived free from business,
> Counted among the masses in the army,
> And have had an equal share?
> For people who are out of the ordinary and busy themselves too much ...[3]

For people do seek their own good, and think that this course of action is what is required. So from this belief has arisen the notion that people like this are practically wise. Nevertheless, one's own good will presumably not exist without the management of a household and without a political system.

Besides, how one should manage one's own affairs is not clear, and ought to be considered. What I have said is supported by the fact that, though the young become proficient in geometry and mathematics, and wise in matters

---

[3] Euripides, *Philoctetes* frr. 787, 788 Nauck.

like these, they do not seem to become practically wise. The reason is that practical wisdom is concerned also with particular facts, and particulars come to be known from experience; and a young person is not experienced, since experience takes a long time to produce.

Indeed, one might ask this question as well: why a boy can become accomplished in mathematics, but not in wisdom or natural science. Surely it is because mathematics is a matter of abstraction, while the first principles of the latter two come from experience? The young speak of them, but without conviction, while the essence of mathematical things is clear enough to them.

Again, error in deliberation can concern either the universal or the particular; for example, thinking that all kinds of water that are heavier than usual are bad, or that this particular water is heavier than usual.

It is obvious that practical wisdom is not scientific knowledge; for, as we have said, it is concerned with the last thing, since this is what is done. It is therefore opposed to intellect, since intellect is concerned with the first terms, of which there is no rational account to be given, while practical wisdom is concerned with the last thing; and this is the object of perception, not of scientific knowledge. This is not the perception concerned with objects peculiar to any particular sense, but like that with which we perceive that the last mathematical object is a triangle; for it will stop here as well. But this is more perception than practical wisdom, though it is another species of perception.

Chapter 9

Inquiry is not the same as deliberation, since deliberation is a kind of inquiry. We must also grasp the nature of good deliberation, and see whether it is some kind of science, or belief, or good guesswork, or some other sort of thing.

1142b   First, it is not scientific knowledge, since people do not inquire about what they know; but good deliberation is a kind of deliberation, and a person who deliberates is engaged in inquiry and calculation.

Nor, moreover, is it good guesswork. Good guesswork does not involve reason and is done quickly, whereas people deliberate for a long time, and say that one should act quickly on the result of one's deliberation, but deliberate slowly. Again, readiness of mind is different from good deliberation, and readiness of mind is a kind of good guesswork.

Nor is good deliberation any kind of belief. But since the person who deliberates badly is in error, while he who deliberates well does things correctly, good deliberation is clearly some kind of correctness; but it is not correctness in knowledge or belief. For there is no such thing as correctness in knowledge, since there is no such thing as error in it either; and correctness of belief is truth. Besides, everything that is an object of belief is already determined.

But excellence in deliberation does involve reason. What remains, then, is that it is correctness in thought, since this is not yet assertion. For belief is not inquiry, but already a kind of assertion, while the person who deliberates, whether he does so well or badly, is inquiring into something and calculating.

But since good deliberation is a kind of correctness in deliberation, we must first inquire into the nature and sphere of deliberation. Since there are various kinds of correctness, it is clear that good deliberation does not consist in every kind. For the incontinent or the bad person will achieve by calculation what he proposes as required, so that, though he will have deliberated correctly, he will have gained a great evil. Having deliberated well, however, seems to be something good, since the sort of correctness in deliberation that comprises good deliberation is the sort that achieves something good. But it is also possible to achieve something good through false inference, that is, to achieve the right result, but not by the right steps, the middle term being false. So this kind of correctness, on the basis of which we achieve the right result, but not by the right steps, is not yet good deliberation either.

Again, one person may achieve the right result after a long period of deliberation, another after a short period. So long deliberation is not enough for good deliberation, which is rather correctness regarding what is beneficial, about the right thing, in the right way, and at the right time.

Again, it is possible to have deliberated well either in an unqualified sense or towards some particular end. Good deliberation in the unqualified sense, then, is what succeeds in relation to the end in the unqualified sense, good deliberation in the particular sense in relation to some particular end.

If, then, it is characteristic of practically wise people to have deliberated well, good deliberation will be correctness with regard to what is useful towards the end, about which practical wisdom is true supposition.

Chapter 10

Judgement, that is good judgement, in virtue of which people are said to have judgement or good judgement, is *1143a* not the same as knowledge in general, or the same as belief (since then everyone would have been a person of judgement); nor is it any one of the particular sciences, such as medicine, which has health as its concern, or geometry, which has spatial dimensions. Judgement is concerned not with what is eternal and unchanging, nor with what comes into being, but with what someone might puzzle and deliberate about. For this reason it is concerned with the same things as practical wisdom.

But judgement and practical wisdom are not the same. Practical wisdom gives commands, since its end is what should or should not be done, while judgement only judges. Judgement and good judgement are the same, as are those with judgement and those with good judgement.

Judgement, then, is neither the possession nor the acquisition of practical wisdom. But just as understanding is called judging, when one employs scientific knowledge, so we also call judging what is involved in employing belief to judge what someone else says about what concerns practical wisdom (and it must judge it nobly, since judging it well is the same as judging it nobly). From this use of the word judgement in the case of understanding is derived the sense in virtue of which people are described as having good judgement, since we often say that understanding is judging.

Chapter 11

What is called discernment, in virtue of which we say that people are discerning and have discernment, is correct judgement of what is equitable. This is indicated by the fact that we say that the equitable person is especially discerning, and that it is equitable to be discerning in certain circumstances. Discernment is correctly discerning judgement of what is equitable; and correct discernment is that which judges what is true.

All these states naturally tend in the same direction. For we attribute discernment, judgement, practical wisdom, and intellect to the same people, saying that they have discernment and thereby intellect, and that they are practically wise and have judgement. For all these audacities are to do with the last things – particular things – and being a person of judgement, a person of sound discernment, or a discerning person, consists in the capacity to judge in those matters that are of concern to the practically wise person. For what is equitable is the common concern of all good people in their relations with others.

Everything that is done is one of the particular and last things; for the practically wise person must understand these, and judgement and discernment are concerned with what is done, and this is one of the last things.

Intellect is also concerned with the last things, and in both directions; there is intellection, not a rational account, *1143b* of both the first terms and the last. The intellect related to demonstrations is concerned with the first and unchanging terms, while in practical questions intellect is concerned with the last term, which can be otherwise, that is, with the minor premise. For these last terms are the first principles for achieving the end, since universals are arrived at from particulars. We ought, then, to have perception of these, and this is intellection.

This is why these states seem to be natural endowments, and why no one is held to be wise by nature, though he may by nature have discernment, judgement and intellect. An indication of this is our thinking that these qualities are related to one's time of life, and the fact that intellect and discernment belong to a particular time of life, which implies that nature is the cause. So we should attend to the undemonstrated words and beliefs of experienced and older people or of practically wise people, no less than to demonstrations, because their experienced eye enables them to see correctly.

We have now stated what practical wisdom and wisdom are, what each is concerned with, and that each is a virtue of a different part of the soul.

Chapter 12

Someone might wonder what use these states are. Wisdom, since it is not concerned with any process of coming into being, will not consider any of the things that make a human being happy, and though practical wisdom does do this, what do we need it for? Practical wisdom is concerned with acts that are just, noble, and good for a human being, but these are characteristic of the good person, and we are no more able to do them through knowing about them, since the virtues are states of character. In the same way, we are no more able to do what is healthy and invigorating – in the sense not of what produces a healthy state but of what results from it – with knowledge alone; for we are no more able to act merely through having scientific knowledge of medicine or of gymnastics.

If we are to say, however, that practical wisdom is useful not for this purpose, but for becoming good, then it will be of no use to those who are good already. Again, it will not actually be useful to people who are not good, since it will make no difference whether they possess it themselves or take the advice of others who possess it; it would be enough for us to do what we do in the case of health – we wish to be healthy, yet we do not learn medicine.

In addition, given that a productive science does govern each product and issue commands about it, it will seem odd if practical wisdom, which is inferior to wisdom, is to be put in control of it.

These, then, are the things we must discuss, since up to now we have only raised the puzzles about them.

1144a   First, then, let us say that these states must be worthy of choice in themselves, even if neither produces anything whatsoever, since each is a virtue of one of the two parts of the soul.

Secondly, they do in fact produce something. Wisdom produces happiness, not as medicine produces health, but as health does. For by being a part of virtue as a whole, it makes a person happy through its being possessed and being exercised.

Again, our characteristic activity is achieved in accordance with practical wisdom and virtue of character; for virtue makes the aim right, and practical wisdom the things towards it. There is no such virtue of the fourth, nutritive part of the soul, because there is nothing it has the power to do or not to do.

As regards the claim that practical wisdom does not increase our capacity for just and noble acts, we should begin a little further back, taking the following as our first principle. We say that some people who do just actions are not yet just; for example, those who do what is laid down by the laws either involuntarily or through ignorance or for some other reason, and not for the sake of the actions themselves (though they do indeed do what they should and what a good person is required to do). Similarly, it seems that there is a way in which a person can do each action so as to be good, namely, as the result of rational choice and for the sake of the actions themselves.

Virtue makes the rational choice right, but the actions of the natural stages in the achievement of that choice are the concern not of virtue but of another capacity – and we must understand these more clearly before proceeding with our discussion.

There is a capacity that people call cleverness. This is such as to be able to do the actions that tend towards the aim we have set before ourselves, and to achieve it. If the aim is noble, then the cleverness is praiseworthy; if it is bad, then it is villainy. This is why both practically wise and villainous people are called clever.

Practical wisdom is not the same as this capacity, though it does involve it. And, as we have said and as is clear, virtue is involved in this eye of the soul's reaching its developed state. For practical syllogisms have a first principle: 'Since such-and-such is the end or chief good', whatever it is (let it be anything you like for the sake of argument). And this is evident to the good person alone, since wickedness distorts our vision and thoroughly deceives us about the first principles of actions.

1144b   Manifestly, then, one cannot be practically wise without being good.

Chapter 13

We must therefore also consider virtue again, because it is related in almost the same way: as practical wisdom is to cleverness – they are not the same, but similar – so natural virtue is to real virtue.

Each of us seems to possess the character he has in some sense by nature, since right from birth we are just, prone to temperance, courageous, and the rest. Nevertheless we expect to find that what is really good is something different, and that we shall possess these qualities in another way. For both children and animals have the natural states, but without intellect they are obviously harmful. This, at least, does seem an observed fact, that just as a strongly built person, if he is deprived of sight, is apt to stumble heavily when he moves around, because he cannot see, so too with virtue. But if the agent acquires intellect, then his action is quite different; his state, while similar to what it was, will then be real virtue.

So, as there are two states, cleverness and practical wisdom, in the part of the soul related to belief, so there are two in the part related to character – natural virtue and real virtue; and of these real virtue does not develop without practical wisdom.

This is why some people say that all the virtues are forms of practical wisdom, and why Socrates was partly right and partly wrong in his inquiry. He was wrong to think that all the virtues are forms of practical wisdom, but correct in saying that they involve practical wisdom. There is evidence for this in the fact that whenever people now define virtue, they all say what state it is and what its objects are, and then add that it is a state in accordance with right reason. Right reason is that which is in accordance with practical wisdom; everyone, then, seems in some way to divine that the state like this, in accordance with practical wisdom, is virtue.

But we need to go a little further. Virtue is not merely the state in accordance with right reason, but that which involves it. And practical wisdom is right reason about such matters. Socrates, then, thought that the virtues were forms of reason (since he believed them all to be forms of knowledge), while we think that they involve reason.

It is clear from what we have said, then, that we cannot be really good without practical wisdom, or practically wise without virtue of character.

(Moreover, on these lines one might also meet the dialectical argument that could be used to suggest that the virtues exist in isolation from one another. The same person, it might be argued, is not best suited by nature for all the virtues, so that he will already have acquired one before he has acquired another. This is possible in respect of the natural virtues, but not in respect of those on the basis of which a person is said to be really good; for he will *1145a* possess all of them as soon as he acquires the one, practical wisdom.)

Clearly, even if practical wisdom were not of value in action, it would be needed, since it is the virtue of this part of the soul; and clearly too rational choice will not be correct in the absence of either practical wisdom or virtue. For the one sets the end, while the other makes us do what is towards the end.

Moreover, practical wisdom is not in control of wisdom or the superior part of the soul, just as medicine is not in control of health. For it does not make use of health, but provides for its coming into being; it therefore issues prescriptions for the sake of health, but not to it. Besides, saying this would be like saying that political science governs the gods, since it issues prescriptions about everything in the city.

Epicurus to Menoeceus and *Principal Doctrines*

Epicurus

hedonism [2 forms] ?

One of Epicurus's central questions is: what is the human good? That is, what is it that makes human life good – or indeed bad – for those living it? On one plausible reading, his answer is a version of hedonism (Letter to Monoeceus 128–9). It is important to distinguish two forms or levels of hedonism. The first level is merely substantive. According to hedonism so understood, the good things in life are pleasurable experiences, and the bad things are painful experiences. An explanatory hedonist will go on to say that what *makes* these things good and bad is, respectively, solely their pleasantness and their painfulness. Other explanatory views are possible. For example, one might think that what makes things good for us is their fulfilling our nature, not their pleasantness, and combine this with the view that what in fact fulfils our nature is our experiencing pleasures. It is not clear whether Epicurus is an explanatory hedonist. He speaks of pleasure as the 'first good', as if there are others, and yet goes on to say that pleasure is the standard for assessing all goods (LM 128–9).

Hedonism then as now was often associated with sensualism, and Epicurus is careful to distance himself from any view putting great weight on bodily pleasures. The pleasantest life is that of philosophy, and there is no extra pleasure in luxury once any pain from fear or want has been removed (LM 122, 130–1; Principal Doctrines 3, 10, 18).

The ancient philosophers were especially exercised by the question of the relation of happiness and virtue. Since egoism – the view that one has strongest or only reason to promote one's own good – was standardly assumed, hedonists were often charged with undermining morality. Why should I be generous or just if I can increase the balance of pleasure over pain in my life by acting viciously? Epicurus insists that not only can one live pleasantly only by living virtuously, but living virtuously will always enable one to live pleasantly (PD 5; see LM 132). Again this enables Epicurus to ward off any charge of sensualism. But it opens him up to objections based on cases in which the virtuous choice seems extremely painful; for example, one may be required to keep some secret while being tortured to death.

The most famous arguments in the passage concern death. Most people think death is an evil and something to be feared. Epicurus thinks this is a terrible error, which causes us to feel ungrounded and unpleasant fear (LM 124–5; PD 2). One of his arguments is connected with hedonism. If only pain is bad, then death cannot be bad, since it involves lack of any sensation. Some hedonists might claim that death is *substantively* a bad thing, although it is not bad in so far as it is painful. This position seems implausible, however. Death for a hedonist really is neither a good nor a bad thing in itself.

Does that mean we have no reason to fear it, then? That, a hedonist might claim, would be a mistake. Being attacked by a savage dog is neither good nor bad in itself; but it is to be feared because of its likely effect on the balance of pleasure over pain in one's life. The same is true of death. For many of us, death is bad in so far as it has a negative effect on the balance of pleasure over pain in our lives as a whole, since it shortens those lives.

History of Ethics – Essential Readings with Commentary, First Edition. Edited by Daniel Star and Roger Crisp.
© 2020 John Wiley & Sons Ltd. Published 2020 by John Wiley & Sons Ltd.

Here Epicurus can introduce his second argument. <u>Death is nothing to us, since while we exist it is absent; and when it is present, we ourselves</u> do not exist. One natural hedonist response employs counterfactuals. If I do not die tomorrow, my life will be more valuable for me overall than were I to die. Dying is hence a worse outcome, and so I fear it. Nevertheless, many have rightly found Epicurus's reflections tantalizing and fascinating, and he raises deep questions about how best to classify goods and bads, when we should claim that such goods and bads affect us, and whether it can be good or bad to be brought into being (after all, if I had not been born, it is hard to see in what sense this could have been worse *for me*, since I would not have existed; and if never having existed could not harm me, Epicurus might ask, how can death – which is just non-existence again – be harmful?).

<u>To be happy</u>, Epicurus believes, <u>requires that one be free from troubles.</u> So for him, <u>security</u> is especially important (PD 6), and he advises living a quiet life to avoid putting one's own security at risk (PD 14). Although <u>friendship is important</u> (PD 27), one should make oneself immune to at least some of the risks of friendship, such as grief at a friend's death, by reflecting philosophically on the fact that death is not bad (PD 40).

morality :

Epicurus also <u>reflects upon the security provided by justice, understood in a broad sense as roughly equivalent to morality as a whole</u> (PD 31–8). Anticipating Hobbes, Epicurus claims that morality is a compact between people to live by certain generally beneficial rules. But what if I can get away with cheating? Epicurus's response here is down to earth: you can never be sure you won't be caught. Nevertheless, what if the benefit of cheating is huge, and the chance of being caught is tiny? Here he will return to the argument discussed earlier, on the relation of virtue and happiness. But there might seem to be something of a tension in Epicurus's position at this point. If people can be brought to see that their greatest happiness lies in virtue, what need will be there for any compact? Perhaps the compact is designed for the unenlightened. But then what does virtue consist of, if justice is *nothing but* a compact (PD 33)? Epicurus's contractualism might be more plausible if understood historically, as an account of how the actual institution of morality came into being.

justice is just a compact '

Epicurus to Menoeceus

LET no one when young delay to study philosophy, nor when he is old grow weary of his study. For no one can come too early or too late to secure the health of his soul. And the man who says that the age for philosophy has either not yet come or has gone by is like the man who says that the age for happiness is not yet come to him, or has passed away. Wherefore both when young and old a man must study philosophy, that as he grows old he may be young in blessings through the grateful recollection of what has been, and that in youth he may be old as well, since he will know no fear of what is to come. We must then meditate on the things that make our happiness, seeing that when that is with us we have all, but when it is absent we do all to win it.

The things which I used unceasingly to commend to you, these do and practice, considering them to be the first principles of the good life. First of all believe that god is a being immortal and blessed, even as the common idea of a god is engraved on men's minds, and do not assign to him anything alien to his immortality or ill-suited to his blessedness: but believe about him everything that can uphold his blessedness and immortality. For gods there are, since the knowledge of them is by clear vision. But they are not such as the many believe them to be: for indeed they do not consistently represent them as they believe them to be. And the impious man is not he who denies the gods of the many, but he who attaches to the gods the beliefs of the many. For the statements of the many about the gods are not conceptions derived from sensation, but false suppositions, according to which the greatest misfortunes befall the wicked and the greatest blessings ⟨the good⟩ by the gift of the gods. For men being accustomed always to their own virtues welcome those like themselves, but regard all that is not of their nature as alien.

Become accustomed to the belief that death is nothing to us. For all good and evil consists in sensation, but death is deprivation of sensation. And therefore a right understanding that death is nothing to us makes the mortality of life enjoyable, not because it adds to it an infinite span of time, but because it takes away the craving for immortality. For there is nothing terrible in life for the man who has truly comprehended that there is nothing terrible in not living. So that the man speaks but idly who says that he fears death not because it will be painful when it comes, but because it is painful in anticipation. For that which gives no trouble when it comes, is but an empty pain in anticipation. So death, the most terrifying of ills, is nothing to us, since so long as we exist, death is not with us; but when death comes, then we do not exist. It does not then concern either the living or the dead, since for the former it is not, and the latter are no more.

But the many at one moment shun death as the greatest of evils, at another ⟨yearn for it⟩ as a respite from the ⟨evils⟩ in life. ⟨But the wise man neither seeks to escape life⟩ nor fears the cessation of life, for neither does life offend him nor does the absence of life seem to be any evil. And just as with food he does not seek simply the larger share and nothing else, but rather the most pleasant, so he seeks to enjoy not the longest period of time, but the most pleasant.

And he who counsels the young man to live well, but the old man to make a good end, is foolish, not merely because of the desirability of life, but also because it is the same training which teaches to live well and to die well. Yet much worse still is the man who says it is good not to be born, but

'once born make haste to pass the gates of Death'.

For if he says this from conviction why does he not pass away out of life? For it is open to him to do so, if he had firmly made up his mind to this. But if he speaks in jest, his words are idle among men who cannot receive them.

We must then bear in mind that the future is neither ours, nor yet wholly not ours, so that we may not altogether expect it as sure to come, nor abandon hope of it, as if it will certainly not come.

We must consider that of desires some are natural, others vain, and of the natural some are necessary and others merely natural; and of the necessary some are necessary for happiness, others for the repose of the body, and others for very life. The right understanding of these facts enables us to refer all choice and avoidance to the health of the body and ⟨the soul's⟩ freedom from disturbance, since this is the aim of the life of blessedness. For it is to obtain this end that we always act, namely, to avoid pain and fear. And when this is once secured for us, all the tempest of the soul is dispersed, since the living creature has not to wander as though in search of something that is missing, and to look for some other thing by which he can fulfil the good of the soul and the good of the body. For it is then that we have need of pleasure, when we feel pain owing to the absence of pleasure; ⟨but when we do not feel pain⟩, we no longer need pleasure. And for this cause we call pleasure the beginning and end of the blessed life. For we recognize pleasure as the first good innate in us, and from pleasure we begin every act of choice and avoidance, and to pleasure we return again, using the feeling as the standard by which we judge every good.

And since pleasure is the first good and natural to us, for this very reason we do not choose every pleasure, but sometimes we pass over many pleasures, when greater discomfort accrues to us as the result of them: and similarly we think many pains better than pleasures, since a greater pleasure comes to us when we have endured pains for a long time. Every pleasure then because of its natural kinship to us is good, yet not every pleasure is to be chosen: even as every pain also is an evil, yet not all are always of a nature to be avoided. Yet by a scale of comparison and by the consideration of advantages and disadvantages we must form our judgement on all these matters. For the good on certain occasions we treat as bad, and conversely the bad as good.

And again independence of desire we think a great good—not that we may at all times enjoy but a few things, but that, if we do not possess many, we may enjoy the few in the genuine persuasion that those have the sweetest pleasure in luxury who least need it, and that all that is natural is easy to be obtained, but that which is superfluous is hard. And so plain savours bring us a pleasure equal to a luxurious diet, when all the pain due to want is removed; and bread and water produce the highest pleasure, when one who needs them puts them to his lips. To grow accustomed therefore to simple and not luxurious diet gives us health to the full, and makes a man alert for the needful employments of life, and when after long intervals we approach luxuries disposes us better towards them, and fits us to be fearless of fortune.

When, therefore, we maintain that pleasure is the end, we do not mean the pleasures of profligates and those that consist in sensuality, as is supposed by some who are either ignorant or disagree with us or do not understand, but freedom from pain in the body and from trouble in the mind. For it is not continuous drinkings and revellings, nor the satisfaction of lusts, nor the enjoyment of fish and other luxuries of the wealthy table, which produce a pleasant life, but sober reasoning, searching out the motives for all choice and avoidance, and banishing mere opinions, to which are due the greatest disturbance of the spirit.

Of all this the beginning and the greatest good is prudence. Wherefore prudence is a more precious thing even than philosophy: for from prudence are sprung all the other virtues, and it teaches us that it is not possible to live pleasantly without living prudently and honourably and justly, ⟨nor, again, to live a life of prudence, honour, and justice⟩ without living pleasantly. For the virtues are by nature bound up with the pleasant life, and the pleasant life is inseparable from them. For indeed who, think you, is a better man than he who holds reverent opinions concerning the gods, and is at all times free from fear of death, and has reasoned out the end ordained by nature? He understands that the limit of good things is easy to fulfil and easy to attain, whereas the course of ills is either short in time or slight in pain: he laughs at ⟨destiny⟩, whom some have introduced as the mistress of all things. ⟨He thinks that with us lies the chief power in determining events, some of which happen by necessity⟩ and some by chance, and some are within our control; for while necessity cannot be called to account, he sees that chance is inconstant, but that which is in our control is subject to no master, and to it are naturally attached praise and blame. For, indeed, it were better to follow the myths about the gods than to become a slave to the destiny of the natural philosophers: for the former suggests a hope of placating the gods by worship, whereas the latter involves a necessity which knows no placation. As to chance, he does not regard it as a god as most men do (for in a god's acts there is no disorder), nor as an uncertain cause ⟨of all things⟩: for he does not believe that good and evil are given by chance to man for the framing of a blessed life, but that opportunities for great good and great evil are afforded by it. He therefore thinks it better to be unfortunate in reasonable action than to prosper in unreason. For it is better in a man's actions that what is well chosen ⟨should fail, rather than that what is ill chosen⟩ should be successful owing to chance.

Meditate therefore on these things and things akin to them night and day by yourself, and with a companion like to yourself, and never shall you be disturbed waking or asleep, but you shall live like a god among men. For a man who lives among immortal blessings is not like to a mortal being.

Principal Doctrines

I. THE blessed and immortal nature knows no trouble itself nor causes trouble to any other, so that it is never constrained by anger or favour. For all such things exist only in the weak.

II. Death is nothing to us: for that which is dissolved is without sensation; and that which lacks sensation is nothing to us.

III. The limit of quantity in pleasures is the removal of all that is painful. Wherever pleasure is present, as long as it is there, there is neither pain of body nor of mind, nor of both at once.

IV. Pain does not last continuously in the flesh, but the acutest pain is there for a very short time, and even that which just exceeds the pleasure in the flesh does not continue for many days at once. But chronic illnesses permit a predominance of pleasure over pain in the flesh.

V. It is not possible to live pleasantly without living prudently and honourably and justly, [nor again to live a life of prudence, honour, and justice] without living pleasantly. And the man who does not possess the pleasant life, is not living prudently and honourably and justly, [and the man who does not possess the virtuous life], cannot possibly live pleasantly.

VI. To secure protection from men anything is a natural good, by which you may be able to attain this end.

VII. Some men wished to become famous and conspicuous, thinking that they would thus win for themselves safety from other men. Wherefore if the life of such men is safe, they have obtained the good which nature craves; but if it is not safe, they do not possess that for which they strove at first by the instinct of nature.

VIII. No pleasure is a bad thing in itself: but the means which produce some pleasures bring with them disturbances many times greater than the pleasures.

IX. If every pleasure could be intensified so that it lasted and influenced the whole organism or the most essential parts of our nature, pleasures would never differ from one another.

X. If the things that produce the pleasures of profligates could dispel the fears of the mind about the phenomena of the sky and death and its pains, and also teach the limits of desires ⟨and of pains⟩, we should never have cause to blame them: for they would be filling themselves full with pleasures from every source and never have pain of body or mind, which is the evil of life.

XI. If we were not troubled by our suspicions of the phenomena of the sky and about death, fearing that it concerns us, and also by our failure to grasp the limits of pains and desires, we should have no need of natural science.

XII. A man cannot dispel his fear about the most important matters if he does not know what is the nature of the universe but suspects the truth of some mythical story. So that without natural science it is not possible to attain our pleasures unalloyed. *natural science 's importance*

XIII. There is no profit in securing protection in relation to men, if things above and things beneath the earth and indeed all in the boundless universe remain matters of suspicion.

XIV. The most unalloyed source of protection from men, which is secured to some extent by a certain force of expulsion, is in fact the immunity which results from a quiet life and the retirement from the world.

XV. The wealth demanded by nature is both limited and easily procured; that demanded by idle imaginings stretches on to infinity.

XVI. In but few things chance hinders a wise man, but the greatest and most important matters reason has ordained and throughout the whole period of life does and will ordain.

XVII. The just man is most free from trouble, the unjust most full of trouble.

XVIII. The pleasure in the flesh is not increased, when once the pain due to want is removed, but is only varied: and the limit as regards pleasure in the mind is begotten by the reasoned understanding of these very pleasures and of the emotions akin to them, which used to cause the greatest fear to the mind.

XIX. Infinite time contains no greater pleasure than limited time, if one measures by reason the limits of pleasure.

XX. The flesh perceives the limits of pleasure as unlimited and unlimited time is required to supply it. But the mind, having attained a reasoned understanding of the ultimate good of the flesh and its limits and having dissipated the fears concerning the time to come, supplies us with the complete life, and we have no further need of infinite time: but neither does the mind shun pleasure, nor, when circumstances begin to bring about the departure from life, does it approach its end as though it fell short in any way of the best life.

XXI.   He who has learned the limits of life knows that that which removes the pain due to want and makes the whole of life complete is easy to obtain; so that there is no need of actions which involve competition.

XXII. We must consider both the real purpose and all the evidence of direct perception, to which we always refer the conclusions of opinion; otherwise, all will be full of doubt and confusion.

XXIII. If you fight against all sensations, you will have no standard by which to judge even those of them which you say are false.

XXIV. If you reject any single sensation and fail to distinguish between the conclusion of opinion as to the appearance awaiting confirmation and that which is actually given by the sensation or feeling, or each intuitive apprehension of the mind, you will confound all other sensations as well with the same groundless opinion, so that you will reject every standard of judgement. And if among the mental images created by your opinion you affirm both that which awaits confirmation and that which does not, you will not escape error, since you will have preserved the whole cause of doubt in every judgement between what is right and what is wrong.

XXV.   If on each occasion instead of referring your actions to the end of nature, you turn to some other nearer standard when you are making a choice or an avoidance, your actions will not be consistent with your principles.

XXVI. Of desires, all that do not lead to a sense of pain, if they are not satisfied, are not necessary, but involve a craving which is easily dispelled, when the object is hard to procure or they seem likely to produce harm.

XXVII. Of all the things which wisdom acquires to produce the blessedness of the complete life, far the greatest is the possession of friendship.

XXVIII. The same conviction which has given us confidence that there is nothing terrible that lasts for ever or even for long, has also seen the protection of friendship most fully completed in the limited evils of this life.

XXIX. Among desires some are natural ⟨and necessary, some natural⟩ but not necessary, and others neither natural nor necessary, but due to idle imagination.

XXX.   Wherever in the case of desires which are physical, but do not lead to a sense of pain, if they are not fulfilled, the effort is intense, such pleasures are due to idle imagination, and it is not owing to their own nature that they fail to be dispelled, but owing to the empty imaginings of the man.

XXXI. The justice which arises from nature is a pledge of mutual advantage to restrain men from harming one another and save them from being harmed.

XXXII. For all living things which have not been able to make compacts not to harm one another or be harmed, nothing ever is either just or unjust; and likewise too for all tribes of men which have been unable or unwilling to make compacts not to harm or be harmed.

XXXIII. Justice never is anything in itself, but in the dealings of men with one another in any place whatever and at any time it is a kind of compact not to harm or be harmed.

XXXIV. Injustice is not an evil in itself, but only in consequence of the fear which attaches to the apprehension of being unable to escape those appointed to punish such actions.

XXXV. It is not possible for one who acts in secret contravention of the terms of the compact not to harm or be harmed, to be confident that he will escape detection, even if at present he escapes a thousand times. For up to the time of death it cannot be certain that he will indeed escape.

XXXVI. In its general aspect justice is the same for all, for it is a kind of mutual advantage in the dealings of men with one another: but with reference to the individual peculiarities of a country or any other circumstances the same thing does not turn out to be just for all.

XXXVII. Among actions which are sanctioned as just by law, that which is proved on examination to be of advantage in the requirements of men's dealings with one another, has the guarantee of justice, whether it is the same for all or not. But if a man makes a law and it does not turn out to lead to advantage in men's dealings with each other, then it no longer has the essential nature of justice. And even if the advantage in the matter of justice shifts from one side to the other, but for a while accords with the general concept, it is none the less just for that period in the eyes of those who do not confound themselves with empty sounds but look to the actual facts.

XXXVIII. Where, provided the circumstances have not been altered, actions which were considered just, have been shown not to accord with the general concept in actual practice, then they are not just. But where, when circumstances have changed, the same actions which were sanctioned as just no longer lead to advantage, there they were just at the time when they were of advantage for the dealings of fellow-citizens with one another; but subsequently they are no longer just, when no longer of advantage.

XXXIX. The man who has best ordered the element of disquiet arising from external circumstances has made those things that he could akin to himself and the rest at least not alien: but with all to which he could not do even this, he has refrained from mixing, and has expelled from his life all which it was of advantage to treat thus.

XL. As many as possess the power to procure complete immunity from their neighbours, these also live most pleasantly with one another, since they have the most certain pledge of security, and after they have enjoyed the fullest intimacy, they do not lament the previous departure of a dead friend, as though he were to be pitied.

The Discourses of Epictetus and *The Manual, or Enchiridion*

Epictetus

Epictetus was a Stoic, and like many Stoics he puts special emphasis on the Socratic idea that the aim of philosophy is not ultimately to understand, but to live well. At Enchiridion 52, he insists that what is most important in philosophy is grasping basic moral principles, such as that lying is wrong. This is less important than understanding *why* lying is wrong, which is itself even less important than elucidation of the nature of moral propositions themselves – whether they are true or false, and so on. Nor is even this first level of philosophical understanding significant in itself; it matters only if you act on your principles, demonstrating their value through your actions (E 46). Epictetus sees philosophy as a potential partial cure for human weakness, and the main aim in his writing is to change us, not merely to change our views. That affects his style: for example, as you will see, he tends to repeat his most fundamental principles.

The key distinction in Epictetus is between what is and what is not in our power (Discourses 1.1; E 1). There is nothing that nonhuman animals can control, but we, because of reason, a spark of divinity within us, have the capacity to will (D 1.22, 2.10, 3.2; E 8). And we should exercise that capacity only over what we can control. Otherwise, we must accept the external world as it is.

This combination of stress on inner autonomy and acceptance of what is external and unavoidable underlies many of Epictetus's ethical views. Our happiness or good consists in, and only in, correct willing (E 2). Only in this way can we attain true freedom (D 1.12). Does that mean that, say, enjoyment is never good for us, or agony never bad for us? Strictly, yes: nothing external is good or bad in itself (E 27). Epictetus also has positive arguments against other alleged goods and bads. For example, pleasure is unreliable and fleeting, and so unsuited to play the role of the good. Nevertheless, it is not a mistake to speak of such things as good or bad, although in fact they are indifferent (that is, neither good nor bad), since nature and virtue sometimes require their pursuit or avoidance (D 1.22; 2.6). The result of focusing on such willing only of what is in our power will be inner peace and tranquillity (E 12). (It is an interesting question whether such contentment is itself merely indifferent.)

There is no point in delaying: we must set ourselves immediately on the path to correct willing, with constant attention to what we are doing (D 4.12; E 51). We will find that this distances ourselves from our emotions, which often mislead us into thinking indifferents are genuinely good or bad. What we might call 'positive thinking' plays an important part here. Don't describe being alone as a wilderness; call it peace and freedom (D 1.12). If someone speaks ill of you, remember that they are merely doing what seems fitting to them, and if they are wrong then that is punishment in itself (E 42). Blame is to be avoided, partly because one does not fully understand the motives of others (E 45). In particular, if you will only what is in your power, you will not be led to blame the gods if you do not get what you want (E 31). That would be a mistake because the universe is designed rationally and providentially (D 1.12): you have to understand it and follow its principles (E 49). By spurning externals such as wealth, you will be mocked by others, but you should ignore them and be a philosopher (E 13, 22). (Epictetus says that eventually you will come to

History of Ethics – Essential Readings with Commentary, First Edition. Edited by Daniel Star and Roger Crisp.
© 2020 John Wiley & Sons Ltd. Published 2020 by John Wiley & Sons Ltd.

be admired by others anyway; but presumably that shouldn't matter to you either.) You should be accepting even of great personal disasters, such as the death of your child, telling yourself that she is just a human being and that you have not lost her, just given her back (E 3; 11).

What matters is only the inner (D 4.12), and the body is external. Nothing harms you except in so far as you *judge* it to be harmful (E 5, 9, 16, 20, 30). And your judgement is something you can control – or at least something you can *try* to control. (One puzzle here is whether the claim about judgement applies to Epictetus's own view. What if I fail to judge that willing what is not in my power harms me?) Other people are part of the external world, and the life Epictetus recommends is one of retreat from social life. In general, you should keep quiet, asking yourself on each occasion, 'What would Socrates have done?' (E 33). (Socrates was of course often rather vocal; but he was talking about things that really matter, which is allowed.)

We must limit our will, but only to a certain point. We must will in accordance with the rational principles governing and ordering the universe (D 1.12; E 49), and these include certain moral principles. One good way to understand such principles is to ask oneself what 'names' one goes by. If one is a son, or a council-member, one is bound by the principles governing those roles (D 2.10). There is a moral truth, and hence grasping the truth is of huge significance (D 2.11, 3.3). We are subject to certain impressions but have control over how we assess them.

Each of us must understand that she is an actor in a divinely authored drama, and we have to play our part appropriately (E 17). That means seeing ourselves as merely parts of a whole, and our moral obligations will be guided by the good of the whole (D 2.5, 2.10). Just as a body may benefit from the loss of a foot, so the whole of which we are a part may benefit from our falling ill, being maimed, or dying. If he really knew that it was ordained for him to be ill, Epictetus tells us (D 2.6), then he would wish to be ill.

The Discourses of Epictetus

Book I

Chapter I: On Things in Our Power and Things Not in Our Power

OF OUR faculties in general you will find that none can take cognizance of itself; none therefore has the power to approve or disapprove its own action. Our grammatical faculty for instance: how far can that take cognizance? Only so far as to distinguish expression. Our musical faculty? Only so far as to distinguish tune. Does any one of these then take cognizance of itself? By no means. If you are writing to your friend, when you want to know what words to write grammar will tell you; but whether you should write to your friend or should not write grammar will not tell you. And in the same way music will tell you about tunes, but whether at this precise moment you should sing and play the lyre or should not sing nor play the lyre it will not tell you. What will tell you then? That faculty which takes cognizance of itself and of all things else. What is this? The reasoning faculty: for this alone of the faculties we have received is created to comprehend even its own nature; that is to say, what it is and what it can do, and with what precious qualities it has come to us, and to comprehend all other faculties as well. For what else is it that tells us that gold is a goodly thing? For the gold does not tell us. Clearly it is the faculty which can deal with our impressions. What else is it which distinguishes the faculties of music, grammar, and the rest, testing their uses and pointing out the due seasons for their use? It is reason and nothing else.

The gods then, as was but right, put in our hands the one blessing that is best of all and master of all, that and nothing else, the power to deal rightly with our impressions, but everything else they did not put in our hands. Was it that they would not? For my part I think that if they could have entrusted us with those other powers as well they would have done so, but they were quite unable. Prisoners on the earth and in an earthly body and among earthly companions, how was it possible that we should not be hindered from the attainment of these powers by these external fetters?

But what says Zeus? 'Epictetus, if it were possible I would have made your body and your possessions (those trifles that you prize) free and untrammelled. But as things are – never forget this – this body is not yours, it is but a clever mixture of clay. But since I could not make it free, I gave you a portion in our divinity, this faculty of impulse to act and not to act, of will to get and will to avoid, in a word the faculty which can turn impressions to right use. If you pay heed to this, and put your affairs in its keeping, you will never suffer let nor hindrance, you will not groan, you will blame no man, you will flatter none.

[…]

But, as things are, though we have it in our power to pay heed to one thing and to devote ourselves to one, yet instead of this we prefer to pay heed to many things and to be bound fast to many – our body, our property, brother and friend, child and slave. Inasmuch then as we are bound fast to many things, we are burdened by them and dragged down. That is why, if the weather is bad for sailing, we sit distracted and keep looking continually and ask, 'What wind is blowing?' 'The north wind.' What have we to do with that? 'When will the west wind blow?' When it so chooses, good sir, or when Aeolus chooses. For God made Aeolus the master of the winds, not you. What follows? We must make the best of those things that are in our power, and take the rest as nature gives it. What do you mean by 'nature'? I mean, God's will.

'What? Am I to be beheaded now, and I alone?'

Why? would you have had all beheaded, to give you consolation? Will you not stretch out your neck as Lateranus did in Rome when Nero ordered his beheadal? For he stretched out his neck and took the blow, and when the blow dealt him was too weak he shrank up a little and then stretched it out again. […]

What then must a man have ready to help him in such emergencies? Surely this: he must ask himself, 'What is mine, and what is not mine? What may I do, what may I not do?'

I must die. But must I die groaning? I must be imprisoned. But must I whine as well? I must suffer exile. Can any one then hinder me from going with a smile, and a good courage, and at peace?

'Tell the secret!'

I refuse to tell, for this is in my power.

'But I will chain you.'

What say you, fellow? Chain me? My leg you will chain – yes, but my will – no, not even Zeus can conquer that.

'I will imprison you.'

My bit of a body, you mean.

'I will behead you.'

Why? When did I ever tell you that I was the only man in the world that could not be beheaded?

These are the thoughts that those who pursue philosophy should ponder, these are the lessons they should write down day by day, in these they should exercise themselves.

[…]

Chapter XII: On Contentment

[…]

The man who is under education ought to approach education with this purpose in his mind: 'How can I follow the gods in everything, and how can I be content with the divine governance and how can I become free?' For he is free, for whom all things happen according to his will and whom no one can hinder.

[…]

Are we to say then that in this sphere alone, the greatest and most momentous of all, the sphere of freedom, it is permitted me to indulge chance desires? By no means: education is just this – learning to frame one's will in accord with events. How do events happen? They happen as the Disposer of events has ordained them. He ordained summer and winter, fruitful and barren seasons, virtue and vice and all such opposites for the sake of the harmony of the universe, and gave to each one of us a body and bodily parts and property and men to associate with.

Remembering then that things are thus ordained we ought to approach education, not that we may change the conditions of life, that is not given to us, nor is it good for us – but that, our circumstances being as they are and as nature makes them, we may conform our mind to events.

I ask you, is it possible to avoid men? How can we? Can we change their nature by our society? Who gives us that power? What is left for us then, or what means do we discover to deal with them? We must so act as to leave them to do as seems good to them, while we remain in accord with nature.

But you are impatient and discontented; if you are alone you call it a wilderness, and if you are with men you describe them as plotters and robbers, and you find fault even with your own parents and children and brothers and neighbours.

Why, when you are alone you ought to call it peace and freedom and consider yourself the equal of the gods; when you are in a large company you should not call it a crowd or a mob or a nuisance, but a high-day and a festival, and so accept all things in a spirit of content.

What punishment is there, you ask, for those who do not accept things in this spirit? Their punishment is to be as they are. Is one discontented with being alone? Let him be deserted. Is one discontented with his parents? Let him be a bad son, and mourn his lot. Is one discontented with his children? Let him be a bad father.

'Cast him into prison.'

What do you mean by prison? he is in prison already; for a man's prison is the place that he is in against his will, just as, conversely, Socrates was not in prison, for he chose to be there.

[…]

Chapter XXII: On Primary Conceptions

PRIMARY conceptions are common to all men, and one does not conflict with another. Who among us, for instance, does not assume that the good is expedient and desirable and that we ought in all circumstances to follow and pursue it? Which of us does not assume that the just is noble and becoming?

At what moment then does conflict arise? It arises in the application of primary conceptions to particular facts; when for instance one says, 'He has done well: he is brave,' and another, 'Nay, he is out of his mind.' Hence arises the conflict of men with one another. Such is the conflict between Jews and. Syrians and Egyptians and Romans – not the question whether holiness must be put before all things and must in all circumstances be pursued, but whether it is holy or unholy to eat of swine's flesh.

[…]

In what then does education consist? In learning to apply the natural primary conceptions to particular occasions in accordance with nature, and further to distinguish between things in our power and things not in our power. In our power are will and all operations of the will, and beyond our power are the body, the parts of the body, possessions, parents, brothers, children, country, in a word – those whose society we share. Where then are we to place 'the good'? To what class of things shall we apply it?

'To what is in our power.'

Does it follow then that health and a whole body, and life are not good, nor children, parents, and country? No one will bear with you if you say that. Let us then transfer the name 'good' to this class of things.

[…]

Book II

Chapter V: How a Careful Life is Compatible with a Noble Spirit

[…]

How is it then that some external things are described as natural and some as unnatural? It is because we regard ourselves as detached from the rest of the universe. For the foot (for instance), I shall say it is natural to be clean, but if you take it as a foot and not as a detached thing, it will be fitting for it to walk in the mud and tread upon thorns and sometimes to be cut off for the sake of the whole body: or else it will cease to be a foot. We must hold exactly the same sort of view about ourselves.

What are you? A man. If you regard man as a detached being, it is natural for him to live to old age, to be rich, to be healthy. But if you regard him as a man and a part of a larger whole, that whole makes it fitting that at one moment you should fall ill, at another go on a voyage and risk your life, and at another be at your wit's end, and, it may be, die before your time. Why then are you indignant? Do you not know that, just as the foot spoke of if viewed apart will cease to be a foot, so you will cease to be a man? For what is a man? A part of a city, first a part of the City in which gods and men are incorporate, and secondly of that city which has the next claim to be called so, which is a small copy of the City universal.

[…]

Chapter VI: On What Is Meant by 'Indifferent' Things

TAKE a given hypothetical proposition. In itself it is indifferent, but your judgement upon it is not indifferent, but is either knowledge, or mere opinion, or delusion. In the same way though life is indifferent, the way you deal with it is not indifferent.

[…]

Therefore Chrysippus well says, 'As long as the consequences are unknown to me, I always hold fast to what is better adapted to secure what is natural, for God Himself created me with the faculty of choosing what is natural.' Nay, if I really knew that it was ordained for me now to be ill, I should wish to be ill; for the foot too, if it had a mind, would wish to get muddy.

[…]

Chapter X: How the Acts Appropriate to Man Are to Be Discovered from the Names He Bears

CONSIDER who you are. First, a Man; that is one who has nothing more sovereign than will, but all else subject to this, and will itself free from slavery or subjection. Consider then from what you are parted by reason. You are parted from wild beasts, you are parted from sheep. On these terms you are a citizen of the universe and a part of it, not one of those marked for service, but of those fitted for command; for you have the faculty to understand the divine governance of the universe and to reason on its sequence. What then is the calling of a Citizen? To have no personal interest, never to think about anything as though he were detached, but to be like the hand or the foot, which, if they had the power of reason and understood the order of nature, would direct every impulse and every process of the will by reference to the whole. That is why it is well said by philosophers that 'if the good man knew coming events beforehand he would help on nature, even if it meant working with disease, and death and maiming,' for he would realize that by the ordering of the universe this task is allotted him, and that the whole is more commanding than the part and the city than the citizen. 'But seeing that we do not know beforehand, it is appropriate that we should hold fast to the things that are by nature more fit to be chosen; for indeed we are born for this.'

Next remember that you are a Son. What part do we expect a son to play? His part is to count all that is his as his father's, to obey him in all things, never to speak ill of him to any, nor to say or do anything to harm him, to give way to him and yield him place in all things, working with him so far as his powers allow.

Next know that you are also a Brother. For this part too you are bound to show a spirit of concession and obedience; [...]

Next, if you are a member of a city council, remember that you are a councillor; if young, that you are young; if old, that you are old; if a father, that you are a father. For each of these names, if properly considered, suggests the acts appropriate to it.

[...]

Chapter XI: What Is the Beginning of Philosophy

THE beginning of philosophy with those who approach it in the right way and by the door is a consciousness of one's own weakness and want of power in regard to necessary things.

[...]

Here you see the beginning of Philosophy, in the discovery of the conflict of men's minds with one another, and the attempt to seek for the reason of this conflict, and the condemnation of mere opinion, as a thing not to be trusted; and a search to determine whether your opinion is true, and an attempt to discover a standard, just as we discover the balance to deal with weights and the rule to deal with things straight and crooked. This is the beginning of Philosophy.

'Are all opinions right which all men hold?'

Nay, how is it possible for contraries to be both right?

'Well, then, not all opinions, but our opinions?'

Why ours, rather than those of the Syrians or the Egyptians, or the personal opinion of myself or of this man or that?

'Why indeed?'

So then, what each man thinks is not sufficient to make a thing so: for in dealing with weights and measures we are not satisfied with mere appearance, but have found a standard to determine each. Is there, then, no standard here beyond opinion? It is impossible surely that things most necessary among men should be beyond discovery and beyond proof?

There is a standard then.

[...]

What subject, I might ask, lies before us for our present discussion?

'Pleasure.'

Submit it to the rule, put it in the balance. Ought the good to be something which is worthy to inspire confidence and trust?

'It ought.'

Is it proper to have confidence in anything which is insecure?

'No.'

Has pleasure, then, any certainty in it?

'No.'

Away with it then! Cast it from the scales and drive it far away from the region of good things. But if your sight is not keen, and you are not satisfied with one set of scales, try another.

Is it proper to be elated at what is good?

'It is.'

Is it proper, then, to be elated at the pleasure of the moment? Be careful how you say that it is proper. If you do, I shall not count you worthy of the scales.

Thus things are judged and weighed if we have standards ready to test them: and in fact the work of philosophy is to investigate and firmly establish such standards; and the duty of the good man is to proceed to apply the decisions arrived at.

[...]

Book III

Chapter II: [1] In What Matters Should the Man Who Is to Make Progress Train Himself: and [2] That We Neglect What Is Most Vital

THERE are three departments in which a man who is to be good and noble must be trained. The first concerns the will to get and will to avoid; he must be trained not to fail to get what he wills to get nor fall into what he wills to avoid. The second is concerned with impulse to act and not to act, and, in a word, the sphere of what is fitting: that we should act in order, with, due consideration, and with proper care. The object of the third is that we may not be deceived, and may not judge at random, and generally it is concerned with assent.

Of these the most important and the most pressing is the first, which is concerned with strong emotions, for such emotion does not arise except when the will to get or the will to avoid fails of its object. This it is which brings with it disturbances, tumults, misfortunes, bad fortunes, mournings, lamentations, envies; which makes men envious and jealous – passions which make us unable to listen to reason.

The second is the sphere of what is fitting: for I must not be without feeling like a statue, but must maintain my natural and acquired relations, as a religious man, as son, brother, father, citizen.

The third department is appropriate only for those who are already making progress, and is concerned with giving certainty in the very things we have spoken of, so that even in sleep or drunkenness or melancholy no untested impression may come upon us unawares.

[…]

Chapter III: What Is the Material With Which the Good Man Deals: And What Should Be the Object of Our Training

[…] just as it is the nature of every soul to assent to what is true and dissent from what is false, and withhold judgement in what is uncertain, so it is its nature to be moved with the will to get what is good and the will to avoid what is evil, and to be neutral towards what is neither good nor evil. For just as neither the banker nor the greengrocer can refuse the Emperor's currency, but, if you show it, he must part, willy-nilly, with what the coin will buy, so it is also with the soul. The very sight of good attracts one towards it, the sight of evil repels. The soul will never reject a clear impression of good, any more than we reject Caesar's currency.

[…]

Book IV

Chapter XII: On Attention

WHEN you relax your attention for a little, do not imagine that you will recover it wherever you wish, but bear this well in mind, that your error of to-day must of necessity put you in a worse position for other occasions. For in the first place – and this is the most serious thing – a habit of inattention is formed, and next a habit of deferring attention: and you get into the way of putting off from one time to another the tranquil and becoming life, the state and behaviour which nature prescribes. Now if such postponement of attention is profitable, it would be still more profitable to abandon it altogether: but if it is not profitable, why do you not keep up your attention continuously?

'I want to play to-day.'

What prevents you, if you attend?

'I want to sing.'

What prevents you, if you attend? Is any part of life excluded, on which attention has no bearing, any that you will make worse by attention, and better by inattention? Nay, is there anything in life generally which is done better by those who do not attend?

[…]

We must set our mind on this object: pursue nothing that is outside us, nothing that is not our own, even as He that is mighty has ordained: pursuing what lies within our will, and all else only so far as it is given us to do so. Further, we must remember who we are, and by what name we are called, and must try to direct our acts to fit each situation and its possibilities.

We must consider what is the time for singing, what the time for play, and in whose presence: what will be unsuited to the occasion; whether our companions are to despise us, or we to despise ourselves: when to jest, and whom to mock at: and on what occasion to be conciliatory and to whom: in a word, how one ought to maintain one's character in society. Wherever you swerve from any of these principles, you suffer loss at once; not loss from without, but issuing from the very act itself.

What then? Is it possible to escape error altogether? No, it is impossible: but it is possible to set one's mind continuously on avoiding error. For it is well worth while to persist in this endeavour, if in the end we escape a few errors, and no more. As it is, you say, 'I will fix my attention to-morrow:' which means, let me tell you, 'To-day I will be shameless, inopportune, abject: others shall have power to vex me: to-day I will harbour anger and envy.' Look what evils you allow yourself. Nay, if it is well to fix my attention to-morrow, how much better to do so to-day! If it is profitable to-morrow, much more so is it to-day: that you may be able to do the same to-morrow, and not put off again to the day after.

The Manual, or Enchiridion

1.   OF ALL existing things some are in our power, and others are not in our power. In our power are thought, impulse, will to get and will to avoid, and, in a word, everything which is our own doing. Things not in our power include the body, property, reputation, office, and, in a word, everything which is not our own doing. Things in our power are by nature free, unhindered, untrammelled; things not in our power are weak, servile, subject to hindrance, dependent on others. Remember then that if you imagine that what is naturally slavish is free, and what is naturally another's is your own, you will be hampered, you will mourn, you will be put to confusion, you will blame gods and men; but if you think that only your own belongs to you, and that what is another's is indeed another's, no one will ever put compulsion or hindrance on you, you will blame none, you will accuse none, you will do nothing against your will, no one will harm you, you will have no enemy, for no harm can touch you.

Aiming then at these high matters, you must remember that to attain them requires more than ordinary effort; you will have to give up some things entirely, and put off others for the moment. And if you would have these also – office and wealth – it may be that you will fail to get them, just because your desire is set on the former, and you will certainly fail to attain those things which alone bring freedom and happiness.

Make it your study then to confront every harsh impression with the words, 'You are but an impression, and not at all what you seem to be.' Then test it by those rules that you possess; and first by this – the chief test of all – 'Is it concerned with what is in our power or with what is not in our power?' And if it is concerned with what is not in our power, be ready with the answer that it is nothing to you.

2.   REMEMBER that the will to get promises attainment of what you will, and the will to avoid promises escape from what you avoid; and he who fails to get what he wills is unfortunate, and he who does not escape what he wills to avoid is miserable. If then you try to avoid only what is unnatural in the region within your control, you will escape from all that you avoid; but if you try to avoid disease or death or poverty you will be miserable.

"Therefore let your will to avoid have no concern with what is not in man's power;" direct it only to things in man's power that are contrary to nature. But for the moment you must utterly remove the will to get; for if you will to get something not in man's power you are bound to be unfortunate; while none of the things in man's power that you could honourably will to get is yet within your reach. Impulse to act and not to act, these are your concern; yet exercise them gently and without strain, and provisionally.

3.   WHEN anything, from the meanest thing upwards, is attractive or serviceable or an object of affection, remember always to say to yourself, 'What is its nature?' If you are fond of a jug, say you are fond of a jug; then you will not be disturbed if it be broken. If you kiss your child or your wife, say to yourself that you are kissing a human being, for then if death strikes it you will not be disturbed.

[…]

5.   "WHAT disturbs men's minds is not events but their judgements on events." For instance, death is nothing dreadful, or else Socrates would have thought it so. No, the only dreadful thing about it is men's judgement that it is dreadful. And so when we are hindered, or disturbed, or distressed, let us never lay the blame on others, but on ourselves, that is on our own judgements. To accuse others for one's own misfortunes is a sign of want of education; to accuse oneself shows that one's education has begun; to accuse neither oneself nor others shows that one's education is complete.

6.   BE NOT elated at an excellence which is not your own. If the horse in his pride were to say, 'I am handsome,' we could bear with it. But when you say with pride, 'I have a handsome horse,' know that the good horse is the ground of your pride. You ask then what you can call your own. The answer is – the way you deal with your impressions. Therefore when you deal with your impressions in accord with nature, then you may be proud indeed, for your pride will be in a good which is your own.

[…]

8.   ASK not that events should happen as you will, but let your will be that events should happen as they do, and you shall have peace.

9.   SICKNESS is a hindrance to the body, but not to the will, unless the will consent. Lameness is a hindrance to the leg, but not to the will. Say this to yourself at each event that happens, for you shall find that though it hinders something else it will not hinder you.

10.   WHEN anything happens to you, always remember to turn to yourself and ask what faculty you have to deal with it. If you see a beautiful boy or a beautiful woman, you will find continence the faculty to exercise there; if trouble is laid on you, you will find endurance; if ribaldry, you will find patience. And if you train yourself in this habit your impressions will not carry you away.

11.   NEVER say of anything, 'I lost it,' but say, 'I gave it back.' Has your child died? It was given back. Has your wife died? She was given back. Has your estate been taken from you? Was not this also given back? But you say, 'He who took it from me is wicked.' What does it matter to you through whom the Giver asked it back? As long as He gives it you, take care of it, but not as your own; treat it as passers-by treat an inn.

12.   IF YOU wish to make progress, abandon reasonings of this sort: 'If I neglect my affairs I shall have nothing to live on;' 'If I do not punish my son, he will be wicked.' For it is better to die of hunger, so that you be free from pain and free from fear, than to live in plenty and be troubled in mind. It is better for your son to be wicked than for you to be miserable. Wherefore begin with little things. Is your drop of oil spilt? Is your sup of wine stolen? Say to yourself, 'This is the price paid for freedom from passion, this is the price of a quiet mind.' Nothing can be had without a price. When you call your slave-boy, reflect that he may not be able to hear you, and if he hears you, he may not be able to do anything you want. But he is not so well off that it rests with him to give you peace of mind.

13.   IF YOU wish to make progress, you must be content in external matters to seem a fool and a simpleton; do not wish men to think you know anything, and if any should think you to be somebody, distrust yourself. For know that it is not easy to keep your will in accord with nature and at the same time keep outward things; if you attend to one you must needs neglect the other.

14.   IT IS silly to want your children and your wife and your friends to live for ever, for that means that you want what is not in your control to be in your control, and what is not your own to be yours. In the same way if you want your servant to make no mistakes, you are a fool, for you want vice not to be vice but something different. But if you want not to be disappointed in your will to get, you can attain to that.

[…] Let him then who wishes to be free not wish for anything or avoid anything that depends on others; or else he is bound to be a slave.

15.   REMEMBER that you must behave in life as you would at a banquet. A dish is handed round and comes to you; put out your hand and take it politely. It passes you; do not stop it. It has not reached you; do not be impatient to get it, but wait till your turn comes. Bear yourself thus towards children, wife, office, wealth, and one day you will be worthy to banquet with the gods. But if when they are set before you, you do not take them but despise them, then you shall not only share the gods' banquet, but shall share their rule. For by so doing Diogenes and Heraclitus and men like them were called divine and deserved the name.

16.   WHEN you see a man shedding tears in sorrow for a child abroad or dead, or for loss of property, beware that you are not carried away by the impression that it is outward ills that make him miserable. Keep this thought by you: 'What distresses him is not the event, for that does not distress another, but his judgement on the event.' Therefore do not hesitate to sympathize with him so far as words go, and if it so chance, even to groan with him; but take heed that you do not also groan in your inner being.

17.   REMEMBER that you are an actor in a play, and the Playwright chooses the manner of it: if he wants it short, it is short; if long, it is long. If he wants you to act a poor man you must act the part with all your powers; and so if your part be a cripple or a magistrate or a plain man. For your business is to act the character that is given you and act it well; the choice of the cast is Another's.

[…]

19.   YOU can be invincible, if you never enter on a contest where victory is not in your power. Beware then that when you see a man raised to honour or great power or high repute you do not let your impression carry you away. For if the reality of good lies in what is in our power, there is no room for envy or jealousy. And you will not wish to be praetor, or prefect or consul, but to be free; and there is but one way to freedom – to despise what is not in our power.

20.   REMEMBER that foul words or blows in themselves are no outrage, but your judgement that they are so. So when any one makes you angry, know that it is your own thought that has angered you. Wherefore make it your first endeavour not to let your impressions carry you away. For if once you gain time and delay, you will find it easier to control yourself.

21.   KEEP before your eyes from day to day death and exile and all things that seem terrible, but death most of all, and then you will never set your thoughts on what is low and will never desire anything beyond measure.

22.   IF YOU set your desire on philosophy you must at once prepare to meet with ridicule and the jeers of many who will say, 'Here he is again, turned philosopher. Where has he got these proud looks?' Nay, put on no proud looks, but hold fast to what seems best to you, in confidence that God has set you at this post. And remember that if you abide where you are, those who first laugh at you will one day admire you, and that if you give way to them, you will get doubly laughed at.

23. IF IT ever happen to you to be diverted to things outside, so that you desire to please another, know that you have lost your life's plan. Be content then always to be a philosopher; if you wish to be regarded as one too, show yourself that you are one and you will be able to achieve it.

24. LET not reflections such as these afflict you: 'I shall live without honour, and never be of any account;' for if lack of honour is an evil, no one but yourself can involve you in evil any more than in shame. Is it your business to get office or to be invited to an entertainment?

Certainly not.

Where then is the dishonour you talk of? How can you be 'of no account anywhere,' when you ought to count for something in those matters only which are in your power, where you may achieve the highest worth?

'But my friends,' you say, 'will lack assistance.'

What do you mean by 'lack assistance'? They will not have cash from you and you will not make them Roman citizens. Who told you that to do these things is in our power, and not dependent upon others? Who can give to another what is not his to give?

'Get them then,' says he, 'that we may have them.'

If I can get them and keep my self-respect, honour, magnanimity, show the way and I will get them. But if you call on me to lose the good things that are mine, in order that you may win things that are not good, look how unfair and thoughtless you are. And which do you really prefer? Money, or a faithful, modest friend? Therefore help me rather to keep these qualities, and do not expect from me actions which will make me lose them.

[…]

'What place then shall I have in the city?'

Whatever place you can hold while you keep your character for honour and self-respect. But if you are going to lose these qualities in trying to benefit your city, what benefit, I ask, would you have done her when you attain to the perfection of being lost to shame and honour?

25. HAS some one had precedence of you at an entertainment or a levée or been called in before you to give advice? If these things are good you ought to be glad that he got them; if they are evil, do not be angry that you did not get them yourself. Remember that if you want to get what is not in your power, you cannot earn the same reward as others unless you act as they do. How is it possible for one who does not haunt the great man's door to have equal shares with one who does, or one who does not go in his train equality with one who does; or one who does not praise him with one who does? You will be unjust then and insatiable if you wish to get these privileges for nothing, without paying their price. What is the price of a lettuce? An obol perhaps. If then a man pays his obol and gets his lettuces, and you do not pay and do not get them, do not think you are defrauded. For as he has the lettuces so you have the obol you did not give. The same principle holds good too in conduct. You were not invited to some one's entertainment? Because you did not give the host the price for which he sells his dinner. He sells it for compliments, he sells it for attentions. Pay him the price then, if it is to your profit. But if you wish to get the one and yet not give up the other, nothing can satisfy you in your folly.

What! you say, you have nothing instead of the dinner?

Nay, you have this, you have not praised the man you did not want to praise, you have not had to bear with the insults of his doorstep.

26. IT IS in our power to discover the will of Nature from those matters on which we have no difference of opinion. For instance, when another man's slave has broken the wine-cup we are very ready to say at once, 'Such things must happen.' Know then that when your own cup is broken, you ought to behave in the same way as when your neighbour's was broken. Apply the same principle to higher matters. Is another's child or wife dead? Not one of us but would say, 'Such is the lot of man;' but when one's own dies, straightway one cries, 'Alas! miserable am I.' But we ought to remember what our feelings are when we hear it of another.

27. AS A MARK is not set up for men to miss it, so there is nothing intrinsically evil in the world.

28. IF ANY one trusted your body to the first man he met, you would be indignant, but yet you trust your mind to the chance comer, and allow it to be disturbed and confounded if he revile you; are you not ashamed to do so?

[…]

29. Man, consider first what it is you are undertaking; then look at your own powers and see if you can bear it. Do you want to compete in the pentathlon or in wrestling? Look to your arms, your thighs, see what your loins are like. For different men are born for different tasks. Do you suppose that if you do this you can live as you do now – eat and drink as you do now, indulge desire and discontent just as before? Nay, you must sit up late, work hard, abandon your own people, be looked down on by a mere slave, be ridiculed by those who meet you, get the worst of it in everything – in honour, in office, in justice, in every possible thing. This is what you have to consider: whether you are willing to pay this price for peace of mind, freedom, tranquillity. If not, do not come near; do not be, like the children, first a philosopher, then a tax-collector, then an orator, then one of Caesar's procurators. These callings do not agree. You must be one man, good or bad; you must develop either your Governing Principle, or your outward endowments; you must study either your inner man, or outward things – in a word, you must choose between the position of a philosopher and that of a mere outsider.

30.   APPROPRIATE acts are in general measured by the relations they are concerned with. 'He is your father.' This means you are called on to take care of him, give way to him in all things, bear with him if he reviles or strikes you.

'But he is a bad father.'

Well, have you any natural claim to a good father? No, only to a father.

'My brother wrongs me.'

Be careful then to maintain the relation you hold to him, and do not consider what he does, but what you must do if your purpose is to keep in accord with nature. For no one shall harm you, without your consent; you will only be harmed, when you think you are harmed. You will only discover what is proper to expect from neighbour, citizen, or praetor, if you get into the habit of looking at the relations implied by each.

31.   FOR piety towards the gods know that the most important thing is this: to have right opinions about them – that they exist, and that they govern the universe well and justly – and to have set yourself to obey them, and to give way to all that happens, following events with a free will, in the belief that they are fulfilled by the highest mind. For thus you will never blame the gods, nor accuse them of neglecting you. But this you cannot achieve, unless you apply your conception of good and evil to those things only which are in our power, and not to those which are out of our power. For if you apply your notion of good or evil to the latter, then, as soon as you fail to get what you will to get or fail to avoid what you will to avoid, you will be bound to blame and hate those you hold responsible. For every living creature has a natural tendency to avoid and shun what seems harmful and all that causes it, and to pursue and admire what is helpful and all that causes it. It is not possible then for one who thinks he is harmed to take pleasure in what he thinks is the author of the harm, any more than to take pleasure in the harm itself.

[…]

33.   LAY down for yourself from the first a definite stamp and style of conduct, which you will maintain when you are alone and also in the society of men. Be silent for the most part, or, if you speak, say only what is necessary and in a few words. Talk, but rarely, if occasion calls you, but do not talk of ordinary things – of gladiators, or horse-races, or athletes, or of meats or drinks – these are topics that arise everywhere – but above all do not talk about men in blame or compliment or comparison. If you can, turn the conversation of your company by your talk to some fitting subject; but if you should chance to be isolated among strangers, be silent.

[…]

Do not go lightly or casually to hear lectures; but if you do go, maintain your gravity and dignity and do not make yourself offensive. When you are going to meet any one, and particularly some man of reputed eminence, set before your mind the thought, 'What would Socrates or Zeno have done?' and you will not fail to make proper use of the occasion.

[…]

34.   WHEN you imagine some pleasure, beware that it does not carry you away, like other imaginations. Wait a while, and give yourself pause. Next remember two things: how long you will enjoy the pleasure, and also how long you will afterwards repent and revile yourself. And set on the other side the joy and self-satisfaction you will feel if you refrain. And if the moment seems come to realize it, take heed that you be not overcome by the winning sweetness and attraction of it; set in the other scale the thought how much better is the consciousness of having vanquished it.

35.   WHEN you do a thing because you have determined that it ought to be done, never avoid being seen doing it, even if the opinion of the multitude is going to condemn you. For if your action is wrong, then avoid doing it altogether, but if it is right, why do you fear those who will rebuke you wrongly?

[…]

37.   IF YOU try to act a part beyond your powers, you not only disgrace yourself in it, but you neglect the part which you could have filled with success.

38. As IN walking you take care not to tread on a nail or to twist your foot, so take care that you do not harm your Governing Principle. And if we guard this in everything we do, we shall set to work more securely.

39. EVERY man's body is a measure for his property, as the foot is the measure for his shoe. If you stick to this limit, you will keep the right measure; if you go beyond it, you are bound to be carried away down a precipice in the end; just as with the shoe, if you once go beyond the foot, your shoe puts on gilding, and soon purple and embroidery. For when once you go beyond the measure there is no limit.

[...]

41. IT is a sign of a dull mind to dwell upon the cares of the body, to prolong exercise, eating, drinking, and other bodily functions. These things are to be done by the way; all your attention must be given to the mind.

42. WHEN a man speaks evil or does evil to you, remember that he does or says it because he thinks it is fitting for him. It is not possible for him to follow what seems good to you, but only what seems good to him, so that, if his opinion is wrong, he suffers, in that he is the victim of deception. In the same way, if a composite judgement which is true is thought to be false, it is not the judgement that suffers, but the man who is deluded about it. If you act on this principle you will be gentle to him who reviles you, saying to yourself on each occasion, 'He thought it right.'

43. EVERYTHING has two handles, one by which you can carry it, the other by which you cannot. If your brother wrongs you, do not take it by that handle, the handle of his wrong, for you cannot carry it by that, but rather by the other handle — that he is a brother, brought up with you, and then you will take it by the handle that you can carry by.

44. IT IS illogical to reason thus, 'I am richer than you, therefore I am superior to you,' 'I am more eloquent than you, therefore I am superior to you.' It is more logical to reason, 'I am richer than you, therefore my property is superior to yours,' 'I am more eloquent than you, therefore my speech is superior to yours.' You are something more than property or speech.

45. IF A MAN wash quickly, do not say that he washes badly, but that he washes quickly. If a man drink much wine, do not say that he drinks badly, but that he drinks much. For till you have decided what judgement prompts him, how do you know that he acts badly? If you do as I say, you will assent to your apprehensive impressions and to none other.

46. ON NO occasion call yourself a philosopher, nor talk at large of your principles among the multitude, but act on your principles. For instance, at a banquet do not say how one ought to eat, but eat as you ought. Remember that Socrates had so completely got rid of the thought of display that when men came and wanted an introduction to philosophers he took them to be introduced; so patient of neglect was he. And if a discussion arise among the multitude on some principle, keep silent for the most part; for you are in great danger of blurting out some undigested thought. And when some one says to you, 'You know nothing,' and you do not let it provoke you, then know that you are really on the right road. For sheep do not bring grass to their shepherds and show them how much they have eaten, but they digest their fodder and then produce it in the form of wool and milk. Do the same yourself; instead of displaying your principles to the multitude, show them the results of the principles you have digested.

47. WHEN you have adopted the simple life, do not pride yourself upon it

[...]

48. THE ignorant man's position and character is this: he never looks to himself for benefit or harm, but to the world outside him. The philosopher's position and character is that he always looks to himself for benefit and harm.

The signs of one who is making progress are: he blames none, praises none, complains of none, accuses none, never speaks of himself as if he were somebody, or as if he knew anything. And if any one compliments him he laughs in himself at his compliment; and if one blames him, he makes no defence. He goes about like a convalescent, careful not to disturb his constitution on its road to recovery, until it has got firm hold. He has got rid of the will to get," and his will to avoid is directed no longer to what is beyond our power but only to what is in our power and contrary to nature. In all things he exercises his will without strain. If men regard him as foolish or ignorant he pays no heed. In one word, he keeps watch and guard on himself as his own enemy, lying in wait for him.

49. WHEN a man prides himself on being able to understand and interpret the books of Chrysippus, say to yourself, 'If Chrysippus had not written obscurely this man would have had nothing on which to pride himself.'

What is my object? To understand Nature and follow her. I look then for some one who interprets her, and having heard that Chrysippus does I come to him. But I do not understand his writings, so I seek an interpreter. So far there is nothing to be proud of. But when I have found the interpreter it remains for me to act on his precepts; that and that alone is a thing to be proud of. But if I admire the mere power of exposition, it comes to this — that I am turned into a grammarian, instead of a philosopher, except that I interpret Chrysippus in place of Homer. Therefore, when some one says to me, 'Read me Chrysippus,' when I cannot point to actions which are in harmony and correspondence with his teaching, I am rather inclined to blush.

50.   WHATEVER principles you put before you, hold fast to them as laws which it will be impious to transgress. But pay no heed to what any one says of you; for this is something beyond your own control.

51.   How long will you wait to think yourself worthy of the highest and transgress in nothing the clear pronouncement of reason? You have received the precepts which you ought to accept, and you have accepted them. Why then do you still wait for a master, that you may delay the amendment of yourself till he comes? You are a youth no longer, you are now a full-grown man. If now you are careless and indolent and are always putting off, fixing one day after another as the limit when you mean to begin attending to yourself, then, living or dying, you will make no progress but will continue unawares in ignorance. Therefore make up your mind before it is too late to live as one who is mature and proficient, and let all that seems best to you be a law that you cannot transgress. And if you encounter anything troublesome or pleasant or glorious or inglorious, remember that the hour of struggle is come, the Olympic contest is here and you may put off no longer, and that one day and one action determines whether the progress you have achieved is lost or maintained.

This was how Socrates attained perfection, paying heed to nothing but reason, in all that he encountered. And if you are not yet Socrates, yet ought you to live as one who would wish to be a Socrates.

52.   THE first and most necessary department of philosophy deals with the application of principles; for instance, 'not to lie.' The second deals with demonstrations; for instance, 'How comes it that one ought not to lie?' The third is concerned with establishing and analysing these processes; for instance, 'How comes it that this is a demonstration? What is demonstration, what is consequence, what is contradiction, what is true, what is false?' It follows then that the third department is necessary because of the second, and the second because of the first. The first is the most necessary part, and that in which we must rest. But we reverse the order: we occupy ourselves with the third, and make that our whole concern, and the first we completely neglect. Wherefore we lie, but are ready enough with the demonstration that lying is wrong.

9

The Enchiridion

[handwritten margin note: God = pure goodness / goodness is required for being]

Saint Augustine

The first main topic discussed in the excerpt from the *Enchiridion* (or *Handbook*) provided here is the nature of evil. For Augustine, evil necessarily involves something that is good being deprived of some, but not all, of its goodness. It is impossible for anything to be wholly evil, as everything that exists contains some goodness. On the other hand, pure goodness can stand alone, in God. So tightly wedded together are good and evil in the world, that Augustine contends that we have here an exception to the general logical rule that no one thing can have contradictory properties (e.g. a particular ball cannot be both red all over and not red all over). Arguably, this is a very bad place to end up, since rules of logic as fundamental as this one do not strike us as being the kind of thing that admit of exceptions. In any case, one might well think Augustine does not need to commit himself to such a strong conclusion. After all, in the section of the text immediately preceding this claim (XIII), we are told: "When we accurately distinguish these two things, we find that … he is good because he is a man, and evil because he is wicked". This suggests that, actually, there are no contradictory properties involved in cases involving evil, but simply different properties attaching to different parts of things (just as there is no contradiction involved in one half of a ball being red and the other half being blue). The fact that Augustine thinks he needs to take a further step here perhaps reveals just how strong a version of the thesis that goodness is required for being he holds to: even an evil *part* of a thing that does not, as a matter of fact, exist in isolation from a good thing (e.g. a human being and his or her will) must itself also be good in order to exist.

In the background here is the so-called *problem of evil*, which Augustine addresses, in one way or another, in a number of different texts. This is the problem of reconciling the idea that God is all-powerful and all-good with the many evils we see in the world as it is (why, we very naturally find ourselves asking, could God not have created a world with significantly less evil in it?). We are not here given a complete solution to this problem, but we are provided with some of the key ingredients of Augustine's (putative) solution. The closely related ideas that evil cannot exist separately from goodness, and that goodness is the ground of everything that exists, are ideas that put some distance between Augustine and the Manichean dualism he flirted with before his conversion to Christianity (the Manicheans believed in two separate, conflicting substances of good and evil), and align him with the Neoplatonist thinkers who positively influenced his views as a Christian philosopher. God is the source of all that exists, and the things that exist must all be good. One of the good things bestowed on human beings is the will, but the will can be put to evil ends, just as bad trees can grow on good, fertile soil (XV). And when we do evil acts, we are responsible for those acts in a way that God is not. Augustine generally downplays bad features of the world that are not due to any human agent's will, elsewhere suggesting that they are part of what makes the whole of creation good; similarly, certain features of an excellent work of art might be bad when considered in isolation.

History of Ethics – Essential Readings with Commentary, First Edition. Edited by Daniel Star and Roger Crisp.
© 2020 John Wiley & Sons Ltd. Published 2020 by John Wiley & Sons Ltd.

The second main topic addressed is error in beliefs and the particular evil of lying. Augustine recognizes that not all false beliefs are due to some error attributable to the believer. Much ignorance is unavoidable, due to our limitations (and ignorance does not entail belief), but people start making mistakes when they take themselves to know what they do not know. This is true, we may assume, even before there is any lying on the scene; but Augustine focuses on a common cause of mistaken beliefs, and that is the evil of lying. Interestingly, Augustine holds that it is possible to commit the sin of lying even if what one says is true, as long as one believes it is false and one intends to deceive (XVIII). Consideration of cases of this kind enables us to see that it is the carrying out of an intention to deceive that is what makes lying evil, and not the mere dissemination of falsehoods. We might agree with this last thought even if we are inclined to think that lies, strictly speaking, must be falsehoods.

This conclusion about the evilness of the intention to deceive is called into question when we consider people who only ever lie to save other people from injury (XXII). It is to Augustine's credit as a philosopher that he also considers this kind of case. His aim here is not to positively recommend that we become liars of some limited kind, but to not shirk from considering a hard case for his view that lying is always wrong. The solution here, he takes it, is to distinguish between a person's deceit and the good intention, in some cases, that leads them to deceive others; the good intention might sometimes be appropriately praised, even though the act is wrong, and it can be an appropriate basis for the wrongness to be pardoned or excused.

The last excerpt is on a third topic, virtue, and is from a different text, *The City of God*. Augustine is adamant that virtue requires belief in the "true" (Christian) God. The contrast with Plato at this point (not to mention Aristotle) is stark. Although one might see a parallel between Plato's idea that the virtuous know the insensible forms, and Augustine's requirement that genuine virtues are capped by belief in God, Augustine's idea that the virtuous are required to see their own wills as subject to the authority of the will of a deity is something that Plato would not have accepted. Augustine contends that (apparent) virtues – which have their basis, we are told, in control over vices that is exercised by reason – when understood without reference to God, and desired simply for themselves, must perforce be ruined by pride and hence fail to be genuine. This claim about pride may strike the contemporary reader as ungrounded, but it makes good sense in the light of Augustine's commitment to the doctrine that God is responsible for good intentions being successfully realized. Failure to recognize that good outcomes are due to God's grace, rather than one's own will, breeds pride (the asymmetry between good and evil here is striking, since we alone are responsible for our sins). Many contemporary readers will not accept this religious doctrine, but we might still agree with Augustine that if some people have *delusional* beliefs about the significance of the effects of their own wills (we might think here of people who believe themselves to be much more important, or much more effective agents of good, than they really are), this may indeed undermine any claim to be virtuous that they might make.

[handwritten notes:]

evil of lying.

virtue requires belief in the true God.

virtuous are required to see their own wills as subject to the authority of the will of a deity.

神是 pure good.

believe in pure good

= seeing own will as a subject of pure good

= virtue ?

Chapter X

The Supremely Good Creator Made All Things Good

By the Trinity, thus supremely and equally and unchangeably good, all things were created; and these are not supremely and equally and unchangeably good, but yet they are good, even taken separately. Taken as a whole, however, they are very good, because their *ensemble* constitutes the universe in all its wonderful order and beauty.

Chapter XI

What Is Called Evil in the Universe Is But the Absence of Good

And in the universe, even that which is called evil, when it is regulated and put in its own place, only enhances our admiration of the good; for we enjoy and value the good more when we compare it with the evil. For the Almighty God, who, as even the heathen acknowledge, has supreme power over all things, being Himself supremely good, would never permit the existence of anything evil among His works, if He were not so omnipotent and good that He can bring good even out of evil. For what is that which we call evil but the absence of good? In the bodies of animals, disease and wounds mean nothing but the absence of health; for when a cure is effected, that does not mean that the evils which were present – namely, the diseases and wounds – go away from the body and dwell elsewhere: they altogether cease to exist; for the wound or disease is not a substance, but a defect in the fleshly substance – the flesh itself being a substance, and therefore something good, of which those evils – that is, privations of the good which we call health – are accidents. Just in the same way, what are called vices in the soul are nothing but privations of natural good. And when they are cured, they are not transferred elsewhere: when they cease to exist in the healthy soul, they cannot exist anywhere else.

Chapter XII

All Beings Were Made Good, but Not Being Made Perfectly Good, Are Liable to Corruption

All things that exist, therefore, seeing that the Creator of them all is supremely good, are themselves good. But because they are not, like their Creator, supremely and unchangeably good, their good may be diminished and increased. But for good to be diminished is an evil, although, however much it may be diminished, it is necessary, if the being is to continue, that some good should remain to constitute the being. For however small or of whatever kind the being may be, the good which makes it a being cannot be destroyed without destroying the being itself. An uncorrupted nature is justly held in esteem. But if, still further, it be incorruptible, it is undoubtedly considered of still higher value. When it is corrupted, however, its corruption is an evil, because it is deprived of some sort of good. For if it be deprived of no good, it receives no injury; but it does receive injury, therefore it is deprived of good. Therefore, so long as a being is in process of corruption, there is in it some good of which it is being deprived; and if a part of the being should remain which cannot be corrupted, this will certainly be an incorruptible being, and accordingly the process of corruption will result in the manifestation of this great good. But if it do not cease to be corrupted, neither can it cease to possess good of which corruption may deprive it. But if it should be thoroughly and completely consumed by corruption, there will then be no good left, because there will be no being. Wherefore corruption can consume the good only by consuming the being. Every being, therefore, is a good; a great good, if it can not be corrupted; a little good, if it can: but in any case, only the foolish or ignorant will deny that it is a good. And if it be wholly consumed by corruption, then the corruption itself must cease to exist, as there is no being left in which it can dwell.

Chapter XIII

There Can Be No Evil Where There Is No Good; and an Evil Man Is an Evil Good

Accordingly, there is nothing of what we call evil, if there be nothing good. But a good which is wholly without evil is a perfect good. A good, on the other hand, which contains evil is a faulty or imperfect good; and there can be no evil where there is no good. From all this we arrive at the curious result: that since every being, so far as it is a being, is good, when we say that a faulty being is an evil being, we just seem to say that what is good is evil, and that nothing but what is good can be evil, seeing that every being is good, and that no evil can exist except in a being. Nothing, then, can be evil except something which is good. And although this, when stated, seems to be a contradiction, yet the strictness of reasoning leaves us no escape from the conclusion. We must, however, beware of incurring the prophetic condemnation: "Woe unto them that call evil good, and good evil: that put darkness for light, and light for darkness: that put bitter for sweet, and sweet for bitter."[1] And yet our Lord says: "An evil man out of the evil treasure of his heart bringeth forth that which is evil."[2] Now, what is an evil man but an evil being? for a man is a being. Now, if a man is a good thing because he is a being, what is an evil man but an evil good? Yet, when we accurately distinguish these two things, we find that it is not because he is a man that he is an evil, or because he is wicked that he is a good; but that he is a good because he is a man, and an evil because he is wicked. Whoever, then, says, "To be a man is an evil," or, "To be wicked is a good," falls under the prophetic denunciation: "Woe unto them that call evil good, and good evil!" For he condemns the work of God, which is the man, and praises the defect of man, which is the wickedness. Therefore every being, even if it be a defective one, in so far as it is a being is good, and in so far as it is defective is evil.

Chapter XIV

Good and Evil Are an Exception to the Rule That Contrary Attributes Cannot Be Predicated of the Same Subject. Evil Springs Up in What Is Good, and Cannot Exist Except in What Is Good

Accordingly, in the case of these contraries which we call good and evil, the rule of the logicians, that two contraries cannot be predicated at the same time of the same thing does not hold. No weather is at the same time dark and bright: no food or drink is at the same time sweet and bitter: no body is at the same time and in the same place black and white: none is at the same time and in the same place deformed and beautiful. And this rule is found to hold in regard to many, indeed nearly all, contraries, that they cannot exist at the same time in any one thing. But although no one can doubt that good and evil are contraries, not only can they exist at the same time, but evil cannot exist without good, or in anything that is not good. Good, however, can exist without evil. For a man or an angel can exist without being wicked; but nothing can be wicked except a man or an angel: and so far as he is a man or an angel, he is good; so far as he is wicked, he is an evil. And these two contraries are so far co-existent, that if good did not exist in what is evil, neither could evil exist; because corruption could not have either a place to dwell in, or a source to spring from, if there were nothing that could be corrupted; and nothing can be corrupted except what is good, for corruption is nothing else but the destruction of good. From what is good, then, evils arose, and except in what is good they do not exist; nor was there any other source from which any evil nature could arise. For if there were, then, in so far as this was a being, it was certainly a good: and a being which was incorruptible would be a great good; and even one which was corruptible must be to some extent a good, for only by corrupting what was good in it could corruption do it harm.

Chapter XV

The Preceding Argument Is in No Wise Inconsistent With the Saying of Our Lord: "A Good Tree Cannot Bring Forth Evil Fruit"

But when we say that evil springs out of good, let it not be thought that this contradicts our Lord's saying: "A good tree cannot bring forth evil fruit."[3] For, as He who is the Truth says, you cannot gather grapes of thorns,[4] because grapes do not grow on thorns. But we see that on good soil both vines and thorns may be grown. And in the same way, just as an evil tree cannot bring forth good fruit, so an evil will cannot produce good works. But from the nature of man, which is good, may spring either a good or an evil will. And certainly there was at first no source from which an evil will could spring, except the nature of angel or of man, which was good. And our Lord Himself clearly shows this in the very same place where He speaks about the tree and its fruit. For He says: "Either make the tree good, and his fruit good; or else make the tree corrupt, and his fruit corrupt"[5] – clearly enough warning us that evil fruits do not grow on a good tree, nor good fruits on an evil tree; but that nevertheless the ground itself, by which He meant those whom He was then addressing, might grow either kind of trees.

[1] Isa. v. 20
[2] Luke vi. 45
[3] Matt. vii. 18
[4] Matt. vii. 16
[5] Matt. xii. 33

Chapter XVI

It Is Not Essential to Man's Happiness That He Should Know the Causes of Physical Convulsions; but It Is, That He Should Know the Causes of Good and Evil

Now, in view of these considerations, when we are pleased with that line of Maro, "Happy the man who has attained to the knowledge of the causes of things,"[6] we should not suppose that it is necessary to happiness to know the causes of the great physical convulsions, causes which lie hid in the most secret recesses of nature's kingdom, "whence comes the earthquake whose force makes the deep seas to swell and burst their barriers, and again to return upon themselves and settle down."[7] But we ought to know the causes of good and evil as far as man may in this life know them, in order to avoid the mistakes and troubles of which this life is so full. For our aim must always be to reach that state of happiness in which no trouble shall distress us, and no error mislead us. If we must know the causes of physical convulsions, there are none which it concerns us more to know than those which affect our own health. But seeing that, in our ignorance of these, we are fain to resort to physicians, it would seem that we might bear with considerable patience our ignorance of the secrets that lie hid in the earth and heavens.

Chapter XVII

why

The Nature of Error. All Error Is Not Hurtful, Though It Is Man's Duty As Far As Possible to Avoid It

For although we ought with the greatest possible care to avoid error, not only in great but even in little things, and although we cannot err except through ignorance, it does not follow that, if a man is ignorant of a thing, he must forthwith fall into error. That is rather the fate of the man who thinks he knows what he does not know. For he accepts what is false as if it were time, and that is the essence of error. But it is a point of very great importance what the subject is in regard to which a man makes a mistake. For on one and the same subject we rightly prefer an instructed man to an ignorant one, and a man who is not in error to one who is. In the case of different subjects, however – that is, when one man knows one thing, and another a different thing, and when what the former knows is useful, and what the latter knows is not so useful, or is actually hurtful – who would not, in regard to the things the latter knows, prefer the ignorance of the former to the knowledge of the latter? For there are points on which ignorance is better than knowledge. And in the same way, it has sometimes been an advantage to depart from the right way – in travelling, however, not in morals. It has happened to myself to take the wrong road where two ways met, so that I did not pass by the place where an armed band of Donatists lay in wait for me. Yet I arrived at the place whither I was bent, though by a roundabout route; and when I heard of the ambush, I congratulated myself on my mistake, and gave thanks to God for it. Now, who would not rather be the traveller who made a mistake like this, than the highwayman who made no mistake? And hence, perhaps, it is that the prince of poets puts these words into the mouth of a lover in misery:[8] "How I am undone, how I have been carried away by an evil error!" for there is an error which is good, as it not merely does no harm, but produces some actual advantage. But when we look more closely into the nature of truth, and consider that to err is just to take the false for the true, and the true for the false, or to hold what is certain as uncertain, and what is uncertain as certain, and that error in the soul is hideous and repulsive just in proportion as it appears fair and plausible when we utter it, or assent to it, saying, "Yea, yea; Nay, nay" – surely this life that we live is wretched indeed, if only on this account, that sometimes, in order to preserve it, it is necessary to fall into error. God forbid that such should be that other life, where truth itself is the life of the soul, where no one deceives, and no one is deceived. But here men deceive and are deceived, and they are more to be pitied when they lead others astray than when they are themselves led astray by putting trust in liars. Yet so much does a rational soul shrink from what is false, and so earnestly does it struggle against error, that even those who love to deceive are most unwilling to be deceived. For the liar does not think that he errs, but that he leads another who trusts him into error. And certainly he does not err in regard to the matter about which he lies, if he himself knows the truth; but he is deceived in this, that he thinks his lie does him no harm, whereas every sin is more hurtful to the sinner than to the sinned against.

[6] Virgil, *Georgics*, ii. 490
[7] *Ibid*.
[8] Virgil, *Eclog*. viii. 41

Chapter XVIII

It Is Never Allowable to Tell a Lie; but Lies Differ Very Much in Guilt, According to the Intention and the Subject

But here arises a very difficult and very intricate question, about which I once wrote a large book, finding it necessary to give it an answer. The question is this: whether at any time it can become the duty of a good man to tell a lie? For some go so far as to contend that there are occasions on which it is a good and pious work to commit perjury even, and to say what is false about matters that relate to the worship of God, and about the very nature of God Himself. To me, however, it seems certain that every lie is a sin, though it makes a great difference with what intention and on what subject one lies. For the sin of the man who tells a lie to help another is not so heinous as that of the man who tells a lie to injure another; and the man who by his lying puts a traveller on the wrong road, does not do so much harm as the man who by false or misleading representations distorts the whole course of a life. No one, of course, is to be condemned as a liar who says what is false, believing it to be true, because such an one does not consciously deceive, but rather is himself deceived. And, on the same principle, a man is not to be accused of lying, though he may sometimes be open to the charge of rashness, if through carelessness he takes up what is false and holds it as true; but, on the other hand, the man who says what is true, believing it to be false, is, so far as his own consciousness is concerned, a liar. For in saying what he does not believe, he says what to his own conscience is false, even though it should in fact be true; nor is the man in any sense free from lying who with his mouth speaks the truth without knowing it, but in his heart wills to tell a lie. And, therefore, not looking at the matter spoken of, but solely at the intention of the speaker, the man who unwittingly says what is false, thinking all the time that it is true, is a better man than the one who unwittingly says what is true, but in his conscience intends to deceive. For the former does not think one thing and say another; but the latter, though his statements may be true in fact, has one thought in his heart and another on his lips: and that is the very essence of lying. But when we come to consider truth and falsehood in respect to the subjects spoken of, the point on which one deceives or is deceived becomes a matter of the utmost importance. For although, as far as a man's own conscience is concerned, it is a greater evil to deceive than to be deceived, nevertheless it is a far less evil to tell a lie in regard to matters that do not relate to religion, than to be led into error in regard to matters the knowledge and belief of which are essential to the right worship of God. To illustrate this by example: suppose that one man should say of some one who is dead that he is still alive, knowing this to be untrue; and that another man should, being deceived, believe that Christ shall at the end of some time (make the time as long as you please) die; would it not be incomparably better to lie like the former, than to be deceived like the latter? and would it not be a much less evil to lead some man into the former error, than to be led by any man into the latter?

Chapter XIX

Men's Errors Vary Very Much in the Magnitude of the Evils They Produce; but Yet Every Error Is in Itself an Evil

In some things, then, it is a great evil to be deceived; in some it is a small evil; in some no evil at all; and in some it is an actual advantage. It is to his grievous injury that a man is deceived when he does not believe what leads to eternal life, or believes what leads to eternal death. It is a small evil for a man to be deceived, when, by taking falsehood for truth, he brings upon himself temporal annoyances; for the patience of the believer will turn even these to a good use, as when, for example, taking a bad man for a good, he receives injury from him. But one who believes a bad man to be good, and yet suffers no injury, is nothing the worse for being deceived, nor does he fall under the prophetic denunciation: "Woe to those who call evil good!"[9] For we are to understand that this is spoken not about evil man, but about the things that make men evil. Hence the man who calls adultery good, falls justly under that prophetic denunciation. But the man who calls the adulterer good, thinking him to be chaste, and not knowing him to be an adulterer, falls into no error in regard to the nature of good and evil, but only makes a mistake as to the secrets of human conduct. He calls the man good on the ground of believing him to be what is undoubtedly good; he calls the adulterer evil, and the pure man good; and he calls this man good, not knowing him to be an adulterer,

---

[9] Isa. v. 20

but believing him to be pure. Further, if by making a mistake one escape death, as I have said above once happened to me, one even derives some advantage from one's mistake. But when I assert that in certain cases a man may be deceived without any injury to himself, or even with some advantage to himself, I do not mean that the mistake in itself is no evil, or is in any sense a good; I refer only to the evil that is avoided, or the advantage that is gained, through making the mistake. For the mistake, considered in itself, is an evil: a great evil if it concern a great matter, a small evil if it concern a small matter, but yet always an evil. For who that is of sound mind can deny that it is an evil to receive what is false as if it were true, and to reject what is true as if it were false, or to hold what is uncertain as certain, and what is certain as uncertain? But it is one thing to think a man good when he is really bad, which is a mistake; it is another thing to suffer no ulterior injury in consequence of the mistake, supposing that the bad man whom we think good inflicts no damage upon us. In the same way, it is one thing to think that we are on the right road when we are not; it is another thing when this mistake of ours, which is an evil, leads to some good, such as saving us from an ambush of wicked men.

[…]

Chapter XXII

A Lie Is Not Allowable, Even to Save Another From Injury

But every lie must be called a sin, because not only when a man knows the truth, but even when, as a man may be, he is mistaken and deceived, it is his duty to say what he thinks in his heart, whether it be true, or whether he only think it to be true. But every liar says the opposite of what he thinks in his heart, with purpose to deceive. Now it is evident that speech was given to man, not that men might therewith deceive one another, but that one man might make known his thoughts to another. To use speech, then, for the purpose of deception, and not for its appointed end, is a sin. Nor are we to suppose that there is any lie that is not a sin, because it is sometimes possible, by telling a lie, to do service to another. For it is possible to do this by theft also, as when we steal from a rich man who never feels the loss, to give to a poor man who is sensibly benefited by what he gets. And the same can be said of adultery also, when, for instance, some woman appears likely to die of love unless we consent to her wishes, while if she lived she might purify herself by repentance; but yet no one will assert that on this account such an adultery is not a sin. And if we justly place so high a value upon chastity, what offense have we taken at truth, that, while no prospect of advantage to another will lead us to violate the former by adultery, we should be ready to violate the latter by lying? It cannot be denied that they have attained a very high standard of goodness who never lie except to save a man from injury; but in the case of men who have reached this standard, it is not the deceit, but their good intention, that is justly praised, and sometimes even rewarded. It is quite enough that the deception should be pardoned, without its being made an object of laudation, especially among the heirs of the new covenant, to whom it is said: "Let your communication be, Yea, yea; Nay, nay: for whatsoever is more than these cometh of evil."[10] And it is on account of this evil, which never ceases to creep in while we retain this mortal vesture, that the co-heirs of Christ themselves say, "Forgive us our debts."[11]

Chapter XXIII

Summary of the Results of the Preceding Discussion

As it is right that we should know the causes of good and evil, so much of them at least as will suffice for the way that leads us to the kingdom, where there will be life without the shadow of death, truth without any alloy of error, and happiness unbroken by any sorrow, I have discussed these subjects with the brevity which my limited space demanded. And I think there cannot now be any doubt, that the only cause of any good that we enjoy is the goodness of God, and that the only cause of evil is the falling away from the unchangeable good of a being made good but changeable, first in the case of an angel, and afterwards in the case of man.

[…]

[10] Matt. v. 37
[11] Matt. vi. 12

Chapter XXV

That Where There Is No True Religion There Are No True Virtues

For though the soul may seem to rule the body admirably, and the reason the vices, if the soul and reason do not themselves obey God, as God has commanded them to serve Him, they have no proper authority over the body and the vices. For what kind of mistress of the body and the vices can that mind be which is ignorant of the true God, and which, instead of being subject to His authority, is prostituted to the corrupting influences of the most vicious demons? It is for this reason that the virtues which it seems to itself to possess, and by which it restrains the body and the vices that it may obtain and keep what it desires, are rather vices than virtues so long as there is no reference to God in the matter. For although some suppose that virtues which have a reference only to themselves, and are desired only on their own account, are yet true and genuine virtues, the fact is that even then they are inflated with pride, and are therefore to be reckoned vices rather than virtues. For as that which gives life to the flesh is not derived from flesh, but is above it, so that which gives blessed life to man is not derived from man, but is something above him; and what I say of man is true of every celestial power and virtue whatsoever.

10

Summa Contra Gentiles and *Summa Theologica*

Saint Thomas Aquinas

Here we have three excerpts from Aquinas's writings. The first is from the *Summa Contra Gentiles*, and the other two are from a later text, the *Summa Theologica*. These are two of Aquinas's best-known works, and the second work is thought to be a descendant of the first. The complete corpus is very large and includes some eleven commentaries on Aristotle, a philosopher who influenced Aquinas in no small measure (this is one thing that sets Aquinas apart from Augustine).

The first excerpt very clearly draws on Aristotle, who, as we have seen, focused in his *Ethics* on the question of what, if anything, human beings aim for as the end of all their activities, since identifying this end, or highest good, is seen to be crucial for answering the closely related, but more general, question of how we should structure our lives. Unlike the Aristotle of Books I through IX of the *Nicomachean Ethics*, at least, Aquinas locates the highest end for human beings (and every 'intellectual substance') not in virtuous activity, but in understanding God. Aquinas's God is himself 'always actually understanding', so in pursuing our end and understanding God we are also like him to the highest degree possible given our finite nature. But the argument of the excerpted text starts at an earlier point: we are first to be persuaded that every agent intends an end, and then, separately, that every agent intends things under the guise of the good. This is an insightful way of proceeding, since it is tempting to think that these things can come apart: that is, one *might* well think (although Aquinas argues this is not the case) that people are capable of pursuing certain ends without conceiving of those ends as good. Here one might have in mind either trivial acts (e.g. twiddling one's thumbs) or particularly malevolent evils.

When Aquinas elsewhere argues that there is an *eternal law*, he tells us that law in general is 'nothing else but a dictate of practical reason emanating from the ruler who governs a perfect community', and that the community that consists of the entire universe is ruled by God, by a law that stands outside of time. *Natural law* is subsequently distinguished from *human law*; we are to think of the former as involving laws that are highly general, essential to our nature, and not chosen by us, while the latter are dictates of our practical reason that are to be derived from natural laws when considering more particular details of the communities that we live in. The natural law in us rational creatures is discoverable through the use of reason and reflects eternal law. It is the basis of our natural inclinations towards various goods.

Aquinas provides us with an account of the most important ethical virtues in the second excerpt. These are the four 'cardinal' virtues, all of which one is required to develop in order to be virtuous: prudence, justice, temperance, and fortitude. All other virtues, we are told, can be described as versions of these virtues (it is interesting to think about how this might or might not work, in relation to a range of other virtues) and have less important subject matters. What distinguishes the cardinal virtues from all others is their crucial role in human judgement and action, given the fact that we are beings who possess both reason and passions that often conflict with reason.

The final excerpt provides a brief, but extremely influential presentation of an idea that has come to be known as *the doctrine of double effect* (in an essay reproduced in the present volume, this doctrine is

History of Ethics – Essential Readings with Commentary, First Edition. Edited by Daniel Star and Roger Crisp.
© 2020 John Wiley & Sons Ltd. Published 2020 by John Wiley & Sons Ltd.

discussed by Philippa Foot in a wholly secular context). Aquinas here begins by distinguishing between effects of our acts that are intended and those that are produced by our acts but not intended. Of course, many of the effects of our acts are not foreseen by us – nor would they be foreseen by us even if we were being as rational as we could possibly be. However, it is clear that it is not unforeseen effects that Aquinas is primarily interested in here. Rather, he is thinking of the effects of our acts that we can foresee or expect to occur, but that we do not *intend* to bring about. It is possible for me not to plan or intend to wear out my shoes by wearing them every day, even though I know that they will, as it happens, be worn out if I wear them every day. And one can defend one's own life by killing an attacker without intending to kill the attacker (his example), and not because one does not think the attacker will die – in certain circumstances, one might reasonably expect an attacker *will* die because of one's act. Still, it is possible not to intend that the attacker die, even as you do something that will kill them. This reasoning enables Aquinas to hold on to the view that carrying out an intention to kill a person is always wrong, whilst very plausibly allowing that some acts that can be expected to lead to the death of others are not wrong (as long as the relevant act of self-defense is not out of proportion to the threat in question); or, at least, to hold on to this idea in relation to ordinary citizens when they are not acting as public authorities. Certain people (e.g. soldiers fighting a just war, and judges) may also have a kind of public authority to kill 'for the common good'. Aquinas is keen to describe even these killings as killings done in self-defense, but here we are to think of the self-defense of our society as the goal of such acts (such killings may be intended means to this end).

Summa Contra Gentiles

Chapter II

That Every Agent Acts for an End

ACCORDINGLY we must first show that every agent, by its action, intends an end.

For in those things which clearly act for an end, we declare the end to be that towards which the movement of the agent tends; for when this is reached, the end is said to be reached, and to fail in this is to fail in the end intended. This may be seen in the physician who aims at health, and in a man who runs towards an appointed goal. Nor does it matter, as to this, whether that which tends to an end be endowed with knowledge or not; for just as the target is the end of the archer, so is it the end of the arrow's flight. Now the movement of every agent tends to something determinate, since it is not from any force that any action proceeds, but heating proceeds from heat, and cooling from cold; and therefore actions are differentiated by their active principles. Action sometimes terminates in something made, as for instance building terminates in a house, and healing in health; while sometimes it does not so terminate, as for instance, in the case of understanding and sensation. And if action terminates in something made, the movement of the agent tends by that action towards the thing made; while if it does not terminate in something made, the movement of the agent tends to the action itself. It follows therefore that every agent intends an end while acting, which end is sometimes the action itself, sometimes a thing made by the action.

Again. In all things that act for an end, that is said to be the last end beyond which the agent seeks nothing further; and thus the physician's action goes as far as health, and when this is attained, his efforts cease. But in the action of every agent, a point can be reached beyond which the agent does not desire to go; or else actions would tend to infinity, which is impossible, for since *it is not possible to pass through an infinite medium*,[1] the agent would never begin to act, because nothing moves towards what it cannot reach. Therefore every agent acts for an end.

Moreover. If the actions of an agent proceed to infinity, these actions must needs result either in something made, or not. If the result is something made, the being of that thing made will follow after an infinity of actions. But that which presupposes an infinity of things cannot possibly be, since *an infinite medium cannot be passed through*. Now impossibility of being argues impossibility of becoming, and that which cannot become, it is impossible to make. Therefore it is impossible for an agent to begin to make a thing for the making of which an infinity of actions is presupposed. – If, however, the result of such actions be not something made, the order of these actions must be either according to the order of active powers (for instance, if a man feels that he may imagine, and imagines that he may understand, and understands that he may will), or according to the order of objects (for instance, I consider the body that I may consider the soul, which I consider in order to consider a separate substance, which again I consider so that I may consider God). Now it is not possible to proceed to infinity, either in active powers (as neither is this possible in the forms of things, as is proved in *Metaph*. ii,[2] since the form is the principle of activity), or in objects (as neither is this possible in beings, since there is one first being, as we have proved above).[3] Therefore it is not possible for agents to proceed to infinity, and consequently there must be something, upon whose attainment the efforts of the agent cease. Therefore every agent acts for an end.

Further. In things that act for an end, whatsoever comes between the first agent and the last end, is an end in respect to what precedes, and an active principle in respect of what follows. Hence if the effort of the agent does not tend to something determinate, and if its action, as stated, proceeds to infinity, the active principles must needs proceed to infinity; which is impossible, as we have shown above. Therefore the effort of the agent must of necessity tend to something determinate.

Again. Every agent acts either by nature or by intellect. Now there can be no doubt that those which act by intellect act for an end, since they act *with* an intellectual preconception of what they attain by their action, and they act *through* such a preconception; for this is to act by intellect. Now just as in the preconceiving intellect there exists the entire likeness of the effect that is attained by the action of the intellectual being, so in the natural agent there pre-exists the likeness of the natural effect, by virtue of which the action is determined to the appointed effect; for

---

[1] Aristotle, *Post. Anal.*, I, 22 (82b 38).
[2] Aristotle, *Metaph.*, I a, 2 (994, 6).
[3] *C. G.*, I, 42.

fire begets fire, and an olive produces an olive. Therefore, even as that which acts by intellect tends by its action to a definite end, so also does that which acts by nature. Therefore every agent acts for an end.

Moreover. Fault is not found save in those things which are for an end, for we do not find fault with one who fails in that to which he is not appointed; and thus we find fault with a physician if he fail to heal, but not with a builder or a grammarian. But we find fault in things done according to art, as when a grammarian fails to speak correctly, and in things that are ruled by nature, as in the case of monstrosities. Therefore every agent, whether according to nature, or according to art, or acting of set purpose, acts for an end.

Again. Were an agent not to act for a definite effect, all effects would be indifferent to it. Now that which is indifferent to many effects does not produce one rather than another. Therefore, from that which is indifferent to either of two effects, no effect results, unless it be determined by something to one of them. Hence it would be impossible for it to act. Therefore every agent tends to some definite effect, which is called its end.

There are, however, certain actions which would seem not to be for an end, such as playful and contemplative actions, and those which are done without attention, such as scratching one's beard, and the like. Whence some might be led to think that there is an agent that acts not for an end. – But we must observe that contemplative actions are not for another end, but are themselves an end. Playful actions are sometimes an end, when one plays for the mere pleasure of play; and sometimes they are for an end, as when we play that afterwards we may study better. Actions done without attention do not proceed from the intellect, but from some sudden act of the imagination, or some natural principle; and thus a disordered humor produces an itching sensation and is the cause of a man scratching his beard, which he does without his intellect attending to it. Such actions do tend to an end, although outside the order of the intellect. Hereby is excluded the error of certain natural philosophers of old, who maintained that all things happen by the necessity of matter, thus utterly banishing the final cause from things.[4]

Chapter III

That Every Agent Acts for a Good

HENCE we must go on to prove that every agent acts for a good.

For that every agent acts for an end clearly follows from the fact that every agent tends to something definite. Now that to which an agent tends definitely must needs be befitting to that agent, since the agent would not tend to it save because of some fittingness thereto. But that which is befitting to a thing is good for it. Therefore every agent acts for a good.

Further. The end is that wherein the appetite of the agent or mover comes to rest, as also the appetite of that which is moved. Now it is the very notion of good to be the term of appetite, since *good is the object of every appetite.*[5] Therefore all action and movement is for a good.

Again. All action and movement would seem to be directed in some way to being, either for the preservation of being in the species or in the individual, or for the acquisition of being. Now this itself, namely, being, is a good; and for this reason all things desire being. Therefore all action and movement is for a good.

Furthermore. All action and movement is for some perfection. For if the action itself be the end, it is clearly a second perfection of the agent. And if the action consist in the transformation of external matter, clearly the mover intends to induce some perfection into the thing moved, towards which perfection the movable also tends, if the movement be natural. Now we say that this is to be good, namely, to be perfect. Therefore every action and movement is for a good.

Also. Every agent acts according as it is actual. Now by acting it tends to something similar to itself. Therefore it tends to an act. But an act has the nature of good, since evil is not found save in a potentiality lacking act. Therefore every action is for a good.

Moreover. The intellectual agent acts for an end, as determining for itself its end; whereas the natural agent, though it acts for an end, as was proved above,[6] does not determine its end for itself, since it knows not the nature of end, but is moved to the end determined for it by another. Now an intellectual agent does not determine the end for itself except under the aspect of good; for the intelligible object does not move except it be considered as

[4] Cf. Aristotle, *Phys.*, II, 8 (198b 12).
[5] Aristotle, *Eth.*, I, 1 (1094a 1).
[6] Ch. 2.

a good, which is the object of the will. Therefore the natural agent also is not moved, nor does it act for an end, except in so far as this end is a good, since the end is determined for the natural agent by some appetite. Therefore every agent acts for a good.

Again. To shun evil and to seek good are of the same nature, even as movement from below and upward are of the same nature. Now we observe that all things shun evil, for intellectual agents shun a thing for the reason that they apprehend it as evil, and all natural agents, in proportion to their strength, resist corruption which is the evil of everything. Therefore all things act for a good.

Again. That which results from the agent's action outside his intention, is said to happen by chance or luck. Now we observe in the works of nature that either always or more often that happens which is best: thus in plants the leaves are so placed as to protect the fruit; and the parts of an animal are so disposed as to conduce to the animal's safety. Therefore, if this happens outside the intention of the natural agent, it will be the result of chance or luck. But that is impossible, because things that happen always, or frequently, are not by chance or fortuitous, but those which occur seldom.[7] Therefore the natural agent tends to that which is best; and much more evidently is this so with the intellectual agent. Therefore every agent intends a good in acting.

Moreover. Whatever is moved is brought to the term of movement by the mover and agent. Therefore mover and moved tend to the same term. Now that which is moved, since it is in potentiality, tends to an act, and consequently to perfection and goodness; for by its movement it passes from potentiality to act. Therefore mover and agent by moving and acting always intend a good.

Hence the philosophers in defining the good said: *The good is the object of every appetite;* and Dionysius says that *all things desire the good and the best.*[8]

[...]

Chapter XXV

That to Know God Is the End of Every Intellectual Substance

Now, seeing that all creatures, even those that are devoid of reason, are directed to God as their last end, and that all reach this end in so far as they have some share of a likeness to Him, the intellectual creature attains to Him in a special way, namely, through its proper operation, by understanding Him. Consequently this must be the end of the intellectual creature, namely, to understand God.

For, as we have shown above,[9] God is the end of each thing, and hence, as far as it is possible to it, each thing intends to be united to God as its last end. Now a thing is more closely united to God by reaching in a way to the very substance of God; which happens when it knows something of the divine substance, rather than when it reaches to a divine likeness. Therefore the intellectual substance tends to the knowledge of God as its last end.

Again. The operation proper to a thing is its end, for it is its second perfection; so that when a thing is well conditioned for its proper operation it is said to be fit and good. Now understanding is the proper operation of the intellectual substance, and consequently is its end. Therefore, whatever is most perfect in this operation is its last end; and especially in those operations which are not directed to some product, such as understanding and sensation. And since operations of this kind take their species from their objects, by which also they are known, it follows that the more perfect the object of any such operation, the more perfect is the operation. Consequently to understand the most perfect intelligible, namely God, is the most perfect in the genus of the operation which consists in understanding. Therefore to know God by an act of understanding is the last end of every intellectual substance.

Someone, however, might say that the last end of an intellectual substance consists indeed in understanding the best intelligible object, but that what is the best intelligible for this or that intellectual substance is not absolutely the best intelligible; and that the higher the intellectual substance, the higher is its best intelligible. So that possibly the supreme intellectual substance has for its best intelligible object that which is best absolutely, and its happiness will consist in understanding God; whereas the happiness of any lower intellectual substance will consist in understanding some lower intelligible object, which however will be the highest thing understood by that substance.

[7] Cf. Aristotle, *Phys.*, II, 5 (196b 11).
[8] *De Div. Nom.*, IV, 4 (PG 3, 699).
[9] Ch. 17.

Especially would it seem not to be in the power of the human intellect to understand that which is absolutely the best intelligible, because of its weakness; for it is as much adapted for knowing the supreme intelligible *as the owl's eye for seeing the sun.*[10]

Nevertheless it is evident that the end of any intellectual substance, even the lowest, is to understand God. For it has been shown above that God is the last end towards which all things tend.[11] And the human intellect, although the lowest in the order of intelligent substances, is superior to all that are devoid of understanding. Since then a more noble substance has not a less noble end, God will be the end also of the human intellect. Now every intelligent being attains to its last end by understanding it, as we have proved. Therefore the human intellect attains to God as its end, by understanding Him.

Again. Just as things devoid of intellect tend to God as their end by way of assimilation, so do intellectual substances by way of knowledge, as clearly appears from what has been said. Now, although things devoid of reason tend towards a likeness to their proximate causes, the intention of nature does not rest there, but has for its end a likeness to the highest good, as we have proved,[12] although they are able to attain to this likeness in a most imperfect manner. Therefore, however little be the knowledge of God to which the intellect is able to attain, this will be the intellect's last end, rather than a perfect knowledge of lower intelligibles.

Moreover. Everything desires most of all its last end. Now the human intellect desires, loves and enjoys the knowledge of divine things, although it can grasp but little about them, more than the perfect knowledge which it has of the lowest things. Therefore man's last end is to understand God in some way.

Further. Everything tends to a divine likeness as its own end. Therefore a thing's last end is that whereby it is most of all like God. Now the intellectual creature is especially likened to God in that it is intellectual, since this likeness belongs to it above other creatures, and includes all other likenesses. And in this particular kind of likeness it is more like God in understanding actually than in understanding habitually or potentially, because God is always actually understanding, as we proved in the First Book.[13] Furthermore, in understanding actually, the intellectual creature is especially like God in understanding God; for by understanding Himself God understands all other things, as we proved in the First Book.[14] Therefore the last end of every intellectual substance is to understand God.

Again. That which is lovable only because of another is for the sake of that which is lovable for its own sake alone; because we cannot go on indefinitely in the appetite of nature, since then nature's desire would be in vain, for it is impossible to pass through an infinite number of things. Now all practical sciences, arts and powers are lovable only for the sake of something else, since their end is not knowledge, but work. But speculative sciences are lovable for their own sake, for their end is knowledge itself. Nor can we find any action in human life that is not directed to some other end, with the exception of speculative consideration. For even playful actions, which seem to be done without any purpose, have some end due to them, namely that the mind may be relaxed, and that thereby we may afterwards become more fit for studious occupations; or otherwise we should always have to be playing, if play were desirable for its own sake, and this is unreasonable. Accordingly, the practical arts are directed to the speculative arts, and again every human operation, to intellectual speculation, as its end. Now, in all sciences and arts that are mutually ordered, the last end seems to belong to the one from which others take their rules and principles. Thus the art of sailing, to which belongs the ship's purpose, namely its use, provides rules and principles to the art of ship-building. And such is the relation of first philosophy to other speculative sciences, for all others depend thereon, since they derive their principles from it, and are directed by it in defending those principles; and moreover first philosophy is wholly directed to the knowledge of God as its last end, and is consequently called the *divine science.*[15] Therefore the knowledge of God is the last end of all human knowledge and activity.

Furthermore. In all mutually ordered agents and movers, the end of the first agent and mover must be the end of all, even as the end of the commander-in-chief is the end of all who are soldiering under him. Now of all the parts of man, the intellect is the highest mover, for it moves the appetite, by proposing its object to it; and the intellective appetite, or will, moves the sensitive appetites, namely the irascible and concupiscible. Hence it is that we do not obey the concupiscence, unless the will command; while the sensitive appetite, when the will has given its

---

[10] Aristotle, *Metaph.*, I *a*, 1 (993b 9).
[11] Ch. 17.
[12] Ch. 19.
[13] *C. G.*, I, 56.
[14] *C. G.*, I, 49.
[15] Aristotle, *Metaph.*, I, 2 (983a 6).

consent, moves the body. Therefore the end of the intellect is the end of all human actions. *Now the intellect's end and good are the true*,[16] and its last end is the first truth. Therefore the last end of the whole man, and of all his deeds and desires, is to know the first truth, namely, God.

Moreover. Man has a natural desire to know the causes of whatever he sees; and so through wondering at what they saw, and not knowing its cause, men first began to philosophize, and when they had discovered the cause they were at rest. Nor do they cease inquiring until they come to the first cause; and *then do we deem ourselves to know perfectly when we know the first cause*.[17] Therefore man naturally desires, as his last end, to know the first cause. But God is the first cause of all things. Therefore man's last end is to know God.

Besides. Man naturally desires to know the cause of any known effect. But the human intellect knows universal being. Therefore it naturally desires to know its cause, which is God alone, as we proved in the Second Book.[18] Now one has not attained to one's last end until the natural desire is at rest. Therefore the knowledge of any intelligible object is not enough for man's happiness, which is his last end, unless he know God also, which knowledge terminates his natural desire as his last end. Therefore this very knowledge of God is man's last end.

Further. A body that tends by its natural appetite to its place is moved all the more vehemently and rapidly the nearer it approaches its end. Hence Aristotle proves that a natural straight movement cannot be towards an indefinite point, because it would not be more moved afterwards than before.[19] Hence that which tends more vehemently to a thing afterwards than before is not moved towards an indefinite point but towards something fixed. Now this we find in the desire of knowledge, for the more one knows, the greater one's desire to know. Consequently, man's natural desire in knowledge tends to a definite end. This can be none other than the highest thing knowable, which is God. Therefore the knowledge of God is man's last end.

Now the last end of man and of any intelligent substance is called *happiness* or *beatitude*, for it is this that every intellectual substance desires as its last end, and for its own sake alone. Therefore the last beatitude or happiness of any intellectual substance is to know God.

Hence it is said (*Matt.* v. 8): *Blessed are the clean of heart, for they shall see God*; and (*Jo.* xvii. 3): *This is eternal life, that they may know thee, the only true God*. Aristotle himself agrees with this judgment when he says that man's ultimate happiness is *speculative, and this with regard to the highest object of speculation*.[20]

Chapter XXVI

Does Happiness Consist in an Act of the Will?

SINCE the intellectual substance attains to God by its operation, not only by an act of understanding but also by an act of the will, through desiring and loving Him, and through delighting in Him, someone might think that man's last end and ultimate happiness consists, not in knowing God, but in loving Him, or in some other act of the will towards Him; [1] especially since the object of the will is the good, which has the nature of an end, whereas the true, which is the object of the intellect, has not the nature of an end except in so far as it also is a good. Therefore, seemingly, man does not attain to his last end by an act of his intellect, but rather by an act of his will.

[2] Further. The ultimate perfection of operation is delight, *which perfects operation as beauty perfects youth*, as the Philosopher says.[21] Hence, if the last end be a perfect operation, it would seem that it must consist in an act of the will rather than of the intellect.

[3] Again. Delight apparently is desired for its own sake, so that it is never desired for the sake of something else; for it is silly to ask of anyone why he seeks to be delighted. Now this is a condition of the ultimate end, namely, that it be sought for its own sake. Therefore, seemingly, the last end consists in an act of the will rather than of the intellect.

[4] Moreover. All agree in their desire of the last end, for it is a natural desire. But more people seek delight than knowledge. Therefore delight would seem to be the last end rather than knowledge.

---

[16] Aristotle, *Eth.*, VI, 2 (1139a 27).
[17] Aristotle, *Metaph.*, I, 3 (983a 25).
[18] *C. G.*, II, 15.
[19] *De Caelo*, I, 8 (277a 18).
[20] *Eth.*, X, 7 (1177a 18).
[21] *Eth.*, X, 4 (1174b 31).

[5] Furthermore. The will is seemingly a higher power than the intellect, for the will moves the intellect to its act; since when a person wills, his intellect considers by an act what he holds by a habit. Therefore, seemingly, the action of the will is more noble than the action of the intellect. Therefore, it would seem that the last end, which is beatitude, consists in an act of the will rather than of the intellect.

But this can be clearly shown to be impossible.

For since happiness is the proper good of the intellectual nature, it must needs become the intellectual nature according to that which is proper thereto. Now appetite is not proper to the intellectual nature, but is in all things, although it is found diversely in diverse things. This diversity, however, arises from the fact that things are diversely related to knowledge. For things wholly devoid of knowledge have only a natural appetite; those that have a sensitive knowledge have also a sensitive appetite, under which the irascible and concupiscible appetites are comprised; and those which have intellectual knowledge have also an appetite proportionate to that knowledge, namely, the will. The will, therefore, in so far as it is an appetite, is not proper to the intellectual nature, but only in so far as it is dependent on the intellect. On the other hand, the intellect is in itself proper to the intellectual nature. Therefore, beatitude or happiness consists principally and essentially in an act of the intellect, rather than in an act of the will.

Again. In all powers that are moved by their objects, the object is naturally prior to the acts of those powers, even as the mover is naturally prior to the movable being moved. Now the will is such a power, for the appetible object moves the appetite. Therefore the will's object is naturally prior to its act, and consequently its first object precedes its every act. Therefore an act of the will cannot be the first thing willed. But this is the last end, which is beatitude. Therefore beatitude or happiness cannot be the very act of the will.

Besides. In all those powers which are able to reflect on their acts, their act must first bear on some other object, and afterwards the power is brought to bear on its own act. For if the intellect understands that it understands, we must suppose first that it understands some particular thing, and that afterwards it understands that it understands; for this very act of understanding, which the intellect understands, must have an object. Hence either we must go on forever, or if we come to some first thing understood, this will not be an act of understanding, but some intelligible thing. In the same way, the first thing willed cannot be the very act of willing, but must be some other good. Now the first thing willed by an intellectual nature is beatitude or happiness; because it is for its sake that we will whatever we will. Therefore happiness cannot consist in an act of the will.

Further. The truth of a thing's nature is derived from those things which constitute its substance; for a true man differs from a man in a picture by the things which constitute man's substance. Now false happiness does not differ from true in an act of the will; because, whatever be proposed to the will as the supreme good, whether truly or falsely, it makes no difference to the will in its desiring, loving, or enjoying that good: the difference is on the part of the intellect, as to whether the good proposed as supreme be truly so or not. Therefore beatitude or happiness consists essentially in an act of the intellect rather than of the will.

Again. If an act of the will were happiness itself, this act would be an act either of desire, or love, or delight. But desire cannot possibly be the last end. For desire implies that the will is tending to what it has not yet; and this is contrary to the very notion of the last end. – Nor can love be the last end. For a good is loved not only while it is in our possession, but even when it is not, because it is through love that we seek by desire what we have not; and if the love of a thing we possess is more perfect, this arises from the fact that we possess the good we love. It is one thing, therefore, to possess the good which is our end, and another to love it; for love was imperfect before we possessed the end, and perfect after we obtained possession. – Nor again is delight the last end. For it is possession of the good that causes delight, whether we are conscious of possessing it actually, or call to mind our previous possession, or hope to possess it in the future. Therefore delight is not the last end. – Therefore no act of the will can be happiness itself essentially.

Furthermore. If delight were the last end, it would be desirable for its own sake. But this is not true. For the desirability of a delight depends on what gives rise to the delight, since that which arises from good and desirable operations is itself good and desirable, but that which arises from evil operations is itself evil and to be avoided. Therefore its goodness and desirability are from something else, and consequently it is not itself the last end or happiness.

Moreover. The right order of things agrees with the order of nature, for in the natural order things are ordered to their end without any error. Now, in the natural order delight is for the sake of operation, and not conversely. For it is to be observed that nature has joined delight with those animal operations which are clearly ordered to necessary ends: for instance, to the use of food that is ordered to the preservation of the individual, and to sexual matters, that are appointed for the preservation of the species; since were there no pleasure, animals would abstain from the use of these necessary things. Therefore delight cannot be the last end.

Again. Delight, seemingly, is nothing else than the quiescence of the will in some becoming good, just as desire is the inclining of the will towards the attaining of some good. Now just as by his will a man is inclined towards an end, and rests in it, so too natural bodies have a natural inclination to their respective ends, and are at rest when they have once attained their end. Now it is absurd to say that the end of the movement of a heavy body is not to be in its proper place, but that it is the quiescence of the inclination towards that place. For if it were nature's chief intent that this inclination should be quiescent, it would not give such an inclination; but it gives the inclination so that the body may tend towards its proper place, and when it has arrived there, as though it were its end, quiescence of the inclination follows. Hence this quiescence is not the end, but accompanies the end. Neither therefore is delight the ultimate end, but accompanies it. Much less therefore is happiness any act of the will.

Besides. If a thing have something extrinsic for its end, the operation whereby it first obtains that thing will be called its last end. Thus, for those whose end is money possession is said to be their end, but not love or desire. Now the last end of the intellectual substance is God. Hence that operation of man whereby he first obtains God is essentially his happiness or beatitude. And this is understanding, since we cannot will what we do not understand. Therefore man's ultimate happiness is essentially to know God by the intellect; it is not an act of the will.

From what has been said we can now solve the arguments that were objected in the contrary sense. For it does not necessarily follow that happiness is essentially the very act of the will, from the fact that it is the object of the will, through being the highest good, as the *first argument* reasoned. On the contrary, the fact that it is the first object of the will shows that it is not an act of the will, as appears from what we have said.

Nor does it follow that whatever perfects a thing in any way whatever must be the end of that thing, as the *second objection* argued. For a thing perfects another in two ways: first, it perfects a thing that has its species; secondly, it perfects a thing that it may have its species. Thus the perfection of a house, considered as already having its species, is that to which the species "house" is directed, namely to be a dwelling; for one would not build a house but for that purpose, and consequently we must include this in the definition of a house, if the definition is to be perfect. On the other hand, the perfection that conduces to the species of a house is both that which is directed to the completion of the species, for instance, its substantial principles; and also that which conduces to the preservation of the species, for instance, the buttresses which are made to support the building; as well as those things which make the house more fit for use, for instance, the beauty of the house. Accordingly, that which is the perfection of a thing, considered as already having its species, is its end; as the end of a house is to be a dwelling. Likewise, the operation proper to a thing, its use, as it were, is its end. On the other hand, whatever perfects a thing by conducing to its species is not the end of that thing; in fact, the thing itself is its end, for matter and form are for the sake of the species. For although the form is the end of generation, it is not the end of the thing already generated and having its species, but is required in order that the species be complete. Again, whatever preserves the thing in its species, such as health and the nutritive power, although it perfects the animal, is not the animal's end, but vice versa. And again, whatever adapts a thing for the perfection of its proper specific operations, and for the easier attainment of its proper end, is not the end of that thing, but vice versa; for instance, a man's comeliness and bodily strength, and the like, of which the Philosopher says that they *conduce to happiness instrumentally*.[22] – Now delight is a perfection of operation, not as though operation were directed thereto in respect of its species, for thus it is directed to other ends (thus, eating, in respect of its species, is directed to the preservation of the individual); but it is like a perfection that is conducive to a thing's species, since for the sake of the delight we perform more attentively and becomingly an operation we delight in. Hence the Philosopher says that *delight perfects operation as beauty perfects youth*,[23] for beauty is for the sake of the one who has youth and not *vice versa*.

Nor is the fact that men seek delight not for the sake of something else but for its own sake a sufficient indication that delight is the last end, as the *third objection* argued. Because delight, though it is not the last end, nevertheless accompanies the last end, since delight arises from the attainment of the end.

Nor do more people seek the pleasure that comes from knowledge than knowledge itself. But more there are who seek sensible delights than intellectual knowledge and the delight consequent thereto; because those things that are outside us are better known to the majority, in that human knowledge takes its beginning from sensible objects.

The suggestion put forward by the *fifth argument*, that the will is a higher power than the intellect, as being the latter's motive power, is clearly untrue. Because the intellect moves the will first and *per se*, for the will, as such, is

---

[22] *Eth.*, I, 8 (1099b 2); 9 (1099b 28).

[23] *Op. cit.*, X, 4 (1174b 31).

moved by its object, which is the apprehended good; whereas the will moves the intellect accidentally as it were, in so far, namely, as the act of understanding is itself apprehended as a good, and on that account is desired by the will, with the result that the intellect understands actually. Even in this, the intellect precedes the will, for the will would never desire understanding, did not the intellect first apprehend its understanding as a good. − And again, the will moves the intellect to actual operation in the same way as an agent is said to move; whereas the intellect moves the will in the same way as the end moves, for the good understood is the end of the will. Now the agent in moving presupposes the end, for the agent does not move except for the sake of the end. It is therefore clear that the intellect is higher than the will absolutely, while the will is higher than the intellect accidentally and in a restricted sense.

Chapter XXVII

That Human Happiness Does Not Consist in Carnal Pleasures

FROM what has been said it is clearly impossible that human happiness consist in pleasures of the body, the chief of which are pleasures of the table and of sex.

It has been shown that according to nature's order pleasure is for the sake of operation, and not conversely.[24] Therefore, if an operation be not the ultimate end, the consequent pleasure can neither be the ultimate end, nor accompany the ultimate end. Now it is manifest that the operations which are followed by the pleasures mentioned above are not the last end; for they are directed to certain manifest ends: eating, for instance, to the preservation of the body, and carnal intercourse to the begetting of children. Therefore the aforesaid pleasures are not the last end, nor do they accompany the last end. Therefore happiness does not consist in them.

Again. The will is higher than the sensitive appetite, for it moves the sensitive appetite, as was stated above.[25] But happiness does not consist in an act of the will, as we have already proved.[26] Much less therefore does it consist in the aforesaid pleasures which are seated in the sensitive appetite.

Moreover. Happiness is a good proper to man, for it is an abuse of terms to speak of brute animals as being happy. Now these pleasures are common to man and brute. Therefore we must not assign happiness to them.

The last end is the most noble of things belonging to a reality, for it has the nature of that which is best. But the aforementioned pleasures do not befit man according to what is most noble in him, namely, the intellect, but according to the sense. Therefore happiness is not to be located in such pleasures.

Besides. The highest perfection of man cannot consist in his being united to things lower than himself, but consists in his being united to something above him; for the end is better than that which tends to the end. Now the above pleasures consist in man's being united through his senses to things beneath him, namely, certain sensible things. Therefore we must not assign happiness to such pleasures.

Further. That which is not good unless it be moderate is not good in itself, but receives its goodness from its moderator. Now the use of the aforesaid pleasures is not good for man unless it be moderate; for otherwise they would frustrate one another. Therefore these pleasures are not in themselves man's good. But the highest good is good of itself, because that which is good of itself is better than what is good through another. Therefore such pleasures are not man's highest good, which is happiness.

Again. In all *per se* predications, if A be predicated of B absolutely, an increase in A will be predicated of an increase in B. Thus if a hot thing heats, a hotter thing heats more, and the hottest thing will heat most. Accordingly, if the pleasures in question were good in themselves, it would follow that to use them very much would be very good. But this is clearly false, because it is considered sinful to use them too much; besides, it is hurtful to the body, and hinders pleasures of the same kind. Therefore they are not *per se* man's good, and human happiness does not consist in them.

Again. Acts of virtue are praiseworthy through being ordered to happiness.[27] If therefore human happiness consisted in the aforesaid pleasures, an act of virtue would be more praiseworthy in acceding to them than in abstaining from them. But this is clearly untrue, for the act of temperance is especially praised in abstinence from pleasures; whence that act takes its name. Therefore man's happiness is not in these pleasures.

---

[24] Ch. 26.
[25] *Ibid.*
[26] *Ibid.*
[27] Cf. Aristotle. *Eth.*, I, 12 (1101b 14).

Furthermore. The last end of everything is God, as was proved above.[28] We must therefore posit as man's last end that by which especially man approaches to God. Now man is hindered by the aforesaid pleasures from his chief approach to God, which is effected by contemplation, to which these same pleasures are a very great hindrance, since more than anything they plunge man into the midst of sensible things, and consequently withdraw him from intelligible things. Therefore human happiness is not to be placed in bodily pleasures.

Hereby is refuted the error of the Epicureans who ascribed man's happiness to pleasures of this kind. In their person Solomon says (*Eccles.* v. 17): *This therefore hath seemed good to me, that a man should eat and drink, and enjoy the fruit, of his labor ... and this is his portion*; and (*Wis.* ii. 9): *Let us everywhere leave tokens of joy, for this is our portion, and this is our lot.*

The error of the Cerinthians is also refuted. For they *pretended that*, in the state of final happiness, *after the resurrection Christ will reign for a thousand years, and men will indulge in the carnal pleasures of the table. Hence they are called 'Chiliastae,'*[29] or believers in the Millennium.

The fables of the Jews and Mohammedans are also refuted, who pretend that the reward of the righteous consists in such pleasures. For happiness is the reward of virtue.

[...]

Chapter XXXII

That Happiness Does Not Consist in Goods of the Body

LIKE arguments avail to prove that man's highest good does not consist in goods of the body, such as health, beauty and strength. For they are common to good and evil, they are unstable, and they are not subject to the will.

Besides. The soul is better than the body, which neither lives nor possesses these goods without the soul. Therefore, the soul's good, such as understanding and the like, is better than the body's good. Therefore the body's good is not man's highest good.

Again. These goods are common to man and other animals, whereas happiness is a good proper to man. Therefore man's happiness does not consist in the things mentioned.

Moreover. Many animals surpass man in goods of the body, for some are fleeter than he, some more sturdy, and so on. Accordingly, if man's highest good consisted in these things, man would not excel all animals; which is clearly untrue. Therefore human happiness does not consist in goods of the body.

Chapter XXXIII

That Human Happiness Is Not Seated in the Senses

BY the same arguments it is evident that neither does man's highest good consist in goods of his sensitive nature. For these goods, again, are common to man and other animals.

Again. Intellect is superior to sense. Therefore the intellect's good is better than that of the sense. Consequently man's supreme good is not seated in the senses.

Besides. The greatest sensual pleasures are those of the table and of sex, wherein the supreme good must needs be, if seated in the senses. But it does not consist in them. Therefore man's highest good is not in the senses.

Moreover. The senses are appreciated for their utility and for knowledge. Now the entire utility of the senses is referred to the goods of the body. Again, sensitive knowledge is ordered to intellectual knowledge, and hence animals devoid of intellect take no pleasure in sensation except in reference to some bodily utility, in so far as by sensitive knowledge they obtain food or sexual intercourse. Therefore, man's highest good which is happiness is not seated in the sensitive part of man.

---

[28] Ch. 17.
[29] St. Augustine, *De Haeres.*, 8 (PL 42, 27).

Chapter XXXIV

That Man's Ultimate Happiness Does Not Consist in Acts of the Moral Virtues

It is clear that man's ultimate happiness does not consist in moral activities.

For human happiness, if ultimate, cannot be directed to a further end. But all moral activities can be directed to something else. This is clear from a consideration of the principal among them. Because deeds of fortitude in time of war are directed to victory and peace; for it were foolish to go to war merely for its own sake.[30] Again, deeds of justice are directed to keeping peace among men, for each man possesses with contentment what is his own. The same applies to all the other virtues. Therefore man's ultimate happiness is not in moral deeds.

Again. The purpose of the moral virtues is that through them we may observe the mean in the passions within us, and in things outside us. Now it is impossible that the moderation of passions or of external things be the ultimate end of man's life, since both passions and external things can be directed to something less. Therefore it is not possible that the practice of moral virtue be man's final happiness.

Further. Since man is man through the possession of reason, his proper good, which is happiness, must needs be in accordance with that which is proper to reason. Now that which reason has in itself is more proper to reason than what it effects in something else. Seeing, then, that the good of moral virtue is a good established by reason in something other than itself, it cannot be the greatest good of man which happiness is; rather this good must be a good that is in reason itself.

Moreover. We have already proved that the last end of all things is to become like God.[31] Therefore that in which man chiefly becomes like God will be his happiness. Now this is not in terms of moral actions, since such actions cannot be ascribed to God, except metaphorically; for it is not befitting to God to have passions, or the like, with which moral virtue is concerned. Therefore man's ultimate happiness, which is his last end, does not consist in moral actions.

Furthermore. Happiness is man's proper good. Therefore that good, which of all goods is most proper to man in comparison with other animals, is the one in which we must seek his ultimate happiness. Now this is not the practice of moral virtue, for animals share somewhat either in liberality or in fortitude, whereas no animal has a share in intellectual activity. Therefore man's ultimate happiness does not consist in moral acts.

Chapter XXXV

That Ultimate Happiness Does Not Consist in the Act of Prudence

It is also evident from the foregoing that neither does man's happiness consist in the act of prudence.

For acts of prudence are solely about matters of moral virtue. But human happiness does not consist in the practice of moral virtue.[32] Neither therefore does it consist in the practice of prudence.

Again. Man's ultimate happiness consists in man's most excellent operation. Now man's most excellent operation, in terms of what is proper to man, is in relation to most perfect objects. But the act of prudence is not concerned with the most perfect objects of intellect or reason; for it is not about necessary things, but about contingent practical matters.[33] Therefore its act is not man's ultimate happiness.

Besides. That which is ordered to another as to its end is not man's ultimate happiness. Now the act of prudence is ordered to another as to its end, both because all practical knowledge, under which prudence is comprised, is ordered to operation, and because prudence disposes a man well in choosing means to an end, as may be gathered from Aristotle.[34] Therefore man's ultimate happiness is not in the practice of prudence.

Furthermore. Irrational animals have no share of happiness, as Aristotle proves.[35] Yet some of them have a certain share of prudence, as may be gathered from the same author.[36] Therefore happiness does not consist in an act of prudence.

[…]

---

[30] Cf. Aristotle, *Eth.*, X, 7 (1177b 9).

[31] Ch. 19.

[32] Ch. 34.

[33] Cf. Aristotle, *Eth.*, VI, 5 (1104a 35).

[34] *Op. cit.*, VI, 13 (1145a 6).

[35] *Op cit.*, I, 9 (1099b 33).

[36] Aristotle, *Metaph.*, I, 1 (980a 30).

Chapter XXXVII

That Man's Ultimate Happiness Consists in Contemplating God

ACCORDINGLY, if man's ultimate happiness does not consist in external things, which are called goods of fortune; nor in goods of the body; nor in goods of the soul, as regards the sensitive part; nor as regards the intellectual part, in terms of the life of moral virtue; nor in terms of the intellectual virtues which are concerned with action, namely, art and prudence: – it remains for us to conclude that man's ultimate happiness consists in the contemplation of truth.

For this operation alone is proper to man, and it is in it that none of the other animals communicates.

Again. This is not directed to anything further as to its end, since the contemplation of the truth is sought for its own sake.

Again. By this operation man is united to beings above him, by becoming like them; because of all human actions this alone is both in God and in the separate substances. Also, by this operation man comes into contact with those higher beings, through knowing them in any way whatever.

Besides, man is more self-sufficing for this operation, seeing that he stands in little need of the help of external things in order to perform it.

Further. All other human operations seem to be ordered to this as to their end. For perfect contemplation requires that the body should be disencumbered, and to this effect are directed all the products of art that are necessary for life. Moreover, it requires freedom from the disturbance caused by the passions, which is achieved by means of the moral virtues and of prudence; and freedom from external disturbance, to which the whole governance of the civil life is directed. So that, if we consider the matter rightly, we shall see that all human occupations appear to serve those who contemplate the truth.

Now, it is not possible that man's ultimate happiness consist in contemplation based on the understanding of first principles; for this is most imperfect, as being most universal, containing potentially the knowledge of things. Moreover, it is the beginning and not the end of human inquiry, and comes to us from nature, and not through the pursuit of the truth. Nor does it consist in contemplation based on the sciences that have the lowest things for their object, since happiness must consist in an operation of the intellect in relation to the most noble intelligible objects. It follows then that man's ultimate happiness consists in wisdom, based on the consideration of divine things.

It is therefore evident also by way of induction that man's ultimate happiness consists solely in the contemplation of God, which conclusion was proved above by arguments.[37]

---

[37] Ch. 25.

Summa Theologica, First Part of the First Part

Question XCI

On the Various Kinds of Law

[…]

Second Article

Whether There Is in Us a Natural Law?

[…]

As we have stated above, law, being a rule and measure, can be in a person in two ways: in one way, as in him that rules and measures; in another way, as in that which is ruled and measured, since a thing is ruled and measured in so far as it partakes of the rule or measure. Therefore, since all things subject to divine providence are ruled and measured by the eternal law, as was stated above, it is evident that all things partake in some way in the eternal law, in so far as, namely, from its being imprinted on them, they derive their respective inclinations to their proper acts and ends. Now among all others, the rational creature is subject to divine providence in a more excellent way, in so far as it itself partakes of a share of providence, by being provident both for itself and for others. Therefore it has a share of the eternal reason, whereby it has a natural inclination to its proper act and end; and this participation of the eternal law in the rational creature is called the natural law. Hence the Psalmist, after saying (*Ps. iv. 6*): *Offer up the sacrifice of justice*, as though someone asked what the works of justice are, adds: *Many say, Who showeth us good things?* in answer to which question he says: *The light of Thy countenance, O Lord, is signed upon us.* He thus implies that the light of natural reason, whereby we discern what is good and what is evil, which is the function of the natural law, is nothing else than an imprint on us of the divine light. It is therefore evident that the natural law is nothing else than the rational creature's participation of the eternal law.

[…]

Question LXI

The Cardinal Virtues (in Five Articles)

[…]

Second Article

Whether There Are Four Cardinal Virtues?

[…]

Things may be numbered either in respect of their formal principles, or according to the subjects in which they are; and in either way we find that there are four cardinal virtues.

For the formal principle of the virtue of which we speak now is the good as defined by reason. This good can be considered in two ways. First, as existing in the consideration itself of reason, and thus we have one principal virtue called *prudence*. – Secondly, according as the reason puts its order into something else, and this either into operations, and then we have *justice*, or into passions, and then we need two virtues. For the need of putting the order of reason into the passions is due to their thwarting reason; and this occurs in two ways. First, when the passions incite to something against reason, and then they need a curb, which we thus call *temperance*; secondly, when the passions withdraw us from following the dictate of reason, *e.g.*, through fear of danger or toil, and then man needs to be strengthened for that which reason dictates, lest he turn back, and to this end there is *fortitude*.

In like manner, we find the same number if we consider the subjects of virtue. For there are four subjects of the virtue of which we now speak, viz., the power which is rational in its essence, and this is perfected by *prudence; and* that which is rational by participation, and is threefold, the will, subject of *justice*, the concupiscible power, subject of *temperance*, and the irascible power, subject of *fortitude*.

[…]

Third Article

Whether Any Other Virtues Should Be Called Principal Rather Than These?

[…]

As was stated above, these four are reckoned as cardinal virtues according to the four formal principles of virtue as we understand it here. These principles are found chiefly in certain acts and passions. Thus the good which exists in the act of reason is found chiefly in reason's command, but not in its counsel or its judgment, as was stated above. Again, good as defined by reason, and put into our operations as something right and due, is found chiefly in commutations and distributions in relation to another person, and on a basis of equality. The good of curbing the passions is found chiefly in those passions which are most difficult to curb, viz., in the pleasures of touch. The good of being firm in holding to the good defined by reason, against the impulse of passion, is found chiefly in perils exposing us to death, which are most difficult to withstand.

Accordingly, the above four virtues may be considered in two ways. First, according to their common formal principles. In this way, they are called principal, being general, as it were, in comparison with all the virtues; so that, for instance, any virtue that causes good in reason's act of consideration may be called prudence; every virtue that causes the good of rectitude and the due in operations, be called justice; every virtue that curbs and represses the passions, be called temperance; and every virtue that strengthens the soul against any passions whatever, be called fortitude. Many, both holy doctors, as also philosophers, speak about these virtues in this sense. It is in this way that the other virtues are contained under them. – Therefore all the objections fail.

Secondly, they may be considered according as each one of them is named from that which is foremost in its respective matter, and thus they are specific virtues, co-divided with the others. Yet they are called principal in comparison with the other virtues because of the importance of their matter. Thus, prudence is the virtue which commands; justice, the virtue which is about due actions between equals; temperance, the virtue which suppresses desires for the pleasures of touch; and fortitude, the virtue which strengthens against dangers of death. – Thus again do the objections fail; because the other virtues may be principal in some other way, but these are called principal by reason of their matter, as was stated above.

Summa Theologica, Second Part of the Second Part

Question 64

Homicide

[…]

Article 7

Is It Legitimate for a Man to Kill Another in Self-Defence?

[…]

A single act may have two effects, of which one alone is intended, whilst the other is incidental to that intention. But the way a moral act is to be classified depends on what is intended, not on what goes beyond such an intention, since this is merely incidental thereto, as we have seen already. In the light of this distinction we can see that an act of self-defence may have two effects: the saving of one's own life, and the killing of the attacker. Now such an act of self-defence is not illegitimate just because the agent intends to save his own life, because it is natural for anything to want to preserve itself in being as far as it can. An act that is properly motivated may, nevertheless, become vitiated if it is not proportionate to the end intended. And this is why somebody who uses more violence than is necessary to defend himself will be doing something wrong. On the other hand, the controlled use of counter-violence constitutes legitimate self-defence, for according to the law *it is legitimate to answer force with force provided it goes no further than due defence requires*. Moreover a person is not obliged under pain of loss of eternal life to renounce the use of proportionate counter-force in order to avoid killing another, for a man is under a greater obligation to care for his own life than for another's.

It remains nevertheless that it is not legitimate for a man actually to intend to kill another in self-defence, since the taking of life is reserved to the public authorities acting for the common good, as we have seen. Killing in self-defence in this sort of way is restricted to somebody who has the public authority to do so; such a man may indeed intend to kill a man in self-defence but he does so for the general good. This is exemplified by the soldier who fights against the enemy, and the official of the court who fights against robbers. And even such men sin if and to the extent that they are moved by some private passion.

Part II

Modern Ethics

1

Leviathan 利維坦

Thomas Hobbes

Thomas Hobbes's *Leviathan* marks a turning point in the history of ethics. When reading the account of the foundations of ethics provided in the following excerpt, the contemporary reader is likely to be struck by how modern, naturalistic, and secular it is. Rather than have us use reason to discover natural laws that reflect divine laws and that wear their substantive moral content on their face, as Aquinas would have us do, Hobbes asks us to use reason to ascertain that there are less substantive, pre-moral laws of nature that would have us each protect and preserve our own wellbeing. Hobbes is not proposing that we live without morality, but rather that we come to see that it is rational for each of us, from the point of view of self-interest, to bind ourselves to a social contract that directs us all to follow moral rules. Indeed, Hobbes contends that it follows from the pre-moral laws of nature, in combination with certain facts about the world outside of us, that the institution of morality must be adhered to.

The institution of morality can come into existence only when we are in a position to be ruled by a strong Sovereign, for it will be rational for each of us properly to commit ourselves to the social contract only if we can be sure that everyone else is also properly committing themselves to it, and the only way that we can count on *this* is if there is a 'common power to keep them [us] all in awe'. This is a power that is able to enforce the social contract and prevent or minimize the breaking of moral rules, through threatening punishment.

In order to convince us that this is the right way of understanding the ground of our moral obligations, Hobbes makes use of the device of the state of nature. Just as it is unnecessary for there to be a piece of paper that we sign for it to be rational for us to commit ourselves to the social contract (for signs of contracts can be 'by inference'), so it is unnecessary to think of the state of nature as a real state our distant ancestors found themselves living in. This is not to deny that Hobbes asserts here that some 'savage people in many places of America' live in the state of nature, but to point out that this claim is not essential to his argument (he also points to the existence of civil wars for examples of what life is like when social institutions break down, and we might look to more recent history to provide other examples of this kind). It is consistent with his main argument to view all stable societies, modern or otherwise, as possessing complex social institutions that prevent people from living in the terrible state of war that Hobbes very plausibly contends all rational people have self-interested reasons to wish to avoid.

Crucially, life in the state of nature is a life of constant competition for resources and of constant anxiety when it comes to protecting one's own life (what Hobbes calls 'diffidence'). It is also a life without the products of culture that we treasure, nor any reliable way of receiving recognition from others for one's accomplishments. The grimness of the picture of the state of nature that Hobbes paints, equating it, as he does, with a state of war, is essential for demonstrating that it is rational, purely in terms of each individual's self-interest, for us all to be willing to give up a great deal of liberty – understood as freedom from external impediments – in order to secure the goods that can come only from living in a society with others.

History of Ethics – Essential Readings with Commentary, First Edition. Edited by Daniel Star and Roger Crisp.
© 2020 John Wiley & Sons Ltd. Published 2020 by John Wiley & Sons Ltd.

An important objection to Hobbes's account of our moral obligations is one addressed here by Hobbes himself, when he considers the 'fool', who lives in society, rather than the state of nature, but who has it that there is no such thing as justice and is happy to break his covenants (that is, depart from the social contract) when it appears to be in his self-interest to do so. If we take it that our entering into the social contract, and the moral reasons that apply to us once we do so, are ultimately grounded in self-interest, it is natural to wonder why we are not rationally permitted (or perhaps even rationally required) to break moral rules when doing so can rationally be expected to benefit, rather than harm us. There is much disagreement amongst commentators when it comes to interpreting Hobbes's response to the fool, but it is worth emphasizing two things here: first, Hobbes's third law of nature has it that, once covenants are made, we *must* follow them (the question of whether it is in one's self-interest to agree to a covenant is crucial when one is first considering it as an option, but it is in the nature of covenants that one cannot be released from them when it is later not in one's self-interest to keep to them); second, Hobbes contends that it cannot, *in the long term*, really be in one's self-interest to turn one's back on the social contract, because anyone who does so will be effectively 'cast out of society' (or will remain in society only because of other people's errors, which cannot be counted on).

One of the biggest practical challenges facing us in the world today illustrates both the continuing relevance of Hobbes's reflections on morality and the limitations of his contractarian theory when it comes to providing us with a full account of morality. The challenge of responding to the crisis of global climate change constitutes a key collective action problem: from the point of view of self-interest, it may well be irrational for individual agents (people, corporations, or national governments) to make economic sacrifices now when other agents are not making the same sacrifices, even though it would clearly be rational to make economic sacrifices if everyone else also committed to making such sacrifices and punishing those who did not. Without the imposition of international laws, and the prospect of significant sanctions for breaking them, it would seem impossible to solve this collective-action problem. At the same time, it also seems to many of us that we have strong reasons to care about climate change that do not depend on the self-interest of presently living adults. When we ask why we should care about either the potential suffering and shorter lives of other animals (whether presently existing or not) or the potential suffering and shorter lives of *future* human beings (people who do not yet exist), social contract theory appears to lack the resources to justify caring about the welfare of such animals and people for *their* sake, for they cannot enter into any kind of social contract with us.

Chapter XIII

Of the Natural Condition of Mankind As Concerning Their Felicity, and Misery

NATURE hath made men so equal, in the faculties of the body, and mind; as that though there be found one man sometimes manifestly stronger in body, or of quicker mind than another; yet when all is reckoned together, the difference between man, and man, is not so considerable, as that one man can thereupon claim to himself any benefit, to which another may not pretend, as well as he. For as to the strength of body, the weakest has strength enough to kill the strongest, either by secret machination, or by confederacy with others, that are in the same danger with himself.

And as to the faculties of the mind, setting aside the arts grounded upon words, and especially that skill of proceeding upon general, and infallible rules, called science; which very few have, and but in few things; as being not a native faculty, born with us; nor attained, as prudence, while we look after somewhat else, I find yet a greater equality amongst men, than that of strength. For prudence, is but experience; which equal time, equally bestows on all men, in those things they equally apply themselves unto. That which may perhaps make such equality incredible, is but a vain conceit of one's own wisdom, which almost all men think they have in a greater degree, than the vulgar; that is, than all men but themselves, and a few others, whom by fame, or for concurring with themselves, they approve. For such is the nature of men, that howsoever they may acknowledge many others to be more witty, or more eloquent, or more learned; yet they will hardly believe there be many so wise as themselves; for they see their own wit at hand, and other men's at a distance. But this proveth rather that men are in that point equal, than unequal. For there is not ordinarily a greater sign of the equal distribution of any thing, than that every man is contented with his share.

From this equality of ability, ariseth equality of hope in the attaining of our ends. And therefore if any two men desire the same thing, which nevertheless they cannot both enjoy, they become enemies; and in the way to their end, which is principally their own conservation, and sometimes their delectation only, endeavour to destroy, or subdue one another. And from hence it comes to pass, that where an invader hath no more to fear, than another man's single power; if one plant, sow, build, or possess a convenient seat, others may probably be expected to come prepared with forces united, to dispossess, and deprive him, not only of the fruit of his labour, but also of his life, or liberty. And the invader again is in the like danger of another.

And from this diffidence of one another, there is no way for any man to secure himself, so reasonable, as anticipation; that is, by force, or wiles, to master the persons of all men he can, so long, till he see no other power great enough to endanger him: and this is no more than his own conservation requireth, and is generally allowed. Also because there be some, that taking pleasure in contemplating their own power in the acts of conquest, which they pursue farther than their security requires; if others, that otherwise would be glad to be at ease within modest bounds, should not by invasion increase their power, they would not be able, long time, by standing only on their defence, to subsist. And by consequence, such augmentation of dominion over men being necessary to a man's conservation, it ought to be allowed him.

Again, men have no pleasure, but on the contrary a great deal of grief, in keeping company, where there is no power able to over-awe them all. For every man looketh that his companion should value him, at the same rate he sets upon himself: and upon all signs of contempt, or undervaluing, naturally endeavours, as far as he dares, (which amongst them that have no common power to keep them in quiet, is far enough to make them destroy each other), to extort a greater value from his contemners, by damage; and from others, by the example.

So that in the nature of man, we find three principal causes of quarrel. First, competition; secondly, diffidence; thirdly, glory.

The first, maketh men invade for gain; the second, for safety; and the third, for reputation. The first use violence, to make themselves masters of other men's persons, wives, children, and cattle; the second, to defend them; the third, for trifles, as a word, a smile, a different opinion, and any other sign of undervalue, either direct in their persons, or by reflection in their kindred, their friends, their nation, their profession, or their name.

Hereby it is manifest, that during the time men live without a common power to keep them all in awe, they are in that condition which is called war; and such a war, as is of every man, against every man. For WAR, consisteth not in battle only, or the act of fighting; but in a tract of time, wherein the will to contend by battle is sufficiently known: and therefore the notion of *time*, is to be considered in the nature of war; as it is in the nature of weather. For as the nature of foul weather, lieth not in a shower or two of rain; but in an inclination thereto of many days together: so the nature of war, consisteth not in actual fighting; but in the known disposition thereto, during all the time there is no assurance to the contrary. All other time is PEACE.

Whatsoever therefore is consequent to a time of war, where every man is enemy to every man; the same is consequent to the time, wherein men live without other security, than what their own strength, and their own invention shall furnish them withal. In such condition, there is no place for industry; because the fruit thereof is uncertain: and consequently no culture of the earth; no navigation, nor use of the commodities that may be imported by sea; no commodious building; no instruments of moving, and removing, such things as require much force; no knowledge of the face of the earth; no account of time; no arts; no letters; no society; and which is worst of all, continual fear, and danger of violent death; and the life of man, solitary, poor, nasty, brutish, and short.

It may seem strange to some man, that has not well weighed these things; that nature should thus dissociate, and render men apt to invade, and destroy one another: and he may therefore, not trusting to this inference, made from the passions, desire perhaps to have the same confirmed by experience. Let him therefore consider with himself, when taking a journey, he arms himself, and seeks to go well accompanied; when going to sleep, he locks his doors; when even in his house he locks his chests; and this when he knows there be laws, and public officers, armed, to revenge all injuries shall be done him; what opinion he has of his fellow-subjects, when he rides armed; of his fellow citizens, when he locks his doors; and of his children, and servants, when he locks his chests. Does he not there as much accuse mankind by his actions, as I do by my words? But neither of us accuse man's nature in it. The desires, and other passions of man, are in themselves no sin. No more are the actions, that proceed from those passions, till they know a law that forbids them: which till laws be made they cannot know: nor can any law be made, till they have agreed upon the person that shall make it.

It may peradventure be thought, there was never such a time, nor condition of war as this; and I believe it was never generally so, over all the world: but there are many places, where they live so now. For the savage people in many places of America, except the government of small families, the concord whereof dependeth on natural lust, have no government at all; and live at this day in that brutish manner, as I said before. Howsoever, it may be perceived what manner of life there would be, where there were no common power to fear, by the manner of life, which men that have formerly lived under a peaceful government, use to degenerate into, in a civil war.

But though there had never been any time, wherein particular men were in a condition of war one against another; yet in all times, kings, and persons of sovereign authority, because of their independency, are in continual jealousies, and in the state and posture of gladiators; having their weapons pointing, and their eyes fixed on one another; that is, their forts, garrisons, and guns upon the frontiers of their kingdoms; and continual spies upon their neighbours; which is a posture of war. But because they uphold thereby, the industry of their subjects; there does not follow from it, that misery, which accompanies the liberty of particular men.

To this war of every man, against every man, this also is consequent; that nothing can be unjust. The notions of right and wrong, justice and injustice have there no place. Where there is no common power, there is no law: where no law, no injustice. Force, and fraud, are in war the two cardinal virtues. Justice, and injustice are none of the faculties neither of the body, nor mind. If they were, they might be in a man that were alone in the world, as well as his senses, and passions. They are qualities, that relate to men in society, not in solitude. It is consequent also to the same condition, that there be no propriety, no dominion, no *mine* and *thine* distinct; but only that to be every man's, that he can get; and for so long, as he can keep it. And thus much for the ill condition, which man by mere nature is actually placed in; though with a possibility to come out of it, consisting partly in the passions, partly in his reason.

The passions that incline men to peace, are fear of death; desire of such things as are necessary to commodious living; and a hope by their industry to obtain them. And reason suggesteth convenient articles of peace, upon which men may be drawn to agreement. These articles, are they, which otherwise are called the Laws of Nature: whereof I shall speak more particularly, in the two following chapters.

Chapter XIV

Of the First and Second Natural Laws, and of Contracts

THE RIGHT OF NATURE, which writers commonly call *jus naturale*, is the liberty each man hath, to use his own power, as he will himself, for the preservation of his own nature; that is to say, of his own life; and consequently, of doing any thing, which in his own judgment, and reason, he shall conceive to be the aptest means thereunto.

By LIBERTY, is understood, according to the proper signification of the word, the absence of external impediments: which impediments, may oft take away part of a man's power to do what he would; but cannot hinder him from using the power left him, according as his judgment, and reason shall dictate to him.

A LAW OF NATURE, *lex naturalis*, is a precept or general rule, found out by reason, by which a man is forbidden to do that, which is destructive of his life, or taketh away the means of preserving the same; and to omit that, by which he thinketh it may be best preserved. For though they that speak of this subject, use to confound *jus*, and *lex*, *right* and *law*: yet they ought to be distinguished; because RIGHT, consisteth in liberty to do, or to forbear; whereas LAW, determineth, and bindeth to one of them: so that law, and right, differ as much, as obligation, and liberty; which in one and the same matter are inconsistent.

And because the condition of man, as hath been declared in the precedent chapter, is a condition of war of every one against every one; in which case every one is governed by his own reason; and there is nothing he can make use of, that may not be a help unto him, in preserving his life against his enemies; it followeth, that in such a condition, every man has a right to every thing; even to one another's body. And therefore, as long as this natural right of every man to every thing endureth, there can be no security to any man, how strong or wise soever he be, of living out the time, which nature ordinarily alloweth men to live. And consequently it is a precept, or general rule of reason, *that every man, ought to endeavour peace, as far as he has hope of obtaining it; and when he cannot obtain it, that he may seek, and use, all helps, and advantages of war.* The first branch of which rule, containeth the first, and fundamental law of nature; which is, *to seek peace, and follow it.* The second, the sum of the right of nature; which is, *by all means we can, to defend ourselves.*

From this fundamental law of nature, by which men are commanded to endeavour peace, is derived this second law; *that a man be willing, when others are so too, as far-forth, as for peace, and defence of himself he shall think it necessary, to lay down this right to all things; and be contented with so much liberty against other men, as he would allow other men against himself.* For as long as every man holdeth this right, of doing any thing he liketh; so long are all men in the condition of war. But if other men will not lay down their right, as well as he; then there is no reason for any one, to divest himself of his: for that were to expose himself to prey, which no man is bound to, rather than to dispose himself to peace. This is that law of the Gospel; *whatsoever you require that others should do to you, that do ye to them.* And that law of all men, *quod tibi fieri non vis, alteri ne feceris.*

To *lay down* a man's *right* to any thing, is to *divest* himself of the *liberty*, of hindering another of the benefit of his own right to the same. For he that renounceth, or passeth away his right, giveth not to any other man a right which he had not before; because there is nothing to which every man had not right by nature: but only standeth out of his way, that he may enjoy his own original right, without hindrance from him; not without hindrance from another. So that the effect which redoundeth to one man, by another man's defect of right, is but so much diminution of impediments to the use of his own right original.

Right is laid aside, either by simply renouncing it; or by transferring it to another. By *simply* RENOUNCING; when he cares not to whom the benefit thereof redoundeth. By TRANSFERRING; when he intendeth the benefit thereof to some certain person, or persons. And when a man hath in either manner abandoned, or granted away his right; then is he said to be OBLIGED, or BOUND, not to hinder those, to whom such right is granted, or abandoned, from the benefit of it: and that he *ought*, and it is his DUTY, not to make void that voluntary act of his own: and that such hindrance is INJUSTICE, and INJURY, as being *sine jure;* the right being before renounced, or transferred. So that *injury*, or *injustice*, in the controversies of the world, is somewhat like to that, which in the disputations of scholars is called *absurdity*. For as it is there called an absurdity, to contradict what one maintained in the beginning: so in the world, it is called injustice, and injury, voluntarily to undo that, which from the beginning he had voluntarily done. The way by which a man either simply renounceth, or transferreth his right, is a declaration, or signification, by some voluntary and sufficient sign, or signs, that he doth so renounce, or transfer; or hath so renounced, or transferred the same, to him that accepteth it. And these signs are either words only, or actions only; or, as it happeneth most often, both words, and actions. And the same are the BONDS, by which men are bound, and obliged: bonds, that have their strength, not from their own nature, for nothing is more easily broken than a man's word, but from fear of some evil consequence upon the rupture.

Whensoever a man transferreth his right, or renounceth it; it is either in consideration of some right reciprocally transferred to himself; or for some other good he hopeth for thereby. For it is a voluntary act: and of the voluntary acts of every man, the object is some *good to himself*. And therefore there be some rights, which no man can be understood by any words, or other signs, to have abandoned, or transferred. As first a man cannot lay down the right of resisting them, that assault him by force, to take away his life; because he cannot be understood to aim thereby, at any good to himself. The same may he said of wounds, and chains, and imprisonment; both because there is no benefit consequent to such patience; as there is to the patience of suffering another to be wounded, or imprisoned: as also because a man cannot tell, when he seeth men proceed against him by violence, whether they intend his death or not. And lastly the motive, and end for which this renouncing, and transferring of right is introduced, is nothing else but the security of a man's person, in his life, and in the means of so preserving life, as not to be weary of it. And therefore if a man by words, or other signs, seem to despoil himself of the end, for which those signs were intended; he is not to be understood as if he meant it, or that it was his will; but that he was ignorant of how such words and actions were to be interpreted.

There is difference between transferring of right to the thing; and transferring, or tradition, that is delivery of the thing itself. For the thing may be delivered together with the translation of the right; as in buying and selling with ready-money; or exchange of goods, or lands: and it may be delivered some time after.

Again, one of the contractors, may deliver the thing contracted for on his part, and leave the other to perform his part at some determinate time after, and in the mean time be trusted; and then the contract on his part, is called PACT, or COVENANT: or both parts may contract now, to perform hereafter: in which cases, he that is to perform in time to come, being trusted, his performance is called *keeping of promise*, or faith; and the failing of performance, if it be voluntary, *violation of faith*.

When the transferring of right, is not mutual: but one of the parties transferreth, in hope to gain thereby friend-ship, or service from another, or from his friends; or in hope to gain the reputation of charity, or magnanimity; or to deliver his mind from the pain of compassion; or in hope of reward in heaven; this is not contract, but GIFT, FREE-GIFT, GRACE: which words signify one and the same thing.

Signs of contract, are either *express*, or *by inference*. Express, are words spoken with understanding of what they signify: and such words are either of the time *present*, or *past*; as, *I give, I grant, I have given, I have granted, I will that this be yours:* or of the future; as, *I will give, I will grant:* which words of the future are called PROMISE.

Signs by inference, are sometimes the consequence of words; sometimes the consequence of silence; sometimes the consequence of actions; sometimes the consequence of forbearing an action: and generally a sign by inference, of any contract, is whatsoever sufficiently argues the will of the contractor.

[…]

If a covenant be made, wherein neither of the parties perform presently, but trust one another; in the condition of mere nature, which is a condition of war of every man against every man, upon any reasonable suspicion, it is void: but if there be a common power set over them both, with right and force sufficient to compel performance, it is not void. For he that performeth first, has no assurance the other will perform after; because the bonds of words are too weak to bridle men's ambition, avarice, anger, and other passions, without the fear of some coercive power; which in the condition of mere nature, where all men are equal, and judges of the justness of their own fears, cannot possibly be supposed. And therefore he which performeth first, does but betray himself to his enemy; contrary to the right, he can never abandon, of defending his life, and means of living.

But in a civil estate, where there is a power set up to constrain those that would otherwise violate their faith, that fear is no more reasonable; and for that cause, he which by the covenant is to perform first, is obliged so to do.

The cause of fear, which maketh such a covenant invalid, must be always something arising after the covenant made; as some new fact, or other sign of the will not to perform: else it cannot make the covenant void. For that which could not hinder a man from promising, ought not to be admitted as a hindrance of performing.

He that transferreth any right, transferreth the means of enjoying it, as far as lieth in his power. As he that selleth land, is understood to transfer the herbage, and whatsoever grows upon it: nor can he that sells a mill turn away the stream that drives it. And they that give to a man the right of government in sovereignty, are understood to give him the right of levying money to maintain soldiers; and of appointing magistrates for the administration of justice.

To make covenants with brute beasts, is impossible; because not understanding our speech, they understand not, nor accept of any translation of right; nor can translate any right to another: and without mutual acceptation, there is no covenant.

[…]

Men are freed of their covenants two ways; by performing; or by being forgiven. For performance, is the natural end of obligation; and forgiveness, the restitution of liberty; as being a retransferring of that right, in which the obligation consisted.

Covenants entered into by fear, in the condition of mere nature, are obligatory. For example, if I covenant to pay a ransom, or service for my life, to an enemy; I am bound by it: for it is a contract, wherein one receiveth the benefit of life; the other is to receive money, or service for it; and consequently, where no other law, as in the condition of mere nature, forbiddeth the performance, the covenant is valid. Therefore prisoners of war, if trusted with the payment of their ransom, are obliged to pay it: and if a weaker prince, make a disadvantageous peace with a stronger, for fear; he is bound to keep it; unless, as hath been said before, there ariseth some new, and just cause of fear, to renew the war. And even in commonwealths, if I be forced to redeem myself from a thief by promising him money, I am bound to pay it, till the civil law discharge me. For whatsoever I may lawfully do without obligation, the same I may lawfully covenant to do through fear: and what I lawfully covenant, I cannot lawfully break.

A former covenant, makes void a later. For a man that hath passed away his right to one man to-day, hath it not to pass to-morrow to another: and therefore the later promise passeth no right, but is null.

[...]

Chapter XV

Of Other Laws of Nature

FROM that law of nature, by which we are obliged to transfer to another, such rights, as being retained, hinder the peace of mankind, there followeth a third; which is this, *that men perform their covenants made:* without which, covenants are in vain, and but empty words; and the right of all men to all things remaining, we are still in the condition of war.

And in this law of nature, consisteth the fountain and original of JUSTICE. For where no covenant hath preceded, there hath no right been transferred, and every man has right to every thing; and consequently, no action can be unjust. But when a covenant is made, then to break it is *unjust:* and the definition of INJUSTICE, is no other than *the not performance of covenant.* And whatsoever is not unjust, is *just*.

But because covenants of mutual trust, where there is a fear of not performance on either part, as hath been said in the former chapter, are invalid; though the original of justice be the making of covenants; yet injustice actually there can be none, till the cause of such fear be taken away; which while men are in the natural condition of war, cannot be done. Therefore before the names of just, and unjust can have place, there must be some coercive power, to compel men equally to the performance of their covenants, by the terror of some punishment, greater than the benefit they expect by the breach of their covenant; and to make good that propriety, which by mutual contract men acquire, in recompense of the universal right they abandon: and such power there is none before the erection of a commonwealth. And this is also to be gathered out of the ordinary definition of justice in the Schools: for they say, that *justice is the constant will of giving to every man his own.* And therefore where there is no *own*, that is no propriety, there is no injustice; and where there is no coercive power erected, that is, where there is no commonwealth, there is no propriety; all men having right to all things: therefore where there is no commonwealth, there nothing is unjust. So that the nature of justice, consisteth in keeping of valid covenants: but the validity of covenants begins not but with the constitution of a civil power, sufficient to compel men to keep them: and then it is also that propriety begins.

The fool hath said in his heart, there is no such thing as justice; and sometimes also with his tongue; seriously alleging, that every man's conservation, and contentment, being committed to his own care, there could be no reason, why every man might not do what he thought conduced thereunto: and therefore also to make, or not make; keep, or not keep covenants, was not against reason, when it conduced to one's benefit. He does not therein deny, that there be covenants; and that they are sometimes broken, sometimes kept; and that such breach of them may be called injustice, and the observance of them justice: but he questioneth, whether injustice, taking away the fear of God, for the same fool hath said in his heart there is no God, may not sometimes stand with that reason, which dictateth to every man his own good; and particularly then, when it conduceth to such a benefit, as shall put a man in a condition, to neglect not only the dispraise, and revilings, but also the power of other men. The kingdom of God is gotten by violence: but what if it could be gotten by unjust violence? were it against reason so to get it, when it is impossible to receive hurt by it? and if it be not against reason, it is not against justice; or else justice is not to be approved for good. From such reasoning as this, successful wickedness hath obtained the name of virtue: and some that in all other things have disallowed the violation of faith; yet have allowed it, when it is for the getting of a kingdom. And the heathen that believed, that Saturn was deposed by his son Jupiter, believed neverthe-less the same Jupiter to be the avenger of injustice: somewhat like to a piece of law in Coke's *Commentaries on Littleton;* where he says, if the right heir of the crown be attainted of treason; yet the crown shall descend to him, and *eo instante* the attainder be void: from which instances a man will be very prone to infer; that when the heir apparent of a kingdom, shall kill him that is in possession, though his father; you may call it injustice, or by what other name you will; yet it can never be against reason, seeing all the voluntary actions of men tend to the benefit of themselves; and those actions are most reasonable, that conduce most to their ends. This specious reasoning is nevertheless false.

For the question is not of promises mutual, where there is no security of performance on either side; as when there is no civil power erected over the parties promising; for such promises are no covenants: but either where one of the parties has performed already; or where there is a power to make him perform; there is the question whether it be against reason, that is, against the benefit of the other to perform, or not. And I say it is not against reason. For the manifestation whereof, we are to consider; first, that when a man doth a thing, which notwithstanding any thing can be foreseen, and reckoned on, tendeth to his own destruction, howsoever some accident which he could not expect, arriving may turn it to his benefit; yet such events do not make it reasonably or wisely done. Secondly, that in a condition of war, wherein every man to every man, for want of a common power to keep them all in awe, is an enemy, there is no man who can hope by his own strength, or wit, to defend himself from destruction, without the help of confederates; where every one expects the same defence by the confederation, that any one else does: and therefore he which declares he thinks it reason to deceive those that help him, can in reason expect no other means of safety, than what can be had from his own single power. He therefore that breaketh his covenant, and consequently declareth that he thinks he may with reason do so, cannot be received into any society, that unite themselves for peace and defence, but by the error of them that receive him; nor when he is received, be retained in it, without seeing the danger of their error; which errors a man cannot reasonably reckon upon as the means of his security: and therefore if he be left, or cast out of society, he perisheth; and if he live in society, it is by the errors of other men, which he could not foresee, nor reckon upon; and consequently against the reason of his preservation; and so, as all men that contribute not to his destruction, forbear him only out of ignorance of what is good for themselves.

As for the instance of gaining the secure and perpetual felicity of heaven, by any way; it is frivolous: there being but one way imaginable; and that is not breaking, but keeping of covenant.

And for the other instance of attaining sovereignty by rebellion; it is manifest, that though the event follow, yet because it cannot reasonably be expected, but rather the contrary; and because by gaining it so, others are taught to gain the same in like manner, the attempt thereof is against reason. Justice therefore, that is to say, keeping of cov-enant, is a rule of reason, by which we are forbidden to do any thing destructive to our life; and consequently a law of nature.

There be some that proceed further; and will not have the law of nature, to be those rules which conduce to the preservation of man's life on earth; but to the attaining of an eternal felicity after death; to which they think the breach of covenant may conduce; and consequently be just and reasonable; such are they that think it a work of merit to kill, or depose, or rebel against, the sovereign power constituted over them by their own consent. But because there is no natural knowledge of man's estate after death; much less of the reward that is then to he given to breach of faith; but only a belief grounded upon other men's saying, that they know it supernaturally, or that they know those, that knew them, that knew others, that knew it supernaturally; breach of faith cannot be called a precept of reason, or nature.

2

Fifteen Sermons Preached at the Rolls Chapel and *Dissertation II*: On the Nature of Virtue

Joseph Butler

Butler suggests that there are two ways to approach ethics (Preface to the Sermons para. 12). The first, which we might call *rationalism*, begins with 'the abstract relations of things' and concludes that vice is contrary to nature; the second, *naturalism*, begins with a natural fact – human nature – and then involves determining which course of life corresponds to this nature, and concludes that vice is contrary to *human* nature. He sees these methods as mutually supportive, claiming that in general, in his *Sermons Preached at the Rolls Chapel*, he tends to adopt naturalism. Rationalism is best understood as the view that we can discover, through rational reflection, certain necessary and a priori truths about morality, such as that it is fitting to thank one's benefactors. One question here is why such truths might not include truths about beings with certain natures, including beings like ourselves. Perhaps Butler is speaking of starting points: naturalists, unlike rationalists, begin with an examination of human nature.

Butler's own version of naturalism revolves around the idea that virtue is natural to human beings, and that vice is more contrary to our nature even than torture or death. As with the ancient moralists he mentions, Butler's position here relies on a form of *teleology*, according to which human beings have a certain natural purpose. A proper understanding of human nature, Butler claims, involves recognizing that humans are wholes consisting of various parts, and that this whole can be seen as a *system*, in which the parts are properly related to one another (P 13–25, 29; D 1). The analogy he uses is a watch. One will understand what a watch is and its purpose only by seeing how the parts, properly related to one another, fulfil a certain purpose – that of telling the time. Humanity's parts include appetites, affections, and passions, which we share with non-human animals, and reflection or conscience, which we don't. It is natural and appropriate for animals to follow their appetites; in human beings it is not, since reflection has natural authority over these other 'principles'. Why? One way to understand Butler here is as pointing out that our reflective capacity is the only capacity able to grasp reasons for action.

At this point, one might imagine a defender of vice saying to Butler, 'I will allow you that vice is unnatural. But I can get more happiness through being immoral than through virtue, so vice is clearly a more reasonable aim for me than virtue'. The ancient philosophers might have responded by equating happiness with virtue or its exercise, or at least by making virtue a necessary condition of happiness. But Butler does not do this. Rather, he turns to a close and deeply insightful study of the relationship between self-love, or self-interest, and acting benevolently: that is, in the interest of others (P 35–42; Sermons 11.2–21).

Consider rational egoism, the view that what you always have strongest reason to do is what will most advance your own good. You might be tempted to think that this principle is in conflict with acting for the sake of others. Butler is at pains to point out that this is not so. First, the principle of self-love is 'contentless'. What it recommends depends on what will in fact most advance your own happiness. Second, your

History of Ethics – Essential Readings with Commentary, First Edition. Edited by Daniel Star and Roger Crisp.
© 2020 John Wiley & Sons Ltd. Published 2020 by John Wiley & Sons Ltd.

happiness will arise from the satisfaction of particular passions. Some of these, such as for food or wealth, will be largely 'private'. But you might also care about others and be motivated to help them in various ways. This is just another particular passion, although of course not a private one, and its satisfaction can bring much enjoyment. Indeed, benevolent people often seem especially cheerful. They are satisfied with their appearance in the eyes of God, and the sources of their happiness are more secure and will not fail them if, say, they become ill. (Further, of course, God will reward the virtuous and punish the vicious in the afterlife, but Butler believes he can make his case without relying on this claim.)

What if – although Butler might think this is impossible – there is a conflict between virtue and my own good? Here Butler argues (P 26–8) that virtue is again more secure, this time at the epistemic level. We can be certain of the obligation of virtue, whereas no one can ever be certain that vice is in their interest.

Butler claims that our moral judgements concern not so much what people *do*, but what they *will* (D 2). Here he might be confronted with the problem of 'moral luck'. Imagine two equally drunk drivers, driving equally badly. If one happens to kill a pedestrian, they will be blamed significantly more than the other. Butler might claim that this common response is irrational. But we might then ask for a fuller account of how we are to tell which of our moral views are rational, and which not. Consider, for example, the notion of desert, which Butler sees as closely bound up with the ideas of moral good and evil (D 3-5). It is true that many of us will think that someone who has committed a moral wrong deserves punishment, independently of that punishment's having good consequences through, for example, deterring the wrongdoer or others from similar action in future. But is it clear that, as Butler believes, this view is based on rational insight, whereas that concerning the greater blameworthiness of the killer driver is not?

Philosophers we now call 'consequentialists' would argue that rightness, wrongness, and the very practice of blaming others all depend only on consequences. According to the *utilitarian* version of consequentialism, all that matters is impartially benefiting others. Butler denies this view (D 8–10), noting, for example, that if it were correct, then apparently great injustice that had no effect on the overall level of happiness would be morally neutral. And even if God is purely benevolent, this does not mean we should follow him: we should follow the non-consequentialist moral law he has laid down for us.

Fifteen Sermons Preached at the Rolls Chapel

Preface to the Sermons

[…]

12. There are two ways in which the subject of morals may be treated. One begins from inquiring into the abstract relations of things: the other from a matter of fact, namely, what the particular nature of man is, its several parts, their economy or constitution; from whence it proceeds to determine what course of life it is, which is correspondent to this whole nature. In the former method the conclusion is expressed thus, that vice is contrary to the nature and reason of things: in the latter, that it is a violation or breaking in upon our own nature. Thus they both lead us to the same thing, our obligations to the practice of virtue; and thus they exceedingly strengthen and enforce each other. The first seems the most direct formal proof, and in some respects the least liable to cavil and dispute: the latter is in a peculiar manner adapted to satisfy a fair mind: and is more easily applicable to the several particular relations and circumstances in life.

13. The following discourses proceed chiefly in this latter method. The three first wholly. They were intended to explain what is meant by the nature of man, when it is said that virtue consists in following, and vice in deviating from it; and by explaining to shew that the assertion is true. That the ancient moralists had some inward feeling or other, which they chose to express in this manner, that man is born to virtue, that it consists in following nature, and that vice is more contrary to this nature than tortures or death, their works in our hands are instances. Now a person who found no mystery in this way of speaking of the ancients; who, without being very explicit with himself, kept to his natural feeling, went along with them, and found within himself a full conviction, that what they laid down was just and true; such an one would probably wonder to see a point, in which he never perceived any difficulty, so laboured as this is, in the second and third sermons; insomuch perhaps as to be at a loss for the occasion, scope, and drift of them. But it need not be thought strange that this manner of expression, though familiar with them, and, if not usually carried so far, yet not uncommon amongst ourselves, should want explaining; since there are several perceptions daily felt and spoken of, which yet it may not be very easy at first view to explicate, to distinguish from all others, and ascertain exactly what the idea or perception is. The many treatises upon the passions are a proof of this; since so many would never have undertaken to unfold their several complications, and trace and resolve them into their principles, if they had thought what they were endeavouring to shew was obvious to every one, who felt and talked of those passions. Thus, though there seems no ground to doubt, but that the generality of mankind have the inward perception expressed so commonly in that manner by the ancient moralists, more than to doubt whether they have those passions; yet it appeared of use to unfold that inward conviction, and lay it open in a more explicit manner, than I had seen done; especially when there were not wanting persons, who manifestly mistook the whole thing, and so had great reason to express themselves dissatisfied with it. A late author of great and deserved reputation says, that to place virtue in following nature, is at best a loose way of talk. And he has reason to say this, if what I think he intends to express, though with great decency, be true, that scarce any other sense can be put upon those words, but acting as any of the several parts, without distinction, of a man's nature happened most to incline him.

14. Whoever thinks it worth while to consider this matter thoroughly, should begin with stating to himself exactly the idea of a system, economy, or constitution of any particular nature, or particular anything: and he will, I suppose, find, that it is an one or a whole, made up of several parts; but yet, that the several parts even considered as a whole do not complete the idea, unless in the notion of a whole you include the relations and respects which those parts have to each other. Every work both of nature and of art is a system: and as every particular thing, both natural and artificial, is for some use or purpose out of and beyond itself, one may add, to what has been already brought into the idea of a system, its conduciveness to this one or more ends. Let us instance in a watch—Suppose the several parts of it taken to pieces, and placed apart from each other: let a man have ever so exact a notion of these several parts, unless he considers the respects and relations which they have to each other, he will not have anything like the idea of a watch. Suppose these several parts brought together and anyhow united: neither will he yet, be the union ever so close, have an idea which will bear any resemblance to that of a watch. But let him view those several parts put together, or consider them as to be put together in the manner of a watch; let him form a notion of the relations which those several parts have to each other—all conducive in their respective ways to this purpose, shewing the hour of the day; and then he has the idea of a watch. Thus it is with regard to the inward frame of man. Appetites, passions, affections, and the principle of reflection, considered merely as the several parts of our

inward nature, do not at all give us an idea of the system or constitution of this nature; because the constitution is formed by somewhat not yet taken into consideration, namely, by the relations which these several parts have to each other; the chief of which is the authority of reflection or conscience. It is from considering the relations which the several appetites and passions in the inward frame have to each other, and, above all, the supremacy of reflection or conscience, that we get the idea of the system or constitution of human nature. And from the idea itself it will as fully appear, that this our nature, *i.e.* constitution, is adapted to virtue, as from the idea of a watch it appears, that its nature, *i.e.* constitution or system, is adapted to measure time. What in fact or event commonly happens is nothing to this question. Every work of art is apt to be out of order: but this is so far from being according to its system, that let the disorder increase, and it will totally destroy it. This is merely by way of explanation, what an economy, system, or constitution is. And thus far the cases are perfectly parallel. If we go further, there is indeed a difference, nothing to the present purpose, but too important a one ever to be omitted. A machine is inanimate and passive: but we are agents. Our constitution is put in our own power. We are charged with it; and therefore are accountable for any disorder or violation of it.

15. Thus nothing can possibly be more contrary to nature than vice: meaning by nature not only the *several parts* of our internal frame, but also the *constitution* of it. Poverty and disgrace, tortures and death, are not so contrary to it. Misery and injustice are indeed equally contrary to some different parts of our nature taken singly: but injustice is moreover contrary to the whole constitution of the nature.

16. If it be asked, whether this constitution be really what those philosophers meant, and whether they would have explained themselves in this manner; the answer is the same, as if it should be asked, whether a person, who had often used the word *resentment*, and felt the thing, would have explained this passion exactly in the same manner, in which it is done in one of these discourses. As I have no doubt, but that this is a true account of that passion, which he referred to, and intended to express by the word *resentment;* so I have no doubt, but that this is the true account of the ground of that conviction which they referred to, when they said, vice was contrary to nature. And though it should be thought that they meant no more than that vice was contrary to the higher and better part of our nature; even this implies such a constitution as I have endeavoured to explain. For the very terms, higher and better, imply a relation or respect of parts to each other; and these relative parts, being in one and the same nature, form a constitution, and are the very idea of it. They had a perception that injustice was contrary to their nature, and that pain was so also. They observed these two perceptions totally different, not in degree, but in kind: and the reflecting upon each of them, as they thus stood in their nature, wrought a full intuitive conviction, that more was due and of right belonged to one of these inward perceptions, than to the other; that it demanded in all cases to govern such a creature as man. So that, upon the whole, this is a fair and true account of what was the ground of their conviction; of what they intended to refer to, when they said, virtue consisted in following nature: a manner of speaking not loose and undeterminate, but clear and distinct, strictly just and true.

17. Though I am persuaded the force of this conviction is felt by almost every one; yet since, considered as an argument and put in words, it appears somewhat abstruse, and since the connexion of it is broken in the three first sermons, it may not be amiss to give the reader the whole argument here in one view.

18. Mankind has various instincts and principles of action, as brute creatures have; some leading most directly and immediately to the good of the community, and some most directly to private good.

19. Man has several which brutes have not; particularly reflection or conscience, an approbation of some principles or actions, and disapprobation of others.

20. Brutes obey their instincts or principles of action, according to certain rules; suppose the constitution of their body, and the objects around them.

21. The generality of mankind also obey their instincts and principles, all of them; those propensions we call good, as well as the bad, according to the same rules; namely, the constitution of their body, and the external circumstances which they are in. (Therefore it is not a true representation of mankind to affirm, that they are wholly governed by self-love, the love of power and sensual appetites: since, as on the one hand they are often actuated by these, without any regard to right or wrong; so on the other it is manifest fact, that the same persons, the generality, are frequently influenced by friendship, compassion, gratitude; and even a general abhorrence of what is base, and liking of what is fair and just, takes its turn amongst the other motives of action. This is the partial inadequate notion of human nature treated of in the first discourse: and it is by this nature, if one may speak so, that the world is in fact influenced, and kept in that tolerable order, in which it is.)

[…]

23. Mankind also in acting thus would act suitably to their whole nature, if no more were to be said of man's nature than what has been now said; if that, as it is a true, were also a complete, adequate account of our nature.

24. But that is not a complete account of man's nature. Somewhat further must be brought in to give us an adequate notion of it; namely, that one of those principles of action, conscience or reflection, compared with the rest as they all stand together in the nature of man, plainly bears upon it marks of authority over all the rest, and claims the absolute direction of them all, to allow or forbid their gratification: a disapprobation of reflection being in itself a principle manifestly superior to a mere propension. And the conclusion is, that to allow no more to this superior principle or part of our nature, than to other parts; to let it govern and guide only occasionally in common with the rest, as its turn happens to come, from the temper and circumstances one happens to be in; this is not to act conformably to the constitution of man: neither can any human creature be said to act conformably to his constitution of nature, unless he allows to that superior principle the absolute authority which is due to it. And this conclusion is abundantly confirmed from hence, that one may determine what course of action the economy of man's nature requires, without so much as knowing in what degrees of *strength* the several principles prevail, or which of them have actually the greatest influence.

25. The practical reason of insisting so much upon this natural authority of the principle of reflection or conscience is, that it seems in great measure overlooked by many, who are by no means the worse sort of men. It is thought sufficient to abstain from gross wickedness, and to be humane and kind to such as happen to come in their way. Whereas in reality the very constitution of our nature requires, that we bring our whole conduct before this superior faculty; wait its determination; enforce upon ourselves its authority, and make it the business of our lives, as it is absolutely the whole business of a moral agent, to conform ourselves to it. This is the true meaning of that ancient precept, *Reverence thyself*.

26. The not taking into consideration this authority, which is implied in the idea of reflex approbation or disapprobation, seems a material deficiency or omission in Lord Shaftesbury's Inquiry concerning Virtue. He has shewn beyond all contradiction, that virtue is naturally the interest or happiness, and vice the misery, of such a creature as man, placed in the circumstances which we are in this world. But suppose there are particular exceptions; a case which this author was unwilling to put, and yet surely it is to be put: or suppose a case which he has put and determined, that of a sceptic not convinced of this happy tendency of virtue, or being of a contrary opinion. His determination is, that it would be *without remedy*. One may say more explicitly, that leaving out the authority of reflex approbation or disapprobation, such an one would be under an obligation to act viciously; since interest, one's own happiness, is a manifest obligation, and there is not supposed to be any other obligation in the case. "But does it much mend the matter, to take in that natural authority of reflection? There indeed would be an obligation to virtue; but would not the obligation from supposed interest on the side of vice remain?" If it should, yet to be under two contrary obligations, *i.e.* under none at all, would not be exactly the same, as to be under a formal obligation to be vicious, or to be in circumstances in which the constitution of man's nature plainly required that vice should be preferred. But the obligation on the side of interest really does not remain. For the natural authority of the principle of reflection is an obligation the most near and intimate, the most certain and known: whereas the contrary obligation can at the utmost appear no more than probable; since no man can be *certain* in any circumstances that vice is his interest in the present world, much less can he be certain against another: and thus the certain obligation would entirely supersede and destroy the uncertain one; which yet would have been of real force without the former.

27. In truth, the taking in this consideration totally changes the whole state of the case; and shews, what this author does not seem to have been aware of, that the greatest degree of scepticism which he thought possible will still leave men under the strictest moral obligations, whatever their opinion be concerning the happiness of virtue. For that mankind upon reflection felt an approbation of what was good, and disapprobation of the contrary, he thought a plain matter of fact, as it undoubtedly is, which none could deny, but from mere affectation. Take in then that authority and obligation, which is a constituent part of this reflex approbation, and it will undeniably follow, though a man should doubt of everything else, yet, that he would still remain under the nearest and most certain obligation to the practice of virtue; an obligation implied in the very idea of virtue, in the very idea of reflex approbation.

28. And how little influence soever this obligation alone can be expected to have in fact upon mankind, yet one may appeal even to interest and self-love, and ask, since for man's nature, condition, and the shortness of life, so little, so very little indeed, can possibly in any case be gained by vice; whether it be so prodigious a thing to sacrifice that little to the most intimate of all obligations; and which a man cannot transgress without being self-condemned, and, unless he has corrupted his nature, without real self-dislike: this question, I say, may be asked, even upon supposition that the prospect of a future life were ever so uncertain.

29. The observation, that man is thus by his very nature a law to himself, pursued to its just consequences, is of the utmost importance; because from it it will follow, that though men should, through stupidity or speculative scepticism, be ignorant of, or disbelieve, any authority in the universe to punish the violation of this law; yet, if there should be such authority, they would be as really liable to punishment, as though they had been beforehand convinced, that such punishment would follow. For in whatever sense we understand justice, even supposing, what I think would be very presumptuous to assert, that the end of Divine punishment is no other than that of civil punishment, namely, to prevent future mischief; upon this bold supposition, ignorance or disbelief of the sanction would by no means exempt even from this justice; because it is not foreknowledge of the punishment which renders us obnoxious to it; but merely violating a known obligation.

[…]

35. The chief design of the eleventh discourse is to state the notion of self-love and disinterestedness, in order to shew that benevolence is not more unfriendly to self-love, than any other particular affection whatever. There is a strange affectation in many people of explaining away all particular affections, and representing the whole of life as nothing but one continued exercise of self-love. Hence arises that surprising confusion and perplexity in the Epicureans of old, Hobbes, the author of *Reflexions, Sentences, et Maximes Morales*, and this whole set of writers; the confusion of calling actions interested which are done in contradiction to the most manifest known interest, merely for the gratification of a present passion. Now all this confusion might easily be avoided, by stating to ourselves wherein the idea of self-love in general consists, as distinguished from all particular movements towards particular external objects; the appetites of sense, resentment, compassion, curiosity, ambition, and the rest. When this is done, if the words *selfish* and *interested* cannot be parted with, but must be applied to everything; yet, to avoid such total confusion of all language, let the distinction be made by epithets: and the first may be called cool or settled selfishness, and the other passionate or sensual selfishness. But the most natural way of speaking plainly is, to call the first only, self-love, and the actions proceeding from it, interested: and to say of the latter, that they are not love to ourselves, but movements towards somewhat external: honour, power, the harm or good of another: and that the pursuit of these external objects, so far as it proceeds from these movements, (for it may proceed from self-love,) is no otherwise interested, than as every action of every creature must, from the nature of the thing, be; for no one can act but from a desire, or choice, or preference of his own.

36. Self-love and any particular passion may be joined together; and from this complication, it becomes impossible in numberless instances to determine precisely, how far an action, perhaps even of one's own, has for its principle general self-love, or some particular passion. But this need create no confusion in the ideas themselves of self-love and particular passions. We distinctly discern what one is, and what the others are: though we may be uncertain how far one or the other influences us. And though, from this uncertainty, it cannot but be that there will be different opinions concerning mankind, as more or less governed by interest; and some will ascribe actions to self-love, which others will ascribe to particular passions: yet it is absurd to say that mankind are wholly actuated by either; since it is manifest that both have their influence. For as, on the one hand, men form a general notion of interest, some placing it in one thing, and some in another, and have a considerable regard to it throughout the course of their life, which is owing to self-love; so, on the other hand, they are often set on work by the particular passions themselves, and a considerable part of life is spent in the actual gratification of them, *i.e.* is employed, not by self-love, but by the passions.

37. Besides, the very idea of an interested pursuit necessarily presupposes particular passions or appetites; since the very idea of interest or happiness consists in this, that an appetite or affection enjoys its object. It is not because we love ourselves that we find delight in such and such objects, but because we have particular affections towards them. Take away these affections, and you leave self-love absolutely nothing at all to employ itself about; no end or object for it to pursue, excepting only that of avoiding pain. Indeed the Epicureans, who maintained that absence of pain was the highest happiness, might, consistently with themselves, deny all affection, and, if they had so pleased, every sensual appetite too: but the very idea of interest or happiness other than absence of pain, implies particular appetites or passions; these being necessary to constitute that interest or happiness.

38. The observation, that benevolence is no more disinterested than any of the common particular passions, seems in itself worth being taken notice of; but is insisted, upon to obviate that scorn, which one sees rising upon the faces of people who are said to know the world, when mention is made of a disinterested, generous, or public-spirited action. The truth of that observation might be made appear in a more formal manner of

proof: for whoever will consider all the possible respects and relations which any particular affection can have to self-love and private interest, will, I think, see demonstrably, that benevolence is not in any respect more at variance with self-love, than any other particular affection whatever, but that it is in every respect, at least, as friendly to it.

39. If the observation be true, it follows, that self-love and benevolence, virtue and interest, are not to be opposed, but only to be distinguished from each other; in the same way as virtue and any other particular affection, love of arts, suppose, are to be distinguished. Everything is what it is, and not another thing. The goodness or badness of actions does not arise from hence, that the epithet, interested or disinterested, may be applied to them, any more than that any other indifferent epithet, suppose inquisitive or jealous, may or may not be applied to them; not from their being attended with present or future pleasure or pain; but from their being what they are; namely, what becomes such creatures as we are, what the state of the case requires, or the contrary. Or in other words, we may judge and determine, that an action is morally good or evil, before we so much as consider, whether it be interested or disinterested. This consideration no more comes in to determine whether an action be virtuous, than to determine whether it be resentful. Self-love in its due degree is as just and morally good, as any affection whatever. Benevolence towards particular persons may be to a degree of weakness, and so be blameable: and disinterestedness is so far from being in itself commendable, that the utmost possible depravity which we can in imagination conceive, is that of disinterested cruelty.

40. Neither does there appear any reason to wish self-love were weaker in the generality of the world than it is. The influence which it has seems plainly owing to its being constant and habitual, which it cannot but be, and not to the degree or strength of it. Every caprice of the imagination, every curiosity of the understanding, every affection of the heart, is perpetually shewing its weakness, by prevailing over it. Men daily, hourly sacrifice the greatest known interest, to fancy, inquisitiveness, love, or hatred, any vagrant inclination. The thing to be lamented is, not that men have so great regard to their own good or interest in the present world, for they have not enough; but that they have so little to the good of others. And this seems plainly owing to their being so much engaged in the gratification of particular passions unfriendly to benevolence, and which happen to be most prevalent in them, much more than to self-love. As a proof of this may be observed, that there is no character more void of friendship, gratitude, natural affection, love to their country, common justice, or more equally and uniformly hard-hearted, than the *abandoned* in, what is called, the way of pleasure——hard-hearted and totally without feeling in behalf of others; except when they cannot escape the sight of distress, and so are interrupted by it in their pleasures. And yet it is ridiculous to call such an abandoned course of pleasure interested, when the person engaged in it knows beforehand, and goes on under the feeling and apprehension, that it will be as ruinous to himself, as to those who depend upon him.

41. Upon the whole, if the generality of mankind were to cultivate within themselves the principle of self-love; if they were to accustom themselves often to set down and consider, what was the greatest happiness they were capable of attaining for themselves in this life, and if self-love were so strong and prevalent, as that they would uniformly pursue this their supposed chief temporal good, without being diverted from it by any particular passion; it would manifestly prevent numberless follies and vices. This was in a great measure the Epicurean system of philosophy. It is indeed by no means the religious or even moral institution of life. Yet, with all the mistakes men would fall into about interest, it would be less mischievous than the extravagances of mere appetite, will, and pleasure: for certainly self-love, though confined to the interest of this life, is, of the two, a much better guide than passion, which has absolutely no bound nor measure, but what is set to it by this self-love, or moral considerations.

42. From the distinction above made between self-love, and the several particular principles or affections in our nature, we may see how good ground there was for that assertion, maintained by the several ancient schools of philosophy against the Epicureans, namely, that virtue is to be pursued as an end, eligible in and for itself. For, if there be any principles or affections in the mind of man distinct from self-love, that the things those principles tend towards, or that the objects of those affections are, each of them, in themselves eligible, to be pursued upon its own account, and to be rested in as an end, is implied in the very idea of such principle or affection. They indeed asserted much higher things of virtue, and with very good reason; but to say thus much of it, that it is to be pursued for itself, is to say no more of it, than may truly be said of the object of every natural affection whatever.

[…]

Sermon XI

Upon the Love of Our Neighbour

And if there be any other commandment, it is briefly comprehended in this saying, namely, Thou shall love thy neighbour as thyself (Romans xiii. 9).

1. It is commonly observed, that there is a disposition in men to complain of the viciousness and corruption of the age in which they live, as greater than that of former ones; which is usually followed with this further observation, that mankind has been in that respect much the same in all times. Now, not to determine whether this last be not contradicted by the accounts of history; thus much can scarce be doubted, that vice and folly takes different turns, and some particular kinds of it are more open and avowed in some ages than in others: and, I suppose, it may be spoken of as very much the distinction of the present to profess a contracted spirit, and greater regards to self-interest, than, appears to have been done formerly. Upon this account it seems worth while to inquire, whether private interest is likely to be promoted in proportion to the degree in which self-love engrosses us, and prevails over all other principles; or whether the contracted affection may not possibly be so prevalent as to disappoint itself, and even contradict its own end, private good.

2. And since, further, there is generally thought to be some peculiar kind of contrariety between self-love and the love of our neighbour, between the pursuit of public and of private good; insomuch that when you are recommending one of these, you are supposed to be speaking against the other; and from hence arises a secret prejudice against, and frequently open scorn of all talk of public spirit, and real goodwill to our fellow-creatures; it will be necessary to inquire what respect benevolence hath to self-love, and the pursuit of private interest to the pursuit of public: or whether there be anything of that peculiar inconsistence and contrariety between them, over and above what there is between self-love and other passions and particular affections, and their respective pursuits.

3. These inquiries, it is hoped, may be favourably attended to: for there shall be all possible concessions made to the favourite passion, which hath so much allowed to it, and whose cause is so universally pleaded: it shall be treated with the utmost tenderness and concern for its interests.

4. In order to this, as well as to determine the fore-mentioned questions, it will be necessary to consider the nature, the object, and end of that self-love, as distinguished from other principles or affections in the mind, and their respective objects.

5. Every man hath a general desire of his own happiness; and likewise a variety of particular affections, passions, and appetites to particular external objects. The former proceeds from, or is self-love; and seems inseparable from all sensible creatures, who can reflect upon themselves and their own interest or happiness, so as to have that interest an object to their minds: what is to be said of the latter is, that they proceed from, or together make up that particular nature, according to which man is made. The object the former pursues is somewhat internal, our own happiness, enjoyment, satisfaction; whether we have, or have not, a distinct particular perception what it is, or wherein it consists: the objects of the latter are this or that particular external thing, which the affections tend towards, and of which it hath always a particular idea or perception. The principle we call self-love never seeks anything external for the sake of the thing, but only as a means of happiness or good: particular affections rest in the external things themselves. One belongs to man as a reasonable creature reflecting upon his own interest or happiness. The other, though quite distinct from reason, are as much a part of human nature.

6. That all particular appetites and passions are towards *external things themselves*, distinct from the *pleasure arising from them*, is manifested from hence; that there could not be this pleasure, were it not for that prior suitableness between the object and the passion: there could be no enjoyment or delight from one thing more than another, from eating food more than from swallowing a stone, if there were not an affection or appetite to one thing more than another.

7. Every particular affection, even the love of our neighbour, is as really our own affection, as self-love; and the pleasure arising from its gratification is as much my own pleasure, as the pleasure self-love would have, from knowing I myself should be happy some time hence, would be my own pleasure. And if, because every particular affection is a man's own, and the pleasure arising from its gratification his own pleasure, or pleasure to himself, such particular affection must be called self-love; according to this way of speaking, no creature whatever can possibly act but merely from self-love; and every action and every affection whatever is to be resolved up into this one principle. But then this is not the language of mankind: or if it were, we should want words to express the difference, between

the principle of an action, proceeding from cool consideration that it will be to my own advantage; and an action, suppose of revenge, or of friendship, by which a man runs upon certain ruin, to do evil or good to another. It is manifest the principles of these actions are totally different, and so want different words to be distinguished by: all that they agree in is, that they both proceed from, and are done to gratify an inclination in a man's self. But the principle or inclination in one case is self-love; in the other, hatred or love of another. There is then a distinction between the cool principle of self-love, or general desire of our happiness, as one part of our nature, and one principle of action; and the particular affections towards particular external objects, as another part of our nature, and another principle of action. How much soever therefore is to be allowed to self-love, yet it cannot be allowed to be the whole of our inward constitution; because, you see, there are other parts or principles which come into it.

8. Further, private happiness or good is all which self-love can make us desire, or be concerned about: in having this consists its gratification: it is an affection to ourselves; a regard to our own interest, happiness, and private good: and in the proportion a man hath this, he is interested, or a lover of himself. Let this be kept in mind; because there is commonly, as I shall presently have occasion to observe, another sense put upon these words. On the other hand, particular affections tend towards particular external things: these are their objects; having these is their end: in this consists their gratification: no matter whether it be, or be not, upon the whole, our interest or happiness. An action done from the former of these principles is called an interested action. An action proceeding from any of the latter has its denomination of passionate, ambitious, friendly, revengeful, or any other, from the particular appetite or affection from which it proceeds. Thus self-love as one part of human nature, and the several particular principles as the other part, are, themselves, their objects and ends, stated and shewn.

9. From hence it will be easy to see, how far, and in what ways, each of these can contribute and be subservient to the private good of the individual. Happiness does not consist in self-love. The desire of happiness is no more the thing itself, than the desire of riches is the possession or enjoyment of them. People may love themselves with the most entire and unbounded affection, and yet be extremely miserable. Neither can self-love any way help them out, but by setting them on work to get rid of the causes of their misery, to gain or make use of those objects which are by nature adapted to afford satisfaction. Happiness or satisfaction consists only in the enjoyment of those objects, which are by nature suited to our several particular appetites, passions, and affections. So that if self-love wholly engrosses us, and leaves no room for any other principle, there can be absolutely no such thing at all as happiness, or enjoyment of any kind whatever; since happiness consists in the gratification of particular passions, which supposes the having of them. Self-love then does not constitute *this* or *that* to be our interest or good; but, our interest or good being constituted by nature and supposed, self-love only puts us upon obtaining and securing it. Therefore, if it be possible, that self-love may prevail and exert itself in a degree or manner which is not subservient to this end; then it will not follow, that our interest will be promoted in proportion to the degree in which that principle engrosses us, and prevails over others. Nay further, the private and contracted affection, when it is not subservient to this end, private good, may, for anything that appears, have a direct contrary tendency and effect. And if we will consider the matter, we shall see that it often really has. *Disengagement* is absolutely necessary to enjoyment; and a person may have so steady and fixed an eye upon his own interest, whatever he places it in, as may hinder him from *attending* to many gratifications within his reach, which others have their minds free and open to. Over-fondness for a child is not generally thought to be for its advantage: and, if there be any guess to be made from appearances, surely that character we call selfish is not the most promising for happiness. Such a temper may plainly be, and exert itself in a degree and manner which may give unnecessary and useless solicitude and anxiety, in a degree and manner which may prevent obtaining the means and materials of enjoyment, as well as the making use of them. Immoderate self-love does very ill consult its own interest: and, how much soever a paradox it may appear, it is certainly true, that even from self-love we should endeavour to get over all inordinate regard to, and consideration of ourselves. Every one of our passions and affections hath its natural stint and bound, which may easily be exceeded; whereas our enjoyments can possibly be but in a determinate measure and degree. Therefore such excess of the affection, since it cannot procure any enjoyment, must in all cases be useless; but is generally attended with inconveniences, and often is downright pain and misery. This holds as much with regard to self-love as to all other affections. The natural degree of it, so far as it sets us on work to gain and make use of the materials of satisfaction, may be to our real advantage; but beyond or besides this, it is in several respects an inconvenience and disadvantage. Thus it appears, that private interest is so far from being likely to be promoted in proportion to the degree in which self-love engrosses us, and prevails over all other principles; that the contracted affection may be so prevalent as to disappoint itself, and even contradict its own end, private good.

10. "But who, except the most sordidly covetous, ever thought there was any rivalship between the love of greatness, honour, power, or between sensual appetites and self-love? No, there is a perfect harmony between them. It is by means of these particular appetites and affections that self-love is gratified in enjoyment, happiness, and satisfaction. The competition and rivalship is between self-love and the love of our neighbour: that affection which leads us out of ourselves, makes us regardless of our own interest, and substitute that of another in its stead." Whether then there be any peculiar competition and contrariety in this case, shall now be considered.

11. Self-love and interestedness was stated to consist in or be an affection to ourselves, a regard to our own private good: it is therefore distinct from benevolence, which is an affection to the good of our fellow-creatures. But that benevolence is distinct from, that is, not the same thing with self-love, is no reason for its being looked upon with any peculiar suspicion; because every principle whatever, by means of which self-love is gratified, is distinct from it; and all things which are distinct from each other are equally so. A man has an affection or aversion to another: that one of these tends to, and is gratified by doing good, that the other tends to, and is gratified by doing harm, does not in the least alter the respect which either one or the other of these inward feelings has to self-love. We use the word *property* so as to exclude any other persons having an interest in that of which we say a particular man has the property. And we often use the word *selfish* so as to exclude in the same manner all regards to the good of others. But the cases are not parallel: for though that exclusion is really part of the idea of property; yet such positive exclusion, or bringing this peculiar disregard to the good of others into the idea of self-love, is in reality adding to the idea, or changing it from what it was before stated to consist in, namely, in an affection to ourselves. This being the whole idea of self-love, it can no otherwise exclude good-will or love of others, than merely by not including it, no otherwise, than it excludes love of arts or reputation, or of anything else. Neither on the other hand does benevolence, any more than love of arts or of reputation, exclude self-love. Love of our neighbour then has just the same respect to, is no more distant from, self-love, than hatred of our neighbour, or than love or hatred of anything else. Thus the principles, from which men rush upon certain ruin for the destruction of an enemy, and for the preservation of a friend, have the same respect to the private affection, and are equally interested, or equally disinterested: and it is of no avail, whether they are said to be one or the other. Therefore to those that are shocked to hear virtue spoken of as disinterested, it may be allowed that it is indeed absurd to speak thus of it; unless hatred, several particular instances of vice, and all the common affections and aversions in mankind, are acknowledged to be disinterested too. Is there any less inconsistence, between the love of inanimate things, or of creatures merely sensitive, and self-love; than between self-love and the love of our neighbour? Is desire of and delight in the happiness of another any more a diminution of self-love, than desire of and delight in the esteem of another? They are both equally desire of and delight in somewhat external to ourselves: either both or neither are so. The object of self-love is expressed in the term *self*: and every appetite of sense, and every particular affection of the heart, are equally interested or disinterested, because the objects of them are all equally self or somewhat else. Whatever ridicule therefore the mention of a disinterested principle or action may be supposed to lie open to, must, upon the matter being thus stated, relate to ambition, and every appetite and particular affection, as much as to benevolence. And indeed all the ridicule, and all the grave perplexity, of which this subject hath had its full share, is merely from words. The most intelligible way of speaking of it seems to be this: that self-love and the actions done in consequence of it (for these will presently appear to be the same as to this question) are interested; that particular affections towards external objects, and the actions done in consequence of those affections, are not so. But every one is at liberty to use words as he pleases. All that is here insisted upon is, that ambition, revenge, benevolence, all particular passions whatever, and the actions they produce, are equally interested or disinterested.

12. Thus it appears that there is no peculiar contrariety between self-love and benevolence; no greater competition between these, than between any other particular affections and self-love. This relates to the affections themselves. Let us now see whether there be any peculiar contrariety between the respective courses of life which these affections lead to; whether there be any greater competition between the pursuit of private and of public good, than between any other particular pursuits and that of private good.

13. There seems no other reason to suspect that there is any such peculiar contrariety, but only that the course of action which benevolence leads to, has a more direct tendency to promote the good of others, than that course of action which love of reputation suppose, or any other particular affection leads to. But that any affection tends to the happiness of another, does not hinder its tending to one's own happiness too. That others enjoy the benefit of the air and the light of the sun, does not hinder but that these are as much one's own private advantage now, as they would be if we had the property of them exclusive of all others. So a pursuit which tends to promote the good of another, yet may have as great tendency to promote private interest, as a pursuit which does not tend to the good

of another at all, or which is mischievous to him. All particular affections whatever, resentment, benevolence, love of arts, equally lead to a course of action for their own gratification, *i.e.* the gratification of ourselves; and the gratification of each gives delight: so far then it is manifest they have all the same respect to private interest. Now take into consideration further, concerning these three pursuits, that the end of the first is the harm, of the second, the good of another, of the last, somewhat indifferent; and is there any necessity, that these additional considerations should alter the respect, which we before saw these three pursuits had to private interest; or render any one of them less conducive to it, than any other? Thus one man's affection is to honour as his end; in order to obtain which he thinks no pains too great. Suppose another, with such a singularity of mind, as to have the same affection to public good as his end, which he endeavours with the same labour to obtain. In case of success, surely the man of benevolence hath as great enjoyment as the man of ambition; they both equally having the end their affections, in the same degree, tended to: but in case of disappointment, the benevolent man has clearly the advantage; since endeavouring to do good considered as a virtuous pursuit, is gratified by its own consciousness, *i.e.* is in a degree its own reward.

14. And as to these two, or benevolence and any other particular passions whatever, considered in a further view, as forming a general temper, which more or less disposes us for enjoyment of all the common blessings of life, distinct from their own gratification: is benevolence less the temper of tranquillity and freedom than ambition or covetousness? Does the benevolent man appear less easy with himself, from his love to his neighbour? Does he less relish his being? Is there any peculiar gloom seated on his face? Is his mind less open to entertainment, to any particular gratification? Nothing is more manifest, than that being in good humour, which is benevolence whilst it lasts, is itself the temper of satisfaction and enjoyment.

15. Suppose then a man sitting down to consider how he might become most easy to himself, and attain the greatest pleasure he could; all that which is his real natural happiness. This can only consist in the enjoyment of those objects, which are by nature adapted to our several faculties. These particular enjoyments make up the sum total of our happiness: and they are supposed to arise from riches, honours, and the gratification of sensual appetites: be it so: yet none profess themselves so completely happy in these enjoyments, but that there is room left in the mind for others, if they were presented to them: nay, these as much as they engage us, are not thought so high, but that human nature is capable even of greater. Now there have been persons in all ages, who have professed that they found satisfaction in the exercise of charity, in the love of their neighbour, in endeavouring to promote the happiness of all they had to do with, and in the pursuit of what is just, and right, and good, as the general bent of their mind, and end of their life; and that doing an action of baseness or cruelty, would be as great violence to *their* self, as much breaking in upon their nature, as any external force. Persons of this character would add, if they might be heard, that they consider themselves as acting in the view of an infinite Being, Who is in a much higher sense the object of reverence and of love, than all the world besides; and therefore they could have no more enjoyment from a wicked action committed under His eye, than the persons to whom they are making their apology could, if all mankind were the spectators of it; and that the satisfaction of approving themselves to His unerring judgment, to Whom they thus refer all their actions, is a more continued settled satisfaction than any this world can afford; as also that they have, no less than others, a mind free and open to all the common innocent gratifications of it, such as they are. And if we go no further, does there appear any absurdity in this? Will any one take it upon him to say, that a man cannot find his account in this general course of life, as much as in the most unbounded ambition, and the excesses of pleasure? Or that such a person has not consulted so well for himself, for the satisfaction and peace of his own mind, as the ambitious or dissolute man? And though the consideration, that God Himself will in the end justify their taste, and support their cause, is not formally to be insisted upon here; yet thus much comes in, that all enjoyments whatever are much more clear and unmixed from the assurance that they will end well. Is it certain then that there is nothing in these pretensions to happiness? especially when there are not wanting persons, who have supported themselves with satisfactions of this kind in sickness, poverty, disgrace, and in the very pangs of death; whereas it is manifest all other enjoyments fail in these circumstances. This surely looks suspicious of having somewhat in it. Self-love methinks should be alarmed. May she not possibly pass over greater pleasures, than those she is so wholly taken up with?

16. The short of the matter is no more than this. Happiness consists in the gratification of certain affections, appetites, passions, with objects which are by nature adapted to them. Self-love may indeed set us on work to gratify these: but happiness or enjoyment has no immediate connexion with self-love, but arises from such gratification alone. Love of our neighbour is one of those affections. This, considered as a *virtuous principle*, is gratified by a consciousness of endeavouring to promote the good of others; but considered as a *natural affection*, its gratification consists in the actual accomplishment of this endeavour. Now indulgence or gratification of this affection, whether

in that consciousness, or this accomplishment, has the same respect to interest, as indulgence of any other affection; they equally proceed from or do not proceed from self-love, they equally include or equally exclude this principle. Thus it appears, that benevolence and the pursuit of public good hath at least as great respect to self-love and the pursuit of private good, as any other particular passions, and their respective pursuits.

17. Neither is covetousness, whether as a temper or pursuit, any exception to this. For if by covetousness is meant the desire and pursuit of riches for their own sake, without any regard to, or consideration of, the uses of them; this hath as little to do with self-love, as benevolence hath. But by this word is usually meant, not such madness and total distraction of mind, but immoderate affection to and pursuit of riches as possessions in order to some further end: namely, satisfaction, interest, or good. This therefore is not a particular affection, or particular pursuit, but it is the general principle of self-love, and the general pursuit of our own interest: for which reason, the word *selfish* is by everyone appropriated to this temper and pursuit. Now as it is ridiculous to assert, that self-love and the love of our neighbour are the same: so neither is it asserted, that following these different affections hath the same tendency and respect to our own interest. The comparison is not between self-love and the love of our neighbour; between pursuit of our own interest, and the interest of others: but between the several particular affections in human nature towards external objects, as one part of the comparison; and the one particular affection to the good of our neighbour, as the other part of it: and it has been shewn, that all these have the same respect to self-love and private interest.

18. There is indeed frequently an inconsistence or interfering between self-love or private interest, and the several particular appetites, passions, affections, or the pursuits they lead to. But this competition or interfering is merely accidental; and happens much oftener between pride, revenge, sensual gratifications, and private interest, than between private interest and benevolence. For nothing is more common, than to see men give themselves up to a passion or an affection to their known prejudice and ruin, and in direct contradiction to manifest and real interest, and the loudest calls of self-love: whereas the seeming competitions and interfering, between benevolence and private interest, relate much more to the materials or means of enjoyment, than to enjoyment itself. There is often an interfering in the former, when there is none in the latter. Thus as to riches: so much money as a man gives away, so much less will remain in his possession. Here is a real interfering. But though a man cannot possibly give without lessening his fortune, yet there are multitudes might give without lessening their own enjoyment; because they may have more than they can turn to any real use or advantage to themselves. Thus, the more thought and time anyone employs about the interests and good of others, he must necessarily have less to attend his own; but he may have so ready and large a supply of his own wants, that such thought might be really useless to himself, though of great service and assistance to others.

19. The general mistake, that there is some greater inconsistence between endeavouring to promote the good of another and self-interest, than between self-interest and pursuing anything else, seems, as hath already been hinted, to arise from our notions of property; and to be carried on by this property's being supposed to be itself our happiness or good. People are so very much taken up with this one subject, that they seem from it to have formed a general way of thinking, which they apply to other things that they have nothing to do with. Hence, in a confused and slight way, it might well be taken for granted, that another's having no interest in an affection, (*i.e.* his good not being the object of it,) renders, as one may speak, the proprietor's interest in it greater; and that if another had an interest in it, this would render his less, or occasion that such affection could not be so friendly to self-love, or conducive to private good, as an affection or pursuit which has not a regard to the good of another. This, I say, might be taken for granted, whilst it was not attended to, that the object of every particular affection is equally somewhat external to ourselves; and whether it be the good of another person, or whether it be any other external thing, makes no alteration with regard to its being one's own affection, and the gratification of it one's own private enjoyment. And so far as it is taken for granted, that barely having the means and materials of enjoyment is what constitutes interest and happiness; that our interest or good consists in possessions themselves, in having the property of riches, houses, lands, gardens, not in the enjoyment of them; so far it will even more strongly be taken for granted, in the way already explained, that an affection's conducing to the good of another, must even necessarily occasion it to conduce less to private good, if not to be positively detrimental to it. For, if property and happiness are one and the same thing, as by increasing the property of another, you lessen your own property, so by promoting the happiness of another, you must lessen your own happiness. But whatever occasioned the mistake, I hope it has been fully proved to be one; as it has been proved, that there is no peculiar rivalship or competition between self-love and benevolence: that as there may be a competition between these two, so there may also between any particular affection whatever and self-love; that every particular affection, benevolence among the rest, is subservient to

self-love by being the instrument of private enjoyment; and that in one respect benevolence contributes more to private interest, *i.e.* enjoyment or satisfaction, than any other of the particular common affections, as it is in a degree its own gratification.

20. And to all these things may be added, that religion, from whence arises our strongest obligation to benevolence, is so far from disowning the principle of self-love, that it often addresses itself to that very principle, and always to the mind in that state when reason presides; and there can no access be had to the understanding, but by convincing men, that the course of life we would persuade them to is not contrary to their interest. It may be allowed, without any prejudice to the cause of virtue and religion, that our ideas of happiness and misery are of all our ideas the nearest and most important to us; that they will, nay, if you please, that they ought to prevail over those of order, and beauty, and harmony, and proportion, if there should ever be, as it is impossible there ever should be, any inconsistence between them: though these last too, as expressing the fitness of actions, are real as truth itself. Let it be allowed, though virtue or moral rectitude does indeed consist in affection to and pursuit of what is right and good, as such; yet, that when we sit down in a cool hour, we can neither justify to ourselves this or any other pursuit, till we are convinced that it will be for our happiness, or at least not contrary to it.

21. Common reason and humanity will have some influence upon mankind, whatever becomes of speculations; but, so far as the interests of virtue depend upon the theory of it being secured from open scorn, so far its very being in the world depends upon its appearing to have no contrariety to private interest and self-love. The foregoing observations, therefore, it is hoped, may have gained a little ground in favour of the precept before us; the particular explanation of which shall be the subject of the next discourse.

Dissertation II

Of the Nature of Virtue

1. That which renders beings capable of moral government, is their having a moral nature, and moral faculties of perception and of action. Brute creatures are impressed and actuated by various instincts and propensions: so also are we. But additional to this, we have a capacity of reflecting upon actions and characters, and making them an object to our thought: and on doing this, we naturally and unavoidably approve some actions, under the peculiar view of their being virtuous and of good desert; and disapprove others, as vicious and of ill desert. That we have this moral approving and disapproving faculty, is certain from our experiencing it in ourselves, and recognising it in each other. It appears from our exercising it unavoidably, in the approbation and disapprobation even of feigned characters: from the words, *right* and *wrong, odious* and *amiable, base* and *worthy*, with many others of like signification in all languages, applied to actions and characters: from the many written systems of morals which suppose it; since it cannot be imagined, that all these authors, throughout all these treatises, had absolutely no meaning at all to their words, or a meaning merely chimerical: from our natural sense of gratitude, which implies a distinction between merely being the instrument of good, and intending it; from the like distinction, every one makes, between injury and mere harm, which, Hobbes says, is peculiar to mankind; and between injury and just punishment, a distinction plainly natural, prior to the consideration of human laws. It is manifest great part of common language, and of common behaviour over the world, is formed upon supposition of such a moral faculty; whether called conscience, moral reason, moral sense, or Divine reason; whether considered as a sentiment of the understanding, or as a perception of the heart; or, which seems the truth, as including both. Nor is it at all doubtful in the general, what course of action this faculty, or practical discerning power within us, approves, and what it disapproves. For, as much as it has been disputed wherein virtue consists, or whatever ground for doubt there may be about particulars; yet, in general, there is in reality a universally acknowledged standard of it. It is that, which all ages and all countries have made profession of in public: it is that, which every man you meet puts on the show of: it is that, which the primary and fundamental laws of all civil constitutions over the face of the earth make it their business and endeavour to enforce the practice of upon mankind: namely, justice, veracity, and regard to common good. It being manifest then, in general, that we have such a faculty or discernment as this, it may be of use to remark some things more distinctly concerning it.

2. First, it ought to be observed, that the object of this faculty is actions, comprehending under that name active or practical principles: those principles from which men would act, if occasions and circumstances gave them power; and which, when fixed and habitual in any person, we call his character. It does not appear, that brutes have the least reflex sense of actions, as distinguished from events: or that will and design, which constitute the very nature of actions as such, are at all an object to their perception. But to ours they are: and they are the object, and the only one, of the approving and disapproving faculty. Acting, conduct, behaviour, abstracted from all regard to what is, in fact and event, the consequence of it, is itself the natural object of the moral discernment; as speculative truth and falsehood is of speculative reason. Intention of such and such consequences, indeed, is always included; for it is part of the action itself: but though the intended good or bad consequences do not follow, we have exactly the same sense of the action as if they did. In like manner we think well or ill of characters, abstracted from all consideration of the good or the evil, which persons of such characters have it actually in their power to do. We never, in the moral way, applaud or blame either ourselves or others, for what we enjoy or what we suffer, or for having impressions made upon us which we consider as altogether out of our power: but only for what we do, or would have done, had it been in our power; or for what we leave undone, which we might have done, or would have left undone, though we could have done it.

3. Secondly, our sense or discernment of actions as morally good or evil, implies in it a sense or discernment of them as of good or ill desert. It may be difficult to explain this perception, so as to answer all the questions which may be asked concerning it: but every one speaks of such and such actions as deserving punishment; and it is not, I suppose, pretended, that they have absolutely no meaning at all to the expression. Now the meaning plainly is not, that we conceive it for the good of society, that the doer of such actions should be made to suffer. For if unhappily it were resolved, that a man, who, by some innocent action, was infected with the plague, should be left to perish, lest, by other people's coming near him, the infection should spread; no one would say he deserved this treatment. Innocence and ill-desert are inconsistent ideas. Ill-desert always supposes guilt: and if one be no part of the other, yet they are evidently and naturally connected in our mind. The sight of a man in misery raises our compassion

towards him; and, if this misery be inflicted on him by another, our indignation against the author of it. But when we are informed, that the sufferer is a villain, and is punished only for his treachery or cruelty; our compassion exceedingly lessens, and in many instances our indignation wholly subsides. Now what produces this effect is the conception of that in the sufferer, which we call ill-desert. Upon considering then, or viewing together, our notion of vice and that of misery, there results a third, that of ill-desert. And thus there is in human creatures an association of the two ideas, natural and moral evil, wickedness and punishment. If this association were merely artificial or accidental, it were nothing: but being most unquestionably natural, it greatly concerns us to attend to it, instead of endeavouring to explain it away.

4. It may be observed further, concerning our perception of good and of ill-desert, that the former is very weak with respect to common instances of virtue. One reason of which may be, that it does not appear to a spectator, how far such instances of virtue proceed from a virtuous principle, or in what degree this principle is prevalent: since a very weak regard to virtue may be sufficient to make men act well in many common instances. And on the other hand, our perception of ill-desert in vicious actions lessens, in proportion to the temptations men are thought to have had to such vices. For, vice in human creatures consisting chiefly in the absence or want of the virtuous principle; though a man be overcome, suppose, by tortures, it does not from thence appear to what degree the virtuous principle was wanting. All that appears is, that he had it not in such a degree, as to prevail over the temptation: but possibly he had it in a degree, which would have rendered him proof against common temptations.

5. Thirdly, our perception of vice and ill-desert arises from, and is the result of, a comparison of actions with the nature and capacities of the agent. For the mere neglect of doing what we ought to do would, in many cases, be determined by all men to be in the highest degree vicious. And this determination must arise from such comparison, and be the result of it; because such neglect would not be vicious in creatures of other natures and capacities, as brutes. And it is the same also with respect to positive vices, or such as consist in doing what we ought not. For, every one has a different sense of harm done by an idiot, madman, or child, and by one of mature and common understanding; though the action of both, including the intention, which is part of the action, be the same: as it may be, since idiots and madmen, as well as children, are capable not only of doing mischief, but also of intending it. Now this difference must arise from somewhat discerned in the nature or capacities of one, which renders the action vicious; and the want of which, in the other, renders the same action innocent or less vicious: and this plainly supposes a comparison, whether reflected upon or not, between the action and capacities of the agent, previous to our determining an action to be vicious. And hence arises a proper application of the epithets, *incongruous, unsuitable, disproportionate, unfit*, to actions which our moral faculty determines to be vicious.

6. Fourthly, it deserves to be considered, whether men are more at liberty, in point of morals, to make themselves miserable without reason, than to make other people so: or dissolutely to neglect their own greater good, for the sake of a present lesser gratification, than they are to neglect the good of others, whom Nature has committed to their care. It should seem, that a due concern about our own interest or happiness, and a reasonable endeavour to secure and promote it, which is, I think, very much the meaning of the word *prudence*, in our language; it should seem, that this is virtue, and the contrary behaviour faulty and blamable; since, in the calmest way of reflection, we approve of the first, and condemn the other conduct, both in ourselves and others. This approbation and disapprobation are altogether different from mere desire of our own, or of their happiness, and from sorrow upon missing it. For the object or occasion of this last kind of perception is satisfaction or uneasiness: whereas the object of the first is active behaviour. In one case, what our thoughts fix upon is our condition: in the other, our conduct. It is true indeed, that Nature has not given us so sensible a dis-approbation of imprudence and folly, either in *ourselves* or *others*, as of falsehood, injustice, and cruelty: I suppose, because that constant habitual sense of private interest and good, which we always carry about with us, renders such sensible disapprobation less necessary, less wanting, to keep us from imprudently neglecting our own happiness, and foolishly injuring ourselves, than it is necessary and wanting to keep us from injuring others, to whose good we cannot have so strong and constant a regard: and also because imprudence and folly, appearing to bring its own punishment more immediately and constantly than injurious behaviour, it less needs the additional punishment, which would be inflicted upon it by others, had they the same sensible indignation against it, as against injustice, and fraud, and cruelty. Besides, unhappiness being in itself the natural object of compassion; the unhappiness which people bring upon themselves, though it be wilfully, excites in us some pity for them: and this of course lessens our displeasure against them. But still it is matter of experience, that we are formed so as to reflect very severely upon the greater instances of imprudent neglects and foolish rashness, both in ourselves and others. In instances of this kind, men often say of themselves with remorse, and of others with some indignation, that they deserved to suffer such calamities, because they brought them upon themselves,

and would not take warning. Particularly when persons come to poverty and distress by a long course of extravagance, and after frequent admonitions, though without falsehood or injustice; we plainly do not regard such people as alike objects of compassion with those, who are brought into the same condition by unavoidable accidents. From these things it appears, that prudence is a species of virtue, and folly of vice: meaning by *folly*, somewhat quite different from mere incapacity; a thoughtless want of that regard and attention to our own happiness, which we had capacity for. And this the word properly includes; and, as it seems, in its usual acceptation: for we scarce apply it to brute creatures.

7. However, if any person be disposed to dispute the matter, I shall very willingly give him up the words Virtue and Vice, as not applicable to prudence and folly: but must beg leave to insist, that the faculty within us, which is the judge of actions, approves of prudent actions, and disapproves imprudent ones; I say prudent and imprudent *actions* as such, and considered distinctly from the happiness or misery which they occasion. And, by the way, this observation may help to determine what justness there is in that objection against religion, that it teaches us to be interested and selfish.

8. Fifthly, without inquiring how far, and in what sense, virtue is resolvable into benevolence, and vice into the want of it; it may be proper to observe, that benevolence, and the want of it, singly considered, are in no sort the whole of virtue and vice. For if this were the case, in the review of one's own character, or that of others, our moral understanding and moral sense would be indifferent to everything, but the degrees in which benevolence prevailed, and the degrees in which it was wanting. That is, we should neither approve of benevolence to some persons rather than to others, nor disapprove injustice and falsehood upon any other account, than merely as an overbalance of happiness was foreseen likely to be produced by the first, and of misery by the second. But now, on the contrary, suppose two men competitors for anything whatever, which would be of equal advantage to each of them; though nothing indeed would be more impertinent, than for a stranger to busy himself to get one of them preferred to the other; yet such endeavour would be virtue, in behalf of a friend or benefactor, abstracted from all consideration of distant consequences: as that examples of gratitude, and the cultivation of friendship, would be of general good to the world. Again, suppose one man should, by fraud or violence, take from another the fruit of his labour, with intent to give it to a third, who he thought would have as much pleasure from it as would balance the pleasure which the first possessor would have had in the enjoyment, and his vexation in the loss of it; suppose also that no bad consequences would follow: yet such an action would surely be vicious. Nay further, were treachery, violence and injustice, no otherwise vicious, than as foreseen likely to produce an overbalance of misery to society; then, if in any case a man could procure to himself as great advantage by an act of injustice, as the whole foreseen inconvenience, likely to be brought upon others by it, would amount to; such a piece of injustice would not be faulty or vicious at all: because it would be no more than, in any other case, for a man to prefer his own satisfaction to another's in equal degrees. The fact then appears to be, that we are constituted so as to condemn falsehood, unprovoked violence, injustice, and to approve of benevolence to some preferably to others, abstracted from all consideration, which conduct is likeliest to produce an overbalance of happiness or misery. And therefore, were the Author of Nature to propose nothing to Himself as an end but the production of happiness, were His moral character merely that of benevolence; yet ours is not so. Upon that supposition indeed the only reason of His giving us the above mentioned approbation of benevolence to some persons rather than others, and disapprobation of falsehood, unprovoked violence, and injustice, must be, that He foresaw this constitution of our nature would produce more happiness, than forming us with a temper of mere general benevolence. But still, since this is our constitution; falsehood, violence, injustice, must be vice in us, and benevolence to some, preferably to others, virtue; abstracted from all consideration of the over-balance of evil or good, which they may appear likely to produce.

9. Now if human creatures are endued with such a moral nature as we have been explaining, or with a moral faculty, the natural object of which is actions; moral government must consist in rendering them happy and unhappy, in rewarding and punishing them, as they follow, neglect, or depart from, the moral rule of action interwoven in their nature, or suggested and enforced by this moral faculty; in rewarding and punishing them upon account of their so doing.

10. I am not sensible that I have, in this fifth observation, contradicted what any author designed to assert. But some of great and distinguished merit have, I think, expressed themselves in a manner, which may occasion some danger, to careless readers, of imagining the whole of virtue to consist in singly aiming, according to the best of their judgment, at promoting the happiness of mankind in the present state; and the whole of vice, in doing what they foresee, or might foresee, is likely to produce an overbalance of unhappiness in it; than which mistakes, none can be conceived more terrible. For it is certain, that some of the most shocking instances of injustice, adultery,

murder, perjury, and even of persecution, may, in many supposable cases, not have the appearance of being likely to produce an overbalance of misery in the present state; perhaps sometimes may have the contrary appearance. For this reflection might easily be carried on, but I forbear –. The happiness of the world is the concern of Him, Who is the Lord and the Proprietor of it: nor do we know what we are about, when we endeavour to promote the good of mankind in any ways, but those which He has directed; that is indeed in all ways not contrary to veracity and justice. I speak thus upon supposition of persons really endeavouring, in some sort, to do good without regard to these. But the truth seems to be, that such supposed endeavours proceed, almost always, from ambition, the spirit of party, or some indirect principle, concealed perhaps in great measure from persons themselves. And though it is our business and our duty to endeavour, within the bounds of veracity and justice, to contribute to the ease, convenience, and even cheerfulness and diversion of our fellow-creatures: yet, from our short views, it is greatly uncertain, whether this endeavour will in particular instances, produce an overbalance of happiness upon the whole; since so many and distant things must come into the account. And that which makes it our duty is, that there is some appearance that it will, and no positive appearance sufficient to balance this, on the contrary side; and also, that such benevolent endeavour is a cultivation of that most excellent of all virtuous principles, the active principle of benevolence.

11. However, though veracity, as well as justice, is to be our rule of life; it must be added, otherwise a snare will be laid in the way of some plain men, that the use of common forms of speech, generally understood, cannot be falsehood; and, in general, that there can be no designed falsehood without designing to deceive. It must likewise be observed, that in numberless cases, a man may be under the strictest obligations to what he foresees will deceive, without his intending it. For it is impossible not to foresee, that the words and actions of men, in different ranks and employments, and of different educations, will perpetually be mistaken by each other; and it cannot but be so, whilst they will judge with the utmost carelessness, as they daily do, of what they are not, perhaps, enough informed to be competent judges of, even though they considered it with great attention.

3

A Treatise of Human Nature and *An Enquiry Concerning the Principles of Morals*: Reason and the Passions

David Hume

According to Hume, the role of reason in ethics is less significant than many of his 'rationalist' contemporaries thought (Treatise of Human Nature 2.3.3.1, 3.1.1.4). They claimed that virtue is a matter of following reason, that reason could discern a priori certain necessary principles concerning what actions are 'fit' to do, and that virtue will often involve the conquering of passions or desires by reason. Hume will have none of this. Reason cannot move us, and it can neither give rise to nor oppose any passion: it is inert.

The role of reason, for Hume, is essentially twofold (T 2.3.3.2–4, 3.1.1.8–9). It is primarily concerned with demonstration, as for example in mathematics, or with assessing the relations between certain ideas or between certain objects (so if I am thirsty, it may tell me that the best means to satisfy my desire is to drink some water). The role of reason is to tell us how things are, not how they 'should' be; it is, as Hume famously says, 'the slave of the passions'. It cannot on its own reach any practical conclusion about what we ought to do; it can tell us only what *is*, and you cannot validly derive a practical conclusion from premises that don't themselves include an 'ought' (T 3.1.2.27).

This analysis applies to the whole of our practical life, including morality (T 3.1.1.5–7). If I judge that lying is wrong, that judgement will motivate me, at least to some extent, to avoid lying. This shows, Hume claims, that morality cannot be derived from reason. Since reason is inert, what lies at the root of morality must be passion. One question to consider here is whether the rationalist could not accept that any action, including any moral action, must be motivated by a desire, but insist that reason can grasp certain principles – that lying is wrong, for example – in such a way that desire, at least in a rational person, will follow understanding, rather than the other way round. Hume will claim this view rests on confusing 'calm' passions – such as a general concern for the welfare of others – with reason (T 2.3.3.8–10). As an empiricist, Hume must base his conclusions on experience; and here the rationalist may insist that Hume is introducing the idea of calm passions as a piece of ad hoc theory to counter the evidence of introspection.

Imagine you are given the choice between your finger's being scratched or the destruction of the world (T 2.3.3.6). Would it not be unreasonable to choose the latter? Again, Hume denies this. Reason cannot assess our passions. We can call some passions unreasonable, but only if they rest on a mistaken judgement about some object, or lead us to choose means unsuited to our ends. I might, for example, desire to experience some fairground ride, falsely believing that I will enjoy it; or take the number 7 bus, which goes north to Kidlington, because I want to get to Kennington, to the south. (One important question here is whether, for Hume, the means-end mistake is merely another example of a false judgement; if reason can itself tell us that we should pursue the right means to our ends, it is not clear why it cannot tell us about other substantive things, such as the wrongness of lying.)

History of Ethics – Essential Readings with Commentary, First Edition. Edited by Daniel Star and Roger Crisp.
© 2020 John Wiley & Sons Ltd. Published 2020 by John Wiley & Sons Ltd.

Moral principles, Hume argues, do not state facts (T 3.1.1.14). Reason does tell us about certain facts, such as the relations between objects, but the kind of relations we find in morality are identical to those between certain natural objects, and so cannot explain moral judgements (T 3.1.1.19, 24–6). Consider, for example, parricide; the relations here are the same whether we are talking about a human child's killing their father, or an oak sapling's causing the death of its parent. Moral properties are not 'out there' in the world for us to discern through reason or rational perception. Rather, they are like 'secondary qualities', such as colour, which we 'project' onto the world on the basis of our experience (T 3.1.1.26, I 1.5.21). The world is not 'really' red, but colourless. Light reflecting from this colourless world gives us certain 'internal' experiences, which lead us to see the world as coloured. The same is true with morality. We feel certain sentiments, which then change our attitudes toward lying and other actions.

The primary sentiments here are pleasure and pain (T 3.1.2.2–3, 3.3.1.1–2; Inquiry concerning the Principles of Morals 1.5.20–1). Because we have a natural sympathy for others, actions that tend to benefit them are agreeable, and those tending to harm them disagreeable (T 3.3.1.6–11). The idea of 'tendency' here is significant. Moral judgements are primarily not about actions, but about characters and their usual or general consequences for others (T 3.1.2.4, 3.3.1.4–5). Further, although our sentiments, such as love of others, are partial, morality itself is, in a sense, impartial, because it relies on our adopting a 'general' point of view, so that we can recognize the equal moral value of, say, justice in our own dealings and in the dealings of distant people many centuries ago.

Morality and virtue can be said to be natural or unnatural in various senses, and it is worth teasing them out; but in one especially important sense, some virtues, such as benevolence, are natural in a way that certain others, in particular justice, are not (T 3.1.2.7–10, 3.3.1.9–13). Feeling sympathy for others is a part of human nature, while, for instance, respecting the property of others is not. The institution of property has been developed by human beings over time. Both natural and artificial virtues, however, are described as virtuous because of their agreeableness to us, and they are agreeable because of their value to society at large. One important difference, according to Hume, is that we will find every naturally virtuous action agreeable, but in the case of justice we will approve only the general system as a whole, regretting individual cases when, say, a judge rules that the fruit of some hard-working person's labour must be given to an idler, because that is what the law requires.

Sympath - human nature

A Treatise of Human Nature

Book II – Of the Passions

Part III – Of the Will and Direct Passions

Section III – Of the Influencing Motives of the Will

Nothing is more usual in philosophy, and even in common life, than to talk of the combat of passion and reason, to give the preference to reason, and assert that men are only so far virtuous as they conform themselves to its dictates. Every rational creature, it is said, is obliged to regulate his actions by reason; and if any other motive or principle challenge the direction of his conduct, he ought to oppose it, till it be entirely subdued, or at least brought to a conformity with that superior principle. On this method of thinking the greatest part of moral philosophy, ancient and modern, seems to be founded; nor is there an ampler field, as well for metaphysical arguments, as popular declamations, than this supposed preeminence of reason above passion. The eternity, in variableness, and divine origin of the former, have been displayed to the best advantage: the blindness, inconstancy, and deceitfulness of the latter, have been as strongly insisted on. In order to show the fallacy of all this philosophy, I shall endeavor to prove *first*, that reason alone can never be a motive to any action of the will; and *secondly*, that it can never oppose passion in the direction of the will. *will. – passion & reason*

The understanding exerts itself after two different ways, as it judges from demonstration or probability; as it regards the abstract relations of our ideas, or those relations of objects of which experience only gives us information. I believe it scarce will be asserted, that the first species of reasoning alone is ever the cause of any action. As its proper province is the world of ideas, and as the will always places us in that of realities, demonstration and volition seem upon that account to be totally removed from each other. Mathematics, indeed, are useful in all mechanical operations, and arithmetic in almost every art and profession: but it is not of themselves they have any influence. Mechanics are the art of regulating the motions of bodies *to some designed end or purpose*; and the reason why we employ arithmetic in fixing the proportions of numbers, is only that we may discover the proportions of their influence and operation. A merchant is desirous of knowing the sum total of his accounts with any person: why? but that he may learn what sum will have the same *effects* in paying his debt, and going to market, as all the particular articles taken together. Abstract or demonstrative reasoning, therefore, never influences any of our actions, but only as it directs our judgment concerning causes and effects; which leads us to the second operation of the understanding.

It is obvious, that when we have the prospect of pain or pleasure from any object, we feel a consequent emotion of aversion or propensity, and are carried to avoid or embrace what will give us this uneasiness or satisfaction. It is also obvious, that this emotion rests not here, but, making us cast our view on every side, comprehends whatever objects are connected with its original one by the relation of cause and effect. Here then reasoning takes place to discover this relation; and according as our reasoning varies, our actions receive a subsequent variation. But it is evident, in this case, that the impulse arises not from reason, but is only directed by it. It is from the prospect of pain or pleasure that the aversion or propensity arises towards any object: and these emotions extend themselves to the causes and effects of that object, as they are pointed out to us by reason and experience. It can never in the least concern us to know, that such objects are causes, and such others effects, if both the causes and effects be indifferent to us. Where the objects themselves do not affect us, their connection can never give them any influence; and it is plain that, as reason is nothing but the discovery of this connection, it cannot be by its means that the objects are able to affect us.

Since reason alone can never produce any action, or give rise to volition, I infer, that the same faculty is as incapable of preventing volition, or of disputing the preference with any passion or emotion. This consequence is necessary. It is impossible reason could have the latter effect of preventing volition, but by giving an impulse in a contrary direction to our passions; and that impulse, had it operated alone, would have been ample to produce volition. Nothing can oppose or retard the impulse of passion, but a contrary impulse; and if this contrary impulse ever arises from reason, that latter faculty must have an original influence on the will, and must be able to cause, as well as hinder, any act of volition. But if reason has no original influence, it is impossible it can withstand any principle which has such an efficacy, or ever keep the mind in suspense a moment. Thus, it appears, that the principle which opposes our passion cannot be the same with reason, and is only called so in an improper sense. We speak not strictly and philosophically, when we talk of the combat of passion and of reason. Reason is, and ought only to be, the slave of the passions, and can never pretend to any other office than to serve and obey them. As this opinion may appear somewhat extraordinary, it may not be improper to confirm it by some other considerations.

A passion is an original existence, or, if you will, modification of existence, and contains not any representative quality, which renders it a copy of any other existence or modification. When I am angry, I am actually possessed with the passion, and in that emotion have no more a reference to any other object, than when I am thirsty, or sick, or more than five feet high. It is impossible, therefore, that this passion can be opposed by, or be contradictory to truth and reason; since this contradiction consists in the disagreement of ideas, considered as copies, with those objects which they represent.

What may at first occur on this head is, that as nothing can be contrary to truth or reason, except what has a reference to it, and as the judgments of our understanding only have this reference, it must follow, that passions can be contrary to reason only, so far as they are *accompanied* with some judgment or opinion. According to this principle, which is so obvious and natural, it is only in two senses that any affection can be called unreasonable. First, when a passion, such as hope or fear, grief or joy, despair or security, is founded on the supposition of the existence of objects, which really do not exist. Secondly, when in exerting any passion in action, we choose means insufficient for the designed end, and deceive ourselves in our judgment of causes and effects. Where a passion is neither founded on false suppositions, nor chooses means insufficient for the end, the understanding can neither justify nor condemn it. It is not contrary to reason to prefer the destruction of the whole world to the scratching of my finger. It is not contrary to reason for me to choose my total ruin, to prevent the least uneasiness of an Indian, or person wholly unknown to me. It is as little contrary to reason to prefer even my own acknowledged lesser good to my greater, and have a more ardent affection for the former than the latter. A trivial good may, from certain circumstances, produce a desire superior to what arises from the greatest and most valuable enjoyment; nor is there any thing more extraordinary in this, than in mechanics to see one pound weight raise up a hundred by the advantage of its situation. In short, a passion must be accompanied with some false judgment, in order to its being unreasonable; and even then, it is not the passion, properly speaking, which is unreasonable, but the judgment.

The consequences are evident. Since a passion can never, in any sense, be called unreasonable, but when founded on a false supposition, or when it chooses means insufficient for the designed end, it is impossible, that reason and passion can ever oppose each other, or dispute for the government of the will and actions. The moment we perceive the falsehood of any supposition, or the insufficiency of any means, our passions yield to our reason without any opposition. I may desire any fruit as of an excellent relish; but whenever you convince me of my mistake, my longing ceases. I may will the performance of certain actions as means of obtaining any desired good; but as my willing of these actions is only secondary, and founded on the supposition that they are causes of the proposed effect; as soon as I discover the falsehood of that supposition, they must become indifferent to me.

It is natural for one, that does not examine objects with a strict philosophic eye, to imagine, that those actions of the mind are entirely the same, which produce not a different sensation, and are not immediately distinguishable to the feeling and perception. Reason, for instance, exerts itself without producing any sensible emotions; and except in the more sublime disquisitions of philosophy, or in the frivolous subtilties of the schools, scarce ever conveys any pleasure or uneasiness. Hence it proceeds, that every action of the mind which operates with the same calmness and tranquillity, is confounded with reason by all those who judge of things from the first view and appearance. Now it is certain there are certain calm desires and tendencies, which, though they be real passions, produce little emotion in the mind, and are more known by their effects than by the immediate feeling or sensation. These desires are of two kinds; either certain instincts originally implanted in our natures, such as benevolence and resentment, the love of life, and kindness to children; or the general appetite to good, and aversion to evil, considered merely as such. When any of these passions are calm, and cause no disorder in the soul, they are very readily taken for the determinations of reason, and are supposed to proceed from the same faculty with that which judges of truth and falsehood. Their nature and principles have been supposed the same, because their sensations are not evidently different.

Beside these calm passions, which often determine the will, there are certain violent emotions of the same kind, which have likewise a great influence on that faculty. When I receive any injury from another, I often feel a violent passion of resentment, which makes me desire his evil and punishment, independent of all considerations of pleasure and advantage to myself. When I am immediately threatened with any grievous ill, my fears, apprehensions, and aversions rise to a great height, and produce a sensible emotion.

The common error of metaphysicians has lain in ascribing the direction of the will entirely to one of these principles, and supposing the other to have no influence. Men often act knowingly against their interest; for which reason, the view of the greatest possible good does not always influence them. Men often counteract a violent passion in prosecution of their interests and designs; it is not, therefore, the present uneasiness alone which determines them. In general we may observe, that both these principles operate on the will; and where they are contrary, that either of them prevails, according to the *general* character or *present* disposition of the person. What we call strength of mind, implies the prevalence of the calm passions above the violent; though we may easily observe, there is no man so constantly possessed of this virtue, as never on any occasion to yield to the solicitations of passion and desire. From these variations of temper proceeds the great difficulty of deciding concerning the actions and resolutions of men, where there is any contrariety of motives and passions.

[…]

Book III – Of Morals

Part I – Of Virtue and Vice in General

Section I – Moral Distinctions Not Derived From Reason

There is an inconvenience which attends all abstruse reasoning, that it may silence, without convincing an antagonist, and requires the same intense study to make us sensible of its force, that was at first requisite for its invention. When we leave our closet, and engage in the common affairs of life, its conclusions seem to vanish like the phantoms of the night on the appearance of the morning; and it is difficult for us to retain even that conviction which we had attained with difficulty. This is still more conspicuous in a long chain of reasoning, where we must preserve to the end the evidence of the first propositions, and where we often lose sight of all the most received maxims, either of philosophy or common life. I am not, however, without hopes, that the present system of philosophy will acquire new force as it advances; and that our reasonings concerning *morals* will corroborate whatever has been said concerning the *understanding* and the *passions*. Morality is a subject that interests us above all others; we fancy the peace of society to be at stake in every decision concerning it; and it is evident that this concern must make our speculations appear more real and solid, than where the subject is in a great measure indifferent to us. What affects us, we conclude can never be a chimera; and, as our passion is engaged on the one side or the other, we naturally think that the question lies within human comprehension; which, in other cases of this nature, we are apt to entertain some doubt of. Without this advantage, I never should have ventured upon a third volume of such abstruse philosophy, in an age wherein the greatest part of men seem agreed to convert reading into an amusement, and to reject every thing that requires any considerable degree of attention to be comprehended.

It has been observed, that nothing is ever present to the mind but its perceptions; and that all the actions of seeing, hearing, judging, loving, hating, and thinking, fall under this denomination. The mind can never exert itself in any action which we may not comprehend under the term of *perception*; and consequently that term is no less applicable to those judgments by which we distinguish moral good and evil, than to every other operation of the mind. To approve of one character, to condemn another, are only so many different perceptions.

Now, as perceptions resolve themselves into two kinds, viz. *impressions* and *ideas*, this distinction gives rise to a question, with which we shall open up our present inquiry concerning morals, *whether it is by means of our ideas or impressions we distinguish betwixt vice and virtue, and pronounce an action blamable or praiseworthy?* This will immediately cut off all loose discourses and declamations, and reduce us to something precise and exact on the present subject.

Those who affirm that virtue is nothing but a conformity to reason; that there are eternal fitnesses and unfitnesses of things, which are the same to every rational being that considers them; that the immutable measure of right and wrong impose an obligation, not only on human creatures, but also on the Deity himself: all these systems concur in the opinion, that morality, like truth, is discerned merely by ideas, and by their juxtaposition and comparison. In order, therefore, to judge of these systems, we need only consider whether it be possible from reason alone, to distinguish betwixt moral good and evil, or whether there must concur some other principles to enable us to make that distinction.

If morality had naturally no influence on human passions and actions, it were in vain to take such pains to inculcate it; and nothing would be more fruitless than that multitude of rules and precepts with which all moralists abound. Philosophy is commonly divided into *speculative* and *practical*; and as morality is always comprehended under the latter division, it is supposed to influence our passions and actions, and to go beyond the calm and indolent judgments of the understanding. And this is confirmed by common experience, which informs us, that men are often governed by their duties, and are deterred from some actions by the opinion of injustice, and impelled to others by that of obligation.

Since morals, therefore, have an influence on the actions and affections, it follows, that they cannot be derived from reason; and that because reason alone, as we have already proved, can never have any such influence. Morals excite passions, and produce or prevent actions. Reason of itself is utterly impotent in this particular. The rules of morality, therefore, are not conclusions of our reason.

No one, I believe, will deny the justness of this inference; nor is there any other means of evading it, than by denying that principle, on which it is founded. As long as it is allowed, that reason has no influence on our passions and actions, it is in vain to pretend that morality is discovered only by a deduction of reason. An active principle can never be founded on an inactive; and if reason be inactive in itself, it must remain so in all its shapes and appearances, whether it exerts itself in natural or moral subjects, whether it considers the powers of external bodies, or the actions of rational beings.

It would be tedious to repeat all the arguments, by which I have proved,[1] that reason is perfectly inert, and can never either prevent or produce any action or affection. It will be easy to recollect what has been said upon that subject. I shall only recall on this occasion one of these arguments, which I shall endeavor to render still more conclusive, and more applicable to the present subject.

Reason is the discovery of truth or falsehood. Truth or falsehood consists in an agreement or disagreement either to the *real* relations of ideas, or to *real* existence and matter of fact. Whatever therefore is not susceptible of this agreement or disagreement, is incapable of being true or false, and can never be an object of our reason. Now, it is evident our passions, volitions, and actions, are not susceptible of any such agreement or disagreement; being original facts and realities, complete in themselves, and implying no reference to other passions, volitions, and actions. It is impossible, therefore, they can be pronounced either true or false, and be either contrary or conformable to reason.

This argument is of double advantage to our present purpose. For it proves *directly*, that actions do not derive their merit from a conformity to reason, nor their blame from a contrariety to it; and it proves the same truth more *indirectly*, by showing us, that as reason can never immediately prevent or produce any action by contradicting or approving of it, it cannot be the source of moral good and evil, which are found to have that influence. Actions may be laudable or blamable; but they cannot be reasonable or unreasonable: laudable or blamable, therefore, are not the same with reasonable or unreasonable. The merit and demerit of actions frequently contradict, and sometimes control our natural propensities. But reason has no such influence. Moral distinctions, therefore, are not the offspring of reason. Reason is wholly inactive, and can never be the source of so active a principle as conscience, or a sense of morals.

But perhaps it may be said, that though no will or action can be immediately contradictory to reason, yet we may find such a contradiction in some of the attendants of the actions, that is, in its causes or effects. The action may cause a judgment, or may be *obliquely* caused by one, when the judgment concurs with a passion; and by an abusive way of speaking, which philosophy will scarce allow of, the same contrariety may, upon that account, be ascribed to the action. How far this truth or falsehood may be the source of morals, it will now be proper to consider.

It has been observed, that reason, in a strict and philosophical sense, can have an influence on our conduct only after two ways: either when it excites a passion, by informing us of the existence of something which is a proper object of it; or when it discovers the connection of causes and effects, so as to afford us means of exerting any passion. These are the only kinds of judgment which can accompany our actions, or can be said to produce them in any manner; and it must be allowed, that these judgments may often be false and erroneous. A person may be affected with passion, by supposing a pain or pleasure to lie in an object which has no tendency to produce either of these sensations, or which produces the contrary to what is imagined. A person may also take false measures for the attaining of his end, and may retard, by his foolish conduct, instead of forwarding the execution of any object. These false judgments may be thought to affect the passions and actions, which are connected with them, and may be said to render them unreasonable, in a figurative and improper way of speaking. But though this be acknowledged, it is easy to observe, that these errors are so far from being the source of all immorality, that they are commonly very innocent, and draw no manner of guilt upon the person who is so unfortunate as to fall into them. They extend not beyond a mistake of *fact*, which moralists have not generally supposed criminal, as being perfectly involuntary. I am more to be lamented than blamed, if I am mistaken with regard to the influence of objects in producing pain or pleasure, or if I know not the proper means of satisfying my desires. No one can ever regard such errors as a defect in my moral character. A fruit, for instance, that is really disagreeable, appears to me at a distance, and, through mistake, I fancy it to be pleasant and delicious. Here is one error. I choose certain means of reaching this fruit, which are not proper for my end. Here is a second error; nor is there any third one, which can ever possibly enter into our reasonings concerning actions. I ask, therefore, if a man in this situation, and guilty of these two errors, is to be regarded as vicious and criminal, however unavoidable they might have been? Or if it be possible to imagine, that such errors are the sources of all immorality?

And here it may be proper to observe, that if moral distinctions be derived from the truth or falsehood of those judgments, they must take place wherever we form the judgments; nor will there be any difference, whether the question be concerning an apple or a kingdom, or whether the error be avoidable or unavoidable.

---

[1] Book II. Part III. Sect. 3.

For as the very essence of morality is supposed to consist in an agreement or disagreement to reason, the other circumstances are entirely arbitrary, and can never either bestow on any action the character of virtuous or vicious, or deprive it of that character. To which we may add, that this agreement or disagreement, not admitting of degrees, all virtues and vices would of course be equal.

Should it be pretended, that though a mistake of *fact* be not criminal, yet a mistake of *right* often is; and that this may be the source of immorality: I would answer, that it is impossible such a mistake can ever be the original source of immorality, since it supposes a real right and wrong; that is, a real distinction in morals, independent of these judgments. A mistake, therefore, of right, may become a species of immorality; but it is only a secondary one, and is founded on some other antecedent to it.

As to those judgments which are the *effects* of our actions, and which, when false, give occasion to pronounce the actions contrary to truth and reason; we may observe, that our actions never cause any judgment, either true or false, in ourselves, and that it is only on others they have such an influence. It is certain that an action, on many occasions, may give rise to false conclusions in others; and that a person, who, through a window, sees any lewd behavior of mine with my neighbor's wife, may be so simple as to imagine she is certainly my own. In this respect my action resembles somewhat a lie or falsehood; only with this difference, which is material, that I perform not the action with any intention of giving rise to a false judgment in another, but merely to satisfy my lust and passion. It causes, however, a mistake and false judgment by accident; and the falsehood of its effects may be ascribed, by some odd figurative way of speaking, to the action itself. But still I can see no pretext of reason for asserting, that the tendency to cause such an error is the first spring or original source of all immorality.[2]

Thus, upon the whole, it is impossible that the distinction betwixt moral good and evil can be made by reason; since that distinction has an influence upon our actions, of which reason alone is incapable. Reason and judgment may, indeed, be the mediate cause of an action, by prompting or by directing a passion; but it is not pretended that a judgment of this kind, either in its truth or falsehood, is attended with virtue or vice. And as to the judgments, which are caused by our judgments, they can still less bestow those moral qualities on the actions which are their causes.

---

[2] One might think it were entirely superfluous to prove this, if a late author, who has had the good fortune to obtain some reputation, had not seriously affirmed, that such a falsehood is the foundation of all guilt and moral deformity. That we may discover the fallacy of his hypothesis, we need only consider, that a false conclusion is drawn from an action, only by means of an obscurity of natural principles, which makes a cause be secretly interrupted in its operation, by contrary causes, and renders the connection betwixt two objects uncertain and variable. Now, as a like uncertainty and variety of causes take place, even in natural objects, and produce a like error in our judgment, if that tendency to produce error were the very essence of vice and immorality, it should follow, that even inanimate objects might be vicious and immoral.

It is in vain to urge, that inanimate objects act without liberty and choice. For as liberty and choice are not necessary to make an action produce in us an erroneous conclusion, they can be, in no respect, essential to morality; and I do not readily perceive, upon this system, how they can ever come to be regarded by it. If the tendency to cause error be the origin of immorality, that tendency and immorality would in every case be inseparable.

Add to this, that if I had used the precaution of shutting the window, while I indulged myself in those liberties with my neighbor's wife, I should have been guilty of no immorality; and that because my action, being perfectly concealed, would have had no tendency to produce any false conclusion.

For the same reason, a thief, who steals in by a ladder at a window, and takes all imaginable care to cause no disturbance, is in no respect criminal. For either he will not be perceived, or if he be it is impossible he can produce any error, nor will any one, from these circumstances, take him to be other than what he really is.

It is well known, that those who are squint-sighted do very readily cause mistakes in others, and that we imagine they salute or are talking to one person, while they address themselves to another. Are they, therefore, upon that account, immoral?

Besides, we may easily observe, that in all those arguments there is an evident reasoning in a circle. A person who takes possession of *another's* goods, and uses them as his *own*, in a manner declares them to be his own; and this falsehood is the source of the immorality of injustice. But is property, or right, or obligation, intelligible without an antecedent morality?

A man that is ungrateful to his benefactor, in a manner affirms that he never received any favors from him. But in what manner? Is it because it is his duty to be grateful? But this supposes that there is some antecedent rule of duty and morals. Is it because human nature is generally grateful, and makes us conclude that a man who does any harm, never receives any favor from the person he harmed? But human nature is not so generally grateful as to justify such a conclusion; or, if it were, is an exception to a general rule in every case criminal, for no other reason than because it is an exception?

But what may suffice entirely to destroy this whimsical system is, that it leaves us under the same difficulty to give a reason why truth is virtuous and falsehood vicious, as to account for the merit or turpitude of any other action. I shall allow, if you please, that all immorality is derived from this supposed falsehood in action, provided you can give me any plausible reason why such a falsehood is immoral. If you consider rightly of the matter, you will find yourself in the same difficulty as at the beginning.

This last argument is very conclusive; because, if there be not an evident merit or turpitude annexed to this species of truth or falsehood, it can never have any influence upon our actions. For who ever thought of forbearing any action, because others might possibly draw false conclusions from it? Or who ever performed any, that he might give rise to true conclusions?

But, to be more particular, and to show that those eternal immutable fitnesses and unfitnesses of things cannot be defended by sound philosophy, we may weigh the following considerations.

If the thought and understanding were alone capable of fixing the boundaries of right and wrong, the character of virtuous and vicious either must lie in some relations of objects, or must be a matter of fact which is discovered by our reasoning. This consequence is evident. As the operations of human understanding divide themselves into two kinds, the comparing of ideas, and the inferring of matter of fact, were virtue discovered by the understanding, it must be an object of one of these operations; nor is there any third operation of the understanding which can discover it. There has been an opinion very, industriously propagated by certain philosophers, that morality is susceptible of demonstration; and though no one has ever been able to advance a single step in those demonstrations, yet it is taken for granted that this science may be brought to an equal certainty with geometry or algebra. Upon this supposition, vice and virtue must consist in some relations; since it is allowed on all hands, that no matter of fact is capable of being demonstrated. Let us therefore begin with examining this hypothesis, and endeavor, if possible, to fix those moral qualities which have been so long the objects of our fruitless researches; point out distinctly the relations which constitute morality or obligation, that we may know wherein they consist, and after what manner we must judge of them.

If you assert that vice and virtue consist in relations susceptible of certainty and demonstration, you must confine yourself to those *four* relations which alone admit of that degree of evidence; and in that case you run into absurdities from which you will never be able to extricate yourself. For as you make the very essence of morality to lie in the relations, and as there is no one of these relations but what is applicable, not only to an irrational but also to an inanimate object, it follows, that even such objects must be susceptible of merit or demerit. *Resemblance, contrariety, degrees in quality, and proportions in quantity and number,* all these relations belong as properly to matter, as to our actions, passions, and volitions. It is unquestionable, therefore, that morality lies not in any of these relations, nor the sense of it in their discovery.[3]

Should it be asserted, that the sense of morality consists in the discovery of some relation distinct from these, and that our enumeration was not complete when we comprehended all demonstrable relations under four general heads; to this I know not what to reply, till some one be so good as to point out to me this new relation. It is impossible to refute a system which has never yet been explained. In such a manner of fighting in the dark, a man loses his blows in the air, and often places them where the enemy is not present.

I must therefore, on this occasion, rest contented with requiring the two following conditions of any one that would undertake to clear up this system. *First,* as moral good and evil belong only to the actions of the mind, and are derived from our situation with regard to external objects, the relations from which these moral distinctions arise must lie only betwixt internal actions and external objects, and must not be applicable either to internal actions, compared among themselves, or to external objects, when placed in opposition to other external objects. For as morality is supposed to attend certain relations, if these relations could belong to internal actions considered singly, it would follow, that we might be guilty of crimes in ourselves, and independent of our situation with respect to the universe; and in like manner, if these moral relations could be applied to external objects, it would follow, that even inanimate beings would be susceptible of moral beauty and deformity. Now, it seems difficult to imagine that any relation can be discovered betwixt our passions, volitions, and actions, compared to external objects, which relation might not belong either to these passions and volitions, or to these external objects, compared among *themselves.*

But it will be still more difficult to fulfil the *second* condition, requisite to justify this system. According to the principles of those who maintain an abstract rational difference betwixt moral good and evil, and a natural fitness and unfitness of things, it is not only supposed, that these relations, being eternal and immutable, are the same, when considered by every rational creature, but their *effects* are also supposed to be necessarily the same; and it is concluded they have no less, or rather a greater, influence in directing the will of the Deity, than in governing the

---

[3] As a proof how confused our way of thinking on this subject commonly is, we may observe, that those who assert that morality is demonstrable, do not say that morality lies in the relations, and that the relations are distinguishable by reason. They only say, that reason can discover such an action, in such relations, to be virtuous, and such another vicious. It seems they thought it sufficient if they could bring the word Relation into the proposition, without troubling themselves whether it was to the purpose or not. But here, I think, is plain argument. Demonstrative reason discovers only relations. But that reason, according to this hypothesis, discovers also vice and virtue. These moral qualities, therefore, must be relations. When we blame any action, in any situation, the whole complicated object of action and situation must form certain relations, wherein the essence of vice consists. This hypothesis is not otherwise intelligible. For what does reason discover, when it pronounces any action vicious? Does it discover a relation or a matter of fact? These questions are decisive, and must not be eluded.

rational and virtuous of our own species. These two particulars are evidently distinct. It is one thing to know virtue, and another to conform the will to it. In order, therefore, to prove that the measures of right and wrong are eternal laws, *obligatory* on every rational mind, it is not sufficient to show the relations upon which they are founded: we must also point out the connection betwixt the relation and the will; and must prove that this connection is so necessary, that in every well-disposed mind, it must take place and have its influence; though the difference betwixt these minds be in other respects immense and infinite. Now, besides what I have already proved, that even in human nature no relation can ever alone produce any action; besides this, I say, it has been shown, in treating of the understanding, that there is no connection of cause and effect, such as this is supposed to be, which is discoverable otherwise than by experience, and of which we can pretend to have any security by the simple consideration of the objects. All beings in the universe, considered in themselves, appear entirely loose and independent of each other. It is only by experience we learn their influence and connection; and this influence we ought never to extend beyond experience.

Thus it will be impossible to fulfil the *first* condition required to the system of eternal rational measures of right and wrong; because it is impossible to show those relations, upon which such a distinction may be founded: and it is as impossible to fulfil the *second* condition; because we cannot prove a priori, that these relations, if they really existed and were perceived, would be universally forcible and obligatory.

But to make these general reflections more clear and convincing, we may illustrate them by some particular instances, wherein this character of moral good or evil is the most universally acknowledged. Of all crimes that human creatures are capable of committing, the most horrid and unnatural is ingratitude, especially when it is committed against parents, and appears in the more flagrant instances of wounds and death. This is acknowledged by all mankind, philosophers as well as the people: the question only arises among philosophers, whether the guilt or moral deformity of this action be discovered by demonstrative reasoning, or be felt by an internal sense, and by means of some sentiment, which the reflecting on such an action naturally occasions. This question will soon be decided against the former opinion, if we can show the same relations in other objects, without the notion of any guilt or iniquity attending them. Reason or science is nothing but the comparing of ideas, and the discovery of their relations; and if the same relations have different characters, it must evidently follow, that those characters are not discovered merely by reason. To put the affair, therefore, to this trial, let us choose any inanimate object, such as an oak or elm; and let us suppose, that, by the dropping of its seed, it produces a sapling below it, which, springing up by degrees, at last overtops and destroys the parent tree: I ask, if, in this instance, there be wanting any relation which is discoverable in parricide or ingratitude? Is not the one tree the cause of the other's existence; and the latter the cause of the destruction of the former, in the same manner as when a child murders his parent? It is not sufficient to reply, that a choice or will is wanting. For in the case of parricide, a will does not give rise to any *different* relations, but is only the cause from which the action is derived; and consequently produces the *same* relations, that in the oak or elm arise from some other principles. It is a will or choice that determines a man to kill his parent: and they are the laws of matter and motion, that determine a sapling to destroy the oak from which it sprung. Here then the same relations have different causes; but still the relations are the same: and as their discovery is not in both cases attended with a notion of immorality, it follows, that that notion does not arise from such a discovery.

But to choose an instance still more resembling; I would fain ask any one, why incest in the human species is criminal, and why the very same action, and the same relations in animals, have not the smallest moral turpitude and deformity? If it be answered, that this action is innocent in animals, because they have not reason sufficient to discover its turpitude; but that man, being endowed with that faculty, which ought to restrain him to his duty, the same action instantly becomes criminal to him. Should this be said, I would reply, that this is evidently arguing in a circle. For, before reason can perceive this turpitude, the turpitude must exist; and consequently is independent of the decisions of our reason, and is their object more properly than their effect. According to this system, then, every animal that has sense and appetite and will, that is, every animal must be susceptible of all the same virtues and vices, for which we ascribe praise and blame to human creatures. All the difference is, that our superior reason may serve to discover the vice or virtue, and by that means may augment the blame or praise: but still this discovery supposes a separate being in these moral distinctions, and a being which depends only on the will and appetite, and which, both in thought and reality, may be distinguished from reason. Animals are susceptible of the same relations with respect to each other as the human species, and therefore would also be susceptible of the same morality, if the essence of morality consisted in these relations. Their want of a sufficient degree of reason may hinder them from perceiving the duties and obligations of morality, but can never hinder these duties from existing; since they must antecedently exist, in order to their being perceived. Reason must find them, and can never produce them. This argument deserves to be weighed, as being, in my opinion, entirely decisive.

Nor does this reasoning only prove, that morality consists not in any relations that are the objects of science; but if examined, will prove with equal certainty, that it consists not in any *matter of fact*, which can be discovered by the understanding. This is the *second* part of our argument; and if it can be made evident, we may conclude, that morality is not an object of reason. But can there be any difficulty in proving, that vice and virtue are not matters of fact, whose existence we can infer by reason? Take any action allowed to be vicious; wilful murder, for instance. Examine it in all lights, and see if you can find that matter of fact, or real existence, which you call *vice*. In whichever way you take it, you find only certain passions, motives, volitions, and thoughts. There is no other matter of fact in the case. The vice entirely escapes you, as long as you consider the object. You never can find it, till you turn your reflection into your own breast, and find a sentiment of disapprobation, which arises in you, towards this action. Here is a matter of fact; but it is the object of feeling, not of reason. It lies in yourself, not in the object. So that when you pronounce any action or character to be vicious, you mean nothing, but that from the constitution of your nature you have a feeling or sentiment of blame from the contemplation of it. Vice and virtue, therefore, may be compared to sounds, colors, heat, and cold, which, according to modern philosophy, are not qualities in objects, but perceptions in the mind: and this discovery in morals, like that other in physics, is to be regarded as a considerable advancement of the speculative sciences; though, like that too, it has little or no influence on practice. Nothing can be more real, or concern us more, than our own sentiments of pleasure and uneasiness; and if these be favorable to virtue, and unfavorable to vice, no more can be requisite to the regulation of our conduct and behavior.

I cannot forbear adding to these reasonings an observation, which may, perhaps, be found of some importance. In every system of morality which I have hitherto met with, I have always remarked, that the author proceeds for some time in the ordinary way of reasoning, and establishes the being of a God, or makes observations concerning human affairs; when of a sudden I am surprised to find, that instead of the usual copulations of propositions, *is*, and *is not*, I meet with no proposition that is not connected with an *ought*, or an *ought not*. This change is imperceptible; but is, however, of the last consequence. For as this *ought*, or *ought not*, expresses some new relation or affirmation, it is necessary that it should be observed and explained; and at the same time that a reason should be given, for what seems altogether inconceivable, how this new relation can be a deduction from others, which are entirely different from it. But as authors do not commonly use this precaution, I shall presume to recommend it to the readers; and am persuaded, that this small attention would subvert all the vulgar systems of morality, and let us see, that the distinction of vice and virtue is not founded merely on the relations of objects, nor is perceived by reason.

Section II – Moral Distinctions Derived From a Moral Sense

Thus the course of the argument leads us to conclude, that since vice and virtue are not discoverable merely by reason, or the comparison of ideas, it must be by means of some impression or sentiment they occasion, that we are able to mark the difference betwixt them. Our decisions concerning moral rectitude and depravity are evidently perceptions; and as all perceptions are either impressions or ideas, the exclusion of the one is a convincing argument for the other. Morality, therefore, is more properly felt than judged of; though this feeling or sentiment is commonly so soft and gentle that we are apt to confound it with an idea, according to our common custom of taking all things for the same which have any near resemblance to each other.

The next question is, of what nature are these impressions, and after what manner do they operate upon us? Here we cannot remain long in suspense, but must pronounce the impression arising from virtue to be agreeable, and that proceeding from vice to be uneasy. Every moment's experience must convince us of this. There is no spectacle so fair and beautiful as a noble and generous action; nor any which gives us more abhorrence than one that is cruel and treacherous. No enjoyment equals the satisfaction we receive from the company of those we love and esteem; as the greatest of all punishments is to be obliged to pass our lives with those we hate or contemn. A very play or romance may afford us instances of this pleasure which virtue conveys to us; and pain, which arises from vice.

Now, since the distinguishing impressions by which moral good or evil is known, are nothing but *particular* pains or pleasures, it follows, that in all inquiries concerning these moral distinctions, it will be sufficient to show the principles which make us feel a satisfaction or uneasiness from the survey of any character, in order to satisfy us why the character is laudable or blamable. An action, or sentiment, or character, is virtuous or vicious; why? because its view causes a pleasure or uneasiness of a particular kind. In giving a reason, therefore, for the pleasure or uneasiness, we sufficiently explain the vice or virtue. To have the sense of virtue, is nothing but to *feel* a satisfaction of a particular kind from the contemplation of a character. The very *feeling* constitutes our praise or admiration. We go no further; nor do we inquire into the cause of the satisfaction. We do not infer a character to be virtuous, because it pleases; but in feeling that it pleases after such a particular manner, we in effect feel that it is virtuous. The case is the same as in our judgments concerning all kinds of beauty, and tastes, and sensations. Our approbation is implied in the immediate pleasure they convey to us.

I have objected to the system which establishes eternal rational measures of right and wrong, that it is impossible to show, in the actions of reasonable creatures, any relations which are not found in external objects; and therefore, if morality always attended these relations, it were possible for inanimate matter to become virtuous or vicious. Now it may, in like manner, be objected to the present system, that if virtue and vice be determined by pleasure and pain, these qualities must, in every case, arise from the sensations; and consequently any object, whether animate or inanimate, rational or irrational, might become morally good or evil, provided it can excite a satisfaction or uneasiness. But though this objection seems to be the very same, it has by no means the same force in the one case as in the other. For, *first*, it is evident that, under the term *pleasure*, we comprehend sensations, which are very different from each other, and which have only such a distant resemblance as is requisite to make them be expressed by the same abstract term. A good composition of music and a bottle of good wine equally produce pleasure; and, what is more, their goodness is determined merely by the pleasure. But shall we say, upon that account, that the wine is harmonious, or the music of a good flavor? In like manner, an inanimate object, and the character or sentiments of any person, may, both of them, give satisfaction; but, as the satisfaction is different, this keeps our sentiments concerning them from being confounded, and makes us ascribe virtue to the one and not to the other. Nor is every sentiment of pleasure or pain which arises from characters and actions, of that peculiar kind which makes us praise or condemn. The good qualities of an enemy are hurtful to us, but may still command our esteem and respect. It is only when a character is considered in general, without reference to our particular interest, that it causes such a feeling or sentiment as denominates it morally good or evil. It is true, those sentiments from interest and morals are apt to be confounded, and naturally run into one another. It seldom happens that we do not think an enemy vicious, and can distinguish betwixt his opposition to our interest and real villany or baseness. But this hinders not but that the sentiments are in themselves distinct; and a man of temper and judgment may preserve himself from these illusions. In like manner, though it is certain a musical voice is nothing but one that naturally gives a *particular* kind of pleasure; yet it is difficult for a man to be sensible that the voice of an enemy is agreeable, or to allow it to be musical. But a person of a fine ear, who has the command of himself, can separate these feelings, and give praise to what deserves it.

Secondly, we may call to remembrance the preceding system of the passions, in order to remark a still more considerable difference among our pains and pleasures. Pride and humility, love and hatred, are excited, when there is any thing presented to us that both bears a relation to the object of the passion, and produces a separate sensation, related to the sensation of the passion. Now, virtue and vice are attended with these circumstances. They must necessarily be placed either in ourselves or others, and excite either pleasure or uneasiness; and therefore must give rise to one of these four passions, which clearly distinguishes them from the pleasure and pain arising from inanimate objects, that often bear no relation to us; and this is, perhaps, the most considerable effect that virtue and vice have upon the human mind.

It may now be asked, *in general*, concerning this pain or pleasure that distinguishes moral good and evil, *From what principle is it derived, and whence does it arise in the human mind?* To this I reply, *first*, that it is absurd to imagine that, in every particular instance, these sentiments are produced by an *original* quality and *primary* constitution. For as the number of our duties is in a manner infinite, it is impossible that our original instincts should extend to each of them, and from our very first infancy impress on the human mind all that multitude of precepts which are contained in the completest system of ethics. Such a method of proceeding is not conformable to the usual maxims by which nature is conducted, where a few principles produce all that variety we observe in the universe, and every thing is carried on in the easiest and most simple manner. It is necessary, therefore, to abridge these primary impulses, and find some more general principles upon which all our notions of morals are founded.

But, in the *second* place, should it be asked, whether we ought to search for these principles in *nature*, or whether we must look for them in some other origin? I would reply, that our answer to this question depends upon the definition of the word Nature, than which there is none more ambiguous and equivocal. If nature be opposed to miracles, not only the distinction betwixt vice and virtue is natural, but also every event which has ever happened in the world, *excepting those miracles on which our religion is founded*. In saying, then, that the sentiments of vice and virtue are natural in this sense, we make no very extraordinary discovery.

But nature may also be opposed to rare and unusual; and in this sense of the word, which is the common one, there may often arise disputes concerning what is natural or unnatural; and one may in general affirm, that we are not possessed of any very precise standard by which these disputes can be decided. Frequent and rare depend upon the number of examples we have observed; and as this number may gradually increase or diminish, it will be impossible to fix any exact boundaries betwixt them. We may only affirm on this head, that if ever there was any thing which could be called natural in this sense, the sentiments of morality certainly may; since there never was any nation of the world, nor any single person in any nation, who was utterly deprived of them, and who never, in any instance, showed the least approbation or dislike of manners. These sentiments are so rooted in our constitution and temper, that, without entirely confounding the human mind by disease or madness, it is impossible to extirpate and destroy them.

But nature may also be opposed to artifice, as well as to what is rare and unusual; and in this sense it may be disputed, whether the notions of virtue be natural or not. We readily forget, that the designs, and projects, and views of men are principles as necessary in their operation as heat and cold, moist and dry; but, taking them to be free and entirely our own, it is usual for us to set them in opposition to the other principles of nature. Should it therefore be demanded, whether the sense of virtue be natural or artificial, I am of opinion that it is impossible for me at present to give any precise answer to this question. Perhaps it will appear afterwards that our sense of some virtues is artificial, and that of others natural. The discussion of this question will be more proper, when we enter upon an exact detail of each particular vice and virtue.[4]

Meanwhile, it may not be amiss to observe, from these definitions of *natural* and *unnatural*, that nothing can be more unphilosophical than those systems which assert, that virtue is the same with what is natural, and vice with what is unnatural. For, in the first sense of the word, nature, as opposed to miracles, both vice and virtue are equally natural; and, in the second sense, as opposed to what is unusual, perhaps virtue will be found to be the most unnatural. At least it must be owned, that heroic virtue, being as unusual, is as little natural as the most brutal barbarity. As to the third sense of the word, it is certain that both vice and virtue are equally artificial and out of nature. For, however it may be disputed, whether the notion of a merit or demerit in certain actions, be natural or artificial, it is evident that the actions themselves are artificial, and performed with a certain design and intention; otherwise they could never be ranked under any of these denominations. It is impossible, therefore, that the character of natural and unnatural can ever, in any sense, mark the boundaries of vice and virtue.

Thus we are still brought back to our first position, that virtue is distinguished by the pleasure, and vice by the pain, that any action, sentiment, or character, gives us by the mere view and contemplation. This decision is very commodious; because it reduces us to this simple question, *Why any action or sentiment, upon the general view or survey, gives a certain satisfaction or uneasiness,* in order to show the origin of its moral rectitude or depravity, without looking for any incomprehensible relations and qualities, which never did exist in nature, nor even in our imagination, by any clear and distinct conception? I flatter myself I have executed a great part of my present design by a state of the question, which appears to me so free from ambiguity and obscurity.

[…]

Part III – Of the Other Virtues and Vices

Section I – Of the Origin of the Natural Virtues and Vices

We come now to the examination of such virtues and vices as are entirely natural, and have no dependence on the artifice and contrivance of men. The examination of these will conclude this system of morals.

The chief spring or actuating principle of the human mind is pleasure or pain; and when these sensations are removed, both from our thought and feeling, we are in a great measure incapable of passion or action, of desire or volition. The most immediate effects of pleasure and pain are the propense and averse motions of the mind; which are diversified into volition, into desire and aversion, grief and joy, hope and fear, according as the pleasure or pain changes its situation, and becomes probable or improbable, certain or uncertain, or is considered as out of our power for the present moment. But when, along with this, the objects that cause pleasure or pain acquire a relation to ourselves or others, they still continue to excite desire and aversion, grief and joy; but cause, at the same time, the

---

[4] In the following discourse, *natural* is also opposed sometimes to *civil*, sometimes to *moral*. The opposition will always discover the sense in which it is taken.

indirect passions of pride or humility, love or hatred, which in this case have a double relation of impressions and ideas to the pain or pleasure.

We have already observed, that moral distinctions depend entirely on certain peculiar sentiments of pain and pleasure, and that whatever mental quality in ourselves or others gives us a satisfaction, by the survey or reflection, is of course virtuous; as every thing of this nature that gives uneasiness is vicious. Now, since every quality in ourselves or others which gives pleasure, always causes pride or love, as every one that produces uneasiness excites humility or hatred, it follows, that these two particulars are to be considered as equivalent, with regard to our mental qualities, virtue and the power of producing love or pride, vice and the power of producing humility or hatred. In every case, therefore, we must judge of the one by the other, and may pronounce any *quality* of the mind virtuous which causes love or pride, and any one vicious which causes hatred or humility.

If any *action* be either virtuous or vicious, it is only as a sign of some quality or character. It must depend upon durable principles of the mind, which extend over the whole conduct, and enter into the personal character. Actions themselves, not proceeding from any constant principle, have no influence on love or hatred, pride or humility; and consequently are never considered in morality.

This reflection is self-evident, and deserves to be attended to, as being of the utmost importance in the present subject. We are never to consider any single action in our inquiries concerning the origin of morals, but only the quality or character from which the action proceeded. These alone are *durable* enough to affect our sentiments concerning the person. Actions are indeed better indications of a character than words, or even wishes and sentiments; but it is only so far as they are such indications, that they are attended with love or hatred, praise or blame.

To discover the true origin of morals, and of that love or hatred which arises from mental qualities, we must take the matter pretty deep, and compare some principles which have been already examined and explained.

We may begin with considering anew the nature and force of *sympathy*. The minds of all men are similar in their feelings and operations; nor can any one be actuated by any affection of which all others are not in some degree susceptible. As in strings equally wound up, the motion of one communicates itself to the rest, so all the affections readily pass from one person to another, and beget correspondent movements in every human creature. When I see the *effects* of passion in the voice and gesture of any person, my mind immediately passes from these effects to their causes, and forms such a lively idea of the passion as is presently converted into the passion itself. In like manner, when I perceive the *causes* of any emotion, my mind is conveyed to the effects, and is actuated with a like emotion. Were I present at any of the more terrible operations of surgery; it is certain that, even before it begun, the preparation of the instruments, the laying of the bandages in order, the heating of the irons, with all the signs of anxiety and concern in the patient and assistants, would have a great effect upon my mind, and excite the strongest sentiments of pity and terror. No passion of another discovers itself immediately to the mind. We are only sensible of its causes or effects. From *these* we infer the passion; and consequently these give rise to our sympathy.

Our sense of beauty depends very much on this principle; and where any object has a tendency to produce pleasure in its possessor, it is always regarded as beautiful; as every object that has a tendency to produce pain, is disagreeable and deformed. Thus, the conveniency of a house, the fertility of a field, the strength of a horse, the capacity, security, and swift-sailing of a vessel, form the principal beauty of these several objects. Here the object, which is denominated beautiful, pleases only by its tendency to produce a certain effect. That effect is the pleasure or advantage of some other person. Now, the pleasure of a stranger for whom we have no friendship, pleases us only by sympathy. To this principle, therefore, is owing the beauty which we find in every thing that is useful. How considerable a part this is of beauty will easily appear upon reflection. Wherever an object has a tendency to produce pleasure in the possessor, or, in other words, is the proper cause of pleasure, it is sure to please the spectator, by a delicate sympathy with the possessor. Most of the works of art are esteemed beautiful, in proportion to their fitness for the use of man; and even many of the productions of nature derive their beauty from that source. Handsome and beautiful, on most occasions, is not an absolute, but a relative quality, and pleases us by nothing but its tendency to produce an end that is agreeable.[5]

The same principle produces, in many instances, our sentiments of morals, as well as those of beauty. No virtue is more esteemed than justice, and no vice more detested than injustice; nor are there any qualities which go further to the fixing the character, either as amiable or odious. Now justice is a moral virtue, merely because it has that tendency to the good of mankind, and indeed is nothing but an artificial invention to that purpose. The same may

---

[5] Decentior equus cujus astricta sunt ilia; sed idem velocior. Pulcher aspectu sit athleta, cujus lacertos exercitatio expressit; idem certamini paratior. Nunquam vero *species ab utilitate* dividitur. Sed hoc quidem discernere, modici judicii est. – Quinct. lib. 8.

be said of allegiance, of the laws of nations, of modesty, and of good manners. All these are mere human contrivances for the interest of society. And since there is a very strong sentiment of morals, which in all nations and all ages has attended them, we must allow that the reflecting on the tendency of characters and mental qualities is sufficient to give us the sentiments of approbation and blame. Now, as the means to an end can only be agreeable where the end is agreeable, and as the good of society, where our own interest is not concerned, or that of our friends, pleases only by sympathy, it follows, that sympathy is the source of the esteem which we pay to all the artificial virtues.

Thus it appears, *that* sympathy is a very powerful principle in human nature, *that* it has a great influence on our taste of beauty, and *that* it produces our sentiment of morals in all the artificial virtues. From thence we may presume, that it also gives rise to many of the other virtues, and that qualities acquire our approbation because of their tendency to the good of mankind. This presumption must become a certainty, when we find that most of those qualities which we *naturally* approve of, have actually that tendency, and render a man a proper member of society; while the qualities which we naturally disapprove of have a contrary tendency, and render any intercourse with the person dangerous or disagreeable. For having found, that such tendencies have force enough to produce the strongest sentiment of morals, we can never reasonably, in these cases, look for any other cause of approbation or blame; it being an inviolable maxim in philosophy, that where any particular cause is sufficient for an effect, we ought to rest satisfied with it, and ought not to multiply causes without necessity. We have happily attained experiments in the artificial virtues, where the tendency of qualities to the good of society is the sole cause of our approbation, without any suspicion of the concurrence of another principle. From thence we learn the force of that principle. And where that principle may take place, and the quality approved of is really beneficial to society, a true philosopher will never require any other principle to account for the strongest approbation and esteem.

That many of the natural virtues have this tendency to the good of society, no one can doubt of. Meekness, beneficence, charity, generosity, clemency, moderation, equity, bear the greatest figure among the moral qualities, and are commonly denominated the social virtues, to mark their tendency to the good of society. This goes so far, that some philosophers have represented all moral distinctions as the effect of artifice and education, when skilful politicians endeavored to restrain the turbulent passions of men, and make them operate to the public good, by the notions of honor and shame. This system, however, is not consistent with experience. For, *first*, there are other virtues and vices beside those which have this tendency to the public advantage and loss. *Secondly*, had not men a natural sentiment of approbation and blame, it could never be excited by politicians; nor would the words *laudable* and *praiseworthy*, *blamable* and *odious*, be any more intelligible than if they were a language perfectly unknown to us, as we have already observed. But though this system be erroneous, it may teach us that moral distinctions arise in a great measure from the tendency of qualities and characters to the interests of society, and that it is our concern for that interest which makes us approve or disapprove of them. Now, we have no such extensive concern for society, but from sympathy; and consequently it is that principle which takes us so far out of ourselves as to give us the same pleasure or uneasiness in the characters of others, as if they had a tendency to our own advantage or loss.

The only difference betwixt the natural virtues and justice lies in this, that the good which results from the former arises from every single act, and is the object of some natural passion; whereas a single act of justice, considered in itself, may often be contrary to the public good; and it is only the concurrence of mankind, in a general scheme or system of action, which is advantageous. When I relieve persons in distress, my natural humanity is my motive; and so far as my succor extends, so far have I promoted the happiness of my fellow-creatures. But if we examine all the questions that come before any tribunal of justice, we shall find that, considering each case apart, it would as often be an instance of humanity to decide contrary to the laws of justice as conformable to them. Judges take from a poor man to give to a rich; they bestow on the dissolute the labor of the industrious; and put into the hands of the vicious the means of harming both themselves and others. The whole scheme, however, of law and justice is advantageous to the society; and it was with a view to this advantage that men, by their voluntary conventions, established it. After it is once established by these conventions, it is naturally attended with a strong sentiment of morals, which can proceed from nothing but our sympathy with the interests of society. We need no other explication of that esteem which attends such of the natural virtues as have a tendency to the public good.

I must further add, that there are several circumstances which render this hypothesis much more probable with regard to the natural than the artificial virtues. It is certain, that the imagination is more affected by what is particular, than by what is general; and that the sentiments are always moved with difficulty, where their objects are in any degree loose and undetermined. Now, every particular act of justice is not beneficial to society, but the whole scheme or system; and it may not perhaps be any individual person for whom we are concerned, who receives benefit from justice, but the whole society alike. On the contrary, every particular act of generosity, or relief of the industrious and indigent, is beneficial, and is beneficial to a particular person, who is not undeserving of it. It is more natural, therefore, to think that the tendencies of the latter virtue will affect our sentiments, and command our approbation, than those of the former; and therefore, since we find that the approbation of the former arises from their tendencies, we may ascribe, with better reason, the same cause to the approbation of the latter. In any number of similar effects, if a cause can be discovered for one, we ought to extend that cause to all the other effects which can be accounted for by it; but much more, if these other effects be attended with peculiar circumstances, which facilitate the operation of that cause.

Before I proceed further, I must observe two remarkable circumstances in this affair, which may seem objections to the present system. The first may be thus explained. When any quality or character has a tendency to the good of mankind, we are pleased with it, and approve of it, because it presents the lively idea of pleasure; which idea affects us by sympathy, and is itself a kind of pleasure. But as this sympathy is very variable, it may be thought that our sentiments of morals must admit of all the same variations. We sympathize more with persons contiguous to us, than with persons remote from us; with our acquaintance, than with strangers; with our countrymen, than with foreigners. But notwithstanding this variation of our sympathy, we give the same approbation to the same moral qualities in China as in England. They appear equally virtuous, and recommend themselves equally to the esteem of a judicious spectator. The sympathy varies without a variation in our esteem. Our esteem, therefore, proceeds not from sympathy.

To this I answer, the approbation of moral qualities most certainly is not derived from reason, or any comparison of ideas; but proceeds entirely from a moral taste, and from certain sentiments of pleasure or disgust, which arise upon the contemplation and view of particular qualities or characters. Now, it is evident that those sentiments, whencever they are derived, must vary according to the distance or contiguity of the objects; nor can I feel the same lively pleasure from the virtues of a person who lived in Greece two thousand years ago, that I feel from the virtues of a familiar friend and acquaintance. Yet I do not say that I esteem the one more than the other; and therefore, if the variation of the sentiment, without a variation of the esteem, be an objection, it must have equal force against every other system, as against that of sympathy. But to consider the matter aright, it has no force at all; and it is the easiest matter in the world to account for it. Our situation with regard both to persons and things is in continual fluctuation; and a man that lies at a distance from us, may in a little time become a familiar acquaintance. Besides, every particular man has a peculiar position with regard to others; and it is impossible we could ever converse together on any reasonable terms, were each of us to consider characters and persons only as they appear from his peculiar point of view. In order, therefore, to prevent those continual *contradictions*, and arrive at a more *stable* judgment of things, we fix on some *steady* and *general* points of view, and always, in our thoughts, place ourselves in them, whatever may be our present situation. In like manner, external beauty is determined merely by pleasure; and it is evident a beautiful countenance cannot give so much pleasure, when seen at a distance of twenty paces, as when it is brought nearer us. We say not, however, that it appears to us less beautiful; because we know what effect it will have in such a position, and by that reflection we correct its momentary appearance.

In general, all sentiments of blame or praise are variable, according to our situation of nearness or remoteness with regard to the person blamed or praised, and according to the present disposition of our mind. But these variations we regard not in our general decisions, but still apply the terms expressive of our liking or dislike, in the same manner as if we remained in one point of view. Experience soon teaches us this method of correcting our sentiments, or at least of correcting our language, where the sentiments are more stubborn and unalterable. Our servant, if diligent and faithful, may excite stronger sentiments of love and kindness than Marcus Brutus, as represented in history; but we say not, upon that account, that the former character is more laudable than the latter. We know that, were we to approach equally near to that renowned patriarch, he would command a much higher degree of affection and admiration. Such corrections are common with regard to all the senses; and indeed it were impossible we could ever make use of language, or communicate our sentiments to one another, did we not correct the momentary appearances of things, and overlook our present situation.

It is therefore from the influence of characters and qualities upon those who have an intercourse with any person, that we blame or praise him. We consider not whether the persons affected by the qualities be our acquaintance or strangers, countrymen or foreigners. Nay, we overlook our own interest in those general judgments, and blame not a man for opposing us in any of our pretensions, when his own interest is particularly concerned. We make allowance for a certain degree of selfishness in men, because we know it to be inseparable from human nature, and inherent in our frame and constitution. By this reflection we correct those sentiments of blame which so naturally arise upon any opposition.

But however the general principle of our blame or praise may be corrected by those other principles, it is certain they are not altogether efficacious, nor do our passions often correspond entirely to the present theory. It is seldom men heartily love what lies at a distance from them, and what no way redounds to their particular benefit; as it is no less rare to meet with persons who can pardon another any opposition he makes to their interest, however justifiable that opposition may be by the general rules of morality. Here we are contented with saying, that reason requires such an impartial conduct, but that it is seldom we can bring ourselves to it, and that our passions do not readily follow the determination of our judgment. This language will be easily understood, if we consider what we formerly said concerning that reason which is able to oppose our passion, and which we have found to be nothing but a general calm determination of the passions, founded on same distant view or reflection. When we form our judgments of persons merely from the tendency of their characters to our own benefit, or to that of our friends, we find so many contradictions to our sentiments in society and conversation, and such an uncertainty from the incessant, changes of our situation, that we seek some other standard of merit and demerit, which may not admit of so great variation. Being thus loosened from our first station, we cannot afterwards fix ourselves so commodiously by any means as by a sympathy with those who have any commerce with the person we consider. This is far from being as lively as when our own interest is concerned, or that of our particular friends; nor has it such an influence on our love and hatred; but being equally conformable to our calm and general principles, it is said to have an equal authority over our reason, and to command our judgment and opinion. We blame equally a bad action which we read of in history, with one performed in our neighborhood the other day; the meaning of which is, that we know from reflection that the former action would excite as strong sentiments of disapprobation as the latter, were it placed in the same position.

I now proceed to the *second* remarkable circumstance which I propose to take notice of. Where a person is possessed of a character that in its natural tendency is beneficial to society, we esteem him virtuous, and are delighted with the view of his character, even though particular accidents prevent its operation, and incapacitate him from being serviceable to his friends and country. Virtue in rags is still virtue; and the love which it procures attends a man into a dungeon or desert, where the virtue can no longer be exerted in action, and is lost to all the world. Now, this may be esteemed an objection to the present system. Sympathy interests us in the good of mankind; and if sympathy were the source of our esteem for virtue, that sentiment of approbation could only take place where the virtue actually attained its end, and was beneficial to mankind. Where it fails of its end, it is only an imperfect means; and therefore can never acquire any merit from that end. The goodness of an end can bestow a merit on such means alone as are complete, and actually produce the end.

To this we may reply, that where any object, in all its parts, is fitted to attain any agreeable end, it naturally gives us pleasure, and is esteemed beautiful, even though some external circumstances be wanting to render it altogether effectual. It is sufficient if every thing be complete in the object itself. A house that is contrived with great judgment for all the commodities of life, pleases us upon that account; though perhaps we are sensible, that no one will ever dwell in it. A fertile soil, and a happy climate, delight us by a reflection on the happiness which they would afford the inhabitants, though at present the country be desert and uninhabited. A man, whose limbs and shape promise strength and activity, is esteemed handsome, though condemned to perpetual imprisonment. The imagination has a set of passions belonging to it, upon which our sentiments of beauty much depend. These passions are moved by degrees of liveliness and strength, which are inferior to *belief*, and independent of the real existence of their objects. Where a character is, in every respect, fitted to be beneficial to society, the imagination passes easily from the cause to the effect, without considering that there are still some circumstances wanting to render the cause a complete one. *General rules* create a species of probability, which sometimes influences the judgment, and always the imagination.

It is true, when the cause is complete, and a good disposition is attended with good fortune, which renders it really beneficial to society, it gives a stronger pleasure to the spectator, and is attended with a more lively sympathy. We are more affected by it; and yet we do not say that it is more virtuous, or that we esteem it more. We know that an alteration of fortune may render the benevolent disposition entirely impotent; and therefore we separate, as much as possible, the fortune from the disposition. The case is the same as when we correct the different sentiments of virtue, which proceed from its different distances from ourselves. The passions do not always follow our corrections; but these corrections serve sufficiently to regulate our abstract notions, and are alone regarded when we pronounce in general concerning the degrees of vice and virtue.

An Enquiry Concerning the Principles of Morals

Appendix I

[…]

V. It appears evident, that the ultimate ends of human actions can never, in any case, be accounted for by reason, but recommend themselves entirely to the sentiments and affections of mankind, without any dependence on the intellectual faculties. Ask a man, why he uses exercise; he will answer, because he desires to keep his health. If you then inquire, why he desires health, he will readily reply, because sickness is painful. If you push your inquiries further, and desire a reason why he hates pain, it is impossible he can ever give any. This is an ultimate end, and is never referred to any other object.

Perhaps to your second question, why he desires health; he may also reply, that it is necessary for the exercise of his calling. If you ask, why he is anxious on that head; he will answer, because he desires to get money. If you demand, Why? It is the instrument of pleasure, says he. And beyond this, it is an absurdity to ask for a reason. It is impossible there can be a progress in infinitum, and that one thing can always be a reason why another is desired. Something must be desirable on its own account, and because of its immediate accord or agreement with human sentiment and affection.

Now, as virtue is an end, and is desirable on its own account, without fee or reward, merely for the immediate satisfaction which it conveys, it is requisite that there should be some sentiment which it touches; some internal taste or feeling, or whatever you please to call it, which distinguishes moral good and evil, and which embraces the one and rejects the other.

Thus the distinct boundaries and offices of reason and of taste are easily ascertained. The former conveys the knowledge of truth and falsehood: the latter gives the sentiment of beauty and deformity, vice and virtue. The one discovers objects, as they really stand in nature, without addition or diminution: the other has a productive faculty; and gilding or staining all natural objects with the colors borrowed from internal sentiment, raises, in a manner, a new creation. Reason, being cool and disengaged, is no motive to action, and directs only the impulse received from appetite or inclination, by showing us the means of attaining happiness or avoiding misery. Taste, as it gives pleasure or pain, and thereby constitutes happiness or misery, becomes a motive to action, and is the first spring or impulse to desire and volition. From circumstances and relations, known or supposed, the former leads us to the discovery of the concealed and unknown. After all circumstances and relations are laid before us, the latter makes us feel from the whole a new sentiment of blame or approbation. The standard of the one, being founded on the nature of things, is eternal and inflexible, even by the will of the Supreme Being: the standard of the other, arising from the internal frame and constitution of animals, is ultimately derived from that Supreme Will, which bestowed on each being its peculiar nature, and arranged the several classes and orders of existence.

4

An Enquiry Concerning the Principles of Morals: Virtue and Utility

David Hume

Philosophical ethics is usually understood to be, at least in part, *prescriptive* or normative: the philosopher is trying to provide reasons to act or live in one way or another. Much of the time, Hume seems rather to be *describing* morality, rather than offering moral judgements. But it is plausible, both from his general tone and because of things he says elsewhere, to think that he is also *recommending* virtue in the form in which he describes it. Further, although most of the time he sounds quite sure of himself, on reflection he is disarmingly aware of the dangers of dogmatism (9.13).

The main aim of section 3 of the *Enquiry* is to show that the only foundation of justice, both as a virtue and as a set of human institutions including property and the law in general, is utility (3.1, 3.12). By 'utility', Hume means the capacity to increase pleasure and decrease pain. And, he believes, justice is, in a sense, a human invention, one that has developed gradually and of its own accord over a long period. That it is merely contingent, he suggests (3.2–9, 17–19), can be seen if we imagine a world without scarcity, or a world in which people are entirely impartial. There are no principles of justice governing the distribution of air, because everyone can get as much as they need; principles of justice, then, have developed in situations in which there are insufficient goods to satisfy everyone. And if we were all entirely impartial, there would be no conflicts to be resolved through the principles of justice. There is no natural 'instinct' to justice, and it is quite clear that complicated individual institutions such as inheritance have been shaped to advance social good overall (3.40–43).

Is Hume right? Consider, for example, the case of production (3.28). Imagine that a group of people are washed up on some desert island. One of them works hard to till a field and grows some nourishing vegetables. The island is large, and the others could have done the same; but they preferred to sunbathe instead. It is tempting to think that the vegetable-grower is entitled to her vegetables, even if the others could prove that it would be more 'useful' for her to share them around.

Here Hume may respond that our view can be explained by the fact that *in general* it promotes happiness for producers to receive what they have produced (see 5.41n). But this may not be enough to satisfy those who think that this entitlement is basic, and does not depend on any further foundation in utility. Take another example: equality. Here again Hume claims that there is no basic principle of egalitarian justice (3.25–7). But consider the following possible outcomes:

I
Group 1: 99
Group 2: 1
II
Group 1: 50
Group 2: 50

History of Ethics – Essential Readings with Commentary, First Edition. Edited by Daniel Star and Roger Crisp.
© 2020 John Wiley & Sons Ltd. Published 2020 by John Wiley & Sons Ltd.

Assume that each group includes 1,000 people, and that the numbers represent happiness. (It doesn't really matter for this argument whether happiness can be measured so precisely.) If all that matters is utility, and not how happiness is shared around, then these outcomes are equally valuable. But many will think that there is non-utility value in outcome II, and that this value may plausibly be described as justice. Indeed, something like this position is found in Butler and in Sidgwick.

In section 5, Hume's concern is not primarily to make the case for utility as the foundation for moral principles such as those of justice. Rather, he is aiming in particular to justify the idea of other-regarding or benevolent concern against the egoistic view that our reasons rest on the advancement of our own self-interest (5.1–2). The 'social virtues', Hume claims, are naturally attractive to us because of their utility, and this utility must be self-interested, other-interested, or both (5.4).

It is not, he goes on to argue (5.5–15), purely a matter of self-interest. Hume believes that there is a good deal of truth in the idea that each of us admires the virtues in part because of the benefit we receive individually from their instantiation in society at large. But we admire the virtues of, for example, individuals in the distant past as much as we do those of our contemporaries who can affect our own self-interest. It is a brute fact about human beings that they, or most of them, have compassion and sympathy for others (5.40, 45), and it is a confusion to think that because they are strongly self-interested they are entirely partial to themselves (5.16–18).

Again, however, a deep hermeneutic question arises here about the status of non-self-regarding virtues. Someone who believes that morality has emerged from, and is based on, self-concern may argue that it is in the interest of each of us to commit to certain other-regarding principles. But on reflection, we can see that our only reason for doing so is egoistic.

Hume might reply with further evidence of the embeddedness of sympathetic concern in our lives (5.19–38). We can see it in our aesthetic responses to buildings, literature, and clothing, for example, or in our interest in news about major events in the world distant from us. Wouldn't any of us, given the choice, avoid stepping on someone else's gouty toes (5.39)? This evidence might still be insufficient for the egoist, or the moral contractualist who sees morality in terms of a self-interested bargain; they will continue to raise the hermeneutic question.

Hume believes that an individual human being will have a natural concern for all others. But he is of course aware that we are especially concerned for certain individuals, such as members of our family. However, we can still compare the virtues of those close to us with those of more remote people with some degree of impartiality. This is because moral discourse itself is based on our adopting a more general point of view, in which judgement can to some degree 'correct' our sentiments.

Section III – Of Justice

Part I

THAT Justice is useful to society, and consequently that *part* of its merit, at least, must arise from that consideration, it would be a superfluous undertaking to prove. That public utility is the *sole* origin of Justice, and that reflections on the beneficial consequences of this virtue are the *sole* foundation of its merit; this proposition being more curious and important, will better deserve our examination and inquiry.

Let us suppose, that nature has bestowed on the human race such profuse *abundance* of all *external* conveniences, that, without any uncertainty in the event, without any care or industry on our part, every individual finds himself fully provided with whatever his most voracious appetites can want, or luxurious imagination wish or desire. His natural beauty, we shall suppose, surpasses all acquired ornaments: the perpetual clemency of the seasons renders useless all clothes or covering: the raw herbage affords him the most delicious fare; the clear fountain the richest beverage. No laborious occupation required: no tillage: no navigation. Music, poetry, and contemplation, form his sole business: conversation, mirth, and friendship, his sole amusement.

It seems evident, that, in such a happy state, every other social virtue would flourish, and receive tenfold increase; but the cautious, jealous virtue of justice, would never once have been dreamed of. For what purpose make a partition of goods, where every one has already more than enough? Why give rise to property, where there cannot possibly be any injury? Why call this object *mine*, when, upon the seizing of it by another, I need but stretch out my hand to possess myself of what is equally valuable? Justice, in that case, being totally USELESS, would be an idle ceremonial, and could never possibly have place in the catalogue of virtues.

We see, even in the present necessitous condition of mankind, that, wherever any benefit is bestowed by nature in an unlimited abundance, we leave it always in common among the whole human race, and make no subdivisions of right and property. Water and air, though the most necessary of all objects, are not challenged as the property of individuals; nor can any man commit injustice by the most lavish use and enjoyment of these blessings. In fertile extensive countries, with few inhabitants, land is regarded on the same footing. And no topic is so much insisted on by those who defend the liberty of the seas, as the unexhausted use of them in navigation. Were the advantages procured by navigation as inexhaustible, these reasoners had never had any adversaries to refute; nor had any claims ever been advanced of a separate, exclusive dominion over the ocean.

It may happen in some countries, at some periods, that there be established a property in water, none in land;* if the latter be in greater abundance than can be used by the inhabitants, and the former be found with difficulty, and in very small quantities.

Again: suppose that, though the necessities of the human race continue the same as at present, yet the mind is so enlarged, and so replete with friendship and generosity, that every man has the utmost tenderness for every man, and feels no more concern for his own interest than for that of his fellows: it seems evident, that the USE of Justice would, in this case, be suspended by such an extensive benevolence, nor would the divisions and barriers of property and obligation have ever been thought of. Why should I bind another, by a deed or promise, to do me any good office, when I know that he is already prompted, by the strongest inclination, to seek my happiness, and would, of himself, perform the desired service; except the hurt he thereby receives be greater than the benefit accruing to me: in which case he knows that, from my innate humanity and friendship, I should be the first to oppose myself to his imprudent generosity? Why raise landmarks between my neighbor's field and mine, when my heart has made no division between our interests, but shares all his joys and sorrows with the same force and vivacity as if originally my own? Every man, upon this supposition, being a second self to another, would trust all his interests to the discretion of every man, without jealousy, without partition, without distinction. And the whole human race would form only one family, where all would lie in common, and be used freely, without regard to property; but cautiously too, with as entire regard to the necessities of each individual, as if our own interests were most intimately concerned.

In the present disposition of the human heart, it would perhaps be difficult to find complete instances of such enlarged affections; but still we may observe, that the case of families approaches towards it; and the stronger the mutual benevolence is among the individuals, the nearer it approaches, till all distinction of property be, in a great measure, lost and confounded among them. Between married persons, the cement of friendship is by the laws

---

* Genesis, chap. xiii. and xxi.

supposed so strong as to abolish all division of possessions, and has often, in reality, the force ascribed to it. And it is observable, that, during the ardor of new enthusiasms, when every principle is inflamed into extravagance, the community of goods has frequently been attempted; and nothing but experience of its inconveniences, from the returning or disguised selfishness of men, could make the imprudent fanatics adopt anew the ideas of justice and of separate property. So true is it that this virtue derives its existence entirely from its necessary *use* to the intercourse and social state of mankind.

To make this truth more evident, let us reverse the foregoing suppositions; and, carrying every thing to the opposite extreme, consider what would be the effect of these new situations. Suppose a society to fall into such want of all common necessaries, that the utmost frugality and industry cannot preserve the greater number from perishing, and the whole from extreme misery: it will readily, I believe, be admitted, that the strict laws of justice are suspended, in such a pressing emergence, and give place to the stronger motives of necessity and self-preservation. Is it any crime, after a shipwreck, to seize whatever means or instrument of safety one can lay hold of, without regard to former limitations of property? Or if a city besieged were perishing with hunger, can we imagine that men will see any means of preservation before them, and lose their lives, from a scrupulous regard to what, in other situations, would be the rules of equity and justice? The USE and TENDENCY of that virtue is to procure happiness and security, by preserving order in society: but where the society is ready to perish from extreme necessity, no greater evil can be dreaded from violence and injustice; and every man may now provide for himself by all the means which prudence can dictate, or humanity permit. The public, even in less urgent necessities, opens granaries without the consent of proprietors, as justly supposing, that the authority of magistracy may, consistent with equity, extend so far: but were any number of men to assemble, without the tie of laws or civil jurisdiction, would an equal partition of bread in a famine, though effected by power and even violence, be regarded as criminal or injurious?

Suppose, likewise, that it should be a virtuous man's fate to fall into the society of ruffians, remote from the protection of laws and government, what conduct must he embrace in that melancholy situation? He sees such a desperate rapaciousness prevail; such a disregard to equity, such contempt of order, such stupid blindness to future consequences, as must immediately have the most tragical conclusions, and must terminate in destruction to the greater number, and in a total dissolution of society to the rest. He, meanwhile, can have no other expedient than to arm himself, to whomever the sword he seizes, or the buckler, may belong: to make provision of all means of defence and security: and his particular regard to justice being no longer of USE to his own safety or that of others, he must consult the dictates of self-preservation alone, without concern for those who no longer merit his care and attention.

When any man, even in political society, renders himself by his crimes obnoxious to the public, he is punished by the laws in his goods and person; that is, the ordinary rules of justice are, with regard to him, suspended for a moment; and it becomes equitable to inflict on him, for the *benefit* of society, what otherwise he could not suffer without wrong or injury.

The rage and violence of public war, what is it but a suspension of justice among the warring parties, who perceive that this virtue is now no longer of any *use* or advantage to them? The laws of war, which then succeed to those of equity and justice, are rules calculated for the *advantage* and *utility* of that particular state in which men are now placed. And were a civilized nation engaged with barbarians, who observed no rules even of war, the former must also suspend their observance of them, where they no longer serve to any purpose, and must render every action or rencounter as bloody and pernicious as possible to the first aggressors.

Thus, the rules of equity or justice depend entirely on the particular state and condition in which men are placed, and owe their origin and existence to that UTILITY, which results to the public from their strict and regular observance. Reverse, in any considerable circumstance, the condition of men: produce extreme abundance or extreme necessity: implant in the human breast perfect moderation and humanity, or perfect rapaciousness and malice: by rendering justice totally *useless*, you thereby totally destroy its essence, and suspend its obligation upon mankind.

The common situation of society is a medium amidst all these extremes. We are naturally partial to ourselves and to our friends, but are capable of learning the advantage resulting from a more equitable conduct. Few enjoyments are given us from the open and liberal hand of nature; but by art, labor, and industry, we can extract them in great abundance. Hence the ideas of property become necessary in all civil society: hence justice derives its usefulness to the public: and hence alone arises its merit and moral obligation.

These conclusions are so natural and obvious, that they have not escaped even the poets in their descriptions of the felicity attending the golden age or the reign of Saturn. The seasons, in that first period of nature, were so temperate, if we credit these agreeable fictions, that there was no necessity for men to provide themselves with clothes and houses, as a security against the violence of heat and cold: the rivers flowed with wine and milk: the oaks yielded honey: and Nature spontaneously produced her greatest delicacies. Nor were these the chief advantages of that happy age. Tempests were not alone removed from nature; but those most furious tempests were unknown to human breasts, which now cause such uproar, and engender such confusion. Avarice, ambition, cruelty, selfishness, was never heard of: cordial affection, compassion, sympathy, were the only movements with which the mind was yet acquainted. Even the punctilious distinction of *mine* and *thine* was banished from among that happy race of mortals, and carried with it the very notion of property and obligation, justice and injustice.

This *poetical* fiction of the *golden age* is, in some respects, of a piece with the *philosophical* fiction of the *state of nature;* only that the former is represented as the most charming and most peaceable condition which can possibly be imagined; whereas the latter is painted out as a state of mutual war and violence, attended with the most extreme necessity. On the first origin of mankind, we are told, their ignorance and savage nature were so prevalent, that they could give no mutual trust, but must each depend upon himself, and his own force or cunning, for protection and security. No law was heard of: no rule of justice known: no distinction of property regarded: power was the only measure of right; and a perpetual war of all against all was the result of men's untamed selfishness and barbarity.*

Whether such a condition of human nature could ever exist, or, if it did, could continue so long as to merit the appellation of a state, may justly be doubted. Men are necessarily born in a family society at least, and are trained up by their parents to some rule of conduct and behavior. But this must be admitted, that, if such a state of mutual war and violence was ever real, the suspension of all laws of justice, from their absolute inutility, is a necessary and infallible consequence.

The more we vary our views of human life, and the newer and more unusual the lights are in which we survey it, the more shall we be convinced, that the origin here assigned for the virtue of justice is real and satisfactory.

Were there a species of creatures intermingled with men, which, though rational, were possessed of such inferior strength, both of body and mind, that they were incapable of all resistance, and could never, upon the highest provocation, make us feel the effects of their resentment: the necessary consequence, I think, is, that we should be bound, by the laws of humanity, to give gentle usage to these creatures, but should not, properly speaking, lie under any restraint of justice with regard to them, nor could they possess any right or property exclusive of such arbitrary lords. Our intercourse with them could not be called society, which supposes a degree of equality; but absolute command on the one side, and servile obedience on the other. Whatever we covet, they must instantly resign. Our permission is the only tenure by which they hold their possessions: our compassion and kindness the only check by which they curb our lawless will: and as no inconvenience ever results from the exercise of a power so firmly established in nature, the restraints of justice and property, being totally *useless*, would never have place in so unequal a confederacy.

This is plainly the situation of men with regard to animals; and how far these may be said to possess reason, I leave it to others to determine. The great superiority of civilized Europeans above barbarous Indians, tempted us to imagine ourselves on the same footing with regard to them, and made us throw off all restraints of justice, and even of humanity, in our treatment of them. In many nations, the female sex are reduced to like slavery, and are rendered incapable of all property, in opposition to their lordly masters. But though the males, when united, have in all countries bodily force sufficient to maintain this severe tyranny, yet such are the insinuations, address, and charms of their fair companions, that women are commonly able to break the confederacy, and share with the other sex in all the rights and privileges of society.

Were the human species so framed by nature as that each individual possessed within himself every faculty requisite both for his own preservation and for the propagation of his kind: were all society and intercourse cut off between man and man, by the primary intention of the Supreme Creator: it seems evident, that so solitary a being would be as much incapable of justice as of social discourse and conversation. Where mutual regards and forbearance serve to no manner of purpose, they would never direct the conduct of any reasonable man. The headlong course of the passions would be checked by no reflection on future consequences. And as each man is here supposed to love himself alone, and to depend only on himself and his own activity for safety and happiness, he would, on every occasion, to the utmost of his power, challenge the preference above every other being, to none of which he is bound by any ties, either of nature or of interest.

But suppose the conjunction of the sexes to be established in nature, a family immediately arises; and particular rules being found requisite for its subsistence, these are immediately embraced, though without comprehending

---

* This fiction of a state of nature, as a state of war, was not first started by Mr. Hobbes, as is commonly imagined. Plato endeavors to refute an hypothesis very like it in the 2d, 3d, and 4th books de Republica. Cicero, on the contrary, supposes it certain and universally acknowledged

the rest of mankind within their prescriptions. Suppose that several families unite together into one society, which is totally disjoined from all others, the rules which preserve peace and order enlarge themselves to the utmost extent of that society; but becoming then entirely useless, lose their force when carried one step further. But again, suppose that several distinct societies maintain a kind of intercourse for mutual convenience and advantage, the boundaries of justice still grow larger, in proportion to the largeness of men's views, and the force of their mutual connection. History, experience, reason, sufficiently instruct us in this natural progress of human sentiments, and in the gradual enlargement of our regards to justice, in proportion as we become acquainted with the extensive utility of that virtue.

Part II

If we examine the *particular* laws by which justice is directed, and property determined, we shall still be presented with the same conclusions. The good of mankind is the only object of all these laws and regulations. Not only is it requisite for the peace and interest of society, that men's possessions should be separated; but the rules which we follow, in making the separation, are such as can best be contrived to serve further the interest of society.

We shall suppose, that a creature possessed of reason, but unacquainted with human nature, deliberates with himself what RULES of justice or property would best promote public interest, and establish peace and security among mankind: his most obvious thought would be, to assign the largest possession to the most extensive virtue, and give every one the power of doing good, proportioned to his inclination. In a perfect theocracy, where a being infinitely intelligent governs by particular volitions, this rule would certainly have place, and might serve to the wisest purposes: but were mankind to execute such a law, so great is the uncertainty of merit, both from its natural obscurity, and from the self-conceit of each individual, that no determinate rule of conduct would ever result from it; and the total dissolution of society must be the immediate consequences. Fanatics may suppose, *that dominion is founded on grace,* and *that saints alone inherit the earth;* but the civil magistrate very justly puts these sublime theorists on the same footing with common robbers, and teaches them, by the severest discipline, that a rule, which in speculation, may seem the most advantageous to society, may yet be found in practice totally pernicious and destructive.

That there were *religious* fanatics of this kind in England during the civil wars, we learn from history; though it is probable that the obvious *tendency* of these principles excited such horror in mankind, as soon obliged the dangerous enthusiasts to renounce, or at least conceal their tenets. Perhaps the *levellers* who claimed an equal distribution of property, were a kind of *political* fanatics, which arose from the religious species, and more openly avowed their pretensions; as carrying a more plausible appearance, of being practicable in themselves, as well as useful to human society.

It must, indeed, be confessed, that nature is so liberal to mankind, that, were all her presents equally divided among the species, and improved by art and industry, every individual would enjoy all the necessaries, and even most of the comforts of life; nor would ever be liable to any ills, but such as might accidentally arise from the sickly frame and constitution of his body. It must also be confessed, that wherever we depart from this equality, we rob the poor of more satisfaction than we add to the rich; and that the slight gratification of a frivolous vanity in one individual, frequently costs more than bread to many families, and even provinces. It may appear withal, that the rule of equality, as it would be highly *useful,* is not altogether *impracticable;* but has taken place, at least in an imperfect degree, in some republics; particularly that of Sparta: where it was attended, it is said, with the most beneficial consequences. Not to mention, that the AGRARIAN laws, so frequently claimed in Rome, and carried into execution in many Greek cities, proceeded, all of them, from the general idea of the utility of this principle.

But historians, and even common sense, may inform us, that however specious these ideas of *perfect* equality may seem, they are really at bottom *impracticable;* and were they not so, would be extremely *pernicious* to human society. Render possessions ever so equal, men's different degrees of art, care, and industry, will immediately break that equality. Or if you check these virtues, you reduce society to the most extreme indigence; and, instead of preventing want and beggary in a few, render it unavoidable to the whole community. The most rigorous inquisition, too, is requisite to watch every inequality on its first appearance; and the most severe jurisdiction, to punish and redress it. But besides that so much authority must soon degenerate into tyranny, and be exerted with great partialities; who can possibly be possessed of it, in such a situation as is here supposed? Perfect equality of possessions, destroying all subordination, weakens extremely the authority of magistracy, and must reduce all power nearly to a level, as well as property.

We may conclude, therefore, that, in order to establish laws for the regulation of property, we must be acquainted with the nature and situation of man; must reject appearances which may be false, though specious; and must search for those rules, which are, on the whole, most *useful* and *beneficial:* vulgar sense and slight experience are sufficient for this purpose, where men give not way to too selfish avidity, or too extensive enthusiasm.

Who sees not, for instance, that whatever, is produced or improved by man's art or industry, ought for ever to be secured to him, in order to give encouragement to such *useful* habits and accomplishments? That the property ought also to descend to children and relations, for the same *useful* purpose? That it may be alienated by consent, in order to beget that commerce and intercourse which is so *beneficial* to human society? And that all contracts and promises ought carefully to be fulfilled, in order to secure mutual trust and confidence, by which the general *interest* of mankind is so much promoted?

Examine the writers on the laws of nature, and you will always find, that, whatever principles they set out with, they are sure to terminate here at last, and to assign, as the ultimate reason for every rule which they establish, the convenience and necessities of mankind. A concession thus extorted, in opposition to systems, has more authority than if it had been made in prosecution of them.

What other reason, indeed, could writers ever give why this must be *mine* and that *yours,* since uninstructed nature, surely, never made any such distinction? The objects which receive these appellations are of themselves foreign to us; they are totally disjoined and separated from us; and nothing but the general interests of society can form the connection.

Sometimes the interests of society may require a rule of justice in a particular case, but may not determine any particular rule, among several, which are all equally beneficial. In that case the *slightest* analogies are laid hold of, in order to prevent that indifference and ambiguity which would be the source of perpetual dissension. Thus, possession alone, and first possession, is supposed to convey property, where nobody else has any preceding claim and pretension. Many of the reasonings of lawyers are of this analogical nature, and depend on very slight connections of the imagination.

Does any one scruple, in extraordinary cases, to violate all regard to the private property of individuals, and sacrifice to public interest a distinction which had been established for the sake of that interest? The safety of the people is the supreme law: all other particular laws are subordinate to it, and dependent on it: and if, in the *common* course of things, they be followed and regarded, it is only because the public safety and interest *commonly* demand so equal and impartial an administration.

Sometimes both *utility* and *analogy* fail, and leave the laws of justice in total uncertainty. Thus, it is highly requisite that prescription or long possession should convey property; but what number of days, or months, or years, should be sufficient for that purpose, it is impossible for reason alone to determine. *Civil laws* here supply the place of the natural *code,* and assign different terms for prescription, according to the different *utilities* proposed by the legislature. Bills of exchange and promissory-notes, by the laws of most countries, prescribe sooner than bonds, and mortgages, and contracts of a more formal nature.

In general, we may observe, that all questions of property are subordinate to the authority of civil laws, which extend, restrain, modify, and alter the rules of natural justice, according to the particular *convenience* of each community. The laws have, or ought to have, a constant reference to the constitution of government, the manners, the climate, the religion, the commerce, the situation of each society. A late author of genius, as well as learning, has prosecuted this subject at large, and has established from these principles a system of political knowledge, which abounds in ingenious and brilliant thoughts, and is not wanting in solidity.*

* The author of *L'Esprit des Loix.* This illustrious writer, however, sets out with a different theory, and supposes all right to be founded on certain *rapports* or relations, which is a system that, in my opinion, never will be reconciled with true philosophy. Father Malebranche, as far as I can learn, was the first that started this abstract theory of morals, which was afterwards adopted by Cudworth, Clarke, and others; and as it excludes all sentiment, and pretends to found every thing on reason, it has not wanted followers in this philosophic age. See *Section 1. Appendix 1.* With regard to justice, the virtue here treated of, the inference against this theory seems short and conclusive. Property is allowed to be dependent on civil laws; civil laws are allowed to have no other object but the interest of society: this therefore must be allowed to be the sole foundation of property and justice. Not to mention, that our obligation itself to obey the magistrate and his laws is founded in nothing but the interests of society.

   If the ideas of justice, sometimes, do not follow the dispositions of civil law, we shall find that these cases, instead of objections, are confirmations of the theory delivered above. Where a civil law is so perverse as to cross all the interests of society, it loses all its authority, and men judge by the ideas of natural justice, which are conformable to those interests. Sometimes also civil laws, for useful purposes, require a ceremony or form to any deed; and where that is wanting, their decrees run contrary to the usual tenor of justice; but one who takes advantage of such chicanes, is not commonly regarded as an honest man. Thus, the interests of society require that contracts be fulfilled; and there is not a more material article either of natural or civil justice: but the omission of a trifling circumstance will often, by law, invalidate a contract *in foro humano,* but not *in foro conscientiae,* as divines express themselves. In these cases, the magistrate is supposed only to withdraw his power of enforcing the right, not to have, altered the right. Where his intention extends to the right, and is conformable to the interests of society, it never fails to alter the right; a clear proof of the origin of justice and of property, as assigned above.

What is a man's property? Any thing which it is lawful for him, and for him alone, to use. *But what rule have we, by which we can distinguish these objects?* Here we must have recourse to statutes, customs, precedents, analogies, and a hundred other circumstances, some of which are constant and inflexible, some variable and arbitrary. But the ultimate point, in which they all professedly terminate, is the interest and happiness of human society. Where this enters not into consideration, nothing can appear more whimsical, unnatural, and even superstitious, than all or most of the laws of justice and of property.

Those who ridicule vulgar superstitions, and expose the folly of particular regards to meats, days, places, postures, apparel, have an easy task; while they consider all the qualities and relations of the objects, and discover no adequate cause for that affection or antipathy, veneration or horror, which have so mighty an influence over a considerable part of mankind. A Syrian would have starved rather than taste pigeons; an Egyptian would not have approached bacon: but if these species of food be examined by the senses of sight, smell, or taste, or scrutinized by the sciences of chemistry, medicine, or physics, no difference is ever found between them and any other species, nor can that precise circumstance be pitched on, which may afford a just foundation for the religious passion. A fowl on Thursday is lawful food; on Friday abominable: eggs, in this house, and in this diocese, are permitted during Lent; a hundred paces further, to eat them is a damnable sin. This earth or building, yesterday, was profane; to-day, by the muttering of certain words, it has become holy and sacred. Such reflections as these, in the mouth of a philosopher, one may safely say, are too obvious to have any influence, because they must always, to every man, occur at first sight; and where they prevail not of themselves, they are surely obstructed by education, prejudice, and passion, not by ignorance or mistake.

It may appear to a careless view, or rather a too abstracted reflection, that there enters a like superstition into all the sentiments of justice; and that, if a man expose its object, or what we call property, to the same scrutiny of sense and science, he will not, by the most accurate inquiry, find any foundation for the difference made by moral sentiment, I may lawfully nourish myself from this tree; but the fruit of another of the same species, ten paces off, it is criminal for me to touch. Had I worn this apparel an hour ago, I had merited the severest punishment; but a man, by pronouncing a few magical syllables, has now rendered it fit for any use and service. Were this house placed in the neighboring territory, it had been immoral for me to dwell in it; but being built on this side of the river, it is subject to a different municipal law, and by its becoming mine, I incur no blame or censure. The same species of reasoning, it may be thought, which so successively exposes superstition, is also applicable to justice; nor is it possible, in the one case, more than in the other, to point out, in the object, that precise quality or circumstance which is the foundation of the sentiment.

But there is this material difference between *superstition* and *justice*, that the former is frivolous, useless, and burdensome; the latter is absolutely requisite to the well-being of mankind, and existence of society. When we abstract from this circumstance (for it is too apparent ever to be overlooked), it must be confessed, that all regards to right and property seem entirely without foundation, as much as the grossest and most vulgar superstition. Were the interests of society nowise concerned, it is as unintelligible why another's articulating certain sounds, implying consent, should change the nature of my actions with regard to a particular object, as why the reciting of a liturgy by a priest, in a certain habit and posture, should dedicate a heap of brick and timber, and render it, thenceforth and for ever, sacred.*

---

* It is evident that the will or consent alone never transfers property, nor causes the obligation of a promise (for the same reasoning extends to both); but the will must be expressed by words or signs, in order to impose a tie upon any man. The expression being once brought in as subservient to the will, soon becomes the principal part of the promise; nor will a man be less bound by his word, though he secretly give a different direction to his intention, and withhold the assent of his mind. But though the expression makes, on most occasions, the whole of the promise, yet it does not always so; and one who should make use of any expression of which he knows not the meaning, and which he uses without any sense of the consequences, would not certainly be bound by it. Nay, though he know its meaning, yet if he uses it in jest only, and with such signs as evidently show that he has no serious intentions of binding himself, he would not lie under any obligation of performance; but it is necessary that the words be a perfect expression of the will, without any contrary signs. Nay, even this we must not carry so far as to imagine, that one whom, by our quickness of understanding, we conjecture, from certain signs, to have an intention of deceiving us, is not bound by his expression or verbal promise, if we accept of it; but must limit this conclusion to those cases where the signs are of a different nature from those of deceit. All these contradictions are easily accounted for, if justice arise entirely from its usefulness to society; but will never be explained on any other hypothesis.

It is remarkable, that the moral decisions of the *Jesuits*, and other relaxed casuists, were commonly formed in prosecution of some such subtilties of reasoning as are here pointed out, and proceed as much from the habit of scholastic refinement as from any corruption of the heart, if we may follow the authority of Mons. Bayle. See his Dictionary, article LOYOLA. And why has the indignation of mankind risen so high against these casuists, but because every one perceived, that human society could not subsist were such practices authorized, and that morals must always be handled with a view to public interest, more than philosophical regularity? If the secret direction of the intention, said every man of sense, could

These reflections are far from weakening; the obligations of justice, or diminishing any thing from the most sacred attention to property. On the contrary, such sentiments must acquire new force from the present reasoning. For what stronger foundation can be desired or conceived for any duty, than to observe, that human society, or even human nature, could not subsist without the establishment of it, and will still arrive at greater degrees of happiness and perfection, the more inviolable the regard is which is paid to that duty?

The dilemma seems obvious: as justice evidently tends to promote public utility, and to support civil society, the sentiment of justice is either derived from our reflecting on that tendency, or, like hunger, thirst, and other appetites, resentment, love of life, attachment to offspring, and other passions, arises from a simple original instinct in the human breast, which nature has implanted for like salutary purposes. If the latter be the case, it follows, that property, which is the object of justice, is also distinguished by a simple, original instinct, and is not ascertained by any argument or reflection. But who is there that ever heard of such an instinct? Or is this a subject in which new discoveries can be made? We may as well expect to discover in the body new senses which had before escaped the observation of all mankind.

But further, though it seems a very simple proposition to say, that nature, by an instinctive sentiment, distinguishes property, yet in reality we shall find, that there are required for that purpose ten thousand different instincts, and these employed about objects of the greatest intricacy and nicest discernment. For when a definition of *property* is required, that relation is found to resolve itself into any possession acquired by occupation, by industry, by prescription, by inheritance, by contract, etc. Can we think that nature, by an original instinct, instructs us in all these methods of acquisition?

These words, too, inheritance and contract, stand for ideas infinitely complicated; and to define them exactly, a hundred volumes of laws, and a thousand volumes of commentators, have not been found sufficient. Does nature, whose instincts in men are all simple, embrace such complicated and artificial objects, and create a rational creature, without trusting any thing to the operation of his reason?

But even though all this were admitted, it would not be satisfactory. Positive laws can certainly transfer property. It is by another original instinct that we recognize the authority of kings and senates, and mark all the boundaries of their jurisdiction. Judges, too, even though their sentence be erroneous and illegal, must be allowed, for the sake of peace and order, to have decisive authority, and ultimately to determine property. Have we original, innate ideas of prætors, and chancellors, and juries? Who sees not, that all these institutions arise merely from the necessities of human society?

All birds of the same species, in every age and country, build their nests alike: in this we see the force of instinct. Men, in different times and places, frame their houses differently: here we perceive the influence of reason and custom. A like inference may be drawn from comparing the instinct of generation and the institution of property.

How great soever the variety of municipal laws, it must be confessed, that their chief outlines pretty regularly concur, because the purposes to which they tend are everywhere exactly similar. In like manner, all houses have a roof and walls, windows and chimneys, though diversified in their shape, figure, and materials. The purposes of the latter, directed to the conveniences of human life, discover not more plainly their origin from reason and reflection, than do those of the former, which point all to a like end.

I need not mention the variations, which all the rules of property receive from the finer turns and connections of the imagination, and from the subtilties and abstractions of law-topics and reasonings. There is no possibility of reconciling this observation to the notion of original instinct.

What alone will beget a doubt concerning the theory on which I insist, is the influence of education and acquired habits, by which we are so accustomed to blame injustice, that we are not, in every instance, conscious of

---

invalidate a contract, where is our security? And yet a metaphysical schoolman might think, that, where an intention was supposed to be requisite, if that intention really had no place, no consequence ought to follow, and no obligation be imposed. The casuistical subtilties may not be, greater than the subtilties of lawyers, hinted at above; but as the former are *pernicious*, and the latter *innocent* and even *necessary*, this is the reason of the very different reception they meet with from the world.

    It is a doctrine of the church of Rome, that the priest, by a secret direction of his intention, can invalidate any sacrament. This position is derived from a strict and regular prosecution of the obvious truth, that empty words alone, without any meaning or intention in the speaker, can never be attended with any effect. If the same conclusion be not admitted in reasonings concerning civil contracts, where the affair is allowed to be, of so much less consequence than the eternal salvation of thousands, it proceeds entirely from men's sense of the danger and inconvenience of the doctrine in the former case: and we may thence observe, that however positive, arrogant, and dogmatical any superstition may appear, it never can convey any thorough persuasion of the reality of its objects, or put them, in any degree, on a balance with the common incidents of life, which we learn from daily observation and experimental reasoning.

any immediate reflection on the pernicious consequences of it. The views the most similar to us are apt, for that very reason, to escape us; and what we have very frequently performed from certain motives, we are apt likewise to continue mechanically, without recalling, on every occasion, the reflections which first determined us. The convenience, or rather necessity, which leads to justice, is so universal, and everywhere points so much to the same rules, that the habit takes place in all societies; and it is not without some scrutiny that we are able to ascertain its true origin. The matter, however, is not so obscure, but that, even in common life, we have every moment recourse to the principle of public utility, and ask, *What must become of the world, if such practices prevail? How could society subsist under such disorders?* Were the distinction or separation of possessions entirely useless, can any one conceive that it ever should have obtained in society?

Thus we seem, upon the whole, to have attained a knowledge of the force of that principle here insisted on, and can determine what degree of esteem or moral approbation may result from reflections on public interest and utility. The necessity of justice to the support of society is the SOLE foundation of that virtue; and since no more excellence is more highly esteemed, we may conclude, that this circumstance of usefulness has, in general, the strongest energy, and most entire command over our sentiments. It must therefore be the source of a considerable part of the merit ascribed to humanity, benevolence, friendship, public spirit, and other social virtues of that stamp; as it is the SOLE source of the moral approbation paid to fidelity, justice, veracity, integrity, and those other estimable and useful qualities and principles. It is entirely agreeable to the rules of philosophy, and even of common reason, where any principle has been found to have a great force and energy in one instance, to ascribe to it a like energy in all similar instances. This indeed is Newton's chief rule of philosophizing.*

[…]

Section V – Why Utility Pleases

Part I

IT seems so natural a thought to ascribe to their utility the praise which we bestow on the social virtues, that one would expect to meet with this principle everywhere in moral writers, as the chief foundation of their reasoning and inquiry. In common life, we may observe, that the circumstance of utility is always appealed to; nor is it supposed that a greater eulogy can be given to any man, than to display his usefulness to the public, and enumerate the services which he has performed to mankind and to society. What praise, even of an inanimate form, if the regularity and elegance of its parts destroy not its fitness for any useful purpose! And how satisfactory an apology for any disproportion or seeming deformity, if we can show the necessity of that particular construction for the use intended! A ship appears more beautiful to an artist, or one moderately skilled in navigation, where its prow is wide and swelling beyond its poop, than if it were framed with a precise geometrical regularity, in contradiction to all the laws of mechanics. A building, whose doors and windows were exact squares, would hurt the eye by that very proportion, as ill adapted to the figure of a human creature, for whose service the fabric was intended. What wonder then that a man, whose habits and conduct are hurtful to society, and dangerous and pernicious to every one who has intercourse with him, should, on that account, be an object of disapprobation, and communicate to every spectator the strongest sentiment of disgust and hatred?*

But perhaps the difficulty of accounting for these effects of usefulness, or its contrary, has kept philosophers from admitting them into their systems of ethics, and has induced them rather to employ any other principle, in

---

* Principia, lib. iii.

* We ought not to imagine, because an inanimate object may be useful as well as a man, that therefore it ought also, according to this system, to merit the appellation of *virtuous*. The sentiments excited by utility are, in the two cases, very different; and the one is mixed with affection, esteem, approbation, etc. and not the other. In like manner, an inanimate object may have good color and proportions as well as a human figure. But can we ever be in love with the former? There are a numerous set of passions and sentiments, of which thinking, rational beings are, by the original constitution of nature, the only proper objects: and though the very same qualities be transferred to an insensible, inanimate being, they will not excite the same sentiment. The beneficial qualities of herbs and minerals are, indeed, sometimes called their *virtues;* but this is an effect of the caprice of language, which ought not to be regarded in reasoning. For though there be a species of approbation attending even inanimate objects, when beneficial, yet this sentiment is so weak, and so different from that which is directed to beneficent magistrates or statesmen, that they ought not to be ranked under the same class or appellation.

A very small variation of the object, even where the same qualities are preserved, will destroy a sentiment. Thus, the same beauty, transferred to a different sex, excites no amorous passion, where nature is not extremely perverted.

explaining the origin of moral good and evil. But it is no just reason for rejecting any principle, confirmed by experience, that we cannot give a satisfactory account of its origin, nor are able to resolve into other more general principles. And if we would employ a little thought on the present subject, we need be at no loss to account for the influence of utility, and to deduce it from principles, the most known and avowed in human nature.

From the apparent usefulness of the social virtues, it has readily been inferred by sceptics, both ancient and modern, that all moral distinctions arise from education, and were at first invented, and afterwards encouraged, by the art of politicians, in order to render men tractable, and subdue their natural ferocity and selfishness, which incapacitated them for society. This principle, indeed, of precept and education, must so far be owned to have a powerful influence, that it may frequently increase or diminish, beyond their natural standard, the sentiments of approbation or dislike; and may even, in particular instances, create, without any natural principle, a new sentiment of this kind, as it is evident in all superstitious practices and observances: but that *all* moral affection or dislike arises from this origin, will never surely be allowed by any judicious inquirer. Had nature made no such distinction, founded on the original constitution of the mind, the words *honorable* and *shameful*, *lovely* and *odious*, *noble* and *despicable*, had never any place in any language; nor could politicians, had they invented these terms, ever have been able to render them intelligible, or make them convey an idea to the audience. So that nothing can be more superficial than this paradox of the sceptics; and it were well if, in the abstruser studies of logic and metaphysics, we could as easily obviate the cavils of that sect, as in the practical and more intelligible sciences of politics and morals.

The social virtues must, therefore, be allowed to have a natural beauty and amiableness, which at first, antecedent to all precept or education, recommends them to the esteem of uninstructed mankind, and engages their affections. And as the public utility of these virtues is the chief circumstance whence they derive their merit, it follows, that the end, which they have a tendency to promote, must be some way agreeable to us, and take hold of some natural affection. It must please, either from considerations of self-interest, or from more generous motives and regards.

It has often been asserted, that as every man has a strong connection with society, and perceives the impossibility of his solitary subsistence, he becomes, on that account, favorable to all those habits or principles which promote order in society, and insure to him the quiet possession of so inestimable a blessing. As much as we value our own happiness and welfare, as much must we applaud the practice of justice and humanity, by which alone the social confederacy can be maintained, and every man reap the fruits of mutual protection and assistance.

This deduction of morals from self-love, or a regard to private interest, is an obvious thought, and has not arisen wholly from the wanton sallies and sportive assaults of the sceptics. To mention no others, Polybius, one of the gravest and most judicious, as well as most moral writers of antiquity, has assigned the selfish origin to all our sentiments of virtue.* But though the solid practical sense of that author, and his aversion to all vain subtilties, render his authority on the present subject very considerable, yet is not this an affair to be decided by authority; and the voice of nature and experience seems plainly to oppose the selfish theory.

We frequently bestow praise on virtuous actions, performed in very distant ages and remote countries, where the utmost subtilty of imagination would not discover any appearance of self-interest, or find any connection of our present happiness and security with events so widely separated from us.

A generous, a brave, a noble deed, performed by an adversary, commands our approbation; while, in its consequences, it may be acknowledged prejudicial to our particular interest.

When private advantage concurs, with general affection for virtue, we readily perceive and avow the mixture of these distinct sentiments, which have a very different feeling and influence on the mind. We praise, perhaps, with more alacrity, where the generous, humane action, contributes to our particular interest: but the topics of praise, which we insist on, are very wide of this circumstance. And we may attempt to bring over others to our sentiments, without endeavoring to convince them that they reap any advantage from the actions which we recommend to their approbation and applause.

Frame the model of a praiseworthy character, consisting of all the most amiable moral virtues: give instances in which these display themselves after an eminent and extraordinary manner: you readily engage the esteem and approbation of all your audience, who never so much as inquire in what age and country the person lived who

---

* Undutifulness to parents is disapproved of by mankind, προορωμένους τὸ μέλλον, καὶ συλλογιζομένους ὅτι τὸ παραπλήσιον ἑκάστοις αὐτν συγκυρήσει. Ingratitude, for a like reason (though he seems there to mix a more generous regard) συναγανακτοῦντας μὲν τῷ πέλας, ἀναφέροντας δ' ἐπ' αὐτοὺς τὸ παραπλήσιον ἐξ ὧν ὑπογίγνεταί τις ἔννοια παρ' ἑκάστῳ τοῦ καθήκοντος δυνάμεως καὶ θεωρίας. Polyb. Lib. vi. cap. iv. Perhaps the historian only meant, that our sympathy and humanity were more enlivened, by our considering the similarity of our case with that of the person suffering; which is a just sentiment.

possessed these noble qualities; a circumstance, however, of all others the most material to self-love, or a concern for our own individual happiness.

Once on a time a statesman, in the shock and contest of parties, prevailed so far as to procure, by his eloquence, the banishment of an able adversary; whom he secretly followed, offering him money for his support during his exile, and soothing him with topics of consolation in his misfortunes. *Alas!* cries the banished statesman, *with what regret must I leave my friends in this city, where even enemies are so generous!* Virtue, though in an enemy, here pleased him: and we also give it the just tribute of praise and approbation; nor do we retract these sentiments, when we hear that the action passed at Athens about two thousand years ago, and that the persons' names were Eschines and Demosthenes.

What is that to me? There are few occasions when this question is not pertinent: and had it that universal, infallible influence supposed, it would turn into ridicule every composition, and almost every conversation, which contain any praise or censure of men and manners.

It is but a weak subterfuge, when pressed by these facts and arguments, to say that we transport ourselves, by the force of imagination, into distant ages and countries, and consider the advantage which we should have reaped from these characters had we been contemporaries, and had any commerce with the persons. It is not conceivable how a *real* sentiment or passion can ever arise from a known *imaginary* interest, especially when our *real* interest is still kept in view, and is often acknowledged to be entirely distinct from the imaginary, and even sometimes opposite to it.

A man brought to the brink of a precipice, cannot look down without trembling; and the sentiment of *imaginary* danger actuates him, in opposition to the opinion and belief of *real* safety. But the imagination is here assisted by the presence of a striking object, and yet prevails not, except it be also aided by novelty, and the unusual appearance of the object. Custom soon reconciles us to heights and precipices, and wears off these false and delusive terrors. The reverse is observable in the estimates which we form of characters and manners; and the more we habituate ourselves to an accurate scrutiny of morals, the more delicate feeling do we acquire of the most minute distinctions between vice and virtue. Such frequent occasion, indeed, have we, in common life, to pronounce all kinds of moral determinations, that no object of this kind can be new or unusual to us; nor could any *false* views or prepossessions maintain their ground against an experience so common and familiar. Experience being chiefly what forms the associations of ideas, it is impossible that any association could establish and support itself in direct opposition to that principle.

Usefulness is agreeable, and engages our approbation. This is a matter of fact, confirmed by daily observation. But *useful?* For what? For somebody's interest surely. Whose interest then? Not our own only, for our approbation frequently extends further. It must therefore be the interest of those who are served by the character or action approved of; and these, we may conclude, however remote, are not totally indifferent to us. By opening up this principle, we shall discover one great source of moral distinctions.

Part II

Self-love is a principle in human nature of such extensive energy, and the interest of each individual is in general so closely connected with that of the community, that those philosophers were excusable who fancied that all our concern for the public might be resolved into a concern for our own happiness and preservation. They saw, every moment, instances of approbation or blame, satisfaction or displeasure, towards characters and actions; they denominated the objects of these sentiments *virtues* or *vices;* they observed, that the former had a tendency to increase the happiness, and the latter the misery of mankind; they asked, whether it were possible that we could have any general concern for society, or any disinterested resentment of the welfare or injury of others; they found it simpler to consider all these sentiments as modifications of self-love; and they discovered a pretence at least for this unity of principle, in that close union of interest which is so observable between the public and each individual.

But notwithstanding this frequent confusion of interests, it is easy to attain what natural philosophers, after Lord Bacon, have affected to call the *experimentum crucis,* or that experiment which points out the right way in any doubt or ambiguity. We have found instances in which private interest was separate from public; in which it was even contrary, and yet we observed the moral sentiment to continue, notwithstanding this disjunction of interests. And wherever these distinct interests sensibly concurred, we always found a sensible increase of the sentiment, and a more warm affection to virtue, and detestation of vice, or what we properly call *gratitude* and *revenge.* Compelled by these instances, we must renounce the theory which accounts for every moral sentiment by the principle of self-love. We must adopt a more public affection, and allow that the interests of society are not, even on their own account, entirely indifferent to us. Usefulness is only a tendency to a certain end; and it is a contradiction in terms, that any thing pleases as means to an end, where the end itself nowise affects us. If usefulness, therefore, be a source of moral sentiment, and if this usefulness be not always considered with a reference to self, it follows, that every thing which contributes to the happiness of society recommends itself directly to our approbation and goodwill. Here is a principle which accounts, in great part, for the origin of morality: and what need we seek for abstruse and remote systems, when there occurs one so obvious and natural?*

Have we any difficulty to comprehend the force of humanity and benevolence? Or to conceive, that the very aspect of happiness, joy, prosperity, gives pleasure; that of pain, suffering, sorrow, communicates uneasiness? The human countenance, says Horace,[†] borrows smiles or tears from the human countenance. Reduce a person to solitude, and he loses all enjoyment, except either of the sensual or speculative kind; and that because the movements of his heart are not forwarded by correspondent movements in his fellow-creatures. The signs of sorrow and mourning, though arbitrary, affect us with melancholy; but the natural symptoms, tears, and cries, and groans, never fail to infuse compassion and uneasiness. And if the effects of misery touch us in so lively a manner, can we be supposed altogether insensible or indifferent towards its causes, when a malicious or treacherous character and behavior are presented to us?

We enter, I shall suppose, into a convenient, warm, well-contrived apartment: we necessarily receive a pleasure from its very survey, because it presents us with the pleasing ideas of ease, satisfaction, and enjoyment. The hospitable, good-humored, humane landlord appears. This circumstance surely must embellish the whole; nor can we easily forbear reflecting, with pleasure, on the satisfaction which results to every one from his intercourse and good offices.

His whole family, by the freedom, ease, confidence, and calm enjoyment diffused over their countenances, sufficiently express their happiness. I have a pleasing sympathy in the prospect of so much joy, and can never consider the source of it without the most agreeable emotions.

He tells me that an oppressive and powerful neighbor had attempted to dispossess him of his inheritance, and had long disturbed all his innocent and social pleasures. I feel an immediate indignation arise in me against such violence and injury.

But it is no wonder, he adds, that a private wrong should proceed from a man who had enslaved provinces, depopulated cities, and made the field and scaffold stream with human blood. I am struck with horror at the prospect of so much misery, and am actuated by the strongest antipathy against its author.

In general, it is certain, that wherever we go, whatever we reflect on or converse about, every thing still presents us with the view of human happiness or misery, and excites in our breast a sympathetic movement of pleasure or uneasiness. In our serious occupations, in our careless amusements, this principle still exerts its active energy.

A man who enters the theatre is immediately struck with the view of so great a multitude participating of one common amusement; and experiences, from their very aspect, a superior sensibility or disposition of being affected with every sentiment which he shares with his fellow-creatures.

He observes the actors to be animated by the appearance of a full audience, and raised to a degree of enthusiasm which they cannot command in any solitary or calm moment.

Every movement of the theatre, by a skilful poet, is communicated, as it were, by magic to the spectators; who weep, tremble, resent, rejoice, and are inflamed with all the variety of passions which actuate the several personages of the drama.

Where any event crosses our wishes, and interrupts the happiness of the favorite characters, we feel a sensible anxiety and concern. But where their sufferings proceed from the treachery, cruelty, or tyranny of an enemy, our breasts are affected with the liveliest resentment against the author of these calamities.

---

* It is needless to push our researches so far as to ask, why we have humanity or a fellow-feeling with others? It is sufficient that this is experienced to be a principle in human nature. We must stop somewhere in our examination of causes; and there are, in every science, some general principles, beyond which we cannot hope to find any principle more general. No man is absolutely indifferent to the happiness and misery of others. The first has a natural tendency to give pleasure, the second pain. This every one may find in himself. It is not probable that these principles can be resolved into principles more simple and universal, whatever attempts may have been made to that purpose. But if it were possible, it belongs not to the present subject; and we may here safely consider these principles as original, – happy if we can render all the consequences sufficiently plain and perspicuous!

† *Uti ridentibus arrident, ita flentibus adflent*
Humani vultus.   HOR.

It is here esteemed contrary to the rules of art to represent any thing cool and indifferent. A distant friend, or a confidant, who has no immediate interest in the catastrophe, ought, if possible, to be avoided by the poet, as communicating a like indifference to the audience, and checking the progress of the passions.

Few species of poetry are more entertaining than *pastoral;* and every one is sensible, that the chief source of its pleasure arises from those images of a gentle and tender tranquillity which it represents in its personages, and of which it communicates a like sentiment to the reader. Sannazarius, who transferred the scene to the sea-shore, though he presented the most magnificent object in nature, is confessed to have erred in his choice. The idea of toil, labor, and danger, suffered by the fishermen, is painful; by an unavoidable sympathy which attends every conception of human happiness or misery.

When I was twenty, says a French poet, Ovid was my favorite: now I am forty, I declare for Horace. We enter, to be sure, more readily into sentiments which resemble those we feel every day: but no passion, when well represented, can be entirely indifferent to us; because there is none of which every man has not with him, at least the seeds and first principles. It is the business of poetry to bring every affection near to us by lively imagery and representation, and make it look like truth and reality; a certain proof that, wherever the reality is found, our minds are disposed to be strongly affected by it.

Any recent event or piece of news, by which the fate of states, provinces, or many individuals is affected, is extremely interesting even to those whose welfare is not immediately engaged. Such intelligence is propagated with celerity, heard with avidity, and inquired into with attention and concern. The interest of society appears, on this occasion, to be in some degree the interest of each individual. The imagination is sure to be affected; though the passions excited may not always be so strong and steady as to have great influence on the conduct and behavior.

The perusal of a history seems a calm entertainment; but would be no entertainment at all, did not our hearts beat with correspondent movements to those which are described by the historian.

Thucydides and Guicciardin support with difficulty our attention; while the former describes the trivial rencounters of the small cities of Greece, and the latter the harmless wars of Pisa. The few persons interested, and the small interest, fill not the imagination, and engage not the affections. The deep distress of the numerous Athenian army before Syracuse; the danger which so nearly threatens Venice; these excite compassion; these move terror and anxiety.

The indifferent, uninteresting style of Suetonius, equally with the masterly pencil of Tacitus, may convince us of the cruel depravity of Nero or Tiberius; but what a difference of sentiment! While the former coldly relates the acts, the latter sets before our eyes the venerable figures of a Soranus and a Thrasea, intrepid in their fate, and only moved by the melting sorrows of their friends and kindred. What sympathy then touches every human heart! What indignation against the tyrant, whose causeless fear or unprovoked malice gave rise to such detestable barbarity!

If we bring these subjects nearer; if we remove all suspicion of fiction and deceit; what powerful concern is excited, and how much superior, in many instances, to the narrow attachments of self-love and private interest! Popular sedition, party zeal, a devoted obedience to factious leaders; these are some of the most visible, though less laudable effects of this social sympathy in human nature.

The frivolousness of the subject, too, we may observe, is not able to detach us entirely from what carries an image of human sentiment and affection.

When a person stutters, and pronounces with difficulty, we even sympathize with this trivial uneasiness, and suffer for him. And it is a rule in criticism, that every combination of syllables or letters, which gives pain to the organs of speech in the recital, appears also, from a species of sympathy, harsh and disagreeable to the ear. Nay, when we run over a book with our eye, we are sensible of such unharmonious composition; because we still imagine, that a person recites it to us, and suffers from the pronunciation of these jarring sounds. So delicate is our sympathy!

Easy and unconstrained postures and motions are always beautiful: an air of health and vigor is agreeable: clothes which warm, without burdening the body; which cover, without imprisoning the limbs, are well-fashioned. In every judgment of beauty, the feelings of the person affected enter into consideration, and communicates to the spectator similar touches of pain or pleasure.* What wonder, then, if we can pronounce no judgment concerning the character and conduct of men, without considering the tendencies of their actions,

---

* "Decentior equus cujus astricta sunt ilia; sed idem velocior. Pulcher aspectu sit athleta, cujus lacertos exercitatio expressit; idem certamini paratior. Nunquam enim *species* ab *utilitate* dividitur. Sed hoc quidem discernere modici judicii est." – Quintilian Inst. lib. viii. cap. 3.

and the happiness or misery which thence arises to society? What association of ideas would ever operate, were that principle here totally inactive?*

If any man, from a cold insensibility, or narrow selfishness of temper, is unaffected with the images of human happiness or misery, he must be equally indifferent to the images of vice and virtue: as, on the other hand, it is always found, that a warm concern for the interests of our species is attended with a delicate feeling of all moral distinctions, a strong resentment of injury done to men, a lively approbation of their welfare. In this particular, though great superiority is observable of one man above another, yet none are so entirely indifferent to the interests of their fellow-creatures, as to perceive no distinctions of moral good and evil, in consequence of the different tendencies of actions and principles. How, indeed, can we suppose it possible in any one, who wears a human heart, that if there be subjected to his censure one character or system of conduct which is beneficial, and another which is pernicious to his species or community, he will not so much as give a cool preference to the former, or ascribe to it the smallest merit or regard? Let us suppose such a person ever so selfish; let private interest have engrossed ever so much his attention, yet in instances where that is not concerned, he must unavoidably feel *some* propensity to the good of mankind, and make it an object of choice, if every thing else be equal. Would any man, who is walking alone, tread as willingly on another's gouty toes, whom he has no quarrel with, as on the hard flint and pavement? There is here surely a difference in the case. We surely take into consideration the happiness and misery of others, in weighing the several motives of actions, and incline to the former, where no private regards draw us to seek our own promotion or advantage by the injury of our fellow-creatures. And if the principles of humanity are capable, in many instances, of influencing our actions, they must, at all times, have *some* authority over our sentiments, and give us a general approbation of what is useful to society, and blame of what is dangerous or pernicious. The degrees of these sentiments may be the subject of controversy; but the reality of their existence, one should think, must be admitted in every theory or system.

A creature, absolutely malicious and spiteful, were there any such in nature, must be worse than indifferent to the images of vice and virtue. All his sentiments must be inverted, and directly opposite to those which prevail in the human species. Whatever contributes to the good of mankind, as it crosses the constant bent of his wishes and desires, must produce uneasiness and disapprobation; and, on the contrary, whatever is the source of disorder and misery in society, must, for the same reason, be regarded with pleasure and complacency. Timon, who probably from his affected spleen, more than any inveterate malice, was denominated the man-hater, embraced Alcibiades with great fondness. *Go on, my boy!* cried he, *acquire the confidence of the people: you will one day, I foresee, be the cause of great calamities to them.** Could we admit the two principles of the Manicheans, it is an infallible consequence, that their sentiments of human actions, as well as of every thing else, must be totally opposite, and that every instance of justice and humanity, from its necessary tendency, must please the one deity and displease the other. All mankind so far resemble the good principle, that where interest, or revenge, or envy, prevents not our disposition, we are always inclined, from our natural philanthropy, to give the preference to the happiness of society, and consequently to virtue above its opposite. Absolute, unprovoked, disinterested malice, has never, perhaps, place in any human breast; or if it had, must there pervert all the sentiments of morals, as well as the feelings of humanity. If the cruelty of Nero be allowed entirely voluntary, and not rather the effect of constant fear and resentment, it is evident that Tigellinus, preferably to Seneca or Burrhus, must have possessed his steady and uniform approbation.

A statesman or patriot, who serves our own country, in our own time, has always a more passionate regard paid to him, than one whose beneficial influence operated on distant ages or remote nations; where the good resulting from his generous humanity, being less connected with us, seems more obscure, and affects us with a less lively sympathy. We may own the merit to be equally great, though our sentiments are not raised to an equal height in

* In proportion to the station which a man possesses, according to the relations in which he is placed, we always expect from him a greater or less degree of good, and, when disappointed, blame his inutility; and much more do we blame him, if any ill or prejudice arises from his conduct and behavior. When the interests of one country interfere with those of another, we estimate the merits of a statesman by the good or ill which results to his own country from his measures and counsels, without regard to the prejudice which he brings on its enemies and rivals. His fellow-citizens are the objects which lie nearest the eye while we determine his character. And as nature has implanted in every one a superior affection to his own country, we never expect any regard to distant nations where à competition arises. Not to mention, that while every man consults the good of his own community, we are sensible that the general interest of mankind is better promoted, than by any loose undeterminate views to the good of a species, whence no beneficial action could ever result, for want of a duly limited object on which they could exert themselves.

* Plutarch in vita Alcib.

both cases. The judgment here corrects the inequalities of our internal emotions and perceptions; in like manner as it preserves us from error, in the several variations of images presented to our external senses. The same object, at a double distance, really throws on the eye a picture of but half the bulk, yet we imagine that it appears of the same size in both situations; because we know that, on our approach to it, its image would expand on the eye, and that the difference consists not in the object itself, but in our position with regard to it. And indeed, without such a correction of appearances, both in internal and external sentiment, men could never think or talk steadily on any subject, while their fluctuating situations produce a continual variation on objects, and throw them into such different and contrary lights and positions.*

The more we converse with mankind, and the greater social intercourse we maintain, the more shall we be familiarized to these general preferences and distinctions, without which our conversation and discourse could scarcely be rendered intelligible to each other. Every man's interest is peculiar to himself, and the aversions and desires which result from it cannot be supposed to affect others in a like degree. General language therefore, being formed for general use, must be moulded on more general views, and must affix the epithets of praise or blame, in conformity to sentiments which arise from the general interests of the community. And if these sentiments, in most men, be not so strong as those which have a reference to private good, yet still they must make some distinction, even in persons the most depraved and selfish, and must attach the notion of good to a beneficent conduct, and of evil to the contrary. Sympathy, we shall allow, is much fainter than our concern for ourselves, and sympathy with persons remote from us much fainter than that with persons near and contiguous; but for this very reason, it is necessary for us, in our calm judgments and discourse concerning the characters of men, to neglect all the differences, and render our sentiments more public and social. Besides, that we ourselves often change our situation in this particular, we every day meet with persons who are in a situation different from us, and who could never converse with us, were we to remain constantly in that position and point of view which is peculiar to ourselves. The intercourse of sentiments, therefore, in society and conversation, makes us form some general unalterable standard, by which we may approve or disapprove of characters and manners. And though the heart takes not part entirely with those general notions, nor regulates all its love and hatred by the universal abstract differences of vice and virtue, without regard to self, or the persons with whom we are more intimately connected, yet have these moral differences a considerable influence; and being sufficient, at least, for discourse, serve all our purposes in company, in the pulpit, in the theatre, and in the schools.*

Thus, in whatever light we take this subject, the merit ascribed to the social virtues appears still uniform, and arises chiefly from that regard which the natural sentiment of benevolence engages us to pay to the interests of mankind and society. If we consider the principles of the human make, such as they appear to daily experience and observation, we must, *à priori*, conclude it impossible for such a creature as man to be totally indifferent to the well or ill being of his fellow-creatures, and not readily, of himself, to pronounce, where nothing gives him any particular bias, that what promotes their happiness is good, what tends to their misery is evil, without any further regard or consideration. Here then are the faint rudiments at least, or outlines, of a *general* distinction between actions; and in proportion as the humanity of the person is supposed to increase, his connection with those who are injured or benefited, and his lively conception of their misery or happiness, his consequent censure or approbation acquires proportionable vigor. There is no necessity that a generous action, barely mentioned in an old history or remote gazette, should communicate any strong feelings of applause and admiration. Virtue, placed at such a distance, is like a fixed star, which, though to the eye of reason it may appear as luminous as the sun in his meridian, is so infinitely

---

* For a like reason, the tendencies of actions and characters, not their real accidental consequences, are alone regarded in our moral determinations or general judgments, though in our real feeling or sentiment we cannot help paying greater regard to one whose station, joined to virtue, renders him really useful to society, than to one who exerts the social virtues only in good intentions and benevolent affections. Separating the character from the fortune, by an easy and necessary effort of thought, we pronounce these persons alike, and give them the same general praise. The judgment corrects, or endeavors to correct, the appearance, but is not able entirely to prevail over sentiment.

Why is this peach-tree said to be better than that other, but because it produces more or better fruit? And would not the same praise be given it, though snails or vermin had destroyed the peaches before they came to full maturity? In morals too, is not *the tree known by the fruit?* And cannot we easily distinguish between nature and accident, in the one case as well as in the other?

* It is wisely ordained by nature, that private connections should commonly prevail over universal views and considerations, otherwise our affections and actions would be dissipated and lost for want of a proper limited object. Thus a small benefit done to ourselves, or our near friends, excites more lively sentiments of love and approbation, than a great benefit done to a distant commonwealth: but still we know here, as in all the senses, to correct these inequalities by reflection, and retain a general standard of vice and virtue, founded chiefly on general usefulness.

removed as to affect the senses neither with light nor heat. Bring this virtue nearer, by our acquaintance or connection with the persons, or even by an eloquent recital of the case, our hearts are immediately caught, our sympathy enlivened, and our cool approbation converted into the warmest sentiments of friendship and regard. These seem necessary and infallible consequences of the general principles of human nature, as discovered in common life and practice.

Again, reverse these views and reasonings: consider the matter *à posteriori*; and, weighing the consequences, inquire if the merit of social virtue be not, in a great measure, derived from the feelings of humanity with which it affects the spectators. It appears to be matter of fact, that the circumstance of *utility*, in all subjects, is a source of praise and approbation: that it is constantly appealed to in all moral decisions concerning the merit and demerit of actions: that it is the *sole* source of that high regard paid to justice, fidelity, honor, allegiance, and chastity: that it is inseparable from all the other social virtues, humanity, generosity, charity, affability, lenity, mercy, and moderation: and, in a word, it is a foundation of the chief part of morals, which has a reference to mankind and our fellow-creatures.

It appears also that, in our general approbation of characters and manners, the useful tendency of the social virtues moves us not by any regards to self-interest, but has an influence much more universal and extensive. It appears that a tendency to public good, and to the promoting of peace, harmony, and order in society, does always, by affecting the benevolent principles of our frame, engage us on the side of the social virtues. And it appears, as an additional confirmation, that these principles of humanity and sympathy enter so deeply into all our sentiments, and have so powerful an influence, as may enable them to excite the strongest censure and applause. The present theory is the simple result of all these inferences, each of which seems founded on uniform experience and observation.

Were it doubtful whether there were any such principle in our nature as humanity or a concern for others, yet when we see, in numberless instances, that whatever has a tendency to promote the interest of society, is so highly approved of, we ought thence to learn the force of the benevolent principle, since it is impossible for any thing to please as means to an end, where the end is totally indifferent. On the other hand, were it doubtful whether there were implanted in our nature any general principle of moral blame and approbation, yet when we see, in numberless instances, the influence of humanity, we ought thence to conclude, that it is impossible but that every thing which promotes the interests of society must communicate pleasure, and what is pernicious give uneasiness. But when these different reflections and observations concur in establishing the same conclusion, must they not bestow an undisputed evidence upon it?

It is however hoped, that the progress of this argument will bring a further confirmation of the present theory, by showing the rise of other sentiments of esteem and regard from the same or like principles.

[…]

Section IX – Conclusion

I cannot, *at present*, be more assured of any truth, which I learn from reasoning and argument, than that personal merit consists entirely in the usefulness or agreeableness of qualities to the person himself possessed of them, or to others who have any intercourse with him. But when I reflect, that though the bulk and figure of the earth have been measured and delineated, though the motions of the tides have been accounted for, the order and economy of the heavenly bodies subjected to their proper laws, and INFINITE itself reduced to calculation; yet men still dispute concerning the foundation of their moral duties: when I reflect on this, I say, I fall back into diffidence and scepticism, and suspect, that an hypothesis, so obvious, had it been a true one, would, long ere now, have been received by the unanimous suffrage and consent of mankind.

5

The Theory of Moral Sentiments

Adam Smith

Adam Smith, a slightly younger Scottish contemporary of David Hume, developed his own version of an ethics based on the sentiments. Smith's view of human nature was more benign than that of some of his predecessors, in particular Thomas Hobbes. He begins his most famous and significant work in ethics, *The Theory of the Moral Sentiments*, with the claim that it is obvious that human beings have the capacity for 'sympathy' – feelings that resonate with, reflect, or arise from those of others. Such sympathy is not even indirectly egoistic. If I am sympathizing with your grief over the death of your son, I am imagining not what I should suffer were my own son to die, but what I should suffer were I you.

One central kind of sympathy is compassion for the suffering of others. But we can sympathize with any kind of feeling: joy, gratitude, resentment, and so on. Sometimes our own feeling spontaneously mirrors another's: consider how seeing someone smile can make you smile. But in standard cases, according to Smith, it operates through imagination. We put ourselves in the position of others and consider not just what their sentiments *are* but what they *should be*. Our sympathy, exercised through imagination, does not merely mimic the sentiments of others, but corresponds to what we think those sentiments *should* be. Sympathy arises, then, not so much from our recognizing another's sentiments, but from our understanding their situation. The object of our sympathy may even be unable to appreciate their situation. When we feel compassion for a person who is demented, though apparently content, Smith suggests, it is the result of our imagining how we would feel in their situation if we were also – per impossibile – able to consider it rationally.

Smith's philosophical ethics, like that of Hume, is sometimes interpreted as purely descriptive. But the sentiments Smith is describing are his own, so when he describes standards of appropriateness for those sentiments, and speaks in favour of normative principles corresponding to them, it is most plausible to understand him as expressing his own moral views rather than as attempting merely to articulate them in a confessional or positivist spirit. The standard by which we judge, and should judge, affections, and the actions they produce, is one of *propriety*. The *merit* and *demerit* of actions consist in the good or bad results which the affection that led to the action aims at or tends to produce, and it is these qualities that ground deserved reward or punishment.

Propriety is a matter of the pure 'fittingness' of some affection or action, and in clearly distinguishing the standard of fittingness from that of utility Smith in effect distances himself from Hume, who tends to ground the virtues in their utility. It is this notion of fittingness that underpins Smith's famous notion of the internal 'impartial spectator', whose deliverances are equivalent to the voice of conscience.

It is significant that the impartial spectator is seen as a human being. His perspective is not that of God, as we learn for example from Smith's discussion of what is now called 'moral luck'. Smith describes as the 'equitable maxim' the view that we should praise or blame others solely for what they intend, independently of how their actions turn out, noting that while everyone will agree with it 'in abstract and general

History of Ethics – Essential Readings with Commentary, First Edition. Edited by Daniel Star and Roger Crisp.
© 2020 John Wiley & Sons Ltd. Published 2020 by John Wiley & Sons Ltd.

terms', in practice our sentiments are greatly influenced by how things turn out. This 'irregularity of sentiment', given to us by 'nature' – that is, by God – has a beneficent purpose. Without it, we would persecute others constantly for mere intentions or suspected intentions, we would be less concerned to avoid negligence, and so on. Now, one might expect the impartial spectator's sentiments to be 'equitable' and 'regular', perhaps as antidote to this further bias within our natural sentiments. But this would of course defeat the purpose of the irregularity itself. So we find, for example, that the spectator will 'feel some indulgence for what may be regarded as the unjust resentment' of someone who has been injured in an accident by someone through no fault of their own.

One has to accept that there is a tension in Smith's position at this point. The correct point of view is that of God, and to that extent in cases of moral luck the view of the spectator is distorted. But Smith can at least allow that there is room for reflection on the equitable maxim, which may moderate our sentiments in accordance with whatever rule is in fact optimum for humanity as a whole.

Does Smith 'solve' the problem of moral luck – the problem of whether we should judge people by their intentions only (which would be fair and just) or also by the effects of those intentions (which are not entirely under the control of the agent)? Consider two equally drunk drivers, one of whom kills a pedestrian, and the other of whom doesn't, just because no pedestrian steps out in front of her car. Should we follow the equitable maxim, and judge them to be equally blameworthy? Or, as Smith would recommend, should we blame and punish the killer more, because of the benefits of such practices of blame and punishment in general?

There is no doubt that Smith sets out the problem of moral luck with great clarity and brilliance. But his own solution lacks a justification of why we should continue to allow ourselves to inflict what amounts to unjust punishment on others because of the good consequences of the practice of so doing. Smith himself may well have believed that any such injustices would be compensated for in the afterlife. There are difficulties internal to that view (wouldn't it be better never to suffer the injustice in the first place?); but of course its usefulness as a support for Smith's solution to the problem of moral luck is these days somewhat limited.

Section I – Of the Sense of Propriety

Chapter I – Of Sympathy

How selfish soever man may be supposed, there are evidently some principles in his nature, which interest him in the fortune of others, and render their happiness necessary to him, though he derives nothing from, it, except the pleasure of seeing it. Of this kind is pity or compassion, the emotion which we feel for the misery of others, when we either see it, or are made to conceive it in a very lively manner. That we often derive sorrow from the sorrow of others, is a matter of fact too obvious to require any instances to prove it; for this sentiment, like all the other original passions of human nature, is by no means confined to the virtuous and humane, though they perhaps may feel it with the most exquisite sensibility. The greatest ruffian, the most hardened violator of the laws of society, is not altogether without it.

As we have no immediate experience of what other men feel, we can form no idea of the manner in which they are affected, but by conceiving what we ourselves should feel in the like situation. Though our brother is upon the rack, as long as we ourselves are at our ease, our senses will never inform us of what he suffers. They never did, and never can, carry us beyond our own person, and it is by the imagination only that we can form any conception of what are his sensations. Neither can that faculty help us to this any other way, than by representing to us what would be our own, if we were in his case. It is the impressions of our own senses only, not those of his, which our imaginations copy. By the imagination we place ourselves in his situation, we conceive ourselves enduring all the same torments, we enter as it were into his body, and become in some measure the same person with him, and thence form some idea of his sensations, and even feel something which, though weaker in degree, is not altogether unlike them. His agonies, when they are thus brought home to ourselves, when we have thus adopted and made them our own, begin at last to affect us, and we then tremble and shudder at the thought of what he feels. For as to be in pain or distress of any kind excites the most excessive sorrow, so to conceive or to imagine that we are in it, excites some degree of the same emotion, in proportion to the vivacity or dulness of the conception.

That this is the source of our fellow-feeling for the misery of others, that it is by changing places in fancy with the sufferer, that we come either to conceive or to be affected by what he feels, may be demonstrated by many obvious observations, if it should not be thought sufficiently evident of itself. When we see a stroke aimed, and just ready to fall upon the leg or arm of another person, we naturally shrink and draw back our own leg or our own arm; and when it does fall, we feel it in some measure, and are hurt by it as well as the sufferer. The mob, when they are gazing at a dancer on the slack rope, naturally writhe and twist and balance their own bodies as they see him do, and as they feel that they themselves must do if in his situation. Persons of delicate fibres and a weak constitution of body complain, that in looking on the sores and ulcers which are exposed by beggars in the streets, they are apt to feel an itching or uneasy sensation in the corresponding part of their own bodies. The horror which they conceive at the misery of those wretches affects that particular part in themselves more than any other; because that horror arises from conceiving what they themselves would suffer, if they really were the wretches whom they are looking upon, and if that particular part in themselves was actually affected in the same miserable manner. The very force of this conception is sufficient, in their feeble frames, to produce that itching or uneasy sensation complained of. Men of the most robust make, observe that in looking upon sore eyes they often feel a very sensible soreness in their own, which proceeds from the same reason; that organ being in the strongest man more delicate than any other part of the body is in the weakest.

Neither is it those circumstances only, which create pain or sorrow, that call forth our fellow-feeling. Whatever is the passion which arises from any object in the person principally concerned, an analogous emotion springs up, at the thought of his situation, in the breast of every attentive spectator. Our joy for the deliverance of those heroes of tragedy or romance who interest us, is as sincere as our grief for their distress, and our fellow-feeling with their misery is not more real than that with their happiness. We enter into their gratitude towards those faithful friends who did not desert them in their difficulties; and we heartily go along with their resentment against those perfidious traitors who injured, abandoned, or deceived them. In every passion of which the mind of man is susceptible, the emotions of the bystander always correspond to what, by bringing the case home to himself, he imagines should be the sentiments of the sufferer.

Pity and compassion are words appropriated to signify our fellow-feeling with the sorrow of others. Sympathy, though its meaning was, perhaps, originally the same, may now, however, without much impropriety, be made use of to denote our fellow-feeling with any passion whatever.

Upon some occasions sympathy may seem to arise merely from the view of a certain emotion in another person. The passions, upon some occasions, may seem to be transfused from one man to another, instantaneously, and antecedent to any knowledge of what excited them in the person principally concerned. Grief and joy, for example, strongly expressed in the look and gestures of any person, at once affect the spectator with some degree of a like painful or agreeable emotion. A smiling face is, to everybody that sees it, a cheerful object; as a sorrowful countenance, on the other hand, is a melancholy one.

This, however, does not hold universally, or with regard to every passion. There are some passions of which the expressions excite no sort of sympathy, but, before we are acquainted with what gave occasion to them, serve rather to disgust and provoke us against them. The furious behaviour of an angry man is more likely to exasperate us against himself than against his enemies. As we are unacquainted with his provocation, we cannot bring his case home to ourselves, nor conceive any thing like the passions which it excites. But we plainly see what is the situation of those with whom he is angry, and to what violence they may be exposed from so enraged an adversary. We readily, therefore, sympathize with their fear or resentment, and are immediately disposed to take part against the man from whom they appear to be in danger.

If the very appearances of grief and joy inspire us with some degree of the like emotions, it is because they suggest to us the general idea of some good or bad fortune that has befallen the person in whom we observe them: and in these passions this is sufficient to have some little influence upon us. The effects of grief and joy terminate in the person who feels those emotions, of which the expressions do not, like those of resentment, suggest to us the idea of any other person for whom we are concerned, and whose interests are opposite to his. The general idea of good or bad fortune, therefore, creates some concern for the person who has met with it; but the general idea of provocation excites no sympathy with the anger of the man who has received it Nature, it seems, teaches us to be more averse to enter into this passion, and, till informed of its cause, to be disposed rather to take part against it.

Even our sympathy with the grief or joy of another, before we are informed of the cause of either, is always extremely imperfect. General lamentations, which express nothing but the anguish of the sufferer, create rather a curiosity to enquire into his situation, along with some disposition to sympathize with him, than any actual sympathy that is very sensible. The first question which we ask is, What has befallen you? Till this be answered, though we are uneasy both from the vague idea of his misfortune, and still more from torturing ourselves with conjectures about what it may be, yet our fellow-feeling is not very considerable.

Sympathy, therefore, does not arise so much from the view of the passion, as from that of the situation which excites it. We sometimes feel for another, a passion of which he himself seems to be altogether incapable; because, when we put ourselves in his case, that passion arises in our breast from the imagination, though it does not in his from the reality. We blush for the impudence and rudeness of another, though he himself appears to have no sense of the impropriety of his own behaviour; because we cannot help feeling with what confusion we ourselves should be covered, had we behaved in so absurd a manner.

Of all the calamities to which the condition of mortality exposes mankind, the loss of reason appears, to those who have the least spark of humanity, by far the most dreadful; and they behold that last stage of human wretchedness with deeper commiseration than any other. But the poor wretch, who is in it, laughs and sings, perhaps, and is altogether insensible to his own misery. The anguish which humanity feels, therefore, at the sight of such an object, cannot be the reflection of any sentiment of the sufferer. The compassion of the spectator must arise altogether from the consideration of what he himself would feel if he was reduced to the same unhappy situation, and, what perhaps is impossible, was at the same time able to regard it with his present reason and judgment.

What are the pangs of a mother, when she hears the moanings of her infant, that, during the agony of disease, cannot express what it feels? In her idea of what it suffers, she joins, to its real helplessness, her own consciousness of that helplessness, and her own terrors for the unknown consequences of its disorder; and out of all these, forms, for her own sorrow, the most complete image of misery and distress. The infant, however, feels only the uneasiness of the present instant, which can never be great. With regard to the future, it is perfectly secure, and in its thoughtlessness and want of foresight, possesses an antidote against fear and anxiety, the great tormentors of the human breast, from which reason and philosophy will in vain attempt to defend it, when it grows up to a man.

We sympathize even with the dead, and overlooking what is of real importance in their situation, that awful futurity which awaits them, we are chiefly affected by those circumstances which strike our senses, but can have no influence upon their happiness. It is miserable, we think, to be deprived of the light of the sun; to be shut out from life and conversation; to be laid in the cold grave, a prey to corruption and the reptiles of the earth; to be no more thought of in this world, but to be obliterated, in a little time, from the affections, and almost from the memory, of their dearest friends and relations. Surely, we imagine, we can never feel too much for those who have suffered so dreadful a calamity. The tribute of our fellow-feeling seems doubly due to them now, when they are in danger of being forgot by every body; and, by the vain honours which we pay to their memory, we endeavour, for our own misery, artificially to keep alive our melancholy remembrance of their misfortune. That our sympathy can afford them no consolation seems to be an addition to their calamity; and to think that all we can do is unavailing, and that, what alleviates all other distress, the regret, the love, and the lamentations of their friends, can yield no comfort to them, serves only to exasperate our sense of their misery. The happiness of the dead, however, most assuredly is affected by none of these circumstances; nor is it the thought of these things which can ever disturb the profound security of their repose. The idea of that dreary and endless melancholy, which the fancy naturally ascribes to their condition, arises altogether from our joining to the change which has been produced upon them, our own consciousness of that change; from our putting ourselves in their situation, and from our lodging, if I may be allowed to say so, our own living souls in their inanimated bodies, and thence conceiving what would be our emotions in this case. It is from this very illusion of the imagination, that the foresight of our own dissolution is so terrible to us, and that the idea of those circumstances, which undoubtedly can give us no pain when we are dead, makes us miserable while we are alive. And from thence arises one of the most important principles in human nature, the dread of death—the great poison to the happiness, but the great restraint upon the injustice of mankind; which, while it afflicts and mortifies the individual, guards and protects the society.

Chapter III – Of the Manner in Which We Judge of the Propriety or Impropriety of the Affections of Other Men, by Their Concord or Dissonance With Our Own

WHEN the original passions of the person principally concerned are in perfect concord with the sympathetic emotions of the spectator, they necessarily appear to this last just and proper, and suitable to their objects; and, on the contrary, when, upon bringing the case home to himself, he finds that they do not coincide with what he feels, they necessarily appear to him unjust and improper, and unsuitable to the causes which excite them. To approve of the passions of another, therefore, as suitable to their objects, is the same thing as to observe that we entirely sympathize with them; and not to approve of them as such, is the same thing as to observe that we do not entirely sympathize with them. The man who resents the injuries that have been done to me, and observes that I resent them precisely as he does, necessarily approves of my resentment. The man whose sympathy keeps time to my grief, cannot but admit the reasonableness of my sorrow. He who admires the same poem or the same picture, and admires them exactly as I do, must surely allow the justness of my admiration. He who laughs at the same joke, and laughs along with me, cannot well deny the propriety of my laughter. On the contrary, the person who, upon these different occasions, either feels no such emotion as that which I feel, or feels none that bears any proportion to mine, cannot avoid disapproving my sentiments, on account of their dissonance with his own. If my animosity goes beyond what the indignation of my friend can correspond to; if my grief exceeds what his most tender compassion can go along with; if my admiration is either too high or too low to tally with his own; if I laugh loud and heartily when he only smiles, or, on the contrary, only smile when he laughs loud and heartily; in all these cases, as soon as he comes, from considering the object, to observe how I am affected by it, according as there is more or less disproportion between his sentiments and mine, I must incur a greater or less degree of his disapprobation: and, upon all occasions, his own sentiments are the standards and measures by which he judges of mine.

To approve of another man's opinions is to adopt those opinions, and to adopt them is to approve of them. If the same arguments which convince you, convince me likewise, I necessarily approve of your conviction; and if they do not, I necessarily disapprove of it; neither can I possibly conceive that I should do the one without the other. To approve or disapprove, therefore, of the opinions of others is acknowledged, by every body, to mean no more than to observe their agreement or disagreement with our own. But this is equally the case with regard to our approbation or disapprobation of the sentiments or passions of others.

There are, indeed, some cases in which we seem to approve, without any sympathy or correspondence of sentiments; and in which, consequently, the sentiment of approbation would seem to be different from the perception of this coincidence. A little attention, however, will convince us, that even in these cases our approbation is ultimately founded upon a sympathy or correspondence of this kind. I shall give an instance in things of a very frivolous nature, because in them the judgments of mankind are less apt to be perverted by wrong systems. We may often approve of a jest, and think the laughter of the company quite just and proper, though we ourselves do not laugh, because, perhaps, we are in a grave humour, or happen to have our attention engaged with other objects. We have learned, however, from experience, what sort of pleasantry is upon most occasions capable of making us laugh, and we observe that this is one of that kind. We approve, therefore, of the laughter of the company, and feel that it is natural and suitable to its object; because, though in our present mood we cannot easily enter into it, we are sensible that upon most occasions we should very heartily join in it.

The same thing often happens with regard to all the other passions. A stranger passes by us in the street with all the marks of the deepest affliction; and we are immediately told that he has just received the news of the death of his father. It is impossible that, in this case, we should not approve of his grief. Yet it may often happen, without any defect of humanity on our part, that, so far from entering into the violence of his sorrow, we should scarce conceive the first movements of concern upon his account. Both he and his father, perhaps, are entirely unknown to us, or we happen to be employed about other things, and do not take time to picture out in our imagination the different circumstances of distress which must occur to him. We have learned, however, from experience, that such a misfortune naturally excites such a degree of sorrow; and we know that if we took time to consider his situation fully, and in all its parts, we should without doubt most sincerely sympathize with him. It is upon the consciousness of this conditional sympathy, that our approbation of his sorrow is founded, even in those cases in which that sympathy does not actually take place; and the general rules derived from our preceding experience of what our sentiments would commonly correspond with, correct, upon this, as upon many other occasions, the impropriety of our present emotions.

The sentiment or affection of the heart, from which any action proceeds, and upon which its whole virtue or vice must ultimately depend, may be considered under two different aspects, or in two different relations; first, in relation to the cause which excites it, or the motive which gives occasion to it; and, secondly, in relation to the end which it proposes, or the effect which it tends to produce.

In the suitableness or unsuitableness, in the proportion or disproportion, which the affection seems to bear to the cause or object which excites it, consists the propriety or impropriety, the decency or ungracefulness, of the consequent action.

In the beneficial or hurtful nature of the effects which the affection aims at, or tends to produce, consists the merit or demerit of the action, the qualities by which it is entitled to reward, or is deserving of punishment.

Philosophers have, of late years, considered chiefly the tendency of affections, and have given little attention to the relation which they stand in to the cause which excites them. In common life, however, when we judge of any person's conduct, and of the sentiments which directed it, we constantly consider them under both these aspects. When we blame in another man the excesses of love, of grief, of resentment, we not only consider the ruinous effects which they tend to produce, but the little occasion which was given for them. The merit of his favourite, we say, is not so great, his misfortune is not so dreadful, his provocation is not so extraordinary, as to justify so violent a passion. We should have indulged, we say, perhaps have approved of the violence of his emotion, had the cause been in any respect proportioned to it.

When we judge in this manner of any affection, as proportioned or disproportioned to the cause which excites it, it is scarce possible that we should make use of any other rule or canon but the correspondent affection in ourselves. If, upon bringing the case home to our own breast, we find that the sentiments which it gives occasion to coincide and tally with our own, we necessarily approve of them, as proportioned and suitable to their objects; if otherwise, we necessarily disapprove of them, as extravagant and out of proportion.

Every faculty in one man is the measure by which he judges of the like faculty in another. I judge of your sight by my sight, of your ear by my ear, of your reason by my reason, of your resentment by my resentment, of your love by my love. I neither have, nor can have, any other way of judging about them.

Chapter IV – The Same Subject Continued

WE may judge of the propriety or impropriety of the sentiments of another person by their correspondence or disagreement with our own, upon two different occasions; either, first, when the objects which excite them are considered without any peculiar relation, either to ourselves or to the person whose sentiments we judge of; or, secondly, when they are considered as peculiarly affecting one or other of us.

1. With regard to those objects which are considered without any peculiar relation either to ourselves or to the person whose sentiments we judge of; wherever his sentiments entirely correspond with our own, we ascribe to

him the qualities of taste and good judgment. The beauty of a plain, the greatness of a mountain, the ornaments of a building, the expression of a picture, the composition of a discourse, the conduct of a third person, the proportions of different quantities and numbers, the various appearances which the great machine of the universe is perpetually exhibiting, with the secret wheels and springs which produce them; all the general subjects of science and taste, are what we and our companions regard as having no peculiar relation to either of us. We both look at them from the same point of view, and we have no occasion for sympathy, or for that imaginary change of situations from which it arises, in order to produce, with regard to these, the most perfect harmony of sentiments and affections. If, notwithstanding, we are often differently affected, it arises either from the different degrees of attention which our different habits of life allow as to give easily to the several parts of those complex objects, or from the different degrees of natural acuteness in the faculty of the mind to which they are addressed.

When the sentiments of our companion coincide with our own in things of this kind, which are obvious and easy, and in which, perhaps, we never found a single person who differed from us, though we, no doubt, must approve of them, yet he seems to deserve no praise or admiration on account of them. But when they not only coincide with our own, but lead and direct our own; when, in forming them, he appears to have attended to many things which we had overlooked, and to have adjusted them to all the various circumstances of their objects; we not only approve of them, but wonder and are surprised at their uncommon and unexpected acuteness and comprehensiveness, and he appears to deserve a very high degree of admiration and applause. For approbation heightened by wonder and surprise, constitutes the sentiment which is properly called admiration, and of which applause is the natural expression. The decision of the man who judges that exquisite beauty is preferable to the grossest deformity, or that twice two are equal to four, must certainly be approved of by all the world, but will not, surely, be much admired. It is the acute and delicate discernment of the man of taste, who distinguishes the minute, and scarce perceptible differences of beauty and deformity; it is the comprehensive accuracy of the experienced mathematician, who unravels with ease the most intricate and perplexed proportions; it is the great leader in science and taste, the man who directs and conducts our own sentiments, the extent and superior justness of whose talents astonish us with wonder and surprise, who excites our admiration, and seems to deserve our applause; and upon this foundation is grounded the greater part of the praise which is bestowed upon what are called the intellectual virtues.

The utility of these qualities, it may be thought, is what first recommends them to us; and, no doubt, the consideration of this, when we come to attend to it, gives them a new value. Originally, however, we approve of another man's judgment, not as something useful, but as right, as accurate, as agreeable to truth and reality; and it is evident we attribute those qualities to it for no other reason but because we find that it agrees with our own. Taste, in the same manner, is originally approved of, not as useful, but as just, as delicate, and as precisely suited to its object. The idea of the utility of all qualities of this kind is plainly an after-thought, and not what first recommends them to our approbation.

2. With regard to those objects, which affect in a particular manner either ourselves or the person whose sentiments we judge of, it is at once more difficult to preserve this harmony and correspondence, and, at the same time, vastly more important. My companion does not naturally look upon the misfortune that has befallen me, or the injury that has been done me, from the same point of view in which I consider them. They affect me much more nearly. We do not view them from the same station, as we do a picture, or a poem, or a system of philosophy; and are therefore apt to be very differently affected by them. But I can much more easily overlook the want of this correspondence of sentiments with regard to such indifferent objects as concern neither me nor my companion, than with regard to what interests me so much as the misfortune that has befallen me, or the injury that has been done me. Though you despise that picture, or that poem, or even that system of philosophy which I admire, there is little danger of our quarrelling upon that account. Neither of us can reasonably be much interested about them. They ought all of them to be matters of great indifference to us both; so that, though our opinions may be opposite, our affections may still be very nearly the same. But it is quite otherwise with regard to those objects by which either you or I are particularly affected. Though your judgments in matters of speculation, though your sentiments in matters of taste, are quite opposite to mine, I can easily overlook this opposition; and if I have any degree of temper, I may still find some entertainment in your conversation, even upon those very subjects. But if you have either no fellow-feeling for the misfortunes I have met with, or none that bears any proportion to the grief which distracts me; or if you have either no indignation at the injuries I have suffered, or none that bears any proportion to the resentment which transports me, we can no longer converse upon these subjects. We become intolerable to one another. I can neither support your company, nor you mine. You are confounded at my violence and passion, and I am enraged at your cold insensibility and want of feeling.

In all such cases, that there may be some correspondence of sentiments between the spectator and the person principally concerned, the spectator must, first of all, endeavour as much as he can to put himself in the situation of the other, and to bring home to himself every little circumstance of distress which can possibly occur to the sufferer. He must adopt the whole case of his companion, with all its minutest incidents; and strive to render as perfect as possible that imaginary change of situation upon which his sympathy is founded.

After all this, however, the emotions of the spectator will still be very apt to fall short of the violence of what is felt by the sufferer. Mankind, though naturally sympathetic, never conceive, for what has befallen another, that degree of passion which naturally animates the person principally concerned. That imaginary change of situation, upon which their sympathy is founded, is but momentary. The thought of their own safety, the thought that they themselves are not really the sufferers, continually intrudes itself upon them; and though it does not hinder them from conceiving a passion somewhat analogous to what is felt by the sufferer, hinders them from conceiving any thing that approaches to the same degree of violence. The person principally concerned is sensible of this, and at the same time passionately desires a more complete sympathy. He longs for that relief which nothing can afford him but the entire concord of the affections of the spectators with his own. To see the emotions of their hearts in every respect beat time to his own, in the violent and disagreeable passions, constitutes his sole consolation. But he can only hope to obtain this by lowering his passion to that pitch, in which the spectators are capable of going along with him. He must flatten, if I may be allowed to say so, the sharpness of its natural tone, in order to reduce it to harmony and concord with the emotions of those who are about him. What they feel will, indeed, always be in some respects different from what he feels, and compassion can never be exactly the same with original sorrow; because the secret consciousness that the change of situations, from which the sympathetic sentiment arises, is but imaginary, not only lowers it in degree, but in some measure varies it in kind, and gives it a quite different modification. These two sentiments, however, may, it is evident, have such a correspondence with one another, as is sufficient for the harmony of society. Though they will never be unisons, they may be concords, and this is all that is wanted or required.

In order to produce this concord, as nature teaches the spectators to assume the circumstances of the person principally concerned, so she teaches this last in some measure to assume those of the spectators. As they are continually placing themselves in his situation, and thence conceiving emotions similar to what he feels; so he is as constantly placing himself in theirs, and thence conceiving some degree of that coolness about his own fortune, with which he is sensible that they will view it. As they are constantly considering what they themselves would feel, if they actually were the sufferers, so he is constantly led to imagine in what manner he would be affected if he was only one of the spectators of his own situation. As their sympathy makes them look at it in some measure with his eyes, so his sympathy makes him look at it, in some measure, with theirs, especially when in their presence, and acting under their observation: and, as the reflected passion which he thus conceives is much weaker than the original one, it necessarily abates the violence of what he felt before he came into their presence, before he began to recollect in what manner they would be affected by it, and to view his situation in this candid and impartial light.

The mind, therefore, is rarely so disturbed, but that the company of a friend will restore it to some degree of tranquillity and sedateness. The breast is, in some measure, calmed and composed the moment we come into his presence. We are immediately put in mind of the light in which he will view our situation, and we begin to view it ourselves in the same light; for the effect of sympathy is instantaneous. We expect less sympathy from a common acquaintance than from a friend; we cannot open to the former all those little circumstances which we can unfold to the latter; we assume, therefore, more tranquillity before him, and endeavour to fix our thoughts upon those general outlines of our situation which he is willing to consider. We expect still less sympathy from an assembly of strangers, and we assume, therefore, still more tranquillity before them, and always endeavour to bring down our passion to that pitch, which the particular company we are in may be expected to go along with. Nor is this only an assumed appearance; for if we are at all masters of ourselves, the presence of a mere acquaintance will really compose us, still more than that of a friend; and that of an assembly of strangers, still more than that of an acquaintance.

Society and conversation, therefore, are the most powerful remedies for restoring the mind to its tranquillity, if, at any time, it has unfortunately lost it; as well as the best preservatives of that equal and happy temper, which is so necessary to self-satisfaction and enjoyment. Men of retirement and speculation, who are apt to sit brooding at home over either grief or resentment, though they may often have more humanity, more generosity, and a nicer sense of honour, yet seldom possess that equality of temper which is so common among men of the world.

Part II – Of Merit and Demerit; or, Of the Objects of Reward and Punishment; Consisting of Three Sections

Section I – Of the Sense of Merit and Demerit

Introduction

THERE is another set of qualities ascribed to the actions and conduct of mankind, distinct from their propriety or impropriety, their decency or ungracefulness, and which are the objects of a distinct species of approbation and disapprobation. These are Merit and Demerit, the qualities of deserving reward, and of deserving punishment.

It has already been observed, that the sentiment or affection of the heart from which any action proceeds, and upon which its whole virtue or vice depends, may be considered under two different aspects, or in two different relations; first, in relation to the cause or object which excites it; and, secondly, in relation to the end which it proposes, or to the effect which it tends to produce: that upon the suitableness or unsuitableness, upon the proportion or disproportion, which the affection seems to bear to the cause or object which excites it, depends the propriety or impropriety, the decency or ungracefulness, of the consequent action; and that upon the beneficial or hurtful effects which the affection proposes or tends to produce depends the merit or demerit, the good or ill desert, of the action to which it gives occasion. Wherein consists our sense of the propriety or impropriety of actions, has been explained in the former part of this discourse. We come now to consider, wherein consists that of their good or ill desert.

[…]

Section III – Of the Influence of Fortune Upon the Sentiments of Mankind, With Regard to the Merit or Demerit of Actions

Introduction

WHATEVER praise or blame can be due to any action, must belong, either, first, to the intention or affection of the heart, from which it proceeds; or, secondly, to the external action or movement of the body, which this affection gives occasion to; or, lastly, to the good or bad consequences, which actually, and in fact, proceed from it. These three different things constitute the whole nature and circumstances of the action, and must be the foundation of whatever quality can belong to it.

That the two last of these three circumstances cannot be the foundation of any praise or blame, is abundantly evident; nor has the contrary ever been asserted by any body. The external action or movement of the body is often the same in the most innocent and in the most blameable actions. He who shoots a bird, and he who shoots a man, both of them perform the same external movement: each of them draws the trigger of a gun. The consequences which actually, and in fact, happen to proceed from any action, are, if possible, still more indifferent either to praise or blame, than even the external movement of the body. As they depend, not upon the agent, but upon fortune, they cannot be the proper foundation for any sentiment, of which his character and conduct are the objects.

The only consequences for which he can be answerable, or by which he can deserve either approbation or disapprobation of any kind, are those which were some way or other intended, or those which, at least, shew some agreeable or disagreeable quality in the intention of the heart, from which he acted. To the intention or affection of the heart, therefore, to the propriety or impropriety, to the beneficence or hurtfulness of the design, all praise or blame, all approbation or disapprobation of any kind, which can justly be bestowed upon any action, must ultimately belong.

When this maxim is thus proposed, in abstract and general terms, there is nobody who does not agree to it. Its self-evident justice is acknowledged by all the world, and there is not a dissenting voice among all mankind. Every body allows, that how different soever the accidental, the unintended, and unforeseen consequences of different actions, yet, if the intentions or affections from which they arose were, on the one hand, equally proper and equally beneficent, or, on the other, equally improper and equally malevolent, the merit or demerit of the actions is still the same, and the agent is equally the suitable object either of gratitude or of resentment.

But how well soever we may seem to be persuaded of the truth of this equitable maxim, when we consider it after this manner, in abstract, yet when we come to particular eases, the actual consequences which happen to proceed from any action, have a very great effect upon our sentiments concerning its merit or demerit, and almost always either enhance or diminish our sense of both. Scarce, in any one instance, perhaps, will our sentiments be found, after examination, to be entirely regulated by this rule, which we all acknowledge ought entirely to regulate them.

This irregularity of sentiment, which every body feels, which scarce any body is sufficiently aware of, and which nobody is willing to acknowledge, I proceed now to explain; and I shall consider, first, the cause which gives occasion to it, or the mechanism by which nature produces it; secondly, the extent of its influence; and, last of all, the end which it answers, or the purpose which the Author of nature seems to have intended by it.

Chapter I – Of the Causes of This Influence of Fortune

THE causes of pain and pleasure, whatever they are, or however they operate, seem to be the objects, which, in all animals, immediately excite those two passions of gratitude and resentment. They are excited by inanimated, as well as by animated objects. We are angry, for a moment, even at the stone that hurts us. A child beats it, a dog barks at it, a choleric man is apt to curse it. The least reflection, indeed, corrects this sentiment, and we soon become sensible, that what has no feeling is a very improper object of revenge. When the mischief, however, is very great, the object which caused it becomes disagreeable to us ever after, and we take pleasure to burn or destroy it. We should treat, in this manner, the instrument which had accidentally been the cause of the death of a friend, and we should often think ourselves guilty of a sort of inhumanity, if we neglected to vent this absurd sort of vengeance upon it.

We conceive, in the same manner, a sort of gratitude for those inanimated objects which have been the causes of great or frequent pleasure to us. The sailor, who, as soon as he got ashore, should mend his fire with the plank upon which he had just escaped from a shipwreck, would seem to be guilty of an unnatural action. We should expect that he would rather preserve it with care and affection, as a monument that was, in some measure, dear to him. A man grows fond of a snuff-box, of a pen-knife, of a staff which he has long made use of, and conceives something like a real love and affection for them. If he breaks or loses them, he is vexed out of all proportion to the value of the damage. The house which we have long lived in, the tree whose verdure and shade we have long enjoyed, are both looked upon with a sort of respect that seems due to such benefactors. The decay of the one, or the ruin of the other, affects us with a kind of melancholy, though we should sustain no loss by it. The dryads and the lares of the ancients, a sort of genii of trees and houses, were probably first suggested by this sort of affection which the authors of those superstitions felt for such objects, and which seemed unreasonable, if there was nothing animated about them.

But, before any thing can be the proper object of gratitude or resentment, it must not only be the cause of pleasure or pain; it must likewise be capable of feeling them. Without this other quality, those passions cannot vent themselves with any sort of satisfaction upon it. As they are excited by the causes of pleasure and pain, so their gratification consists in retaliating those sensations upon what gave occasion to them; which it is to no purpose to attempt upon what has no sensibility. Animals, therefore, are less improper objects of gratitude and resentment than inanimated objects. The dog that bites, the ox that gores, are both of them punished. If they have been the causes of the death of any person, neither the public, nor the relations of the slain, can be satisfied, unless they are put to death in their turn: nor is this merely for the security of the living, but, in some measure, to revenge the injury of the dead. Those animals, on the contrary, that have been remarkably serviceable to their masters, become the objects of a very lively gratitude. We are shocked at the brutality of that officer, mentioned in the Turkish Spy, who stabbed the horse that had carried him across an arm of the sea, lest that animal should afterwards distinguish some other person by a similar adventure.

But, though animals are not only the causes of pleasure and pain, but are also capable of feeling those sensations they are still far from being complete and perfect objects either of gratitude or resentment; and those passions still feel, that there is something wanting to their entire gratification. What gratitude chiefly desires, is not only to make the benefactor feel pleasure in his turn, but to make him conscious that he meets with this reward on account of his past conduct, to make him pleased with that conduct, and to satisfy him that the person upon whom he bestowed his good offices was not unworthy of them. What most of all charms us in our benefactor, is the concord between his sentiments and our own, with regard to what interests us so nearly as the worth of our own character, and the esteem that is due to us. We are delighted to find a person who values us as we value ourselves, and distinguishes us from the rest of mankind, with an attention not unlike that with which we distinguish ourselves. To maintain in him these agreeable and flattering sentiments, is one of the chief ends proposed by the returns we are disposed to make to him. A generous mind often disdains the interested thought of extorting new favours from its benefactor, by what may be called the importunities of its gratitude. But to preserve and to increase his esteem, is an interest which the greatest mind does not think unworthy of its attention. And this is the foundation of what I formerly observed, that when we cannot enter into the motives of our benefactor, when his conduct and character appear unworthy of our approbation, let his services have been ever so great, our gratitude is always sensibly diminished. We are less flattered by the distinction; and to preserve the esteem of so weak, or so worthless a patron, seems to be an object which does not deserve to be pursued for its own sake.

The object, on the contrary, which resentment is chiefly intent upon, is not so much to make our enemy feel pain in his turn, as to make him conscious that he feels it upon account of his past conduct, to make him repent of that conduct, and to make him sensible, that the person whom he injured did not deserve to be treated in that manner. What chiefly enrages us against the man who injures or insults us, is the little account which he seems to make of us, the unreasonable preference which he gives to himself above us, and that absurd self-love, by which he seems to imagine, that other people may be sacrificed at any time, to his conveniency or his humour. The glaring impropriety of this conduct, the gross insolence and injustice which it seems to involve in it, often shock and exasperate us more than all the mischief which we have suffered. To bring him back to a more just sense of what is due to other people, to make him sensible of what he owes us, and of the wrong that he has done to us, is frequently the principal end proposed in our revenge, which is always imperfect when it cannot accomplish this. When our enemy appears to have done us no injury, when we are sensible that he acted quite properly, that, in his situation, we should have done the same thing, and that we deserved from him all the mischief we met with; in that case, if we have the least spark either of candour or justice, we can entertain no sort of resentment.

Before any thing, therefore, can be the complete and proper object, either of gratitude or resentment, it must possess three different qualifications. First, it must be the cause of pleasure in the one case, and of pain in the other. Secondly, it must be capable of feeling those sensations. And, thirdly, it must not only have produced those sensations, but it must have produced them from design, and from a design that is approved of in the one case, and disapproved of in the other. It is by the first qualification that any object is capable of exciting those passions: it is by the second, that it is in any respect capable of gratifying them: the third qualification is not only necessary for their complete satisfaction, but, as it gives a pleasure or pain that is both exquisite and peculiar, it is likewise an additional exciting cause of those passions.

As what gives pleasure or pain, therefore, either in one way or another, is the sole exciting cause of gratitude and resentment; though the intentions of any person should be ever so proper and beneficent, on the one hand, or ever so improper and malevolent on the other; yet, if he has failed in producing either the good or the evil which he intended, as one of the exciting causes is wanting in both cases, less gratitude seems due to him in the one, and less resentment in the other. And, on the contrary, though in the intentions of any person, there was either no laudable degree of benevolence on the one hand, or no blameable degree of malice on the other; yet, if his actions should produce either great good or great evil, as one of the exciting causes takes place upon both these occasions, some gratitude is apt to arise towards him in the one, and some resentment in the other. A shadow of merit seems to fall upon him in the first, a shadow of demerit in the second. And, as the consequences of actions are altogether under the empire of fortune, hence arises her influence upon the sentiments of mankind with regard to merit and demerit.

Chapter II – Of the Extent of This Influence of Fortune

THE effect of this influence of fortune, is, first, to diminish our sense of the merit or demerit of those actions which arose from the most laudable or blameable intentions, when they fail of producing their proposed effects: and, secondly, to increase our sense of the merit or demerit of actions, beyond what, is due to the motives or affections from which they proceed, when they accidentally give occasion either to extraordinary pleasure or pain.

1. First, I say, though the intentions of any person should be ever so proper and beneficent on the one hand, or ever so improper or malevolent on the other, yet, if they fail in producing their effects, his merit seems imperfect in the one case, and his demerit incomplete in the other. Nor is this irregularity of sentiment felt only by those who are immediately affected by the consequences of any action. It is felt, in some measure, even by the impartial spectator. The man who solicits an office for another, without obtaining it, is regarded as his friend, and seems to deserve his love and affection. But the man who not only solicits, but procures it, is more peculiarly considered as his patron and benefactor, and is entitled to his respect and gratitude. The person obliged, we are apt to think, may with some justice, imagine himself on a level with the first: but we cannot enter into his sentiments, if he does not feel himself inferior to the second. It is common indeed to say, that we are equally obliged to the man who has endeavoured to serve us, as to him who actually did so. It is the speech which we constantly make upon every unsuccessful attempt

of this kind; but which, like all other fine speeches, must be understood with a grain of allowance. The sentiments which a man of generosity entertains for the friend who fails, may often indeed be nearly the same with those which he conceives for him who succeeds: and the more generous he is, the more nearly will those sentiments approach to an exact level. With the truly generous, to be beloved, to be esteemed by those whom they themselves think worthy of esteem, gives more pleasure, and thereby excites more gratitude, than all the advantages which they can ever expect from those sentiments. When they lose those advantages, therefore, they seem to lose but a trifle, which is source worth regarding. They still, however, lose something. Their pleasure, therefore, and consequently their gratitude, is not perfectly complete: and accordingly, if between the friend who fails, and the friend who succeeds, all other circumstances are equal, there will, even in the noblest and best mind, be some little difference of affection in favour of him who succeeds. Nay, so unjust are mankind in this respect, that though the intended benefit should be procured, yet if it is not procured by the means of a particular benefactor, they are apt to think that less gratitude is due to the man, who with the best intentions in the world could do no more than help it a little forward. As their gratitude is in this case divided among the different persons who contributed to their pleasure, a smaller share of it seems due to any one. Such a person, we hear men commonly say, intended no doubt reserve us; and we really believe exerted himself to the utmost of his abilities for that purpose. We are not, however, obliged to him for this benefit; since, had it not been for the concurrence of others, all that he could have done would never have brought it about. This consideration, they imagine, should even in the eyes of the impartial spectator diminish the debt which they owe to him. The person himself who has unsuccessfully endeavoured to confer a benefit, has by no means the same dependency upon the gratitude of the man whom he meant to oblige, nor the same sense of his own merit towards him, which he would have had in the case of success.

Even the merit of talents and abilities which some accident has hindered from producing their effects, seems in some measure imperfect, even to those who are fully convinced of their capacity to produce them. The general who has been hindered by the envy of ministers from gaining some great advantage over the enemies of his country, regrets the loss of the opportunity for ever after. Nor is it only upon account of the public that he regrets it. He laments that he was hindered from performing an action which would have added a new lustre to his character in his own eyes, as well as in those of every other person. It satisfies neither himself nor others to reflect that the plan or design was all that depended on him: that no greater capacity was required to execute it than what was necessary to concert it: that he was allowed to be every way capable of executing it, and that had he been permitted to go on, success was infallible. He still did not execute it; and though he might deserve all the approbation which is due to a magnanimous and great design, he still wanted the actual merit of having performed a great action. To take the management of any affair of public concern from the man who has almost brought it to a conclusion, is regarded as the most invidious injustice. As he had done so much, he should, we think, have been allowed to acquire the complete merit of putting an end to it. It was objected to Pompey, that he came in upon the victories of Lucullus, and gathered those laurels which were due to the fortune and valour of another. The glory of Lucullus, it seems, was less complete even in the opinion of his own friends, when he was not permitted to finish that conquest which his conduct and courage had put in the power of almost any man to finish. It mortifies an architect when his plans are either not executed at all, or when they are so far altered as to spoil the effect of the building. The plan, however, is all that depends upon the architect. The whole of his genius is, to good judges, as completely discovered in that as in the actual execution. But a plan does not, even to the most intelligent, give the same pleasure as a noble and magnificent building. They may discover as much both of taste and genius in the one as in the other. But their effects are still vastly different, and the amusement derived from the first never approaches to the wonder and admiration which are sometimes excited by the second. We may believe of many men, that their talents are superior to those of Cæsar and Alexander; and that in the same situations they would perform still greater actions. In the meantime, however, we do not behold them with that astonishment and admiration with which those two heroes have been regarded in all ages and nations. The calm judgments of the mind may approve of them more, but they want the splendour of great actions to dazzle and transport it. The superiority of virtues and talents has not, even upon those who acknowledge that superiority, the same effect with the superiority of achievements.

As the merit of an unsuccessful attempt to do good seems thus, in the eyes of ungrateful mankind, to be diminished by the miscarriage, so does likewise the demerit of an unsuccessful attempt to do evil. The design to commit a crime, how clearly soever it may be proved, is scarce ever punished with the same severity as the actual commission of it. The case of treason is perhaps the only exception. That crime immediately affecting the being of the government itself, the government is naturally more jealous of it than of any other. In the punishment of treason, the sovereign resents the injuries which are immediately done to himself: in the punishment of other crimes, he resents those which are done to other men. It is his own resentment which he indulges in the one case: it is that of his subjects which by sympathy he enters into in the other. In the first case, therefore, as he judges in his own cause, he is very apt to be more violent and sanguinary in his punishments than the impartial spectator can approve of. His resentment too rises here upon smaller occasions, and does not always, as in other cases, wait for the perpetration of the crime, or even for the attempt to commit it. A treasonable concert, though nothing has been done, or even attempted in consequence of it, nay, a treasonable conversation, is in many countries punished in the same manner as the actual commission of treason. With regard to all other crimes, the mere design, upon which no attempt has followed, is seldom punished at all, and is never punished severely. A criminal design, and a criminal action, it may be said, indeed, do not necessarily suppose the same degree of depravity, and ought not therefore to be subjected to the same punishment. We are capable, it may be said, of resolving, and even of taking measures to execute, many things which, when it comes to the point, we feel ourselves altogether incapable of executing. But this reason can have no place when the design has been carried the length of the last attempt. The man, however, who fires a pistol at his enemy but misses him, is punished with death by the laws of scarce any country. By the old law of Scotland, though he should wound him, yet, unless death ensues within a certain time, the assassin, is not liable to the last punishment. The resentment of mankind, however, runs so high against this crime, their terror for the man who shews himself capable of committing it, is so great, that the mere attempt to commit it ought in all countries to be capital. The attempt to commit smaller crimes is almost always punished very lightly, and sometimes is not punished at all. The thief, whose hand has been caught in his neighbour's pocket before he had taken any thing out of it, is punished with ignominy only. If he had got time to take away a handkerchief, he would have been put to death. The house-breaker, who has been found setting a ladder to his neighbour's window, but had not got into it, is not exposed to the capital punishment The attempt to ravish is not punished as a rape. The attempt to seduce a married woman is not punished at all, though seduction is punished severely. Our resentment against the person who only attempted to do a mischief, is seldom so strong as to bear us out in inflicting the same punishment upon him, which we should have thought due if he had actually done it. In the one case, the joy of our deliverance alleviates our sense of the atrocity of his conduct; in the other, the grief of our misfortune increases it. His real demerit, however, is undoubtedly the same in both cases, since his intentions were equally criminal; and there is in this respect, therefore, an irregularity in the sentiments of all men, and a consequent relaxation of discipline, in the laws of, I believe, all nations, of the most civilized, as well as of the most barbarous. The humanity of a civilised people disposes them either to dispense with, or to mitigate punishments wherever their natural indignation is not goaded on by the consequences of the crime. Barbarians, on the other hand, when no actual consequence has happened from any action, are not apt to be very delicate or inquisitive about the motives.

The person himself who, either from passion or from the influence of bad company, has resolved, and perhaps taken measures, to perpetrate some crime, but who has fortunately been prevented by an accident which put it out of his power, is sure, if he has any remains of conscience, to regard this event all his life after as a great and signal deliverance. He can never think of it without returning thanks to Heaven for having been thus graciously pleased to save him from the guilt in which he was just ready to plunge himself, and to hinder him from rendering all the rest of his life a scene of horror, remorse, and repentance. But though his hands are innocent, he is conscious that his heart is equally guilty as if he had actually executed what he was so fully resolved upon. It gives great ease to his conscience, however, to consider that the crime was not executed, though he knows that the failure arose from no virtue in him. He still considers himself as less deserving of punishment and resentment; and this good fortune either diminishes, or takes away altogether, all sense of guilt. To remember how much he was resolved upon it, has no other effect than to make him regard his escape as the greater and more miraculous: for he still fancies that he has escaped, and he looks back upon the danger to which his peace of mind was exposed, with that terror, with which one who is in safety may sometimes remember the hazard he was in of falling over a precipice, and shudder with horror at the thought.

2. The second effect of this influence of fortune, is to increase our sense of the merit or demerit of actions beyond what is due to the motives or affection from which they proceed, when they happen to give occasion to extraordinary pleasure or pain. The agreeable or disagreeable effects of the action often throw a shadow of merit or demerit upon the agent, though in his intention there was nothing that deserved either praise or blame, or at least that deserved them in the degree in which we are apt to bestow them. Thus, even the messenger of bad news is disagreeable to us; and, on the contrary, we feel a sort of gratitude for the man who brings us good tidings. For a moment we look upon them both as the authors, the one of our good, the other of our bad fortune, and regard them in some measure as if they had really brought about the events which they only give an account of. The first

author of our joy is naturally the object of a transitory gratitude: we embrace him with warmth and affection, and should be glad, during the instant of our prosperity, to reward him as for some signal service. By the custom of all courts, the officer who brings the news of a victory is entitled to considerable preferments, and the general always chooses one of his principal favourites to go upon so agreeable an errand. The first author of our sorrow is, on the contrary, just as naturally the object of a transitory resentment. We can scarce avoid looking upon him with chagrin and uneasiness; and the rude and brutal are apt to vent upon him that spleen which his intelligence gives occasion to. Tigranes, King of Armenia, struck off the head of the man who brought him the first account of the approach of a formidable enemy. To punish in this manner the author of bad tidings, seems barbarous and inhuman: yet, to reward the messenger of good news, is not disagreeable to us; we think it suitable to the bounty of kings. But why do we make this difference, since, if there is no fault in the one, neither is there any merit in the other? It is because any sort of reason seems sufficient to authorize the exertion of the social and benevolent affections; but it requires the most solid and substantial to make us enter into that of the unsocial and malevolent.

But though in general we are averse to enter into the unsocial and malevolent affections, though we lay it down for a rule that we ought never to approve of their gratification, unless so far as the malicious and unjust intention of the person against whom they are directed renders him their proper object; yet, upon some occasions, we relax of this severity. When the negligence of one man has occasioned some unintended damage to another, we generally enter so far into the resentment of the sufferer, as to approve of his inflicting a punishment upon the offender much beyond what the offence would have appeared to deserve, had no such unlucky consequence followed from it.

There is a degree of negligence, which would appear to deserve some chastisement though it should occasion no damage to any body. Thus, if a person should throw a large stone over a wall into a public street without giving warning to those who might be passing by, and without regarding where it was likely to fall, he would undoubtedly deserve some chastisement. A very accurate police would punish so absurd an action, even though it had done no mischief. The person who has been guilty of it, shews an insolent contempt of the happiness and safety of others. There is real injustice in his conduct. He wantonly exposes his neighbour to what no man in his senses would choose to expose himself, and evidently wants that sense of what is due to his fellow-creatures, which is the basis of justice and of society. Gross negligence, therefore, is, in the law, said to be almost equal to malicious design. When any unlucky consequences happen from such carelessness, the person who has been guilty of it is often punished as if he had really intended those consequences; and his conduct, which was only thoughtless and insolent, and what deserved some chastisement, is considered as atrocious, and as liable to the severest punishment. Thus if, by the imprudent action above mentioned, he should accidentally kill a man, he is, by the laws of many countries, particularly by the old law of Scotland, liable to the last punishment. And though this is no doubt excessively severe, it is not altogether inconsistent with our natural sentiments. Our just indignation against the folly and inhumanity of his conduct is exasperated by our sympathy with the unfortunate sufferer. Nothing, however, would appear more shocking to our natural sense of equity, than to bring a man to the scaffold merely for having thrown a stone carelessly into the street without hurting anybody. The folly and inhumanity of his conduct, however, would in this case be the same; but still our sentiments would be very different. The consideration of this difference may satisfy us how much the indignation even of the spectator is apt to be animated by the actual consequences of the action. In cases of this kind there will, if I am not mistaken, be found a great degree of severity in the laws of almost all nations; as I have already observed that in those of an opposite kind there was a very general relaxation of discipline.

There is another degree of negligence which does not involve in it any sort of injustice. The person who is guilty of it treats his neighbour as he treats himself, means no harm to any body, and is far from entertaining any insolent contempt for the safety and happiness of others. He is not, however, so careful and circumspect in his conduct as he ought to be, and deserves upon this account some degree of blame and censure, but no sort of punishment Yet if, by a negligence of this kind, he should occasion some damage to another person, he is by the laws of, I believe, all countries, obliged to compensate it. And though this is no doubt a real punishment, and what no mortal would have thought of inflicting upon him, had it not been for the unlucky accident which his conduct gave occasion to; yet this decision of the law is approved of by the natural sentiments of all mankind. Nothing, we think, can be more just than that one man should not suffer by the carelessness of another; and that the damage occasioned by blameable negligence, should be made up by the person who was guilty of it.

There is another species of negligence, which consists merely in a want of the most anxious timidity and circumspection with regard to all the possible consequences of our actions. The want of this painful attention, when no bad consequences follow from it, is so far from being regarded as blameable, that the contrary quality is rather considered as such. That timid circumspection which is afraid of every thing, is never regarded as a virtue, but as a quality which, more than any other, incapacitates for action and business. Yet when, from a want of this excessive care, a person happens to occasion some damage to another, he is often by the law obliged to compensate it. Thus, by the Aquilian law, the man, who not being able to manage a horse that had accidentally taken fright, should happen to ride down his neighbour's slave, is obliged to compensate the damage. When an accident of this kind happens, we are apt to think that he ought not to have rode such a horse, and to regard his attempting it as an unpardonable levity; though without this accident we should not only have made no such reflection, but should have regarded his refusing it as the effect of timid weakness, and of an anxiety about merely possible events, which it is to no purpose to be aware of. The person himself who by an accident even of this kind has involuntarily hurt another, seems to have some sense of his own ill desert with regard to him. He naturally runs up to the sufferer to express his concern for what has happened, and to make every acknowledgment in his power. If he has any sensibility, he necessarily desires to compensate the damage, and to do every thing he can to appease that animal resentment, which he is sensible will be apt to arise in the breast of the sufferer. To make no apology, to offer no atonement, is regarded as the highest brutality. Yet why should he make an apology more than any other person? Why should he, since he was equally innocent with any other by-stander, be thus singled out from among all mankind, to make up for the bad fortune of another? This task would surely never be imposed upon him, did not even the impartial spectator feel some indulgence for what may be regarded as the unjust resentment of that other.

Chapter III – Of the Final Cause of This Irregularity of Sentiments

SUCH is the effect of the good or bad consequence of actions upon the sentiments both of the person who performs them, and of others; and thus, fortune, which governs the world, has some influence where we should be least willing to allow her any, and directs in some measure the sentiments of mankind, with regard to the character and conduct both of themselves and others. That the world judges by the event, and not by the design, has been in all ages the complaint, and is the great discouragement of virtue. Every body agrees to the general maxim, that as the event does not depend on the agent, it ought to have no influence upon our sentiments, with regard to the merit or propriety of his conduct. But when we come to particulars, we find that our sentiments are scarce in any one instance exactly conformable to what this equitable maxim would direct. The happy or unprosperous event of any action, is not only apt to give us a good or bad opinion of the prudence with which it was conducted, but almost always too animates our gratitude or resentment, our sense of the merit or demerit of the design.

Nature, however, when she implanted the seeds of this irregularity in the human breast, seems, as upon all other occasions, to have intended the happiness and perfection of the species. If the hurtfulness of the design, if the malevolence of the affection, were alone the causes which excited our resentment, we should feel all the furies of that passion against any person in whose breast we suspected or believed such designs or affections were harboured, though they had never broken out into any actions. Sentiments, thoughts, intentions, would become the objects of punishment; and if the indignation of mankind run as high against them as against actions; if the baseness of the thought which had given birth to no action, seemed in the eyes of the world as much to call aloud for vengeance as the baseness of the action, every court of judicature would become a real inquisition. There would be no safety for the most innocent and circumspect conduct. Bad wishes, bad views, bad designs, might still be suspected; and while these excited the same indignation with bad conduct, while bad intentions were as much resented as bad actions, they would equally expose the person to punishment and resentment. Actions, therefore, which either produce actual evil, or attempt to produce it, and thereby put us in the immediate fear of it, are by the Author of nature rendered the only proper and approved objects of human punishment and resentment. Sentiments, designs, affections, though it is from these that according to cool reason human actions derive their whole merit or demerit, are placed by the great Judge of hearts beyond the limits of every human jurisdiction, and are reserved for the cognizance of his own unerring tribunal. That necessary rule of justice, therefore, that men in this life are liable to punishment for their actions only, not for their designs and intentions, is founded upon this salutary and useful irregularity in human sentiments concerning merit or demerit, which at first sight appears so absurd and unaccountable. But every part of nature, when attentively surveyed, equally demonstrates the providential care of its Author; and we may admire the wisdom and goodness of God even in the weakness and folly of men.

Nor is that irregularity of sentiments altogether without its utility, by which the merit of an unsuccessful attempt to serve, and much more that of mere good inclinations and kind wishes, appears to be imperfect. Man was made for action, and to promote by the exertion of his faculties such changes in the external circumstances both of himself and others, as may seem most favourable to the happiness of all. He must not be satisfied with indolent benevolence, nor fancy himself the friend of mankind, because in his heart he wishes well to the prosperity of the world. That he may call forth the whole vigour of his soul, and strain every nerve, in order to produce those ends which it is the purpose of his being to advance, Nature has taught him, that neither himself nor mankind can be fully satisfied with his conduct, nor bestow upon it the full measure of applause, unless he has actually produced them. He is made to know, that the praise of good intentions, without the merit of good offices, will be but of little avail to excite either the loudest acclamations of the world, or even the highest degree of self-applause. The man who has performed no single action of importance, but whose whole conversation and deportment express the justest, the noblest, and most generous sentiments, can be entitled to demand no very high reward, even though his inutility should be owing to nothing but the want of an opportunity to serve. We can still refuse it him without blame. We can still ask him, What have you done? What actual service can you produce, to entitle you to so great a recompence? We esteem you and love you; but we owe you nothing. To reward indeed that latent virtue which has been useless only for want of on opportunity to serve, to bestow upon it those honours and preferments, which, though in some measure it may be said to deserve them, it could not with propriety have insisted upon, is the effect of the most divine benevolence. To punish, on the contrary, for the affections of the heart only, where no crime has been committed, is the most insolent and barbarous tyranny. The benevolent affections seem to deserve most praise, when they do not wait till it becomes almost a crime for them not to exert themselves. The malevolent, on the contrary, can scarce be too tardy, too slow, or deliberate.

It is even of considerable importance that the evil which is done without design should be regarded as a misfortune to the doer as well as to the sufferer. Man is thereby taught to reverence the happiness of his brethren, to tremble lest he should, even unknowingly, do any thing that can hurt them, and to dread that animal resentment which, he feels, is ready to burst out against him, if he should, without design, be the unhappy instrument of their calamity. As, in the ancient heathen religion, that holy ground which had been consecrated to some god, was not to be trod upon but upon solemn and necessary occasions, and the man who had even ignorantly violated it, became piacular from that moment, and, until proper atonement should be made, incurred the vengeance of that powerful and invisible being to whom it had been set apart; so, by the wisdom of Nature, the happiness of every innocent man is, in the same manner, rendered holy, consecrated, and hedged round against the approach of every other man; not to be wantonly trod upon, not even to be, in any respect, ignorantly and involuntarily violated, without requiring some expiation, some atonement in proportion to the greatness of such undesigned violation. A man of humanity, who accidentally, and without the smallest degree of blameable negligence, has been the cause of the death of another man, feels himself piacular, though not guilty. During his whole life he considers this accident as one of the greatest misfortunes that could have befallen him. If the family of the slain is poor, and he himself in tolerable circumstances, he immediately takes them under his protection, and without any other merit, thinks them entitled to every degree of favour and kindness. If they are in better circumstances, he endeavours by every submission, by every expression of sorrow, by rendering them every good office which he can devise, or they accept of, to atone for what has happened, and to propitiate, as much as possible, their, perhaps natural, though no doubt meat unjust resentment for the great, though involuntary, offence which he has given them.

The distress which an innocent person feels, who, by some accident, has been led to do something which, if it had been done with knowledge and design, would have justly exposed him to the deepest reproach, has given occasion to some of the finest and most interesting scenes both of the ancient and of the modern drama. It is this fallacious sense of guilt, if I may call it so, which constitutes the whole distress of Œdipus and Jocasta upon the Greek, of Monimia and Isabella upon the English, theatre. They are all of them in the highest degree piacular, though not one of them is in the smallest degree guilty.

Notwithstanding, however, all these seeming irregularities of sentiment, if man should unfortunately either give occasion to those evils which he did not intend, or fail in producing that good which he intended, Nature has not left his innocence altogether without consolation, nor his virtue altogether without reward. He then calls to his assistance that just and equitable maxim, that those events which did not depend upon our conduct, ought not to diminish the esteem that is due to us. He summons up his whole magnanimity and firmness of soul, and strives to regard himself, not in the light in which he at present appears, but in that in which he ought to appear, in which he would have appeared had his generous designs been crowned with success, and in which he would still appear, not-withstanding their miscarriage, if the sentiments of mankind were either altogether candid and equitable, or even perfectly consistent with themselves. The more candid and humane part of mankind entirely go along with the efforts which he thus makes to support himself in his own opinion. They exert their whole generosity and greatness of mind, to correct in themselves this irregularity of human nature, and endeavour to regard his unfortunate magnanimity in the same light in which, had it been successful, they would, without any such generous exertion, have naturally been disposed to consider it.

[…]

In such paroxysms of distress, if I may be allowed to call them so, the wisest and firmest man, in order to preserve his equanimity, is obliged, I imagine, to make a considerable, and even a painful exertion. His own natural feeling of his own distress, his own natural view of his own situation, presses hard upon him, and he cannot, without a very great effort, fix his attention upon that of the impartial spectator. Both views present themselves to him at the same time. His sense of honour, his regard to his own dignity, directs him to fix his whole attention upon the one view. His natural, his untaught and undisciplined feelings, are continually calling it off to the other. He does not, in this case, perfectly identify himself with the ideal man within the breast, he does not become himself the impartial spectator of his own conduct. The different views of both characters exist in his mind separate and distinct from one another, and each directing him to a behaviour different from that to which the other directs him. When he follows that view which honour and dignity point out to him, Nature does not, indeed, leave him without a recompense. He enjoys his own complete self-approbation, and the applause of every candid and impartial spectator. By her unalterable laws, however, he still suffers; and the recompense which she bestows, though very considerable, is not sufficient completely to compensate the sufferings which those laws inflict. Neither is it fit that it should. If it did completely compensate them, he could, from self-interest, have no motive for avoiding an accident which must necessarily diminish his utility both to himself and to society; and Nature, from her parental care of both, meant that he should anxiously avoid all such accidents. He suffers, therefore, and though, in the agony of the paroxysm, he maintains not only the manhood of his countenance but the sedateness and sobriety of his judgment, it requires his utmost and most fatiguing exertions to do so.

[…]

By nature, the events which immediately affect that little department in which we ourselves have some little management and direction, which immediately affect ourselves, our friends, our country, are the events which interest us the most, and which chiefly excite our desires and aversions, our hopes and fears, our joys and sorrows. Should those passions be, what they are very apt to be, too vehement, nature has provided a proper remedy and correction. The real or even the imaginary presence of the impartial spectator, the authority of the man within the breast, is always at hand to overawe them into the proper tone and temper of moderation.

If, notwithstanding our most faithful exertions, all the events which can affect this little department should turn out the most unfortunate and disastrous, nature has by no means left us without consolation. That consolation may be drawn, not only from the complete approbation of the man within the breast, but, if possible, from a still nobler and more generous principle—from a firm reliance upon, and a reverential submission to, that benevolent wisdom which directs all the events of human life, and which, we may be assured, would never have suffered those misfortunes to happen had they not been indispensably necessary for the good of the whole.

Nature has not prescribed to us this sublime contemplation as the great business and occupation of our lives. She only points it out to us as the consolation of our misfortunes.

6

Groundwork of the Metaphysics of Morals and *The Metaphysics of Morals*: Reason and the Good Will

Immanuel Kant

Kant states in the preface to the *Groundwork of the Metaphysics of Morals* that the overall aim of the book is to search for and establish the 'supreme principle of morality' (the preface is not reproduced here). He begins, in Section I, by analyzing the concepts of the will and of duty. Amongst other things, we learn the following in Section I: (i) that there is only one thing that is unconditionally good, and that is the good will; (ii) that the good will is the will that acts *for* duty, where this involves transcending one's desires; (iii) through reflection on the concept of duty itself, we can know a priori that our duties (if there are any) must be universal and categorical; and (iv) such reflection can also reveal to us that the subjective rules or policies ('maxims') that rational beings like us consider whenever we make choices must, if we are to act for duty, be fit to be used by everyone.

In Kant's view, actions always incorporate a goal for which they are done (e.g. I do not just raise my arm, but raise my arm to wave to you, or raise my arm to get a book from a bookshelf, or raise my arm to wave it about in the air in order to attempt to demonstrate that actions do not always incorporate a goal). Moral judgement can be appropriate not only in relation to actions, but also in relation to the attitudes that partly constitute our actions; it can be wrong to have various intentions, independent of any effect that acting on such intentions will have. And when we ask whether an act is done *from* duty, we are asking whether the intention or maxim that lies behind more external aspects of the act was such that it respected moral laws. Only acts done from duty are products of the good will and therefore morally praiseworthy. Still, Kant allows that many acts that fail to meet this standard – such as those of the merely prudent shopkeeper who does not overcharge customers – do, nonetheless, *conform* with duty.

The general distinction between acting from duty and acting in conformity with duty is useful, for we do generally wish to discriminate between cases where people deserve moral credit or praise for doing the right thing and cases where they do not deserve moral credit or praise. However, Kant's interpretation of this distinction is controversial, and many find it unattractive. We are told that a person who acts in a way that beneficence recommends, but from a motive of natural sympathy, deserves no moral credit for their good deeds, while a person who is 'cold and indifferent' but forces themselves to do a beneficent act does deserve such credit (4:398). We are not responsible for those aspects of our psychologies that we are born with, and reflection on this fact *might* lead us to agree with Kant regarding these two types of people. Still, we can make progress here if we distinguish between *three* types of people: people who are simply born with a sympathetic nature, people who are born cold and indifferent and remain that way, and people who are born cold and indifferent but, over time, develop warm, sympathetic characters as a result of actively working at developing genuinely sympathetic emotions and motives. Kant does not consider this third kind of person, but even if we were to agree with him that the second kind of person deserves moral praise

History of Ethics – Essential Readings with Commentary, First Edition. Edited by Daniel Star and Roger Crisp.
© 2020 John Wiley & Sons Ltd. Published 2020 by John Wiley & Sons Ltd.

when she acts charitably whereas the first does not, it seems extremely attractive to also think that the charitable acts of the third kind of person, many of which will, in the end, be quite spontaneous (for they need not be fixated on thoughts of duty) are much more deserving of moral praise than the acts of the second kind of person.

Kant recognizes that practical deliberation is not always moral. He distinguishes between hypothetical imperatives and categorical imperatives. Hypothetical imperatives are the types of directives we are faced with when we engage in instrumental reasoning; such reasoning may have a moral end in mind, such as when, having decided to help someone in need, I find it makes most sense to do so by giving them money, but it need not (it is just as indispensable when deliberating about morally neutral ends, or evil ends). Whether or not a claim about a hypothetical imperative makes sense will depend on whether or not I have a relevant desire or intention (e.g. if I plan to fly to Berlin for a holiday, I must intend to buy an airplane ticket, at risk of being irrational; but if I change my mind and no longer plan to fly to Berlin, then there is no longer any rational pressure on me to buy an airplane ticket to Berlin, to say the least). But the demands of morality are different: I cannot escape them by changing my desires.

In an important paragraph here, Kant presents the first formulation of what he will call 'the categorical imperative' in Section II (emphasis added): 'I ought never to act except in such a way that I could also will that my maxim should become a universal law.' This represents the culmination of an argument in the preceding paragraphs. This argument is complex, and the details contentious, but we might attempt to summarize it as follows: reflection on our ordinary commitments about what is involved in acting from moral duty leads us to exclude our individual desires and prudential considerations, as well as considerations concerning the actual effects of our actions on the world, as at all relevant, and to include reverence for the moral law as crucial; the only thing then left for the good will to be acting on when we act for duty is the idea of making one's own maxims conform with universal moral laws. Hence, the fundamental moral law must itself be one that directs each of us to act only on maxims that are such that we could will that they become laws for everyone (putting this fundamental law into action would not involve coming to believe that such maxims will, in fact, become laws that others act on, but only that there would be nothing inconceivable or incoherent in them becoming universal laws). It is not obvious that this conclusion follows from the premises that precede it. In any case, Kant also helpfully follows the presentation of the argument with an example of the reasoning he has in mind when applying the fundamental principle, involving the duty not to lie. To avoid misunderstanding, note that the principle does *not* say that one must always use the recommended form of reasoning if one is to act in a morally praiseworthy way; it merely says that one should act on maxims that one *could* (coherently) will be universal laws. Although this form of reasoning is a priori available to everyone, it need not be utilized when making ordinary moral decisions.

Also included here are two excerpts from a later text, *The Metaphysics of Morals*. The first excerpt begins with a discussion of inclinations and choices. It is included because it is helpful in understanding the moral psychology already largely in place in the *Groundwork*. The second excerpt provides us with a discussion of virtue. Following the revival of virtue ethics in the second half of the twentieth century, Kantian ethicists have been keen to point out that Kant was interested not only in duty, but also in virtue. That being said, on Kant's account of virtue, virtues are very closely connected to duty, since the virtuous person is always freely doing his or her duty. There is an important proviso here: many ordinary acts are morally permissible; hence doing one's duty provides one with much leeway in the choice of particular ends (we are told that the virtuous person is not an overly moralistic busybody). The fact that wide or imperfect duties provide us with flexibility in our choice of good ends is said to explain how there is a diverse range of particular virtues, although Kant does not go into details here. Virtue itself is equated with strength of will, where this is not to be understood in terms of (strong) feelings or desire. The virtuous person has a tranquil mind. To be precise, 'virtue is the strength of a human being's maxims in fulfilling his duty.' It involves constraining contingent features of one's psychology in order to be able to act freely through rationally selecting the correct principles of action. Virtue is precarious, and the person who is on his or her way to being virtuous must be vigilant (being virtuous is an ideal that may not be able to be realized in practice); virtue cannot become habitual, as autonomous reason must always be in play if we are to be truly acting from duty.

Groundwork of the Metaphysics of Morals

Section I

Transition from Common Rational to Philosophic Moral Cognition

It is impossible to think of anything at all in the world, or indeed even beyond it, that could be considered good without limitation except a **good will**. Understanding, wit, judgment[3] and the like, whatever such *talents* of mind may be called, or courage, resolution, and perseverance in one's plans, as qualities of *temperament*, are undoubtedly good and desirable for many purposes, but they can also be extremely evil and harmful if the will which is to make use of these gifts of nature, and whose distinctive constitution is therefore called *character*, is not good. It is the same with *gifts of fortune*. Power, riches, honor, even health and that complete well-being and satisfaction with one's condition called *happiness*, produce boldness and thereby often arrogance as well unless a good will is present which corrects the influence of these on the mind and, in so doing, also corrects the whole principle of action and brings it into conformity with universal ends – not to mention that an impartial rational spectator can take no delight in seeing the uninterrupted prosperity of a being graced with no feature of a pure and good will, so that a good will seems to constitute the indispensable condition even of worthiness to be happy.

Some qualities are even conducive to this good will itself and can make its work much easier; despite this, however, they have no inner unconditional worth but always presuppose a good will, which limits the esteem one *4:394* otherwise rightly has for them and does not permit their being taken as absolutely good. Moderation in affects and passions, self-control, and calm reflection are not only good for all sorts of purposes but even seem to constitute a part of the *inner* worth of a person; but they lack much that would be required to declare them good without limitation (however unconditionally they were praised by the ancients); for, without the basic principles of a good will they can become extremely evil, and the coolness of a scoundrel makes him not only far more dangerous but also immediately more abominable in our eyes than we would have taken him to be without it.

A good will is not good because of what it effects or accomplishes, because of its fitness to attain some proposed end, but only because of its volition, that is, it is good in itself and, regarded for itself, is to be valued incomparably higher than all that could merely be brought about by it in favor of some inclination and indeed, if you will, of the sum of all inclinations. Even if, by a special disfavor of fortune or by the niggardly provision of a stepmotherly nature, this will should wholly lack the capacity to carry out its purpose – if with its greatest efforts it should yet achieve nothing and only the good will were left (not, of course, as a mere wish but as the summoning of all means insofar as they are in our control) – then, like a jewel, it would still shine by itself, as something that has its full worth in itself. Usefulness or fruitlessness can neither add anything to this worth nor take anything away from it. Its usefulness would be, as it were, only the setting to enable us to handle it more conveniently in ordinary commerce or to attract to it the attention of those who are not yet expert enough, but not to recommend it to experts or to determine its worth.

There is, however, something so strange in this idea of the absolute worth of a mere will, in the estimation of which no allowance is made for any usefulness, that, despite all the agreement even of common understanding with this idea, a suspicion must yet arise that its covert basis is perhaps mere high-flown fantasy and that we may have misunderstood the purpose of nature in assigning reason to our will as its governor. Hence we shall put this idea to *4:395* the test from this point of view.

In the natural constitution of an organized being, that is, one constituted purposively for life, we assume as a principle that there will be found in it no instrument for some end other than what is also most appropriate to that end and best adapted to it. Now in a being that has reason and a will, if the proper end of nature were its *preservation*, its *welfare*, in a word its *happiness*, then nature would have hit upon a very bad arrangement in selecting the reason of the creature to carry out this purpose. For all the actions that the creature has to perform for this purpose, and the whole rule of its conduct, would be marked out for it far more accurately by instinct, and that end would have thereby been attained much more surely than it ever can be by reason; and if reason should have been given, over and above, to this favored creature, it must have served it only to contemplate the fortunate constitution of its nature, to admire this, to delight in it, and to be grateful for it to the beneficent cause, but not to submit its faculty of desire to that weak and deceptive guidance and meddle with nature's purpose. In a word, nature would have taken care that reason should not break forth into *practical use* and have the presumption, with its weak insight, to think out for itself a plan for happiness and for the means of attaining it. Nature would have taken upon itself the choice not only of ends but also of means and, with wise foresight, would have entrusted them both simply to instinct.

And, in fact, we find that the more a cultivated reason purposely occupies itself with the enjoyment of life and with happiness, so much the further does one get away from true satisfaction; and from this there arises in many, and indeed in those who have experimented most with this use of reason, if only they are candid enough to admit it, a certain degree of *misology*, that is, hatred of reason; for, after calculating all the advantages they draw – I do not say from the invention of all the arts of common luxury, but even from the sciences (which seem to them to be, at bottom, only a luxury of the understanding) – they find that they have in fact only brought more trouble upon

4:396 themselves instead of gaining in happiness; and because of this they finally envy rather than despise the more common run of people, who are closer to the guidance of mere natural instinct and do not allow their reason much influence on their behavior. And to this extent we must admit that the judgment of those who greatly moderate, and even reduce below zero, eulogies extolling the advantages that reason is supposed to procure for us with regard to the happiness and satisfaction of life is by no means surly or ungrateful to the goodness of the government of the world; we must admit, instead, that these judgments have as their covert basis the idea of another and far worthier purpose of one's existence, to which therefore, and not to happiness, reason is properly destined, and to which, as supreme condition, the private purpose of the human being must for the most part defer.

Since reason is not sufficiently competent to guide the will surely with regard to its objects and the satisfaction of all our needs (which it to some extent even multiplies) – an end to which an implanted natural instinct would have led much more certainly; and since reason is nevertheless given to us as a practical faculty, that is, as one that is to influence the *will*; then, where nature has everywhere else gone to work purposively in distributing its capacities, the true vocation of reason must be to produce a will that is good, not perhaps *as a means* to other purposes, but *good in itself*, for which reason was absolutely necessary. This will need not, because of this, be the sole and complete good, but it must still be the highest good and the condition of every other, even of all demands for happiness. In this case it is entirely consistent with the wisdom of nature if we perceive that the cultivation of reason, which is requisite to the first and unconditional purpose, limits in many ways – at least in this life – the attainment of the second, namely happiness, which is always conditional; indeed it may reduce it below zero without nature proceeding unpurposively in the matter, because reason, which cognizes its highest practical vocation in the establishment of a good will, in attaining this purpose is capable only of its own kind of satisfaction, namely from fulfilling an end which in turn only reason determines, even if this should be combined with many infringements upon the ends of inclination.

4:397 We have, then, to explicate the concept of a will that is to be esteemed in itself and that is good apart from any further purpose, as it already dwells in natural sound understanding and needs not so much to be taught as only to be clarified – this concept that always takes first place in estimating the total worth of our actions and constitutes the condition of all the rest. In order to do so, we shall set before ourselves the concept of **duty**, which contains that of a good will though under certain subjective limitations and hindrances, which, however, far from concealing it and making it unrecognizable, rather bring it out by contrast and make it shine forth all the more brightly.

I here pass over all actions that are already recognized as contrary to duty, even though they may be useful for this or that purpose; for in their case the question whether they might have been done *from duty* never arises, since they even conflict with it. I also set aside actions that are really in conformity with duty but to which human beings have *no inclination* immediately and which they still perform because they are impelled to do so through another inclination. For in this case it is easy to distinguish whether an action in conformity with duty is done *from duty* or from a self-seeking purpose. It is much more difficult to note this distinction when an action conforms with duty and the subject has, besides, an *immediate* inclination to it. For example, it certainly conforms with duty that a shopkeeper not overcharge an inexperienced customer, and where there is a good deal of trade a prudent merchant does not overcharge but keeps a fixed general price for everyone, so that a child can buy from him as well as everyone else. People are thus served *honestly;* but this is not nearly enough for us to believe that the merchant acted in this way from duty and basic principles of honesty; his advantage required it; it cannot be assumed here that he had, besides, an immediate inclination toward his customers, so as from love, as it were, to give no one preference over another in the matter of price. Thus the action was done neither from duty nor from immediate inclination but merely for purposes of self-interest.

On the other hand, to preserve one's life is a duty, and besides everyone has an immediate inclination to do so. But on this account the often anxious care that most people take of it still has no inner worth and their maxim has

4:398 no moral content. They look after their lives *in conformity with duty* but not *from duty*. On the other hand, if adversity and hopeless grief have quite taken away the taste for life; if an unfortunate man, strong of soul and more indignant about his fate than despondent or dejected, wishes for death and yet preserves his life without loving it, not from inclination or fear but from duty, then his maxim has moral content.

To be beneficent where one can is a duty, and besides there are many souls so sympathetically attuned that, without any other motive of vanity or self-interest they find an inner satisfaction in spreading joy around them and can take delight in the satisfaction of others so far as it is their own work. But I assert that in such a case an action of this kind, however it may conform with duty and however amiable it may be, has nevertheless no true moral worth but is on the same footing with other inclinations, for example, the inclination to honor, which, if it fortunately lights upon what is in fact in the common interest and in conformity with duty and hence honorable, deserves praise and encouragement but not esteem; for the maxim lacks moral content, namely that of doing such actions not from inclination but *from duty*. Suppose, then, that the mind of this philanthropist were overclouded by his own grief, which extinguished all sympathy with the fate of others, and that while he still had the means to benefit others in distress their troubles did not move him because he had enough to do with his own; and suppose that now, when no longer incited to it by any inclination, he nevertheless tears himself out of this deadly insensibility and does the action without any inclination, simply from duty; then the action first has its genuine moral worth. Still further: if nature had put little sympathy in the heart of this or that man; if (in other respects an honest man) he is by temperament cold and indifferent to the sufferings of others, perhaps because he himself is provided with the special gift of patience and endurance toward his own sufferings and presupposes the same in every other or even requires it; if nature had not properly fashioned such a man (who would in truth not be its worst product) for a philanthropist, would he not still find within himself a source from which to give himself a far higher worth than what a mere good-natured temperament might have? By all means! It is just then that the worth of character comes out, which *4:399* is moral and incomparably the highest, namely that he is beneficent not from inclination but from duty.

To assure one's own happiness is a duty (at least indirectly); for, want of satisfaction with one's condition, under pressure from many anxieties and amid unsatisfied needs, could easily become a great *temptation to transgression of duty*. But in addition, without looking to duty here, all people have already, of themselves, the strongest and deepest inclination to happiness because it is just in this idea that all inclinations unite in one sum. However, the precept of happiness is often so constituted that it greatly infringes upon some inclinations, and yet one can form no determinate and sure concept of the sum of satisfaction of all inclinations under the name of happiness. Hence it is not to be wondered at that a single inclination, determinate both as to what it promises and as to the time within which it can be satisfied, can often outweigh a fluctuating idea, and that a man – for example, one suffering from gout – can choose to enjoy what he likes and put up with what he can since, according to his calculations, on this occasion at least he has not sacrificed the enjoyment of the present moment to the perhaps groundless expectation of a happiness that is supposed to lie in health. But even in this case, when the general inclination to happiness did not determine his will; when health, at least for him, did not enter as so necessary into this calculation, there is still left over here, as in all other cases, a law, namely to promote his happiness not from inclination but from duty; and it is then that his conduct first has properly moral worth.

It is undoubtedly in this way, again, that we are to understand the passages from scripture in which we are commanded to love our neighbor, even our enemy. For, love as an inclination cannot be commanded, but beneficence from duty – even though no inclination impels us to it and, indeed, natural and unconquerable aversion opposes it – is *practical* and not *pathological* love, which lies in the will and not in the propensity of feeling, in principles of action and not in melting sympathy; and it alone can be commanded.

The second proposition is this: an action from duty has its moral worth *not in the purpose* to be attained by it but in the maxim in accordance with which it is decided upon, and therefore does not depend upon the realization of the object of the action but merely upon the *principle of volition* in accordance with which the action is done with- *4:400* out regard for any object of the faculty of desire. That the purposes we may have for our actions, and their effects as ends and incentives of the will, can give actions no unconditional and moral worth is clear from what has gone before. In what, then, can this worth lie, if it is not to be in the will in relation to the hoped for effect of the action? It can lie nowhere else *than in the principle of the will* without regard for the ends that can be brought about by such an action. For, the will stands between its a priori principle, which is formal, and its a posteriori incentive, which is material, as at a crossroads; and since it must still be determined by something, it must be determined by the formal principle of volition as such when an action is done from duty, where every material principle has been withdrawn from it.

The third proposition, which is a consequence of the two preceding, I would express as follows: *duty is the necessity of an action from respect for law*. For an object as the effect of my proposed action I can indeed have *inclination* but *never respect*, just because it is merely an effect and not an activity of a will. In the same way I cannot have respect for inclination as such, whether it is mine or that of another; I can at most in the first case approve it and in the second sometimes even love it, that is, regard it as favorable to my own advantage. Only what is connected with my will merely as ground and never as effect, what does not serve my inclination but outweighs it or at least excludes it altogether from calculations in making a choice – hence the mere law for itself – can be an object of respect and so a command. Now, an action from duty is to put aside entirely the influence of inclination and with it every object of the will; hence there is left for the will nothing that could determine it except objectively the *law* and 4:401 subjectively *pure respect* for this practical law, and so the maxim★ of complying with such a law even if it infringes upon all my inclinations.

Thus the moral worth of an action does not lie in the effect expected from it and so too does not lie in any principle of action that needs to borrow its motive from this expected effect. For, all these effects (agreeableness of one's condition, indeed even promotion of others' happiness) could have been also brought about by other causes, so that there would have been no need, for this, of the will of a rational being, in which, however, the highest and unconditional good alone can be found. Hence nothing other than the *representation of the law* in itself, *which can of course occur only in a rational being*, insofar as it and not the hoped-for effect is the determining ground of the will, can constitute the preeminent good we call moral, which is already present in the person himself who acts in accordance with this representation and need not wait upon the effect of his action.†

4:402   But what kind of law can that be, the representation of which must determine the will, even without regard for the effect expected from it, in order for the will to be called good absolutely and without limitation? Since I have deprived the will of every impulse that could arise for it from obeying some law, nothing is left but the conformity of actions as such with universal law, which alone is to serve the will as its principle, that is, *I ought never to act except in such a way that I could also will that my maxim should become a universal law*. Here mere conformity to law as such, without having as its basis some law determined for certain actions, is what serves the will as its principle, and must so serve it, if duty is not to be everywhere an empty delusion and a chimerical concept. Common human reason also agrees completely with this in its practical appraisals and always has this principle before its eyes. Let the question be, for example: may I, when hard pressed, make a promise with the intention not to keep it? Here I easily distinguish two significations the question can have: whether it is prudent or whether it is in conformity with duty to make a false promise. The first can undoubtedly often be the case. I see very well that it is not enough to get out of a present difficulty by means of this subterfuge but that I must reflect carefully whether this lie may later give rise to much greater inconvenience for me than that from which I now extricate myself; and since, with all my supposed *cunning*, the results cannot be so easily foreseen but that once confidence in me is lost this could be far more prejudicial to me than all the troubles I now think to avoid, I must reflect whether the matter might be handled *more prudently* by proceeding on a general maxim and making it a habit to promise nothing except with the intention of keeping it. But it is soon clear to me that such a maxim will still be based only on results feared. To be truthful from duty, however, is something entirely different from being truthful from anxiety about detrimental results, since in the first case the concept of the action in itself already contains a law for me while in the second I must first look about elsewhere to see what effects on me might be combined with it. For, if I deviate from the principle of duty this is quite certainly evil; but if I am 4:403 unfaithful to my maxim of prudence this can sometimes be very advantageous to me, although it is certainly safer to abide by it. However, to inform myself in the shortest and yet infallible way about the answer to this problem, whether a lying promise is in conformity with duty, I ask myself: would I indeed be content that my maxim

---

★ A *maxim* is the subjective principle of volition; the objective principle (i.e., that which would also serve subjectively as the practical principle for all rational beings if reason had complete control over the faculty of desire) is the practical *law*.

† It could be objected that I only seek refuge, behind the word *respect*, in an obscure feeling, instead of distinctly resolving the question by means of a concept of reason. But though respect is a feeling, it is not one *received* by means of influence; it is, instead, a feeling *self-wrought* by means of a rational concept and therefore specifically different from all feelings of the first kind, which can be reduced to inclination or fear. What I cognize immediately as a law for me I cognize with respect, which signifies merely consciousness of the *subordination* of my will to a law without the mediation of other influences on my sense. Immediate determination of the will by means of the law and consciousness of this is called *respect*, so that this is regarded as the *effect* of the law on the subject, and not as the *cause* of the law. Respect is properly the representation of a worth that infringes upon my self-love. Hence there is something that is regarded as an object neither of inclination nor of fear, though it has something analogous to both. The *object* of respect is therefore simply the *law*, and indeed the law that we impose upon *ourselves* and yet as necessary in itself. As a law we are subject to it without consulting self-love; as imposed upon us by ourselves it is nevertheless a result of our will; and in the first respect it has an analogy with fear, in the second with inclination. Any respect for a person is properly only respect for the law (of integrity and so forth) of which he gives us an example. Because we also regard enlarging our talents as a duty, we represent a person of talents also as, so to speak, an *example of the law* (to become like him in this by practice), and this is what constitutes our respect. All so-called moral *interest* consists simply in *respect* for the law.

(to get myself out of difficulties by a false promise) should hold as a universal law (for myself as well as for others)? and could I indeed say to myself that every one may make a false promise when he finds himself in a difficulty he can get out of in no other way? Then I soon become aware that I could indeed will the lie, but by no means a universal law to lie; for in accordance with such a law there would properly be no promises at all, since it would be futile to avow my will with regard to my future actions to others who would not believe this avowal or, if they rashly did so, would pay me back in like coin; and thus my maxim, as soon as it were made a universal law, would have to destroy itself.

I do not, therefore, need any penetrating acuteness to see what I have to do in order that my volition be morally good. Inexperienced in the course of the world, incapable of being prepared for whatever might come to pass in it, I ask myself only: can you also will that your maxim become a universal law? If not, then it is to be repudiated, and that not because of a disadvantage to you or even to others forthcoming from it but because it cannot fit as a principle into a possible giving of universal law, for which lawgiving reason, however, forces from me immediate respect. Although I do not yet *see* what this respect is based upon (this the philosopher may investigate), I at least understand this much: that it is an estimation of a worth that far outweighs any worth of what is recommended by inclination, and that the necessity of my action from *pure* respect for the practical law is what constitutes duty, to which every other motive must give way because it is the condition of a will good *in itself*, the worth of which surpasses all else.

Thus, then, we have arrived, within the moral cognition of common human reason, at its principle, which it admittedly does not think so abstractly in a universal form but which it actually has always before its eyes and uses as the norm for its appraisals. Here it would be easy to show how common human reason, with this compass in *4:404* hand, knows very well how to distinguish in every case that comes up what is good and what is evil, what is in conformity with duty or contrary to duty, if, without in the least teaching it anything new, we only, as did Socrates, make it attentive to its own principle; and that there is, accordingly, no need of science and philosophy to know what one has to do in order to be honest and good, and even wise and virtuous. We might even have assumed in advance that cognizance of what it is incumbent upon everyone to do, and so also to know, would be the affair of every human being, even the most common. Yet we cannot consider without admiration how great an advantage the practical faculty of appraising has over the theoretical in common human understanding. In the latter, if common reason ventures to depart from laws of experience and perceptions of the senses it falls into sheer incomprehensibilities and self-contradictions, at least into a chaos of uncertainty, obscurity, and instability. But in practical matters, it is just when common understanding excludes all sensible incentives from practical laws that its faculty of appraising first begins to show itself to advantage. It then becomes even subtle, whether in quibbling tricks with its own conscience or with other claims regarding what is to be called right, or in sincerely wanting to determine the worth of actions for its own instruction; and, what is most admirable, in the latter case it can even have as good a hope of hitting the mark as any philosopher can promise himself; indeed, it is almost more sure in this matter, because a philosopher, though he cannot have any other principle than that of common understanding, can easily confuse his judgment by a mass of considerations foreign and irrelevant to the matter and deflect it from the straight course. Would it not therefore be more advisable in moral matters to leave the judgment of common reason as it is and, at most, call in philosophy only to present the system of morals all the more completely and apprehensibly and to present its rules in a form more convenient for use (still more for disputation), but not to lead common human understanding, even in practical matters, away from its fortunate simplicity and to put it, by means of philosophy, on a new path of investigation and instruction?

There is something splendid about innocence; but what is bad about it, in turn, is that it cannot protect itself very well and is easily seduced. Because of this, even wisdom — which otherwise consists more in conduct than in *4:405* knowledge — still needs science, not in order to learn from it but in order to provide access and durability for its precepts. The human being feels within himself a powerful counterweight to all the commands of duty, which reason represents to him as so deserving of the highest respect — the counterweight of his needs and inclinations, the entire satisfaction of which he sums up under the name happiness. Now reason issues its precepts unremittingly, without thereby promising anything to the inclinations, and so, as it were, with disregard and contempt for those claims, which are so impetuous and besides so apparently equitable (and refuse to be neutralized by any command). But from this there arises a *natural dialectic*, that is, a propensity to rationalize against those strict laws of duty and to cast doubt upon their validity, or at least upon their purity and strictness, and, where possible, to make them better suited to our wishes and inclinations, that is, to corrupt them at their basis and to destroy all their dignity — something that even common practical reason cannot, in the end, call good.

In this way *common human reason* is impelled, not by some need of speculation (which never touches it as long as it is content to be mere sound reason), but on practical grounds themselves, to go out of its sphere and to take a step into the field of *practical philosophy*, in order to obtain there information and distinct instruction regarding the source of its principle and the correct determination of this principle in comparison with maxims based on need and inclination, so that it may escape from its predicament about claims from both sides and not run the risk of being deprived of all genuine moral principles through the ambiguity into which it easily falls. So there develops unnoticed in common practical reason as well, when it cultivates itself, a *dialectic* that constrains it to seek help in philosophy, just as happens in its theoretical use; and the first will, accordingly, find no more rest than the other except in a complete critique of our reason.

The Metaphysics of Morals

Part I – Metaphysical First Principles of the Doctrine of Right

Introduction to the Metaphysics of Morals

[…]

II.   On the Relation of the Faculties of the Human Mind to Moral Laws   *6:211*

The *faculty of desire* is the faculty to be, by means of one's representations, the cause of the objects of these representations. The faculty of a being to act in accordance with its representations is called *life*.

First, *pleasure* or *displeasure*, susceptibility to which is called *feeling*, is always connected with desire or aversion; but the converse does not always hold, since there can be a pleasure that is not connected with any desire for an object but is already connected with a mere representation that one forms of an object (regardless of whether die object of the representation exists or not). *Second*, pleasure or displeasure in an object of desire does not always precede the desire and need not always be regarded as the cause of the desire but can also be regarded as the effect of it.

[…]

Although where a merely pure interest of reason must be assumed no interest of inclination can be substituted for it, yet in order to conform to ordinary speech we can speak of an inclination for what can be an object only of an intellectual pleasure as a habitual desire from a pure interest of reason; but an inclination of this sort would not be the cause but rather the effect of this pure interest of reason, and we could call it a *sense-free inclination* (*propensio intellectualis*).

[…]

The faculty of desire in accordance with concepts, insofar as the ground determining it to action lies within itself and not in its object, is called a faculty to *do or to refrain from doing as one pleases*. Insofar as it is joined with one's consciousness of the ability to bring about its object by one's action it is called *choice*; if it is not joined with this consciousness its act is called a *wish*. The faculty of desire whose inner determining ground, hence even what pleases it, lies within the subject's reason is called the *will*. The will is therefore the faculty of desire considered not so much in relation to action (as choice is) but rather in relation to the ground determining choice to action. The will itself, strictly speaking, has no determining ground; insofar as it can determine choice, it is instead practical reason itself.

Insofar as reason can determine the faculty of desire as such, not only *choice* but also mere *wish* can be included under the will. That choice which can be determined by *pure reason* is called *free choice*. That which can be determined only by *inclination* (sensible impulse, *stimulus*) would be animal choice (*arbitrium brutum*). Human choice, however, is a choice that can indeed be *affected* but not *determined* by impulses, and is therefore of itself (apart from an acquired proficiency of reason) not pure but can still be determined to actions by pure will. *Freedom* of choice is this independence from being *determined* by sensible impulses; this is the negative concept of freedom. The positive concept of freedom is that of the ability of pure reason to be of itself practical. But this *6:214* is not possible except by the subjection of the maxim of every action to the condition of its qualifying as universal law. For as pure reason applied to choice irrespective of its objects, it does not have within it the matter of the law; so, as a faculty of principles (here practical principles, hence a lawgiving faculty), there is nothing it can make the supreme law and determining ground of choice except the form, the fitness of maxims of choice to be universal law. And since the maxims of human beings, being based on subjective causes, do not of themselves conform with those objective principles, reason can prescribe this law only as an imperative that commands or prohibits absolutely.

In contrast to laws of nature, these laws of freedom are called *moral* laws.

[…]

Part II – Metaphysical First Principles of the Doctrine of Virtue

Introduction to the Doctrine of Virtue

[…]

III.   On the Basis for Thinking of an End That Is Also a Duty

6:385   An **end** is an *object* of free choice, the representation of which determines it to an action (by which the object is brought about). Every action, therefore, has its end; and since no one can have an end without *himself* making the object of his choice into an end, to have any end of action whatsoever is an act of *freedom* on the part of the acting subject, not an effect of *nature*.

[…]

IV.   What Are the Ends That Are Also Duties?

They are *one's own perfection* and *the happiness of others*.

Perfection and happiness cannot be interchanged here, so that *one's own happiness* and *the perfection of others* would be made ends that would be in themselves duties of the same person.

6:386   For *his own happiness* is an end that every human being has (by virtue of the impulses of his nature), but this end can never without self-contradiction be regarded as a duty. What everyone already wants unavoidably, of his own accord, does not come under the concept of *duty*, which is *constraint* to an end adopted reluctantly. Hence it is self-contradictory to say that he is *under obligation* to promote his own happiness with all his powers.

So too, it is a contradiction for me to make another's *perfection* my end and consider myself under obligation to promote this. For the *perfection* of another human being, as a person, consists just in this: that he *himself* is able to set his end in accordance with his own concepts of duty; and it is self-contradictory to require that I do (make it my duty to do) something that only the other himself can do.

[…]

V.   Clarification of These Two Concepts

A. One's Own Perfection

[…]

1)   A human being has a duty to raise himself from the crude state of his nature, from his animality (*quoad actum*), more and more toward humanity, by which he alone is capable of setting himself ends; he has a duty to diminish his ignorance by instruction and to correct his errors. And it is not merely that technically practical reason *counsels* him to do this as a means to his further purposes (of art); morally practical reason *commands* it absolutely and makes this end his duty, so that he may be worthy of the humanity that dwells within him. 2) A human being has a duty to carry the cultivation of his *will* up to the purest virtuous disposition, in which the *law* becomes also the incentive to his actions that conform with duty and he obeys the law from duty. This disposition is inner morally practical perfection. Since it is a feeling of the effect that the lawgiving will within the human being exercises on his capacity to act in accordance with his will, it is called *moral feeling*, a special *sense* (*sensus moralis*), as it were. It is true that moral sense is often misused in a visionary way, as if (like Socrates' daimon) it could precede reason or even dispense with reason's judgment. Yet it is a moral perfection, by which one makes one's object every particular end that is also a duty.

[…]

IX.   What Is a Duty of Virtue?

Virtue is the strength of a human being's maxims in fulfilling his duty. – Strength of any kind can be recognized only by the obstacles it can overcome, and in the case of virtue these obstacles are natural inclinations, which can come into conflict with the human being's moral resolution; and since it is the human being *himself* who puts these obstacles in the way of his maxims, virtue is not merely a self-constraint (for then one natural inclination could strive to overcome another), but also a self-constraint in accordance with a principle of inner freedom, and so through the mere representation of one's duty in accordance with its formal law.

All duties involve a concept of *constraint* through a law. *Ethical* duties involve a constraint for which only internal lawgiving is possible, whereas duties of right involve a constraint for which external lawgiving is also possible. Both, therefore, involve constraint, whether it be self-constraint or constraint by another. Since the moral capacity to constrain oneself can be called virtue, action springing from such a disposition (respect for law) can be called virtuous (ethical) action, even though the law lays down a duty of right; for it is the *doctrine of virtue* that commands us to hold the right of human beings sacred.

But what it is virtuous to do is not necessarily a *duty of virtue* strictly speaking. What it is virtuous to do may concern only *what is formal* in maxims, whereas a duty of virtue has to do with their matter, that is to say, with an   *6:395* end that is thought as also a duty. – But since ethical obligation to ends, of which there can be several, is only *wide* obligation – because it involves a law only for *maxims* of actions, and an end is the matter (object) of choice – there are many different duties, corresponding to the different ends prescribed by the law, which are called *duties of virtue* (*officia honestatis*) just because they are subject only to free self-constraint, not constraint by other human beings, and because they determine an end that is also a duty.

Like anything *formal*, virtue as the will's conformity with every duty, based on a firm disposition, is merely one and the same. But with respect to the *end* of actions that is also a duty, that is, what one *ought* to make one's *end* (what is material), there can be several virtues; and since obligation to the maxim of such an end is called a duty of virtue, there are many duties of virtue.

The supreme principle of the doctrine of virtue is: act in accordance with a maxim of *ends* that it can be a universal law for everyone to have. – In accordance with this principle a human being is an end for himself as well as for others, and it is not enough that he is not authorized to use either himself or others merely as means (since he could then still be indifferent to them); it is in itself his duty to make the human being as such his end.

This basic principle of the doctrine of virtue, as a categorical imperative, cannot be proved, but it can be given a deduction from pure practical reason. – What, in the relation of a human being to himself and others, *can* be an end *is* an end for pure practical reason; for, pure practical reason is a faculty of ends generally, and for it to be indifferent to ends, that is, to take no interest in them, would therefore be a contradiction, since then it would not determine maxims for actions either (because every maxim of action contains an end) and so would not be practical reason. But pure reason can prescribe no ends a priori without setting them forth as also duties, and such duties are then called duties of virtue.

X.   The Supreme Principle of the Doctrine of Right Was *Analytic*; That of the Doctrine   *6:396*
of Virtue Is *Synthetic*

[…]

The highest, unconditional end of pure practical reason (which is still a duty) consists in this: that virtue be its own end and, despite the benefits it confers on human beings, also its own reward. Virtue so shines as an ideal that it seems, by human standards, to eclipse *holiness* itself, which is never tempted to break the law.* Nevertheless, this   *6:397* is an illusion arising from the fact that, having no way to measure the degree of a strength except by the magnitude of the obstacles it could overcome (in us, these are inclinations), we are led to mistake the *subjective* conditions by which we assess the magnitude for the *objective* conditions of the magnitude itself. Yet in comparison with *human ends*, all of which have their obstacles to be contended with, it is true that the worth of virtue itself, as its own end, far exceeds the worth of any usefulness and any empirical ends and advantages that virtue may still bring in its wake.

It is also correct to say that the human being is under obligation *to virtue* (as moral strength). For while the capacity (*facultas*) to overcome all opposing sensible impulses can and must be simply *presupposed* in man on account of his freedom, yet this capacity as *strength* (*robur*) is something he must acquire; and the way to acquire it is to enhance the moral *incentive* (the thought of the law), both by contemplating the dignity of the pure rational law in us (*contemplatione*) and by *practicing* virtue (*exercitio*).

[…]

---

* Man with all his faults
 Is better than a host of angels without will. Haller

XVI. Virtue Necessarily Presupposes Apathy (Regarded As Strength)

The word "apathy" has fallen into disrepute, as if it meant lack of feeling and so subjective indifference with respect to objects of choice; it is taken for weakness. This misunderstanding can be prevented by giving the name "*moral apathy*" to that absence of affects which is to be distinguished from indifference because in cases of moral apathy feelings arising from sensible impressions lose their influence on moral feeling only because respect for the law is more powerful than all such feelings together. – Only the apparent strength of someone feverish lets a lively sympathy even for *what is good* rise into an affect, or rather degenerate into it. An affect of this kind is called *enthusiasm*, and the *moderation* that is usually recommended even for the practice of virtue is to be interpreted as referring to it (*insani sapiens nomen habeat[;] aequus iniqui* – **ultra quam satis est** *virtutem si petat ipsam. Horat.*); for otherwise it is absurd to suppose that one could be *too wise, too virtuous*. An affect always belongs to sensibility, no matter by what kind of object it is aroused. The true strength of virtue is a *tranquil mind* with a considered and firm resolution to put the law of virtue into practice. That is the state of *health* in the moral life, whereas an affect, even one aroused by the thought of *what is good*, is a momentary, sparkling phenomenon that leaves one exhausted. – But that the human being can be called fantastically virtuous who allows *nothing to be morally indifferent* (*adiaphora*) and strews all his steps with duties, as with mantraps; it is not indifferent to him whether I eat meat or fish, drink beer or wine, supposing that both agree with me. Fantastic virtue is a concern with petty details which, were it admitted into the doctrine of virtue, would turn the government of virtue into tyranny.

6:409

Remark

Virtue is always *in progress* and yet always starts *from the beginning*. – It is always in progress because, considered *objectively*, it is an ideal and unattainable, while yet constant approximation to it is a duty. That it always starts from the beginning has a *subjective* basis in human nature, which is affected by inclinations because of which virtue can never settle down in peace and quiet with its maxims adopted once and for all but, if it is not rising, is unavoidably sinking. For, moral maxims, unlike technical ones, cannot be based on habit (since this belongs to the natural constitution of the will's determination); on the contrary, if the practice of virtue were to become a habit the subject would suffer loss to that *freedom* in adopting his maxims which distinguishes an action done from duty.

7

Groundwork of the Metaphysics of Morals (Continued): The Categorical Imperative

Immanuel Kant

It is tempting to treat the different formulations of the categorical imperative that Kant discusses in Section II of the *Groundwork* as separate and distinct moral principles. This is perhaps the best way to proceed if one is aiming to contribute to contemporary ethical discussions, rather than study the history of philosophy, but Kant himself took it that there can be only one fundamental principle of morality, and that the various formulae that he articulates are to be approached as multiple versions of this one principle.

Kant begins here with a formulation of the categorical imperative that is often referred to as the Formula of Universal Law (it is essentially the same formula he discussed in Section I): 'act only in accordance with that maxim through which you can at the same time will that it become a universal law.' He quickly argues that this is equivalent to the formula 'act as if the maxim of your actions were to become by your will a universal law of nature' (some commentators distinguish this from the first formula by calling it the Formula of the Universal Law of Nature). The idea here is that for any policy one might adopt when acting (and every action is done for some purpose, we have seen), one might consider whether it would be possible for everyone to actively follow this policy. Permissible policies must be such that one is not making an exception for oneself in adopting them (here one may think of the commonsense moral query, 'What if everyone did that?').

With respect to some maxims, it is not even conceivable (hence possible) that everyone might follow the maxim. With respect to other maxims, one might rightly judge it possible for everyone to act on the maxim, but still judge that one could not rationally *will* that one act on the policy when considering a world where everyone is acting on the policy. If a maxim fails the first, stronger test, then it is strictly impermissible to proceed with any course of action that follows the maxim, while if a maxim only fails the second test, then it is impermissible to adopt it as a general policy, but the duty that one has thus located is 'imperfect' rather than 'perfect'. This may seem rather obscure, but things become clearer when one considers the two most straightforward of the four examples that Kant provides.

First, a person who is thinking of making a false promise (a promise he has no intention of keeping) in order to obtain money might ask himself: can I conceive of a world where *everyone* obtains money by making false promises to return money? Kant contends that we cannot conceive of such a world because promises (of this kind) could not be trusted in such a world, and hence would not even be possible. The conscientious person can thus reason he has a perfect duty not to make false promises (that is, he must never do so). In the second example, a person of means is confronted by someone contending with great hardships and is tempted not to extend any help to this person. He might ask whether it is conceivable that everyone not help others when they are in need. Sadly, it seems all too easy to imagine a world where it is true that no one helps anyone else (even though they can afford to). So, if there is a duty of charity, it is

History of Ethics – Essential Readings with Commentary, First Edition. Edited by Daniel Star and Roger Crisp.

not a perfect duty. However, it is not possible, Kant says, rationally to *will* that the maxim that one not help others when they are in need (even though one can afford to) be a universal law. This is because a will that set itself to act in this way would be in conflict with itself, due to the fact that one's own wellbeing depends on the assistance of others (at the very least, there is always a significant risk that it may do so in the future). For this reason, we are to think of the duty of charity as an imperfect duty; it is not required of us to aid others on each and every occasion that we might do so, but it is required of us to help others, in general. Since charity is an imperfect duty, it is left up to us to decide when exactly to help others, but if one does too little to help others during the course of one's life, one will not be fulfilling this duty.

The Formula of Universal Law, considered alone, is notoriously susceptible to counterexamples: there are actions it appears to rule impermissible that are not impermissible (e.g. institutional activities dedicated to ending slavery), as well as actions it appears to fail to rule impermissible that are clearly impermissible (e.g. it fails to tell us that we have a perfect duty not to commit murderous acts that do not involve theft or deception). It is also very difficult to interpret and defend, and there is much disagreement about how best to do so. Kant's second formula, the Formula of Humanity, is generally thought to fare better. It locates final value in our rational nature and directs us always to respect this foundational end: 'So act that you use humanity, whether in your own person or in the person of any other, always at the same time as an end, never merely as a means.'

It is not necessarily wrong to treat people as means, e.g. when asking a stranger the time, or purchasing a product from a shopkeeper; but it is intuitively wrong to treat people as *mere* means (part of the point of saying 'thank you' in such ordinary interactions is to indicate that one is dealing with a person, and not a tool). When he returns to the four examples he discussed earlier, Kant argues that making a false promise always involves treating people as mere means, as it purposely circumvents their rational nature, for people cannot consent to being lied to. This is a way of explaining why we have a perfect duty not to lie. With respect to the imperfect duty of charity, the explanation takes a different form: to fail to attempt to further the ends of others is to fail to properly positively value their rational nature (as beings who pursue ends, and happiness, in particular), even though it does not involve circumventing or actively interfering with their nature.

Finally, the Formula of the Kingdom of Ends asks us to consider what moral laws we would prescribe in a world where we properly respect the value of people (i.e. our rational nature). Where the Formula of Universal Law directs us to consider whether our maxims are universalizable, this final formula ask us to imagine being in the driving seat: 'act only so that the will could regard itself as at the same time giving universal law through its maxim.' In this final part of the text we are also told more about what is involved in treating people *as* ends, and not just as a means: it is to recognize that they are not entities whose value consists in having a *price* (they are not exchangeable), but rather that they have a dignity that is 'raised above all price and therefore admits of no equivalent.' The extent to which Kant is opposed to utilitarianism is particularly apparent here.

Section II – Transition from Popular Moral Philosophy to Metaphysics of Morals

If we have so far drawn our concept of duty from the common use of our practical reason, it is by no means to be inferred from this that we have treated it as a concept of experience. On the contrary, if we attend to experience of people's conduct we meet frequent and, as we ourselves admit, just complaints that no certain example can be cited of the disposition to act from pure duty; that, though much may be done *in conformity with* what *duty* commands, still it is always doubtful whether it is really done *from duty* and therefore has moral worth. Hence there have at all times been philosophers who have absolutely denied the reality of this disposition in human actions and ascribed everything to more or less refined self-love. They did not, on account of this, call into doubt the correctness of the concept of morality but rather spoke with deep regret of the frailty and impurity of human nature, which is indeed noble enough to take as its precept an idea so worthy of respect but at the same time is too weak to follow it, and uses reason, which should serve it for giving law, only to look after the interests of the inclinations, whether singly or, at most, in their greatest compatibility with one another.

In fact, it is absolutely impossible by means of experience to make out with complete certainty a single case in which the maxim of an action otherwise in conformity with duty rested simply on moral grounds and on the representation of one's duty. It is indeed sometimes the case that with the keenest self-examination we find nothing besides the moral ground of duty that could have been powerful enough to move us to this, or that good action and to so great a sacrifice; but from this it cannot be inferred with certainty that no covert impulse of self-love, under the mere pretense of that idea, was not actually the real determining cause of the will; for we like to flatter ourselves by falsely attributing to ourselves a nobler motive, whereas in fact we can never, even by the most strenuous self-examination, get entirely behind our covert incentives, since, when moral worth is at issue, what counts is not actions, which one sees, but those inner principles of actions that one does not see.

Moreover, one cannot better serve the wishes of those who ridicule all morality as the mere phantom of a human imagination overstepping itself through self-conceit than by granting them that concepts of duty must be drawn solely from experience (as, from indolence, people like to persuade themselves is the case with all other concepts as well); for then one prepares a sure triumph for them. From love of humankind I am willing to admit that even most of our actions are in conformity with duty; but if we look more closely at the intentions and aspirations in them we everywhere come upon the dear self, which is always turning up; and it is on this that their purpose is based, not on the strict command of duty, which would often require self-denial. One need not be an enemy of virtue but only a cool observer, who does not take the liveliest wish for the good straight-away as its reality, to become doubtful at certain moments (especially with increasing years, when experience has made one's judgment partly more shrewd and partly more acute in observation) whether any true virtue is to be found in the world. And then nothing can protect us against falling away completely from our ideas of duty and can preserve in our soul a well-grounded respect for its law than the clear conviction that, even if there never have been actions arising from such pure sources, what is at issue here is not whether this or that happened; that, instead, reason by itself and independently of all appearances commands what ought to happen; that, accordingly, actions of which the world has perhaps so far given no example, and whose very practicability might be very much doubted by one who bases everything on experience, are still inflexibly commanded by reason; and that, for example, pure sincerity in friendship can be no less required of everyone even if up to now there may never have been a sincere friend, because this duty – as duty in general – lies, prior to all experience, in the idea of a reason determining the will by means of a priori grounds.

If we add further that, unless we want to deny to the concept of morality any truth and any relation to some possible object, we cannot dispute that its law is so extensive in its import that it must hold not only for human beings but for all *rational beings as such*, not merely under contingent conditions and with exceptions but with *absolute necessity*, then it is clear that no experience could give occasion to infer even the possibility of such apodictic laws. For, by what right could we bring into unlimited respect, as a universal precept for every rational nature, what is perhaps valid only under the contingent conditions of humanity? And how should laws of the determination of *our* will be taken as laws of the determination of the will of rational beings as such, and for ours only as rational beings, if they were merely empirical and did not have their origin completely a priori in pure but practical reason?

Nor could one give worse advice to morality than by wanting to derive it from examples. For, every example of it represented to me must itself first be appraised in accordance with principles of morality, as to whether it is also worthy to serve as an original example, that is, as a model; it can by no means authoritatively provide the concept of morality. Even the Holy One of the Gospel must first be compared with our ideal of moral perfection before he is cognized as such; even he says of himself: why do you call me (whom you see) good? none is good (the archetype of the good) but God only (whom you do not see). But whence have we the concept of God as the highest good? Solely from the *idea* of moral perfection that reason frames a priori and connects inseparably with the concept of a free will. Imitation has no place at all in matters of morality, and examples serve only for encouragement, that is, they put beyond doubt the practicability of what the law commands and make intuitive what the practical rule expresses more generally, but they can never justify setting aside their true original, which lies in reason, and guiding oneself by examples.

If there is, then, no genuine supreme basic principle of morality that does not have to rest only on pure reason independently of all experience, I believe it unnecessary even to ask whether it is a good thing to set forth in their generality (*in abstracto*) these concepts as they, along with the principles belonging to them, are fixed a priori, if this cognition is to be distinguished from the common and called philosophic. But in our day it may well be necessary to ask this. For if votes were collected as to which is to be preferred – pure rational cognition separated from anything empirical, hence metaphysics of morals, or popular practical philosophy – one can guess at once on which side the preponderance would fall.

This descending to popular concepts is certainly very commendable, provided the ascent to the principles of pure reason has first taken place and has been carried through to complete satisfaction. That would mean that the doctrine of morals is first *grounded* on metaphysics and afterwards, when it has been firmly established, is provided with *access* by means of popularity. But it is quite absurd to want to comply with popularity in the first investigation, on which all correctness of basic principles depends. Not only can this procedure never lay claim to the very rare merit of a true *philosophic popularity*, since there is no art in being commonly understandable if one thereby renounces any well-grounded insight; it also produces a disgusting hodge-podge of patchwork observations and half-rationalized principles, in which shallow pates revel because it is something useful for everyday chitchat, but the insightful, feeling confused and dissatisfied without being able to help themselves, avert their eyes – although philosophers, who see quite well through the deception, get little hearing when they call [moralists] away for a time from this alleged popularity, so that they may be rightly popular only after having acquired determinate insight.

One need only look at attempts at morality in that popular taste. One will find now the special determination of human nature (but occasionally the idea of a rational nature as such along with it), now perfection, now happiness, here moral feeling, there fear of God, a bit of this and also a bit of that in a marvellous mixture, without its occurring to them to ask whether the principles of morality are to be sought at all in acquaintance with human nature (which we can get only from experience) and, if this is not the case – if these principles are to be found altogether a priori, free from anything empirical, solely in pure rational concepts and nowhere else even to the slightest extent – instead to adopt the plan of quite separating this investigation as pure practical philosophy or (if one may use a name so decried) as metaphysics of morals,* of bringing it all by itself to its full completeness, and of putting off the public, which demands popularity, pending the outcome of this undertaking.

But such a completely isolated metaphysics of morals, mixed with no anthropology, theology, physics, or hyperphysics and still less with occult qualities (which could be called hypophysical), is not only an indispensable substratum of all theoretical and surely determined cognition of duties; it is also a desideratum of utmost importance to the actual fulfillment of their precepts. For, the pure thought of duty and in general of the moral law, mixed with no foreign addition of empirical inducements, has by way of reason alone (which with this first becomes aware that it can of itself also be practical) an influence on the human heart so much more powerful than all other incentives,† which may be summoned from the empirical field, that reason, in the consciousness of its dignity, despises the latter

---

* One can, if one wants to, distinguish pure philosophy of morals (metaphysics) from applied (namely to human nature), (just as pure mathematics is distinguished from applied, and pure logic from applied). By using this name one is also reminded at once that moral principles are not based on what is peculiar to human nature but must be fixed a priori by themselves, while from such principles it must be possible to derive practical rules for every rational nature, and accordingly for human nature as well.

† I have a letter from the late excellent Sulzer in which he asks me what the cause might be that the teachings of virtue, however much they contain that is convincing to reason, accomplish so little. By trying to prepare a complete answer I delayed too long. However, my answer is simply that the teachers themselves have not brought their concepts to purity, but, since they want to do too well by hunting everywhere for motives to moral goodness, in trying to make their medicine really strong they spoil it. For the most ordinary observation shows that if we represent, on the one hand, an action of integrity done with steadfast soul, apart from every view to advantage of any kind in this world or another and even under the greatest temptations of need or allurement, it leaves far behind and eclipses any similar act that was affected in the least by an extraneous incentive; it elevates the soul and awakens a wish to be able to act in like manner oneself. Even children of moderate age feel this impression, and one should never represent duties to them in any other way.

and can gradually become their master; on the other hand a mixed doctrine of morals, put together from incentives of feeling and inclination and also of rational concepts, must make the mind waver between motives that cannot be brought under any principle, that can lead only contingently to what is good and can very often also lead to what is evil.

From what has been said it is clear that all moral concepts have their seat and origin completely a priori in reason, [...]

However, in order to advance by natural steps in this study – not merely from common moral appraisal (which is here very worthy of respect) to philosophic, as has already been done, but – from a popular philosophy, which goes no further than it can by groping with the help of examples, to metaphysics (which no longer lets itself be held back by anything empirical and, since it must measure out the whole sum of rational cognition of this kind, goes if need be all the way to ideas, where examples themselves fail us), we must follow and present distinctly the practical faculty of reason, from its general rules of determination to the point where the concept of duty arises from it.

Everything in nature works in accordance with laws. Only a rational being has the capacity to act *in accordance with the representation* of laws, that is, in accordance with principles, or has a *will*. Since *reason* is required for the derivation of actions from laws, the will is nothing other than practical reason. If reason infallibly determines the will, the actions of such a being that are cognized as objectively necessary are also subjectively necessary, that is, the will is a capacity to choose *only that* which reason independently of inclination cognizes as practically necessary, that is, as good. However, if reason solely by itself does not adequately determine the will; if the will is exposed also to subjective conditions (certain incentives) that are not always in accord with the objective ones; in a word, if the will is not *in itself* completely in conformity with reason (as is actually the case with human beings), then actions that are cognized as objectively necessary are subjectively contingent, and the determination of such a will in conformity with objective laws is *necessitation:* that is to say, the relation of objective laws to a will that is not thoroughly good is represented as the determination of the will of a rational being through grounds of reason, indeed, but grounds to which this will is not by its nature necessarily obedient.

The representation of an objective principle, insofar as it is necessitating for a will, is called a command (of reason), and the formula of the command is called an **imperative**.

All imperatives are expressed by an *ought* and indicate by this the relation of an objective law of reason to a will that by its subjective constitution is not necessarily determined by it (a necessitation). They say that to do or to omit something would be good, but they say it to a will that does not always do something just because it is represented to it that it would be good to do that thing. Practical good, however, is that which determines the will by means of representations of reason, hence not by subjective causes but objectively, that is, from grounds that are valid for every rational being as such. It is distinguished from the *agreeable*, as that which influences the will only by means of feeling from merely subjective causes, which hold only for the senses of this or that one, and not as a principle of reason, which holds for everyone.*

A perfectly good will would, therefore, equally stand under objective laws (of the good), but it could not on this account be represented as *necessitated* to actions in conformity with law since of itself, by its subjective constitution, it can be determined only through the representation of the good. Hence no imperatives hold for the *divine* will and in general for a *holy* will: the "ought" is out of place here, because volition is of itself necessarily in accord with the law. Therefore imperatives are only formulae expressing the relation of objective laws of volition in general to the subjective imperfection of the will of this or that rational being, for example, of the human will.

Now, all imperatives command either *hypothetically* or *categorically*. The former represent the practical necessity of a possible action as a means to achieving something else that one wills (or that it is at least possible for one to will). The categorical imperative would be that which represented an action as objectively necessary of itself, without reference to another end.

---

* The dependence of the faculty of desire upon feelings is called inclination, and this accordingly always indicates a *need*. The dependence of a contingently determinable will on principles of reason, however, is called an *interest*. This, accordingly, is present only in the case of a dependent will, which is not of itself always in conformity with reason; in the case of the divine will we cannot think of any interest. But even the human will can *take an interest* in something without therefore *acting from interest*. The first signifies *practical* interest in the action, the second, *pathological* interest in the object of the action. The former indicates only dependence of the will upon principles of reason *in themselves;* the second, dependence upon principles of reason for the sake of inclination, namely where reason supplies only the practical rule as to how to remedy the need of inclination. In the first case the action interests me; in the second, the object of the action (insofar as it is agreeable to me). We have seen in the first Section that in the case of an action from duty we must look not to interest in the object but merely to that in die action itself and its principle in reason (the law).

Since every practical law represents a possible action as good and thus as necessary for a subject practically determinable by reason, all imperatives are formulae for the determination of action that is necessary in accordance with the principle of a will which is good in some way. Now, if the action would be good merely as a means *to something else* the imperative is *hypothetical;* if the action is represented as *in itself* good, hence as necessary in a will in itself conforming to reason, as its principle, *then it is categorical.*

The imperative thus says which action possible by me would be good, and represents a practical rule in relation to a will that does not straightaway do an action just because it is good, partly because the subject does not always know that it is good, partly because, even if he knows this, his maxims could still be opposed to the objective principles of a practical reason.

Hence the hypothetical imperative says only that the action is good for some *possible* or *actual* purpose. In the first case it is a **problematically** practical principle, in the second an **assertorically** practical principle. The categorical imperative, which declares the action to be of itself objectively necessary without reference to some purpose, that is, even apart from any other end, holds as an **apodictically** practical principle.

One can think of what is possible only through the powers of some rational being as also a possible purpose of some will; accordingly, principles of action, insofar as this is represented as necessary for attaining some possible purpose to be brought about by it, are in fact innumerable. All sciences have some practical part, consisting of problems [which suppose] that some end is possible for us and of imperatives as to how it can be attained. These can therefore be called, in general, imperatives of skill. Whether the end is rational and good is not at all the question here, but only what one must do in order to attain it. The precepts for a physician to make his man healthy in a well-grounded way, and for a poisoner to be sure of killing his, are of equal worth insofar as each serves perfectly to bring about his purpose. Since in early youth it is not known what ends might occur to us in the course of life, parents seek above all to have their children learn *a great many things* and to provide for *skill* in the use of means to all sorts of *discretionary* ends, about none of which can they determine whether it might in the future actually become their pupil's purpose, though it is always *possible* that he might at some time have it; and this concern is so great that they commonly neglect to form and correct their children's judgment about the worth of the things that they might make their ends.

There is, however, *one* end that can be presupposed as actual in the case of all rational beings (insofar as imperatives apply to them, namely as dependent beings), and therefore one purpose that they not merely *could* have but that we can safely presuppose they all actually *do have* by a natural necessity, and that purpose is *happiness.* The hypothetical imperative that represents the practical necessity of an action as a means to the promotion of happiness is **assertoric**. It may be set forth not merely as necessary to some uncertain, merely possible purpose but to a purpose that can be presupposed surely and a priori in the case of every human being, because it belongs to his essence. Now, skill in the choice of means to one's own greatest well-being can be called *prudence** in the narrowest sense. Hence the imperative that refers to the choice of means to one's own happiness, that is, the precept of prudence, is still always *hypothetical;* the action is not commanded absolutely but only as a means to another purpose.

Finally there is one imperative that, without being based upon and having as its condition any other purpose to be attained by certain conduct, commands this conduct immediately. This imperative is **categorical**. It has to do not with the matter of the action and what is to result from it, but with the form and the principle from which the action itself follows; and the essentially good in the action consists in the disposition, let the result be what it may. This imperative may be called the imperative **of morality**.

Volition in accordance with these three kinds of principles is also clearly distinguished by *dissimilarity* in the necessitation of the will. In order to make this dissimilarity evident, I think they would be most suitably named in their order by being said to be either *rules* of skill, or *counsels* of prudence, or *commands* (*laws*) of morality. For, only law brings with it the concept of an *unconditional* and objective and hence universally valid *necessity*, and commands are laws that must be obeyed, that is, must be followed even against inclination. *Giving counsel* does involve necessity, which, however, can hold only under a subjective and contingent condition, whether this or that man counts this or that in his happiness; the categorical imperative, on the contrary, is limited by no condition and, as absolutely

---

* The word "prudence" is taken in two senses: in the one it may bear the name of "knowledge of the world," in the other that of "private prudence." The first is a human being's skill in influencing others so as to use them for his own purposes. The second is the insight to unite all these purposes to his own enduring advantage. The latter is properly that to which the worth even of the former is reduced, and if someone is prudent in the first sense but not in the second, we might better say of him that he is clever and cunning but, on the whole, nevertheless imprudent.

although practically necessary, can be called quite strictly a command. The first imperative could also be called *technical* (belonging to art), the second pragmatic* (belonging to welfare), the third moral (belonging to free conduct as such, that is, to morals).

Now the question arises: how are all these imperatives possible? This question does not inquire how the performance of the action that the imperative commands can be thought, but only how the necessitation of the will, which the imperative expresses in the problem, can be thought. How an imperative of skill is possible requires no special discussion. Whoever wills the end also wills (insofar as reason has decisive influence on his actions) the indispensably necessary means to it that are within his power. This proposition is, as regards the volition, analytic; for in the volition of an object as my effect, my causality as acting cause, that is, the use of means, is already thought, and the imperative extracts the concept of actions necessary to this end merely from the concept of a volition of this end (synthetic propositions no doubt belong to determining the means themselves to a purpose intended, but they do not have to do with the ground for actualizing the act of will but for actualizing the object). That in order to divide a line into two equal parts on a sure principle I must make two intersecting arcs from its ends, mathematics admittedly teaches only by synthetic propositions; but when I know that only by such an action can the proposed effect take place, then it is an analytic proposition that if I fully will the effect I also will the action requisite to it; for, it is one and the same thing to represent something as an effect possible by me in a certain way and to represent myself as acting in this way with respect to it.

If only it were as easy to give a determinate concept of happiness, imperatives of prudence would agree entirely with those of skill and would be just as analytic. For it could be said, here just as there: who wills the end also wills (necessarily in conformity with reason) the sole means to it that are within his control. But it is a misfortune that the concept of happiness is such an indeterminate concept that, although every human being wishes to attain this, he can still never say determinately and consistently with himself what he really wishes and wills. The cause of this is that all the elements that belong to the concept of happiness are without exception empirical, that is, they must be borrowed from experience, and that nevertheless for the idea of happiness there is required an absolute whole, a maximum of well-being in my present condition and in every future condition. Now, it is impossible for the most insightful and at the same time most powerful but still finite being to frame for himself a determinate concept of what he really wills here. If he wills riches, how much anxiety, envy and intrigue might he not bring upon himself in this way! If he wills a great deal of cognition and insight, that might become only an eye all the more acute to show him, as all the more dreadful, ills that are now concealed from him and that cannot be avoided, or to burden his desires, which already give him enough to do, with still more needs. If he wills a long life, who will guarantee him that it would not be a long misery? If he at least wills health, how often has not bodily discomfort kept someone from excesses into which unlimited health would have let him fall, and so forth. In short, he is not capable of any principle by which to determine with complete certainty what would make him truly happy, because for this omniscience would be required. One cannot therefore act on determinate principles for the sake of being happy, but only on empirical counsels, for example, of a regimen, frugality, courtesy, reserve and so forth, which experience teaches are most conducive to well-being on the average. From this it follows that imperatives of prudence cannot, to speak precisely, command at all, that is, present actions objectively as practically *necessary;* that they are to be taken as counsels (*consilia*) rather than as commands (*praecepta*) of reason; that the problem of determining surely and universally which action would promote the happiness of a rational being is completely insoluble, so that there can be no imperative with respect to it that would, in the strict sense, command him to do what would make him happy; for happiness is not an ideal of reason but of imagination, resting merely upon empirical grounds, which it is futile to expect should determine an action by which the totality of a series of results in fact infinite would be attained. This imperative of prudence would, nevertheless, be an analytic practical proposition if it is supposed that the means to happiness can be assigned with certainty; for it is distinguished from the imperative of skill only in this: that in the case of the latter the end is merely possible, whereas in the former it is given; but since both merely command the means to what it is presupposed one wills as an end, the imperative that commands volition of the means for him who wills the end is in both cases analytic. Hence there is also no difficulty with respect to the possibility of such an imperative.

---

* It seems to me that the proper meaning of the word *pragmatic* can be most accurately determined in this way. For *sanctions* are called "pragmatic" that do not flow strictly from the right of *states* as necessary laws but from *provision* for the general welfare. A *history* is composed pragmatically when it makes us *prudent*, that is, instructs the world how it can look after its advantage better than, or at least as well as, the world of earlier times.

On the other hand, the question of how the imperative of *morality* is possible is undoubtedly the only one needing a solution, since it is in no way hypothetical and the objectively represented necessity can therefore not be based on any presupposition, as in the case of hypothetical imperatives. Only we must never leave out of account, here, that it cannot be made out *by means of any example*, and so empirically, whether there is any such imperative at all, but it is rather to be feared that all imperatives which seem to be categorical may yet in some hidden way be hypothetical. For example, when it is said "you ought not to promise anything deceitfully," and one assumes that the necessity of this omission is not giving counsel for avoiding some other ill – in which case what is said would be "you ought not to make a lying promise lest if it comes to light you destroy your credit" – but that an action of this kind must be regarded as in itself evil and that the imperative of prohibition is therefore categorical: one still cannot show with certainty in any example that the will is here determined merely through the law, without another incentive, although it seems to be so; for it is always possible that covert fear of disgrace, perhaps also obscure apprehension of other dangers, may have had an influence on the will. Who can prove by experience the nonexistence of a cause when all that experience teaches is that we do not perceive it? In such a case, however, the so-called moral imperative, which as such appears to be categorical and unconditional, would in fact be only a pragmatic precept that makes us attentive to our advantage and merely teaches us to take this into consideration.

We shall thus have to investigate entirely a priori the possibility of a *categorical* imperative, since we do not here have the advantage of its reality being given in experience, so that the possibility would be necessary not to establish it but merely to explain it. In the meantime, however, we can see this much: that the categorical imperative alone has the tenor of a practical **law**; all the others can indeed be called *principles* of the will but not laws, since what it is necessary to do merely for achieving a discretionary purpose can be regarded as in itself contingent and we can always be released from the precept if we give up the purpose; on the contrary, the unconditional command leaves the will no discretion with respect to the opposite, so that it alone brings with it that necessity which we require of a law.

Second, in the case of this categorical imperative or law of morality the ground of the difficulty (of insight into its possibility) is also very great. It is an a priori synthetic practical proposition;* and since it is so difficult to see the possibility of this kind of proposition in theoretical cognition, it can be readily gathered that the difficulty will be no less in practical cognition.

In this task we want first to inquire whether the mere concept of a categorical imperative may not also provide its formula containing the proposition which alone can be a categorical imperative. For, how such an absolute command is possible, even if we know its tenor, will still require special and difficult toil, which, however, we postpone to the last section.

When I think of a *hypothetical* imperative in general I do not know beforehand what it will contain; I do not know this until I am given the condition. But when I think of a *categorical* imperative I know at once what it contains. For, since the imperative contains, beyond the law, only the necessity that the maxim† be in conformity with this law, while the law contains no condition to which it would be limited, nothing is left with which the maxim of action is to conform but the universality of a law as such; and this conformity alone is what the imperative properly represents as necessary.

There is, therefore, only a single categorical imperative and it is this: *act only in accordance with that maxim through which you can at the same time will that it become a universal law.*

Now, if all imperatives of duty can be derived from this single imperative as from their principle, then, even though we leave it undecided whether what is called duty is not as such an empty concept, we shall at least be able to show what we think by it and what the concept wants to say.

Since the universality of law in accordance with which effects take place constitutes what is properly called *nature* in the most general sense (as regards its form) – that is, the existence of things insofar as it is determined in accordance with universal laws – the universal imperative of duty can also go as follows: *act as if the maxim of your action were to become by your will a* **universal law of nature**.

---

* I connect the deed with the will, without a presupposed condition from any inclination, a priori and hence necessarily (though only objectively, i.e., under the idea of a reason having complete control over all subjective motives). This is, therefore, a practical proposition that does not derive the volition of an action analytically from another volition already presupposed (for we have no such perfect will), but connects it immediately with the concept of the will of a rational being as something that is not contained in it.

† A *maxim* is the subjective principle of acting, and must be distinguished from the *objective* principle, namely the practical law. The former contains the practical rule determined by reason conformably with the conditions of the subject (often his ignorance or also his inclinations), and is therefore the principle in accordance with which the subject *acts;* but the law is the objective principle valid for every rational being, and the principle in accordance with which he *ought to act,* i.e., an imperative.

We shall now enumerate a few duties in accordance with the usual division of them into duties to ourselves and to other human beings and into perfect and imperfect duties.*

1)   Someone feels sick of life because of a series of troubles that has grown to the point of despair, but is still so far in possession of his reason that he can ask himself whether it would not be contrary to his duty to himself to take his own life. Now he inquires whether the maxim of his action could indeed become a universal law of nature. His maxim, however, is: from self-love I make it my principle to shorten my life when its longer duration threatens more troubles than it promises agreeableness. The only further question is whether this principle of self-love could become a universal law of nature. It is then seen at once that a nature whose law it would be to destroy life itself by means of the same feeling whose destination is to impel toward the furtherance of life would contradict itself and would therefore not subsist as nature; thus that maxim could not possibly be a law of nature and, accordingly, altogether opposes the supreme principle of all duty.

2)   Another finds himself urged by need to borrow money. He well knows that he will not be able to repay it but sees also that nothing will be lent him unless he promises firmly to repay it within a determinate time. He would like to make such a promise, but he still has enough conscience to ask himself: is it not forbidden and contrary, to duty to help oneself out of need in such a way? Supposing that he still decided to do so, his maxim of action would go as follows: when I believe myself to be in need of money I shall borrow money and promise to repay it, even though I know that this will never happen. Now this principle of self-love or personal advantage is perhaps quite consistent with my whole future welfare, but the question now is whether it is right. I therefore turn the demand of self-love into a universal law and put the question as follows: how would it be if my maxim became a universal law? I then see at once that it could never hold as a universal law of nature and be consistent with itself, but must necessarily contradict itself. For, the universality of a law that everyone, when he believes himself to be in need, could promise whatever he pleases with the intention of not keeping it would make the promise and the end one might have in it itself impossible, since no one would believe what was promised him but would laugh at all such expressions as vain pretenses.

3)   A third finds in himself a talent that by means of some cultivation could make him a human being useful for all sorts of purposes. However, he finds himself in comfortable circumstances and prefers to give himself up to pleasure than to trouble himself with enlarging and improving his fortunate natural predispositions. But he still asks himself whether his maxim of neglecting his natural gifts, besides being consistent with his propensity to amusement, is also consistent with what one calls duty. He now sees that a nature could indeed always subsist with such a universal law, although (as with the South Sea Islanders) the human being should let his talents rust and be concerned with devoting his life merely to idleness, amusement, procreation – in a word, to enjoyment; only he cannot possibly **will** that this become a universal law or be put in us as such by means of natural instinct. For, as a rational being he necessarily wills that all the capacities in him be developed, since they serve him and are given to him for all sorts of possible purposes.

Yet a *fourth*, for whom things are going well while he sees that others (whom he could very well help) have to contend with great hardships, thinks: what is it to me? let each be as happy as heaven wills or as he can make himself; I shall take nothing from him nor even envy him; only I do not care to contribute anything to his welfare or to his assistance in need! Now, if such a way of thinking were to become a universal law the human race could admittedly very well subsist, no doubt even better than when everyone prates about sympathy and benevolence and even exerts himself to practice them occasionally, but on the other hand also cheats where he can, sells the right of human beings or otherwise infringes upon it. But although it is possible that a universal law of nature could very well subsist in accordance with such a maxim, it is still impossible to will that such a principle hold everywhere as a law of nature. For, a will that decided this would conflict with itself, since many cases could occur in which one would need the love and sympathy of others and in which, by such a law of nature arisen from his own will, he would rob himself of all hope of the assistance he wishes for himself.

These are a few of the many actual duties, or at least of what we take to be such, whose derivation from the one principle cited above is clear. We must *be able to will* that a maxim of our action become a universal law: this is the canon of moral appraisal of action in general. Some actions are so constituted that their maxim cannot even

* It must be noted here that I reserve the division of duties entirely for a future *Metaphysics of Morals*, so that the division here stands only as one adopted at my discretion (for the sake of arranging my examples). For the rest, I understand here by a perfect duty one that admits no exception in favor of inclination, and then I have not merely external but also internal *perfect duties;* although this is contrary to the use of the work adopted in the schools, I do not intend to justify it here, since for my purpose it makes no difference whether or not it is granted me.

be *thought* without contradiction as a universal law of nature, far less could one *will* that it *should* become such. In the case of others that inner impossibility is indeed not to be found, but it is still impossible to *will* that their maxim be raised to the universality of a law of nature because such a will would contradict itself. It is easy to see that the first is opposed to strict or narrower (unremitting) duty, the second only to wide (meritorious) duty; and so all duties, as far as the kind of obligation (not the object of their action) is concerned, have by these examples been set out completely in their dependence upon the one principle.

If we now attend to ourselves in any transgression of a duty, we find that we do not really will that our maxim should become a universal law, since that is impossible for us, but that the opposite of our maxim should instead remain a universal law, only we take the liberty of making an *exception* to it for ourselves (or just for this once) to the advantage of our inclination. Consequently, if we weighed all cases from one and the same point of view, namely that of reason, we would find a contradiction in our own will, namely that a certain principle be objectively necessary as a universal law and yet subjectively not hold universally but allow exceptions. Since, however, we at one time regard our action from the point of view of a will wholly conformed with reason but then regard the very same action from the point of view of a will affected by inclination, there is really no contradiction here but instead a resistance of inclination to the precept of reason (*antagonismus*), through which the universality of the principle (*universalitas*) is changed into mere generality (*generalitas*) and the practical rational principle is to meet the maxim half way. Now, even though this cannot be justified in our own impartially rendered judgment, it still shows that we really acknowledge the validity of the categorical imperative and permit ourselves (with all respect for it) only a few exceptions that, as it seems to us, are inconsiderable and wrung from us.

We have therefore shown at least this much: that if duty is a concept that is to contain significance and real lawgiving for our actions it can be expressed only in categorical imperatives and by no means in hypothetical ones; we have also – and this is already a great deal – set forth distinctly and as determined for every use the content of the categorical imperative, which must contain the principle of all duty (if there is such a thing at all). But we have not yet advanced so far as to prove a priori that there really is such an imperative, that there is a practical law, which commands absolutely of itself and without any incentives, and that the observance of this law is duty.

For the purpose of achieving this it is of the utmost importance to take warning that we must not let ourselves think of wanting to derive the reality of this principle from the *special property of human nature*. For, duty is to be practical unconditional necessity of action and it must therefore hold for all rational beings (to which alone an imperative can apply at all) and *only because of this* be also a law for all human wills. On the other hand, what is derived from the special natural constitution of humanity – what is derived from certain feelings and propensities and even, if possible, from a special tendency that would be peculiar to human reason and would not have to hold necessarily for the will of every rational being – that can indeed yield a maxim for us but not a law; it can yield a subjective principle on which we might act if we have the propensity and inclination, but not an objective principle on which we would be *directed* to act even though every propensity, inclination, and natural tendency of ours were against it – so much so that the sublimity and inner dignity of the command in a duty is all the more manifest the fewer are the subjective causes in favor of it and the more there are against it, without thereby weakening in the least the necessitation by the law or taking anything away from its validity.

Here, then, we see philosophy put in fact in a precarious position, which is to be firm even though there is nothing in heaven or on earth from which it depends or on which it is based. Here philosophy is to manifest its purity as sustainer of its own laws, not as herald of laws that an implanted sense or who knows what tutelary nature whispers to it, all of which – though they may always be better than nothing at all – can still never yield basic principles that reason dictates and that must have their source entirely and completely a priori and, at the same time, must have their commanding authority from this: that they expect nothing from the inclination of human beings but everything from the supremacy of the law and the respect owed it or, failing this, condemn the human being to contempt for himself and inner abhorrence.

Hence everything empirical, as an addition to the principle of morality, is not only quite inept for this; it is also highly prejudicial to the purity of morals, where the proper worth of an absolutely good will – a worth raised above all price – consists just in the principle of action being free from all influences of contingent grounds, which only experience can furnish. One cannot give too many or too frequent warnings against this laxity, or even mean cast of mind, which seeks its principle among empirical motives and laws; for, human reason in its weariness gladly rests on this pillow and in a dream of sweet illusions (which allow it to embrace a cloud instead of Juno) it substitutes for morality a bastard patched up from limbs of quite diverse ancestry, which looks like whatever one wants to see in it but not like virtue for him who has once seen virtue in her true form.*

The question is therefore this: is it a necessary law *for all rational beings* always to appraise their actions in accordance with such maxims as they themselves could will to serve as universal laws? If there is such a law, then it must already be connected (completely a priori) with the concept of the will of a rational being as such. But in order to discover this connection we must, however reluctantly, step forth, namely into metaphysics, although into a domain of it that is distinct from speculative philosophy, namely into metaphysics of morals. In a practical philosophy, where we have to do not with assuming grounds for what *happens* but rather laws for what *ought to happen* even if it never does, that is, objective practical laws, we do not need to undertake an investigation into the grounds on account of which something pleases or displeases; how the satisfaction of mere sensation differs from taste, and whether the latter differs from a general satisfaction of reason; upon what the feeling of pleasure of displeasure rests, and how from it desires and inclinations arise, and from them, with the cooperation of reason, maxims; for, all that belongs to an empirical doctrine of the soul, which would constitute the second part of the doctrine of nature when this is regarded as *philosophy of nature* insofar as it is based *on empirical laws*. Here, however, it is a question of objective practical laws and hence of the relation of a will to itself insofar as it determines itself only by reason; for then everything that has reference to the empirical falls away of itself, since if reason entirely by itself determines conduct (and the possibility of this is just what we want now to investigate), it must necessarily do so a priori.

The will is thought as a capacity to determine itself to acting in conformity with the *representation of certain laws*. And such a capacity can be found only in rational beings. Now, what serves the will as the objective ground of its self-determination is an end, and this, if it is given by reason alone, must hold equally for all rational beings. What, on the other hand, contains merely the ground of the possibility of an action the effect of which is an end is called a *means*. The subjective ground of desire is an *incentive;* the objective ground of volition is a *motive;* hence the distinction between subjective ends, which rest on incentives, and objective ends, which depend on motives, which hold for every rational being. Practical principles are *formal* if they abstract from all subjective ends, whereas they are *material* if they have put these, and consequently certain incentives, at their basis. The ends that a rational being proposes at his discretion as *effects* of his actions (material ends) are all only relative; for only their mere relation to a specially constituted faculty of desire on the part of the subject gives them their worth, which can therefore furnish no universal principles, no principles valid and necessary for all rational beings and also for every volition, that is, no practical laws. Hence all these relative ends are only the ground of hypothetical imperatives.

But suppose there were something the *existence of which in itself* has an absolute worth, something which as *an end in itself* could be a ground of determinate laws; then in it, and in it alone, would lie the ground of a possible categorical imperative, that is, of a practical law.

Now I say that the human being and in general every rational being *exists* as an end in itself, *not merely as a means* to be used by this or that will at its discretion; instead he must in all his actions, whether directed to himself or also to other rational beings, always be regarded *at the same time as an end*. All objects of the inclinations have only a conditional worth; for, if there were not inclinations and the needs based on them, their object would be without worth. But the inclinations themselves, as sources of needs, are so far from having an absolute worth, so as to make one wish to have them, that it must instead be the universal wish of every rational being to be altogether free from them. Thus the worth of any object *to be acquired* by our action is always conditional. Beings the existence of which rests not on our will but on nature, if they are beings without reason, still have only a relative worth, as means, and are therefore called *things*, whereas rational beings are called *persons* because their nature already marks them out as and end in itself, that is, as something that may not be used merely as a means, and hence so far limits all choice (and is an object of respect). These, therefore, are not merely subjective ends, the existence of which as an effect of our action has a worth *for us*, but rather *objective ends*, that is, beings the existence of which is in itself an end, and indeed one such that no other end, to which they would serve *merely* as means, can be put in its place, since without it nothing of *absolute worth* would be found anywhere; but if all worth were conditional and therefore contingent, then no supreme practical principle for reason could be found anywhere.

---

* To behold virtue in her proper form is nothing other than to present morality stripped of any admixture of the sensible and of any spurious adornments of reward or self-love. By means of the least effort of his reason everyone can easily become aware of how much virtue then eclipses everything else that appears charming to the inclinations, provided his reason is not altogether spoiled for abstraction.

If, then, there is to be a supreme practical principle and, with respect to the human will, a categorical imperative, it must be one such that, from the representation of what is necessarily an end for everyone because it is an *end in itself*, it constitutes an *objective* principle of the will and thus can serve as a universal practical law. The ground of this principle is: *rational nature exists as an end in itself.* The human being necessarily represents his own existence in this way; so far it is thus a *subjective* principle of human actions. But every other rational being also represents his existence in this way consequent on just the same rational ground that also holds for me;* thus it is at the same time an *objective* principle from which, as a supreme practical ground, it must be possible to derive all laws of the will. The practical imperative will therefore be the following: *So act that you use humanity, whether in your own person or in the person of any other, always at the same time as an end, never merely as a means.* We shall see whether this can be carried out.

To keep to the preceding examples:

First, as regards the concept of necessary duty to oneself, someone who has suicide in mind will ask himself whether his action can be consistent with the idea of humanity *as an end in itself.* If he destroys himself in order to escape from a trying condition he makes use of a person *merely as a means* to maintain a tolerable condition up to the end of life. A human being, however, is not a thing and hence not something that can be used *merely* as a means, but must in all his actions always be regarded as an end in itself. I cannot, therefore, dispose of a human being in my own person by maiming, damaging or killing him. (I must here pass over a closer determination of this principle that would prevent any misinterpretation, e.g., as to having limbs amputated in order to preserve myself, or putting my life in danger in order to preserve my life, and so forth; that belongs to morals proper.)

Second, as regards necessary duty to others or duty owed them, he who has it in mind to make a false promise to others sees at once that he wants to make use of another human being *merely as a means*, without the other at the same time containing in himself the end. For, he whom I want to use for my purposes by such a promise cannot possibly agree to my way of behaving toward him, and so himself contain the end of this action. This conflict with the principle of other human beings is seen more distinctly if examples of assaults on the freedom and property of others are brought forward. For then it is obvious that he who transgresses the rights of human beings intends to make use of the person of others merely as means, without taking into consideration that, as rational beings, they are always to be valued at the same time as ends, that is, only as beings who must also be able to contain in themselves the end of the very same action.†

Third, with respect to contingent (meritorious) duty to oneself, it is not enough that the action does not conflict with humanity in our person as an end in itself; it must also *harmonize with it.* Now there are in humanity predispositions to greater perfection, which belong to the end of nature with respect to humanity in our subject; to neglect these might admittedly be consistent with the *preservation* of humanity as an end in itself but not with the *furtherance* of this end.

Fourth, concerning meritorious duty to others, the natural end that all human beings have is their own happiness. Now, humanity might indeed subsist if no one contributed to the happiness of others but yet did not intentionally withdraw anything from it; but there is still only a negative and not a positive agreement with *humanity as an end in itself* unless everyone also tries, as far as he can, to further the ends of others. For, the ends of a subject who is an end in itself must as far as possible be also *my* ends, if that representation is to have its *full* effect in me.

This principle of humanity, and in general of every rational nature, *as an end in itself* (which is the supreme limiting condition of the freedom of action of every human being) is not borrowed from experience; first because of its universality, since it applies to all rational beings as such and no experience is sufficient to determine anything about them; second because in it humanity is represented not as an end of human beings (subjectively), that is, not as an object that we of ourselves actually make our end, but as an objective end that, whatever ends we may have, ought as law to constitute the supreme limiting condition of all subjective ends, so that the principle must arise from pure reason. That is to say, the ground of all practical lawgiving lies (in accordance with the first principle) *objectively in the rule* and the form of universality which makes it fit to be a law (possibly a law of nature); *subjectively*, however, it

---

* Here I put forward this proposition as a postulate. The grounds for it will be found in the last Section.
† Let it not be thought that the trite *quod tibi non vis fieri* etc. can serve as norm of principle here. For it is, though with various limitations, only derived from the latter. It can be no universal law because it contains the ground neither of duties to oneself nor of duties of love to others (for many a man would gladly agree that others should not benefit him if only he might be excused from showing them beneficence), and finally it does not contain the ground of duties owed to others; for a criminal would argue on this ground against the judge punishing him, and so forth.

lies in the *end;* but the subject of all ends is every rational being as an end in itself (in accordance with the second principle); from this there follows now the third practical principle of the will, as supreme condition of its harmony with universal practical reason, the idea *of the will of every rational being as a will giving universal law.*

In accordance with this principle all maxims are repudiated that are inconsistent with the will's own giving of universal law. Hence the will is not merely subject to the law but subject to it in such a way that it must be viewed as also giving the law to itself and just because of this as first subject to the law (of which it can regard itself as the author).

Imperatives as they were represented above – namely in terms of the conformity of actions with universal law similar to a *natural order* or of the universal *supremacy as ends* of rational beings in themselves – did exclude from their commanding authority any admixture of interest as incentive, just by their having been represented as categorical; but they were only *assumed* to be categorical because we had to make such an assumption if we wanted to explain the concept of duty. But that there are practical propositions which command categorically could not itself be proved, any more than it could be proved either here or anywhere else in this section; one thing, however, could still have been done: namely, to indicate in the imperative itself the renunciation of all interest, in volition from duty, by means of some determination the imperative contains, as the specific mark distinguishing categorical from hypothetical imperatives; and this is done in the present third formula of the principle, namely the idea of the will of every rational being as a *will giving universal law.*

For when we think a will of this kind, then although a will that *stands under law* may be bound to this law by means of some interest, a will that is itself the supreme lawgiver cannot possibly, as such, depend upon some interest; for, a will that is dependent in this way would itself need yet another law that would limit the interest of its self-love to the condition of a validity for universal law.

Thus the *principle* of every human will as *a will giving universal law through all its maxims,** provided it is otherwise correct, would be very *well suited* to be the categorical imperative by this: that just because of the idea of giving universal law *it is based on no interest* and therefore, among all possible imperatives, can alone be *unconditional;* or still better, by converting the proposition, if there is a categorical imperative (i.e., a law for every will of a rational being) it can only command that everything be done from the maxim of one's will as a will that could at the same time have as its object itself as giving universal law; for only then is the practical principle, and the imperative that the will obeys, unconditional, since it can have no interest as its basis.

If we look back upon all previous efforts that have ever been made to discover the principle of morality, we need not wonder now why all of them had to fail. It was seen that the human being is bound to laws by his duty, but it never occurred to them that he is subject *only to laws given by himself but still universal* and that he is bound only to act in conformity with his own will, which, however, in accordance with nature's end is a will giving universal law. For, if one thought of him only as subject to a law (whatever it may be), this law had to carry with it some interest by way of attraction or constraint, since it did not as a law arise from *his* will; in order to conform with the law, his will had instead to be constrained by *something else* to act in a certain way. By this quite necessary consequence, however, all the labor to find a supreme ground of duty was irretrievably lost. For, one never arrived at duty but instead at the necessity of an action from a certain interest. This might be one's own or another's interest. But then the imperative had to turn out always conditional and could not be fit for a moral command. I will therefore call this basic principle the principle of the **autonomy** of the will in contrast with every other, which I accordingly count as **heteronomy**.

The concept of every rational being as one who must regard himself as giving universal law through all the maxims of his will, so as to appraise himself and his actions from this point of view, leads to a very fruitful concept dependent upon it, namely that *of a kingdom of ends.*

By a *kingdom* I understand a systematic union of various rational beings through common laws. Now since laws determine ends in terms of their universal validity, if we abstract from the personal differences of rational beings as well as from all the content of their private ends we shall be able to think of a whole of all ends in systematic connection (a whole both of rational beings as ends in themselves and of the ends of his own that each may set himself), that is, a kingdom of ends, which is possible in accordance with the above principles.

For, all rational beings stand under the *law* that each of them is to treat himself and all others *never merely as means* but always *at the same time as ends in themselves.* But from this there arises a systematic union of rational beings through

---

* I may be excused from citing examples to illustrate this principle, since those that have already illustrated the categorical imperative and its formula can all serve for the same end here.

common objective laws, that is, a kingdom, which can be called a kingdom of ends (admittedly only an ideal) because what these laws have as their purpose is just the relation of these beings to one another as ends and means.

A rational being belongs as a *member* to the kingdom of ends when he gives universal laws in it but is also himself subject to these laws. He belongs to it *as sovereign* when, as lawgiving, he is not subject to the will of any other.

A rational being must always regard himself as lawgiving in a kingdom of ends possible through freedom of the will, whether as a member or as sovereign. He cannot, however, hold the position of sovereign merely by the maxims of his will but only in case he is a completely independent being, without needs and with unlimited resources adequate to his will.

Morality consists, then, in the reference of all action to the lawgiving by which alone a kingdom of ends is possible. This lawgiving must, however, be found in every rational being himself and be able to arise from his will, the principle of which is, accordingly: to do no action on any other maxim than one such that it would be consistent with it to be a universal law, and hence to act only *so that the will could regard itself as at the same time giving universal law through its maxim.* Now, if maxims are not already of their nature in agreement with this objective principle of rational beings as givers of universal law, the necessity of an action in accordance with this principle is called practical necessitation, that is, *duty.* Duty does not apply to the sovereign in the kingdom of ends, but it does apply to every member of it and indeed to all in equal measure.

The practical necessity of acting in accordance with this principle, that is, duty, does not rest at all on feelings, impulses, and inclinations but merely on the relation of rational beings to one another, in which the will of a rational being must always be regarded as at the same time *lawgiving,* since otherwise it could not be thought as an *end in itself.* Reason accordingly refers every maxim of the will as giving universal law to every other will and also to every action toward oneself, and does so not for the sake of any other practical motive or any future advantage but from the idea of the *dignity* of a rational being, who obeys no law other than that which he himself at die same time gives.

In the kingdom of ends everything has either a *price* or a *dignity.* What has a price can be replaced by something else as its *equivalent;* what on the other hand is raised above all price and therefore admits of no equivalent has a dignity.

What is related to general human inclinations and needs has a *market price;* that which, even without presupposing a need, conforms with a certain taste, that is, with a delight in the mere purposeless play of our mental powers, has a *fancy price;* but that which constitutes the condition under which alone something can be an end in itself has not merely a relative worth, that is, a price, but an inner worth, that is, *dignity.*

Now, morality is the condition under which alone a rational being can be an end in itself, since only through this is it possible to be a lawgiving member in the kingdom of ends. Hence morality, and humanity insofar as it is capable of morality, is that which alone has dignity. Skill and diligence in work have a market price; wit, lively imagination and humor have a fancy price; on the other hand, fidelity in promises and benevolence from basic principles (not from instinct) have an inner worth. Nature, as well as art, contains nothing that, lacking these, it could put in their place; for their worth does not consist in the effects arising from them, in the advantage and use they provide, but in dispositions, that is, in maxims of the will that in this way are ready to manifest themselves through actions, even if success does not favor them. Such actions also need no recommendation from any subjective disposition or taste, so as to be looked upon with immediate favor and delight, nor do they need any immediate propensity or feeling for them; they present the will that practices them as the object of an immediate respect, and nothing but reason is required to *impose* them upon the will, not to *coax* them from it, which latter would in any case be a contradiction in the case of duties. This estimation therefore lets the worth of such a cast of mind be cognized as dignity and puts it infinitely above all price, with which it cannot be brought into comparison or competition at all without, as it were, assaulting its holiness.

And what is it, then, that justifies a morally good disposition, or virtue, in making such high claims? It is nothing less than the *share* it affords a rational being *in the giving of universal laws,* by which it makes him fit to be a member of a possible kingdom of ends, which he was already destined to be by his own nature as an end in itself and, for that very reason, as lawgiving in the kingdom of ends – as free with respect to all laws of nature, obeying only those which he himself gives and in accordance with which his maxims can belong to a giving of universal law (to which at the same time he subjects himself). For, nothing can have a worth other than that which the law determines for it. But the lawgiving itself, which determines all worth, must for that very reason have a dignity, that is, an unconditional, incomparable worth; and the word *respect* alone provides a becoming expression for the estimate of it that a rational being must give. *Autonomy* is therefore the ground of the dignity of human nature and of every rational nature.

The above three ways of representing the principle of morality are at bottom only so many formulae of the very same law, and any one of them of itself unites the other two in it. There is nevertheless a difference among them, which is indeed subjectively rather than objectively practical, intended namely to bring an idea of reason closer to intuition (by a certain analogy) and thereby to feeling. All maxims have, namely,

1. a *form*, which consists in universality; and in this respect the formula of the moral imperative is expressed thus: that maxims must be chosen as if they were to hold as universal laws of nature;
2. a *matter*, namely an end, and in this respect the formula says that a rational being, as an end by its nature and hence as an end in itself, must in every maxim serve as the limiting condition of all merely relative and arbitrary ends;
3. a *complete determination* of all maxims by means of that formula, namely that all maxims from one's own lawgiving are to harmonize with a possible kingdom of ends as with a kingdom of nature.* A progression takes place here, as through the categories of the *unity* of the form of the will (its universality), the *plurality* of the matter (of objects, i.e., of ends), and the *allness* or totality of the system of these. But one does better always to proceed in moral *appraisal* by the strict method and put at its basis the universal formula of the categorical imperative: *act in accordance with a maxim that can at the same time make itself a universal law*. If, however, one wants also to provide *access* for the moral law, it is very useful to bring one and the same action under the three concepts mentioned above and thereby, as far as possible, bring it closer to intuition.

We can now end where we set out from at the beginning, namely with the concept of a will unconditionally good. *That will is absolutely good* which cannot be evil, hence whose maxim, if made a universal law, can never conflict with itself. This principle is, accordingly, also its supreme law: act always on that maxim whose universality as a law you can at the same time will; this is the sole condition under which a will can never be in conflict with itself, and such an imperative is categorical. Since the validity of the will as a universal law for possible actions has an analogy with the universal connection of the existence of things in accordance with universal laws, which is the formal aspect of nature in general, the categorical imperative can also be expressed thus: *act in accordance with maxims that can at the same time have as their object themselves as universal laws of nature*. In this way, then, the formula of an absolutely good will is provided.

Rational nature is distinguished from the rest of nature by this, that it sets itself an end. This end would be the matter of every good will. But since, in the idea of a will absolutely good without any limiting condition (attainment of this or that end) abstraction must be made altogether from every end to be *effected* (this would make every will only relatively good), the end must here be thought not as an end to be effected but as an *independently existing* end, and hence thought only negatively, that is, as that which must never be acted against and which must therefore in every volition be estimated never merely as a means but always at the same time as an end. Now, this end can be nothing other than the subject of all possible ends itself, because this subject is also the subject of a possible absolutely good will; for, such a will cannot without contradiction be subordinated to any other object. The principle, so act with reference to every rational being (yourself and others) that in your maxim it holds at the same time as an end in itself, is thus at bottom the same as the basic principle, act on a maxim that at the same time contains in itself its own universal validity for every rational being. For, to say that in the use of means to any end I am to limit my maxim to the condition of its universal validity as a law for every subject is tantamount to saying that the subject of ends, that is, the rational being itself, must be made the basis of all maxims of actions, never merely as a means but as the supreme limiting condition in the use of all means, that is, always at the same time as an end.

Now, from this it follows incontestably that every rational being, as an end in itself, must be able to regard himself as also giving universal laws with respect to any law whatsoever to which he may be subject; for, it is just this fitness of his maxims for giving universal law that marks him out as an end in itself; it also follows that this dignity (prerogative) he has over all merely natural beings brings with it that he must always take his maxims from the point of view of himself, and likewise every other rational being, as lawgiving beings (who for this reason are also called persons). Now in this way a world of rational beings (*mundus intelligibilis*) as a kingdom of ends is possible, through the giving of their own laws by all persons as members. Consequently, every rational being must act as if he were by his maxims at all times a lawgiving member of the universal kingdom of ends. The formal principle of these

---

* *Teleology* considers nature as a kingdom of ends, *morals* considers a possible kingdom of ends as a kingdom of nature. In the former the kingdom of ends is a theoretical idea for explaining what exists. In the latter, it is a practical idea for the sake of bringing about, in conformity with this very idea, that which does not exist but which can become real by means of our conduct.

maxims is, act as if your maxims were to serve at the same time as a universal law (for all rational beings). A kingdom of ends is thus possible only by analogy with a kingdom of nature; the former, however, is possible only through maxims, that is, rules imposed upon oneself, the latter only through laws of externally necessitated efficient causes. Despite this, nature as a whole, even though it is regarded as a machine, is still given the name "a kingdom of nature" insofar as and because it has reference to rational beings as its ends. Now, such a kingdom of ends would actually come into existence through maxims whose rule the categorical imperative prescribes to all rational beings *if they were universally followed*. It is true that, even though a rational being scrupulously follows this maxim himself, he cannot for that reason count upon every other to be faithful to the same maxim nor can he count upon the kingdom of nature and its purposive order to harmonize with him, as a fitting member, toward a kingdom of ends possible through himself, that is, upon its favoring his expectation of happiness; nevertheless that law, act in accordance with the maxims of a member giving universal laws for a merely possible kingdom of ends, remains in its full force because it commands categorically. And just in this lies the paradox that the mere dignity of humanity as rational nature, without any other end or advantage to be attained by it – hence respect for a mere idea – is yet to serve as an inflexible precept of the will, and that it is just in this independence of maxims from all such incentives that their sublimity consists, and the worthiness of every rational subject to be a lawgiving member in the kingdom of ends; for otherwise he would have to be represented only as subject to the natural law of his needs. Even if the kingdom of nature as well as the kingdom of ends were thought as united under one sovereign, so that the latter would no longer remain a mere idea but would obtain true reality, it would no doubt gain the increment of a strong incentive but never any increase of its inner worth; for, even this sole absolute lawgiver would, despite this, still have to be represented as appraising the worth of rational beings only by their disinterested conduct, prescribed to themselves merely from that idea. The essence of things is not changed by their external relations; and that which, without taking account of such relations, alone constitutes the worth of a human being is that in terms of which he must also be appraised by whoever does it, even by the supreme being. *Morality* is thus the relation of actions to the autonomy of the will, that is, to a possible giving of universal law through its maxims. An action that can coexist with the autonomy of the will is *permitted;* one that does not accord with it is *forbidden.* A will whose maxims necessarily harmonize with the laws of autonomy is a *holy,* absolutely good will. The dependence upon the principle of autonomy of a will that is not absolutely good (moral necessitation) is *obligation.* This, accordingly, cannot be attributed to a holy being. The objective necessity of an action from obligation is called *duty.*

From what has just been said it is now easy to explain how it happens that, although in thinking the concept of duty we think of subjection to the law, yet at the same time we thereby represent a certain sublimity and *dignity* in the person who fulfills all his duties. For there is indeed no sublimity in him insofar as he is *subject* to the moral law, but there certainly is insofar as he is at the same time *lawgiving* with respect to it and only for that reason subordinated to it. We have also shown above how neither fear nor inclination but simply respect for the law is that incentive which can give actions a moral worth. Our own will insofar as it would act only under the condition of a possible giving of universal law through its maxims – this will possible for us in idea – is the proper object of respect; and the dignity of humanity consists just in this capacity to give universal law, though with the condition of also being itself subject to this very lawgiving.

8

An Introduction to the Principles of Morals and Legislation

Jeremy Bentham

Bentham begins with two quite different sorts of claim (1.1–6). The first is *descriptive* and may be understood as a form of what is known as *psychological egoistic hedonism*. According to this view, human beings act with the aim of maximizing the balance of pleasure over pain in their own lives. Note that nothing is being said here about what people *ought* to do. That is the subject of Bentham's second, *prescriptive* claim. According to the 'principle of utility', 'the greatest happiness principle', or *utilitarianism*, each of us ought to act to promote the greatest balance of pleasure over pain of the relevant 'party'. If the party in question is oneself, there will be no practical conflict between what I ought to do and what I will do. But it is clear that Bentham believes that we should take into account *all* parties – that is, maximize the balance of pleasure over pain among all sentient beings. This in part explains the emphasis Bentham puts on legislation (1.7, 2.19). The task of the legislator is to create a legal system that will provide incentives for people to do what they ought, for example by threatening punishment for deviation from the course of action required by morality.

Many have found each of these views plausible; but they do face some challenging objections. The psychological egoist will find it hard to explain cases of apparent self-sacrifice. For example, in a war, a soldier might volunteer for a mission they know will result in their own death, fully believing that if they were not to volunteer, then their life would probably include more happiness overall. The hedonist version of this view will face problems with cases in which people appear to aim for non-hedonic goods. Someone might undergo much hardship to achieve posthumous fame, for instance. The possibility of non-hedonic goods is also a problem for a hedonist version of the principle of utility such as Bentham's. If, as many have thought, a person's well-being can be advanced through accomplishment, understanding, or friendship, then these goods have as strong a claim to be promoted as pleasure. There are also difficulties for utilitarianism in its denying certain potential 'moral' goods, such as justice. Consider a case in which, for example, the population of some town is going to riot because of a series of violent crimes, the perpetrator of which the police have failed to find. It may produce the best outcome in utilitarian terms to frame and punish some innocent person; but many would object that this is unjust and forbidden by morality.

Philosophers sometimes distinguish between *metaethics* and *normative ethics*. Utilitarianism is a normative ethical view, as is the view that there is a principle of justice. Bentham makes claims at both levels, suggesting that any normative view other than utilitarianism is a mere expression of sentiment and 'capricious' in the sense that the only reason anyone proposing such a view can offer for their position is that they themselves approve of it (1.14, 2.11–12). The only genuine justification for any view must appeal to the hedonic consequences of actions. Bentham even goes so far as to claim that moral words can be given a sense only if understood in utilitarian terms (1.10).

Here the anti-utilitarian proponent of justice may offer various responses. First, it is not clear why any metaethical claim about non-utilitarian principles should not apply also to utilitarianism. Second, justifications

History of Ethics – Essential Readings with Commentary, First Edition. Edited by Daniel Star and Roger Crisp.
© 2020 John Wiley & Sons Ltd. Published 2020 by John Wiley & Sons Ltd.

for non-utilitarian principles need not appeal to their proponents' own approval. It may be claimed, for example, that there is an ultimate or basic principle, on all fours with the utility principle, according to which it is wrong or unjust to punish an innocent person (1.11). Finally, Bentham's claim about moral language seems to make the principle of utility tautologous: if 'right' *means* 'utility-maximizing', then the claim that it is right to maximize utility amounts to the claim that maximizing utility is maximizing utility.

The first two responses here, if they are correct, raise an important question about moral epistemology. If Bentham is right that a moral theory must rest on a fundamental principle which cannot itself be proved by reference to some further principle, where does this leave the debate between the utilitarian and the non-utilitarian? How can they continue to argue with one another if they have reached theoretical bedrock?

Bentham is famous for claiming that pleasure and pain can be measured in terms of what is sometimes called his *felicific calculus*. He lists seven relevant properties, but only the first two – intensity and duration – actually determine the value of any particular pleasure. The other properties are relevant to decision-making; for example, even if one knows that some course of action will not lead to the greatest possible balance of pleasure over pain, one may choose it because the chance of achieving that greatest possible balance is very small, and the chance of achieving some smaller balance is significantly greater.

Bentham does not distinguish between types of pleasure. Some philosophers, such as Mill, have claimed that this is a mistake, since the source of certain pleasures (for example, in intellectual activity) makes them more valuable than certain others (such as basic sensual pleasures). There are also important and puzzling questions about whether intensity and duration can be traded off against one another. Consider 10 years of the most horrible agony imaginable. The intensity of this pain of course makes the whole experience very bad. Twenty years of only slightly less bad agony is even worse. But now consider the discomfort of a mild twinge in one's finger. In Bentham's view, there must be some length of time of such a twinge that would make the experience worse than that of the 10 years of agony. But most people, if they imagine being given the choice, would greatly prefer the twinge to the agony, perhaps however long that twinge lasted.

Chapter I

Of the Principle of Utility

1.   Nature has placed mankind under the governance of two sovereign masters, *pain* and *pleasure*. It is for them alone to point out what we ought to do, as well as to determine what we shall do. On the one hand the standard of right and wrong, on the other the chain of causes and effects, are fastened to their throne. They govern us in all we do, in all we say, in all we think: every effort we can make to throw off our subjection, will serve but to demonstrate and confirm it. In words a man may pretend to abjure their empire: but in reality he will remain subject to it all the while. The *principle of utility*[1] recognises this subjection, and assumes it for the foundation of that system, the object of which is to rear the fabric of felicity by the hands of reason and of law. Systems which attempt to question it, deal in sounds instead of senses, in caprice instead of reason, in darkness instead of light.

But enough of metaphor and declamation: it is not by such means that moral science is to be improved.

2.   The principle of utility is the foundation of the present work: it will be proper therefore at the outset to give an explicit and determinate account of what is meant by it. By the principle[2] of utility is meant that principle which approves or disapproves of every action whatsoever, according to the tendency which it appears to have to augment or diminish the happiness of the party whose interest is in question: or, what is the same thing in other words, to promote, or to oppose that happiness. I say of every action whatsoever; and therefore not only of every action of a private individual, but of every measure of government.

3.   By utility is meant that property in any object, whereby it tends to produce benefit, advantage, pleasure, good, or happiness, (all this in the present case comes to the same thing) or (what comes again to the same thing) to prevent the happening of mischief, pain, evil, or unhappiness to the party whose interest is considered: if that party be the community in general, then the happiness of the community: if a particular individual, then the happiness of that individual.

4.   The interest of the community is one of the most general expressions that can occur in the phraseology of morals: no wonder that the meaning of it is often lost. When it has a meaning, it is this. The community is a fictitious *body*, composed of the individual persons who are considered as constituting as it were its *members*. The interest of the community then is, what? − the sum of the interests of the several members who compose it.

5.   It is in vain to talk of the interest of the community, without understanding what is the interest of the individual.[3] A thing is said to promote the interest, or to be *for* the interest, of an individual, when it tends to add to the sum total of his pleasures: or, what comes to the same thing, to diminish the sum total of his pains.

6.   An action then may be said to be conformable to the principle of utility, or, for shortness sake, to utility, (meaning with respect to the community at large) when the tendency it has to augment the happiness of the community is greater than any it has to diminish it.

---

[1] Note by the Author, July 1822.

  To this denomination has of late been added, or substituted, the *greatest happiness* or *greatest felicity* principle: this for shortness, instead of saving at length *that principle* which states the greatest happiness of all those whose interest is in question, as being the right and proper, and only right and proper and universally desirable, end of human action: of human action in every situation, and in particular in that of a functionary or set of functionaries exercising the powers of Government. The word *utility* does not so clearly point to the ideas of *pleasure* and *pain* as the words *happiness* and *felicity* do: nor does it lead us to the consideration of the *number*, of the interests affected; to the *number*, as being the circumstance, which contributes, in the largest proportion, to the formation of the standard here in question, the *standard of right and wrong*, by which alone the propriety of human conduct, in every situation, can with propriety be tried. This want of a sufficiently manifest connexion between the ideas of *happiness* and *pleasure* on the one hand, and the idea of *utility* on the other, I have every now and then found operating, and with but too much efficiency, as a bar to the acceptance, that might otherwise have been given, to this principle.

[2] The word principle is derived from the Latin principium: which seems to be compounded of the two words primus, first, or chief, and cipium, a termination which seems to be derived from capio, to take, as in manicipium, municipium; to which are analogous, auceps, forceps, and others. It is a term of very vague and very extensive signification: it is applied to any thing which is conceived to serve as a foundation or beginning to any series of operations: in some cases, of physical operations; but of mental operations in the present case.

  The principle here in question may be taken for an act of the mind; a sentiment; a sentiment of approbation; a sentiment which, when applied to an action, approves of its utility, as that quality of it by which the measure of approbation or disapprobation bestowed upon it ought to be governed.

[3] Interest is one of those words, which not having any superior *genus*, cannot in the ordinary way be defined.

7.   A measure of government (which is but a particular kind of action, performed by a particular person or persons) may be said to be conformable to or dictated by the principle of utility, when in like manner the tendency which it has to augment the happiness of the community is greater than any which it has to diminish it.

8.   When an action, or in particular a measure of government, is supposed by a man to be conformable to the principle of utility, it may be convenient, for the purposes of discourse, to imagine a kind of law or dictate, called a law or dictate of utility; and to speak of the action in question, as being conformable to such law or dictate.

9.   A man may be said to be a partisan of the principle of utility, when the approbation or disapprobation he annexes to any action, or to any measure, is determined by and proportioned to the tendency which he conceives it to have to augment or to diminish the happiness of the community: or in other words, to its conformity or uncomformity to the laws or dictates of utility.

10.   Of an action that is conformable to the principle of utility one may always say either that it is one that ought to be done, or at least that it is not one that ought not to be done. One may say also, that it is right it should be done; at least that it is not wrong it should be done: that it is a right action; at least that it is not a wrong action. When thus interpreted, the words *ought*, and *right* and *wrong*, and others of that stamp, have a meaning: when otherwise, they have none.

11.   Has the rectitude of this principle been ever formally contested? It should seem that it had, by those who have not known what they have been meaning. Is it susceptible of any direct proof? it should seem not: for that which is used to prove every thing else, cannot itself be proved: a chain of proofs must have their commencement somewhere. To give such proof is as impossible as it is needless.

12.   Not that there is or ever has been that human creature breathing, however stupid or perverse, who has not on many, perhaps on most occasions of his life, deferred to it. By the natural constitution of the human frame, on most occasions of their lives men in general embrace this principle, without thinking of it: if not for the ordering of their own actions, yet for the trying of their own actions, as well as of those of other men. There have been, at the same time, not many, perhaps, even of the most intelligent, who have been disposed to embrace it purely and without reserve. There are even few who have not taken some occasion or other to quarrel with it, either on account of their not understanding always how to apply it, or on account of some prejudice or other which they were afraid to examine into, or could not bear to part with. For such is the stuff that man is made of: in principle and in practice, in a right track and in a wrong one, the rarest of all human qualities is consistency.

13.   When a man attempts to combat the principle of utility, it is with reasons drawn, without his being aware of it, from that very principle itself.[4] His arguments, if they prove any thing, prove not that the principle is *wrong*, but that, according to the applications he supposes to be made of it, it is *misapplied*. Is it possible for a man to move the earth? Yes; but he must first find out another earth to stand upon.

---

[4] 'The principle of utility, (I have heard it said) is a dangerous principle: it is dangerous on certain occasions to consult it.' This is as much as to say, what? that it is not consonant to utility, to consult utility: in short, that it is *not* consulting it, to consult it.

Addition by the Author, July 1822.

Not long after the publication of the Fragment on Government, anno 1776, in which, in the character of an all-comprehensive and all-commanding principle, the principle of *utility* was brought to view, one person by whom observation to the above effect was made was *Alexander Wedderburn*, at that time Attorney or Solicitor General, afterwards successively Chief Justice of the Common Pleas, and Chancellor of England, under the successive titles of Lord Loughborough and Earl of Rosslyn. It was made – not indeed in my hearing, but in the hearing of a person by whom it was almost immediately communicated to me. So far from being self-contradictory, it was a shrewd and perfectly true one. By that distinguished functionary, the state of the Government was thoroughly understood: by the obscure individual, at that time not so much as supposed to be so: his disquisitions had not been as yet applied, with any thing like a comprehensive view, to the field of Constitutional Law, nor therefore to those features of the English Government, by which the greatest happiness of the ruling *one* with or without that of a favoured few, are now so plainly seen to be the only ends to which the course of it has at any time been directed. The *principle of utility* was an appellative, at that time employed – employed by me, as it had been by others, to designate that which in a more perspicuous and instructive manner, may, as above, be designated by the name of the *greatest happiness principle*. 'This principle (said Wedderburn) is a dangerous one.' Saying so, he said that which, to a certain extent, is strictly true: a principle, which lays down, as the only *right* and justifiable end of Government, the greatest happiness of the greatest number – how can it be denied to be a dangerous one? dangerous it unquestionably is, to every government which has for its *actual* end or object, the greatest happiness of a certain *one*, with or without the addition of some comparatively small number of others, whom it is a matter of pleasure or accommodation to him to admit, each of them, to a share in the concern, on the footing of so many junior partners. *Dangerous* it

14. To disprove the propriety of it by arguments is impossible; but, from the causes that have been mentioned, or from some confused or partial view of it, a man may happen to be disposed not to relish it. Where this is the case, if he thinks the settling of his opinions on such a subject worth the trouble, let him take the following steps and at length, perhaps, he may come to reconcile himself to it.

1. Let him settle with himself, whether he would wish to discard this principle altogether; if so, let him consider what it is that all his reasonings (in matters of politics especially) can amount to?
2. If he would, let him settle with himself, whether he would judge and act without any principle, or whether there is any other he would judge and act by?
3. If there be, let him examine and satisfy himself whether the principle he thinks he has found is really any separate intelligible principle; or whether it be not a mere principle in words, a kind of phrase, which at bottom expresses neither more nor less than the mere averment of his own unfounded sentiments; that is, what in another person he might be apt to call caprice?
4. If he is inclined to think that his own approbation or disapprobation, annexed to the idea of an act, without any regard to its consequences, is a sufficient foundation for him to judge and act upon, let him ask himself whether his sentiment is to be a standard of right and wrong, with respect to every other man, or whether every man's sentiment has the same privilege of being a standard to itself?
5. In the first case, let him ask himself whether his principle is not despotical, and hostile to all the rest of the human race?
6. In the second case, whether it is not anarchical, and whether at this rate there are not as many different standards of right and wrong as there are men? and whether even to the sane man, the same thing, which is right to-day, may not (without the least change in its nature) be wrong to-morrow? and whether the same thing is not right and wrong in the same place at the same time? and in either case, whether all argument is not at an end? and whether, when two men have said, 'I like this,' and 'I don't like it,' they can (upon such a principle) have any thing more to say?
7. If he should have said to himself, No: for that the sentiment which he proposes as a standard must be grounded on reflection, let him say on what particulars the reflection is to turn? if on particulars having relation to the utility of the act, then let him say whether this is not deserting his own principle, and borrowing assistance from that very one in opposition to which he sets it up: or if not on those particulars, on what other particulars?
8. If he should be for compounding the matter, and adopting his own principle in part, and the principle of utility in part, let him say how far he will adopt it?
9. When he has settled with himself where he will stop, then let him ask himself how he justifies to himself the adopting it so far? and why he will not adopt it any farther?
10. Admitting any other principle than the principle of utility to be a right principle, a principle that it is right for a man to pursue; admitting (what is not true) that the word *right* can have a meaning without reference to utility, let him say whether there is any such thing as a *motive* that a man can have to pursue the dictates of it: if there is, let him say what that motive is, and how it is to be distinguished from those which enforce the dictates of utility: if not, then lastly let him say what it is this other principle can be good for?

[…]

---

therefore really was, to the interest – the sinister interest – of all those functionaries, himself included, whose interest it was, to maximise delay, vexation, and expense, in judicial and other modes of procedure, for the sake of the profit, extractible out of the expense. In a Government which had for its end in view the greatest happiness of the greatest number, Alexander Wedderburn might have been Attorney General and then Chancellor: but he would not have been Attorney General with £15,000 a year, nor Chancellor, with a peerage with a veto upon all justice, with £25,000 a year, and with 500 sinecures at his disposal, under the name of Ecclesiastical Benefices, besides *et cæteras*.

Chapter II

Of Principles Adverse to that of Utility

[...]

11.   Among principles adverse[5] to that of utility, that which at this day seems to have most influence in matters of government, is what may be called the principle of sympathy and antipathy. By the principle of sympathy and antipathy, I mean that principle which approves or disapproves of certain actions, not on account of their tending to augment the happiness, nor yet on account of their tending to diminish the happiness of the party whose interest is in question, but merely because a man finds himself disposed to approve or disapprove of them: holding up that approbation or disapprobation as a sufficient reason for itself, and disclaiming the necessity of looking out for any extrinsic ground. Thus for in the general department of morals: and in the particular department of politics, measuring out the quantum (as well as determining the ground) of punishment, by the degree of the disapprobation.

12.   It is manifest, that this is rather a principle in name than in reality: it is not a positive principle of itself, so much as a term employed to signify the negation of all principle. What one expects to find in a principle is something that points out some external consideration, as a means of warranting and guiding; the internal sentiments of approbation and disapprobation: this expectation is but ill fulfilled by a proposition, which does neither more nor less than hold up each of those sentiments as a ground and standard for itself.

[...]

19.   There are two things which are very apt to be confounded, but which it imports us carefully to distinguish: – the motive or cause, which, by operating on the mind of an individual, is productive of any act: and the ground or reason which warrants a legislator, or other by-stander, in regarding that act with an eye of approbation. When the act happens, in the particular instance in question, to be productive of effects which we approve of, much more if we happen to observe that the same motive may frequently be productive, in other instances, of the like effects, we are apt to transfer our approbation to the motive itself, and to assume, as the just ground for the approbation we bestow on the act, the circumstance of its originating from that motive. It is in this way that the sentiment of antipathy has often been considered as a just ground of action. Antipathy, for instance, in such or such a case, is the cause of an action which is attended with good effects: but this does not make it a right ground of action in that case, any more than in any other. Still farther. Not only the effects are good, but the agent sees beforehand that they will be so. This may make the action indeed a perfectly right action: but it does not make antipathy a right ground of action. For the same sentiment of antipathy, if implicitly deferred to, may be, and very frequently is, productive of the very worst effects. Antipathy, therefore, can never be a right ground of action. No more, therefore, can resentment, which, as will be seen more particularly hereafter, is but a modification of antipathy. The only right ground of action, that can possibly subsist, is, after all, the consideration of utility, which if it is a right principle of action, and of approbation, in any one case, is so in every other. Other principles in abundance, that is, other motives, may be the reasons why such and such an act *has* been done: that is, the reasons or causes of its being done: but it is this alone that can be the reason why it might or ought to have been done. Antipathy or resentment requires always to be regulated, to prevent its doing mischief: to be regulated by what? always by the principle of utility. The principle of utility neither requires nor admits of any other regulator than itself.

[...]

---

[5]   The following Note was first printed in January 1789.

It ought rather to have been styled, more extensively, the principle of *caprice*. Where it applies to the choice of actions to be marked out for injunction or prohibition, for reward or punishment, (to stand, in a word, as subjects for *obligations* to be imposed,) it may indeed with propriety be termed, as in the text, the principle of *sympathy* and *antipathy*. But this appellative does not so well apply to it, when occupied in the choice of the *events* which are to serve as sources of *title* with respect to *rights*: where the actions prohibited and allowed, the obligations and rights, being already fixed, the only question is, under what circumstances a man is to be invested with the one or subjected to the other? from what incidents occasion is to be taken to invest a man, or to refuse to invest him, with the one, or to subject him to the other? In the latter case it may more appositely be characterised by the name of the *phantastic principle*. Sympathy and antipathy are affections of the *sensible* faculty. But the choice of *titles* with respect to *rights*, especially with respect to proprietary rights, upon grounds unconnected with utility, has been in many instances the work, not of the affections hut of the imagination.

Chapter IV

Value of a Lot of Pleasure or Pain, How to Be Measured   √

1.   Pleasures then, and the avoidance of pains, are the *ends* which the legislator has in view: it behoves him therefore to understand their *value*. Pleasures and pains are the *instruments* he has to work with: it behoves him therefore to understand their force, which is again, in other words, their value.

2.   To a person considered *by himself*, the value of a pleasure or pain considered *by itself*, will be greater or less, according to the four following circumstances:[6]

(1) Its *intensity*.
(2) Its *duration*.
(3) Its *certainty* or *uncertainty*.
(4) Its *propinquity* or *remoteness*.

3.   These are the circumstances which are to be considered in estimating a pleasure or a pain considered each of them by itself. But when the value of any pleasure or pain is considered for the purpose of estimating the tendency of any *act* by which it is produced, there are two other circumstances to be taken into account; these are,

(5) Its *fecundity*, or the chance it has of being followed by sensations of the *same* kind: that is, pleasures, if it be a pleasure: pains, if it be a pain.
(6) Its *purity*, or the chance it has of *not* being followed by sensations of the *opposite* kind: that is, pains, if it be a pleasure: pleasures, if it be a pain.

These two last, however, are in strictness scarcely to be deemed properties of the pleasure or the pain itself; they are not, therefore, in strictness to be taken into the account of the value of that pleasure or that pain. They are in strictness to be deemed properties only of the act, or other event, by which such pleasure or pain has been produced; and accordingly are only to be taken into the account of the tendency of such act or such event.

4.   To a *number* of persons, with reference to each of whom the value of a pleasure or a pain is considered, it will be greater or less, according to seven circumstances: to wit, the six preceding ones; *viz.*

(1) Its *intensity*.
(2) Its *duration*.
(3) Its *certainty* or *uncertainty*.
(4) Its *propinquity* or *remoteness*.
(5) Its *fecundity*.
(6) Its *purity*.

And one other; to wit:

(7) Its *extent*; that is, the number of persons to whom it *extends*; or (in other words) who are affected by it.

5.   To take an exact account then of the general tendency of any act, by which the interests of a community are affected, proceed as follows. Begin with any one person of those whose interests seem most immediately to be affected by it: and take an account,

---

[6] These circumstances have since been denominated *elements* or *dimensions* of *value* in a pleasure or a pain. √

Not long after the publication of the first edition, the following memoriter verses were framed, in the view of lodging more effectually, in the memory, these points, on which the whole fabric of morals and legislation may be seen to rest.

> *Intense, long, certain, speedy, fruitful, pure* —
> Such marks in *pleasures* and in *pains* endure.
> Such pleasures seek if *private* be thy end:
> If it be *public*, wide let them *extend*.
> Such *pains* avoid, whichever be thy view:
> If pains *must* come, let them *extend* to few.

(1) Of the value of each distinguishable *pleasure* which appears to be produced by it in the *first* instance.

(2) Of the value of each *pain* which appears to be produced by it in the *first* instance.

(3) Of the value of each pleasure which appears to be produced by it *after* the first. This constitutes the *fecundity* of the first *pleasure* and the *impurity* of the first *pain*.

(4) Of the value of each *pain* which appears to be produced by it after the first. This constitutes the *fecundity* of the first *pain*, and the *impurity* of the first pleasure.

(5) Sum up all the values of all the *pleasures* on the one side, and those of all the pains on the other. The balance, if it be on the side of pleasure, will give the *good* tendency of the act upon the whole, with respect to the interests of that *individual* person; if on the side of pain, the *bad* tendency of it upon the whole.

(6) Take an account of the *number* of persons whose interests appear to be concerned; and repeat the above process with respect to each. *Sum up* the numbers expressive of the degrees of *good* tendency, which the act has, with respect to each individual, in regard to whom the tendency of it is *good* upon the whole: do this again with respect to each individual, in regard to whom the tendency of it is *bad* upon the whole. Take the *balance*; which, if on the side of *pleasure*, will give the general *good tendency* of the act, with respect to the total number or community of individuals concerned; if on the side of pain, the general *evil tendency*, with respect to the same community.

6. It is not to be expected that this process should be strictly pursued previously to every moral judgment, or to every legislative or judicial operation. It may, however, be always kept in view: and as near as the process actually pursued on these occasions approaches to it, so near will such process approach to the character of an exact one.

7. The same process is alike applicable to pleasure and pain, in whatever shape they appear: and by whatever denomination they are distinguished: to pleasure, whether it be called *good* (which is properly the cause or instrument of pleasure) or *profit* (which is distant pleasure, or the cause or instrument of distant pleasure,) or *convenience*, or *advantage, benefit, emolument, happiness*, and so forth: to pain, whether it be called *evil*, (which corresponds to *good*) or *mischief*, or *inconvenience*, or *disadvantage*, or *loss*, or *unhappiness*, and so forth.

8. Nor is this a novel and unwarranted, any more than it is a useless theory. In all this there is nothing but what the practice of mankind, wheresoever they have a clear view of their own interest, is perfectly conformable to. An article of property, an estate in land, for instance, is valuable, on what account? On account of the pleasures of all kinds which it enables a man to produce, and what comes to the same thing the pains of all kinds which it enables him to avert. But the value of such an article of property is universally understood to rise or fall according to the length or shortness of the time which a man has in it: the certainty or uncertainty of its coming into possession: and the nearness or remoteness of the time at which, if at all, it is to come into possession. As to the *intensity* of the pleasures which a man may derive from it, this is never thought of, because it depends upon the use which each particular person may come to make of it; which cannot be estimated till the particular pleasures he may come to derive from it, or the particular pains he may come to exclude by means of it, are brought to view. For the same reason, neither does he think of the *fecundity* or *purity* of those pleasures.

Thus much for pleasure and pain, happiness and unhappiness, in *general*.

9

Utilitarianism and *The Subjection of Women*

John Stuart Mill

Mill is the most famous defender of the moral theory known as *utilitarianism*. 'Utility' is another word for happiness, and Mill defines utilitarianism as the view that 'actions are right as they tend to promote happiness, wrong as they tend to promote the reverse of happiness' (Utilitarianism 2.2). Mill is best understood not to be suggesting that rightness and wrongness come in degrees. Rather, the right action is that which promotes the greatest balance of pleasure over pain overall, and any other action is wrong; and the further its consequences are from the best, the worse it is, morally speaking. Nor need we think that the mention of 'tendencies' in Mill's definition is important. He is using the verb 'to tend' in the way that one might speak of an overloaded ship tending to starboard, and not saying that the rightness of any individual action depends on the general consequences of the class of actions to which it belongs.

There are two central components to a utilitarian theory: a theory of utility, and a theory about its distribution (i.e. the theory that it be maximized impartially). Mill's theory of happiness is *hedonist*: the only thing good for anyone is pleasure, and the only bad thing is pain. As Mill points out (U 2.3–8), hedonism has often been criticized as the 'philosophy of swine', on the ground that the goods in a normal human life set us apart from the other animals. We can engage, for example, in intellectual and aesthetic activities. Mill's response is to distinguish between 'higher' and 'lower' pleasures. If we compare some intellectual pleasure, such as appreciating Shakespeare, with a lower pleasure such as a massage, it is not inconsistent with hedonism to claim that the intellectual pleasure is discontinuously more valuable than the bodily, in the sense that no amount of the lower can be as valuable as a finite amount of the former.

This raises some difficult questions about thresholds (how much Shakespeare are we talking about – the collected works, one play, one sonnet, or a well-turned phrase?). In the end, Mill leaves such questions to be answered by 'competent judges' who have experienced both of the pleasures in question. But even in Mill's time, many thought that Mill's view was in effect a denial of hedonism. He speaks for example of the 'nobility' of higher pleasures; but nobility is quite different from pleasantness. Or consider accomplishment, knowledge, or friendship. Many will think these add to the value of life independently of pleasure.

Much of the second chapter of *Utilitarianism* is taken up with responses to further objections, such as the claim that happiness is unattainable (Mill plausibly says that it isn't), that it should be renounced (again plausibly, Mill says that sacrifice of one's happiness is justified only for the sake of the happiness of others), or that it is godless (Mill notes that God might be a utilitarian). Some of the most important objections are related: that utilitarianism is too demanding, that it alienates us from our feelings and relationships, and that we don't have the time to work out the value of the consequences of every action we perform (2.19–20, 24). Mill's response is to distinguish utilitarianism as a theory of right action from a claim about the kind of life recommended by utilitarianism. Just because actions are made right by their maximizing utility does not mean that we have constantly to be aiming at doing just that. In fact, Mill claims, given the kind of beings we are, with limited capacities for prediction and impartiality, it will be more valuable if we

History of Ethics – Essential Readings with Commentary, First Edition. Edited by Daniel Star and Roger Crisp.
© 2020 John Wiley & Sons Ltd. Published 2020 by John Wiley & Sons Ltd.

live according to common-sense principles, according to which, for example, lying is wrong, and if we are motivated by partial concern for those close to us.

One of the most important such common-sense principles concerns justice, which concerns several important areas of life -- legal rights, desert, contracts, and so on (U 5.4–10). In a long examination of justice, Mill claims that our sentiment of justice has evolved from a generalized desire to punish those who harm us, and that its ground is utilitarian (U 16–23). In particular, respect for justice gives us basic security (U 5.24–5, 32–4). This does go some way toward answering the objection that utilitarianism has no room for justice. But anti-utilitarians will continue to argue that utilitarians cannot recognize the intrinsic significance of justice. Just as accomplishment matters independently of pleasure, so equality or the respecting of rights matters independently of overall happiness.

In Chapter 4, Mill seeks to justify utilitarianism. His argument has three stages:

1. Happiness is desirable (U 4.2).
2. The greatest happiness is desirable (U 4.2).
3. Only happiness is desirable (U 4.4–8).

His argument for the first stage involves a somewhat regrettable analogy between the visible (what can be seen) and the desirable (what *ought* to be desired). But Mill's claim is not especially radical, and he may just be asking the reader to consult their own desires. If we do that, however, we may find that we desire non-hedonic goods, which will be a problem for stage (3). And we may accept that we have reason to promote our own happiness but not see why this requires us to promote the happiness of all sentient beings impartially (see U 2.10, 18).

Earlier, I noted that Mill believed much of our everyday morality can be justified in utilitarian terms. But he saw the morality governing relations between the sexes, in which women are praised for, for example, their meekness or devotion to looking after their family, as a clear exception. Here the correct principle is equality, both within the home and beyond (S 1.1, 3.1).

In Mill's day, as now, it was often said that it was natural for women to stay at home with their children. Mill objects that we cannot *know* that this is women's nature, since women have been constantly subjected to indoctrination by a male-dominated society (S 1.2–9). But – and here there is perhaps some tension in his view – he also claims that the contemporary position of women, because of this indoctrination, is not natural. Perhaps Mill sets his standards for knowledge too high. Given his plausible debunking account of the view that it is unnatural for women to work, and given our experience of women in the workplace, I suggest that we do know that such work is not inconsistent with human nature. Further, as Mill points out (S 3.1), even if women were somehow less naturally suited for certain occupations, this would not justify restricting those occupations to men. Jobs should be open to the talented, whether the talents in question are possessed by men or women.

Utilitarianism

2

What Utilitarianism Is

1. A passing remark is all that needs be given to the ignorant blunder of supposing that those who stand up for utility as the test of right and wrong, use the term in that restricted and merely colloquial sense in which utility is opposed to pleasure. An apology is due to the philosophical opponents of utilitarianism, for even the momentary appearance of confounding them with anyone capable of so absurd a misconception; which is the more extraordinary, inasmuch as the contrary accusation, of referring everything to pleasure, and that too in its grossest form, is another of the common charges against utilitarianism: and, as has been pointedly remarked by an able writer, the same sort of persons, and often the very same persons, denounce the theory 'as impracticably dry when the word utility precedes the word pleasure, and as too practically voluptuous when the word pleasure precedes the word utility.' Those who know anything about the matter are aware that every writer, from Epicurus to Bentham, who maintained the theory of utility, meant by it, not something to be contradistinguished from pleasure, but pleasure itself, together with exemption from pain; and instead of opposing the useful to the agreeable or the ornamental, have always declared that the useful means these, among other things. Yet the common herd, including the herd of writers, not only in newspapers and periodicals, but in books of weight and pretension, are perpetually falling into this shallow mistake. Having caught up the word utilitarian, while knowing nothing whatever about it but its sound, they habitually express by it the rejection, or the neglect, of pleasure in some of its forms; of beauty, of ornament, or of amusement. Nor is the term thus ignorantly misapplied solely in disparagement, but occasionally in compliment; as though it implied superiority to frivolity and the mere pleasures of the moment. And this perverted use is the only one in which the word is popularly known, and the one from which the new generation are acquiring their sole notion of its meaning. Those who introduced the word, but who had for many years discontinued it as a distinctive appellation, may well feel themselves called upon to resume it, if by doing so they can hope to contribute anything towards rescuing it from this utter degradation.*

2. The creed which accepts as the foundation of morals, Utility, or the Greatest Happiness Principle, holds that actions are right in proportion as they tend to promote happiness, wrong as they tend to produce the reverse of happiness. By happiness is intended pleasure, and the absence of pain; by unhappiness, pain, and the privation of pleasure. To give a clear view of the moral standard set up by the theory, much more requires to be said; in particular, what things it includes in the ideas of pain and pleasure; and to what extent this is left an open question. But these supplementary explanations do not affect the theory of life on which this theory of morality is grounded – namely, that pleasure, and freedom from pain, are the only things desirable as ends; and that all desirable things (which are as numerous in the utilitarian as in any other scheme) are desirable either for the pleasure inherent in themselves, or as means to the promotion of pleasure and the prevention of pain.

3. Now, such a theory of life excites in many minds, and among them in some of the most estimable in feeling and purpose, inveterate dislike. To suppose that life has (as they express it) no higher end than pleasure – no better and nobler object of desire and pursuit – they designate as utterly mean and grovelling; as a doctrine worthy only of swine, to whom the followers of Epicurus were, at a very early period, contemptuously likened; and modern holders of the doctrine are occasionally made the subject of equally polite comparisons by its German, French and English assailants.

4. When thus attacked, the Epicureans have always answered, that it is not they, but their accusers, who represent human nature in a degrading light; since the accusation supposes human beings to be capable of no pleasures except those of which swine are capable. If this supposition were true, the charge could not be gainsaid, but would then be no longer an imputation; for if the sources of pleasure were precisely the same to human beings and to swine, the rule of life which is good enough for the one would be good enough for the other. The comparison of the

* The author of this essay has reason for believing himself to be the first person who brought the word utilitarian into use. He did not invent it, but adopted it from a passing expression in Mr Galt's *Annals of the Parish*. After using it as a designation for several years, he and others abandoned it from a growing dislike to anything resembling a badge or watchword of sectarian distinction. But as a name for one single opinion not a set of opinions – to denote the recognition of utility as a standard, nor any particular way of applying it – the term supplies a want in the language, and offers, in many cases, a convenient mode of avoiding tiresome circumlocution.

Epicurean life to that of beasts is felt as degrading, precisely because a beast's pleasures do not satisfy a human being's conceptions of happiness. Human beings have faculties more elevated than the animal appetites, and when once made conscious of them, do not regard anything as happiness which does not include their gratification. I do not, indeed, consider the Epicureans to have been by any means faultless in drawing out their scheme of consequences from the utilitarian principle. To do this in any sufficient manner, many Stoic, as well as Christian elements require to be included. But there is no known Epicurean theory of life which does not assign to the pleasures of the intellect, of the feelings and imagination, and of the moral sentiments, a much higher value as pleasures than to those of mere sensation. It must be admitted, however, that utilitarian writers in general have placed the superiority of mental over bodily pleasures chiefly in the greater permanency, safety, uncostliness, &c., of the former – that is, in their circumstantial advantages rather than in their intrinsic nature. And on all these points utilitarians have fully proved their case; but they might have taken the other, and, as it may be called, higher ground, with entire consistency. It is quite compatible with the principle of utility to recognize the fact, that some *kinds* of pleasure are more desirable and more valuable than others. It would be absurd that while, in estimating all other things, quality is considered as well as quantity, the estimation of pleasures should be supposed to depend on quantity alone.

5. If I am asked, what I mean by difference of quality in pleasures, or what makes one pleasure more valuable than another, merely as a pleasure, except its being greater in amount, there is but one possible answer. Of two pleasures, if there be one to which all or almost all who have experience of both give a decided preference, irrespective of any feeling of moral obligation to prefer it, that is the more desirable pleasure. If one of the two is, by those who are competently acquainted with both, placed so far above the other that they prefer it, even though knowing it to be attended with a greater amount of discontent, and would not resign it for any quantity of the other pleasure which their nature is capable of, we are justified in ascribing to the preferred enjoyment a superiority in quality, so far outweighing quantity as to render it, in comparison, of small account.

6. Now it is an unquestionable fact that those who are equally acquainted with, and equally capable of appreciating and enjoying, both, do give a most marked preference to the manner of existence which employs their higher faculties. Few human creatures would consent to be changed into any of the lower animals, for a promise of the fullest allowance of a beast's pleasures; no intelligent human being would consent to be a fool, no instructed person would be an ignoramus, no person of feeling and conscience would be selfish and base, even though they should be persuaded that the fool, the dunce, or the rascal is better satisfied with his lot than they are with theirs. They would not resign what they possess more than he, for the most complete satisfaction of all the desires which they have in common with him. If they ever fancy they would, it is only in cases of unhappiness so extreme, that to escape from it they would exchange their lot for almost any other, however undesirable in their own eyes. A being of higher faculties requires more to make him happy, is capable probably of more acute suffering, and is certainly accessible to it at more points, than one of an inferior type; but in spite of these liabilities, he can never really wish to sink into what he feels to be a lower grade of existence. We may give what explanation we please of this unwillingness; we may attribute it to pride, a name which is given indiscriminately to some of the most and to some of the least estimable feelings of which mankind arc capable; we may refer it to the love of liberty and personal independence, an appeal to which was with the Stoics one of the most effective means for the inculcation of it; to the love of power, or to the love of excitement, both of which do really enter into and contribute to it: but its most appropriate appellation is a sense of dignity, which all human beings possess in one form or other, and in some, though by no means in exact, proportion to their higher faculties, and which is so essential a part of the happiness of those in whom it is strong, that nothing which conflicts with it could be, otherwise than momentarily, an object of desire to them. Whoever supposes that this preference takes place at a sacrifice of happiness – that the superior being, in anything like equal circumstances, is not happier than the inferior – confounds the two very different ideas, of happiness, and content, It is indisputable that the being whose capacities of enjoyment are low, has the greatest chance of having them fully satisfied; and a highly endowed being will always feel that any happiness which he can look for, as the world is constituted, is imperfect. But he can learn to bear its imperfections, if they are at all bearable; and they will not make him envy the being who is indeed unconscious of the imperfections, but only because he feels not at all the good which those imperfections qualify. It is better to be a human being dissatisfied than a pig satisfied; better to be Socrates dissatisfied than a fool satisfied. And if the fool, or the pig, is of a different opinion, it is because they only know their own side of the question. The other party to the comparison knows both sides.

7. It may be objected, that many who are capable of the higher pleasures, occasionally, under the influence of temptation, postpone them to the lower. But this is quite compatible with a full appreciation of the intrinsic

superiority of the higher. Men often, from infirmity of character, make their election for the nearer good, though they know it to be the less valuable; and this no less when the choice is between two bodily pleasures, than when it is between bodily and mental. They pursue sensual indulgences to the injury of health, though perfectly aware that health is the greater good. It may be further objected, that many who begin with youthful enthusiasm for everything noble, as they advance in years sink into indolence and selfishness. But I do not believe that those who undergo this very common change, voluntarily choose the lower description of pleasures in preference to the higher. I believe that before they devote themselves exclusively to the one, they have already become incapable of the other. Capacity for the nobler feelings is in most natures a very tender plant, easily killed, not only by hostile influences, but by mere want of sustenance; and in the majority of young persons it speedily dies away if the occupations to which their position in life has devoted them, and the society into which it has thrown them, are not favourable to keeping that higher capacity in exercise. Men lose their high aspirations as they lose their intellectual tastes, because they have not time or opportunity for indulging them; and they addict themselves to inferior pleasures, not because they deliberately prefer them, but because they are either the only ones to which they have access, or the only ones which they are any longer capable of enjoying. It may be questioned whether any one who has remained equally susceptible to both classes of pleasures, ever knowingly and calmly preferred the lower; though many, in all ages, have broken down in an ineffectual attempt to combine both.

8. From this verdict of the only competent judges, I apprehend there can be no appeal. On a question which is the best worth having of two pleasures, or which of two modes of existence is the most grateful to the feelings, apart from its moral attributes and from its consequences, the judgment of those who are qualified by knowledge of both, or, if they differ, that of the majority among them, must be admitted as final. And there needs be the less hesitation to accept this judgment respecting the quality of pleasures, since there is no other tribunal to be referred to even on the question of quantity. What means are there of determining which is the acutest of two pains, or the intensest of two pleasurable sensations, except the general suffrage of those who are familiar with both? Neither pains nor pleasures are homogeneous, and pain is always heterogeneous with pleasure. What is there to decide whether a particular pleasure is worth purchasing at the cost of a particular pain, except the feelings and judgment of the experienced? When, therefore, those feelings and judgment declare the pleasures derived from the higher faculties to be preferable *in kind*, apart from the question of intensity, to those of which the animal nature, disjoined from the higher faculties, is susceptible, they are entitled on this subject to the same regard.

9. I have dwelt on this point, as being a necessary part of a perfectly just conception of Utility or Happiness, considered as the directive rule of human conduct. But it is by no means an indispensable condition to the acceptance of the utilitarian standard; for that standard is not the agent's own greatest happiness, but the greatest amount of happiness altogether; and if it may possibly be doubted whether a noble character is always the happier for its nobleness, there can be no doubt that it makes other people happier, and that the world in general is immensely a gainer by it. Utilitarianism, therefore, could only attain its end by the general cultivation of nobleness of character, even if each individual were only benefited by the nobleness of others, and his own, so far as happiness is concerned, were a sheer deduction from the benefit. But the bare enunciation of such an absurdity as this last, renders refutation superfluous.

10. According to the Greatest Happiness Principle, as above explained, the ultimate end, with reference to and for the sake of which all other things are desirable (whether we are considering our own good or that of other people), is an existence exempt as far as possible from pain, and as rich as possible in enjoyments, both in point of quantity and quality; the test of quality, and the rule for measuring it against quantity, being the preference felt by those who, in their opportunities of experience, to which must be added their habits of self-consciousness and self-observation, are best furnished with the means of comparison. This, being, according to the utilitarian opinion, the end of human action, is necessarily also the standard of morality; which may accordingly be defined, the rules and precepts for human conduct, by the observance of which an existence such as has been described might be, to the greatest extent possible, secured to all mankind; and not to them only, but, so far as the nature of things admits, to the whole sentient creation.

11. Against this doctrine, however, arises another class of objectors, who say that happiness, in any form, cannot be the rational purpose of human life and action; because, in the first place, it is unattainable: and they contemptuously ask, What right hast thou to be happy? a question which Mr Carlyle clenches by the addition, What right, a short time ago, hadst thou even *to be*? Next, they say, that men can do *without* happiness; that all noble human beings have felt this, and could not have become noble but by learning the lesson of Entsagen, or renunciation; which lesson, thoroughly learnt and submitted to, they affirm to be the beginning and necessary condition of all virtue.

12. The first of these objections would go to the root of the matter were it well founded; for if no happiness is to be had at all by human beings, the attainment of it cannot be the end of morality, or of any rational conduct. Though, even in that case, something might still be said for the utilitarian theory; since utility includes not solely the pursuit of happiness, but the prevention or mitigation of unhappiness; and if the former aim be chimerical, there will be all the greater scope and more imperative need for the latter, so long at least as mankind think fit to live, and do not take refuge in the simultaneous act of suicide recommended under certain conditions by Novalis. When, however, it is thus positively asserted to be impossible that human life should be happy, the assertion, if not something like a verbal quibble, is at least an exaggeration. If by happiness be meant a continuity of highly pleasurable excitement, it is evident enough that this is impossible. A state of exalted pleasure lasts only moments, or in some cases, and with some intermissions, hours or days, and is the occasional brilliant flash of enjoyment, not its permanent and steady flame. Of this the philosophers who have taught that happiness is the end of life were as fully aware as those who taunt them. The happiness which they meant was not a life of rapture; but moments of such, in an existence made up of few and transitory pains, many and various pleasures, with a decided predominance of the active over the passive, and having as the foundation of the whole, not to expect more from life than it is capable of bestowing. A life thus composed, to those who have been fortunate enough to obtain it, has always appeared worthy of the name of happiness. And such an existence is even now the lot of many, during some considerable portion of their lives. The present wretched education, and wretched social arrangements, are the only real hindrance to its being attainable by almost all.

13. The objectors perhaps may doubt whether human beings, if taught to consider happiness as the end of life, would be satisfied with such a moderate share of it. But great numbers of mankind have been satisfied with much less. The main constituents of a satisfied life appear to be two; either of which by itself is often found sufficient for the purpose: tranquillity, and excitement. With much tranquillity many find that they can be content with very little pleasure: with much excitement, many can reconcile themselves to a considerable quantity of pain. There is assuredly no inherent impossibility in enabling even the mass of mankind to unite both; since the two are so far from being incompatible that they are in natural alliance, the prolongation of either being a preparation for, and exciting a wish for, the other. It is only those in whom indolence amounts to a vice, that do not desire excitement after an interval of repose; it is only those in whom the need of excitement is a disease, that feel the tranquillity which follows excitement dull and insipid, instead of pleasurable in direct proportion to the excitement which preceded it. When people who are tolerably fortunate in their outward lot do not find in life sufficient enjoyment to make it valuable to them, the cause generally is, caring for nobody but themselves. To those who have neither public nor private affections, the excitements of life are much curtailed, and in any case dwindle in value as the time approaches when all selfish interests must be terminated by death: while those who leave after them objects of personal affection, and especially those who have also cultivated a fellow feeling with the collective interests of mankind, retain as lively an interest in life on the eve of death as in the vigour of youth and health. Next to selfishness, the principal cause which makes life unsatisfactory, is want of mental cultivation. A cultivated mind – I do not mean that of a philosopher, but any mind to which the fountains of knowledge have been opened, and which has been taught, in any tolerable degree, to exercise its faculties – finds sources of inexhaustible interest in all that surrounds it; in the objects of nature, the achievements of art, the imaginations of poetry, the incidents of history, the ways of mankind past and present, and their prospects in the future. It is possible, indeed, to become indifferent to all this and that too without having exhausted a thousandth part of it; but only when one has had from the beginning no moral or human interest in these things, and has sought in them only the gratification of curiosity.

14. Now there is absolutely no reason in the nature of things why an amount, of mental culture sufficient to give an intelligent interest in these objects of contemplation, should not be the inheritance of every one born in a civilized country. As little is there an inherent necessity that any human being should be a selfish egotist, devoid of every feeling or care but those which centre in his own miserable individuality. Something far superior to this is sufficiently common even now, to give ample earnest of what the human species may be made. Genuine private affections, and a sincere interest in the public good, are possible, though in unequal degrees, to every rightly brought up human being. In a world in which there is so much to interest, so much to enjoy, and so much also to correct and improve, every one who has this moderate amount of moral and intellectual requisites is capable of an existence which may be called enviable; and unless such a person, through bad laws, or subjection to the will of others, is denied the liberty to use the sources of happiness within his reach, he will not fail to find this enviable existence, if he escape the positive evils of life, the great sources of physical and mental suffering – such as indigence, disease, and the unkindness, worthiessness, or premature loss of objects of affection. The main stress of the problem lies,

therefore, in the contest with these calamities, from which it is a rare good fortune entirely to escape; which, as things now are, cannot be obviated, and often cannot be in any material degree mitigated. Yet no one whose opinion deserves a moment's consideration can doubt that most of the great positive evils of the world are in themselves removable, and will, if human affairs continue to improve, be in the end reduced within narrow limits. Poverty, in any sense implying suffering, may be completely extinguished by the wisdom of society, combined with the good sense and providence of individuals. Even that most intractable of enemies, disease, may be indefinitely reduced in dimensions by good physical and moral education, and proper control of noxious influences; while the progress of science holds out a promise for the future of still more direct conquests over this detestable foe. And every advance in that direction relieves us from some, not only of the chances which cut short our own lives, but, what concerns us still more, which deprive us of those in whom our happiness is wrapt up. As for vicissitudes of fortune, and other disappointments connected with worldly circumstances, these are principally the effect either of gross imprudence, of ill-regulated desires, or of bad or imperfect social institutions. All the grand sources, in short, of human suffering are in a great degree, many of them almost entirely, conquerable by human care and effort; and though their removal is grievously slow – though a long succession of generations will perish in the breach before the conquest is completed, and this world becomes all that, if will and knowledge were not wanting, it might easily be made – yet every mind sufficiently intelligent and generous to bear a part, however small and unconspicuous, in the endeavour, will draw a noble enjoyment from the contest itself, which he would not for any bribe in the form of selfish indulgence consent to be without.

15. And this leads to the true estimation of what is said by the objectors concerning the possibility, and the obligation, of learning to do without happiness. Unquestionably it is possible to do without happiness; it is done involuntarily by nineteen twentieths of mankind, even in those parts of our present world which are least deep in barbarism; and it often has to be done voluntarily by the hero or the martyr, for the sake of something which he prizes more than his individual happiness. But this something, what is it, unless the happiness of others, or some of the requisites of happiness? It is noble to be capable of resigning entirely one's own portion of happiness, or chances of it; but, after all, this self-sacrifice must be for some end; it is not its own end; and if we are told that its end is not happiness, but virtue, which is better than happiness, I ask, would the sacrifice be made if the hero or martyr did not believe that it would earn for others immunity from similar sacrifices? Would it be made, if he thought that his renunciation of happiness for himself would produce no fruit for any of his fellow creatures, but to make their lot like his, and place them also in the condition of persons who have renounced happiness? All honour to those who can abnegate for themselves the personal enjoyment of life, when by such renunciation they contribute worthily to increase the amount of happiness in the world; but he who does it, or professes to do it, for any other purpose, is no more deserving of admiration than the ascetic mounted on his pillar. He may be an inspiriting proof of what men *can* do, but assuredly not an example of what they *should*.

16. Though it is only in a very imperfect state of the world's arrangements that any one can best serve the happiness of others by the absolute sacrifice of his own, yet so long as the world is in that imperfect state, I fully acknowledge that the readiness to make such a sacrifice is the highest virtue which can be found in man. I will add, that in this condition of the world, paradoxical as the assertion may be, the conscious ability to do without happiness gives the best prospect of realizing such happiness as is attainable. For nothing except that consciousness can raise a person above the chances of life, by making him feel that, let fate and fortune do their worst, they have not power to subdue him: which, once felt, frees him from excess of anxiety concerning the evils of life, and enables him, like many a Stoic in the worst times of the Roman Empire, to cultivate in tranquillity the sources of satisfaction accessible to him, without concerning himself about the uncertainty of their duration, any more than about their inevitable end.

17. Meanwhile, let utilitarians never cease to claim the morality of self-devotion as a possession which belongs by as good a right to them, as either to the Stoic or to the Transcendentalist. The utilitarian morality does recognize in human beings the power of sacrificing their own greatest good for the good of others. It only refuses to admit that the sacrifice is itself a good. A sacrifice which does not increase, or tend to increase, the sum total of happiness, it considers as wasted. The only self-renunciation which it applauds, is devotion to the happiness, or to some of the means of happiness, of others; either of mankind collectively, or of individuals within the limits imposed by the collective interests of mankind.

18. I must again repeat, what the assailants of utilitarianism seldom have the justice to acknowledge, that the happiness which forms the utilitarian standard of what is right in conduct, is not the agent's own happiness, but that of all concerned. As between his own happiness and that of others, utilitarianism requires him to be as strictly impartial

as a disinterested and benevolent spectator. In the golden rule of Jesus of Nazareth, we read the complete spirit of the ethics of utility. To do as one would be done by, and to love one's neighbour as oneself constitute the ideal perfection of utilitarian morality. As the means of making the nearest approach to this ideal, utility would enjoin, first, that laws and social arrangements should place the happiness, or (as speaking practically it may be called) the interest, of every individual, as nearly as possible in harmony with the interest of the whole; and secondly, that education and opinion, which have so vast a power over human character, should so use that power as to establish in the mind of every individual an indissoluble association between his own happiness and the good of the whole; especially between his own happiness and the practice of such modes of conduct, negative and positive, as regard for the universal happiness prescribes: so that not only he may be unable to conceive the possibility of happiness to himself, consistently with conduct opposed to the general good, but also that a direct impulse to promote the general good may be in every individual one of the habitual motives of action, and the sentiments connected therewith may fill a large and prominent place in every human being's sentient existence. If the impugners of the utilitarian morality represented it to their own minds in this its true character, I know not what recommendation possessed by any other morality they could possibly affirm to be wanting to it: what more beautiful or more exalted developments of human nature any other ethical system can be supposed to foster, or what springs of action, not accessible to the utilitarian, such systems rely on for giving effect to their mandates.

19. The objectors to utilitarianism cannot always be charged with representing it in a discreditable light. On the contrary, those among them who entertain anything like a just idea of its disinterested character, sometimes find fault with its standard as being too high for humanity. They say it is exacting too much to require that people shall always act from the inducement of promoting the general interests of society. But this is to mistake the very meaning of a standard of morals, and to confound the rule of action with the motive of it. It is the business of ethics to tell us what are our duties, or by what test we may know them; but no system of ethics requires that the sole motive of all we do shall be a feeling of duty; on the contrary, ninety-nine hundredths of all our actions are done from other motives, and rightly so done, if the rule of duty-does not condemn them. It is the more unjust to utilitarianism that this particular misapprehension should be made a ground of objection to it, inasmuch as utilitarian moralists have gone beyond almost all others in affirming that the motive has nothing to do with the morality of the action, though much with the worth of the agent. He who saves a fellow creature from drowning does what is morally right, whether his motive be duty, or the hope of being paid for his trouble: he who betrays the friend that trusts him, is guilty of a crime, even if his object be to serve another friend to whom he is under greater obligations*. But to speak only of actions done from the motive of duty, and in direct obedience to principle: it is a misapprehension of the utilitarian mode of thought, to conceive it as implying that people should fix their minds upon so wide a generality as the world, or society at large. The great majority of good actions are intended, not for the benefit of the world, but for that of individuals, of which the good of the world is made up: and the thoughts of the most virtuous man need not on these occasions travel beyond the particular persons concerned, except so far as is necessary to assure himself that in benefiting them he is not violating the rights – that is, the legitimate and authorized expectations – of any one else. The multiplication of happiness is, according to the utilitarian ethics, the object of virtue: the occasions on which any person (except one in a thousand) has it in his power to do this on an extended scale, in other words, to be a public benefactor, are but exceptional; and on these occasions alone is he called on to

* An opponent, whose intellectual and moral fairness it is a pleasure to acknowledge (the Rev. J. Llewellyn Davies), has objected to this passage, saying. 'Surely the rightness or wrongness of saving a man from drowning does depend very much upon the motive with which it is done. Suppose that a tyrant, when his enemy jumped into the sea to escape from him, saved him from drowning simply in order that he might inflict upon him more exquisite tortures, would it tend to clearness to speak of that rescue as "a morally right action?" Or suppose again, according to one of the stock illustrations of ethical inquiries, that a man betrayed a trust received from a friend, because the discharge of it would fatally injure that friend himself or some one belonging to him, would utilitarianism compel one to call the betrayal "a crime" as much as if it had been done from the meanest motive?'

I submit, that he who saves another from drowning in order to kill him by torture afterwards, does not differ only in motive from him who does the same thing from duty or benevolence; the act itself is different. The rescue of the man is, in the case supposed, only the necessary first step of an act far more atrocious than leaving him to drown would have been. Had Mr Davies said, 'The rightness or wrongness of saving a man from drowning does depend very much' – not upon the motive, but – 'upon the *intention*,' no utilitarian would have differed from him. Mr Davies, by an oversight too common not to be quite venial, has in this case confounded the very different ideas of Motive and Intention. There is no point which utilitarian thinkers (and Bentham pre-eminently) have taken more pains to illustrate than this. The morality of the action depends entirely upon the intention – that is, upon what the agent *wills to do*. But the motive, chat is, the feeling which makes him will so to do, when it makes no difference in the act, makes none in the morality: though it makes a great difference in our moral estimation of the agent, especially if it indicates a good or a bad habitual *disposition* – a bene of character from which useful, or from which hurtful actions are likely to arise.

consider public utility; in every other case, private utility, the interest or happiness of some few persons, is all he has to attend to. Those alone the influence of whose actions extends to society in general, need concern themselves habitually about so large an object. In the case of abstinences indeed – of things which people forbear to do, from moral considerations, though the consequences in the particular case might be beneficial – it would be unworthy of an intelligent agent not to be consciously aware that the action is of a class which, if practised generally, would be generally injurious, and that this is the ground of the obligation to abstain from it. The amount of regard for the public interest implied in this recognition, is no greater than is demanded by every system of morals, for they all enjoin to abstain from whatever is manifestly pernicious to society.

20. The same considerations dispose of another reproach against the doctrine of utility, founded on a still grosser misconception of the purpose of a standard of morality, and of the very meaning of the words right and wrong. It is often affirmed that utilitarianism renders men cold and unsympathizing; that it chills their moral feelings towards individuals; that it makes them regard only the dry and hard consideration, of the consequences of actions, not taking into their moral estimate the qualities from which those actions emanate. If the assertion means that they do not allow their judgment respecting the rightness or wrongness of an action to be influenced by their opinion of the qualities of the person who does it, this is a complaint not against utilitarianism, but against having any standard of morality at all; for certainly no known ethical standard decides an action to be good or bad because it is done by a good or a bad man, still less because done by an amiable, a brave, or a benevolent man, or the contrary. These considerations are relevant, not to the estimation of actions, but of persons; and there is nothing in the utilitarian theory inconsistent with the fact that there are other things which interest us in persons besides the rightness and wrongness of their actions. The Stoics, indeed, with the paradoxical misuse of language which was part of their system, and by which they strove to raise themselves above all concern about anything but virtue, were fond of saying that he who has that has everything; that he, and only he, is rich, is beautiful, is a king. But no claim of this description is made for the virtuous man by the utilitarian doctrine. Utilitarians are quite aware that there are other desirable possessions and qualities besides virtue, and are perfectly willing to allow to all of them their full worth. They are also aware, that a right action does not necessarily indicate a virtuous character, and that actions which are blameable often proceed from qualities entitled to praise. When this is apparent in any particular case, it modifies their estimation, not certainly of the act, but of the agent. I grant that they are, notwithstanding, of opinion, that in the long run the best proof of a good character is good actions; and resolutely refuse to consider any mental disposition as good, of which the predominant tendency is to produce bad conduct. This makes them unpopular with many people; but it is an unpopularity which they must share with every one who regards the distinction between right and wrong in a serious light; and the reproach is not one which a conscientious utilitarian need be anxious to repel.

21. If no more be meant by the objection than that many utilitarians look on the morality of actions, as measured by the utilitarian standard, with too exclusive a regard, and do not lay sufficient stress upon the other beauties of character which go towards making a human being lovable or admirable, this may be admitted. Utilitarians who have cultivated their moral feelings, but not their sympathies nor their artistic perceptions, do fall into this mistake; and so do all other moralists under the same conditions. What can be said in excuse for other moralists is equally available for them, namely, that if there is to be any error, it is better that it should be on that side. As a matter of fact, we may affirm that among utilitarians as among adherents of other systems, there is every imaginable degree of rigidity and of laxity in the application of their standard: some are even puritanically rigorous, while others are as indulgent as can possibly be desired by sinner or by sentimentalist. But on the whole, a doctrine which brings prominently forward the interest that mankind have in the repression and prevention of conduct which violates the moral law, is likely to be inferior to no other in turning the sanctions of opinion against such violations. It is true, the question, What does violate the moral law? is one on which those who recognize different standards of morality are likely now and then to differ. But difference of opinion on moral questions was not first introduced into the world by utilitarianism, while that doctrine does supply, if not always an easy, at all events a tangible and intelligible mode of deciding such differences.

22. It may not be superfluous to notice a few more of the common misapprehensions of utilitarian ethics, even those which are so obvious and gross that it might appear impossible for any person of candour and intelligence to fall into them: since persons, even of considerable mental endowments, often give themselves so little trouble to understand the bearings of any opinion against which they entertain a prejudice, and men are in general so little conscious of this voluntary ignorance as a defect, that the vulgarest misunderstandings of ethical doctrines are continually met with in the deliberate writings of persons of the greatest pretensions both to high principle and

to philosophy. We not uncommonly hear the doctrine of utility inveighed against as a *godless* doctrine. If it be necessary to say anything at all against so mere an assumption, we may say that the question depends upon what idea we have formed of the moral character of the Deity. If it be a true belief that God desires, above all things, the happiness of his creatures, and that this was his purpose in their creation, utility is not only not a godless doctrine, but more profoundly religious than any other. If it be meant that utilitarianism does not recognize the revealed will of God as the supreme law of morals, I answer, that an utilitarian who believes in the perfect goodness and wisdom of God, necessarily believes that whatever God has thought fit to reveal on the subject of morals, must fulfil the requirements of utility in a supreme degree. But others besides utilitarians have been of opinion that the Christian revelation was intended, and is fitted, to inform the hearts and minds of mankind with a spirit which should enable them to find for themselves what is right, and incline them to do it when found, rather than to tell them, except in a very general way, what it is: and that we need a doctrine of ethics, carefully followed out, to *interpret* to us the will of God. Whether this opinion is correct or not, it is superfluous here to discuss; since whatever aid religion, either natural or revealed, can afford to ethical investigation, is as open to the utilitarian moralist as to any other. He can use it as the testimony of God to the usefulness or hurtfulness of any given course of action, by as good a right as others can use it for the indication of a transcendental law, having no connexion with usefulness or with happiness.

23. Again, Utility is often summarily stigmatized as an immoral doctrine by giving it the name of Expediency, and taking advantage of the popular use of that term to contrast it with Principle. But the Expedient, in the sense in which it is opposed to the Right, generally means that which is expedient for the particular interest of the agent himself; as when a minister sacrifices the interest of his country to keep himself in place. When it means anything better than this, it means that which is expedient for some immediate object, some temporary purpose, but which violates a rule whose observance is expedient in a much higher degree. The Expedient, in this sense, instead of being the same thing with the useful, is a branch of the hurtful. Thus, it would often be expedient, for the purpose of getting over some momentary embarrassment, or attaining some object immediately useful to ourselves or others, to tell a lie. But inasmuch as the cultivation in ourselves of a sensitive feeling on the subject of veracity, is one of the most useful, and the enfeeblement of that feeling one of the most hurtful, things to which our conduct can be instrumental; and inasmuch as any, even unintentional, deviation from truth does that much towards weakening the trustworthiness of human assertion, which is not only the principal support of all present social well-being, but the insufficiency of which does more than any one thing that can be named to keep back civilization, virtue, everything on which human happiness on the largest scale depends; we feel that the violation, for a present advantage, of a rule of such transcendent expediency, is not expedient, and that he who, for the sake of a convenience to himself or to some other individual, does what depends on him to deprive mankind of the good, and inflict upon them the evil, involved in the greater or less reliance which they can place, in each other's word, acts the part of one of their worst enemies. Yet that even this rule, sacred as it is, admits of possible exceptions, is acknowledged by all moralists; the chief of which is when the withholding of some fact (as of information from a malefactor, or of bad news from a person dangerously ill) would preserve some one (especially a person other than oneself) from great and unmerited evil, and when the withholding can only be effected by denial. But in order that the exception may not extend itself beyond the need, and may have the least possible effect in weakening reliance on veracity, it ought to be recognised, and, if possible, its limits defined; and if the principle of utility is good for anything, it must be good for weighing these conflicting utilities against one another, and marking out the region within which one or the other preponderates.

24. Again, defenders of utility often find themselves called upon to reply to such objections as this – that there is not time, previous to action, for calculating and weighing the effects of any line of conduct on the general happiness. This is exactly as if any one were to say that it is impossible to guide our conduct by Christianity, because there is not time, on every occasion on which anything has to be done, to read through the Old and New Testaments. The answer to the objection is, that there has been ample time, namely, the whole past duration of the human species. During all that time mankind have been learning by experience the tendencies of actions; on which experience all the prudence, as well as all the morality of life, is dependent. People talk as if the commencement of this course of experience had hitherto been put off, and as if, at the moment when some man feels tempted to meddle with the property or life of another, he had to begin considering for the first time whether murder and theft are injurious to human happiness. Even then I do not think that he would find the question very puzzling, but, at all events, the matter is now done to his hand. It is truly a whimsical supposition that if mankind were agreed in considering utility to be the test of morality, they would remain without any agreement as to what *is* useful, and would

take no measures for having their notions on the subject taught to the young, and enforced by law and opinion. There is no difficulty in proving any ethical standard whatever to work ill, if we suppose universal idiocy to be conjoined with it; but on any hypothesis short of that, mankind must by this time have acquired positive beliefs as to the effects of some actions on their happiness; and the beliefs which have thus come down are the rules of morality for the multitude, and for the philosopher until he has succeeded in finding better. That philosophers might easily do this, even now, on many subjects; that the received code of ethics is by no means of divine right; and that mankind have still much to learn as to the effects of actions on the general happiness, I admit, or rather, earnestly maintain. The corollaries from the principle of utility, like the precepts of every practical art, admit of indefinite improvement, and, in a progressive state of human mind, their improvement is perpetually going on. But to consider the rules of morality as improvable, is one thing; to pass over the intermediate generalizations entirely, and endeavour to test each individual action directly by the first principle, is another. It is a strange notion that the acknowledgment of a first principle is inconsistent with the admission of secondary ones. To inform a traveller respecting the place of his ultimate destination, is not to forbid the use of landmarks and direction-posts on the way. The proposition that happiness is the end and aim of morality, does not mean that no road ought to be laid down to that goal, or that persons going thither should not be advised to take one direction rather than another. Men really ought to leave off talking a kind of nonsense on this subject, which they would neither talk nor listen to on other matters of practical concernment. Nobody argues that the art of navigation is not founded on astronomy, because sailors cannot wait to calculate the Nautical Almanack. Being rational creatures, they go to sea with it ready calculated; and all rational creatures go out upon the sea of life with their minds made up on the common questions of right and wrong, as well as on many of the far more difficult questions of wise and foolish. And this, as long as foresight is a human quality, it is to be presumed they will continue to do. Whatever we adopt as the fundamental principle of morality, we require subordinate principles to apply it by: the impossibility of doing without them, being common to all systems, can afford no argument against any one in particular: but gravely to argue as if no such secondary principles could be had, and as if mankind had remained till now, and always must remain, without drawing any general conclusions from the experience of human life, is as high a pitch, I think, as absurdity has ever reached in philosophical controversy.

25. The remainder of the stock arguments against utilitarianism mostly consist in laying to its charge the common infirmities of human nature, and the general difficulties which embarrass conscientious persons in shaping their course through life. We are told that an utilitarian will be apt to make his own particular case an exception to moral rules, and, when under temptation, will see an utility in the breach of a rule, greater than he will see in its observance. But is utility the only creed which is able to furnish us with excuses for evil doing, and means of cheating our own conscience? They are afforded in abundance by all doctrines which recognize as a fact in morals the existence of conflicting considerations; which all doctrines do, that have been believed by sane persons. It is not the fault of any creed, but of the complicated nature of human affairs, that rules of conduct cannot be so framed as to require no exceptions, and that hardly any kind of action can safely be laid down as either always obligatory or always condemnable. There is no ethical creed which does not temper the rigidity of its laws, by giving a certain latitude, under the moral responsibility of the agent, for accommodation to peculiarities of circumstances; and under every creed, at the opening thus made, self-deception and dishonest casuistry get in. There exists no moral system under which there do not arise unequivocal cases of conflicting obligation. These are the real difficulties, the knotty points both in the theory of ethics, and in the conscientious guidance of personal conduct. They are overcome practically with greater or with less success according to the intellect and virtue of the individual; but it can hardly be pretended that anyone will be the less qualified for dealing with them, from possessing an ultimate standard to which conflicting rights and duties can be referred. If utility is the ultimate source of moral obligations, utility may be invoked to decide between them when their demands are incompatible. Though the application of the standard may be difficult, it is better than none at all: while in other systems, the moral laws all claiming independent authority, there is no common umpire entitled to interfere between them; their claims to precedence one over another rest on little better than sophistry, and unless determined, as they generally are, by the unacknowledged influence of considerations of utility, afford a free scope for the actions of personal desires and partialities. We must remember that only in these cases of conflict between secondary principles is it requisite that first principles should be appealed to. There is no case of moral obligation in which some secondary principle is not involved; and if only one, there can seldom be any real doubt which one it is in the mind of any person by whom the principle itself is recognized.

[…]

4

Of What Sort of Proof the Principle of Utility Is Susceptible

1. […] questions of ultimate ends do not admit of proof, in the ordinary acceptation of the term. To be incapable of proof by reasoning is common to all first principles; to the first premises of our knowledge, as well as to those of our conduct. But the former, being matters of fact, may be the subject of a direct appeal to the faculties which judge of fact – namely, our senses, and our internal consciousness. Can an appeal be made to the same faculties on questions of practical ends? Or by what other faculty is cognizance taken of them?

2. Questions about ends are, in other words, questions what things are desirable. The utilitarian doctrine is, that happiness is desirable, and the only thing desirable, as an end; all other things being only desirable as means to that end. What ought to be required of this doctrine – what conditions is it requisite that the doctrine should fulfil – to make good its claim to be believed?

3. The only proof capable of being given that an object is visible, is that people actually see it. The only proof that a sound is audible, is that people hear it: and so of the other sources of our experience. In like manner, I apprehend, the sole evidence it is possible to produce that anything is desirable, is that people do actually desire it. If the end which the utilitarian doctrine proposes to itself were not, in theory and in practice, acknowledged to be an end, nothing could ever convince any person that it was so. No reason can be given why the general happiness is desirable, except that each person, so far as he believes it to be attainable, desires his own happiness. This, however, being a fact, we have not only all the proof which the case admits of, but all which it is possible to require, that happiness is a good: that each person's happiness is a good to that person, and the general happiness, therefore, a good to the aggregate of all persons. Happiness has made out its title as *one* of the ends of conduct, and consequently one of the criteria of morality.

4. But it has not, by this alone, proved itself to be the sole criterion. To do that, it would seem, by the same rule, necessary to show, not only that people desire happiness, but that they never desire anything else. Now it is palpable that they do desire things which, in common language, are decidedly distinguished from happiness. They desire, for example, virtue and the absence of vice, no less really than pleasure and the absence of pain. The desire of virtue is not as universal, but it is as authentic a fact, as the desire of happiness. And hence the opponents of the utilitarian standard deem that they have a right to infer that there are other ends of human action besides happiness, and that happiness is not the standard of approbation and disapprobation.

5. But does the utilitarian doctrine deny that people desire virtue, or maintain that virtue is not a thing to be desired? The very reverse. It maintains not only that virtue is to be desired, but that it is to be desired disinterestedly, for itself. Whatever may be the opinion of utilitarian moralists as to the original conditions by which virtue is made virtue; however they may believe (as they do) that actions and dispositions are only virtuous because they promote another end than virtue; yet this being granted, and it having been decided, from considerations of this description, what *is* virtuous, they not only place virtue at the very head of the things which are good as means to the ultimate end, but they also recognize as a psychological fact the possibility of its being, to the individual, a good in itself, without looking to any end beyond it; and hold, that the mind is not in a right state, not in a state conformable to Utility, not in the state most conducive to the general happiness, unless it does love virtue in this manner – as a thing desirable in itself, even although, in the individual instance, it should not produce those other desirable consequences which it tends to produce, and on account of which it is held to be virtue. This opinion is not, in the smallest degree, a departure from the Happiness principle. The ingredients of happiness are very various, and each of them is desirable in itself, and not merely when considered as swelling an aggregate. The principle of utility does not mean that any given pleasure, as music, for instance, or any given exemption from pain, as for example health, are to be looked upon as means to a collective something termed happiness, and to be desired on that account. They are desired and desirable in and for themselves; besides being means, they are a part of the end. Virtue, according to the utilitarian doctrine, is not naturally and originally part of the end, but it is capable of becoming so; and is desired and cherished, not as a means to happiness, but as a part of their happiness.

6. To illustrate this farther, we may remember that virtue is not the only thing, originally a means, and which if it were not a means to anything else, would be and remain indifferent, but which by association with what it is a means to, comes to be desired for itself, and that too with the utmost intensity. What, for example, shall we say of the love of money? There is nothing originally more desirable about money than about any heap of glittering

pebbles. Its worth is solely that of the things which it will buy; the desires for other things than itself, which it is a means of gratifying. Yet the love of money is not only one of the strongest moving forces of human life, but money is, in many cases, desired in and for itself; the desire to possess it is often stronger than the desire to use it, and goes on increasing when all the desires which point to ends beyond it, to be compassed by it, are falling off. It may be then said truly, that money is desired not for the sake of an end, but as part of the end. From being a means to happiness, it has come to be itself a principal ingredient of the individual's conception of happiness. The same may be said of the majority of the great objects of human life – power, for example, or fame; except that to each of these there is a certain amount of immediate pleasure annexed, which has at least the semblance of being naturally inherent in them; a thing which cannot be said of money. Still, however, the strongest natural attraction, both of power and of fame, is the immense aid they give to the attainment of our other wishes; and it is the strong association thus generated between them and all our objects of desire, which gives to the direct desire of them the intensity it often assumes, so as in some characters to surpass in strength all other desires. In these cases the means have become a part of the end, and a more important part of it than any of the things which they are means to. What was once desired as an instrument for the attainment of happiness, has come to be desired for its own sake. In being desired for its own sake it is, however, desired as *part* of happiness. The person is made, or thinks he would be made, happy by its mere possession; and is made unhappy by failure to obtain it. The desire of it is not a different thing from the desire of happiness, any more than the love of music, or the desire of health. They are included in happiness. They are some of the elements of which the desire of happiness is made up. Happiness is not an abstract idea, but a concrete whole; and these are some of its parts. And the utilitarian standard sanctions and approves their being so. Life would be a poor thing, very ill provided with sources of happiness, if there were not this provision of nature, by which things originally indifferent, but conducive to, or otherwise associated with, the satisfaction of our primitive desires, become in themselves sources of pleasure more valuable than the primitive pleasures, both in permanency, in the space of human existence that they are capable of covering, and even in intensity.

7. Virtue, according to the utilitarian conception, is a good of this description. There was no original desire of it, or motive to it, save its conduciveness to pleasure, and especially to protection from pain. But through the association thus formed, it may be felt a good in itself, and desired as such with as great intensity as any other good; and with this difference between it and the love of money, of power, or of fame, that all of these may, and often do, render the individual noxious to the other members of the society to which he belongs, whereas there is nothing which makes him so much a blessing to them as the cultivation of the disinterested love of virtue. And consequently, the utilitarian standard, while it tolerates and approves those other acquired desires, up to the point beyond which they would be more injurious to the general happiness than promotive of it, enjoins and requires the cultivation of the love of virtue up to the greatest strength possible, as being above all things important to the general happiness.

8. It results from the preceding considerations, that there is in reality nothing desired except happiness. Whatever is desired otherwise than as a means to some end beyond itself, and ultimately to happiness, is desired as itself a part of happiness, and is not desired for itself until it has become so. Those who desire virtue for its own sake, desire it either because the consciousness of it is a pleasure, or because the consciousness of being without it is a pain, or for both reasons united; as in truth the pleasure and pain seldom exist separately, but almost always together, the same person feeling pleasure in the degree of virtue attained, and pain in not having attained more. If one of these gave him no pleasure, and the other no pain, he would not love or desire virtue, or would desire it only for the other benefits which it might produce to himself or to persons whom he cared for.

9. We have now, then, an answer to the question, of what sort of proof the principle of utility is susceptible. If the opinion which I have now stated is psychologically true – if human nature is so constituted as to desire nothing which is not either a part of happiness or a means of happiness, we can have no other proof, and we require no other, that these are the only things desirable. If so, happiness is the sole end of human action, and the promotion of it the test by which to judge of all human conduct; from whence it necessarily follows that it must be the criterion of morality, since a part is included in the whole.

10. And now to decide whether this is really so; whether mankind do desire nothing for itself but that which is a pleasure to them, or of which the absence is a pain; we have evidently arrived at a question of fact and experience, dependent, like all similar questions, upon evidence. It can only be determined by practised self-consciousness and self-observation, assisted by observation of others. I believe that these sources of evidence, impartially consulted, will declare that desiring a thing and finding it pleasant, aversion to it and thinking of it as painful, are phenomena entirely inseparable, or rather two parts of the same phenomenon; in strictness of language, two different modes of

naming the same psychological fact: that to think of an object as desirable (unless for the sake of its consequences), and to think of it as pleasant are one and the same thing; and that to desire anything, except in proportion as the idea of it is pleasant, is a physical and metaphysical impossibility.

5

On the Connexion Between Justice and Utility

1. In all ages of speculation, one of the strongest obstacles to the reception of the doctrine that Utility or Happiness is the criterion of right and wrong, has been drawn from the idea of Justice. The powerful sentiment, and apparently clear perception, which that word recalls with a rapidity and certainty resembling an instinct, have seemed to the majority of thinkers to point to an inherent quality in things; to show that the Just must have an existence in Nature as something absolute – generically distinct from every variety of the Expedient, and, in idea, opposed to it, though (as is commonly acknowledged) never, in the long run, disjoined from it in fact.

2. In the case of this, as of our other moral sentiments, there is no necessary connexion between the question of its origin, and that of its binding force. That a feeling is bestowed on us by Nature, does not necessarily legitimate all its promptings. The feeling of justice might be a peculiar instinct, and might yet require, like our other instincts, to be controlled and enlightened by a higher reason. If we have intellectual instincts, leading us to judge in a particular way, as well as animal instincts that prompt us to act in a particular way, there is no necessity that the former should be more infallible in their sphere than the latter in theirs: it may as well happen that wrong judgments are occasionally suggested by those, as wrong actions by these. But though it is one thing to believe that we have natural feelings of justice, and another to acknowledge them as an ultimate criterion of conduct, these two opinions are very closely connected in point of fact. Mankind are always predisposed to believe that any subjective feeling, not otherwise accounted for, is a revelation of some objective reality. Our present object is to determine whether the reality, to which the feeling of justice corresponds, is one which needs any such special revelation; whether the justice or injustice of an action is a thing intrinsically peculiar, and distinct from all its other qualities, or only a combination of certain of those qualities, presented under a peculiar aspect. For the purpose of this inquiry, it is practically important to consider whether the feeling itself, of justice and injustice, is *sui generis* like our sensations of colour and taste, or a derivative feeling, formed by a combination of others. And this it is the more essential to examine, as people are in general willing enough to allow, that objectively the dictates of justice coincide with a part of the field of General Expediency; but inasmuch as the subjective mental feeling of Justice is different from that which commonly attaches to simple expediency, and, except in extreme cases of the latter, is far more imperative in its demands, people find it difficult to see, in Justice, only a particular kind or branch of general utility, and think that its superior binding force requires a totally different origin.

3. To throw light upon this question, it is necessary to attempt to ascertain what is the distinguishing character of justice, or of injustice: what is the quality, or whether there is any quality, attributed in common to all modes of conduct designated as unjust (for justice, like many other moral attributes, is best defined by its opposite), and distinguishing them from such modes of conduct as are disapproved, but without having that particular epithet of disapprobation applied to them. If, in everything which men are accustomed to characterize, as just or injust, some, one common attribute or collection of attributes is always present, we may judge whether this particular attribute or combination of attributes would be capable of gathering round it a sentiment of that peculiar character and intensity by virtue of the general laws of our emotional constitution, or whether the sentiment is inexplicable, and requires to be regarded as a special provision of Nature. If we find the former to be the case, we shall, in resolving this question, have resolved also the main problem: if the latter, we shall have to seek for some other mode of investigating it.

4. To find the common attributes of a variety of objects, it is necessary to begin by surveying the objects themselves in the concrete. Let us therefore advert successively to the various modes of action, and arrangements of human affairs, which are classed, by universal or widely spread opinion, as Just or as Unjust. The things well known to excite the sentiments associated with those names, are of a very multifarious character. I shall pass them rapidly in review, without studying any particular arrangement.

5. In the first place, it is mostly considered unjust to deprive any one of his personal liberty, his property, or any other thing which belongs to him by law. Here, therefore, is one instance of the application of the terms just and unjust in a perfectly definite sense, namely, that it is just to respect, unjust to violate, the *legal rights* of anyone.

But this judgment admits of several exceptions, arising from the other forms in which the notions of justice and injustice present themselves. For example, the person who suffers the deprivation may (as the phrase is) have *forfeited* the rights which he is so deprived of: a case to which we shall return presently. But, also,

6. Secondly; the legal rights of which he is deprived, may be rights which *ought* not to have belonged to him; in other words, the law winch confers on him these rights, may be a bad law. When it is so, or when (which is the same thing for our purpose) it is supposed to be so, opinions will differ as to the justice or injustice of infringing it. Some maintain that no law, however bad, ought to be disobeyed by an individual citizen: that his opposition to it, if shown at all, should only be shown in endeavouring to get it altered by competent authority. This opinion (which condemns many of the most illustrious benefactors of mankind, and would often protect pernicious institutions against the only weapons which, in the state of things existing at the time, have any chance of succeeding against them) is defended by those who hold it, on grounds of expediency; principally on that of the importance, to the common interest of mankind, of maintaining inviolate the sentiment of submission to law. Other persons, again, hold the directly contrary opinion, that any law, judged to be bad, may blamelessly be disobeyed, even though it be not judged to be unjust, but only inexpedient; while others would confine the licence of disobedience to the case of unjust laws: but again, some say, that all laws which are inexpedient are unjust; since every law imposes some restriction on the natural liberty of mankind, which restriction is an injustice, unless legitimated by tending to their good. Among these diversities of opinion, it seems to be universally admitted that there may be unjust laws, and that law, consequently, is not the ultimate criterion of justice, but may give to one person a benefit, or impose on another an evil, which justice condemns. When, however, a law is thought to be unjust, it seems always to be regarded as being so in the same way in which a breach of law is unjust, namely, by infringing somebody's right; which, as it cannot in this case be a legal right, receives a different appellation, and is called a moral right. We may say, therefore, that a second case of injustice consists in taking or withholding from any person that to which he has a *moral right*.

7. Thirdly, it is universally considered just that each person should obtain that (whether good or evil) which he *deserves*; and unjust that he should obtain a good, or be made to undergo an evil, which he does not deserve. This is, perhaps, the clearest and most emphatic form in which the idea of injustice is conceived by the general mind. As it involves the notion of desert, the question arises, what constitutes desert? Speaking in a general way, a person is understood to deserve good if he does right, evil if he does wrong; and in a more particular sense, to deserve good from those to whom he does or has done good, and evil from those to whom he does or has done evil. The precept of returning good for evil has never been regarded as a case of the fulfilment of justice, but as one in which the claims of justice are waved, in obedience to other considerations.

8. Fourthly, it is confessedly unjust to *break faith* with any one: to violate an engagement, either express or implied, or disappoint expectations raised by our own conduct, at least if we have raised those expectations knowingly and voluntarily. Like the other obligations of justice already spoken of, this one is not regarded as absolute, but as capable of being overruled by a stronger obligation of justice on the other side; or by such conduct on the part of the person concerned as is deemed to absolve us from our obligation to him, and to constitute a *forfeiture* of the benefit which he has been led to expect.

9. Fifthly, it is, by universal admission, inconsistent with justice to be *partial*; to show favour or preference to one person over another, in matters to which favour and preference do not properly apply. Impartiality, however, does not seem to be regarded as a duty in itself, but rather as instrumental to some other duty; for it is admitted that favour and preference are not always censurable, and indeed the cases in which they are condemned are rather the exception than the rule. A person would be more likely to be blamed than applauded for giving his family or friends no superiority in good offices over strangers, when he could do so without violating any other duty; and no one thinks it unjust to seek one person in preference to another as a friend, connexion, or companion. Impartiality where rights are concerned is of course obligatory, but this is involved in the more general obligation of giving to every one his right. A tribunal, for example, must be impartial, because it is bound to award, without regard to any other consideration, a disputed object to the one of two parties who has the right to it. There are other cases in which impartiality means, being solely influenced by desert; as with those who, in the capacity of judges, preceptors, or parents, administer reward and punishment as such. There are cases, again, in which it means, being solely influenced by consideration for the public interest; as in making a selection among candidates for a government employment. Impartiality, in short, as an obligation of justice, may be said to mean, being exclusively influenced by the considerations which it is supposed ought to influence the particular case in hand; and resisting the solicitation of any motives which prompt to conduct different from what those considerations would dictate.

10. Nearly allied to the idea of impartiality, is that of *equality*; which often enters as a component part both into the conception of justice and into the practice of it, and, in the eyes of many persons, constitutes its essence. But in this, still more than in any other case, the notion of justice varies in different persons, and always conforms in its variations to their notion of utility. Each person maintains that equality is the dictate of justice, except where he thinks that expediency requires inequality. The justice of giving equal protection to the rights of all, is maintained by those who support the most outrageous inequality in the rights themselves. Even in slave countries it is theoretically admitted that the rights of the slave, such as they are, ought to be as sacred as those of the master; and that a tribunal which fails to enforce them with equal strictness is wanting in justice; while, at the same time, institutions which leave to the slave scarcely any rights to enforce, are not deemed unjust, because they are not deemed inexpedient. Those who think that utility requires distinctions of rank, do not consider it unjust that riches and social privileges should be unequally dispensed; but those who think this inequality inexpedient, think it unjust also. Whoever thinks that government is necessary, sees no injustice in as much inequality as is constituted by giving to the magistrate powers not granted to other people. Even among those who hold levelling doctrines, there are as many questions of justice as there are differences of opinion about expediency. Some Communists consider it unjust that the produce of the labour of the community should be shared on any other principle than that of exact equality; others think it just that those should receive most whose needs are greatest; while others hold that those who work harder, or who produce more, or whose services are more valuable to the community, may justly claim a larger quota in the division of the produce. And the sense of natural justice may be plausibly appealed to on behalf of every one of these opinions.

11. Among so many diverse applications of the term Justice, which yet is not regarded as ambiguous, it is a matter of some difficulty to seize the mental link which holds them together, and on which the moral sentiment adhering to the term essentially depends. Perhaps, in this embarrassment, some help may be derived from the history of the word, as indicated by its etymology.

12. In most, if not in all, languages, the etymology of the word which corresponds to Just, points to an origin connected either with positive law, or with that which was in most cases the primitive form of law – authoritative custom. *Justum* is a form of *jussum*, that which has been ordered. *Jus* is of the same origin. Δίκαιον comes from δίκη, of which the principal meaning, at least in the historical ages of Greece, was a suit at law. Originally, indeed, it meant only the mode or *manner* of doing things, but it early came to mean the *prescribed* manner; that which the recognized authorities, patriarchal, judicial, or political, would enforce. *Recht*, from which came *right*, and *righteous*, is synonymous with law. The original meaning indeed of *rech!* did not point to law, but to physical straightness; as *wrong* and its Latin equivalents meant twisted or *tortuous*; and from this it is argued that right did not originally mean law, but on the contrary law meant right. But however this may be, the fact that *recht* and *droit* became restricted in their meaning to positive law although much which is not required by law is equally necessary to moral straightness or rectitude, is as significant of the original character of moral ideas as if the derivation had been the reverse way. The courts of justice, the administration of justice, are the courts and the administration of law. *La justice*, in French, is the established term for judicature. There can, I think, be no doubt that the *idée mère*, the primitive element, in the formation of the notion of justice, was conformity to law. It constituted the entire idea among the Hebrews, up to the birth of Christianity; as might be expected in the case of a people whose laws attempted to embrace all subjects on which precepts were required, and who believed those laws to be a direct emanation from the Supreme Being. But other nations, and in particular the Greeks and Romans, who knew that their laws had been made originally, and still continued to be made, by men, were not afraid to admit that those men might make bad laws; might do, by law, the same things, and from the same motives, which, if done by individuals without the sanction of law, would be called unjust. And hence the sentiment of injustice came to be attached, not to all violations of law, but only to violations of such laws as *ought* to exist, including such as ought to exist but do not; and to laws themselves, if supposed to be contrary to what ought to be law. In this manner the idea of law and of its injunctions was still predominant in the notion of justice, even when the laws actually in force ceased to be accepted as the standard of it.

13. It is true that mankind consider the idea of justice and its obligations as applicable to many things which neither are, nor is it desired that they should be, regulated by law. Nobody desires that laws should interfere with the whole detail of private life; yet every one allows that in all daily conduct a person may and does show himself to be either just or unjust. But even here, the idea of the breach of what ought to be law, still lingers in a modified shape. It would always give us pleasure, and chime in with our feelings of fitness, that acts which we deem unjust should be punished, though we do not always think it expedient that this should be done by the tribunals. We forego that gratification on account of incidental inconveniences. We should be glad to see just conduct enforced

and injustice repressed, even in the minutest details, if we were not, with reason, afraid of trusting the magistrate with so unlimited an amount of power over individuals. When we think that a person is bound in justice to do a thing, it is an ordinary form of language to say, that he ought to be compelled to do it. We should be gratified to see the obligation enforced by anybody who had the power. If we see that its enforcement by law would be inexpedient, we lament the impossibility, we consider the impunity given to injustice as an evil, and strive to make amends for it by bringing a strong expression of our own and the public disapprobation to bear upon the offender. Thus the idea of legal constraint is still the generating idea of the notion of justice, though undergoing several transformations before that notion, as it exists in an advanced state of society, becomes complete.

14. The above is, I think, a true account, as far as it goes, of the origin and progressive growth of the idea of justice. But we must observe, that it contains, as yet, nothing to distinguish that obligation from moral obligation in general. For the truth is, that the idea of penal sanction, which is the essence of law, enters not only into the conception of injustice, but into that of any kind of wrong. We do not call anything wrong, unless we mean to imply that a person ought to be punished in some way or other for doing it; if not by law, by the opinion of his fellow creatures; if not by opinion, by the reproaches of his own conscience. This seems the real turning point of the distinction between morality and simple expediency. It is a part of the notion of Duty in every one of its forms, that a person may rightfully be compelled to fulfil it. Duty is a thing which may be *exacted* from a person, as one exacts a debt. Unless we think that it might be exacted from him, we do not call it his duty. Reasons of prudence, or the interest of other people, may militate against actually exacting it; but the person himself, it is clearly understood, would not be entitled to complain. There are other things, on the contrary, which we wish that people should do, which we like or admire them for doing, perhaps dislike or despise them for not doing, but yet admit that they are not bound to do; it is not a case of moral obligation; we do not blame them, that is, we do not think that they are proper objects of punishment. How we come by these ideas of deserving and not deserving punishment, will appear, perhaps, in the sequel; but I think there is no doubt that this distinction lies at the bottom of the notions of right and wrong; that we call any conduct wrong, or employ, instead, some other term of dislike or disparagement, according as we think that the person ought, or ought not, to be punished for it; and we say that it would be right to do so and so, or merely that it would be desirable or laudable, according as we would wish to see the person whom it concerns, compelled, or only persuaded and exhorted, to act in that manner.*

15. This, therefore, being the characteristic difference which marks off, not justice, but morality in general, from the remaining provinces of Expediency and Worthiness; the character is still to be sought which distinguishes justice from other branches of morality. Now it is known that ethical writers divide moral duties into two classes, denoted by the ill-chosen expressions, duties of perfect and of imperfect obligation; the latter being those in which, though the act is obligatory, the particular occasions of performing it are left to our choice; as in the case of charity or beneficence, which we are indeed bound to practise, but not towards any definite person, nor at any prescribed time. In the more precise language of philosophic jurists, duties of perfect obligation are those duties in virtue of which a correlative *right* resides in some person or persons; duties of imperfect obligation are those moral obligations which do not give birth to any right. I think it will be found that this distinction exactly coincides with that which exists between justice and the other obligations of morality. In our survey of the various popular acceptations of justice, the term appeared generally to involve the idea of a personal right – a claim on the part of one or more individuals, like that which the law gives when it confers a proprietary or other legal right. Whether the injustice consists in depriving a person of a possession, or in breaking faith with him, or in treating him worse than he deserves, or worse than other people who have no greater claims, in each case the supposition implies two things – a wrong done, and some assignable person who is wronged. Injustice may also be done by treating a person better than others; but the wrong in this case is to his competitors, who are also assignable persons. It seems to me that this feature in the case – a right in some person, correlative to the moral obligation – constitutes the specific difference between justice, and generosity or beneficence. Justice implies something which it is not only right to do, and wrong not to do, but which some individual person can claim from us as his moral right. No one has a moral right to our generosity or beneficence, because we are not morally bound to practise those virtues towards any given individual. And it will be found with respect to this as with respect to every correct definition, that the instances which seem to conflict with it are those which most confirm it. For if a moralist attempts, as some have done, to

---

* See this point enforced and illustrated by Professor Bain in an admirable chapter (entitled 'The Ethical Emotions, or the Moral Sense'), of the second of the two treatises composing his elaborate and profound work on the Mind.

make out that mankind generally, though not any given individual, have a right to all the good we can do them, he at once, by that thesis, includes generosity and beneficence within the category of justice. He is obliged to say, that our utmost exertions are *due* to our fellow creatures, thus assimilating them to a debt; or that nothing less can be a sufficient *return* for what society does for us, thus classing the case as one of gratitude; both of which are acknowledged cases of justice. Wherever there is a right, the case is one of justice, and not of the virtue of beneficence: and whoever does not place the distinction between justice and morality in general where we have now placed it, will be found to make no distinction between them at all, but to merge all morality in justice.

16. Having thus endeavoured to determine the distinctive elements which enter into the composition of the idea of justice, we are ready to enter on the inquiry, whether the feeling, which accompanies the idea, is attached to it by a special dispensation of nature, or whether it could have grown up, by any known laws, out of the idea itself, and in particular, whether it can have originated in considerations of general expediency.

17. I conceive that the sentiment itself does not arise from anything which would commonly, or correctly, be termed an idea of expediency; but that though, the sentiment does not, whatever is moral in it does.

18. We have seen that the two essential ingredients in the sentiment of justice are, the desire to punish a person who has done harm, and the knowledge or belief that there is some definite individual or individuals to whom harm has been done.

19. Now it appears to me, that the desire to punish a person who has done harm to some individual, is a spontaneous outgrowth from two sentiments, both in the highest degree natural, and which either are or resemble instincts; the impulse of self-defence, and the feeling of sympathy.

20. It is natural to resent, and to repel or retaliate, any harm done or attempted against ourselves, or against those with whom we sympathize. The origin of this sentiment it is not necessary here to discuss. Whether it be an instinct or a result of intelligence, it is, we know, common to all animal nature; for every animal tries to hurt those who have hurt, or who it thinks are about to hurt, itself or its young. Human beings, in this point, only differ from other animals in two particulars. First, in being capable of sympathizing, not solely with their offspring, or, like some of the more noble animals, with some superior animal who is kind to them, but with all human, and even with all sentient, beings. Secondly, in having a more developed intelligence, which gives a wider range to the whole of their sentiments, whether self-regarding or sympathetic. By virtue of his superior intelligence, even apart from his superior range of sympathy, a human being is capable of apprehending a community of interest between himself and the human society of which he forms a part, such that any conduct which threatens the security of the society generally, is threatening to his own, and calls forth his instinct (if instinct it be) of self-defence. The same superiority of intelligence, joined to the power of sympathizing with human beings generally, enables him to attach himself to the collective idea of his tribe, his country, or mankind, in such a manner that any act hurtful to them rouses his instinct of sympathy, and urges him to resistance.

21. The sentiment of justice, in that one of its elements which consists of the desire to punish, is thus, I conceive, the natural feeling of retaliation or vengeance, rendered by intellect and sympathy applicable to those injuries, that is, to those hurts, which wound us through, or in common with, society at large, This sentiment, in itself, has nothing moral in it; what is moral is, the exclusive subordination of it to the social sympathies, so as to wait on and obey their call. For the natural feeling tends to make us resent indiscriminately whatever any one does that is disagreeable to us; but when moralized by the social feeling, it only acts in the directions conformable to the general good: just persons resenting a hurt to society, though not otherwise a hurt to themselves, and not resenting a hurt to themselves, however painful, unless it be of the kind which society has a common interest with them in the repression of.

22. It is no objection against this doctrine to say, that when we feel our sentiment of justice outraged, we are not thinking of society at large, or of any collective interest, but only of the individual case. It is common enough certainly, though the reverse of commendable, to feel resentment merely because we have suffered pain; but a person whose resentment is really a moral feeling, that is, who considers whether an act is blameable before he allows himself to resent it – such a person, though he may not say expressly to himself that he is standing up for the interest of society, certainly does feel that he is asserting a rule which is for the benefit of others as well as for his own. If he is not feeling this – if he is regarding the act solely as it affects him individually – he is not consciously just; he is not concerning himself about the justice of his actions. This is admitted even by anti-utilitarian moralists. When Kant (as before remarked) propounds as the fundamental principle of morals, 'So act, that thy rule of conduct might be adopted as a law by all rational beings,' he virtually acknowledges that the interest of mankind collectively, or at least of mankind indiscriminately, must be in the mind of the agent when conscientiously deciding on the morality of the act. Otherwise he uses words without a meaning: for, that a rule even of utter selfishness could not *possibly*

be adopted by all rational beings – that there is any insuperable obstacle, in the nature of things to its adoption – cannot be even plausibly maintained. To give any meaning to Kant's principle, the sense put upon it must be, that we ought to shape our conduct by a rule which all rational beings might adopt *with benefit, to their collective interest.*

23. To recapitulate: the idea of justice supposes two things; a rule of conduct, and a sentiment which sanctions the rule. The first must be supposed common to all mankind, and intended for their good. The other (the sentiment) is a desire that punishment may be suffered by those who infringe the rule. There is involved, in addition, the conception of some definite person who suffers by the infringement; whose rights (to use the expression appropriated to the case) are violated by it. And the sentiment of justice appears to me to be, the animal desire to repel or retaliate a hurt or damage to oneself, or to those with whom one sympathizes, widened so as to include all persons, by the human capacity of enlarged sympathy, and the human conception of intelligent self-interest. From the latter elements, the feeling derives its morality; from the former, its peculiar impressiveness, and energy of self-assertion.

24. I have, throughout, treated the idea of a *right*, residing in the injured person, and violated by the injury, not as a separate element in the composition of the idea and sentiment, but as one of the forms in which the other two elements clothe themselves. These elements are, a hurt to some assignable person or persons on the one hand, and a demand for punishment on the other. An examination of our own minds, I think, will show, that these two things include all that we mean when we speak of violation of a right. When we call anything a person's right, we mean that he has a valid claim on society to protect him in the possession of it, either by the force of law, or by that of education and opinion. If he has what we consider a sufficient claim, on whatever account, to have something guaranteed to him by society, we say that he has a right to it. If we desire to prove that anything does not belong to him by right, we think this done as soon as it is admitted that society ought not to take measures for securing it to him, but should leave it to chance, or to his own exertions. Thus, a person is said to have a right to what he can earn in fair professional competition; because society ought not to allow any other person to hinder him from endeavouring to earn in that manner as much as he can. But he has not a right to three hundred a-year, though he may happen to be earning it; because society is not called on to provide that he shall earn that sum. On the contrary, if he owns ten thousand pounds three per cent stock, he *has* a right to three hundred a-year; because society has come under an obligation to provide him with an income of that amount.

25. To have a right, then, is, I conceive, to have something which society ought to defend me in the possession of. If the objector goes on to ask why it ought, I can give him no other reason than general utility. If that expression does not seem to convey a sufficient feeling of the strength of the obligation, nor to account for the peculiar energy of the feeling, it is because there goes to the composition of the sentiment, not a rational only but also an animal element, the thirst for retaliation; and this thirst derives its intensity, as well as its moral justification, from the extraordinarily important and impressive kind of utility which is concerned. The interest involved is that of security, to every one's feelings the most vital of all interests. Nearly all other earthly benefits are needed by one person, not needed by another; and many of them can, if necessary, be cheerfully foregone, or replaced by something else; but security no human being can possibly do without; on it Ave depend for all our immunity from evil, and for the whole value of all and every good, beyond the passing moment; since nothing but the gratification of the instant could be of any worth to us, if we could be deprived of everything the next instant by whoever was momentarily stronger than ourselves. Now this most indispensable of all necessaries, after physical nutriment, cannot be had, unless the machinery for providing it is kept unintermittedly in active play. Our notion, therefore, of the claim we have on our fellow-creatures to join in making safe for us the very groundwork of our existence, gathers feelings round it so much more intense than those concerned in any of the more common cases of utility, that the difference in degree (as is often the case in psychology) becomes a real difference in kind. The claim assumes that character of absoluteness, that apparent infinity, and incommensurability with all other considerations, which constitute the distinction between the feeling of right and wrong and that of ordinary expediency and inexpediency. The feelings concerned are so powerful, and we count so positively on finding a responsive feeling in others (all being alike interested), that *ought* and *should* grow into *must*, and recognized indispensability becomes a moral necessity; analogous to physical, and often not inferior to it in binding force.

[…]

32. Is, then, the difference between the Just and the Expedient a merely imaginary distinction? Have mankind been under a delusion in thinking that justice is a more sacred thing than policy, and that the latter ought only to be listened to after the former has been satisfied? By no means. The exposition we have given of the nature and origin of the sentiment, recognizes a real distinction; and no one of those who profess the most sublime contempt

for the consequences of actions as an element in their morality, attaches more importance to the distinction than I do. While I dispute the pretensions of any theory which sets up an imaginary standard of justice not grounded on utility, I account the justice which is grounded on utility to be the chief part, and incomparably the most sacred and binding part, of all morality. Justice is a name for certain classes of moral rules, which concern the essentials of human well-being more nearly, and are therefore of more absolute obligation, than any other rules for the guidance of life; and the notion which we have found to be of the essence of the idea of justice, that of a right residing in an individual, implies and testifies to this more binding obligation.

33. The moral rules which forbid mankind to hurt one another (in which we must never forget to include wrongful interference with each other's freedom) are more vital to human well-being than any maxims, however important, which only point out the best mode of managing some department of human affairs. They have also the peculiarity, that they are the main element in determining the whole of the social feelings of mankind. It is their observance which alone preserves peace among human beings: if obedience to them were not the rule, and diso-bedience the exception, every one would see in every one else a probable enemy, against whom he must be per-petually guarding himself. What is hardly less important, these are the precepts which mankind have the strongest and the most direct inducements for impressing upon one another. By merely giving to each other prudential instruction or exhortation, they may gain, or think they gain, nothing: in inculcating on each other the duty of posi-tive beneficence they have an unmistakeable interest, but far less in degree: a person may possibly not need the benefits of others; but he always needs that they should not do him hurt. Thus the moralities which protect every individual from being harmed by others, either directly or by being hindered in his freedom of pursuing his own good, are at once those which he himself has most at heart, and those which he has the strongest interest in publish-ing and enforcing by word and deed. It is by a person's observance of these, that his fitness to exist as one of the fellowship of human beings, is tested and decided; for on that depends his being a nuisance or not to those with whom he is in contact. Now it is these moralities primarily, which compose the obligations of justice. The most marked cases of injustice, and those which give the tone to the feeling of repugnance which characterizes the senti-ment; are acts of wrongful aggression, or wrongful exercise of power over some one; the next are those, which consist in wrongfully withholding from him something which is his due; in both cases, inflicting on him a positive hurt, either in the form of direct suffering, or of the privation of some good which he had reasonable ground, either of a physical or of a social kind, for counting upon.

34. The same powerful motives which command the observance of these primary moralities, enjoin the punish-ment of those who violate them; and as the impulses of self-defence, of defence of others, and of vengeance, are all called forth against such persons, retribution, or evil for evil, becomes closely connected with the sentiment of justice, and is universally included in the idea. Good for good is also one of the dictates of justice; and this, though its social utility is evident, and though it carries with it a natural human feeling, has not at first sight that obvious connexion with hurt or injury, which, existing in the most elementary cases of just and unjust, is the source of the characteristic intensity of the sentiment. But the connexion, though less obvious, is not less real. He who accepts benefits, and denies a return of them when needed, inflicts a real hurt, by disappointing one of the most natural and reasonable of expectations, and one which he must at least tacitly have encouraged, otherwise the benefits would seldom have been conferred. The important rank, among human evils and wrongs, of the disappointment of expec-tation, is shown in the fact that it constitutes the principal criminality of two such highly immoral acts as a breach of friendship and a breach of promise. Few hurts which human beings can sustain are greater, and none wound more, than when that on which they habitually and with full assurance relied, fails them in the hour of need; and few wrongs are greater than this mere withholding of good; none excite more resentment, either in the person suffering, or in a sympathizing spectator. The principle, therefore, of giving to each what they deserve, that is, good for good as well as evil for evil, is not only included within the idea of Justice as we have defined it, but is a proper object of that intensity of sentiment, which places the Just, in human estimation, above the simply Expedient.

35. Most of the maxims of justice current in the world, and commonly appealed to in its transactions, are simply instrumental to carrying into effect the principles of justice which we have now spoken of. That a person is only respon-sible for what he has done voluntarily, or could voluntarily have avoided; that it is unjust to condemn any person unheard; that the punishment ought to be proportioned to the offence, and the like, are maxims intended to prevent the just principle of evil for evil from being perverted to the infliction of evil without that justification. The greater part of these common maxims have come into use from the practice of courts of justice, which have been naturally led to a more complete recognition and elaboration than was likely to suggest itself to others, of the rules necessary to enable them to fulfil their double function, of inflicting punishment when due, and of awarding to each person his right.

36. That first of judicial virtues, impartiality, is an obligation of justice, partly for the reason last mentioned; as being a necessary condition of the fulfilment of the other obligations of justice. But this is not the only source of the exalted rank, among human obligations, of those maxims of equality and impartiality, which, both in popular estimation and in that of the most enlightened, are included among the precepts of justice. In one point of view, they may be considered as corollaries from the principles already laid down. If it is a duty to do to each according to his deserts, returning good for good as well as repressing evil by evil, it necessarily follows that we should treat all equally well (when no higher duty forbids) who have deserved equally well of us, and that society should treat all equally well who have deserved equally well of it, that is, who have deserved equally well absolutely. This is the highest abstract standard of social and distributive justice; towards which all institutions, and the efforts of all virtuous citizens, should be made in the utmost possible degree to converge. But this great moral duty rests upon a still deeper foundation, being a direct emanation from the first principle of morals, and not a mere logical corollary from secondary or derivative doctrines. It is involved in the very meaning of Utility; or the Greatest-Happiness Principle. That principle is a mere form of words without rational signification, unless one person's happiness, supposed equal in degree (with the proper allowance made for kind), is counted for exactly as much as another's. Those conditions being supplied, Bentham's dictum 'everybody to count for one, nobody for more than one,' might be written under the principle of utility as an explanatory commentary. The equal claim of everybody to happiness in the estimation of the moralist and the legislator, involves an equal claim to all the means of happiness, except in so far as the inevitable conditions of human life, and the general interest, in which that of every individual is included, set limits to the maxim; and those limits ought to be strictly construed. As every other maxim of justice, so this, is by no means applied or held applicable universally; on the contrary, as I have already remarked, it bends to every person's ideas of social expediency. But in whatever case it is deemed applicable at all, it is held to be the dictate of justice. All persons are deemed to have a *right* to equality of treatment, except when some recognized social expediency requires the reverse. And hence all social inequalities which have ceased to be considered expedient, assume the character not of simple inexpediency, but of injustice, and appear so tyrannical, that people are apt to wonder how they ever could have been tolerated; forgetful that they themselves perhaps tolerate other inequalities under an equally mistaken notion of expediency, the correction of which would make that which they approve seem quite as monstrous as what they have at last learnt to condemn. The entire history of social improvement has been a series of transitions, by which one custom or institution after another, from being a supposed primary necessity of social existence, has passed into the rank of an universally stigmatized injustice and tyranny. So it has been with the distinctions of slaves and freemen, nobles and serfs, patricians and plebeians; and so it will be, and in part already is, with the aristocracies of colour, race, and sex.

37. It appears from what has been said, that justice is a name for certain moral requirements, which, regarded collectively, stand higher in the scale of social utility, and are therefore of more paramount obligation, than any others; though particular cases may occur in which some other social duty is so important, as to overrule any one of the general maxims of justice. Thus, to save a life, it may not only be allowable, but a duty, to steal, or take by force, the necessary food or medicine, or to kidnap, and compel to officiate the only qualified medical practitioner. In such cases, as we do not call anything justice which is not a virtue, we usually say, not that justice must give way to some other moral principle, but that what is just in ordinary cases is, by reason of that other principle, not just in the particular case. By this useful accommodation of language, the character of indefeasibility attributed to justice is kept up, and we are saved from the necessity of maintaining that there can be laudable injustice.

38. The considerations which have now been adduced resolve, I conceive, the only real difficulty in the utilitarian theory of morals. It has always been evident that all cases of justice are also cases of expediency: the difference is in the peculiar sentiment which attaches to the former, as contradistinguished from the latter. If this characteristic sentiment has been sufficiently accounted for; if there is no necessity to assume for it any peculiarity of origin; if it is simply the natural feeling of resentment, moralized by being made coextensive with the demands of social good; and if this feeling not only does but ought to exist in all the classes of cases to which the idea of justice corresponds; that idea no longer presents itself as a stumbling-block to the utilitarian ethics. Justice remains the appropriate name for certain social utilities which are vastly more important, and therefore more absolute and imperative, than any others are as a class (though not more so than others may be in particular cases); and which, therefore, ought to be, as well as naturally are, guarded by a sentiment not only different in degree, but also in kind; distinguished from the milder feeling which attaches to the mere idea of promoting human pleasure or convenience, at once by the more definite nature of its commands, and by the sterner character of its sanctions.

The Subjection of Women

Chapter I

THE object of this Essay is to explain, as clearly as I am able, the grounds of an opinion which I have held from the very earliest period when I had formed any opinions at all on social or political matters, and which, instead of being weakened or modified, has been constantly growing stronger by the progress of reflection and the experience of life: That the principle which regulates the existing social relations between the two sexes – the legal subordination of one sex to the other – is wrong in itself, and now one of the chief hindrances to human improvement; and that it ought to be replaced by a principle of perfect equality, admitting no power or privilege on the one side, nor disability on the other.

[…]

If the authority of men over women, when first established, had been the result of conscientious comparison between different modes of constituting the government of society; if, after trying various other modes of social organization – the government of women over men, equality between the two, and such mixed and divided modes of government as might be invented – it had been decided, on the testimony of experience, that the mode in which women are wholly under the rule of men, having no share at all in public concerns, and each in private being under the legal obligation of obedience to the man with whom she has associated her destiny, was the arrangement most conducive to the happiness and well-being of both; its general adoption might then be fairly thought to be some evidence that, at the time when it was adopted, it was the best: though even then the considerations which recommended it may, like so many other primeval social facts of the greatest importance, have subsequently, in the course of ages, ceased to exist. But the state of the case is in every respect the reverse of this. In the first place, the opinion in favor of the present system, which entirely subordinates the weaker sex to the stronger, rests upon theory only; for there never has been trial made of any other: so that experience, in the sense in which it is vulgarly opposed to theory, cannot be pretended to have pronounced any verdict. And in the second place, the adoption of this system of inequality never was the result of deliberation, or forethought, or any social ideas, or any notion whatever of what conduced to the benefit of humanity or the good order of society. It arose simply from the fact that from the very earliest twilight of human society, every woman (owing to the value attached to her by men, combined with her inferiority in muscular strength) was found in a state of bondage to some man. Laws and systems of polity always begin by recognizing the relations they find already existing between individuals. They convert what was a mere physical fact into a legal right, give it the sanction of society, and principally aim at the substitution of public and organized means of asserting and protecting these rights, instead of the irregular and lawless conflict of physical strength. Those who had already been compelled to obedience became in this manner legally bound to it. Slavery, from being a mere affair of force between the master and the slave, became regularized and a matter of compact among the masters, who, binding themselves to one another for common protection, guaranteed by their collective strength the private possessions of each, including his slaves. In early times, the great majority of the male sex were slaves, as well as the whole of the female. And many ages elapsed, some of them ages of high cultivation, before any thinker was bold enough to question the rightfulness, and the absolute social necessity, either of the one slavery or of the other. By degrees such thinkers did arise: and (the general progress of society assisting) the slavery of the male sex has, in all the countries of Christian Europe at least (though, in one of them, only within the last few years), been at length abolished, and that of the female sex has been gradually changed into a milder form of dependence. But this dependence, as it exists at present, is not an original institution, taking a fresh start from considerations of justice and social expediency – it is the primitive state of slavery lasting on, through successive mitigations and modifications occasioned by the same causes which have softened the general manners, and brought all human relations more under the control of justice and the influence of humanity. It has not lost the taint of its brutal origin. No presumption in its favor, therefore, can be drawn from the fact of its existence. The only such presumption which it could be supposed to have, must be grounded on its having lasted till now, when so many other things which, came down from the same odious source have been done away with. And this, indeed, is what makes it strange to ordinary ears, to hear it asserted that the inequality of rights between men and women has no other source than the law of the strongest.

That this statement should have the effect of a paradox, is in some respects creditable to the progress of civilization, and the improvement of the moral sentiments of mankind. We now live – that is to say, one or two of the most advanced nations of the world now live – in a state in which the law of the strongest seems to be entirely abandoned as the regulating principle of the world's affairs: nobody professes it, and, as regards most of the relations between human beings, nobody is permitted to practice it. When anyone succeeds in doing so, it is under cover of some pretext which gives him the semblance of having some general social interest on his side. This being the ostensible state of things, people flatter themselves that the rule of mere force is ended; that the law of the strongest cannot be the reason of existence of anything which, has remained in full operation down to the present time. However any of our present institutions may have begun, it can only, they think, have been preserved to this period of advanced civilization by a well-grounded feeling of its adaptation to human nature, and conduciveness to the general good. They do not understand the great vitality and durability of institutions which place right on the side of might; how intensely they are clung to; how the good as well as the bad propensities and sentiments of those who have power in their hands, become identified with retaining it; how slowly these bad institutions give way, one at a time, the weakest first, beginning with those which are least interwoven with the daily habits of life; and how very rarely those who have obtained legal power because they first had physical, have ever lost their hold of it until the physical power had passed over to the other side.

[...]

All causes, social and natural, combine to make it unlikely that women should be collectively rebellious to the power of men. They are so far in a position different from all other subject classes, that their masters require something more from them than actual service. Men do not want solely the obedience of women, they want their sentiments. All men, except the most brutish, desire to have, in the woman most nearly connected with them, not a forced slave but a willing one, not a slave merely, but a favorite. They have therefore put everything in practice to enslave their minds. The masters of all other slaves rely, for maintaining obedience, on fear, – either fear of themselves, or religious fears. The masters of women wanted more than simple obedience, and they turned the whole force of education to effect their purpose. All women are brought up from the very earliest years in the belief that their ideal of character is the very opposite to that of men; not self-will and government by self-control, but submission and yielding to the control of others. All the moralities tell them that it is the duty of women, and all the current sentimentalities that it is their nature, to live for others, to make complete abnegation of themselves, and to have no life but in their affections. And by their affections are meant the only ones they are allowed to have – those to the men with whom they are connected, or to the children who constitute an additional and indefeasible tie between them and a man. When we put together three things – first, the natural attraction between opposite sexes; secondly, the wife's entire dependence on the husband, every privilege or pleasure she has being either his gift, or depending entirely on his will; and lastly, that the principal object of human pursuit, consideration, and all objects of social ambition, can in general be sought or obtained by her only through him, it would be a miracle if the object of being attractive to men had not become the polar star of feminine education and formation of character. And this great means of influence over the minds of women having been acquired, an instinct of selfishness made men avail themselves of it to the utmost as a means of holding women in subjection, by representing to them meekness, submissiveness, and resignation of all individual will into the hands of a man, as an essential part of sexual attractiveness. Can it be doubted that any of the other yokes which mankind have succeeded in breaking, would have subsisted till now if the same means had existed, and had been as sedulously used, to bow down their minds to it? If it had been made the object of the life of every young plebeian to find personal favor in the eyes of some patrician, of every young serf with some seigneur; if domestication with him, and a share of his personal affections, had been held out as the prize which they all should look out for, the most gifted and aspiring being able to reckon on the most desirable prizes; and if, when this prize had been obtained, they had been shut out by a wall of brass from all interests not centering in him, all feelings and desires but those which he shared or inculcated; would not serfs and seigneurs, plebeians and patricians, have been as broadly distinguished at this day as men and women are? And would not all but a thinker here and there have believed the distinction to be a fundamental and unalterable fact in human nature?

The preceding considerations are amply sufficient to show that custom, however universal it may be, affords in this case no presumption, and ought not to create any prejudice, in favor of the arrangements which place women in social and political subjection to men. But I may go further, and maintain that the course of history, and the tendencies of progressive human society, afford not only no presumption in favor of this system of inequality of rights, but a strong one against it; and that, so far as the whole course of human improvement up to this time, the whole stream of modern tendencies, warrants any inference on the subject, it is, that this relic of the past is discordant with the future, and must necessarily disappear.

For, what is the peculiar character of the modern world – the difference which chiefly distinguishes modern institutions, modern social ideas, modern life itself, from those of times long past? It is, that human beings are no longer born to their place in life, and chained down by an inexorable bond to the place they are born to, but are free to employ their faculties, and such favorable chances as offer, to achieve the lot which may appear to them most desirable.

[...]

Neither does it avail anything to say that the *nature* of the two sexes adapts them to their present functions and position, and renders these appropriate to them. Standing on the ground of common sense and the constitution of the human mind, I deny that anyone knows, or can know, the nature of the two sexes, as long as they have only been seen in their present relation to one another. If men had ever been found in society without women, or women without men, or if there had been a society of men and women in which the women were not under the control of the men, something might have been positively known about the mental and moral differences which may be inherent in the nature of each. What is now called the nature of women is an eminently artificial thing – the result of forced repression in some directions, unnatural stimulation in others. It may be asserted without scruple, that no other class of dependents have had their character so entirely distorted from its natural proportions by their relation with their masters; for, if conquered and slave races have been, in some respects, more forcibly repressed, whatever in them has not been crushed down by an iron heel has generally been let alone, and if left with any liberty of development it has developed itself according to its own laws; but in the case of women, a hot-house and stove cultivation has always been carried on of some of the capabilities of their nature, for the benefit and pleasure of their masters. Then, because certain products of the general vital force sprout luxuriantly and reach a great development in this heated atmosphere and under this active nurture and watering, while other shoots from the same root, which are left outside in the wintry air, with ice purposely heaped all round them, have a stunted growth, and some are burnt off with fire and disappear; men, with that inability to recognize their own work which distinguishes the unanalytic mind, indolently believe that the tree grows of itself in the way they have made it grow, and that it would die if one-half of it were not kept in a vapor-bath and the other half in the snow.

Of all difficulties which impede the progress of thought, and the formation of well-grounded opinions on life and social arrangements, the greatest is now the unspeakable ignorance and inattention of mankind in respect to the influences which form human character. Whatever any portion of the human species now are, or seem to be, such, it is supposed, they have a natural tendency to be: even when the most elementary knowledge of the circumstances in which they have been placed, clearly points out the causes that made them what they are. Because the Greeks cheated the Turks, and the Turks only plundered the Greeks, there are persons who think that the Turks are naturally more sincere: and because women, as is often said, care nothing about politics except their personalities, it is supposed that the general good is naturally less interesting to women than to men. History, which is now so much better understood than formerly, teaches another lesson: if only by showing the extraordinary susceptibility of human nature to external influences, and the extreme variableness of those of its manifestations which are supposed to be most universal and uniform. But in history, as in traveling, men usually see only what they already had in their own minds; and few learn much from history, who do not bring much with them to its study.

Hence, in regard to that most difficult question, what are the natural differences between the two sexes – a subject on which it is impossible in the present state of society to obtain complete and correct knowledge – while almost everybody dogmatizes upon it, almost all neglect and make light of the only means by which any partial insight can be obtained into it. This is, an analytic study of the most important department of psychology, the laws of the influence of circumstances on character. For, however great and apparently ineradicable the moral and intellectual differences between men and women might be, the evidence of their being natural differences could only be negative. Those only could be inferred to be natural which could not possibly be artificial – the residuum, after deducting every characteristic of either sex which can admit of being explained from education or external circumstances. The profoundest knowledge of the laws of the formation of character is indispensable to entitle anyone to affirm even that there is any difference, much more what the difference is, between the two sexes considered as moral and rational beings; and since no one, as yet, has that knowledge (for there is hardly any subject which, in proportion to its importance, has been so little studied), no one is thus far entitled to any positive opinion on the subject. Conjectures are all that can at present be made; conjectures more or less probable, according as more or less authorized by such knowledge as we yet have of the laws of psychology, as applied to the formation of character.

[...]

Chapter II

[...]

Even the commonest men reserve the violent, the sulky, the undisguisedly selfish side of their character for those who have no power to withstand it. The relation of superiors to dependents is the nursery of these vices of character, which, wherever else they exist, are an overflowing from that source. A man who is morose or violent to his equals, is sure to be one who has lived among inferiors, whom he could frighten or worry into submission. If the family in its best forms is, as it is often said to be, a school of sympathy, tenderness, and loving forgetfulness of self, it is still oftener, as respects its chief, a school of wilfulness, overbearingness, unbounded self-indulgence, and a double-dyed and idealized selfishness, of which sacrifice itself is only a particular form: the care for the wife and children being only care for them as parts of the man's own interests and belongings, and their individual happiness being immolated in every shape to his smallest preferences. What better is to be looked for under the existing form of the institution? We know that the bad propensities of human nature are only kept within bounds when they are allowed no scope for their indulgence. We know that from impulse and habit, when not from deliberate purpose, almost everyone to whom others yield, goes on encroaching upon them, until a point is reached at which they are compelled to resist. Such being the common tendency of human nature; the almost unlimited power which present social institutions give to the man over at least one human being – the one with whom he resides, and whom he has always present – this power seeks out and evokes the latent germs of selfishness in the remotest corners of his nature – fans its faintest sparks and smoldering embers – offers to him a license for the indulgence of those points of his original character which in all other relations he would have found it necessary to repress and conceal, and the repression of which would in time have become a second nature.

[...]

Chapter III

ON the other point which is involved in the just equality of women, their admissibility to all the functions and occupations hitherto retained as the monopoly of the stronger sex, I should anticipate no difficulty in convincing anyone who has gone with me on the subject of the equality of women in the family. I believe that their disabilities elsewhere are only clung to in order to maintain their subordination in domestic life; because the generality of the male sex cannot yet tolerate the idea of living with an equal. Were it not for that, I think that almost everyone, in the existing state of opinion in politics and political economy, would admit the injustice of excluding half the human race from the greater number of lucrative occupations, and from almost all high social functions; ordaining from their birth either that they are not, and cannot by any possibility become, fit for employments which are legally open to the stupidest and basest of the other sex, or else that however fit they may be, those employments shall be interdicted to them, in order to be preserved for the exclusive benefit of males. In the last two centuries, when (which was seldom the case) any reason beyond the mere existence of the fact was thought to be required to justify the disabilities of women, people seldom assigned as a reason their inferior mental capacity; which, in times when there was a real trial of personal faculties (from which all women were not excluded) in the struggles of public life, no one really believed in. The reason given in those days was not women's unfitness, but the interest of society, by which was meant the interest of men: just as the *raison d'état*, meaning the convenience of the government, and the support of existing authority, was deemed a sufficient explanation and excuse for the most flagitious crimes. In the present day, power holds a smoother language, and whomsoever it oppresses, always pretends to do so for their own good: accordingly, when anything is forbidden to women, it is thought necessary to say, and desirable to believe, that they are incapable of doing it, and that they depart from their real path of success and happiness when they aspire to it. But to make this reason plausible (I do not say valid), those by whom it is urged must be prepared to carry it to a much greater length than anyone ventures to do in the face of present experience. It is not sufficient to maintain that women on the average are less gifted than men on the average, with certain of the higher mental faculties, or that a smaller number of women than of men are fit for occupations and functions of the highest intellectual character. It is necessary to maintain that no women at all are fit for them, and that the most eminent women are inferior in mental faculties to the most mediocre of the men on whom those functions at present devolve. For if the performance of the function is decided either by competition, or by any mode of choice which secures regard to the public interest, there needs be no apprehension that any important employments will fall into the hands of women inferior to average men, or to the average of their male competitors.

10

On the Genealogy of Morality

Friedrich Nietzsche

The *Genealogy of Morality* is a notoriously difficult text to interpret. An insufficiently cautious reading may leave the reader with the impression that Nietzsche is a nihilist who believes that no ethical system is better than any other, and that ethical theory is best avoided altogether. To avoid such a misunderstanding, it is crucial to bear in mind that when Nietzsche refers to morality and writes of his own skepticism regarding morality, he has in mind a particular package of substantive commitments that have a long, contingent history. He believes we have inherited this package in an insufficiently critical manner. A genealogical approach to this package – an approach where we step back from our moral commitments and think afresh about what the *functions* of various elements of morality were at various times – is necessary if we are to get ourselves into a position of endorsing the best framework of values available to us (a 'higher morality'). We need, he thinks, a 'revaluation of all values'.

In Section I of the present text, Nietzsche provides the main elements of his account of this genealogy. In particular, we are provided with a story of a progression from an aristocratic Greek and Roman framework, central to which is said to be a contrast between 'good' and 'bad', to a Judeo-Christian framework, central to which is said to be a contrast between 'good' and 'evil'. The first rests on a distinction between a class of noble people and the rest of humankind (that is, those who are not in a position to be good), while the second is egalitarian, cutting across social classes. It is tempting for the contemporary reader to think of the change that has occurred to morality historically as involving in particular a positive, outward expansion in the circle of those who are thought to deserve equal treatment; this circle has now expanded to include all human beings. Nietzsche would say that such a description does not get at the essence of the change that has occurred, both because it fails to appreciate the way in which the second framework was constructed by *ressentiment*, and because it leaves behind something worth valuing in the first framework (however, Nietzsche does not think we can or should simply return to the first framework).

We are told that the crucial turning point in the way in which we now understand morality came about because of a slave revolt against the aristocratic order that was powered by *ressentiment*, initially merely present in a priestly class frustrated with their inability to dominate the social order, and only then possessed more generally by those who lacked power in that order (those outside of the ruling class were initially content with the good/bad moral system). At the risk of oversimplifying a complex text, one might summarize Nietzsche here as saying that those who did not belong to the aristocracy came to resent their status in that order, and so were strongly motivated to adopt a strategy of holding everyone accountable to universal moral standards that enable us to distinguish between good and evil people very generally. Such a framework was eventually adopted by the ruling classes in Europe, and this represented victory for the 'slaves' (we should understand Nietzsche to be using this term very broadly, just as we should understand his talk of the Jewish people to be very broad, as it is meant to extend to Christians; and we should understand his talk of 'English psychologists' to refer to certain views that are not directly connected to the

History of Ethics – Essential Readings with Commentary, First Edition. Edited by Daniel Star and Roger Crisp.
© 2020 John Wiley & Sons Ltd. Published 2020 by John Wiley & Sons Ltd.

work of any particular English psychologists or philosophers). How exactly this victory was achieved is a complex issue, although it seems clear, at least, that Nietzsche takes the priestly class, present in the higher echelons of society both before and after the slave revolt, to have played a crucial role in effecting change (here we might naturally think of the motivating power of the idea that sins in this world will be punished in the next).

Are we to think of the slave revolt and the *ressentiment* that powered it merely as phenomena that lie in the distant past, but not the present? Nietzsche thinks not. In the conclusion to Section I, we are told that the battle between the framework of 'good' and 'bad' and 'good' and 'evil' still goes on in many places. More importantly, Section II of the *Genealogy* aims to show how it is that key moral concepts we now make much use of, especially 'conscience' and 'guilt', are much less innocent than we are inclined to think (and Section III of the text, none of which is reproduced here, similarly criticizes the priestly ascetic ideal for glorifying suffering rather than everything that is life affirming).

In Section II, Nietzsche begins by considering responsibility, suggesting that the arrival of the belief that we are responsible for our actions, and our promises in particular, provided us with a sense of power over things. And he tells us that our consciousness of the privilege of being responsible for the fate of ourselves and others is what we call *conscience*. The rest of the section then focuses on 'bad conscience' or *guilt*. He will conclude here that, at its heart, guilt involves cruelty – that, in having each person feel guilty about their actions, the modern moral framework has each treat themself cruelly. He does this in two stages. First, he provides a 'preliminary' account (as he says in section 16), which offers a very general, naturalistic explanation for our tendency to direct cruelty at ourselves, and which does not yet refer to the shift from the ancient to the Christian world: here the tendency is traced to the way in which human beings became reflective social animals. Second, we are told that this tendency is transformed by Christian morality in such a way that it takes a particularly brutal form: 'that suppressed cruelty of the animal-human who has been made inward … this man of bad conscience has taken over the religious presupposition in order to drive his self-torture to its most gruesome severity and sharpness. Guilt before *God*: this thought becomes.' If Nietzsche is right about the nature of guilt, we are very much still causally under the influence of the shift from 'good' and 'bad' to 'good' and 'evil', in a way that seems highly problematic.

3

Given a skepticism that is characteristic of me, to which I reluctantly admit – for it is directed towards *morality*, towards everything on earth that has until now been celebrated as morality – a skepticism that first appeared so early in my life, so spontaneously, so irrepressibly, so much in contradiction to my environment, age, models, origins, that I almost have the right to call it my "*a priori*[1]" – it was inevitable that early on my curiosity and my suspicion as well would stop at the question: what, in fact, is the *origin* of our good and evil? In fact, the problem of the origin of evil haunted me as a thirteen-year-old lad: at an age when one has "half child's play, half God in one's heart," I devoted my first literary child's play to it, my first philosophic writing exercise – and as to my "solution" to the problem back then, well, I gave the honor to God, as is fitting, and made him the *father* of evil. Was *this* what my "a priori" wished of me? that new, immoral, at least immoralistic "a priori" and the, alas! so anti-Kantian, so mysterious "categorical imperative" speaking through it, to which I have since increasingly lent my ear, and not just my ear? ... Fortunately I learned early on to distinguish theological from moral prejudice, and no longer sought the origin of evil *behind* the world. A little historical and philological schooling, combined with an innate sense of discrimination in all psychological questions, soon transformed my problem into a different one: under what conditions did man invent those value judgments good and evil? *and what value do they themselves have?* Have they inhibited or furthered human flourishing up until now? Are they a sign of distress, of impoverishment, of the degeneration of life? Or, conversely do they betray the fullness, the power, the will of life, its courage, its confidence, its future? – In response I found and ventured a number of answers; I distinguished ages, peoples, degrees of rank among individuals; I divided up my problem; out of the answers came new questions, investigations, conjectures, probabilities: until I finally had a land of my own, a ground of my own, an entire unspoken growing blossoming world, secret gardens as it were, of which no one was permitted even an inkling ... O how we are *happy*, we knowers, provided we simply know how to be silent long enough! ...

[...]

5

Actually there was something much more important on my mind just then than my own or anyone else's hypothesizing about the origin of morality (or, more precisely: the latter concerned me solely for the sake of an end to which it is one means among many). The issue for me was the *value* of morality – and over this I had to struggle almost solely with my great teacher Schopenhauer, to whom that book, the passion and the secret contradiction of that book, is directed, as if to a contemporary (– for that book, too, was a "polemic"). In particular the issue was the value of the unegoistic, of the instincts of compassion, self-denial, self-sacrifice, precisely the instincts that Schopenhauer had gilded, deified, and made otherworldly until finally they alone were left for him as the "values in themselves," on the basis of which he *said* "*no*" to life, also to himself. But against precisely *these* instincts there spoke from within me an ever more fundamental suspicion, an ever deeper-delving skepticism! Precisely here I saw the *great* danger to humanity, its most sublime lure and temptation – and into what? into nothingness? – precisely here I saw the beginning of the end, the standstill, the backward-glancing tiredness, the will turning *against* life, the last sickness gently and melancholically announcing itself: I understood the ever more widely spreading morality of compassion – which seized even the philosophers and made them sick – as the most uncanny symptom of our now uncanny European culture, as its detour to a new Buddhism? to a Buddhism for Europeans? to – *nihilism?* ... For this preferential treatment and overestimation of compassion on the part of modern philosophers is something new: until this point philosophers had agreed precisely on the *worthlessness* of compassion. I name only Plato, Spinoza, La Rochefoucauld, and Kant, four spirits as different from each other as possible, but united on one point: their low regard for compassion. –

---

[1] "*a priori*"] nonempirical or independent of experience; literally: from what is before.

6

This problem of the *value* of compassion and of the morality of compassion (– I am an opponent of the disgraceful modern softening of feelings –) appears at first to be only an isolated matter, a lone question mark; whoever sticks here for once, however, and *learns* to ask questions here, will fare as I have fared; – an immense new vista opens up to him, a possibility takes hold of him like a dizziness, every sort of mistrust, suspicion, fear springs forth, the belief in morality, in all morality totters, – finally a new challenge is heard. Let us speak it aloud, this *new challenge*: we need a *critique* of moral values, *for once the value of these values must itself he called into question* – and for this we need a knowledge of the conditions and circumstances out of which they have grown, under which they have developed and shifted (morality as consequence, as symptom, as mask, as Tartuffery, as sickness, as misunderstanding; but also morality as cause, as medicine, as stimulus, as inhibitor, as poison), knowledge of a kind that has neither existed up until now nor even been desired. One has taken the *value* of these "values" as given, as a fact, as beyond all calling-into-question; until now one has not had even the slightest doubt or hesitation in ranking "the good" as of higher value than "the evil," of higher value in the sense of its furtherance, usefulness, beneficiality – with respect to man *in general* (taking into account the future of man). What? if the opposite were true? What? if a symptom of regression also lay in the "good," likewise a danger, a temptation, a poison, a narcotic through which perhaps the present were living *at the expense of the future?* Perhaps more comfortably, less dangerously, but also in a reduced style, on a lower level? … So that precisely morality would be to blame if a *highest power and splendor* of the human type – in itself possible – were never attained? So that precisely morality were the danger of dangers? …

     […]

First Treatise: "Good and Evil," "Good and Bad"

1

– These English psychologists whom we also have to thank for the only attempts so far to produce a history of the genesis of morality – they themselves are no small riddle for us; I confess, in fact, that precisely as riddles in the flesh they have something substantial over their books – *they themselves are interesting!* These English psychologists – what do they actually want? One finds them, whether voluntarily or involuntarily, always at the same task, namely of pushing the *partie honteuse*[2] of our inner world into the foreground and of seeking that which is actually effective, leading, decisive for our development, precisely where the intellectual pride of man would least of all *wish* to find it (for example in the *vis inertiae*[3] of habit or in forgetfulness or in a blind and accidental interlacing and mechanism of ideas or in anything purely passive, automatic, reflexive, molecular, and fundamentally mindless) – what is it actually that always drives these psychologists in precisely *this* direction? Is it a secret, malicious, base instinct to belittle mankind, one that perhaps cannot be acknowledged even to itself? Or, say, a pessimistic suspicion, the mistrust of disappointed, gloomy idealists who have become poisonous and green? Or a little subterranean animosity and rancor against Christianity (and Plato) that has perhaps not yet made it past the threshold of consciousness? Or even a lascivious taste for the disconcerting, for the painful-paradoxical, for the questionable and nonsensical aspects of existence? Or finally – a little of everything, a little meanness, a little gloominess, a little anti-Christianity, a little tickle and need for pepper? … But I am told that they are simply old, cold, boring frogs who creep and hop around on human beings, into human beings, as if they were really in their element there, namely in a *swamp*. I resist this, still more, I don't believe it; and if one is permitted to wish where one cannot know, then I wish from my heart that the reverse may be the case with them – that these explorers and microscopists of the soul are basically brave, magnanimous, and proud animals who know how to keep a rein on their hearts as well as their pain and have trained themselves to sacrifice all desirability to truth, to *every* truth, even plain, harsh, ugly, unpleasant, unchristian, immoral truth … For there are such truths. –

---

[2] *partie honteuse*] shameful part (in the plural, this expression is the equivalent of the English "private parts").
[3] *vis inertiae*] force of inactivity. In Newtonian physics, this term denotes the resistance offered by matter to any force tending to alter its state of rest or motion.

2

Hats off then to whatever good spirits may be at work in these historians of morality! Unfortunately, however, it is certain that they lack the *historical spirit* itself, that they have been left in the lurch precisely by all the good spirits of history! As is simply the age-old practice among philosophers, they all think *essentially* ahistorically; of this there is no doubt. The ineptitude of their moral genealogy is exposed right at the beginning, where it is a matter of determining the origins of the concept and judgment "good." "Originally" – so they decree – "unegoistic actions were praised and called good from the perspective of those to whom they were rendered, hence for whom they were *useful*; later one *forgot* this origin of the praise and, simply because unegoistic actions were *as a matter of habit* always praised as good, one also felt them to be good – as if they were something good in themselves." One sees immediately: this first derivation already contains all the characteristic traits of the idiosyncrasy of English psychologists – we have "usefulness," "forgetting," "habit," and in the end "error," all as basis for a valuation of which the higher human being has until now been proud as if it were some kind of distinctive prerogative of humankind. This pride *must* be humbled, this valuation devalued: has this been achieved? … Now in the first place it is obvious to me that the actual genesis of the concept "good" is sought and fixed in the wrong place by this theory: the judgment "good" does *not* stem from those to whom "goodness" is rendered! Rather it was "the good" themselves, that is the noble, powerful, higher-ranking, and high-minded who felt and ranked themselves and their doings as good, which is to say, as of the first rank, in contrast to everything base, low-minded, common, and vulgar. Out of this *pathos of distance* they first took for themselves the right to create values, to coin names for values: what did they care about usefulness! The viewpoint of utility is as foreign and inappropriate as possible, especially in relation to so hot an outpouring of highest rank-ordering, rank-distinguishing value judgments: for here feeling has arrived at an opposite of that low degree of warmth presupposed by every calculating prudence, every assessment of utility – and not just for once, for an hour of exception, but rather for the long run. As was stated, the pathos of nobility and distance, this lasting and dominant collective and basic feeling of a higher ruling nature in relation to a lower nature, to a "below" – *that* is the origin of the opposition "good" and "bad." (The right of lords to give names goes so far that we should allow ourselves to comprehend the origin of language itself as an expression of power on the part of those who rule: they say "this *is* such and such," they seal each thing and happening with a sound and thus, as it were, take possession of it.) It is because of this origin that from the outset the word "good" does *not* necessarily attach itself to "unegoistic" actions – as is the superstition of those genealogists of morality. On the contrary, only when aristocratic value judgments begin to *decline* does this entire opposition "egoistic" "unegoistic" impose itself more and more on the human conscience – to make use of my language, it is *the herd instinct* that finally finds a voice (also *words*) in this opposition. And even then it takes a long time until this instinct becomes dominant to such an extent that moral valuation in effect gets caught and stuck at that opposition (as is the case in present-day Europe: today the prejudice that takes "moral," "unegoistic," "*désintéressé*"[4] to be concepts of equal value already rules with the force of an "*idée fixe*"[5] and sickness in the head).

3

In the second place, however: quite apart from the historical untenability of that hypothesis concerning the origins of the value judgment "good," it suffers from an inherent psychological absurdity. The usefulness of the unegoistic action is supposed to be the origin of its praise, and this origin is supposed to have been *forgotten*: – how is this forgetting even *possible*? Did the usefulness of such actions cease at some point? The opposite is the case: this usefulness has been the everyday experience in all ages, something therefore that was continually underscored anew; accordingly, instead of disappearing from consciousness, instead of becoming forgettable, it could not help but impress itself upon consciousness with ever greater clarity. How much more reasonable is that opposing theory (it is not therefore truer –) advocated for example by Herbert Spencer – which ranks the concept "good" as essentially identical with the concept "useful," "purposive," so that in the judgments "good" and "bad" humanity has summed up and sanctioned its *unforgotten* and *unforgettable* experiences concerning what is useful-purposive, what is injurious-nonpurposive. Good, according to this theory, is whatever has proved itself as useful from time immemorial: it

---

[4] désintéressé] disinterested, unselfish, selfless.
[5] "idée fixe"] obsession; literally: a fixed idea.

may thus claim validity as "valuable in the highest degree," as "valuable in itself." This path of explanation is also false, as noted above, but at least the explanation is in itself reasonable and psychologically tenable.

4

– The pointer to the *right* path was given to me by the question: what do the terms coined for "good" in the various languages actually mean from an etymological viewpoint? Here I found that they all lead back to the *same conceptual transformation* – that everywhere the basic concept is "noble," "aristocratic" in the sense related to the estates, out of which "good" in the sense of "noble of soul," "high-natured of soul," "privileged of soul" necessarily develops: a development that always runs parallel to that other one which makes "common," "vulgar," "base" pass over finally into the concept "bad." The most eloquent example of the latter is the German word "*schlecht*" [bad] itself: which is identical with "*schlecht*" [plain, simple] – compare "*schlechtweg*," "*schlechterdings*" [simply or downright] – and originally designated the plain, the common man, as yet without a suspecting sideward glance, simply in opposition to the noble one. Around the time of the Thirty-Years' War, in other words late enough, this sense shifts into the one now commonly used. – With respect to morality's genealogy this appears to me to be an *essential* insight; that it is only now being discovered is due to the inhibiting influence that democratic prejudice exercises in the modern world with regard to all questions of origins. And this influence extends all the way into that seemingly most objective realm of natural science and physiology, as I shall merely hint at here. But the nonsense that this prejudice – once unleashed to the point of hate – is able to inflict, especially on morality and history, is shown by Buckle's notorious case; the *plebeianism* of the modern spirit, which is of English descent, sprang forth there once again on its native ground, vehemently like a muddy volcano and with that oversalted, overloud, common eloquence with which until now all volcanoes have spoken. –

[…]

7

– One will already have guessed how easily the priestly manner of valuation can branch off from the knightly-aristocratic and then develop into its opposite; this process is especially given an impetus every time the priestly caste and the warrior caste confront each other jealously and are unable to agree on a price. The knightly-aristocratic value judgments have as their presupposition a powerful physicality, a blossoming, rich, even overflowing health, together with that which is required for its preservation: war, adventure, the hunt, dance, athletic contests, and in general everything which includes strong, free, cheerful-hearted activity. The priestly-noble manner of valuation – as we have seen – has other presuppositions: too bad for it when it comes to war! Priests are, as is well known, the *most evil enemies* – why is that? Because they are the most powerless. Out of their powerlessness their hate grows into something enormous and uncanny, into something most spiritual and most poisonous. The truly great haters in the history of the world have always been priests, also the most ingenious haters: – compared with the spirit of priestly revenge all the rest of spirit taken together hardly merits consideration. Human history would be much too stupid an affair without the spirit that has entered into it through the powerless: – let us turn right to the greatest example. Of all that has been done on earth against "the noble," "the mighty," "the lords," "the power-holders," nothing is worthy of mention in comparison with that which the *Jews* have done against them: the Jews, that priestly people who in the end were only able to obtain satisfaction from their enemies and conquerors through a radical revaluation of their values, that is, through an act of *spiritual revenge*. This was the only way that suited a priestly people, the people of the most suppressed priestly desire for revenge. It was the Jews who in opposition to the aristocratic value equation (good = noble = powerful = beautiful = happy = beloved of God) dared its inversion, with fear-inspiring consistency, and held it fast with teeth of the most unfathomable hate (the hate of powerlessness), namely: "the miserable alone are the good; the poor, powerless, lowly alone are the good; the suffering, deprived, sick, ugly are also the only pious, the only blessed in God, for them alone is there blessedness, – whereas you, you noble and powerful ones, you are in all eternity the evil, the cruel, the lustful, the insatiable, the godless, you will eternally be the wretched, accursed, and damned!" … We know *who* inherited this Jewish revaluation … In connection with the enormous and immeasurably doom-laden initiative provided by the Jews with this most fundamental of all declarations of war, I call attention to the proposition which I arrived at on another occasion ("Beyond Good and Evil" section 195) – namely, that with the Jews *the slave revolt in morality* begins: that revolt which has a two-thousand-year history behind it and which has only moved out of our sight today because it – has been victorious …

8

– But you don't understand that? You don't have eyes for something that has taken two thousand years to achieve victory? ... There is nothing to wonder at in this: all *lengthy* things are difficult to see, to see in their entirety. *This* however is what happened: out of the trunk of that tree of revenge and hate, Jewish hate – the deepest and most sublime hate, namely an ideal-creating, value-reshaping hate whose like has never before existed on earth – grew forth something just as incomparable, a *new love*, the deepest and most sublime of all kinds of love: – and from what other trunk could it have grown? ... But by no means should one suppose it grew upwards as, say, the true negation of that thirst for revenge, as the opposite of Jewish hate! No, the reverse is the truth! This love grew forth out of it, as its crown, as the triumphant crown unfolding itself broadly and more broadly in purest light and sunny fullness, reaching out, as it were, in the realm of light and of height, for the goals of that hate – for victory, for booty, for seduction – with the same drive with which the roots of that hate sunk themselves ever more thoroughly and greedily down into everything that had depth and was evil. This Jesus of Nazareth, as the embodied Gospel of Love, this "Redeemer" bringing blessedness and victory to the poor, the sick, the sinners – was he not precisely seduction in its most uncanny and irresistible form, the seduction and detour to precisely those *Jewish* values and reshapings of the ideal? Has not Israel reached the final goal of its sublime desire for revenge precisely via the detour of this "Redeemer," this apparent adversary and dissolver of Israel? Does it not belong to the secret black art of a truly *great* politics of revenge, of a far-seeing, subterranean, slow-working and pre-calculating revenge, that Israel itself, before all the world, should deny as its mortal enemy and nail to the cross the actual tool of its revenge, so that "all the world," namely all the opponents of Israel, could take precisely this bait without thinking twice? And, out of all sophistication of the spirit, could one think up any more *dangerous* bait? Something that in its enticing, intoxicating, anesthetizing, destructive power might equal that symbol of the "holy cross," that gruesome paradox of a "god on the cross," that mystery of an inconceivable, final, extreme cruelty and self-crucifixion of God *for the salvation of man?* ... What is certain, at least, is that *sub hoc signo*[6] Israel, with its revenge and revaluation of all values, has thus far again and again triumphed over all other ideals, over all *more noble* ideals. – –

9

– "But why are you still talking about *nobler* ideals! Let's submit to the facts: the people were victorious – or 'the slaves,' or 'the mob,' or 'the herd,' or whatever you like to call them – if this happened through the Jews, so be it! then never has a people had a more world-historic mission. 'The lords' are cast off; the morality of the common man has been victorious. One may take this victory to be at the same time a blood poisoning (it mixed the races together) – I won't contradict; in any event it is beyond doubt that this toxication *succeeded*. The 'redemption' of the human race (namely from 'the lords') is well under way; everything is jewifying or christifying or mobifying as we watch (what do the words matter!).

    [...]

10

The slave revolt in morality begins when *ressentiment* itself becomes creative and gives birth to values: the *ressentiment* of beings denied the true reaction, that of the deed, who recover their losses only through an imaginary revenge. Whereas all noble morality grows out of a triumphant yes-saying to oneself, from the outset slave morality says "no" to an "outside," to a "different," to a "not-self": and *this* "no" is its creative deed. This reversal of the value-establishing glance – this *necessary* direction toward the outside instead of back onto oneself – belongs to the very nature of *ressentiment*: in order to come into being, slave-morality always needs an opposite and external world; it needs, psychologically speaking, external stimuli in order to be able to act at all, – its action is, from the ground up, reaction. The reverse is the case with the noble manner of valuation: it acts and grows spontaneously, it seeks out its opposite only in order to say "yes" to itself still more gratefully and more jubilantly – its negative concept "low" "common" "bad" is only an after-birth, a pale contrast-image in relation to its positive basic concept, saturated through and through with life and passion: "we noble ones, we good ones, we beautiful ones, we happy ones!" When the noble manner of valuation lays a hand on reality and sins against it, this occurs relative to the sphere with

---

[6] sub hoc signo] under this sign.

which it is *not* sufficiently acquainted, indeed against a real knowledge of which it rigidly defends itself: in some cases it forms a wrong idea of the sphere it holds in contempt, that of the common man, of the lower people; on the other hand, consider that the affect of contempt, of looking down on, of the superior glance – assuming that it does *falsify* the image of the one held in contempt – will in any case fall far short of the falsification with which the suppressed hate, the revenge of the powerless, lays a hand on its opponent – in effigy, of course. Indeed there is too much carelessness in contempt, too much taking-lightly, too much looking-away and impatience mixed in, even too much of a feeling of cheer in oneself, for it to be capable of transforming its object into a real caricature and monster. Do not fail to hear the almost benevolent nuances that, for example, the Greek nobility places in all words by which it distinguishes the lower people from itself; how they are mixed with and sugared by a kind of pity, considerateness, leniency to the point that almost all words that apply to the common man ultimately survive as expressions for "unhappy" "pitiful" (compare *deilos, deilaios, poneros, mochtheros*,[7] the latter two actually designating the common man as work-slave and beast of burden) – and how, on the other hand, to the Greek ear "bad" "low" "unhappy" have never ceased to end on the same note, with a tone color in which "unhappy" predominates: this as inheritance of the old, nobler aristocratic manner of valuation that does not deny itself even in its contempt (let philologists be reminded of the sense in which *oizyrns, anolbos, tlemon, dystychein, xymphora*[8] are used). The "well-born" simply *felt* themselves to be the "happy"; they did not first have to construct their happiness artificially by looking at their enemies, to talk themselves into it, to *lie themselves into it* (as all human beings of *ressentiment* tend to do); and as full human beings, overloaded with power and therefore *necessarily* active, they likewise did not know how to separate activity out from happiness, – for them being active is of necessity included in happiness (whence *eu prattein*[9] takes its origins) – all of this very much in opposition to "happiness" on the level of the powerless, oppressed, those festering with poisonous and hostile feelings, in whom it essentially appears as narcotic, anesthetic, calm, peace, "Sabbath," relaxation of mind and stretching of limbs, in short, *passively*. While the noble human being lives with himself in confidence and openness (*gennaias*[10] "noble-born" underscores the nuance "sincere" and probably also "naive") the human being of *ressentiment* is neither sincere, nor naive, nor honest and frank with himself. His soul *looks obliquely* at things; his spirit loves hiding places, secret passages and backdoors, everything hidden strikes him as *his* world, *his* security, *his* balm; he knows all about being silent, not forgetting, waiting, belittling oneself for the moment, humbling oneself. A race of such human beings of *ressentiment* in the end necessarily becomes *more prudent* than any noble race, it will also honor prudence in an entirely different measure: namely as a primary condition of existence. With noble human beings, in contrast, prudence is likely to have a refined aftertaste of luxury and sophistication about it: – here it is not nearly as essential as the complete functional reliability of the regulating *unconscious* instincts or even a certain imprudence, for example the gallant making-straight-for-it, be it toward danger, be it toward the enemy, or that impassioned suddenness of anger, love, reverence, gratitude, and revenge by which noble souls in all ages have recognized each other. For the *ressentiment* of the noble human being, when it appears in him, runs its course and exhausts itself in an immediate reaction, therefore it does *not poison* – on the other hand it does not appear at all in countless cases where it is unavoidable in all the weak and powerless. To be unable for any length of time to take his enemies, his accidents, his *misdeeds* themselves seriously – that is the sign of strong, full natures in which there is an excess of formative, reconstructive, healing power that also makes one forget (a good example of this from the modern world is Mirabeau, who had no memory for insults and base deeds committed against him and who was only unable to forgive because he – forgot). Such a human is simply able to shake off with a single shrug a collection of worms that in others would dig itself in; here alone is also possible – assuming that it is at all possible on earth – the true "*love* of one's enemies." What great reverence for his enemies a noble human being has! – and such reverence is already a bridge to love ... After all, he demands his enemy for himself, as his distinction; he can stand no other enemy than one in whom there is nothing to hold in contempt and *a very great deal* to honor! On the other hand, imagine "the enemy" as the human being of *ressentiment*

---

[7] deilos, deilaios, poneros, mochtheros] deilos: cowardly, worthless, low-born, miserable, wretched; deilaios: wretched, sorry, paltry; poneros: wretched, oppressed by toils, worthless, base, cowardly; mochtheros: wretched, suffering hardship, miserable, worthless, knavish.

[8] oizyros, anolbos, tlemon, dystychein, xymphora] oizyros: woeful, pitiable, miserable, sorry, poor; anolbos: unblest, wretched, luckless, poor; tlemon: suffering, enduring; hence: "steadfast, stouthearted," but also "wretched, miserable"; dystychein: to be unlucky, unhappy, unfortunate; xymphora: originally "chance," then usually in a bad sense, that is, "misfortune."

[9] eu prattein] to do well, to fare well, or to do good.

[10] gennaios] high-born, noble, high-minded.

conceives of him – and precisely here is his deed, his creation: he has conceived of "the evil enemy," "*the evil one*," and this indeed as the basic concept, starting from which he now also thinks up, as reaction and counterpart, a "good one" – himself!...

11

Precisely the reverse, therefore, of the case of the noble one, who conceives the basic concept "good" in advance and spontaneously, starting from himself that is, and from there first creates for himself an idea of "bad"! This "bad" of noble origin and that "evil" out of the brewing cauldron of unsatiated hate – the first, an after-creation, something on the side, a complementary color; the second, in contrast, the original, the beginning, the true *deed* in the conception of a slave morality – how differently the two words "bad" and "evil" stand there, seemingly set in opposition to the same concept "good"! But it is *not* the same concept "good": on the contrary, just ask yourself *who* is actually "evil" in the sense of the morality of *ressentiment*. To answer in all strictness: *precisely* the "good one" of the other morality, precisely the noble, the powerful, the ruling one, only recolored, only reinterpreted, only reseen through the poisonous eye of *ressentiment*. There is one point we wish to deny least of all here: whoever encounters those "good ones" only as enemies encounters nothing but *evil enemies*, and the same humans who are kept so strictly within limits *inter pares*,[11] by mores, worship, custom, gratitude, still more by mutual surveillance, by jealousy, and who on the other hand in their conduct towards each other prove themselves so inventive in consideration, self-control, tact, loyalty, pride, and friendship, – they are not much better than uncaged beasts of prey toward the outside world, where that which is foreign, the foreign world, begins. There they enjoy freedom from all social constraint; in the wilderness they recover the losses incured through the tension that comes from a long enclosure and fencing-in within the peace of the community; they step *back* into the innocence of the beast-of-prey conscience, as jubilant monsters, who perhaps walk away from a hideous succession of murder, arson, rape, torture with such high spirits and equanimity that it seems as if they have only played a student prank, convinced that for years to come the poets will again have something to sing and to praise. At the base of all these noble races one cannot fail to recognize the beast of prey, the splendid *blond beast* who roams about lusting after booty and victory; from time to time this hidden base needs to discharge itself, the animal must get out, must go back into the wilderness: [...]

12

[...] grant me just one glimpse of something perfect, completely formed, happy, powerful, triumphant, in which there is still something to fear! Of a human being who justifies man *himself;* a human being who is a stroke of luck, completing and redeeming man, and for whose sake one may hold fast to *belief in man*! ... For things stand thus: the reduction and equalization of the European human conceals *our* greatest danger, for this sight makes tired ... We see today nothing that wishes to become greater, we sense that things are still going downhill, downhill – into something thinner, more good-natured, more prudent, more comfortable, more mediocre, more apathetic, more Chinese, more Christian – man, there is no doubt, is becoming ever "better" ... Precisely here lies Europe's doom – with the fear of man we have also forfeited the love of him, the reverence toward him, the hope for him, indeed the will to him. The sight of man now makes tired – what is nihilism today if it is not *that*? ... We are tired of *man* ...

13

– But let us come back: the problem of the *other* origin of "good," of the good one as conceived by the man of *ressentiment*, demands its conclusion. – That the lambs feel anger toward the great birds of prey does not strike us as odd: but that is no reason for holding it against the great birds of prey that they snatch up little lambs for themselves. And when the lambs say among themselves "these birds of prey are evil; and whoever is as little as possible a bird of prey but rather its opposite, a lamb, – isn't he good?" there is nothing to criticize in this setting up of an ideal, even if the birds of prey should look on this a little mockingly and perhaps say to themselves; "*we* do not feel any anger towards them, these good lambs, as a matter of fact, we love them: nothing is more tasty than a tender lamb." – To

---

[11] inter pares] among equals; here, "among themselves."

demand of strength that it *not* express itself as strength, that it *not* be a desire to overwhelm, a desire to cast down, a desire to become lord, a thirst for enemies and resistances and triumphs, is just as nonsensical as to demand of weakness that it express itself as strength. A quantum of power is just such a quantum of drive, will, effect – more precisely, it is nothing other than this very driving, willing, effecting, and only through the seduction of language (and the basic errors of reason petrified therein), which understands and misunderstands all effecting as conditioned by an effecting something, by a "subject," can it appear otherwise. For just as common people separate the lightning from its flash and take the latter as a *doing*, as an effect of a subject called lightning, so popular morality also separates strength from the expressions of strength as if there were behind the strong an indifferent substratum that is free to express strength – or not to. But there is no such substratum; there is no "being" behind the doing, effecting, becoming; "the doer" is simply fabricated into the doing – the doing is everything. Common people basically double the doing when they have the lightning flash; this is a doing-doing: the same happening is posited first as cause and then once again as its effect. Natural scientists do no better when they say "force moves, force causes," and so on – our entire science, despite all its coolness, its freedom from affect, still stands under the seduction of language and has not gotten rid of the changelings slipped over on it, the "subjects" (the atom, for example, is such a changeling, likewise the Kantian "thing in itself"): small wonder if the suppressed, hiddenly glowing affects of revenge and hate exploit this belief and basically even uphold no other belief more ardently than this one, that *the strong one is free* to be weak, and the bird of prey to be a lamb: – they thereby gain for themselves the right to hold the bird of prey *accountable* for being a bird of prey ... When out of the vengeful cunning of powerlessness the oppressed, downtrodden, violated say to themselves: "let us be different from the evil ones, namely good! And good is what everyone is who does not do violence, who injures no one, who doesn't attack, who doesn't retaliate, who leaves vengeance to God, who keeps himself concealed, as we do, who avoids all evil, and in general demands very little of life, like us, the patient, humble, righteous" – it means, when listened to coldly and without prejudice, actually nothing more than: "we weak ones are simply weak; it is good if we do nothing *for which we are not strong enough*" – but this harsh matter of fact, this prudence of the lowest order, which even insects have (presumably playing dead when in great danger in order not to do "too much"), has, thanks to that counterfeiting and self-deception of powerlessness, clothed itself in the pomp of renouncing, quiet, patiently waiting virtue, as if the very weakness of the weak – that is to say, his *essence*, his effecting, his whole unique, unavoidable, undetachable reality – were a voluntary achievement, something willed, something chosen, a *deed*, a *merit*. This kind, of human *needs* the belief in a neutral "subject" with free choice, out of an instinct of self-preservation, self-affirmation, in which every lie tends to hallow itself. It is perhaps for this reason that the subject (or, to speak more popularly, the *soul*) has until now been the best article of faith on earth, because it made possible for the majority of mortals, the weak and oppressed of every kind, that sublime self-deception of interpreting weakness itself as freedom, of interpreting their being-such-and-such as a *merit*.

[...]

16

Let us conclude. The two *opposed* values 'good and bad,' 'good and evil,' have fought a terrible millennia-long battle on earth; and as certainly as the second value has had the upper hand for a long time, even so there is still no shortage of places where the battle goes on, undecided. One could even say that it has in the meantime been borne up ever higher and precisely thereby become ever deeper, ever more spiritual: so that today there is perhaps no more decisive mark of the "*higher nature*," of the more spiritual nature, than to be conflicted in that sense and still a real battle-ground for those opposites. The symbol of this battle, written in a script that has so far remained legible across all of human history, is "Rome against Judea, Judea against Rome": – so far there has been no greater-event than *this* battle, *this* formulation of the problem, *this* mortally hostile contradiction. Rome sensed in the Jew something like anti-nature itself, its antipodal monstrosity as it were; in Rome the Jew was held to have been "*convicted of hatred against the entire human race*": rightly so, insofar as one has a right to tie the salvation and the future of the human race to the unconditional rule of aristocratic values, of Roman values. What the Jews on the other hand felt towards Rome? One can guess it from a thousand indications; but it will suffice to recall again the Johannine Apocalypse, that most immoderate of all written outbursts that revenge has on its conscience. (Do not underestimate, by the way, the profound consistency of the Christian instinct when it gave precisely this book of hate the name of the disciple of love, the same one to whom it attributed that enamored-rapturous gospel –: therein lies a piece of truth, however much literary counterfeiting may have been needed for this purpose.) The Romans were after all the strong and noble ones, such that none stronger and nobler have ever existed, ever even been dreamt of; everything that remains of them, every inscription thrills, supposing that one can guess *what* is doing the writing there. The Jews, conversely, were that priestly-people of *ressentiment* par excellence, in whom there dwelt a popular-moral genius without parallel: just compare the peoples with related talents – for instance the Chinese or the Germans – with the Jews in order to feel what is first and what fifth rank. Which of them has been victorious in the meantime, Rome or Judea? But there is no doubt at all: just consider before whom one bows today in Rome itself as before the quintessence of all the highest values – and not only in Rome, but over almost half the earth, everywhere that man has become tame or wants to become tame, – before *three Jems*, as everyone knows, and *one Jewess* (before Jesus of Nazareth, the fisher Peter, the carpet-weaver Paul, and the mother of the aforementioned Jesus, called Mary). This is very remarkable: Rome has succumbed without any doubt.

[…]

Second Treatise: "Guilt," "Bad Conscience," and Related Matters

2

Precisely this is the long history of the origins of *responsibility*. As we have already grasped, the task of breeding an animal that is permitted to promise includes, as condition and preparation, the more specific task of first *making* man to a certain degree necessary, uniform, like among like, regular, and accordingly predictable. The enormous work of what I have called "morality of custom" (cf. *Daybreak* 9, 14, 16) – the true work of man on himself for the longest part of the duration of the human race, his entire *prehistoric* work, has in this its meaning, its great justification – however much hardness, tyranny, mindlessness, and idiocy may be inherent in it: with the help of the morality of custom and the social straightjacket man was *made* truly calculable. If, on the other hand, we place ourselves at the end of the enormous process, where the tree finally produces its fruit, where society and its morality of custom finally brings to light that *to which* it was only the means: then we will find as the ripest fruit on its tree the *sovereign individual*, the individual resembling only himself, free again from the morality of custom, autonomous and super-moral (for "autonomous" and "moral" are mutually exclusive), in short, the human being with his own independent long will, the human being who *is permitted to promise* – and in him a proud consciousness, twitching in all his muscles, of *what* has finally been achieved and become flesh in him, a true consciousness of power and freedom, a feeling of the completion of man himself. This being who has become free, who is really *permitted* to promise, this lord of the *free* will, this sovereign – how could he not know what superiority he thus has over all else that is not permitted to promise and vouch for itself, how much trust, how much fear, how much reverence he awakens – he "*earns*" all three – and how this mastery over himself also necessarily brings with it mastery over circumstances, over nature and all lesser-willed and more unreliable creatures? The "free" human being, the possessor of a long, unbreakable will, has in this possession his *standard of value* as well: looking from himself toward the others, he honors or holds in contempt; and just as necessarily as he honors the ones like him, the strong and reliable (those who are *permitted* to promise), – that is, everyone who promises like a sovereign, weightily, seldom, slowly, who is stingy with his trust, who *conveys a mark of distinction* when he trusts, who gives his word as something on which one can rely because he knows himself to be strong enough to uphold it even against accidents, even "against fate" –: just as necessarily he will hold his kick in readiness for the frail dogs who promise although they are not permitted to do so, and his switch for the liar who breaks his word already the moment it leaves his mouth. The proud knowledge of the extraordinary privilege of *responsibility*, the consciousness of this rare freedom, this power over oneself and fate, has sunk into his lowest depth and has become instinct, the dominant instinct: – what will he call it, this dominant instinct, assuming that he feels the need to have a word for it? But there is no doubt: this sovereign human being calls it his *conscience* …

[…]

4

But how then did that other "gloomy thing," the consciousness of guilt, the entire "bad conscience" come into the world? – And thus we return to our genealogists of morality. To say it once more – or haven't I said it at all yet? – they aren't good for anything. Their own five-span-long, merely "modern" experience; no knowledge, no will to knowledge of the past; still less an instinct for history, a "second sight" necessary precisely here – and nonetheless doing history of morality: this must in all fairness end with results that stand in a relation to truth that is not even flirtatious. Have these previous genealogists of morality even remotely dreamt, for example, that that central moral concept "guilt" had its origins in the very material concept "debt"? Or that punishment as *retribution* developed completely apart from any presupposition concerning freedom or lack of freedom of the will? – and to such a degree that in fact a *high* level of humanization is always necessary before the animal "man" can begin to make those much more primitive distinctions "intentional," "negligent," "accidental," "accountable," and their opposites, and to take them into account when measuring out punishment. The thought, now so cheap and apparently so natural, so unavoidable, a thought that has even had to serve as an explanation of how the feeling of justice came into being at all on earth – "the criminal has earned his punishment *because* he could have acted otherwise" – is in fact a sophisticated form of human judging and inferring that was attained extremely late; whoever shifts it to the beginnings lays a hand on the psychology of older humanity in a particularly crude manner. Throughout the greatest part of human history punishment was definitely *not* imposed *because* one held the evil-doer responsible for his deed, that is, *not* under the presupposition that only the guilty one is to be punished: – rather, as parents even today punish their children, from anger over an injury suffered, which is vented on the agent of the injury – anger held within bounds, however, and modified through the idea that every injury has its *equivalent* in something and can really be paid off, even if only through the *pain* of its agent. Whence has this age-old, deeply-rooted, perhaps now no longer eradicable idea taken its power – the idea of an equivalence between injury and pain? I have already given it away: in the contractual relationship between *creditor* and *debtor*, which is as old as the existence of "legal subjects" and in turn points back to the basic forms of purchase, sale, exchange, trade, and commerce.

[…]

8

The feeling of guilt, of personal obligation – to take up the train of our investigation again – had its origin, as we have seen, in the oldest and most primitive relationship among persons there is, in the relationship between buyer and seller, creditor and debtor: here for the first time person stepped up against person, here for the first time a person *measured himself* by another person. No degree of civilization however low has yet been discovered in which something of this relationship was not already noticeable. Making prices, gauging values, thinking out equivalents, exchanging – this preoccupied man's very first thinking to such an extent that it is in a certain sense thinking *itself*: here that oldest kind of acumen was bred, here likewise we may suspect the first beginnings of human pride, man's feeling of pre-eminence with respect to other creatures. Perhaps our word "man" (*manas*)[12] still expresses precisely something of this self-esteem: man designated himself as the being who measures values, who values and measures, as the "appraising animal in itself." Purchase and sale, together with their psychological accessories, are older than even the beginnings of any societal associations and organizational forms: it was out of the most rudimentary form of personal legal rights that the budding feeling of exchange, contract, guilt, right, obligation, compensation first *transferred* itself onto the coarsest and earliest communal complexes (in their relationship to similar complexes), together with the habit of comparing, measuring, and calculating power against power. The eye was simply set to this perspective: and with that clumsy consistency characteristic of earlier humanity's thinking – which has difficulty moving but then continues relentlessly in the same direction – one arrived straightaway at the grand generalization "every thing has its price; *everything* can be paid off" – at the oldest and most naive moral canon of *justice*, at the beginning of all "good-naturedness," all "fairness," all "good will," all "objectivity" on earth. Justice at this first stage is the good will among parties of approximately equal power to come to terms with one another, to reach an "understanding" again by means of a settlement – and in regard to less powerful parties, to *force* them to a settlement among themselves. –

9

Always measured by the standard of an earlier time (which earlier time is, by the way, at all times present or again possible): the community, too, thus stands to its members in that important basic relationship, that of the creditor to his debtor. One lives in a community, one enjoys the advantages of a community (oh what advantages! we sometimes

---

[12] (manas)] Sanskrit: mind; understanding or the conscious will.

underestimate this today), one lives protected, shielded, in peace and trust, free from care with regard to certain injuries and hostilities to which the human *outside*, the "outlaw," is exposed – a German understands what "Elend," *êlend*[13] originally means –, since one has pledged and obligated oneself to the community precisely in view of these injuries and hostilities. What happens *in the other case?* The community, the deceived creditor, will exact payment as best it can, one can count on that. Here it is least of all a matter of the direct injury inflicted by the injuring party; quite apart from this, the criminal is above all a "breaker," one who breaks his contract and word *with the whole*, in relation to all goods and conveniences of communal life in which he has until this point had a share. The criminal is a debtor who not only fails to pay back the advantages and advances rendered him, but also even lays a hand on his creditor: he therefore not only forfeits all of these goods and advantages from now on, as is fair, – he is also now reminded *how much there is to these goods*. The anger of the injured creditor, of the community, gives him back again to the wild and outlawed condition from which he was previously protected: it expels him from itself, – and now every kind of hostility may vent itself on him. At this level of civilization "punishment" is simply the copy, the *mimus* of normal behavior toward the hated, disarmed, defeated enemy, who has forfeited not only every right and protection, but also every mercy; in other words, the law of war and the victory celebration of *vae victis!*[14] in all their ruthlessness and cruelty: – which explains why war itself (including the warlike cult of sacrifice) has supplied all the *forms* in which punishment appears in history.

10

As its power grows, a community no longer takes the transgressions of the individual so seriously because they can no longer count as dangerous and subversive for the continued existence of the whole to the same extent as formerly: the evildoer is no longer "made an outlaw" and cast out; the general anger is no longer allowed to vent itself in the same unbridled manner as formerly – rather, from now on, the evildoer is carefully defended against this anger, particularly that of the ones directly injured, and taken under the protection of the whole. Compromise with the anger of the one immediately affected by the misdeed; a striving to localize the case and prevent a further or indeed general participation and unrest; attempts to find equivalents and to settle the entire affair (the *compositio*[15]); above all the increasingly more resolute will to understand every offense as in some sense *capable of being paid off*, hence, at least to a certain extent, to *isolate* the criminal and his deed from each other – these are the traits that are imprinted with increasing clarity onto the further development of penal law. If the power and the self-confidence of a community grow, the penal law also always becomes milder; every weakening and deeper endangering of the former brings the latter's harsher forms to light again. The "creditor" has always become more humane to the degree that he has become richer; finally the amount of injury he can bear without suffering from it even becomes the *measure* of his wealth. It would not be impossible to imagine a *consciousness of power* in society such that society might allow itself the noblest luxury there is for it – to leave the one who injures it *unpunished*. "What concern are my parasites to me?" it might then say. "Let them live and prosper: I am strong enough for that!" ... The justice that began with "everything can be paid off, everything must be paid off," ends by looking the other way and letting the one unable to pay go free, – it ends like every good thing on earth, by *cancelling itself*. This self-cancellation of justice: we know what pretty name it gives itself – *mercy*; as goes without saying, it remains the privilege of the most powerful, better still, his beyond-the-law.

   [...]

16

At this point I can no longer avoid helping my own hypothesis on the origin of the "bad conscience" to a first, preliminary expression: it is not easy to present and needs to be considered, guarded, and slept over for a long time. I take bad conscience to be the deep sickness into which man had to fall under the pressure of that most fundamental of all changes he ever experienced – the change of finding himself enclosed once and for all within the sway

---

[13] "Elend," êlend] The New High German Elend (misery) derives from the Old High German adjective elilenti (in another land or country; banished) via the shortened Middle High German ellende or êlend (foreign, miserable).

[14] vae victis!] Woe to the conquered! Livy, Ab urbe condita, Book V, 48, 9.

[15] compositio] term from Roman law referring to the settlement in a case of injury or damage caused by an illegal act.

of society and peace. Just as water animals must have fared when they were forced either to become land animals or to perish, so fared these half animals who were happily adapted to wilderness, war, roaming about, adventure – all at once all of their instincts were devalued and "disconnected." From now on they were to go on foot and "carry themselves" where they had previously been carried by the water: a horrible heaviness lay upon them. They felt awkward doing the simplest tasks; for this new, unfamiliar world they no longer had their old leaders, the regulating drives that unconsciously guided them safely – they were reduced to thinking, inferring, calculating, connecting cause and effect, these unhappy ones, reduced to their "consciousness," to their poorest and most erring organ! I do not believe there has ever been such a feeling of misery on earth, such a leaden discomfort – and yet those old instincts had not all at once ceased to make their demands! It's just that it was difficult and seldom possible to yield to them: for the most part they had to seek new and as it were subterranean gratifications. All instincts that do not discharge themselves outwardly *turn themselves inwards* – this is what I call the *internalizing* of man: thus first grows in man that which he later calls his "soul." The entire inner world, originally thin as if inserted between two skins, has spread and unfolded, has taken on depth, breadth, height to the same extent that man's outward discharging has been *obstructed*. Those terrible bulwarks with which the organization of the state protects itself against the old instincts of freedom – punishments belong above all else to these bulwarks – brought it about that all those instincts of the wild free roaming human turned themselves backwards *against man himself*. Hostility, cruelty, pleasure in persecution, in assault, in change, in destruction – all of that turning itself against the possessors of such instincts: *that* is the origin of "bad conscience." The man who, for lack of external enemies and resistance, and wedged into an oppressive narrowness and regularity of custom, impatiently tore apart, persecuted, gnawed at, stirred up, maltreated himself; this animal that one wants to "tame" and that beats itself raw on the bars of its cage; this deprived one, consumed by homesickness for the desert, who had to create out of himself an adventure, a place of torture, an uncertain and dangerous wilderness – this fool, this longing and desperate prisoner became the inventor of "bad conscience." In him, however, the greatest and most uncanny of sicknesses was introduced, one from which man has not recovered to this day, the suffering of man *from man*, from *himself* – as the consequence of a forceful separation from his animal past, of a leap and plunge, as it were, into new situations and conditions of existence, of a declaration of war against the old instincts on which his energy, desire, and terribleness had thus far rested. Let us immediately add that, on the other hand, with the appearance on earth of an animal soul turned against itself, taking sides against itself, something so new, deep, unheard of, enigmatic, contradictory, *and full of future* had come into being that the appearance of the earth was thereby essentially changed. Indeed, divine spectators were necessary to appreciate the spectacle that thus began and whose end is still by no means in sight – a spectacle too refined, too wonderful, too paradoxical to be permitted to play itself out senselessly-unnoticed on some ridiculous star! Since that time man is *included* among the most unexpected and exciting lucky throws in the game played by the "big child" of Heraclitus, whether called Zeus or chance – he awakens for himself an interest, an anticipation, a hope, almost a certainty, as if with him something were announcing itself, something preparing itself, as if man were not a goal but only a path, an incident, a bridge, a great promise …

17

To the presupposition of this hypothesis on the origin of bad conscience belongs first, that this change was not gradual, not voluntary, and that it presented itself not as an organic growing into new conditions, but rather as a break, a leap, a compulsion, an inescapable doom, against which there was no struggle and not even any *ressentiment*. Second, however, that this fitting of a previously unrestrained and unformed population into a fixed form, given its beginning in an act of force, could be brought to its completion only by acts of force – that the oldest "state" accordingly made its appearance as a terrible tyranny, as a crushing and ruthless machinery, and continued to work until finally such a raw material of people and half-animals was not only thoroughly kneaded and pliable but also *formed*. I use the word "state": it goes without saying who is meant by this – some pack of blond beasts of prey, a race of conquerors and lords, which, organized in a warlike manner and with the power to organize, unhesitatingly lays its terrible paws on a population enormously superior in number perhaps, but still formless, still roaming about. It is in this manner, then, that the "state" begins on earth: I think the flight of fancy that had it beginning with a "contract" has been abandoned. Whoever can give orders, whoever is "lord" by nature, whoever steps forth violently, in deed and gesture – what does he have to do with contracts! With such beings one does not reckon, they come like fate, without basis, reason, consideration, pretext; they are there like lightning is there: too terrible, too sudden, too convincing, too "different" even to be so much as hated. Their work is an instinctive creating of forms, impressing of forms; they are the most involuntary, unconscious artists there are: – where they appear, in a short time something new stands there, a ruling structure that *lives*, in which parts and functions are delimited and related to one another, in which nothing at all finds a place that has not first had placed into it a "meaning" with respect to the whole. They do not know what guilt, what responsibility, what consideration is, these born organizers; in them that terrible artists' egoism rules, that has a gaze like bronze and that knows itself already justified to all eternity in its "work," like the mother in her child. *They* are not the ones among whom "bad conscience" grew, that is clear from the outset – but it would not have grown *without them*, this ugly growth, it would be missing, if an enormous quantity of freedom had not been banished from the world, at least from visibility, and made *latent* as it were, under the pressure of the blows of their hammers, of their artist's violence. This *instinct for freedom*, forcibly made latent – we have already grasped it – this instinct for freedom, driven back, suppressed, imprisoned within, and finally discharging and venting itself only on itself: this, only this, is *bad conscience* in its beginnings.

18

One should guard against forming a low opinion of this entire phenomenon just because it is ugly and painful from the outset. After all, the active force that is at work on a grander scale in those violence-artists and organizers and that builds states, is basically the same force that here – inwardly, on a smaller, pettier scale, in a backwards direction, in the "labyrinth of the breast," to use Goethe's words – creates for itself the bad conscience and builds negative ideals: namely that *instinct for freedom* (speaking in my language: the will to power). Only here the matter on which this force's formative and violating nature vents itself is precisely man himself, his entire animal old self – and *not*, as in that larger and more conspicuous phenomenon, the *other* human, the *other* humans. This secret self-violation, this artists' cruelty, this pleasure in giving oneself – as heavy resisting suffering matter – a form, in burning into oneself a will, a critique, a contradiction, a contempt, a "no"; this uncanny and horrifying-pleasurable work of a soul compliant-conflicted with itself, that makes itself suffer out of pleasure in making-suffer, this entire *active* "bad conscience," as the true womb of ideal and imaginative events, finally brought to light – one can guess it already – a wealth of new disconcerting beauty and affirmation and perhaps for the first time beauty *itself* ... For what would be "beautiful" if contradiction had not first come to a consciousness of itself, if the ugly had not first said to itself "I am ugly"? ... After this hint, that enigma will at the least be less enigmatic, namely, to what extent an ideal, a beauty can be suggested by contradictory concepts like *selflessness, self-denial, self-sacrifice*; and we know one thing henceforth, this I do not doubt – namely what kind of *pleasure* it is that the selfless, the self-denying, the self-sacrificing feel from the very start: this pleasure belongs to cruelty. – So much for the present on the origins of the "unegoistic" as a *moral* value and toward Staking out the ground from which this value has grown: bad conscience, the will to self-maltreatment, first supplies the presupposition for the *value* of the unegoistic. –

19

It is a sickness, bad conscience – this admits of no doubt – but a sickness as pregnancy is a sickness. Let us seek out the conditions under which this sickness has come to its most terrible and most sublime pinnacle: – we shall see just what it was that thus first made its entry into the world. For this we need a long breath, – and to start off we must return once again to an earlier viewpoint. The civil-law relationship of the debtor to his creditor, of which I have already spoken at length, was once again – and indeed in a manner that is historically exceedingly curious and questionable – interpreted into a relationship in which it is for us modern humans perhaps at its most incomprehensible: namely the relationship of *those presently living* to their *ancestors*. Within the original clan association – we are speaking of primeval times – the living generation always acknowledges a juridical obligation to the earlier generation, and particularly to the earliest one, which founded the clan (and by no means a mere sentimental obligation: one might with good reason even deny the latter altogether for the longest part of the existence of the human race). Here the conviction holds sway that it is only through the sacrifices and achievements of the ancestors that the clan *exists* at all, – and that one has to *repay* them through sacrifices and achievements: one thereby acknowledges a *debt* that is continually growing, since these ancestors, in their continued existence as powerful spirits, do not cease to use their strength to bestow on the clan new benefits and advances. For nothing perhaps? But to those brutal and "soul-poor" ages there is no "for nothing." What can one give back to them? Sacrifices (initially only nourishment, in the coarsest sense), festivals, shrines, tributes, above all obedience – for all customs, as works of the ancestors, are also their statutes and commands –: does one ever give them enough? This suspicion remains and grows: from time to time it forces a great redemption, lock, stock, and barrel, some enormity of a counter-payment to the "creditor" (the notorious sacrifice of the firstborn, for example; blood, human blood in any case). The fear of the progenitor and his power, the consciousness of debts toward him necessarily increases, according to this kind of logic, to exactly the same degree that the power of the clan itself increases, that the clan itself stands ever more victorious, independent, honored, feared. By no means the other way around! Rather every step toward the atrophying of the clan, all miserable chance occurrences, all signs of degeneration, of approaching dissolution always *diminish* the fear of the spirit of the founder and give an ever more reduced notion of his shrewdness, his foresightedness, and his presence as power. If one imagines this brutal kind of logic carried through to its end: finally, through the imagination of growing fear the progenitors of the *most powerful* clans must have grown into enormous proportions and have been pushed back into the darkness of a divine uncanniness and unimaginability: – in the end the progenitor is necessarily transfigured into a *god*. This may even be the origin of the gods, an origin, that is, out of *fear*! … And those who think it necessary to add: "but also out of piety!" would hardly be right with regard to the longest period of the human race, its primeval period. All the more, admittedly, for the *middle* period in which the noble clans take shape: – who in fact returned, with interest, to their originators, the ancestors (heroes, gods) all of the qualities that had in the meantime become apparent in them, the *noble* qualities. Later we will take another look at the aristocratizing and ennobling of the gods (which is by no means their "hallowing"): for the present let us simply bring the course of this whole development of guilt consciousness to a conclusion.

20

As history teaches, the consciousness of having debts to the deity by no means came to an end even after the decline of the "community" organized according to blood-relationships; in the same way that it inherited the concepts "good and bad" from the clan nobility (together with its basic psychological propensity for establishing orders of rank), humanity also inherited, along with the deities of the clan and tribe, the pressure of the still unpaid debts and of the longing for the redemption of the same. (The transition is made by those broad slave and serf populations who adapted themselves to the cult of the gods practiced by their lords, whether through force or through submissiveness and mimicry: starting from them, this inheritance then overflows in all directions.) For several millennia the feeling of guilt toward the deity did not stop growing and indeed grew ever onward in the same proportion as the concept of god and the feeling for god grew on earth and was borne up on high. (The whole history of ethnic fighting, triumphing, reconciling, merging – everything that precedes the final rank-ordering of all ethnic elements in every great racial synthesis – is reflected in the genealogical confusion of their gods, in the legends of their fights, triumphs, and reconciliations; development toward universal empires is also always development toward universal deities; despotism with its overpowering of the independent nobility also always prepares the way for some kind of monotheism.) The rise of the Christian god as the maximum god that has been attained thus far therefore also brought a maximum of feelings of guilt into appearance on earth. Assuming that we have by now entered into the *reverse* movement, one might with no little probability deduce from the unstoppable decline of faith in the Christian god that there would already be a considerable decline in human consciousness of guilt as well; indeed the prospect cannot be dismissed that the perfect and final victory of atheism might free humanity from this entire feeling of having debts to its beginnings, its *causa prima*.[16] Atheism and a kind of *second innocence* belong together. –

21

So much for the present, in short and roughly speaking, on the connection of the concepts "guilt," "duty" to religious presuppositions: I have until now intentionally left aside the actual moralization of these concepts (their being pushed back into conscience, more precisely the entanglement of *bad* conscience with the concept of god) and at the end of the previous section even spoke as if there were no such moralization, consequently, as if those concepts were now necessarily coming to an end now that their presupposition, the faith in our "creditor," in God, has fallen. The facts of the case diverge from this in a terrible manner. With the moralization of the concepts guilt and duty,

---

[16] causa prima] first cause.

with their being pushed back into *bad* conscience, we have in actual fact the attempt to *reverse* the direction of the development just described, at least to bring its movement to a standstill: precisely the prospect of a conclusive redemption *shall* now pessimistically close itself off once and for all; the gaze *shall* now bleakly deflect off, deflect back from a brazen impossibility; those concepts "guilt" and "duty" *shall* now turn themselves backwards – and against whom? There can be no doubt: first against the "debtor," in whom bad conscience now fixes itself firmly, eats into him, spreads out, and grows like a polyp in every breadth and depth until finally, with the impossibility of discharging the debt, the impossibility of discharging penance is also conceived of, the idea that it cannot be paid off ("*eternal* punishment") –; finally, however, even against the "creditor," think here of the *causa prima* of man, of the beginning of the human race, of its progenitor, who is now burdened with a curse ("Adam," "Original Sin," "unfreedom of the will") or of nature, from whose womb man arises and into which the evil principle is now placed ("demonizing of nature") or of existence generally, which is left as *valueless in itself* (nihilistic turning away from it, longing into nothingness or longing into its "opposite," a being-other, Buddhism and related things) – until all at once we stand before the paradoxical and horrifying remedy in which tortured humanity found temporary relief, *Christianity's* stroke of genius: God sacrificing himself for the guilt of man, God himself exacting payment of himself, God as the only one who can redeem from man what has become irredeemable for man himself – the creditor sacrificing himself for his debtor, out of *love* (is that credible? –), out of love for his debtor!...

22

One will already have guessed *what* actually happened with all of this and *under* all of this: that will to self-torment, that suppressed cruelty of the animal-human who had been made inward, scared back into himself, of the one locked up in the "state" for the purpose of taming, who invented the bad conscience in order to cause himself pain after the *more natural* outlet for this *desire to cause pain* was blocked, – this man of bad conscience has taken over the religious presupposition in order to drive his self-torture to its most gruesome severity and sharpness. Guilt before *God*: this thought becomes an instrument of torture for him. In "God" he captures the most extreme opposites he can find to his actual and inescapable animal instincts; he reinterprets these animal instincts themselves as guilt before God (as hostility, rebellion, insurrection against the "lord," the "father," the primal ancestor and beginning of the world); he harnesses himself into the contradiction "God" and "devil"; he takes all the "no" that he says to himself, to nature, naturalness, the facticity of his being and casts it out of himself as a "yes," as existing, corporeal, real, as God, as holiness of God, as judgeship of God, as executionership of God, as beyond, as eternity, as torture without end, as hell, as immeasurability of punishment and guilt. This is a kind of madness of the will in psychic cruelty that has absolutely no equal: the *will* of man to find himself guilty and reprehensible to the point that it cannot be atoned for; his *will* to imagine himself punished without the possibility of the punishment ever becoming equivalent to the guilt; his *will* to infect and make poisonous the deepest ground of things with the problem of punishment and guilt in order to cut off the way out of this labyrinth of "*idées fixes*" once and for all; his *will* to erect an ideal – that of the "holy God" – in order, in the face of the same, to be tangibly certain of his absolute unworthiness. Oh, this insane sad beast man! What ideas occur to it, what anti-nature, what paroxysms of nonsense; what *bestiality of idea* immediately breaks forth when it is hindered only a little from being a *beast of deed*! … All of this is interesting to the point of excess, but also of such black gloomy unnerving sadness that one must forcibly forbid oneself to look too long into these abysses. Here there is *sickness*, beyond all doubt, the most terrible sickness that has thus far raged in man: – and whoever is still capable of hearing (but one no longer has the ears for it today! –) how in this night of torture and absurdity the cry *love* resounded, the cry of the most longing delight, of redemption in *love*, will turn away, seized by an invincible horror … There is so much in man that is horrifying! … The earth has been a madhouse for too long! …

23

Let this suffice once and for all concerning the origins of the "holy God." – That *in itself* the conception of gods does not necessarily lead to this degradation of the imagination, which we could not spare ourselves from calling to mind for a moment, that there are *more noble* ways of making use of the fabrication of gods than for this self-crucifixion and self-defilement of man in which Europe's last millennia have had their mastery – this can fortunately be read from every glance one casts on the *Greek gods*, these reflections of noble and autocratic human beings in whom the *animal* in man felt itself deified and *did not* tear itself apart, *did not* rage against itself! For the longest time these Greeks used their gods precisely to keep "bad conscience" at arm's length, to be able to remain cheerful about their freedom of soul: that is, the reverse of the use which Christianity made of its god. They took this to *great lengths*, these splendid and lionhearted childish ones; and no lesser authority than that of the Homeric Zeus himself gives them to understand here and there that they make it too easy for themselves. "A wonder!" he says once – it concerns the case of Aegisthus, a *very* bad case –

> A wonder, how much the mortals complain against the gods!
> *Only from us is there evil*, they think; but they themselves
> Create their own misery through lack of understanding, even counter to fate.

But one hears and sees at the same time that even this Olympian spectator and judge is far from being angry at them for this and from thinking evil of them: "how *foolish* they are!" so he thinks in the face of the misdeeds of the mortals, – and "foolishness," "lack of understanding," a little "disturbance in the head," this much even the Greeks of the strongest, bravest age *allowed* themselves as the reason for much that was bad and doom-laden: – foolishness, *not* sin! do you understand that? ... But even this disturbance in the head was a problem – "indeed, how is it even possible? whence could it actually have come, given heads such as *we* have, we men of noble descent, of happiness, of optimal form, of the best society, of nobility, of virtue?" – thus the noble Greek wondered for centuries in the face of every incomprehensible atrocity and wanton act with which one of his equals had sullied himself. "A god must have beguiled him," he said to himself finally, shaking his head ... This way out is *typical* of the Greeks ... In this manner the gods served in those days to justify humans to a certain degree even in bad things, they served as causes of evil – in those days it was not the punishment they took upon themselves but rather, as is *more noble*, the guilt ...

11

The Methods of Ethics

Henry Sidgwick

Sidgwick's book *The Methods of Ethics* is among the greatest philosophical books on ethics; many have thought it the greatest. Sidgwick aims for clarity over style or persuasiveness in his writing; but, because his project was so ambitious and covers so much ground, it is not always easy to grasp the point of particular claims or arguments. So getting an overview of the *Methods* is important.

Sidgwick himself explains his motivation for writing the book in a helpful preface, published with the 6th edition. He tells us here that, influenced by J.S. Mill, he began as a hedonistic utilitarian, believing that utility or the good consists only in happiness, or the balance of pleasure over pain, and that this should be maximized. He was inclined to accept psychological hedonistic egoism – that each person aims for their own greatest happiness – but then recognized that there might be a conflict between one's good and the promotion of happiness overall. Having re-read Joseph Butler, he gave up psychological egoism and saw that utilitarianism would require a fundamental *intuition*, or basic and self-evident belief. Wondering whether the everyday morality of his time might provide some insight, he first wrote book 3 of the *Methods*, the most brilliant discussion of 'common-sense morality' since Aristotle. Finding common-sense morality inadequate, Sidgwick nevertheless thought utilitarianism could be provided with an intuitionist basis. But he could not reject egoism, which left him with his so-called *dualism of the practical reason*, unable to decide between egoism and utilitarianism.

Sidgwick begins the *Methods* (1.1) with a definition of what he means by 'a method: 'any rational procedure by which we determine what individual human beings "ought" … to do'. A method is similar to what we might now call a 'normative theory' – a theory about our ultimate reasons for action. Sidgwick plausibly sees philosophical ethics primarily as a debate between egoism, common-sense morality, and utilitarianism – these are his three 'methods'. (Note that Sidgwick understands 'ethics' in a broad sense, as concerning ultimate reasons. These reasons need not be 'moral' in any narrower sense.)

Sidgwick is careful to distinguish the notions of the right and the good, and recognizes that philosophers vary in the role they assign to each in their theories. Sidgwick's own view of the good remained hedonistic (1.9, 3.14). He points out that 'the good' cannot literally be defined as 'pleasure' without tautology, anticipating G.E. Moore's famous 1903 'open question argument'. Many will accept that pleasure is *a* good. The difficulty for hedonism is that many will also claim that there are non-hedonic goods. Sidgwick rules out such goods as irrational early in the *Methods* (1.1), which throws some doubt on his claim in the preface and elsewhere to strict scientific impartiality. Later he seeks to undermine the claims of non-hedonic goods, noting for example that pleasure often arises when one aims for objects other than pleasure (so aiming to win a tennis match can make it more enjoyable than explicitly aiming to enjoy oneself). But the fact remains that many serious thinkers will be unconvinced, and it could be that Sidgwick is required by his own epistemic principles concerning disagreement to suspend judgement (more on this shortly).

History of Ethics – Essential Readings with Commentary, First Edition. Edited by Daniel Star and Roger Crisp.
© 2020 John Wiley & Sons Ltd. Published 2020 by John Wiley & Sons Ltd.

Sidgwick is deliberately modest in his claims *about* ethical judgements. He assumes from the start (preface to 1st edn.) that there is a truth about what we have reason to do, and that this may be known. But in 1.1 he insists that his arguments are also relevant to non-rationalists, as long as they are ready to make judgements about ultimate reasons. Nevertheless he is prepared to insist that, as far as he is concerned, the notion of 'ought' is irreducible to mere desire, so the conflict that many of us seem to feel between desire and reason is a genuine one (1.3).

Sidgwick speaks often of intuition and intuitionism, and it is useful to be clear on the differences between the different forms (1.8). He groups them together because they all, in different ways, rely on an 'immediate' judgement. According to the first kind, *perceptional intuitionism*, moral agents can, in the situation they are in, immediately see what is right or wrong. Sidgwick calls this view 'ultra-intuitional', and notes its unsatisfactoriness. People often demand reasons for decisions, for example, and they also often disagree with one another. This takes us to what he calls *dogmatic intuitionism*, which is the moral theory based on development of common-sense morality. This rests on the idea that certain actions can be seen as right or wrong immediately, without reference to their consequences, and is the view discussed in the longest of the four 'books' in the *Methods*, book 3 (book 1 is an introduction, 2 is on egoism, and 4 on utilitarianism). The problem with this view, as Sidgwick sees it, is exemplified in his discussion of promising (3.6). It may seem intuitively plausible to claim that we have an ultimate reason to keep our promises. But there seem to be cases where this isn't so (for example, if my promise is extracted by force), and that means any principle governing promises will have to be extremely long and complicated, to the point that it is no longer self-evident. Again, however, as in the case of non-hedonic goods, we have to admit that many *will* find such a principle self-evident.

This takes us to the final *philosophical* 'phase' of intuitionism, a level where we can avoid the 'accidental aggregate' of principles alleged by dogmatic intuitionists. Here we seek principles that meet certain epistemic conditions (3.11): clarity, reflectiveness, consistency, and non-dissensus (this is the condition that requires us to suspend judgement in cases of disagreement). Sidgwick himself finds three such principles (3.13): 'justice' – that our moral judgements must apply to all relevantly similar cases; 'prudence' (which underlies egoism); and 'rational benevolence' (which underlies utilitarianism). (It is worth noting that Sidgwick later suggests that utilitarians, who base their view on rational benevolence, will also give weight to equality as a tie-breaker when two outcomes contain the same amount of happiness overall.)

Utilitarianism (defined in 4.1 as the view that objectively right action will maximize overall happiness) has support, then, from philosophical intuitionism. But it also gains support from its providing 'harmony' for the aggregate of common-sense principles (4.2–5): most of them can be seen as devices developed for the promotion of happiness, and those that are not should be considered, with some care, for reform. But Sidgwick finds that he cannot give up rational egoism, and despite his best efforts cannot make egoism consistent with utilitarianism (2.5; Concluding Chapter). So his great book ends in indecision. There is a hint that there may be epistemological theories that would allow us to assume harmony between egoism and utilitarianism, but Sidgwick never developed any such theory himself.

Preface to the First Edition

IN offering to the public a new book upon a subject so trite as Ethics, it seems desirable to indicate clearly at the outset its plan and purpose. Its distinctive characteristics may be first given negatively. It is not, in the main, metaphysical or psychological: at the same time it is not dogmatic or directly practical: it does not deal, except by way of illustration, with the history of ethical thought: in a sense it might be said to be not even critical, since it is only quite incidentally that it offers any criticism of the systems of individual moralists. It claims to be an examination, at once expository and critical, of the different methods of obtaining reasoned convictions as to what ought to be done which are to be found – either explicit or implicit – in the moral consciousness of mankind generally: and which, from time to time, have been developed, either singly or in combination, by individual thinkers, and worked up into the systems now historical.

I have avoided the inquiry into the Origin of the Moral Faculty – which has perhaps occupied a disproportionate amount of the attention of modern moralists – by the simple assumption (which seems to be made implicitly in all ethical reasoning) that there is something[1] under any given circumstances which it is right or reasonable to do, and that this may be known. If it be admitted that we now have the faculty of knowing this, it appears to me that the investigation of the historical antecedents of this cognition, and of its relation to other elements of the mind, no more properly belongs to Ethics than the corresponding questions as to the cognition of Space belong to Geometry.[2] I make, however, no further assumption as to the nature of the object of ethical knowledge: and hence my treatise is not dogmatic: all the different methods developed in it are expounded and criticised from a neutral position, and as impartially as possible. And thus, though my treatment of the subject is, in a sense, more practical than that of many moralists, since I am occupied from first to last in considering how conclusions are to be rationally reached in the familiar matter of our common daily life and actual practice; still, my immediate object – to invert Aristotle's phrase – is not Practice but Knowledge. I have thought that the predominance in the minds of moralists of a desire to edify has impeded the real progress of ethical science: and that this would be benefited by an application to it of the same disinterested curiosity to which we chiefly owe the great discoveries of physics. It is in this spirit that I have endeavoured to compose the present work: and with this view I have desired to concentrate the reader's attention, from first to last, not on the practical results to which our methods lead, but on the methods themselves. I have wished to put aside temporarily the urgent need which we all feel of finding and adopting the true method of determining what we ought to do; and to consider simply what conclusions will be rationally reached if we start with certain ethical premises, and with what degree of certainty and precision.

[…]

Preface to the Second Edition

[…]

In revising my work, I have endeavoured to profit as much as possible by all the criticisms on it that have been brought to my notice, whether public or private. I have frequently deferred to objections, even when they appeared to me unsound, if I thought I could avoid controversy by alterations to which I was myself indifferent. Where I have been unable to make the changes required, I have usually replied, in the text or the notes, to such criticisms as have appeared to me plausible, or in any way instructive. […] I have generally left unnoticed such criticisms as have been due to mere misapprehensions, against which I thought I could effectually guard in the present edition. There is, however, one fundamental misunderstanding, on which it seems desirable to say a few words. I find that more than one critic has overlooked or disregarded the account of the plan of my treatise, given in the original preface and in § 5 of the introductory chapter: and has consequently supposed me to be writing as an assailant of two of the methods which I chiefly examine, and a defender of the third. Thus one of my reviewers seems to regard Book iii. (on Intuitionism) as containing mere hostile criticism from the outside: another has constructed an article on the supposition that my principal object is the 'suppression of Egoism': a third has gone to the length of a pamphlet under the impression (apparently) that the 'main argument' of my treatise is a demonstration of Universalistic Hedonism.

---

[1] I did not mean to exclude the supposition that two or more alternatives might under certain circumstances be equally right (1884).

[2] This statement now appears to me to require a slight modification (1884).

I am concerned to have caused so much misdirection of criticism: and I have carefully altered in this edition the passages which I perceive to have contributed to it. The morality that I examine in Book iii. is my own morality as much as it is any man's: it is, as I say, the 'Morality of Common Sense,' which I only attempt to represent in so far as I share it; I only place myself outside it either (1) temporarily, for the purpose of impartial criticism, or (2) in so far as I am forced beyond it by a practical consciousness of its incompleteness. I have certainly criticised this morality unsparingly: but I conceive myself to have exposed with equal unreserve the defects and difficulties of the hedonistic method (cf. especially chaps, iii., iv. of Book ii., and chap. v. of Book iv.). And as regards the two hedonistic principles, I do not hold the reasonableness of aiming at happiness generally with any stronger conviction than I do that of aiming at one's own. It was no part of my plan to call special attention to this "Dualism of the Practical Reason" as I have elsewhere called it: but I am surprised at the extent to which my view has perplexed even those of my critics who have understood it. I had imagined that they would readily trace it to the source from which I learnt it, Butler's well-known Sermons. I hold with Butler that "Reasonable Self-love and Conscience are the two chief or superior principles in the nature of man," each of which we are under a "manifest obligation" to obey: and I do not (I believe) differ materially from Butler in my view either of reasonable self-love, or – theology apart – of its relation to conscience. Nor, again, do I differ from him in regarding conscience as essentially a function of the practical Reason: "moral precepts," he says in the *Analogy* (Part II. chap, viii.), "are precepts the reason of which we see." My difference only begins when I ask myself, 'What among the precepts of our common conscience do we really see to be ultimately reasonable?' a question which Butler does not seem to have seriously put, and to which, at any rate, he has given no satisfactory answer. The answer that I found to it supplied the rational basis that I had long perceived to be wanting to the Utilitarianism of Bentham, regarded as an ethical doctrine: and thus enabled me to transcend the commonly received antithesis between Intuitionists and Utilitarians.

[…]

Preface to the Sixth Edition

[…]

Among the MS. material which Professor Sidgwick intended to be referred to, in preparing this edition for the press, there occurs, as part of the MS. notes for a lecture, a brief history of the development in his thought of the ethical view which he has set forth in the *Methods of Ethics*. This, though not in a finished condition, is in essentials complete and coherent, and since it cannot fail to have peculiar value and interest for students of the book, it has been decided to insert it here.

[…]

In the account referred to Professor Sidgwick says: –

"My first adhesion to a definite Ethical system was to the Utilitarianism of Mill: I found in this relief from the apparently external and arbitrary pressure of moral rules which I had been educated to obey, and which presented themselves to me as to some extent doubtful and confused; and sometimes, even when clear, as merely dogmatic, unreasoned, incoherent. My antagonism to this was intensified by the study of Whewell's *Elements of Morality* which was prescribed for the study of undergraduates in Trinity. It was from that book that I derived the impression – which long remained uneffaced – that Intuitional moralists were hopelessly loose (as compared to mathematicians) in their definitions and axioms.

The two elements of Mill's view which I am accustomed to distinguish as Psychological Hedonism [that each man does seek his own Happiness] and Ethical Hedonism [that each man ought to seek the general Happiness] both attracted me, and I did not at first perceive their incoherence.

Psychological Hedonism – the law of universal pleasure-seeking – attracted me by its frank naturalness. Ethical Hedonism, as expounded by Mill, was morally inspiring by its dictate of readiness for absolute self - sacrifice. They appealed to different elements of my nature, but they brought these into apparent harmony: they both used the same words "pleasure," "happiness," and the persuasiveness of Mill's exposition veiled for a time the profound discrepancy between the natural end of action – private happiness, and the end of duty – general happiness. Or if a doubt assailed me as to the coincidence of private and general happiness, I was inclined to hold that it ought to be cast to the winds by a generous resolution.

But a sense grew upon me that this method of dealing with the conflict between Interest and Duty, though perhaps proper for practice could not be final for philosophy. For practical men who do not philosophise, the maxim of subordinating self-interest, as commonly conceived, to "altruistic" impulses and sentiments which they feel to be higher and nobler is, I doubt not, a commendable maxim; but it is surely the business of Ethical Philosophy to find and make explicit the rational ground of such action.

I therefore set myself to examine methodically the relation of Interest and Duty.

This involved a careful study of Egoistic Method, to get the relation of Interest and Duty clear. Let us suppose that my own Interest is paramount. What really is my Interest, how far can acts conducive to it be known, how far does the result correspond with Duty (or Wellbeing of Mankind)? This investigation led me to feel very strongly *this* opposition, rather than that which Mill and the earlier Utilitarians felt between so-called Intuitions or Moral Sense Perceptions, and Hedonism, whether Epicurean or Utilitarian. Hence the arrangement of my book – ii., iii., iv. [Book ii. Egoism, Book iii. Intuitionism, Book iv. Utilitarianism].

The result was that I concluded that no complete solution of the conflict between my happiness and the general happiness was possible on the basis of mundane experience. This [conclusion I] slowly and reluctantly accepted – cf. Book ii. chap., v., and last chapter of treatise [Book ii. chap. v. is on "Happiness and Duty," and the concluding chapter is on "The Mutual Relations of the Three Methods"]. This [was] most important to me.

In consequence of this perception, moral choice of the general happiness or acquiescence in self-interest as ultimate, became practically necessary. But on what ground?

I put aside Mill's phrases that such sacrifice was "heroic": that it was not "well" with me unless I was in a disposition to make it. I put to him in my mind the dilemma: – Either it is for my own happiness or it is not. If not, why [should I do it]? – It was no use to say that if I was a moral hero I should have formed a habit of willing actions beneficial to others which would remain in force, even with my own pleasure in the other scale. I knew that at any rate I was not the kind of moral hero who does this without reason; from *blind* habit. Nor did I even wish to be that kind of hero: for it seemed to me that that kind of hero, however admirable, was certainly not a philosopher. I must somehow *see* that it was right for me to sacrifice my happiness for the good of the whole of which I am a part.

Thus, in spite of my early aversion to Intuitional Ethics, derived from the study of Whewell, and in spite of my attitude of discipleship to Mill, I was forced to recognise the need of a fundamental ethical intuition.

The utilitarian method – which I had learnt from Mill – could not, it seemed to me, be made coherent and harmonious without this fundamental intuition.

In this state of mind I read Kant's Ethics again: I had before read it somewhat unintelligently, under the influence of Mill's view as to its "grotesque failure."[3] I now read it more receptively and was impressed with the truth and importance of its fundamental principle: – *Act from a principle or maxim that you can will to be a universal law* – cf. Book iii. chap. i. § 3 [of *The Methods of Ethics*]. It threw the "golden rule" of the gospel ("Do unto others as ye would that others should do unto you") into a form that commended itself to my reason.

Kant's resting of morality on Freedom did not indeed commend itself to me,[4] though I did not at first see, what I now seem to see clearly, that it involves the fundamental confusion of using "freedom" in two distinct senses – "freedom" that is realised only when we do right, when reason triumphs over inclination, and "freedom" that is realised equally when we choose to do wrong, and which is apparently implied in the notion of ill-desert. What commended itself to me, in short, was Kant's ethical principle rather than its metaphysical basis. This I briefly explain in Book iii. chap. i. § 3 [of *The Methods of Ethics*]. I shall go into it at more length when we come to Kant.

That whatever is right for me must be right for all persons in similar circumstances – which was the form in which I accepted the Kantian maxim – seemed to me certainly fundamental, certainly true, and not without practical importance.

But the fundamental principle seemed to me inadequate for the construction of a system of duties; and the more I reflected on it the more inadequate it appeared.

On reflection it did not seem to me really to meet the difficulty which had led me from Mill to Kant: it did not settle finally the subordination of Self-interest to Duty.

For the Rational Egoist – a man who had learnt from Hobbes that Self-preservation is the first law of Nature and Self-interest the only rational basis of social morality – and in fact, its actual basis, so far as it is effective – such a thinker might accept the Kantian principle and remain an Egoist.

He might say, "I quite admit that when the painful necessity comes for another man to choose between his own happiness and the general happiness, he must as a reasonable being prefer his own, *i.e.* it is right for him to do this on my principle. No doubt, as I probably do not sympathise with him in particular any more than with other

---

[3] Kant's *Fundamental Principles* (*Grundlegung zur Metaphysik der Sitten*), §§ 1, 2. Mill, *Utilitarianism*, pp. 5, 6 [7th edition (large print), 1879].

[4] Book i. chap. v. of *The Methods of Ethics*.

persons, I as a disengaged spectator should like him to sacrifice himself to the general good: but I do not expect him to do it, any more than I should do it myself in his place."

It did not seem to me that this reasoning could be effectively confuted. No doubt it was, from the point of view of the universe, reasonable to prefer the greater good to the lesser, even though the lesser good was the private happiness of the agent. Still, it seemed to me also undeniably reasonable for the individual to prefer his own. The rationality of self-regard seemed to me as undeniable as the rationality of self-sacrifice. I could not give up this conviction, though neither of my masters, neither Kant nor Mill, seemed willing to admit it: in different ways, each in his own way, they refused to admit it.

I was, therefore, [if] I may so say, a disciple on the loose, in search of a master – or, if the term 'master' be too strong, at any rate I sought for sympathy and support, in the conviction which I had attained in spite of the opposite opinions of the thinkers from whom I had learnt most.

It was at this point then that the influence of Butler came in. For the stage at which I had thus arrived in search of an ethical creed, at once led me to understand Butler, and to find the support and intellectual sympathy that I required in his view.

I say to understand him, for hitherto I had misunderstood him, as I believe most people then misunderstood, and perhaps still misunderstand, him. He had been presented to me as an advocate of the authority of Conscience; and his argument, put summarily, seemed to be that because reflection on our impulses showed us Conscience claiming authority therefore we ought to obey it. Well, I had no doubt that my conscience claimed authority, though it was a more utilitarian conscience than Butler's: for, through all this search for principles I still adhered for practical purposes to the doctrine I had learnt from Mill, *i.e.* I still held to the maxim of aiming at the general happiness as the supreme directive rule of conduct, and I thought I could answer the objections that Butler brought against this view (in the "Dissertation on Virtue" at the end of the *Analogy*). My difficulty was, as I have said, that this claim of conscience, whether utilitarian or not, had to be harmonised with the claim of Rational Self-love; and that I vaguely supposed Butler to avoid or override [the latter claim].

But reading him at this stage with more care, I found in him, with pleasure and surprise, a view very similar to that which had developed itself in my own mind in struggling to assimilate Mill and Kant. I found he expressly admitted that "interest, my own happiness, is a manifest obligation," and that "Reasonable Self-love" [is "one of the two chief or superior principles in the nature of man"]. That is, he recognised a "Dualism of the Governing Faculty" – or as I prefer to say "Dualism of the Practical Reason," since the 'authority' on which Butler laid stress must present itself to my mind as the authority of reason, before I can admit it.

Of this more presently: what I now wish to make clear is that it was on this side – if I may so say – that I entered into Butler's system and came under the influence of his powerful and cautious intellect. But the effect of his influence carried me a further step away from Mill: for I was led by it to abandon the doctrine of Psychological Hedonism, and to recognise the existence of 'disinterested' or 'extra-regarding' impulses to action, [impulses] not directed towards the agent's pleasure [cf. chap iv. of Book i. of *The Methods of Ethics*]. In fact as regards what I may call a Psychological basis of Ethics, I found myself much more in agreement with Butler than Mill.

And this led me to reconsider my relation to Intuitional Ethics. The strength and vehemence of Butler's condemnation of pure Utilitarianism, in so cautious a writer, naturally impressed me much. And I had myself become, as I had to admit to myself, an Intuitionist to a certain extent. For the supreme rule of aiming at the general happiness, as I had come to see, must rest on a fundamental moral intuition, if I was to recognise it as binding at all. And in reading the writings of the earlier English Intuitionists, More and Clarke, I found the axiom I required for my Utilitarianism [That a rational agent is bound to aim at Universal Happiness], in one form or another, holding a prominent place (cf. *History of Ethics*, pp. 172, 181).

I had then, theoretically as well as practically, accepted this fundamental moral intuition; and there was also the Kantian principle, which I recognised as irresistibly valid, though not adequate to give complete guidance. – I was then an "intuitional" moralist to this extent: and if so, why not further? The orthodox moralists such as Whewell (then in vogue) said that there was a whole intelligible system of intuitions: but how were they to be learnt? I could not accept Butler's view as to the sufficiency of a plain man's conscience: for it appeared to me that plain men agreed rather verbally than really.

In this state of mind I had to read Aristotle again; and a light seemed to dawn upon me as to the meaning and drift of his procedure – especially in Books ii., iii., iv. of the *Ethics* – (cf. *History of Ethics*, chap. ii. § 9, p. 58, read to end of section).

What he gave us there was the Common Sense Morality of Greece, reduced to consistency by careful comparison: given not as something external to him but as what "we" – he and others – think, ascertained by reflection. And was not this really the Socratic induction, elicited by interrogation?

Might I not imitate this: do the same for *our* morality here and now, in the same manner of impartial reflection on current opinion?

Indeed *ought* I not to do this before deciding on the question whether I had or had not a system of moral intuitions? At any rate the result would be useful, whatever conclusion I came to.

So this was the part of my book first written (Book iii., chaps, i.-xi.), and a certain imitation of Aristotle's manner was very marked in it at first, and though I have tried to remove it where it seemed to me affected or pedantic, it still remains to some extent.

But the result of the examination was to bring out with fresh force and vividness the difference between the maxims of Common Sense Morality (even the strongest and strictest, *e.g.* Veracity and Good Faith) and the intuitions which I had already attained, *i.e.* the Kantian Principle (of which I now saw the only certain element in Justice – "treat similar cases similarly" – to be a particular application), and the Fundamental Principle of Utilitarianism. And this latter was in perfect harmony with the Kantian Principle. I certainly could will it to be a universal law that men should act in such a way as to promote universal happiness; in fact it was the only law that it was perfectly clear to me that I could thus decisively will, from a universal point of view.

I was then a Utilitarian again, but on an Intuitional basis.

But further, the reflection on Common Sense Morality which I had gone through, had continually brought home to me its character as a system of rules tending to the promotion of general happiness (cf. [*Methods of Ethics*] pp. 470, 471).

Also the previous reflection on hedonistic method for Book ii. had shown me its weaknesses. What was then to be done? [The] conservative attitude [to be observed] towards Common Sense [is] given in chapter v. of Book iv.: "Adhere generally, deviate and attempt reform only in exceptional cases in which, – notwithstanding the roughness of hedonistic method, – the argument against Common Sense is decisive."

In this state of mind I published my book: I tried to say what I had found: that the opposition between Utilitarianism and Intuitionism was due to a misunderstanding. There was indeed a fundamental opposition between the individual's interest and either morality, which I could not solve by any method I had yet found trustworthy, without the assumption of the moral government of the world: so far I agreed with both Butler and Kant.

But I could find no real opposition between Intuitionism and Utilitarianism. … The Utilitarianism of Mill and Bentham seemed to me to want a basis: that basis could only be supplied by a fundamental intuition; on the other hand the best examination I could make of the Morality of Common Sense showed me no clear and self-evident principles except such as were perfectly consistent with Utilitarianism.

Still, investigation of the Utilitarian method led me to see defects [in it]: the merely empirical examination of the consequences of actions is unsatisfactory; and being thus conscious of the practical imperfection in many cases of the guidance of the Utilitarian calculus, I remained anxious to treat with respect, and make use of, the guidance afforded by Common Sense in these cases, on the ground of the general presumption which evolution afforded that moral sentiments and opinions would point to conduct conducive to general happiness; though I could not admit this presumption as a ground for overruling a strong probability of the opposite, derived from utilitarian calculations."

[…]

BOOK I

Chapter I

Introduction

§ 1.   THE boundaries of the study called Ethics are variously and often vaguely conceived: but they will perhaps be sufficiently defined, at the outset, for the purposes of the present treatise, if a 'Method of Ethics' is explained to mean any rational procedure by which we determine what individual human beings 'ought' – or what it is 'right' for them – to do, or to seek to realise by voluntary action.[5]

[…]

---

[5] The exact relation of the terms 'right' and 'what ought to be' is discussed in chap. iii. of this Book. I here assume that they may be used as convertible, for most purposes.

§ 2.   In the language of the preceding section I could not avoid taking account of two different forms in which the fundamental problem of Ethics is stated; the difference between which leads, as we shall presently see, to rather important consequences. Ethics is sometimes considered as an investigation of the true Moral laws or rational precepts of Conduct; sometimes as an inquiry into the nature of the Ultimate End of reasonable human action – the Good or 'True Good' of man – and the method of attaining it. Both these views are familiar, and will have to be carefully considered: but the former seems most prominent in modern ethical thought, and most easily applicable to modern ethical systems generally. For the Good investigated in Ethics is limited to Good in some degree attainable by human effort; accordingly knowledge of the end is sought in order to ascertain what actions are the right means to its attainment. Thus however prominent the notion of an Ultimate Good – other than voluntary action of any kind – may be in an ethical system, and whatever interpretation may be given to this notion, we must still arrive finally, if it is to be practically useful, at some determination of precepts or directive rules, of conduct.

On the other hand, the conception of Ethics as essentially an investigation of the 'Ultimate Good' of Man and the means of attaining it is not universally applicable, without straining, to the view of Morality which we may conveniently distinguish as the Intuitional view; according to which conduct is held to be right when conformed to certain precepts or principles of Duty, intuitively known to be unconditionally binding. In this view the conception of Ultimate Good is not necessarily of fundamental importance in the determination of Right conduct except on the assumption that Right conduct itself – or the character realised in and developed through Right conduct – is the sole Ultimate Good for man. But this assumption is not implied in the Intuitional view of Ethics: nor would it, I conceive, accord with the moral common sense of modern Christian communities. For we commonly think that the complete notion of human Good or Well-being must include the attainment of Happiness as well as the performance of Duty; even if we hold with Butler that "the happiness of the world is the concern of Him who is the Lord and the Proprietor of it," and that, accordingly, it is not right for men to make their performance of Duty conditional on their knowledge of its conduciveness to their Happiness. For those who hold this, what men ought to take as the *practically* ultimate end of their action and standard of Right conduct, may in some cases have no logical connexion with the conception of Ultimate Good for man: so that, in such cases, however indispensable this latter conception may be to the completeness of an ethical system, it would still not be important for the methodical determination of Right conduct.

It is on account of the prevalence of the Intuitional view just mentioned, and the prominent place which it consequently occupies in my discussion, that in defining Ethics I have avoided the term 'Art of Conduct' which some would regard as its more appropriate designation. For the term 'Art' – when applied to the contents of a treatise – seems to signify systematic express knowledge (as distinguished from the implicit knowledge or organised habit which we call skill) of the right means to a given end. Now if we assume that the rightness of action depends on its conduciveness to some ulterior end, then no doubt – when this end has been clearly ascertained – the process of determining the right rules of conduct for human beings in different relations and circumstances would naturally come under the notion of Art. But on the view that the practically ultimate end of moral action is often the Rightness of the action itself – or the Virtue realised in and confirmed by such action – and that this is known intuitively in each case or class of cases, we can hardly regard the term 'Art' as properly applicable to the systematisation of such knowledge. Hence, as I do not wish to start with any assumption incompatible with this latter view, I prefer to consider Ethics as the science or study of what is right or what ought to be, so far as this depends upon the voluntary action of individuals.[6]

§ 3.   If, however, this view of the scope of Ethics is accepted, the question arises why it is commonly taken to consist, to a great extent, of psychological discussion as to the 'nature of the moral faculty'; especially as I have myself thought it right to include some discussion of this kind in the present treatise. For it does not at first appear why this should belong to Ethics, any more than discussions about the mathematical faculty or the faculty of sense-perception belong to mathematics and physics respectively. Why do we not simply start with certain premises, stating what ought to be done or sought, without considering the faculty by which we apprehend their truth?

One answer is that the moralist has a practical aim: we desire knowledge of right conduct in order to act on it. Now we cannot help believing what we see to be true, but we can help doing what we see to be right or wise, and in fact often do what we know to be wrong or unwise: thus we are forced to notice the existence in us of irrational

[6] The relation of the notion of 'Good' to that of 'Right' or 'what ought to be' will be further considered in a subsequent chapter of this Book (ix.).

springs of action, conflicting with our knowledge and preventing its practical realisation: and the very imperfectness of the connexion between our practical judgment and our will impels us to seek for more precise knowledge as to the nature of that connexion.

But this is not all. Men never ask, 'Why should I believe what I see to be true?' but they frequently ask, 'Why should I do what I see to be right?' It is easy to reply that the question is futile, since it could only be answered by a reference to some other recognised principle of right conduct, and the question might just as well be asked as regards that again, and so on. But still we do ask the question widely and continually, and therefore this demonstration of its futility is not completely satisfactory; we require besides some explanation of its persistency.

One explanation that may be offered is that, since we are moved to action not by moral judgment alone, but also by desires and inclinations that operate independently of moral judgment, the answer which we really want to the question 'Why should I do it?' is one which does not merely prove a certain action to be right, but also stirs in us a predominant inclination to do the action.

That this explanation is true for some minds in some moods I would not deny. Still I think that when a man seriously asks 'why he should do' anything, he commonly assumes in himself a determination to pursue whatever conduct may be shown by argument to be reasonable, even though it be very different from that to which his non-rational inclinations may prompt. And we are generally agreed that reasonable conduct in any case has to be determined on principles, in applying which the agent's inclination – as it exists apart from such determination – is only one element among several that have to be considered, and commonly not the most important element. But when we ask what these principles are, the diversity of answers which we find manifestly declared in the systems and fundamental formulæ of professed moralists seems to be really present in the common practical reasoning of men generally; with this difference, that whereas the philosopher seeks unity of principle, and consistency of method at the risk of paradox, the unphilosophic man is apt to hold different principles at once, and to apply different methods in more or less confused combination. If this be so, we can offer another explanation of the persistent unsatisfied demand for an ultimate reason, above noticed. For if there are different views of the ultimate reasonableness of conduct, implicit in the thought of ordinary men, though not brought into clear relation to each other, – it is easy to see that any single answer to the question 'why' will not be completely satisfactory, as it will be given only from one of these points of view, and will always leave room to ask the question from some other.

I am myself convinced that this is the main explanation of the phenomenon: and it is on this conviction that the plan of the present treatise is based. We cannot, of course, regard as valid reasonings that lead to conflicting conclusions; and I therefore assume as a fundamental postulate of Ethics, that so far as two methods conflict, one or other of them must be modified or rejected. But I think it fundamentally important to recognise, at the outset of Ethical inquiry, that there is a diversity of methods applied in ordinary practical thought.

§ 4.   What then are these different methods? what are the different practical principles which the common sense of mankind is *prima facie* prepared to accept as ultimate? Some care is needed in answering this question: because we frequently prescribe that this or that 'ought' to be done or aimed at without any express reference to an ulterior end, while yet such an end is tacitly presupposed. It is obvious that such prescriptions are merely, what Kant calls them, Hypothetical Imperatives; they are not addressed to any one who has not first accepted the end.

For instance: a teacher of any art assumes that his pupil wants to produce the product of the art, or to produce it excellent in quality: he tells him that he *ought* to hold the awl, the hammer, the brush differently. A physician assumes that his patient wants health: he tells him that he *ought* to rise early, to live plainly, to take hard exercise. If the patient deliberately prefers ease and good living to health, the physician's precepts fall to the ground: they are no longer addressed to him. So, again, a man of the world assumes that his hearers wish to get on in society, when he lays down rules of dress, manner, conversation, habits of life. A similar view may be plausibly taken of many rules prescribing what are sometimes called "duties to oneself": it may be said that they are given on the assumption that a man regards his own Happiness as an ultimate end: that if any one should be so exceptional as to disregard it, he does not come within their scope: in short, that the '*ought*' in such formulæ is still implicitly relative to an *optional* end.

It does not, however, seem to me that this account of the matter is exhaustive. We do not all look with simple indifference on a man who declines to take the right means to attain his own happiness, on no other ground than that he does not care about happiness. Most men would regard such a refusal as irrational, with a certain disapprobation; they would thus implicitly assent to Butler's statement[7] that "interest, one's own happiness, is a manifest obligation."

---

[7] See the Preface to Butler's *Sermons on Human Nature*.

In other words, they would think that a man *ought* to care for his own happiness. The word 'ought' thus used is no longer relative: happiness now appears as an ultimate end, the pursuit of which – at least within the limits imposed by other duties – appears to be prescribed by reason 'categorically,' as Kant would say, *i.e.* without any tacit assumption of a still ulterior end. And it has been widely held by even orthodox moralists that all morality rests ultimately on the basis of "reasonable self-love";[8] *i.e.* that its rules are ultimately binding on any individual only so far as it is his interest on the whole to observe them.

Still, common moral opinion certainly regards the duty or virtue of Prudence as only a part – and not the most important part – of duty or virtue in general. Common moral opinion recognises and inculcates other fundamental rules – *e.g.* those of Justice, Good Faith, Veracity – which, in its ordinary judgments on particular cases, it is inclined to treat as binding without qualification and without regard to ulterior consequences. And, in the ordinary form of the Intuitional view of Ethics, the "categorical" prescription of such rules is maintained explicitly and definitely, as a result of philosophical reflection: and the realisation of Virtue in act – at least in the case of the virtues just mentioned – is held to consist in strict and unswerving conformity to such rules.

On the other hand it is contended by many Utilitarians that all the rules of conduct which men prescribe to one another as moral rules are really – though in part unconsciously – prescribed as means to the general happiness of mankind, or of the whole aggregate of sentient beings; and it is still more widely held by Utilitarian thinkers that such rules, however they may originate, are only valid so far as their observance is conducive to the general happiness. This contention I shall hereafter examine with due care. Here I wish only to point out that, if the duty of aiming at the general happiness is thus taken to include all other duties, as subordinate applications of it, we seem to be again led to the notion of Happiness as an ultimate end categorically prescribed, – only it is now General Happiness and not the private happiness of any individual. And this is the view that I myself take of the Utilitarian principle.

At the same time, it is not necessary, in the methodical investigation of right conduct, considered relatively to the end either of private or of general happiness, to assume that the end itself is determined or prescribed by reason: we only require to assume, in reasoning to cogent practical conclusions, that it is adopted as ultimate and paramount. For if a man accepts any end as ultimate and paramount, he accepts implicitly as his "method of ethics" whatever process of reasoning enables him to determine the actions most conducive to this end.[9] Since, however, to every difference in the end accepted at least some difference in method will generally correspond: if all the ends which men are found practically to adopt as ultimate (subordinating everything else to the attainment of them under the influence of 'ruling passions'), were taken as principles for which the student of Ethics is called upon to construct rational methods, his task would be very complex and extensive. But if we confine ourselves to such ends as the common sense of mankind appears to accept as rational ultimate ends, the task is reduced, I think, within manageable limits; since this criterion will exclude at least many of the objects which men practically seem to regard as paramount. Thus many men sacrifice health, fortune, happiness, to Fame; but no one, so far as I know, has deliberately maintained that Fame is an object which it is reasonable for men to seek for its own sake. It only commends itself to reflective minds either (1) as a source of Happiness to the person who gains it, or (2) a sign of his Excellence, moral or intellectual, or (3) because it attests the achievement by him of some important benefit to society, and at the same time stimulates him and others to further achievement in the future: and the conception of "benefit" would, when examined in its turn, lead us again to Happiness or Excellence of human nature, – since a man is commonly thought to benefit others either by making them happier or by making them wiser and more virtuous.

Whether there are any ends besides these two, which can be reasonably regarded as ultimate, it will hereafter[10] be part of our business to investigate: but we may perhaps say that *prima facie* the only two ends which have a strongly and widely supported claim to be regarded as rational ultimate ends are the two just mentioned, Happiness and Perfection or Excellence of human nature – meaning here by 'Excellence' not primarily superiority to others, but a partial realisation of, or approximation to, an ideal type of human Perfection. And we must observe that the adoption of the former of these ends leads us to two *prima facie* distinct methods, according as it is sought to be

---

[8] The phrase is Butler's.

[9] See the last paragraph of chap. iii. of this Book.

[10] See chap. ix. of this Book, and Book iii. chap. xiv.

realised universally, or by each individual for himself alone. For though doubtless a man may often best promote his own happiness by labouring and abstaining for the sake of others, it seems to be implied in our common notion of self-sacrifice that actions most conducive to the general happiness do not – in this world at least – always tend also to the greatest happiness of the agent.[11] And among those who hold that "happiness is our being's end and aim" we seem to find a fundamental difference of opinion as to whose happiness it is that it is ultimately reasonable to aim at. For to some it seems that "the constantly proper end of action on the part of any individual at the moment of action is his real greatest happiness from that moment to the end of his life";[12] whereas others hold that the view of reason is essentially universal, and that it cannot be reasonable to take as an ultimate and paramount end the happiness of any one individual rather than that of any other – at any rate if equally deserving and susceptible of it – so that general happiness must be the "true standard of right and wrong, in the field of morals" no less than of politics.[13] It is, of course, possible to adopt an end intermediate between the two, and to aim at the happiness of some limited portion of mankind, such as one's family or nation or race: but any such limitation seems arbitrary, and probably few would maintain it to be reasonable *per se*, except as the most practicable way of aiming at the general happiness, or of indirectly securing one's own.

The case seems to be otherwise with Excellence or Perfection.[14] At first sight, indeed, the same alternatives present themselves:[15] it seems that the Excellence aimed at may be taken either individually or universally; and circumstances are conceivable in which a man is not unlikely to think that he could best promote the Excellence of others by sacrificing his own. But no moralist who takes Excellence as an ultimate end has ever approved of such sacrifice, at least so far as Moral Excellence is concerned; no one has ever directed an individual to promote the virtue of others except in so far as this promotion is compatible with, or rather involved in, the complete realisation of Virtue in himself.[16] So far, then, there seems to be no need of separating the method of determining right conduct which takes the Excellence or Perfection of the individual as the ultimate aim from that which aims at the Excellence or Perfection of the human community. And since Virtue is commonly conceived as the most valuable element of human Excellence – and an element essentially preferable to any other element that can come into competition with it as an alternative for rational choice – any method which takes Perfection or Excellence of human nature as ultimate End will *prima facie* coincide to a great extent with that based on what I called the Intuitional view: and I have accordingly decided to treat it as a special form of this latter.[17] The two methods which take happiness as an ultimate end it will be convenient to distinguish as Egoistic and Universalistic Hedonism: and as it is the latter of these, as taught by Bentham and his successors, that is more generally understood under the term 'Utilitarianism,' I shall always restrict that word to this signification. For Egoistic Hedonism it is somewhat hard to find a single perfectly appropriate term. I shall often call this simply Egoism: but it may sometimes be convenient to call it Epicureanism: for though this name more properly denotes a particular historical system, it has come to be commonly used in the wider sense in which I wish to employ it.

§ 5.   The last sentence suggests one more explanation, which, for clearness' sake, it seems desirable to make: an explanation, however, rather of the plan and purpose of the present treatise than of the nature and boundaries of the subject of Ethics as generally understood.

There are several recognised ways of treating this subject, none of which I have thought it desirable to adopt. We may start with existing systems, and either study them historically, tracing the changes in thought through the

---

[11] For a full discussion of this question, see Book ii. chap. v. and the concluding chapter of the work.

[12] Bentham, *Memoirs* (vol. x. of Bowring's edition), p. 560.

[13] Bentham again, *Memoirs*, p. 79. See note at the end of Book i. chap. vi. The Utilitarians since Bentham have sometimes adopted one, sometimes the other, of these two principles as paramount.

[14] I use the terms 'Excellence' and 'Perfection' to denote the same ultimate end regarded in somewhat different aspects: meaning by either an ideal complex of mental qualities, of which we admire and approve the manifestation in human life: but using 'Perfection' to denote the ideal as such, while 'Excellence' denotes such partial realisation of or approximation to the ideal as we actually find in human experience.

[15] It may be said that even more divergent views of the reasonable end are possible here than in the case of happiness: for we are not necessarily limited (as in that case) to the consideration of sentient beings: inanimate things also seem to have a perfection and excellence of their own and to be capable of being made better or worse in their kind; and this perfection, or one species of it, appears to be the end of the Fine Arts. But reflection I think shows that neither beauty nor any other quality of inanimate objects can be regarded as good or desirable in itself, out of relation to the perfection or happiness of sentient beings. Cf. *post*, chap. ix. of this Book.

[16] Kant roundly denies that it can be my duty to take the Perfection of others for my end: but his argument is not, I think, valid. Cf. *post*, Book iii. chap. iv. § 1.

[17] See Book iii. chap. xiv., where I explain my reasons for only giving a subordinate place to the conception of Perfection as Ultimate End.

centuries, or compare and classify them according to relations of resemblance, or criticise their internal coherence. Or we may seek to add to the number of these systems: and claim after so many unsuccessful efforts to have at last attained the one true theory of the subject, by which all others may be tested. The present book contains neither the exposition of a system nor a natural or critical history of systems. I have attempted to define and unfold not one Method of Ethics, but several: at the same time these are not here studied historically, as methods that have actually been used or proposed for the regulation of practice; but rather as alternatives between which – so far as they cannot be reconciled – the human mind seems to me necessarily forced to choose, when it attempts to frame a complete synthesis of practical maxims and to act in a perfectly consistent manner. Thus, they might perhaps be called natural methods rationalised; because men commonly seem to guide themselves by a mixture of different methods, more or less disguised under ambiguities of language. The impulses or principles from which the different methods take their rise, the different claims of different ends to be rational, are admitted, to some extent, by all minds: and as along with these claims is felt the need of harmonising them – since it is, as was said, a postulate of the Practical Reason, that two conflicting rules of action cannot both be reasonable – the result is ordinarily either a confused blending, or a forced and premature reconciliation, of different principles and methods. Nor have the systems framed by professed moralists been free from similar defects. The writers have usually proceeded to synthesis without adequate analysis; the practical demand for the former being more urgently felt than the theoretical need of the latter. For here as in other points the development of the theory of Ethics would seem to be somewhat impeded by the preponderance of practical considerations; and perhaps a more complete detachment of the theoretical study of right conduct from its practical application is to be desired for the sake even of the latter itself: since a treatment which is a compound between the scientific and the hortatory is apt to miss both, the results that it would combine; the mixture is bewildering to the brain and not stimulating to the heart. So again, I am inclined to think that here, as in other sciences, it would be an advantage to draw as distinct a line as possible between the known and the unknown; as the clear indication of an unsolved problem is at any rate a step to its solution. In ethical treatises, however, there has been a continual tendency to ignore and keep out of sight the difficulties of the subject; either unconsciously, from a latent conviction that the questions which the writer cannot answer satisfactorily must be questions which ought not to be asked; or consciously, that he may not shake the sway of morality over the minds of his readers. This last well-meant precaution frequently defeats itself: the difficulties thus concealed in exposition are liable to reappear in controversy: and then they appear not carefully limited, but magnified for polemical purposes. Thus we get on the one hand vague and hazy reconciliation, on the other loose and random exaggeration of discrepancies; and neither process is effective to dispel the original vagueness and ambiguity which lurks in the fundamental notions of our common practical reasonings. To eliminate or reduce this indefiniteness and confusion is the sole immediate end that I have proposed to myself in the present work. In order better to execute this task, I have refrained from expressly attempting any such complete and final solution of the chief ethical difficulties and controversies as would convert this exposition of various methods into the development of a harmonious system. At the same time I hope to afford aid towards the construction of such a system; because it seems easier to judge of the mutual relations and conflicting claims of different modes of thought, after an impartial and rigorous investigation of the conclusions to which they logically lead. It is not uncommon to find in reflecting on practical principles, that – however unhesitatingly they seem to command our assent at first sight, and however familiar and apparently clear the notions of which they are composed – nevertheless when we have carefully examined the consequences of adopting them they wear a changed and somewhat dubious aspect. The truth seems to be that most of the practical principles that have been seriously put forward are more or less satisfactory to the common sense of mankind, so long as they have the field to themselves. They all find a response in our nature: their fundamental assumptions are all such as we are disposed to accept, and such as we find to govern to a certain extent our habitual conduct. When I am asked, "Do you not consider it ultimately reasonable to seek pleasure and avoid pain for yourself?" "Have you not a moral sense?" "Do you not intuitively pronounce some actions to be right and others wrong?" "Do you not acknowledge the general happiness to be a paramount end?" I answer 'yes' to all these questions. My difficulty begins when I have to choose between the different principles or inferences drawn from them. We admit the necessity, when they conflict, of making this choice, and that it is irrational to let sometimes one principle prevail and sometimes another; but the necessity is a painful one. We cannot but hope that all methods may ultimately coincide: and at any rate, before making our election we may reasonably wish to have the completest possible knowledge of each.

My object, then, in the present work, is to expound as clearly and as fully as my limits will allow the different methods of Ethics that I find implicit in our common moral reasoning; to point out their mutual relations; and where they seem to conflict, to define the issue as much as possible. In the course of this endeavour I am led to discuss the considerations which should, in my opinion, be decisive in determining the adoption of ethical first principles: but it is not my primary aim to establish such principles; nor, again, is it my primary aim to supply a set of practical directions for conduct. I have wished to keep the reader's attention throughout directed to the processes rather than the results of ethical thought: and have therefore never stated as my own any positive practical conclusions unless by way of illustration: and have never ventured to decide dogmatically any controverted points, except where the controversy seemed to arise from want of precision or clearness in the definition of principles, or want of consistency in reasoning.

Chapter III

Ethical Judgments

§ 1. IN the first chapter I spoke of actions that we judge to be right and what ought to be done as being "reasonable," or "rational," and similarly of ultimate ends as "prescribed by Reason": and I contrasted the motive to action supplied by the recognition of such reasonableness with "non-rational" desires and inclinations. This manner of speaking is employed by writers of different schools, and seems in accordance with the common view and language on the subject. For we commonly think that wrong conduct is essentially irrational, and can be shown to be so by argument; and though we do not conceive that it is by reason alone that men are influenced to act rightly, we still hold that appeals to the reason are an essential part of all moral persuasion, and that part which concerns the moralist or moral philosopher as distinct from the preacher or moral rhetorician. On the other hand it is widely maintained that, as Hume says, "Reason, meaning the judgment of truth and falsehood, can never of itself be any motive to the Will"; and that the motive to action is in all cases some Non-rational Desire, including under this term the impulses to action given by present pleasure and pain. It seems desirable to examine with some care the grounds of this contention before we proceed any further.

Let us begin by defining the issue raised as clearly as possible. Every one, I suppose, has had experience of what is meant by the conflict of non-rational or irrational desires with reason: most of us (*e.g.*) occasionally feel bodily appetite prompting us to indulgences which we judge to be imprudent, and anger prompting us to acts which we disapprove as unjust or unkind. It is when this conflict occurs that the desires are said to be irrational, as impelling us to volitions opposed to our deliberate judgments; sometimes we yield to such seductive impulses, and sometimes not; and it is perhaps when we do *not* yield that the impulsive force of such irrational desires is most definitely felt, as we have to exert in resisting them a voluntary effort somewhat analogous to that involved in any muscular exertion. Often, again, – since we are not always thinking either of our duty or of our interest, – desires of this kind take effect in voluntary actions without our having judged such actions to be either right or wrong, either prudent or imprudent; as (*e.g.*) when an ordinary healthy man eats his dinner. In such cases it seems most appropriate to call the desires "non-rational" rather than "irrational." Neither term is intended to imply that the desires spoken of – or at least the more important of them – are not normally accompanied by intellectual processes. It is true that some impulses to action seem to take effect, as we say "blindly" or "instinctively," without any definite consciousness either of the end at which the action is aimed, or of the means by which the end is to be attained: but this, I conceive, is only the case with impulses that do not occupy consciousness for an appreciable time, and ordinarily do not require any but very familiar and habitual actions for the attainment of their proximate ends. In all other cases – that is, in the case of the actions with which we are chiefly concerned in ethical discussion – the result aimed at, and some part at least of the means by which it is to be realised, are more or less distinctly represented in consciousness, previous to the volition that initiates the movements tending to its realisation. Hence the resultant forces of what I call "non-rational" desires, and the volitions to which they prompt, are continually modified by intellectual processes in two distinct ways; first by new perceptions or representations of means conducive to the desired ends, and secondly by new presentations or representations of facts actually existing or in prospect – especially more or less probable consequences of contemplated actions – which rouse new impulses of desire and aversion.

The question, then, is whether the account just given of the influence of the intellect on desire and volition is not exhaustive; and whether the experience which is commonly described as a "conflict of desire with reason" is not more properly conceived as merely a conflict among desires and aversions; the sole function of reason being to bring before the mind ideas of actual or possible facts, which modify in the manner above described the resultant force of our various impulses.

I hold that this is not the case; that the ordinary moral or prudential judgments which, in the case of all or most minds, have some – though often an inadequate – influence on volition, cannot legitimately be interpreted as judgments respecting the present or future existence of human feelings or any facts of the sensible world; the fundamental notion represented by the word "ought" or "right,"[18] which such judgments contain expressly or by implication, being essentially different from all notions representing facts of physical or psychical experience. The question is one on which appeal must ultimately be made to the reflection of individuals on their practical judgments and reasonings: and in making this appeal it seems most convenient to begin by showing the inadequacy of all attempts to explain the practical judgments or propositions in which this fundamental notion is introduced, without recognising its unique character as above negatively defined. There is an element of truth in such explanations, in so far as they bring into view feelings which undoubtedly accompany moral or prudential judgments, and which ordinarily have more or less effect in determining the will to actions judged to be right; but so far as they profess to be interpretations of what such judgments mean, they appear to me to fail altogether.

[...]

It is absurd to say that a mere statement of my approbation of truth-speaking is properly given in the proposition 'Truth ought to be spoken'; otherwise the fact of another man's disapprobation might equally be expressed by saying 'Truth ought not to be spoken'; and thus we should have two coexistent facts stated in two mutually contradictory propositions. This is so obvious, that we must suppose that those who hold the view which I am combating do not really intend to deny it: but rather to maintain that this subjective fact of my approbation is all that there is any *ground* for stating, or perhaps that it is all that any reasonable person is prepared on reflection to affirm. And no doubt there is a large class of statements, in form objective, which yet we are not commonly prepared to maintain as more than subjective if their validity is questioned. If I say that 'the air is sweet,' or 'the food disagreeable,' it would not be exactly true to say that I mean no more than that I like the one or dislike the other: but if my statement is challenged, I shall probably content myself with affirming the existence of such feelings in my own mind. But there appears to me to be a fundamental difference between this case and that of moral feelings. The peculiar emotion of moral approbation is, in my experience, inseparably bound up with the conviction, implicit or explicit, that the conduct approved is 'really' right – *i.e.* that it cannot, without error, be disapproved by any other mind. If I give up this conviction because others do not share it, or for any other reason, I may no doubt still retain a sentiment prompting to the conduct in question, or – what is perhaps more common – a sentiment of repugnance to the opposite conduct: but this sentiment will no longer have the special quality of 'moral sentiment' strictly so called. This difference between the two is often overlooked in ethical discussion: but any experience of a change in moral opinion produced by argument may afford an illustration of it.

[...]

§ 3.   [...] It is important to note and distinguish two different implications with which the word "ought" is used; in the narrowest ethical sense what we judge 'ought to be' done, is always thought capable of being brought about by the volition of any individual to whom the judgment applies. I cannot conceive that I 'ought' to do anything which at the same time I judge that I cannot do. In a wider sense, however, – which cannot conveniently be discarded – I sometimes judge that I 'ought' to know what a wiser man would know, or feel as a better man would feel, in my place, though I may know that I could not directly produce in myself such knowledge or feeling by any effort of will. In this case the word merely implies an ideal or pattern which I 'ought' – in the stricter sense – to seek to imitate as far as possible. And this wider sense seems to be that in which the word is normally used in the precepts of Art generally, and in political judgments: when I judge that the laws and constitution of my country 'ought to be' other than they are, I do not of course imply that my own or any other individual's single volition can directly bring about the change.[19]

Chapter VIII

Intuitionism

§ 1.   I HAVE used the term 'Intuitional' to denote the view of ethics which regards as the practically ultimate end of moral actions their conformity to certain rules or dictates of Duty unconditionally prescribed.
[...]

---

[18] The difference between the significations of the two words is discussed later.

[19] I do not even imply that any combination of individuals could completely realise the state of political relations which I conceive 'ought to' exist. My conception would be futile if it had no relation to practice: but it may merely delineate a pattern to which no more than an approximation is practically possible.

§ 2.   […] In the popular view of Conscience it seems to be often implied that particular judgments are the most trustworthy. 'Conscience' is the accepted popular term for the faculty of moral judgment, as applied to the acts and motives of the person judging; and we most commonly think of the dictates of conscience as relating to particular actions. Thus when a man is bidden, in any particular case, to 'trust to his conscience,' it commonly seems to be meant that he should exercise a faculty of judging morally this particular case without reference to general rules, and even in opposition to conclusions obtained by systematic deduction from such rules. And it is on this view of Conscience that the contempt often expressed for 'Casuistry' may be most easily justified: for if the particular case can be satisfactorily settled by conscience without reference to general rules, 'Casuistry,' which consists in the application of general rules to particular cases, is at best superfluous. But then, on this view, we shall have no practical need of any such general rules, or of scientific Ethics at all. We may of course form general propositions by induction from these particular conscientious judgments, and arrange them systematically: but any interest which such a system may have will be purely speculative. And this accounts, perhaps, for the indifference or hostility to systematic morality shown by some conscientious persons. For they feel that they can at any rate do without it: and they fear that the cultivation of it may place the mind in a wrong attitude in relation to practice, and prove rather unfavourable than otherwise to the proper development of the practically important faculty manifested or exercised in particular moral judgments.

The view above described may be called, in a sense, 'ultra-intuitional,' since, in its most extreme form, it recognises simple immediate intuitions alone and discards as superfluous all modes of reasoning to moral conclusions: and we may find in it one phase or variety of the Intuitional method, – if we may extend the term 'method' to include a procedure that is completed in a single judgment.

§ 3.   But though probably all moral agents have experience of such particular intuitions, and though they constitute a great part of the moral phenomena of most minds, comparatively few are so thoroughly satisfied with them, as not to feel a need of some further moral knowledge even from a strictly practical point of view. For these particular intuitions do not, to reflective persons, present themselves as quite indubitable and irrefragable: nor do they always find when they have put an ethical question to themselves with all sincerity, that they are conscious of clear immediate insight in respect of it. Again, when a man compares the utterances of his conscience at different times, he often finds it difficult to make them altogether consistent: the same conduct will wear a different moral aspect at one time from that which it wore at another, although our knowledge of its circumstances and conditions is not materially changed. Further, we become aware that the moral perceptions of different minds, to all appearance equally competent to judge, frequently conflict: one condemns what another approves. In this way serious doubts are aroused as to the validity of each man's particular moral judgments: and we are led to endeavour to set these doubts at rest by appealing to general rules, more firmly established on a basis of common consent.

And in fact, though the view of conscience above discussed is one which much popular language seems to suggest, it is not that which Christian and other moralists have usually given. They have rather represented the process of conscience as analogous to one of jural reasoning, such as is conducted in a Court of Law. Here we have always a system of universal rules given, and any particular action has to be brought under one of these rules before it can be pronounced lawful or unlawful. Now the rules of positive law are usually not discoverable by the individual's reason: this may teach him that law ought to be obeyed, but what law is must, in the main, be communicated to him from some external authority. And this is not unfrequently the case with the conscientious reasoning of ordinary persons when any dispute or difficulty forces them to reason: they have a genuine impulse to conform to the right rules of conduct, but they are not conscious, in difficult or doubtful cases, of seeing for themselves what these are: they have to inquire of their priest, or their sacred books, or perhaps the common opinion of the society to which they belong. In so far as this is the case we cannot strictly call their method Intuitional. They follow rules generally received, not intuitively apprehended. Other persons, however (or perhaps all to some extent), do seem to see for themselves the truth[20] and bindingness of all or most of these current rules. They may still put forward 'common consent' as an argument for the validity of these rules: but only as supporting the individual's intuition, not as a substitute for it or as superseding it.

Here then we have a second Intuitional Method: of which the fundamental assumption is that we can discern certain general rules with really clear and finally valid intuition. It is held that such general rules are implicit in the moral reasoning of ordinary men, who apprehend them adequately for most practical purposes, and are able to enunciate them roughly; but that to state them with proper precision requires a special habit of contemplating clearly and steadily abstract moral notions. It is held that the moralist's function then is to perform this process of

[20] Strictly speaking, the attributes of truth and falsehood only belong formally to Rules when they are changed from the imperative mood ("Do X") into the indicative ("X ought to be done").

abstract contemplation, to arrange the results as systematically as possible, and by proper definitions and explanations to remove vagueness and prevent conflict. It is such a system as this which seems to be generally intended when Intuitive or *a priori* morality is mentioned, and which will chiefly occupy us in Book iii.

§ 4.   By philosophic minds, however, the 'Morality of Common Sense' (as I have ventured to call it), even when made as precise and orderly as possible, is often found unsatisfactory as a system, although they have no disposition to question its general authority. It is found difficult to accept as scientific first principles the moral generalities that we obtain by reflection on the ordinary thought of mankind, even though we share this thought. Even granting that these rules can be so defined as perfectly to fit together and cover the whole field of human conduct, without coming into conflict and without leaving any practical questions unanswered, – still the resulting code seems an accidental aggregate of precepts, which stands in need of some rational synthesis. In short, without being disposed to deny that conduct commonly judged to be right is so, we may yet require some deeper explanation *why* it is so. From this demand springs a third species or phase of Intuitionism, which, while accepting the morality of common sense as in the main sound, still attempts to find for it a philosophic basis which it does not itself offer: to get one or more principles more absolutely and undeniably true and evident, from which the current rules might be deduced, either just as they are commonly received or with slight modifications and rectifications.[21]

The three phases of Intuitionism just described may be treated as three stages in the formal development of Intuitive Morality: we may term them respectively Perceptional, Dogmatic, and Philosophical. The last-mentioned I have only defined in the vaguest way: in fact, as yet I have presented it only as a problem, of which it is impossible to foresee how many solutions may be attempted: but it does not seem desirable to investigate it further at present, as it will be more satisfactorily studied after examining in detail the Morality of Common Sense.

It must not be thought that these three phases are sharply distinguished in the moral reasoning of ordinary men: but then no more is Intuitionism of any sort sharply distinguished from either species of Hedonism. A loose combination or confusion of methods is the most common type of actual moral reasoning. Probably most moral men believe that their moral sense or instinct in any case will guide them fairly right, but also that there are general rules for determining right action in different departments of conduct: and that for these again it is possible to find a philosophical explanation, by which they may be deduced from a smaller number of fundamental principles. Still for systematic direction of conduct, we require to know on what judgments we are to rely as ultimately valid.

Chapter IX

Good

§ 2.   [...] When we pass from the *adjective* to the *substantive* 'good,' it is at once evident that this latter cannot be understood as equivalent to 'pleasure' or 'happiness' by any persons who affirm – as a significant proposition and not as a mere tautology – that the Pleasure or Happiness of human beings is their Good or Ultimate Good. Such affirmation, which would, I think, be ordinarily made by Hedonists, obviously implies that the *meaning* of the two terms is different, however closely their denotation may coincide. And it does not seem that any fundamental difference of meaning is implied by the grammatical variation from adjective to substantive.

Book II

Chapter V

Happiness and Duty

[...]

§ 4.   We must conclude, then, that if the conduct prescribed to the individual by the avowedly accepted morality of the community of which he is a member, can be shown to coincide with that to which Rational Self-love would prompt, it must be, in many cases, solely or chiefly on the score of the internal sanctions. In considering the force

---

[21] It should be observed that such principles will not necessarily be "intuitional" in the narrower sense that excludes consequences; but only in the wider sense as being self-evident principles relating to 'what ought to be.'

of these sanctions, I shall eliminate those pleasures and pains which lie in the anticipation of rewards and punishments in a future life: for as we are now supposing the calculations of Rational Egoism to be performed without taking into account any feelings that are beyond the range of experience, it will be more consistent to exclude also the pleasurable or painful anticipations of such feelings.

Let us, then, contemplate by itself the satisfaction that attends the performance of duty as such (without taking into consideration any ulterior consequences), and the pain that follows on its violation. After the discussions of the two preceding chapters I shall not of course attempt to weigh exactly these pleasures and pains against others; but I see no empirical grounds for believing that such feelings are always sufficiently intense to turn the balance of prospective happiness in favour of morality. This will hardly be denied if the question is raised in respect of isolated acts of duty. Let us take an extreme case, which is yet quite within the limits of experience. The call of duty has often impelled a soldier or other public servant, or the adherent of a persecuted religion, to face certain and painful death, under circumstances where it might be avoided with little or no loss even of reputation. To prove such conduct always reasonable from an egoistic point of view, we have to assume that, in all cases where such a duty could exist and be recognised, the mere pain[22] that would follow on evasion of duty would be so great as to render the whole remainder of life hedonistically worthless. Surely such an assumption would be paradoxical and extravagant. Nothing that we know of the majority of persons in any society would lead us to conclude that their moral feelings taken alone form so preponderant an element of their happiness. And a similar conclusion seems irresistible even in more ordinary cases, where a man is called on to give up, for virtue's sake, not life, but a considerable share of the ordinary sources of human happiness. Can we say that all, or even most, men are so constituted that the satisfactions of a good conscience are certain to repay them for such sacrifices, or that the pain and loss involved in them would certainly be outweighed by the remorse that would follow the refusal to make them?[23]

Perhaps, however, so much as this has scarcely ever been expressly maintained. What Plato in his *Republic* and other writers on the same side have rather tried to prove, is not that at any particular moment duty will be, to every one on whom it may devolve, productive of more happiness than any other course of conduct; but rather that it is every one's interest on the whole to choose the life of the virtuous man. But even this it is very difficult even to render probable: as will appear, I think, if we examine the lines of reasoning by which it is commonly supported.

To begin with Plato's argument. He represents the soul of the virtuous man as a well-ordered polity of impulses, in which every passion and appetite is duly obedient to the rightful sovereignty of reason, and operates only within the limits laid down by the latter. He then contrasts the tranquil peace of such a mind with the disorder of one where a succession of baser impulses, or some ruling passion, lords it over reason: and asks which is the happiest, even apart from external rewards and punishments. But we may grant all that Plato claims, and yet be no further advanced towards the solution of the question before us. For here the issue does not lie between Reason and Passion, but rather – in Butler's language – between Rational Self-love and Conscience. We are supposing the Egoist to have all his impulses under control, and are only asking how this control is to be exercised. Now we have seen that the regulation and organisation of life best calculated to attain the end of self-interest appears *prima facie* divergent at certain points from that to which men in general are prompted by a sense of duty. In order to maintain Plato's position it has to be shown that this appearance is false; and that a system of self-government, which under certain circumstances leads us to pain, loss, and death, is still that which self-interest requires. It can scarcely be said that our nature is such that only this anti-egoistic kind of regulation is possible; that the choice lies between this and none at all. It is easy to imagine a rational egoist, strictly controlling each of his passions and impulses – including

---

[22] Under the notion of 'moral pain' (or pleasure) I intend to include, in this argument, all pain (or pleasure) that is due to sympathy with the feelings of others. It is not convenient to enter, at this stage of the discussion, into a full discussion of the relation of Sympathy to Moral Sensibility; but I may say that it seems to me certain, on the one hand, that these two emotional susceptibilities are actually distinct in most minds, whatever they may have been originally; and on the other hand that sympathetic and strictly moral feelings are almost inextricably blended in the ordinary moral consciousness: so that, for the purposes of the present argument it is not of fundamental importance to draw a distinction between them. I have, however, thought it desirable to undertake a further examination of sympathy—as the internal sanction on which Utilitarians specially lay stress—in the concluding chapter of this treatise: to which, accordingly, the reader may refer.

[23] A striking confirmation of this is furnished by those Christian writers of the last century who treat the *moral* unbeliever as a fool who sacrifices his happiness both here and hereafter. These men were, for the most part, earnestly engaged in the practice of virtue, and yet this practice had not made them love virtue so much as to prefer it, even under ordinary circumstances, to the sensual and other enjoyments that it excludes. It seems then absurd to suppose that, in the case of persons who have not developed and strengthened by habit their virtuous impulses, the pain that might afterwards result from resisting the call of duty would always be sufficient to neutralise all other sources of pleasure.

his social sentiments – within such limits that its indulgence should not involve the sacrifice of some greater gratification: and experience seems to show us many examples of persons who at least approximate as closely to this type
as any one else does to the ideal of the orthodox moralist. Hence if the regulation of Conscience be demonstrably
the best means to the individual's happiness, it must be because the order kept by Self-love involves a sacrifice of
pleasure on the whole, as compared with the order kept by Conscience. And if this is the case, it would seem that
it can only be on account of the special emotional pleasure attending the satisfaction of the moral sentiments, or
special pain or loss of happiness consequent on their repression and violation.

Before, however, we proceed further, a fundamental difficulty must be removed which has probably some time
since suggested itself to the reader. If a man thinks it reasonable to seek his own interest, it is clear that he cannot
himself disapprove of any conduct that comes under this principle or approve of the opposite. And hence it may
appear that the pleasures and pains of conscience cannot enter into the calculation whether a certain course of
conduct is or is not in accordance with Rational Egoism, because they cannot attach themselves in the egoist's mind
to any modes of action which have not been already decided, on other grounds, to be reasonable or the reverse.
And this is to a certain extent true; but we must here recur to the distinction (indicated in Book i. chap. iii. § 1)
between the general impulse to do what we believe to be reasonable, and special sentiments of liking or aversion
for special kinds of conduct, independent of their reasonableness. In the moral sentiments as they exist in ordinary
men, these two kinds of feeling are indistinguishably blended; because it is commonly believed that the rules of
conduct to which the common moral sentiments are attached are in some way or other reasonable. We can, however, conceive the two separated: and in fact, as was before said, we have experience of such separation whenever a
man is led by a process of thought to adopt a different view of morality from that in which he has been trained; for
in such a case there will always remain in his mind some quasi-moral likings and aversions, no longer sustained by
his deliberate judgment of right and wrong. And thus there is every reason to believe that most men, however firmly
they might adopt the principles of Egoistic Hedonism, would still feel sentiments prompting to the performance of
social duty, as commonly recognised in their society, independently of any conclusion that the actions prompted by
such sentiments were reasonable and right. For such sentiments would always be powerfully supported by the sympathy of others, and their expressions of praise and blame, liking and aversion: and since it is agreed that the conduct
commonly recognised as virtuous is *generally* coincident with that which enlightened self-love would dictate, a
rational egoist's habits of conduct will be such as naturally to foster these (for him) 'quasi-moral' feelings. The question, therefore arises – not whether the egoist should cherish and indulge these sentiments up to a certain point,
which all would admit; – but whether be can consistently encourage them to grow to such a pitch that they will
always prevail over the strongest opposing considerations; or, to put it otherwise, whether prudence requires him to
give them the rein and let them carry him whither they will. We have already seen ground for believing that
Rational Self-love will best attain its end by limiting its conscious operation and allowing free play to disinterested
impulses: can we accept the further paradox that it is reasonable for it to abdicate altogether its supremacy over some
of these impulses?

On a careful consideration of the matter, it will appear, I think, that this abdication of self-love is not really a
possible occurrence in the mind of a sane person, who still regards his own interest as the reasonable ultimate end
of his actions. Such a man may, no doubt, resolve that he will devote himself unreservedly to the practice of virtue,
without any particular consideration of what appears to him to be his interest: he may perform a series of acts in
accordance with this resolution, and these may gradually form in him strong habitual tendencies to acts of a similar
kind. But it does not seem that these habits of virtue can ever become so strong as to gain irresistible control over
a sane and reasonable will. When the occasion comes on which virtue demands from such a man an extreme
sacrifice – the imprudence of which must force itself upon his notice, however little he may be in the habit of
weighing his own pleasures and pains – he must always be able to deliberate afresh, and to act (as far as the control
of his will extends) without reference to his past actions. It may, however, be said that, though an egoist retaining
his belief in rational egoism cannot thus abandon his will to the sway of moral enthusiasm, still, supposing it possible
for him to change his conviction and prefer duty to interest, – or supposing we compare him with another man
who makes this choice, – we shall find that a gain in happiness on the whole results from this preference. It may be
held that the pleasurable emotions attendant upon such virtuous or quasi-virtuous habits as are compatible with
adhesion to egoistic principles are so inferior to the raptures that attend the unreserved and passionate surrender of
the soul to virtue, that it is really a man's interest – even with a view to the present life only – to obtain, if he can,
the convictions that render this surrender possible; although under certain circumstances it must necessarily lead

him to act in a manner which, considered by itself, would be undoubtedly imprudent. This is certainly a tenable proposition, and I am quite disposed to think it true of persons with specially refined moral sensibilities. But – though from the imperfections of the hedonistic calculus the proposition cannot in any case be conclusively disproved – it seems, as I have said, to be opposed to the broad results of experience, so far as the great majority of mankind are concerned. Observation would lead me to suppose that most men are so constituted as to feel far more keenly pleasures (and pains) arising from some other source than the conscience; either from the gratifications of sense, or from the possession of power and fame, or from strong human affections, or from the pursuit of science, art, etc.; so that in many cases perhaps not even early training could have succeeded in giving to the moral feelings the requisite predominance: and certainly where this training has been wanting, it seems highly improbable that a mere change of ethical conviction could develop their moral susceptibilities so far as to make it clearly their earthly interest to resolve on facing all sacrifices for the fulfilment of duty.

To sum up: although the performance of duties towards others and the exercise of social virtue seem to be *generally* the best means to the attainment of the individual's happiness, and it is easy to exhibit this coincidence between Virtue and Happiness rhetorically and popularly; still, when we carefully analyse and estimate the consequences of Virtue to the virtuous agent, it appears improbable that this coincidence is complete and universal. We may conceive the coincidence becoming perfect in a Utopia where men were as much in accord on moral as they are now on mathematical questions, where Law was in perfect harmony with Moral Opinion, and all offences were discovered and duly punished: or we may conceive the same result attained by intensifying the moral sentiments of all members of the community, without any external changes (which indeed would then be unnecessary). But just in proportion as existing societies and existing men fall short of this ideal, rules of conduct based on the principles of Egoistic Hedonism seem liable to diverge from those which most men are accustomed to recognise as prescribed by Duty and Virtue.

BOOK III

Chapter VI

Laws and Promises

[…]

§ 9. I have laid down that a promise is binding in so far as it is understood on both sides similarly: and such an understanding is ordinarily attained with sufficient clearness, as far as the apprehension of express words or signs is concerned. Still, even here obscurity and misapprehension sometimes occur; and in the case of the tacit understandings with which promises are often complicated, a lack of definite agreement is not improbable; It becomes, therefore, of practical importance to decide the question previously raised: What duty rests on the promiser of satisfying expectations which he did not intend to create? I called this a duty not so much of Good Faith as of Justice, which prescribes the fulfilment of normal expectations. How then shall we determine what these are? The method by which we commonly ascertain them seems to be the following. We form the conception of an average or normal man, and consider what expectations he would form under the circumstances, inferring this from the beliefs and expectations which men generally entertain under similar circumstances. We refer, therefore, to the customary use of language, and customary tacit understandings current among persons in the particular relations in which promiser and promisee stand. Such customary interpretations and understandings are of course not obligatory upon persons entering into an engagement: but they constitute a standard which we think we may presume to be known to all men, and to be accepted by them, except in so for as it is explicitly rejected. If one of the parties to an engagement has deviated from this common standard without giving express notice, we think it right that he should suffer any loss that may result from the misunderstanding. This criterion then is generally applicable: but if custom is ambiguous or shifting it cannot be applied; and then the just claims of the parties become a problem, the solution of which is very difficult, if not strictly indeterminate.

So far we have supposed that the promiser can choose his own words, and that if the promisee finds them ambiguous he can get them modified, or (what comes to the same thing) explained, by the promiser. But we have now to observe that in the case of promises made to the community, as a condition of obtaining some office or emolument, a certain unalterable form of words has to be used if the promise is made at all. Here the difficulties of moral interpretation are much increased. It may be said, indeed, that the promise ought to be interpreted in the sense in which its terms are understood by the community: and, no doubt, if their usage is quite uniform and unambiguous, this rule of interpretation is sufficiently obvious and simple. But since words are often used in different ways by different members of the same society, and especially with different degrees of strictness and laxity, it often happens that a promise to the community cannot strictly be said to be understood in any one sense: the question therefore arises, whether the promiser is bound to keep it in the sense in which it will be most commonly interpreted, or whether he may select any of its possible meanings. And if the formula is one of some antiquity, it is further questioned, whether it ought to be interpreted in the sense which its words would now generally bear, or in that which they bore when it was drawn up; or, if they were then ambiguous, in the sense which appears to have been attached to them by the government that imposed the promise. On all these points it is difficult to elicit any clear view from Common Sense. And the difficulty is increased by the fact that there are usually strong inducements to make these formal engagements, which cause even tolerably conscientious persons to take them in a strained and unnatural sense. When this has been done continually by many persons, a new general understanding grows up as to the meaning of the engagements: sometimes they come to be regarded as 'mere forms,' or, if they do not reach this point of degradation, they are at least understood in a sense differing indefinitely from their original one. The question then arises, how far this process of gradual illegitimate relaxation or perversion can modify the moral obligation of the promise for a thoroughly conscientious person. It seems clear that when the process is complete, we are right in adopting the new understanding as far as Good Faith is concerned, even if it palpably conflicts with the natural meaning of language; although it is always desirable in such cases that the form of the promise should be changed to correspond with the changed substance. But when, as is ordinarily the case, the process is incomplete, since a portion of the community understands the engagement in the original strict sense, the obligation becomes difficult to determine, and the judgments of conscientious persons respecting it become divergent and perplexed.

To sum up the results of the discussion: it appears that a clear *consensus* can only be claimed for the principle that a promise, express or tacit, is binding, if a number of conditions are fulfilled: viz. if the promiser has a clear belief as to the sense in which it was understood by the promisee, and if the latter is still in a position to grant release from it, but unwilling to do so, if it was not obtained by force or fraud, if it does not conflict with definite prior obligations, if we do not believe that its fulfilment will be harmful to the promisee, or will inflict a disproportionate sacrifice on the promiser, and if circumstances have not materially changed since it was made. If any of these conditions fails, the *consensus* seems to become evanescent, and the common moral perceptions of thoughtful persons fall into obscurity and disagreement.

Chapter XI

Review of the Morality of Common Sense

[…]

§ 2.   There seem to be four conditions, the complete fulfilment of which would establish a significant proposition, apparently self-evident, in the highest degree of certainty attainable: and which must be approximately realised by the premises of our reasoning in any inquiry, if that reasoning is to lead us cogently to trustworthy conclusions.

I.   The terms of the proposition must be clear and precise. The rival originators of modern Methodology, Descartes and Bacon, vie with each other in the stress that they lay on this point: and the latter's warning against the "notiones male terminatæ" of ordinary thought is peculiarly needed in ethical discussion. In fact my chief business in the preceding survey has been to free the common terms of Ethics, as far as possible, from objection on this score.

II.   The self-evidence of the proposition must be ascertained by careful reflection. It is needful to insist on this, because most persons are liable to confound intuitions, on the one hand with mere impressions or impulses, which to careful observation do not present themselves as claiming to be dictates of Reason; and on the other hand, with mere opinions, to which the familiarity that comes from frequent hearing and repetition often gives a false appearance of self-evidence which attentive reflection disperses. In such cases the Cartesian method of testing the ultimate premises of our reasonings, by asking ourselves if we clearly and distinctly apprehend them to be true, may be of real use; though it does not, as Descartes supposed, afford a complete protection against error. A rigorous demand for self-evidence in our premises is a valuable protection against the misleading influence of our own irrational impulses on our judgments: while at the same time it not only distinguishes as inadequate the mere external support of authority and tradition, but also excludes the more subtle and latent effect of these in fashioning our minds to a facile and unquestioning admission of common but unwarranted assumptions.

And we may observe that the application of this test is especially needed in Ethics. For, on the one hand, it cannot be denied that any strong sentiment, however purely subjective, is apt to transform itself into the semblance of an intuition; and it requires careful contemplation to detect the illusion. Whatever we desire we are apt to pronounce desirable: and we are strongly tempted to approve of whatever conduct gives us keen pleasure.[24] And on the other hand, among the rules of conduct to which we customarily conform, there are many which reflection shows to be really derived from some external authority: so that even if their obligation be unquestionable, they cannot be intuitively ascertained. This is of course the case with the Positive Law of the community to which we belong. There is no doubt that we ought, – at least generally speaking, – to obey this: but what it is we cannot of course ascertain by any process of abstract reflection, but only by consulting Reports and Statutes. Here, however, the sources of knowledge are so definite and conspicuous, that we are in no danger of confounding the knowledge gained from studying them with the results of abstract contemplation. The case is somewhat different with the traditional and customary rules of behaviour which exist in every society, supplementing the regulative operation of Law proper: here it is much more difficult to distinguish the rules which a moral man is called upon to define for himself, by the application of intuitively known principles, from those as to which some authority external to the individual is recognised as the final arbiter.[25]

[...]

It must be observed that each individual in any society commonly finds in himself a knowledge not obviously incomplete of the rules of Honour and Etiquette, and an impulse to conform to them without requiring any further reason for doing so. Each often seems to see at a glance what is honourable and polite just as clearly as he sees what is right: and it requires some consideration to discover that in the former cases custom and opinion are generally the final authority from which there is no appeal. And even in the case of rules regarded as distinctly moral, we can generally find an element that seems to us as clearly conventional as the codes just mentioned, when we contemplate the morality of other men, even in our own age and country. Hence we may reasonably suspect a similar element in our own moral code: and must admit the great importance of testing rigorously any rule which we find that we have a habitual impulse to obey; to see whether it really expresses or can be referred to a clear intuition of rightness.

III.   The propositions accepted as self-evident must be mutually consistent. Here, again, it is obvious that any collision between two intuitions is a proof that there is error in one or the other, or in both. Still, we frequently find ethical writers treating this point very lightly. They appear to regard a conflict of ultimate rules as a difficulty that may be ignored or put aside for future solution, without any slur being thrown on the scientific character of the conflicting formulæ. Whereas such a collision is absolute proof that at least one of the formulæ needs qualification: and suggests a doubt whether the correctly qualified proposition will present itself with the same self-evidence as the simpler but inadequate one; and whether we have not mistaken for an ultimate and independent axiom one that is really derivative and subordinate.

IV.   Since it is implied in the very notion of Truth that it is essentially the same for all minds, the denial by another of a proposition that I have affirmed has a tendency to impair my confidence in its validity. And in fact 'universal' or 'general' consent has often been held to constitute by itself a sufficient evidence of the truth of the most important beliefs; and is practically the only evidence upon which the greater part of mankind can rely. A proposition accepted as true upon this ground alone has, of course, neither self-evidence nor demonstrative evidence for the mind that so accepts it; still, the secure acceptance that we commonly give to the generalisations of the empirical sciences rests – even in the case of experts – largely on the belief that other experts have seen for themselves the evidence for these generalisations, and do not materially disagree as to its adequacy. And it will be easily seen that the absence of such disagreement must remain an indispensable negative condition of the certainty of our beliefs. For if I find any of my judgments, intuitive or inferential, in direct conflict with a judgment of some other mind, there must be error somewhere: and if I have no more reason to suspect error in the other mind than in my own, reflective comparison between the two judgments necessarily reduces me temporarily to a state of

---

[24] Hence the practical importance of the Formal test of Rightness, on which Kant insists: cf. *ante*, chap. i. § 3 of this Book.

[25] The final arbiter, that is, on the question what the rule is: of course the moral obligation to conform to any rule laid down by an external authority must rest on some principle which the individual's reason has to apply.

neutrality. And though the total result in my mind is not exactly suspense of judgment, but an alternation and conflict between positive affirmation by one act of thought and the neutrality that is the result of another, it is obviously something very different from scientific certitude.

Now if the account given of the Morality of Common Sense in the preceding chapters be in the main correct, it seems clear that, generally speaking, its maxims do not fulfil the conditions just laid down. So long as they are left in the state of somewhat vague generalities, as we meet them in ordinary discourse, we are disposed to yield them unquestioning assent, and it may be fairly claimed that the assent is approximately universal – in the sense that any expression of dissent is eccentric and paradoxical. But as soon as we attempt to give them the definiteness which science requires, we find that we cannot do this without abandoning the universality of acceptance. We find, in some cases, that alternatives present themselves, between which it is necessary that we should decide; but between which we cannot pretend that Common Sense does decide, and which often seem equally or nearly equally plausible. In other cases the moral notion seems to resist all efforts to obtain from it a definite rule: in others it is found to comprehend elements which we have no means of reducing to a common standard, except by the application of the Utilitarian – or some similar – method. Even where we seem able to educe from Common Sense a more or less clear reply to the questions raised in the process of definition, the principle that results is qualified in so complicated a way that its self-evidence becomes dubious or vanishes altogether. And thus in each case what at first seemed like an intuition turns out to be either the mere expression of a vague impulse, needing regulation and limitation which it cannot itself supply, but which must be drawn from some other source: or a current opinion, the reasonableness of which has still to be shown by a reference to some other principle.

Chapter XIII

Philosophical Intuitionism

§ 1.   Is there, then, no possibility of attaining, by a more profound and discriminating examination of our common moral thought, to real ethical axioms – intuitive propositions of real clearness and certainty?

This question leads us to the examination of that third phase of the intuitive method, which was called Philosophical Intuitionism.[26] For we conceive it as the aim of a philosopher, as such, to do somewhat more than define and formulate the common moral opinions of mankind. His function is to tell men what they ought to think, rather than what they do think: he is expected to transcend Common Sense in his premises, and is allowed a certain divergence from Common Sense in his conclusions. It is true that the limits of this deviation are firmly, though indefinitely, fixed: the truth of a philosopher's premises will always be tested by the acceptability of his conclusions: if in any important point he be found in flagrant conflict with common opinion, his method is likely to be declared invalid. Still, though he is expected to establish and concatenate at least the main part of the commonly accepted moral rules, he is not necessarily bound to take them as the basis on which his own system is constructed. Rather, we should expect that the history of Moral Philosophy – so far at least as those whom we may call orthodox thinkers are concerned – would be a history of attempts to enunciate, in full breadth and clearness, those primary intuitions of Reason, by the scientific application of which the common moral thought of mankind may be at once systematised and corrected.

And this is to some extent the case. But Moral Philosophy, or philosophy as applied to Morality, has had other tasks to occupy it, even more profoundly difficult than that of penetrating to the fundamental principles of Duty. In modern times especially, it has admitted the necessity of demonstrating the harmony of Duty with Interest; that is, with the Happiness or Welfare of the agent on whom the duty in each case is imposed. It has also undertaken to determine the relation of Right or Good generally to the world of actual existence: a task which could hardly be satisfactorily accomplished without an adequate explanation of the existence of Evil. It has further been distracted by questions which, in my view, are of psychological rather than ethical importance, as to the 'innateness' of our notions of Duty, and the origin of the faculty that furnishes them. With their attention concentrated on these difficult subjects, each of which has been mixed up in various ways with the discussion of fundamental moral intuitions, philosophers have too easily been led to satisfy themselves with ethical formulæ, which implicitly accept the morality of Common Sense *en bloc*, ignoring its defects; and merely express a certain view of the relation of

---

[26] Cf. *ante*, Book i. chap. viii. § 4.

this morality to the individual mind or to the universe of actual existence. Perhaps also they have been hampered by the fear (not, as we have seen, unfounded) of losing the support given by 'general assent' if they set before themselves and their readers too rigid a standard of scientific precision. Still, in spite of all these drawbacks, we find that philosophers have provided us with a considerable number of comprehensive moral propositions, put forward as certain and self-evident, and such as at first sight may seem well adapted to serve as the first principles of scientific morality.

§ 2.   But here a word of caution seems required, which has been somewhat anticipated in earlier chapters, but on which it is particularly needful to lay stress at this point of our discussion: against a certain class of sham-axioms, which are very apt to offer themselves to the mind that is earnestly seeking for a philosophical synthesis of practical rules, and to delude the unwary with a tempting aspect of clear self-evidence. These are principles which appear certain and self-evident because they are substantially tautological: because, when examined, they are found to affirm no more than that it is right to do that which is – in a certain department of life, under certain circumstances and conditions – right to be done. One important lesson which the history of moral philosophy teaches is that, in this region, even powerful intellects are liable to acquiesce in tautologies of this kind; sometimes expanded into circular reasonings, sometimes hidden in the recesses of an obscure notion, often lying so near the surface that, when once they have been exposed, it is hard to understand how they could ever have presented themselves as important.

Let us turn, for illustration's sake, to the time-honoured Cardinal Virtues. If we are told that the dictates of Wisdom and Temperance may be summed up in clear and certain principles, and that these are respectively,

1.   It is right to act rationally,
2.   It is right that the Lower parts of our nature should be governed by the Higher,

we do not at first feel that we are not obtaining valuable information. But when we find (cf. *ante*, chap. xi. § 3) that "acting rationally" is merely another phrase for "doing what we see to be right," and, again, that the "higher part" of our nature to which the rest are to submit is explained to be Reason, so that "acting temperately" is only "acting rationally" under the condition of special non-rational impulses needing to be resisted, the tautology of our "principles" is obvious. Similarly when we are asked to accept as the principle of Justice "that we ought to give every man his own," the definition seems plausible – until it appears that we cannot define "his own" except as equivalent to "that which it is right he should have."

The definitions quoted may be found in modern writers: but it seems worthy of remark that throughout the ethical speculation of Greece,[27] such universal affirmations as are presented to us concerning Virtue or Good conduct seem almost always to be propositions which can only be defended from the charge of tautology, if they are understood as definitions of the problem to be solved, and not as attempts at its solution. For example, Plato and Aristotle appear to offer as constructive moralists the scientific knowledge on ethical matters of which Socrates proclaimed the absence; knowledge, that is, of the Good and Bad in human life. And they seem to be agreed that such Good as can be realised in the concrete life of men and communities is chiefly Virtue, – or (as Aristotle more precisely puts it) the *exercise* of Virtue: so that the practical part of ethical science must consist mainly in the knowledge of Virtue. If, however, we ask how we are to ascertain the kind of conduct which is properly to be called Virtuous, it does not seem that Plato can tell us more of each virtue in turn than that it consists in (1) the knowledge of what is Good in certain circumstances and relations, and (2) such a harmony of the different elements of man's appetitive nature, that their resultant impulse may be always in accordance with this knowledge. But it is just this knowledge (or at least its principles and method) that we are expecting him to give us: and to explain to us instead the different exigencies under which we need it, in no way satisfies our expectation. Nor, again, does Aristotle bring us much nearer such knowledge by telling us that the Good in conduct is to be found somewhere between different kinds of Bad. This at best only indicates the *whereabouts* of Virtue: it does not give us a method for finding it.

[…]

---

[27] I am fully sensible of the peculiar interest and value of the ethical thought of ancient Greece. Indeed through a large part of the present work the influence of Plato and Aristotle on my treatment of this subject has been greater than that of any modern writer. But I am here only considering the value of the general principles for determining what ought to be done, which the ancient systems profess to supply.

The most characteristic formula of Stoicism seems to have been that declaring 'Life according to Nature' to be the ultimate end of action. The spring of the motion that sustained this life was in the vegetable creation a mere unfelt impulse: in animals it was impulse accompanied with sensation: in man it was the direction of Reason, which in him was naturally supreme over all merely blind irrational impulses. What then does Reason direct? 'To live according to Nature' is one answer: and thus we get the circular exposition of ethical doctrine in its simplest form. Sometimes, however, we are told that it is 'Life according to Virtue': which leads us into the circle already noticed in the Platonic-Aristotelian philosophy; as Virtue, by the Stoics also, is only defined as knowledge of Good and Bad in different circumstances and relations. Indeed, this latter circle is given by the Stoics more neatly and perfectly: for with Plato and Aristotle Virtue was not the *sole*, but only the *chief* content of the notion Good, in its application to human life: but in the view of Stoicism the two notions are absolutely coincident. The result, then, is that Virtue is knowledge of what is good and ought to be sought or chosen, and of what is bad and ought to be shunned or rejected: while at the same time there is nothing good or properly choice-worthy, nothing bad or truly formidable, except Virtue and Vice respectively. But if Virtue is thus declared to be a science that has no object except itself, the notion is inevitably emptied of all practical content. In order, therefore, to avoid this result and to reconcile their system with common sense, the Stoics explained that there were other things in human life which were in a manner preferable, though not strictly good, including in this class the primary objects of men's normal impulses. On what principle then are we to select these objects when our impulses are conflicting or ambiguous? If we can get an answer to this question, we shall at length have come to something practical. But here again the Stoic could find no other general answer except either that we were to choose what was Reasonable, or that we were to act in accordance with Nature: each of which answers obviously brings us back into the original circle at a different point.[28]

In Butler's use of the Stoic formula, this circular reasoning seems to be avoided: but it is so only so long as the intrinsic reasonableness of right conduct is ignored or suppressed. Butler assumes with his opponents that it is reasonable to live according to Nature, and argues that Conscience or the faculty that imposes moral rules is naturally supreme in man. It is therefore reasonable to obey Conscience. But are the rules that Conscience lays down merely known to us as the dictates of arbitrary authority, and not as in themselves reasonable? This would give a surely dangerous absoluteness of authority to the possibly unenlightened conscience of any individual: and Butler is much too cautious to do this: in fact, in more than one passage of the *Analogy*[29] he expressly adopts the doctrine of Clarke, that the true rules of morality are essentially reasonable. But if Conscience is, after all, Reason applied to Practice, then Butler's argument seems to bend itself into the old circle: 'it is reasonable to live according to Nature, and it is natural to live according to Reason.'

In the next chapter I shall have to call attention to another logical circle into which we are liable to slide, if we refer to the Good or Perfection, whether of the agent or of others, in giving an account of any special virtue; if we allow ourselves, in explaining Good or Perfection, to use the general notion of virtue (which is commonly regarded as an important element of either). Meanwhile I have already given, perhaps, more than sufficient illustration of one of the most important dangers that beset the students of Ethics. In the laudable attempt to escape from the doubtfulness, disputableness, and apparent arbitrariness of current moral opinions, he is liable to take refuge in principles that are incontrovertible but tautological and insignificant.

§ 3.   Can we then, between this Scylla and Charybdis of ethical inquiry, avoiding on the one hand doctrines that merely bring us back to common opinion with all its imperfections, and on the other hand doctrines that lead us round in a circle, find any way of obtaining self-evident moral principles of real significance? It would be disheartening to have to regard as altogether illusory the strong instinct of Common Sense that points to the existence of such principles, and the deliberate convictions of the long line of moralists who have enunciated them. At the same time, the more we extend our knowledge of man and his environment, the more we realise the vast variety of human natures and circumstances that have existed in different ages and countries, the less disposed we are to believe that there is any definite code of absolute rules, applicable to all human beings without exception.

---

[28] It should be observed that in determining the particulars of external duty the Stoics to some extent used the notion 'nature' in a different way: they tried to derive guidance from the complex adaptation of means to ends exhibited in the organic world. But since in their view the whole course of the Universe was both perfect and completely predetermined, it was impossible for them to obtain from any observation of actual existence a clear and consistent principle for preferring and rejecting alternatives of conduct: and in fact their most characteristic practical precepts show a curious conflict between the tendency to accept what was customary as 'natural,' and the tendency to reject what seemed arbitrary as unreasonable.

[29] Cf. *Analogy*, Part ii, chap. i. and chap. viii.

And we shall find, I think, that the truth lies between these two conclusions. There are certain absolute practical principles, the truth of which, when they are explicitly stated, is manifest; but they are of too abstract a nature, and too universal in their scope, to enable us to ascertain by immediate application of them what we ought to do in any particular case; particular duties have still to be determined by some other method.

One such principle was given in chap. i. § 3 of this Book; where I pointed out that whatever action any of us judges to be right for himself, he implicitly judges to be right for all similar persons in similar circumstances. Or, as we may otherwise put it, 'if a kind of conduct that is right (or wrong) for me is not right (or wrong) for some one else, it must be on the ground of some difference between the two cases, other than the fact that I and he are different persons.' A corresponding proposition may be stated with equal truth in respect of what ought to be done *to* – not *by* – different individuals. These principles have been most widely recognised, not in their most abstract and universal form, but in their special application to the situation of two (or more) individuals similarly related to each other: as so applied, they appear in what is popularly known as the Golden Rule, 'Do to others as you would have them do to you.' This formula is obviously unprecise in statement; for one might wish for another's co-operation in sin, and be willing to reciprocate it. Nor is it even true to say that we ought to do to others only what we think it right for them to do to us; for no one will deny that there may be differences in the circumstances – and even in the natures – of two individuals, A and B, which would make it wrong for A to treat B in the way in which it is right for B to treat A. In short the self-evident principle strictly stated must take some such negative form as this; 'it cannot be right for A to treat B in a manner in which it would be wrong for B to treat A, merely on the ground that they are two different individuals, and without there being any difference between the natures or circumstances of the two which can be stated as a reasonable ground for difference of treatment.' Such a principle manifestly does not give complete guidance – indeed its effect, strictly speaking, is merely to throw a definite *onus, probanda* on the man who applies to another a treatment of which he would complain if applied to himself; but Common Sense has amply recognised the practical importance of the maxim: and its truth, so far as it goes, appears to me self-evident.

A somewhat different application of the same fundamental principle that individuals in similar conditions should be treated similarly finds its sphere in the ordinary administration of Law, or (as we say) of 'Justice.' Accordingly in § 1 of chap. v. of this Book I drew attention to 'impartiality in the application of general rules,' as an important element in the common notion of Justice; indeed, there ultimately appeared to be no other element which could be intuitively known with perfect clearness and certainty. Here again it must be plain that this precept of impartiality is insufficient for the complete determination of just conduct, as it does not help us to decide what kind of rules should be thus impartially applied; though all admit the importance of excluding from government, and human conduct generally, all conscious partiality and 'respect of persons.'

[...] The proposition 'that one ought to aim at one's own good' is sometimes given as the maxim of Rational Self-love or Prudence: but as so stated it does not clearly avoid tautology; since we may define 'good' as 'what one ought to aim at.' If, however, we say 'one's good on the whole,' the addition suggests a principle which, when explicitly stated, is, at any rate, not tautological. I have already referred to this principle[30] as that 'of impartial concern for all parts of our conscious life': – we might express it concisely by saying 'that Hereafter *as such* is to be regarded neither less nor more than Now.' It is not, of course, meant that the good of the present may not reasonably be preferred to that of the future on account of its greater certainty: or again, that a week ten years hence may not be more important to us than a week now, through an increase in our means or capacities of happiness. All that the principle affirms is that the mere difference of priority and posteriority in time is not a reasonable ground for having more regard to the consciousness of one moment than to that of another. The form in which it practically presents itself to most men is 'that a smaller present good is not to be preferred to a greater future good' (allowing for difference of certainty): since Prudence is generally exercised in restraining a present desire (the object or satisfaction of which we commonly regard as *pro tanto* 'a good'), on account of the remoter consequences of gratifying it. The commonest view of the principle would no doubt be that the present *pleasure* or *happiness* is reasonably to be foregone with the view of obtaining greater pleasure or happiness hereafter: but the principle need not be restricted to a hedonistic application; it is equally applicable to any other interpretation of 'one's own good,' in which good is conceived as a mathematical whole, of which the integrant parts are realised in different parts or moments of a lifetime. And therefore it is perhaps better to distinguish it here from the principle 'that Pleasure is the sole Ultimate Good,' which does not seem to have any logical connexion with it.

---

[30] Cf. *ante;* note to p. 124.

So far we have only been considering the 'Good on the Whole' of a single individual: but just as this notion is constructed by comparison and integration of the different 'goods' that succeed one another in the series of our conscious states, so we have formed the notion of Universal Good by comparison and integration of the goods of all individual human – or sentient – existences. And here again, just as in the former case, by considering the relation of the integrant parts to the whole and to each other, I obtain the self-evident principle that the good of any one individual is of no more importance, from the point of view (if I may say so) of the Universe, than the good of any other; unless, that is, there are special grounds for believing that more good is likely to be realised in the one case than in the other. And it is evident to me that as a rational being I am bound to aim at good generally, – so far as it is attainable by my efforts, – not merely at a particular part of it.

From these two rational intuitions we may deduce, as a necessary inference, the maxim of Benevolence in an abstract form: viz. that each one is morally bound to regard the good of any other individual as much as his own, except in so far as he judges it to be less, when impartially viewed, or less certainly knowable or attainable by him. I before observed that the duty of Benevolence as recognised by common sense seems to fall somewhat short of this. But I think it may be fairly urged in explanation of this that *practically* each man, even with a view to universal Good, ought chiefly to concern himself with promoting the good of a limited number of human beings, and that generally in proportion to the closeness of their connexion with him. I think that a 'plain man,' in a modern civilised society, if his conscience were fairly brought to consider the hypothetical question, whether it would be morally right for him to seek his own happiness on any occasion if it involved a certain sacrifice of the greater happiness of some other human being, – without any counterbalancing gain to any one else, – would answer unhesitatingly in the negative.

I have tried to show how in the principles of Justice, Prudence, and Rational Benevolence as commonly recognised there is at least a self-evident element, immediately cognisable by abstract intuition; depending in each case on the relation which individuals and their particular ends bear as parts to their wholes, and to other parts of these wholes. I regard the apprehension, with more or less distinctness, of these abstract truths, as the permanent basis of the common conviction that the fundamental precepts of morality are essentially reasonable. No doubt these principles are often placed side by side with other precepts to which custom and general consent have given a merely illusory air of self-evidence: but the distinction between the two kinds of maxims appears to me to become manifest by merely reflecting upon them. I know by direct reflection that the propositions, 'I ought to speak the truth,' 'I ought to keep my promises' – however true they may be – are not self-evident to me; they present themselves as propositions requiring rational justification of some kind. On the other hand, the propositions, 'I ought not to prefer a present lesser good to a future greater good,' and 'I ought not to prefer my own lesser good to the greater good of another,'[31] do present themselves as self-evident; as much (*e.g.*) as the mathematical axiom that 'if equals be added to equals the wholes are equal.'

It is on account of the fundamental and manifest importance, in my view, of the distinction above drawn between (1) the moral maxims which reflection shows not to possess ultimate validity, and (2) the moral maxims which are or involve genuine ethical axioms, that I refrained at the outset of this investigation from entering at length into the psychogonical question as to the origin of apparent moral intuitions. For no psychogonical theory has ever been put forward professing to discredit the propositions that I regard as really axiomatic, by showing that the causes which produced them were such as had a tendency to make them false: while as regards the former class of maxims, a psychogonical proof that they are untrustworthy when taken as absolutely and without qualification true is in my view, superfluous: since direct reflection shows me they have no claim to be so taken. On the other hand, so far as psychogonical theory represents moral rules as, speaking broadly and generally, means to the ends of individual and social good or well-being, it obviously tends to give a general support to the conclusions to which the preceding discussion has brought us by a different method: since it leads us to regard other moral rules as subordinate to the principles of Prudence and Benevolence.[32]

[...]

---

[31] To avoid misapprehension I should state that in these propositions the consideration of the different degrees of *certainty* of Present and Future Good, Own and Others' Good respectively, is supposed to have been fully taken into account *before* the future or alien Good is judged to be greater.

[32] It may, however, be thought that in exhibiting this aspect of the morality of Common Sense, psychogonical theory leads us to define in a particular way the general notion of 'good' or 'well-being,' regarded as a result which morality has a demonstrable natural tendency to produce. This point will be considered subsequently (chap. xiv. § 1 of this Book: and Book iv. chap. iv.).

§ 5.   I must now point out – if it has not long been apparent to the reader – that the self-evident principles laid down in § 3 do not specially belong to Intuitionism in the restricted sense which, for clear distinction of methods, I gave to this term at the outset of our investigation. The axiom of Prudence, as I have given it, is a self-evident principle, implied in Rational Egoism as commonly accepted.[33] Again, the axiom of Justice or Equity as above stated – 'that similar cases ought to be treated similarly' – belongs in all its applications to Utilitarianism as much as to any system commonly called Intuitional: while the axiom of Rational Benevolence is, in my view, required as a rational basis for the Utilitarian system.

Accordingly, I find that I arrive, in my search for really clear and certain ethical intuitions, at the fundamental principle of Utilitarianism. I must, however, admit that the thinkers who in recent times have taught this latter system, have not, for the most part, expressly tried to exhibit the truth of their first principle by means of any such procedure as that above given. Still, when I examine the "proof" of the "principle of Utility" presented by the most persuasive and probably the most influential among English expositors of Utilitarianism, – J. S, Mill, – I find the need of some such procedure to complete the argument very plain and palpable.

Mill begins by explaining[34] that though "questions of ultimate ends are not amenable" to "proof in the ordinary and popular meaning of the term," there is a "larger meaning of the word proof" in which they are amenable to it. "The subject," he says, is "within the cognisance of the rational faculty. ... Considerations may be presented capable of determining the intellect to" accept "the Utilitarian formula." He subsequently makes clear that by "acceptance of the Utilitarian formula" he means the acceptance, not of the agent's own greatest happiness, but of "the greatest amount of happiness altogether" as the ultimate "end of human action" and "standard of morality": to promote which is, in the Utilitarian view, the supreme "directive rule of human conduct." Then when he comes to give the "proof" – in the larger sense before explained – of this rule or formula, he offers the following argument. "The sole evidence it is possible to produce that anything is desirable, is that people do actually desire it. ... No reason can be given why the general happiness is desirable, except that each person, so far as he believes it to be attainable, desires his own happiness. This, however, being a fact, we have not only all the proof which the case admits of, but all which it is possible to require, that happiness is a good: that each person's happiness is a good to that person, and the general happiness, therefore, a good to the aggregate of persons."[35] He then goes on to argue that pleasure, and pleasure alone, is what all men actually do desire.

Now, as we have seen, it is as a "standard of right and wrong," or "directive rule of conduct," that the utilitarian principle is put forward by Mill: hence, in giving as a statement of this principle that "the general happiness is *desirable*," he must be understood to mean (and his whole treatise shows that he does mean) that it is what each individual *ought* to desire, or at least – in the stricter sense of 'ought' – to aim at realising in action.[36] But this proposition is not established by Mill's reasoning, even if we grant that what is actually desired may be legitimately inferred to be in this sense desirable. For an aggregate of actual desires, each directed towards a different part of the general happiness, does not constitute an actual desire for the general happiness, existing in any individual; and Mill would certainly not contend that a desire which does not exist in any individual can possibly exist in an aggregate of individuals. There being therefore no actual desire – so far as this reasoning goes – for the general happiness, the proposition that the general happiness is desirable cannot be in this way established: so that there is a gap in the expressed argument, which can, I think, only be filled by some such proposition as that which I have above tried to exhibit as the intuition of Rational Benevolence.

Utilitarianism is thus presented as the final form into which Intuitionism tends to pass, when the demand for really self-evident first principles is rigorously pressed. In order, however, to make this transition logically complete, we require to interpret 'Universal Good' as 'Universal Happiness.' And this interpretation cannot, in my view, be justified by arguing, as Mill does, from the psychological fact that Happiness is the sole object of men's actual desires, to the ethical conclusion that it alone is desirable or good; because in Book i. chap. iv. of this treatise I have attempted to show that Happiness or Pleasure is not the only object that each for himself actually desires.

---

[33] On the relation of Rational Egoism to Rational Benevolence – which I regard as the profoundest problem of Ethics – my final view is given in the last chapter of this treatise.

[34] *Utilitarianism*, chap. i. pp. 6, 7, and chap. ii. pp. 16, 17.

[35] *l.c.* chap. iv. pp. 52, 53.

[36] It has been suggested that I have overlooked a confusion in Mill's mind between two possible meanings of the term 'desirable,' (1) what can be desired and (2) what ought to be desired. I intended to show by the two first sentences of this paragraph that I was aware of this confusion, but thought it unnecessary for my present purpose to discuss it.

The identification of Ultimate Good with Happiness is properly to be reached, I think, by a more indirect mode of reasoning; which I will endeavour to explain in the next Chapter.

Chapter XIV

Ultimate Good

§ 1. AT the outset of this treatise[37] I noticed that there are two forms in which the object of ethical inquiry is considered; it is sometimes regarded as a Rule or Rules of Conduct, 'the Right,' sometimes as an end or ends, 'the Good.' I pointed out that in the moral consciousness of modern Europe the two notions are *prima facie* distinct; since while it is commonly thought that the obligation to obey moral rules is absolute, it is not commonly held that the whole Good of man lies in such obedience; this view, we may say, is – vaguely and respectfully but unmistakably – repudiated as a Stoical paradox. The ultimate Good or Well-being of man is rather regarded as an ulterior result, the connexion of which with his Right Conduct is indeed commonly held to be certain, but is frequently conceived as supernatural, and so beyond the range of independent ethical speculation. But now, if the conclusions of the preceding chapters are to be trusted, it would seem that the practical determination of Right Conduct depends on the determination of Ultimate Good. For we have seen (*a*) that most of the commonly received maxims of Duty – even of those which at first sight appear absolute and independent – are found when closely examined to contain an implicit subordination to the more general principles of Prudence and Benevolence: and (*b*) that no principles except these, and the formal principle of Justice or Equity can be admitted as at once intuitively clear and certain; while, again, these principles themselves, so far as they are self-evident, may be stated as precepts to seek (1) one's own good on the whole, repressing all seductive impulses prompting to undue preference of particular goods, and (2) others' good no less than one's own, repressing any undue preference for one individual over another. Thus we are brought round again to the old question with which ethical speculation in Europe began, 'What is the Ultimate Good for man?' – though not in the egoistic form in which the old question was raised. When, however, we examine the controversies to which this question originally led, we see that the investigation which has brought us round to it has tended definitely to exclude one of the answers which early moral reflection was disposed to give to it. For to say that 'General Good' consists solely in general Virtue, – if we mean by Virtue conformity to such prescriptions and prohibitions as make up the main part of the morality of Common Sense – would obviously involve us in a logical circle; since we have seen that the exact determination of these prescriptions and prohibitions must depend on the definition of this General Good.

Nor, I conceive, can this argument be evaded by adopting the view of what I have called 'Æsthetic Intuitionism' and regarding Virtues as excellences of conduct clearly discernible by trained insight, although their nature does not admit of being stated in definite formulæ. For our notions of special virtues do not really become more independent by becoming more indefinite: they still contain, though perhaps more latently, the same reference to 'Good' or 'Wellbeing' as an ultimate standard. This appears clearly when we consider any virtue in relation to the cognate vice – or at least *non-virtue* – into which it tends to pass over when pushed to an extreme, or exhibited under inappropriate conditions. For example, Common Sense may seem to regard Liberality, Frugality, Courage, Placability, as intrinsically desirable: but when we consider their relation respectively to Profusion, Meanness, Foolhardiness, Weakness, we find that Common Sense draws the line in each case not by immediate intuition, but by reference either to some definite maxim of duty, or to the general notion of 'Good' or Wellbeing: and similarly when we ask at what point Candour, Generosity, Humility cease to be virtues by becoming 'excessive.' Other qualities commonly admired, such as Energy, Zeal, Self-control, Thoughtfulness, are obviously regarded as virtues only when they are directed to good ends. In short, the only so-called Virtues which can be thought to be essentially and always such, and incapable of excess, are such qualities as Wisdom, Universal Benevolence, and (in a sense) Justice; of which the notions manifestly involve this notion of Good, supposed already determinate. Wisdom is insight into Good and the means to Good; Benevolence is exhibited in the purposive actions called "doing Good": Justice (when regarded as essentially and always a Virtue) lies in distributing Good (or evil) impartially according to right rules. If then we are asked what is this Good which it is excellent to know, to bestow on others,

---

[37] See Book i. chap. i. § 2.

to distribute impartially, it would be obviously absurd to reply that it is just this knowledge, these beneficent purposes, this impartial distribution.

Nor, again, can I perceive that this difficulty is in any way met by regarding Virtue as a quality of "character" rather than of "conduct," and expressing the moral law in the form, "Be this," instead of the form "Do this."[38] From a practical point of view, indeed, I fully recognise the importance of urging that men should aim at an ideal of character, and consider action in its effects on character. But I cannot infer from this that character and its elements – faculties, habits, or dispositions of any kind – are the constituents of Ultimate Good. It seems to me that the opposite is implied in the very conception of a faculty or disposition; it can only be defined as a tendency to act or feel in a certain way under certain conditions; and such a tendency appeal's to me clearly not valuable in itself but for the acts and feelings in which it takes effect, or for the ulterior consequences of these, – which consequences, again, cannot be regarded as Ultimate Good, so long as they are merely conceived as modifications of faculties, dispositions, etc. When, therefore, I say that effects on character are important, it is a summary way of saying that by the laws of our mental constitution the present act or feeling is a cause tending to modify importantly our acts and feelings in the indefinite future: the comparatively permanent result supposed to be produced in the mind or soul, being a tendency that will show itself in an indefinite number of particular acts and feelings, may easily be more important, in relation to the ultimate end, than a single act or the transient feeling of a single moment: but its comparative permanence appears to me no ground for regarding it as itself a constituent of ultimate good.

§ 2.   So far, however, I have been speaking only of particular virtues, as exhibited in conduct judged to be objectively right: and it may be argued that this is too external a view of the Virtue that claims to constitute Ultimate Good. It may be said that the difficulty that I have been urging vanishes if we penetrate beyond the particular virtues to the root and essence of virtue in general, – the determination of the will to do whatever is judged to be right and to aim at realising whatever is judged to be best –; since this subjective rightness or goodness of will, being independent of knowledge of what is objectively right or good, is independent of that presupposition of Good as already known and determined, which we have seen to be implied in the common conceptions of virtue as manifested in outward acts. I admit that if subjective rightness or goodness of Will is affirmed to be the Ultimate Good, the affirmation does not exactly involve the logical difficulty that I have been urging. None the less is it fundamentally opposed to Common Sense; since the very notion of subjective rightness or goodness of will implies an objective standard, which it directs us to seek, but does not profess to supply. It would be a palpable and violent paradox to set before the right-seeking mind no end except this right-seeking itself, and to affirm this to be the sole Ultimate Good, denying that any effects of right volition can be in themselves good, except the subjective rightness of future volitions, whether of self or of others. It is true that no rule can be recognised, by any reasonable individual, as more authoritative than the rule of doing what he judges to be right; for, in deliberating with a view to my own immediate action, I cannot distinguish between doing what is objectively right, and realising my own subjective conception of rightness. But we are continually forced to make the distinction as regards the actions of others and to judge that conduct may be objectively wrong though subjectively right: and we continually judge conduct to be objectively wrong because it tends to cause pain and loss of happiness to others, – apart from any effect on the subjective rightness of their volitions. It is as so judging that we commonly recognise the mischief and danger of fanaticism: – meaning by a fanatic a man who resolutely and unswervingly carries out his own conception of rightness, when it is a plainly mistaken conception.

The same result may be reached even without supposing so palpable a divorce between subjective and objective rightness of volition as is implied in the notion of fanaticism. As I have already pointed out,[39] though the 'dictates of Reason' are always to be obeyed, it does not follow that 'the dictation of Reason' – the predominance of consciously moral over non-moral motives – is to be promoted without limits; and indeed Common Sense appears to hold that some things are likely to be better done, if they are done from other motives than conscious obedience to practical Reason or Conscience. It thus becomes a practical question how far the dictation of Reason, the predominance of moral choice and moral effort in human life, is a result to be aimed at: and the admission of this question implies that conscious rightness of volition is not the sole ultimate good. On the whole, then, we may conclude that neither (1) subjective rightness or goodness of volition, as distinct from objective, nor (2) virtuous character, except as manifested or realised in virtuous conduct, can be regarded as constituting

---

[38] Cf. Stephen, *Science of Ethics*, chap. iv. § 16.
[39] Chap. xi. § 3; see also chap, xii. § 3.

Ultimate Good: while, again, we are precluded from identifying Ultimate Good with virtuous conduct, because our conceptions of virtuous conduct, under the different heads or aspects denoted by the names of the particular virtues, have been found to presuppose the prior determination of the notion of Good – that Good which virtuous conduct is conceived as producing or promoting or rightly distributing.

And what has been said of Virtue, seems to me still more manifestly true of the other talents, gifts, and graces which make up the common notion of human excellence or Perfection. However immediately the excellent quality of such gifts and skills may be recognised and admired, reflection shows that they are only valuable on account of the good or desirable conscious life in which they are or will be actualised, or which will be somehow promoted by their exercise.

[…]

§ 4.   If then Ultimate Good can only be conceived as Desirable Consciousness – including the Consciousness of Virtue as a part but only as a part – are we to identify this notion with Happiness or Pleasure, and say with the Utilitarians that General Good is general happiness? Many would at this point of the discussion regard this conclusion as inevitable: to say that all other things called good are only means to the end of making conscious life better or more desirable, seems to them the same as saying that they are means to the end of happiness. But very important distinctions remain to be considered. According to the view taken in a previous chapter,[40] in affirming Ultimate Good to be Happiness or Pleasure, we imply (1) that nothing is desirable except desirable feelings, and (2) that the desirability of each feeling is only directly cognisable by the sentient individual at the time of feeling it, and that therefore this particular judgment of the sentient individual must be taken as final[41] on the question how far each element of feeling has the quality of Ultimate Good. Now no one, I conceive, would estimate in any other way the desirability of feeling considered merely as feeling: but it may be urged that our conscious experience includes besides Feelings, Cognitions and Volitions, and that the desirability of these must be taken into account, and is not to be estimated by the standard above stated. I think, however, that when we reflect on a cognition as a transient fact of an individual's psychical experience, – distinguishing it on the one hand from the feeling that normally accompanies it, and on the other hand from that relation of the knowing mind to the object known which is implied in the term "true" or "valid cognition"[42] – it is seen to be an element of consciousness quite neutral in respect of desirability: and the same may be said of Volitions, when we abstract from their concomitant feelings, and their relation to an objective norm or ideal, as well as from all their consequences. It is no doubt true, that in ordinary thought certain states of consciousness – such as Cognition of Truth, Contemplation of Beauty, Volition to realise Freedom or Virtue – are sometimes judged to be preferable on other grounds than their pleasantness: but the general explanation of this seems to be that what in such cases we really prefer is not the present consciousness itself, but either effects on future consciousness more or less distinctly foreseen, or else something in the objective relations of the conscious being, not strictly included in his present consciousness.

[…]

§ 5.   It must be allowed that we find in Common Sense an aversion to admit Happiness (when explained to mean a sum of pleasures) to be the sole ultimate end and standard of right conduct. But this, I think, can be fully accounted for by the following considerations.

I.   The term Pleasure is not commonly used so as to include clearly *all* kinds of consciousness which we desire to retain or reproduce: in ordinary usage it suggests too prominently the coarser and commoner kinds of such feelings; and it is difficult even for those who are trying to use it scientifically to free their minds altogether from the associations of ordinary usage, and to mean by Pleasure only Desirable Consciousness or Feeling of whatever kind. Again, our knowledge of human life continually suggests to us instances of pleasures which will inevitably involve as concomitant or consequent either a greater amount of pain or a loss of more important pleasures: and we naturally shrink from including even hypothetically in our conception of ultimate good these – in Bentham's phrase – "impure" pleasures; especially since we have, in many cases, moral or æsthetic instincts warning us against such pleasures.

---

[40] Book ii. chap. ii.

[41] Final, that is, so far as the quality of the present feeling is concerned. I have pointed out that so far as any estimate of the desirability or pleasantness of a feeling involves comparison with feelings only represented in idea, it is liable to be erroneous through imperfections in the representation

[42] The term "cognition" without qualification more often implies what is signified by "true" or "valid": but for the present purpose it is necessary to eliminate this implication.

II.   We have seen[43] that many important pleasures can only be felt on condition of our experiencing desires for other things than pleasure. Thus the very acceptance of Pleasure as the ultimate end of conduct involves the practical rule that it is not always to be made the conscious end. Hence, even if we are considering merely the good of one human being taken alone, excluding from our view all effects of his conduct on others, still the reluctance of Common Sense to regard pleasure as the sole thing ultimately desirable may be justified by the consideration that human beings tend to be less happy if they are exclusively occupied with the desire of personal happiness. *E.g.* (as was before shown) we shall miss the valuable pleasures which attend the exercise of the benevolent affections if we do not experience genuinely disinterested impulses to procure happiness for others (which are, in fact, implied in the notion of 'benevolent affections').

III.   But again, I hold, as was expounded in the preceding chapter, that disinterested benevolence is not only thus generally in harmony with rational Self-love, but also in another sense and independently rational: that is, Reason shows me that if my happiness is desirable and a good, the equal happiness of any other person must be equally desirable. Now, when Happiness is spoken of as the sole ultimate good of man, the idea most commonly suggested is that each individual is to seek his own happiness at the expense (if necessary) or, at any rate, to the neglect of that of others: and this offends both our sympathetic and our rational regard for others' happiness. It is, in fact, rather the end of Egoistic than of Universalistic Hedonism, to which Common Sense feels an aversion. And certainly one's individual happiness is, in many respects, an unsatisfactory mark for one's supreme aim, apart from any direct collision into which the exclusive pursuit of it may bring us with rational or sympathetic Benevolence. It does not possess the characteristics which, as Aristotle says, we "divine" to belong to Ultimate Good: being (so far, at least, as it can be empirically foreseen) so narrow and limited, of such necessarily brief duration, and so shifting and insecure while it lasts. But Universal Happiness, desirable consciousness or feeling for the innumerable multitude of sentient beings, present and to come, seems an End that satisfies our imagination by its vastness, and sustains our resolution by its comparative security.

It may, however, be said that if we require the individual to sacrifice his own happiness to the greater happiness of others on the ground that it is reasonable to do so, we really assign to the individual a different ultimate end from that which we lay down as the ultimate Good of the universe of sentient beings: since we direct him to take, as ultimate, Happiness for the Universe, but Conformity to Reason for himself. I admit the substantial truth of this statement, though I should avoid the language as tending to obscure the distinction before explained between "obeying the dictates" and "promoting the dictation" of reason. But granting the alleged difference, I do not see that it constitutes an argument against the view here maintained, since the individual is essentially and fundamentally different from the larger whole – the universe of sentient beings – of which he is conscious of being a part; just because he has a known relation to similar parts of the same whole, while the whole itself has no such relation. I accordingly see no inconsistency in holding that while it *would* be reasonable for the aggregate of sentient beings, if it could act collectively, to aim at its own happiness only as an ultimate end – and would be reasonable for any individual to do the same, if he were the only sentient being in the universe – it may yet be *actually* reasonable for an individual to sacrifice his own Good or happiness for the greater happiness of others.[44]

At the same time I admit that, in the earlier age of ethical thought which Greek philosophy represents, men sometimes judged an act to be 'good' *for the agent*, even while recognising that its consequences would be on the whole painful to him, – as (*e.g.*) a heroic exchange of a life full of happiness for a painful death at the call of duty. I attribute this partly to a confusion of thought between what it is reasonable for an individual to desire, when he considers his own existence alone, and what he must recognise as reasonably to be desired, when he takes the point of view of a larger whole: partly, again, to a faith deeply rooted in the moral consciousness of mankind, that there cannot be really and ultimately any conflict between the two kinds of reasonableness.[45] But when 'Reasonable Self-love' has been clearly distinguished from Conscience, as it is by Butler and his followers, we find it is naturally understood to mean desire for one's own Happiness: so that in fact the interpretation of 'one's own good,' which was almost peculiar in ancient thought to the Cyrenaic and Epicurean heresies, is adopted by some of the most

---

[43] Book i. chap, iv.; cf. Book ii. chap. iii.

[44] I ought at the same time to say that I hold it no less reasonable for an individual to take his own happiness as his ultimate end. This "Dualism of the Practical Reason" will be further discussed in the concluding chapter of the treatise.

[45] We may illustrate this double explanation by a reference to some of Plato's Dialogues, such as the *Gorgias*, where the ethical argument has a singularly mixed effect on the mind. Partly, it seems to us more or less dexterous sophistry, playing on a confusion of thought latent in the common notion of good: partly a noble and stirring expression of a profound moral faith.

orthodox of modern moralists. Indeed it often does not seem to have occurred to these latter that this notion can have any other interpretation.[46] If, then, when any one hypothetically concentrates his attention on himself, Good is naturally and almost inevitably conceived to be Pleasure, we may reasonably conclude that the Good of any number of similar beings, whatever their mutual relations may be, cannot be essentially different in quality.

IV. But lastly, from the universal point of view no less than from that of the individual, it seems true that Happiness is likely to be better attained if the extent to which we set ourselves consciously to aim at it be carefully restricted. And this not only because action is likely to be more effective if our effort is temporarily concentrated on the realisation of more limited ends – though this is no doubt an important reason: – but also because the fullest development of happy life for each individual seems to require that he should have other external objects of interest besides the happiness of other conscious beings. And thus we may conclude that the pursuit of the ideal objects before mentioned, Virtue, Truth, Freedom, Beauty, etc., *for their own sakes*, is indirectly and secondarily, though not primarily and absolutely, rational; on account not only of the happiness that will result from their attainment, but also of that which springs from their disinterested pursuit. While yet if we ask for a final criterion of the comparative value of the different objects of men's enthusiastic pursuit, and of the limits within which each may legitimately engross the attention of mankind, we shall none the less conceive it to depend upon the degree in which they respectively conduce to Happiness.

If, however, this view be rejected, it remains to consider whether we can frame any other coherent account of Ultimate Good. If we are not to systematise human activities by taking Universal Happiness as their common end, on what other principles are we to systematise them? It should be observed that these principles must not only enable us to compare among themselves the values of the different non-hedonistic ends which we have been considering, but must also provide a common standard for comparing these values with that of Happiness; unless we are prepared to adopt the paradoxical position of rejecting happiness as absolutely valueless. For we have a practical need of determining not only whether we should pursue Truth rather than Beauty, or Freedom or some ideal constitution of society rather than either, or perhaps desert all of these for the life of worship and religious contemplation; but also how far we should follow any of these lines of endeavour, when we foresee among its consequences the pains of human or other sentient beings, or even the loss of pleasures that might otherwise have been enjoyed by them.[47]

I have failed to find – and am unable to construct – any systematic answer to this question that appears to me deserving of serious consideration: and hence I am finally led to the conclusion (which at the close of the last chapter seemed to be premature) that the Intuitional method rigorously applied yields as its final result the doctrine of pure Universalistic Hedonism, – which it is convenient to denote by the single word, Utilitarianism.

---

[46] Cf. Stewart, *Philosophy of the Active and Moral Powers*, Book ii. chap, i.

[47] The controversy on vivisection, to which I referred just now, affords a good illustration of the need that I am pointing out. I do not observe that any one in this controversy has ventured on the paradox that the pain of sentient beings is not *per se* to be avoided.

Part III

Foundations of Contemporary Ethics

_____

1

Principia Ethica

G. E. Moore

When contemporary philosophers discuss Chapter 1 of Moore's *Principia Ethica*, they very often focus on Moore's 'open question argument'. This argument is presented toward the end of the text reproduced here (in section 13), and it very much deserves to be discussed, but it is worth pointing out that Moore himself takes his time getting to the argument. His primary aims in this chapter are to argue that 'good' is an undefinable notion of fundamental importance to ethics, and to diagnose the 'naturalistic fallacy' that he contends is committed by philosophers who think they are able to define goodness in other terms (note that naturalism, as it is understood in twentieth century metaethics, should not be confused with the view that we ought to act as nature would have us act; rather, it is the view that moral properties and facts, if they exist at all, are not something additional to the natural 'furniture of the world').

For Moore, to say that 'good' is incapable of being defined amounts to saying that there are no parts to goodness, such that the parts compose a whole (sections 8 and 10). It can be confusing to talk of parts and wholes in this fashion, but we can use examples to illustrate what is at issue here. If 'brother' is simply definable as 'male sibling', then there are two conceptual parts that make up the whole of the concept 'brother'. In this example, it's clear that the parts are not all individual physical things, since the relation of sibling is not itself something physical (we cannot point to it), even if being of a certain sex is (perhaps). Moore's discussion of his example of the definition of 'horse' is a little confusing in this respect, since it moves from a definition that makes essential reference to a particular genus, to talk of the exact physical parts that make up a horse (perhaps these parts and the physical relations they stand in are metaphysically equivalent to being a hoofed quadruped of the genus *equus*, but this is far from obvious). Finally, consider the definition of 'triangle' as 'a figure with three straight sides and three angles'; here it is really a stretch to think of the part/whole relation as physical.

The naturalistic fallacy, Moore tells us, is the mistake whereby philosophers confuse definitions of 'good' with statements about properties that things that are 'good' always possess (section 10). His target is not the view that good things, in addition to being good, are always desired by rational people. But he is concerned to argue that 'good' does not mean 'desired'. He calls this mistake *naturalistic* as he is intent on considering examples that involve attempts to define 'good' by reference to natural properties, such as pleasure and desire; but, in fact, the fallacy (if it is a fallacy) extends to super-natural definitions as well, e.g. the view that 'good' is definable as 'loved by God'.

The open question argument is an argument to the effect that the mistake Moore calls the naturalistic fallacy is being committed in cases where people attempt to define good (and, if the argument works, it will be generalizable to other mistaken attempts at definition, as well). It can be traced back to Sidgwick's *Methods*, as Moore notes. The argument proceeds (in section 13) by first taking a purported definition and recasting it as a question about a particular example, e.g. by recasting 'to be good … [is] to be that which we desire to desire' as 'Is it good to desire to desire A?' Next, we ask ourselves whether this question is 'as

History of Ethics – Essential Readings with Commentary, First Edition. Edited by Daniel Star and Roger Crisp.
© 2020 John Wiley & Sons Ltd. Published 2020 by John Wiley & Sons Ltd.

intelligible as' (that is, we might alternatively say, on all fours with) the simpler question 'Is A good?' It would appear that we are at least as much inclined to be left wanting an answer to the question 'Is it good to desire to desire A?' as we are to the question 'Is A good?', and it is this fact that tells us we have before us an open question and not a successful definition. Moore adds that, if the definition were a good one, we should be able to recast 'Is it good to desire to desire A?' as 'Is the desire to desire A one of the things which we desire to desire?' Moore is right that this second question does not strike us as equivalent to the first, but he later conceded that this in itself does not show us very much; after all, 'brother' may be definable as 'male sibling', yet if I think to myself that a brother is a male sibling I am not simply thinking to myself that a brother is a brother.

We leave criticism of Moore's account of the naturalistic fallacy to our commentary on Frankena's critical article. Here, let us point out that a particularly odd feature of the rest of Moore's book is that, after endorsing use of the open question argument when considering goodness, he asks the reader to accept that "right" does and can mean nothing but "cause of a good result"' (section 89). Moore contends that it is an analytic truth concerning rightness (understood as permissibility) that acts that are right will be acts that will not cause there to be any less good in the universe than any alternative acts (and acts that are obligatory will be such that they produce more good in the universe than any alternative acts). Yet it seems to many of us, even those of us who find consequentialism attractive, that the following question is an open question: 'is it always true that an act that, of any of the alternatives available to an agent, produces the most good in the universe is right?'

To be fair to Moore, he does consider how deontologists might respond to his claim about the meaning of 'right' (section 17). He offers an interpretation of deontology according to which, in those cases where it would appear that we must follow our duties, or respect people's rights, in ways that appear not to maximize the production of good states of affairs, what is really occurring is that we are taking it that more that is of intrinsic value will exist in the universe if we stick to our duties or respect people's rights than would exist if we failed to do so. We might interpret Moore as thus committed to the idea that deontological theories really have a consequentialist structure. The idea that deontological theories are susceptible to 'consequentialization' has proven to be a popular idea in recent defenses of consequentialism, although it is not generally thought necessary to follow Moore in thinking that the connections between rightness and goodness of the kind he discusses are analytic. In any case, deontologists tend to think that moves of the consequentializing kind, even if they lead to consequentialist theories that can mimic the judgements regarding particular cases that are delivered by deontological theories, still offer the wrong kind of account of the relation between goodness and our moral duties.

[…] **5.** This question, how 'good' is to be defined, is the most fundamental question in all Ethics. That which is meant by 'good' is, in fact, except its converse 'bad,' the *only* simple object of thought which is peculiar to Ethics. Its definition is, therefore, the most essential point in the definition of Ethics: and moreover a mistake with regard to it entails a far larger number of erroneous ethical judgments than any other. Unless this first question be fully understood, and its true answer clearly recognised, the rest of Ethics is as good as useless from the point of view of systematic knowledge. True ethical judgments, of the two kinds last dealt with, may indeed be made by those who do not know the answer to this question as well as by those who do; and it goes without saying that the two classes of people may lead equally good lives. But it is extremely unlikely that the *most general* ethical judgments will be equally valid, in the absence of a true answer to this question: I shall presently try to shew that the gravest errors have been largely due to beliefs in a false answer. And, in any case, it is impossible that, till the answer to this question be known, any one should know *what is the evidence* for any ethical judgment whatsoever. But the main object of Ethics, as a systematic science, is to give correct *reasons* for thinking that this or that is good; and, unless this question he answered, such reasons cannot be given. Even, therefore, apart from the fact that a false answer leads to false conclusions, the present enquiry is a most necessary and important part of the science of Ethics.

6. What, then, is good? How is good to be defined? Now, it may be thought that this is a verbal question. A definition does indeed often mean the expressing of one word's meaning in other words. But this is not the sort of definition I am asking for. Such a definition can never be of ultimate importance in any study except lexicography. If I wanted that kind of definition I should have to consider in the first place how people generally used the word 'good'; but my business is not with its proper usage, as established by custom. I should, indeed, be foolish, if I tried to use it for something which it did not usually denote: if, for instance, I were to announce that, whenever I used the word 'good,' I must be understood to be thinking of that object which is usually denoted by the word 'table.' I shall, therefore, use the word in the sense in which I think it is ordinarily used; but at the same time I am not anxious to discuss whether I am right in thinking that it is so used. My business is solely with that object or idea, which I hold, rightly or wrongly, that the word is generally used to stand for. What I want to discover is the nature of that object or idea, and about this I am extremely anxious to arrive at an agreement.

But, if we understand the question in this sense, my answer to it may seem a very disappointing one. If I am asked 'What is good?' my answer is that good is good, and that is the end of the matter. Or if I am asked 'How is good to be defined?' my answer is that it cannot be defined, and that is all I have to say about it. But disappointing as these answers may appear, they are of the very last importance. To readers who are familiar with philosophic terminology, I can express their importance by saying that they amount to this: That propositions about the good are all of them synthetic and never analytic; and that is plainly no trivial matter. And the same thing may be expressed more popularly, by saying that, if I am right, then nobody can foist upon us such an axiom as that 'Pleasure is the only good' or that 'The good is the desired' on the pretence that this is 'the very meaning of the word.'

7. Let us, then, consider this position. My point is that 'good' is a simple notion, just as 'yellow' is a simple notion; that, just as you cannot, by any manner of means, explain to any one who does not already know it, what yellow is, so you cannot explain what good is. Definitions of the kind that I was asking for, definitions which describe the real nature of the object or notion denoted by a word, and which do not merely tell us what the word is used to mean, are only possible when the object or notion in question is something complex. You can give a definition of a horse, because a horse has many different properties and qualities, all of which you can enumerate. But when you have enumerated them all, when you have reduced a horse to his simplest terms, then you can no longer define those terms. They are simply something which you think of or perceive, and to any one who cannot think of or perceive them, you can never, by any definition, make their nature known. It may perhaps be objected to this that we are able to describe to others, objects which they have never seen or thought of. We can, for instance, make a man understand what a chimaera is, although he has never heard of one or seen one. You can tell him that it is an animal with a lioness's head and body, with a goat's head growing from the middle of its back, and with a snake in place of a tail. But here the object which you are describing is a complex object; it is entirely composed of parts, with which we are all perfectly familiar – a snake, a goat, a lioness; and we know, too, the manner in which those parts are to be put together, because we know what is meant by the middle of a lioness's back, and where her tail is wont to grow. And so it is with all objects, not previously known, which we are able to define: they are all complex; all composed of parts, which may themselves, in the first instance, be capable of similar definition, but which must in the end be reducible to simplest parts, which can no longer be defined. But yellow and good, we say, are not complex: they are notions of that simple kind, out of which definitions are composed and with which the power of further defining ceases.

8.   When we say, as Webster says, 'The definition of horse is "A hoofed, quadruped of the genus Equus,"' we may, in fact, mean three different things. (1) We may mean merely: 'When I say "horse," you are to understand that I am talking about a hoofed quadruped of the genus Equus.' This might be called the arbitrary verbal definition: and I do not mean that good is indefinable in that sense. (2) We may mean, as Webster ought to mean: 'When most English people say "horse," they mean a hoofed quadruped of the genus Equus.' This may be called the verbal definition proper, and I do not say that good is indefinable in this sense either; for it is certainly possible to discover how people use a word: otherwise, we could never have known that 'good' may be translated by 'gut' in German and by 'bon' in French. But (3) we may, when we define horse, mean something much more important. We may mean that a certain object, which we all of us know, is composed in a certain manner: that it has four legs, a head, a heart, a liver, etc., etc., all of them arranged in definite relations to one another. It is in this sense that I deny good to be definable. I say that it is not composed of any parts, which we can substitute for it in our minds when we are think-ing of it. We might think just as clearly and correctly about a horse, if we thought of all its parts and their arrange-ment instead of thinking of the whole: we could. I say, think how a horse differed from a donkey just as well, just as truly, in this way, as now we do, only not so easily; but there is nothing whatsoever which we could so substitute for good; and that is what I mean, when I say that good is indefinable.

9.   But I am afraid I have still not removed the chief difficulty which may prevent acceptance of the proposition that good is indefinable. I do not mean to say that *the* good, that which is good, is thus indefinable; if I did think so, I should not be writing on Ethics, for my main object is to help towards discovering that definition. It is just because I think there will be less risk of error in our search for a definition of 'the good,' that I am now insisting that *good* is indefinable. I must try to explain the difference between these two. I suppose it may be granted that 'good' is an adjec-tive. Well 'the good,' 'that which is good,' must therefore be the substantive to which the adjective 'good' will apply: it must be the whole of that to which the adjective will apply, and the adjective must *always* truly apply to it. But if it is that to which the adjective will apply, it must be something different from that adjective itself; and the whole of that something different, whatever it is, will he our definition of *the* good. Now it may be that this something will have other adjectives, beside 'good,' that will apply to it. It may be full of pleasure, for example; it may be intelligent: and if these two adjectives are really part of its definition, then it will certainly be true, that pleasure and intelligence are good. And many people appear to think that, if we say 'Pleasure and intelligence are good,' or if we say 'Only pleasure and intelligence are good,' we are defining 'good.' Well, I cannot deny that propositions of this nature may sometimes be called definitions; I do not know well enough how the word is generally used to decide upon this point. I only wish it to be understood that that is not what I mean when I say there is no possible definition of good, and that I shall not mean this if I use the word again. I do most fully believe that some true proposition of the form 'Intelligence is good and intelligence alone is good' can be found; if none could be found, our definition of *the* good would be impossible. As it is, I believe *the* good to be definable; and yet I still say that good itself is indefinable.

10.   'Good,' then, if we mean by it that quality which we assert to belong to a thing, when we say that the thing is good, is incapable of any definition, in the most important sense of that word. The most important sense of 'defi-nition' is that in which a definition states what are the parts which invariably compose a certain whole; and in this sense 'good' has no definition because it is simple and has no parts. It is one of those innumerable objects of thought which are themselves incapable of definition, because they are the ultimate terms by reference to which whatever *is* capable of definition must be defined. That there must be an indefinite number of such terms is obvious, on reflection; since we cannot define anything except by an analysis, which, when carried as far as it will go, refers us to something, which is simply different from anything else, and which by that ultimate difference explains the peculiarity of the whole which we are defining: for every whole contains some parts which are common to other wholes also. There is, therefore, no intrinsic difficulty in the contention that 'good' denotes a simple and indefinable quality. There are many other instances of such qualities.

Consider yellow, for example. We may try to define it, by describing its physical equivalent; we may state what kind of light-vibrations must stimulate the normal eye, in order that we may perceive it. But a moment's reflection is sufficient to shew that those light-vibrations are not themselves what we mean by yellow. *They* are not what we perceive. Indeed we should never have been able to discover their existence, unless we had first been struck by the patent difference of quality between the different colours. The most we can be entitled to say of those vibrations is that they are what corresponds in space to the yellow which we actually perceive.

Yet a mistake of this simple kind has commonly been made about 'good.' It may be true that all things which are good are *also* something else, just as it is true that all things which are yellow produce a certain kind of vibration in the light. And it is a fact, that Ethics aims at discovering what are those other properties belonging to all things which are good. But far too many philosophers have thought that when they named those other properties they were actually defining good; that these properties, in fact, were simply not 'other,' but absolutely and entirely the same with goodness. This view I propose to call the 'naturalistic fallacy' and of it I shall now endeavour to dispose.

11.   Let us consider what it is such philosophers say. And first it is to be noticed that they do not agree among themselves. They not only say that they are right as to what good is, but they endeavour to prove that other people who say that it is something else, are wrong. One, for instance, will affirm that good is pleasure, another, perhaps, that good is that which is desired; and each of these will argue eagerly to prove that the other is wrong. But, how is that possible? One of them says that good is nothing but the object of desire, and at the same time tries to prove that it is not pleasure. But from his first assertion, that good just means the object of desire, one of two things must follow as regards his proof:

1.   He may be trying to prove that the object of desire is not pleasure. But, if this be all, where is his Ethics? The position he is maintaining is merely a psychological one. Desire is something which occurs in our minds, and pleasure is something else which so occurs; and our would-be ethical philosopher is merely holding that the latter is not the object of the former. But what has that to do with the question in dispute? His opponent held the ethical proposition that pleasure was the good, and although he should prove a million times over the psychological proposition that pleasure is not the object of desire, he is no nearer proving his opponent to be wrong. The position is like this. One man says a triangle is a circle: another replies 'A triangle is a straight line, and I will prove to you that I am right: *for*' (this is the only argument) 'a straight line is not a circle.' 'That is quite true,' the other may reply; 'but nevertheless a triangle is a circle, and you have said nothing whatever to prove the contrary. What is proved is that one of us is wrong, for we agree that a triangle cannot be both a straight line and a circle: but which is wrong, there can be no earthly means of proving, since you define triangle as straight line and I define it as circle.' – Well, that is one alternative which any naturalistic Ethics has to face; if good is *defined* as something else, it is then impossible either to prove that any other definition is wrong or even to deny such definition.

2.   The other alternative will scarcely be more welcome. It is that the discussion is after all a verbal one. When A says 'Good means pleasant' and B says 'Good means desired,' they may merely wish to assert that most people have used the word for what is pleasant and for what is desired respectively. And this is quite an interesting subject for discussion: only it is not a whit more an ethical discussion than the last was. Nor do I think that any exponent of naturalistic Ethics would be willing to allow that this was all he meant. They are all so anxious to persuade us that what they call the good is what we really ought to do. 'Do, pray, act so, because the word "good" is generally used to denote actions of this nature': such, on this view, would be the substance of their teaching. And in so far as they tell us how we ought to act, their teaching is truly ethical, as they mean it to be. But how perfectly absurd is the reason they would give for it! 'You are to do this, because most people use a certain word to denote conduct such as this.' 'You are to say the thing which is not, because most people call it lying.' That is an argument just as good! – My dear sirs, what we want to know from you as ethical teachers, is not how people use a word; it is not even, what kind of actions they approve, which the use of this word 'good' may certainly imply; what we want to know is simply what *is* good. We may indeed agree that what most people do think good, is actually so; we shall at all events be glad to know their opinions: but when we say their opinions about what *is* good, we do mean what we say; we do not care whether they call that thing which they mean 'horse' or 'table' or 'chair,' 'gut' or 'bon' or '*ἀγαθός*'; we want to know what it is that they so call. When they say 'Pleasure is good.' we cannot, believe that they merely mean 'Pleasure is pleasure' and nothing more than that.

12.   Suppose a man says 'I am pleased'; and suppose that is not a lie or a mistake but the truth. Well, if it is true, what does that mean? It means that his mind, a certain definite mind, distinguished by certain definite marks from all others, has at this moment a certain definite feeling called pleasure. 'Pleased' *means* nothing but having pleasure, and though we may be more pleased or less pleased, and even, we may admit for the present, have one or another kind of pleasure; yet in so far as it is pleasure we have, whether there be more or less of it, and whether it be of one kind or another, what we have is one definite thing, absolutely indefinable, some one thing that is the same in all the various degrees and in all the various kinds of it that there may be. We may be able to say how it is related to other things: that, for example, it is in the mind, that it causes desire, that we are conscious of it, etc., etc. We can, I say, describe its relations to other things, but define it we can *not*. And if anybody tried to define pleasure for us as being any other natural object; if anybody were to say, for instance, that pleasure *means* the sensation of red, and were to proceed to deduce from that that pleasure is a colour, we should be entitled to laugh at him and to distrust his future statements about pleasure. Well, that would be the same fallacy which I have called the naturalistic fallacy. That 'pleased' does not mean 'having the sensation of red.' or anything else whatever, does not prevent us from understanding what it does mean. It is enough for us to know that 'pleased' does mean 'having the sensation of pleasure,' and though pleasure is absolutely indefinable, though pleasure is pleasure and nothing else whatever, yet we feel no difficulty in saying that we are pleased. The reason is, of course, that when I say 'I am pleased,' I do *not* mean that 'I' am the same thing as 'having pleasure.' And similarly no difficulty need be found in my saying that 'pleasure is good' and yet not meaning that 'pleasure' is the same thing as 'good,' that pleasure *means* good, and that good *means* pleasure. If I were to imagine that when I said 'I am pleased,' I meant that I was exactly the same thing as 'pleased,' I should not indeed call that a naturalistic fallacy, although it would be the same fallacy as I have called naturalistic with reference to Ethics. The reason of this is obvious enough. When a man confuses two natural objects with one another, defining the one by the other, if for instance, he confuses himself, who is one natural object, with 'pleased' or with 'pleasure' which are others, then there is no reason to call the fallacy naturalistic. But if he confuses 'good,' which is not in the same sense a natural object, with any natural object whatever, then there is a reason for calling that a naturalistic fallacy; its being made with regard to 'good' marks it as something quite specific, and this specific mistake deserves a name because it is so common. As for the reasons why good is not to be considered a natural object, they may be reserved for discussion in another place. But, for the present, it is sufficient to notice this: Even if it were a natural object, that would not alter the nature of the fallacy nor diminish its importance one whit. All that I have said about it would remain quite equally true: only the name which I have called it would not be so appropriate as I think it is. And I do not care about the name: what I do care about is the fallacy. It does not matter what we call it, provided we recognise it when we meet with it. It is to be met with in almost every book on Ethics; and yet it is not recognised: and that is why it is necessary to multiply illustrations of it, and convenient to give it a name. It is a very simple fallacy indeed. When we say that an orange is yellow, we do not think our statement binds us to hold that 'orange' means nothing else than 'yellow,' or that nothing can be yellow but an orange. Supposing the orange is also sweet! Does that bind us to say that 'sweet' is exactly the same thing as 'yellow,' that 'sweet' must be defined as 'yellow'? And supposing it be recognised that 'yellow' just means 'yellow' and nothing else whatever, does that make it any more difficult to hold that oranges are yellow? Most certainly it does not: on the contrary, it would be absolutely meaningless to say that oranges were yellow, unless yellow did in the end mean just 'yellow' and nothing else whatever – unless it was absolutely indefinable. We should not get any very clear notion about things, which are yellow – we should not get very far with our science, if we were bound to hold that everything which was yellow, *meant* exactly the, same thing as yellow. We should find we had to hold that an orange was exactly the same thing as a stool, a piece of paper, a lemon, anything you like. We could prove any number of absurdities: but should we be the nearer to the truth? Why, then, should it be different with 'good'? Why, if good is good and indefinable, should I be held to deny that pleasure, is good? Is there any difficulty in holding both to be true at once? On the contrary, there is no meaning in saying that pleasure is good, unless good is something different from pleasure. It is absolutely useless, so far as Ethics is concerned, to prove, as Mr Spencer tries to do, that increase of pleasure coincides with increase of life, unless good *means* something different from either life or pleasure. He might just as well try to prove that an orange is yellow by shewing that it always is wrapped up in paper.

13.   In fact, if it is not the case that 'good' denotes something simple and indefinable, only two alternatives are possible: either it is a complex, a given whole, about the correct analysis of which there may be disagreement; or else it means nothing at all, and there is no such subject as Ethics. In general, however, ethical philosophers have attempted to define good, without recognising what such an attempt must mean. They actually use arguments which involve one or both of the absurdities considered in § 11. We are, therefore, justified in concluding that the attempt to define good is chiefly due to want of clearness as to the possible nature of definition. There are, in fact, only two serious alternatives to be considered, in order to establish the conclusion that 'good' does denote a simple and indefinable notion. It might possibly denote a complex, as 'horse' does: or it might have no meaning at all. Neither of these possibilities has, however, been clearly conceived and seriously maintained, as such, by those who presume to define good; and both may be dismissed by a simple appeal to facts.

1.   The hypothesis that disagreement about the meaning of good is disagreement with regard to the correct analysis of a given whole, may be most plainly seen to be incorrect by consideration of the fact that, whatever definition be offered, it may be always asked, with significance, of the complex so defined, whether it is itself good. To take, for instance, one of the more plausible, because one of the more complicated, of such proposed definitions, it may easily be thought, at first sight, that to be good may mean to be that which we desire to desire.

Thus if we apply this definition to a particular instance and say 'When we think that A is good, we are think-ing that A is one of the things which we desire to desire,' our proposition may seem quite plausible. But, if we carry the investigation further, and ask ourselves 'Is it good to desire to desire A?' it is apparent, on a little reflection, that this question is itself as intelligible, as the original question 'Is A good?' – that we are, in fact, now asking for exactly the same information about the desire to desire A, for which we formerly asked with regard to A itself. But it is also apparent that the meaning of this second question cannot be, correctly ana-lysed into 'Is the desire to desire A one of the things which we desire to desire?': we have not before our minds anything so complicated as the question 'Do we desire to desire to desire to desire A?' Moreover any one can easily convince himself by inspection that the predicate of this proposition – 'good' – is positively different from the notion of 'desiring to desire' which enters into its subject: 'That we should desire to desire A is good' is *not* merely equivalent to 'That A should be good is good.' It may indeed be true that what we desire to desire is always also good; perhaps, even the converse may be true: but it is very doubtful whether this is the case, and the mere fact that we understand very well what is meant by doubting it, shews clearly that we have two different notions before our minds.

2. And the same consideration is sufficient to dismiss the hypothesis that 'good' has no meaning whatsoever. It is very natural to make the mistake of supposing that what is universally true is of such a nature that its negation would be self-contradictory: the importance which has been assigned to analytic propositions in the history of philosophy shews how easy such a mistake is. And thus it is very easy to conclude that what seems to be a universal ethical principle is in fact an identical proposition; that, if, for example, whatever is called 'good' seems to be pleasant, the proposition 'Pleasure is the good' does not assert a connection between two different notions, but involves only one, that of pleasure, which is easily recognised as a distinct entity. But whoever will attentively consider with himself what is actually before his mind when he asks the question 'Is pleasure (or whatever it may be) after all good?' can easily satisfy himself that he is not merely wondering whether pleasure is pleasant. And if he will try this experiment with each suggested definition in succession, he may become expert enough to recognise that in every case he has before his mind a unique object, with regard to the con-nection of which with any other object, a distinct question may be asked. Every one does in fact understand the question 'Is this good?' When he thinks of it, his state of mind is different from what it would be, were he asked 'Is this pleasant, or desired, or approved?' It has a distinct meaning for him, even though he may not recognise in what respect it is distinct. Whenever he thinks of 'intrinsic value,' or 'intrinsic worth,' or says that a thing 'ought to exist,' he has before his mind the unique object – the unique property of things – which I mean by 'good.' Everybody is constantly aware of this notion, although he may never become aware at all that it is different from other notions of which he is also aware. But, for correct ethical reasoning, it is extremely important that he should become aware of this fact; and, as soon as the nature of the problem is clearly under-stood, there should be little difficulty in advancing so far in analysis.

14. 'Good,' then, is indefinable; and yet, so far as I know, there is only one ethical writer, Prof. Henry Sidgwick, who has clearly recognised and stated this fact. We shall see, indeed, how far many of the most reputed ethical sys-tems fall short of drawing the conclusions which follow from such a recognition. At present I will only quote one instance, which will serve to illustrate the meaning and importance of this principle that 'good' is indefinable, or, as Prof. Sidgwick says, an 'unanalysable notion.' It is an instance to which Prof. Sidgwick himself refers in a note on the passage, in which he argues that 'ought' is unanalysable[1].

'Bentham,' says Sidgwick, 'explains that his fundamental principle "states the greatest happiness of all those whose interest is in question as being the right and proper end of human action"'; and yet 'his language in other passages of the same chapter would seem to imply' that he *means* by the word 'right' 'conducive to the general happiness.' Prof. Sidgwick sees that, if you take these two statements together, you get the absurd result that 'greatest happiness is the end of human action, which is conducive to the general happiness'; and so absurd does it seem to him to call this result, as Bentham calls it, 'the fundamental principle of a moral system,' that he suggests that Bentham cannot have meant it. Yet Prof. Sidgwick himself states elsewhere[2] that Psychological Hedonism is 'not seldom confounded with Egoistic Hedonism'; and that confusion, as we shall see, rests chiefly on that same fallacy, the naturalistic fallacy, which is implied in Bentham's statements. Prof. Sidgwick admits therefore that this fallacy is sometimes committed, absurd as it is; and

I am inclined to think that Bentham may really have been one of those who committed it. Mill, as we shall see, certainty did commit it. In any case, whether Bentham committed it or not, his doctrine, as above quoted, will serve as a very good illustration of this fallacy, and of the importance of the contrary proposition that good is indefinable.

Let us consider this doctrine. Bentham seems to imply, so Prof. Sidgwick says, that the word 'right' *means* 'conducive to general happiness.' Now this, by itself, need not necessarily involve the naturalistic fallacy. For the word 'right' is very commonly appropriated to actions which lead to the attainment of what is good; which are regarded as *means* to the ideal and not as ends-in-themselves. This use of 'right,' as denoting what is good as a means, whether or not it be also good as an end, is indeed the use to which I shall confine the word. Had Bentham been using 'right' in this sense, it might be perfectly consistent for him to *define* right as 'conducive to the general happiness,' *provided only* (and notice this proviso) he had already proved, or laid down as an axiom, that general happiness was *the* good, or (what is equivalent to this) that general happiness alone was good. For in that case he would have already defined *the* good as general happiness (a position perfectly consistent, as we have seen, with the contention that 'good' is indefinable), and, since right was to be defined as 'conducive to *the* good,' it would actually *mean* 'conducive to general happiness.' But this method of escape from the charge of having committed the naturalistic fallacy has been closed by Bentham himself. For his fundamental principle is, we see, that the greatest happiness of all concerned is the *right* and proper *end* of human action. He applies the word 'right,' therefore, to the end, as such, not only to the means which are conducive to it; and, that being so, right can no longer be defined as 'conducive to the general happiness,' without involving the fallacy in question. For now it is obvious that the definition of right as conducive to general happiness can be used by him in support of the fundamental principle that general happiness is the right end; instead of being itself derived from that principle. If right, by definition, means conducive to general happiness, then it is obvious that general happiness is the right end. It is not necessary now first to prove or assert that general happiness is the right end, before right is defined as conducive to general happiness – a perfectly valid procedure; but on the contrary the definition of right as conducive to general happiness proves general happiness to be the right end – a perfectly invalid procedure, since in this case the statement that 'general happiness is the right end of human action' is not an ethical principle at all, but either, as we have seen, a proposition about the meaning of words, or else a proposition about the *nature* of general happiness, not about its rightness or goodness.

Now, I do not wish the importance I assign to this fallacy to be misunderstood. The discovery of it does not at all refute Bentham's contention that greatest happiness is the proper end of human action, if that be understood as an ethical proposition, as he undoubtedly intended it. That principle may be true all the same; we shall consider whether it is so in succeeding chapters. Bentham might have maintained it, as Prof. Sidgwick does, even if the fallacy had been pointed out to him. What I am maintaining is that the *reasons* which he actually gives for his ethical proposition are fallacious ones so far as they consist in a definition of right. What I suggest is that he did not perceive them to be fallacious; that, if he had done so, he would have been led to seek for other reasons in support of his Utilitarianism; and that, had he sought for other reasons, he *might* have found none which he thought to be sufficient. In that case he would have changed his whole system – a most important consequence. It is undoubtedly also possible that he would have thought other reasons to be sufficient, and in that case his ethical system, in its main results, would still have stood. But, even in this latter case, his use of the fallacy would be a serious objection to him as an ethical philosopher. For it is the business of Ethics, I must insist, not only to obtain true results, but also to find valid reasons for them. The direct object of Ethics is knowledge and not practice; and any one who uses the naturalistic fallacy has certainly not fulfilled this first object, however correct his practical principles may be.

My objections to Naturalism are then, in the first place, that it offers no reason at all, far less any valid reason, for any ethical principle whatever; and in this it already fails to satisfy the requirements of Ethics, as a scientific study. But in the second place I contend that, though it gives a reason for no ethical principle, it is a *cause* of the acceptance of false principles – it deludes the mind into accepting ethical principles, which are false; and in this it is contrary to every aim of Ethics. It is easy to see that if we start with a definition of right conduct as conduct conducive to general happiness; then, knowing that right conduct is universally conduct conducive to the good, we very easily arrive at the result that the good is general happiness. If, on the other hand, we once recognise that we must start our Ethics without a definition, we shall be much more apt to look about us, before we adopt any ethical principle whatever; and the more we look about us, the less likely are we to adopt a false one. It may be replied to this: Yes, but we shall look about us just as much, before we settle on our definition, and are therefore just as likely to be right. But I will try to shew that this is not the case. If we start with the conviction that a definition of good can be found, we start with the conviction that good *can mean* nothing else than some one property of things; and our only business will then be to discover what that property is. But if we recognise that, so far as the meaning of good goes, anything whatever may be good, we start with a much more open mind. Moreover, apart from the fact that, when we think we have a definition, we cannot logically defend our ethical principles in any way whatever, we shall also be much less apt to defend them well, even if illogically. For we shall start with the conviction that good must mean so and so, and shall therefore be inclined either to misunderstand our opponent's arguments or to cut them short with the reply, 'This is not an open question: the very meaning of the word decides it; no one can think otherwise except through confusion.'

15.   Our first conclusion as to the subject-matter of Ethics is, then, that there is a simple, indefinable, unanalysable object of thought by reference to which it must be defined. By what name we call this unique object is a matter of indifference, so long as we clearly recognise what it is and that it does differ from other objects. The words which are commonly taken as the signs of ethical judgments all do refer to it; and they are expressions of ethical judgments solely because they do so refer. But they may refer to it in two different ways, which it is very important to distinguish, if we are to have a complete definition of the range of ethical judgments. [...] They may either assert that this unique property does always attach to the thing in question, or else they may assert only that the thing in question is *a cause or necessary condition* for the existence of other things to which this unique property does attach. The nature of these two species of universal ethical judgments is extremely different; and a great part of the difficulties, which are met with in ordinary ethical speculation, are due to the failure to distinguish them clearly. Their difference has, indeed, received expression in ordinary language by the contrast between the terms 'good as means' and. 'good in itself,' 'value as a means' and 'intrinsic value.' But these terms are apt to be applied correctly only in the more obvious instances; and this seems to be due to the fact that the distinction between the conceptions which they denote has not been made a separate object of investigation.

2

The Right and the Good

W. D. Ross

Notice first the title of Ross's chapter. He is interested not just in the substantive question of which acts are right, but also in the explanatory issue of which properties of acts *make* them right or wrong.

Ross begins by rejecting hedonism, the view that the only good is pleasure (1, 3). According to him, virtue and the possession of the type of knowledge that constitutes understanding, for example, are also good. He also quickly rejects rational egoism – the view that one's strongest, or only, reason is to advance one's own good – with the claim that it is obvious that we have other-regarding reasons that can override our own good (2). Ross could afford to be brief because when he wrote, there were few serious defenders of egoism; there are certainly responses the egoist can make, including the mere counter-assertion that egoism is obvious.

Ross spends more time arguing against utilitarianism – the view that what makes an act right is its being 'optimific', i.e. its maximizing the good or utility overall (5, 34–9). He first notes that the 'plain man' – the unphilosophical moral agent – will, say, fulfil some promise he has made without reference to the consequences of doing so: he is inclined to see the act as right in itself. As we shall see, Ross believes that such unreflective views must be taken very seriously. But he goes on also to argue in more detail against utilitarianism. Consider the following example (34): if you fulfil your promise to A, this will produce 1000 units of good for A; but if you break your promise, you can produce 1001 units for B. Ross claims that you should fulfil your promise, and that it is far from self-evident that the properties of rightness and being optimific are co-extensive.

The utilitarian might respond that we have to take into account the value of the practice of promising as a whole (39–40). If you break your promise to B, this might have some effect, for example, on the level of confidence people in general place in promises, and this may itself cause a decrease in overall goodness. Ross responds that, even when the utility-consequences of these effects are factored in, we *still* think that there is a reason to keep the promise, even at some cost to the overall good.

Ross's view is that utilitarians have grasped part of the truth about ethics: the fact that an action promotes the overall good is *one* of the factors determining whether some action is right (41). What are the others? Here we meet one of Ross's most important contributions to ethical theory: the idea of *prima facie* duty (7–15, 16–24, 25–6, 45–54).

Ross is not entirely happy with his terminology (8). He does not mean that these duties are merely apparent; nor are they really 'duties' in the most obvious sense, but merely related to duties in that sense. He calls duties in the more obvious, overall sense 'duty proper'. A *prima facie* duty is the characteristic an act has of being an act that *would* be a duty proper if it were not at the same time of another kind which is morally significant. Imagine that I promise to meet you for tea at 3:00 p.m., but on my way I have an opportunity to help someone injured in a serious accident. I have a *prima facie* duty to keep promises and a *prima facie* duty to help others, which in this case conflict. The second duty outweighs the first, so that

History of Ethics – Essential Readings with Commentary, First Edition. Edited by Daniel Star and Roger Crisp.
© 2020 John Wiley & Sons Ltd. Published 2020 by John Wiley & Sons Ltd.

344 HISTORY OF ETHICS

my absolute or overall duty is to help the injured person. What Ross appears to be talking about here could be captured using the distinction between *a reason* and *overall reason*. I have a reason to keep my promise and a reason to help. The second reason is stronger, and so my overall reason is to help.

Prima facie duties are to perform (or to refrain from) certain actions – to fulfil a promise, for example, not to pack up and send off a book that I have promised to return (since it may not get there) (46–50). (Ross considers other possibilities, but not the plausible idea common in eighteenth-century ethics that our duty is to *will* certain actions.) Such duties can be placed in different categories, depending on their ground (10). They include fidelity, reparation, gratitude, justice, beneficence, self-improvement, and non-maleficence. Duty is 'personal' and depends on the relation in which I stand to those affected by my actions (7, 11). Relevant relations include that of promisor to promisee, or friend to friend. And because there are several such significant relations, there is no reason to assume that ethics must be captured in a single principle (15). Some systematization is possible (so some duties are broadly grounded on the good, others on special relations (16–22)), but in the end we must decide what to do in each situation for ourselves, using our own capacity for judgement (45).

Ross was heavily influenced by Prichard, and this influence can be seen clearly in his *intuitionism* (27–33, 42–4). Ross claims that it is self-evident that, for example, there is a *prima facie* duty to keep promises – that the property of being a keeping of a promise is a 'right-making' property. Ethics is, in this respect, like mathematics. We first grasp the relevant property in particular cases, and then later grasp the overall principle.

Ross claims that this view of promising not only stands up to reflection in his own case, but is held by 'thoughtful and well-educated people' (44). The moral views of such people are, for philosophers, like the empirical experiences on which scientists base their theories. But Ross never fully confronts the fact that there have been many thoughtful and well-educated utilitarians, and indeed egoists. Perhaps all one can do in the face of such disagreement is to articulate one's own position as carefully, calmly, and clearly as one can; certainly few moral philosophers have achieved that to the same degree as Ross.

II

What Makes Right Acts Right?

THE real point at issue between hedonism and utilitarianism on the one hand and their opponents on the other is not whether 'right' means 'productive of so and so'; for it cannot with any plausibility be maintained that it does. The point at issue is that to which we now pass, viz. whether there is any general character which makes right acts right, and if so, what it is. Among the main historical attempts to state a single characteristic of all right actions which is the foundation of their rightness are those made by egoism and utilitarianism. But I do not propose to discuss these, not because the subject is unimportant, but because it has been dealt with so often and so well already, and because there has come to be so much agreement among moral philosophers that neither of these theories is satisfactory. A much more attractive theory has been put forward by Professor Moore: that what makes actions right is that they are productive of more *good* than could have been produced by any other action open to the agent.[1]

This theory is in fact the culmination of all the attempts to base rightness on productivity of some sort of result. The first form this attempt takes is the attempt to base rightness on conduciveness to the advantage or pleasure of the agent. This theory comes to grief over the fact, which stares us in the face, that a great part of duty consists in an observance of the rights and a furtherance of the interests of others, whatever the cost to ourselves may be. Plato and others may be right in holding that a regard for the rights of others never in the long run involves a loss of happiness for the agent, that 'the just life profits a man'. But this, even if true, is irrelevant to the rightness of the act. As soon as a man does an action *because* he thinks he will promote his own interests thereby, he is acting not from a sense of its rightness but from self-interest.

To the egoistic theory hedonistic utilitarianism supplies a much-needed amendment. It points out correctly that the fact that a certain pleasure will be enjoyed by the agent is no reason why he *ought* to bring it into being rather than an equal or greater pleasure to be enjoyed by another, though, human nature being what it is, it makes it not unlikely that he *will* try to bring it into being. But hedonistic utilitarianism in its turn needs a correction. On reflection it seems clear that pleasure is not the only thing in life that we think good in itself, that for instance we think the possession of a good character, or an intelligent understanding of the world, as good or better. A great advance is made by the substitution of 'productive of the greatest good' for 'productive of the greatest pleasure'.

Not only is this theory more attractive than hedonistic utilitarianism, but its logical relation to that theory is such that the latter could not be true unless *it* were true, while it might be true though hedonistic utilitarianism were not. It is in fact one of the logical bases of hedonistic utilitarianism. For the view that what produces the maximum pleasure is right has for its bases the views (1) that what produces the maximum good is right, and (2) that pleasure is the only thing good in itself. If they were not assuming that what produces the maximum *good* is right, the utilitarians' attempt to show that pleasure is the only thing good in itself, which is in fact the point they take most pains to establish, would have been quite irrelevant to their attempt to prove that only what produces the maximum *pleasure* is right. If, therefore, it can be shown that productivity of the maximum good is not what makes all right actions right, we shall *a fortiori* have refuted hedonistic utilitarianism.

When a plain man fulfils a promise because he thinks he ought to do so, it seems clear that he does so with no thought of its total consequences, still less with any opinion that these are likely to be the best possible. He thinks in fact much more of the past than of the future. What makes him think it right to act in a certain way is the fact that he has promised to do so – that and, usually, nothing more. That his act will produce the best possible consequences is not his reason for calling it right. What lends colour to the theory we are examining, then, is not the actions (which form probably a great majority of our actions) in which some such reflection as 'I have promised' is the only reason we give ourselves for thinking a certain action right, but the exceptional cases in which the consequences of fulfilling a promise (for instance) would be so disastrous to others that we judge it right not to do so. It must of course be admitted that such cases exist. If I have promised to meet a friend at a particular time for some trivial purpose, I should certainly think myself justified in breaking my engagement if by doing so I could prevent a serious accident or bring relief to the victims of one. And the supporters of the view we are examining hold that my thinking so is due to my thinking that I shall bring more good into existence by the one action than by the

---

[1] I take the theory which, as I have tried to show, seems to be put forward in *Ethics* rather than the earlier and less plausible theory put forward in *Principia Ethica*.

other. A different account may, however, be given of the matter, an account which will, I believe, show itself to be the true one. It may be said that besides the duty of fulfilling promises I have and recognize a duty of relieving distress,[2] and that when I think it right to do the latter at the cost of not doing the former, it is not because I think I shall produce more good thereby but because I think it the duty which is in the circumstances more of a duty. This account surely corresponds much more closely with what we really think in such a situation. If, so far as I can see, I could bring equal amounts of good into being by fulfilling my promise and by helping some one to whom I had made no promise, I should not hesitate to regard the former as my duty. Yet on the view that what is right is right because it is productive of the most good I should not so regard it.

There are two theories, each in its way simple, that offer a solution of such cases of conscience. One is the view of Kant, that there are certain duties of perfect obligation, such as those of fulfilling promises, of paying debts, of telling the truth, which admit of no exception whatever in favour of duties of imperfect obligation, such as that of relieving distress. The other is the view of, for instance, Professor Moore and Dr. Rashdall, that there is only the duty of producing good, and that all 'conflicts of duties' should be resolved by asking 'by which action will most good be produced?' But it is more important that our theory fit the facts than that it be simple, and the account we have given above corresponds (it seems to me) better than either of the simpler theories with what we really think, viz. that normally promise-keeping, for example, should come before benevolence, but that when and only when the good to be produced by the benevolent act is very great and the promise comparatively trivial, the act of benevolence becomes our duty.

In fact the theory of 'ideal utilitarianism', if I may for brevity refer so to the theory of Professor Moore, seems to simplify unduly our relations to our fellows. It says, in effect, that the only morally significant relation in which my neighbours stand to me is that of being possible beneficiaries by my action.[3] They do stand in this relation to me, and this relation is morally significant. But they may also stand to me in the relation of promisee to promiser, of creditor to debtor, of wife to husband, of child to parent, of friend to friend, of fellow countryman to fellow countryman, and the like; and each of these relations is the foundation of a *prima facie* duty, which is more or less incumbent on me according to the circumstances of the case. When I am in a situation, as perhaps I always am, in which more than one of these *prima facie* duties is incumbent on me, what I have to do is to study the situation as fully as I can until I form the considered opinion (it is never more) that in the circumstances one of them is more incumbent than any other; then I am bound to think that to do this *prima facie* duty is my duty *sans phrase* in the situation.

I suggest '*prima facie* duty' or 'conditional duty' as a brief way of referring to the characteristic (quite distinct from that of being a duty proper) which an act has, in virtue of being of a certain kind (e.g. the keeping of a promise), of being an act which would be a duty proper if it were not at the same time of another kind which is morally significant. Whether an act is a duty proper or actual duty depends on *all* the morally significant kinds it is an instance of. The phrase '*prima facie* duty' must be apologized for, since (1) it suggests that what we are speaking of is a certain kind of duty, whereas it is in fact not a duty, but something related in a special way to duty. Strictly speaking, we want not a phrase in which duty is qualified by an adjective, but a separate noun. (2) '*Prima*' *facie* suggests that one is speaking only of an appearance which a moral situation presents at first sight, and which may turn out to be illusory; whereas what I am speaking of is an objective fact involved in the nature of the situation, or more strictly in an element of its nature, though not, as duty proper does, arising from its *whole* nature. I can, however, think of no term which fully meets the case. 'Claim' has been suggested by Professor Prichard. The word 'claim' has the advantage of being quite a familiar one in this connexion, and it seems to cover much of the ground. It would be quite natural to say, 'a person to whom I have made a promise has a claim on me', and also, 'a person whose distress I could relieve (at the cost of breaking the promise) has a claim on me'. But (1) while 'claim' is appropriate from *their* point of view, we want a word to express the corresponding fact from the agent's point of view – the fact of his being subject to claims that can be made against him; and ordinary language provides us with no such correlative to 'claim'. And (2) (what is more important) 'claim' seems inevitably to suggest two persons, one of whom might make a claim on the other; and while this covers the ground of

---

[2] These are not strictly speaking duties, but things that tend to be our duty, or *prima facie* duties.

[3] Some will think it, apart from other considerations, a sufficient refutation of this view to point out that I also stand in that relation to myself, so that for this view the distinction of oneself from others is morally insignificant.

social duty, it is inappropriate in the case of that important part of duty which is the duty of cultivating a certain kind of character in oneself. It would be artificial, I think, and at any rate metaphorical, to say that one's character has a claim on oneself.

There is nothing arbitrary about these *prima facie* duties. Each rests on a definite circumstance which cannot seriously be held to be without moral significance. Of *prima facie* duties I suggest, without claiming completeness or finality for it, the following division.[4]

(1) Some duties rest on previous acts of my own. These duties seem to include two kinds, (*a*) those resting on a promise or what may fairly be called an implicit promise, such as the implicit undertaking not to tell lies, which seems to be implied in the act of entering into conversation (at any rate by civilized men), or of writing books that purport to be history and not fiction. These may be called the duties of fidelity. (*b*) Those resting on a previous wrongful act. These may be called the duties of reparation. (2) Some rest on previous acts of other men, i.e. services done by them to me. These may be loosely described as the duties of gratitude. (3) Some rest on the fact or possibility of a distribution of pleasure or happiness (or of the means thereto) which is not in accordance with the merit of the persons concerned; in such cases there arises a duty to upset or prevent such a distribution. These are the duties of justice. (4) Some rest on the mere fact that there are other beings in the world whose condition we can make better in respect of virtue, or of intelligence, or of pleasure. These are the duties of beneficence. (5) Some rest on the fact that we can improve our own condition in respect of virtue or of intelligence. These are the duties of self-improvement. (6) I think that we should distinguish from (4) the duties that may be summed up under the title of 'not injuring others'. No doubt to injure others is incidentally to fail to do them good; but it seems to me clear that non-maleficence is apprehended as a duty distinct from that of beneficence, and as a duty of a more stringent character. It will be noticed that this alone among the types of duty has been stated in a negative way. An attempt might no doubt be made to state this duty, like the others, in a positive way. It might be said that it is really the duty to prevent ourselves from acting either from an inclination to harm others or from an inclination to seek our own pleasure, in doing which we should incidentally harm them. But on reflection it seems clear that the primary duty here is the duty not to harm others, this being a duty whether or not we have an inclination that if followed would lead to our harming them; and that when we have such an inclination the primary duty not to harm others gives rise to a consequential duty to resist the inclination. The recognition of this duty of non-maleficence is the first step on the way to the recognition of the duty of beneficence; and that accounts for the prominence of the commands 'thou shalt not kill', 'thou shalt not commit adultery', 'thou shalt not steal', 'thou shalt not bear false witness', in so early a code as the Decalogue. But even when we have come to recognize the duty of beneficence, it appears to me that the duty of non-maleficence is recognized as a distinct one, and as *prima facie* more binding. We should not in general consider it justifiable to kill one person in order to keep another alive, or to steal from one in order to give alms to another.

The essential defect of the 'ideal utilitarian' theory is that it ignores, or at least does not do full justice to, the highly personal character of duty. If the only duty is to produce the maximum of good, the question who is to have the good – whether it is myself, or my benefactor, or a person to whom I have made a promise to confer that good on him, or a mere fellow man to whom I stand in no such special relation – should make no difference to my having a duty to produce that good. But we are all in fact sure that it makes a vast difference.

One or two other comments must be made on this provisional list of the divisions of duty. (1) The nomenclature is not strictly correct. For by 'fidelity' or 'gratitude' we mean, strictly, certain states of motivation; and, as I have urged, it is not our duty to have certain motives, but to do certain acts. By 'fidelity', for instance, is meant, strictly, the disposition to fulfil promises and implicit promises *because we have made them*. We have no general word to cover the actual fulfilment of promises and implicit promises *irrespective of motive*; and I use 'fidelity', loosely but perhaps conveniently, to fill this gap. So too I use 'gratitude' for the returning of services, irrespective of motive. The term 'justice' is not so much confined, in ordinary usage, to a certain state of motivation, for we should often talk of a

---

[4] I should make it plain at this stage that I am *assuming* the correctness of some of our main convictions as to *prima facie* duties, or, more strictly, am claiming that we *know* them to be true. To me it seems as self-evident as anything could be, that to make a promise, for instance, is to create a moral claim on us in someone else. Many readers will perhaps say that they do *not* know this to be true. If so, I certainly cannot prove it to them; I can only ask them to reflect again, in the hope that they will ultimately agree that they also know it to be true. The main moral convictions of the plain man seem to me to be, not opinions which it is for philosophy to prove or disprove, but knowledge from the start; and in my own case I seem to find little difficulty in distinguishing these essential convictions from other moral convictions which I also have, which are merely fallible opinions based on an imperfect study of the working for good or evil of certain institutions or types of action.

man as acting justly even when we did not think his motive was the wish to do what was just simply for the sake of doing so. Less apology is therefore needed for our use of 'justice' in this sense. And I have used the word 'benefi-cence' rather than 'benevolence', in order to emphasize the fact that it is our duty to do certain things, and not to do them from certain motives.

(2)   If the objection be made, that this catalogue of the main types of duty is an unsystematic one resting on no logical principle, it may be replied, first, that it makes no claim to being ultimate. It is a *prima facie* classification of the duties which reflection on our moral convictions seems actually to reveal. And if these convictions are, as I would claim that they are, of the nature of knowledge, and if I have not misstated them, the list will be a list of authentic conditional duties, correct as far as it goes though not necessarily complete. The list of *goods* put forward by the rival theory is reached by exactly the same method – the only sound one in the circumstances – viz. that of direct reflection on what we really think. Loyalty to the facts is worth more than a symmetrical architectonic or a hastily reached simplicity. If further reflection discovers a perfect logical basis for this or for a better classification, so much the better.

(3)   It may, again, be objected that our theory that there are these various and often conflicting types of *prima facie* duty leaves us with no principle upon which to discern what is our actual duty in particular circumstances. But this objection is not one which the rival theory is in a position to bring forward. For when we have to choose between the production of two heterogeneous goods, say knowledge and pleasure, the 'ideal utilitarian' theory can only fall back on an opinion, for which no logical basis can be offered, that one of the goods is the greater; and this is no better than a similar opinion that one of two duties is the more urgent. And again, when we consider the infinite variety of the effects of our actions in the way of pleasure, it must surely be admitted that the claim which *hedonism* sometimes makes, that it offers a readily applicable criterion of right conduct, is quite illusory.

I am unwilling, however, to content myself with an *argumentum ad hominem*, and I would contend that in princi-ple there is no reason to anticipate that every act that is our duty is so for one and the same reason. Why should two sets of circumstances, or one set of circumstances, *not* possess different characteristics, any one of which makes a certain act our *prima facie* duty? When I ask what it is that makes me in certain cases sure that I have a *prima facie* duty to do so and so, I find that it lies in the fact that I have made a promise; when I ask the same question in another case, I find the answer lies in the fact that I have done a wrong. And if on reflection I find (as I think I do) that neither of these reasons is reducible to the other, I must not on any *a priori* ground assume that such a reduction is possible.

An attempt may be made to arrange in a more systematic way the main types of duty which we have indicated. In the first place it seems self-evident that if there are things that are intrinsically good, it is *prima facie* a duty to bring them into existence rather than not to do so, and to bring as much of them into existence as possible. It will be argued in our fifth chapter that there are three main things that are intrinsically good – virtue, knowledge, and, with certain limitations, pleasure. And since a given virtuous disposition, for instance, is equally good whether it is realized in myself or in another, it seems to be my duty to bring it into existence whether in myself or in another. So too with a given piece of knowledge.

The case of pleasure is difficult; for while we clearly recognize a duty to produce pleasure for others, it is by no means so clear that we recognize a duty to produce pleasure for ourselves. This appears to arise from the following facts. The thought of an act as our duty is one that presupposes a certain amount of reflection about the act; and for that reason does not normally arise in connexion with acts towards which we are already impelled by another strong impulse. So far, the cause of our not thinking of the promotion of our own pleasure as a duty is analogous to the cause which usually prevents a highly sympathetic person from thinking of the promotion of the pleasure of others as a duty. He is impelled so strongly by direct interest in the well-being of others towards promoting their pleasure that he does not stop to ask whether it is his duty to promote it; and we are all impelled so strongly towards the promotion of our own pleasure that we do not stop to ask whether it is a duty or not. But there is a further reason why even when we stop to think about the matter it does not usually present itself as a duty: viz. that, since the performance of most of our duties involves the giving up of some pleasure that we desire, the doing of duty and the getting of pleasure for ourselves come by a natural association of ideas to be thought of as incompatible things. This association of ideas is in the main salutary in its operation, since it puts a check on what but for it would be much too strong, the tendency to pursue one's own pleasure without thought of other considerations. Yet if pleasure is good, it seems in the long run clear that it is right to get it for ourselves as well as to produce it for others, when this does not involve the failure to discharge some more stringent *prima facie* duty. The question is a very difficult one, but it seems that this conclusion can be denied only on one or other of three grounds: (1) that pleasure is not *prima facie* good (i.e. good when it is neither the actualization of a bad disposition nor undeserved), (2) that there is no *prima facie* duty to produce as much that is good as we can, or (3) that though there is a *prima facie* duty to produce other things that are good, there is no *prima facie* duty to produce pleasure which will be enjoyed by ourselves. I give reasons later for not accepting the first contention. The second hardly admits of argument but seems to me plainly false. The third seems plausible only if we hold that an act that is pleasant or brings pleasure to ourselves must for that reason not be a duty; and this would lead to paradoxical consequences, such as that if a man enjoys giving pleasure to others or working for their moral improvement, it cannot be his duty to do so. Yet it seems to be a very stubborn fact, that in our ordinary consciousness we are not aware of a duty to get pleasure for ourselves; and by way of partial explanation of this I may add that though, as I think, one's own pleasure is a good and there is a duty to produce it, it is only if we *think* of our own pleasure not as simply our own pleasure, but as an objective good, something that an impartial spectator would approve, that we can think of the getting it as a duty; and we do not habitually think of it in this way.

If these contentions are right, what we have called the duty of beneficence and the duty of self-improvement rest on the same ground. No different principles of duty are involved in the two cases. If we feel a special responsibility for improving our own character rather than that of others, it is not because a special principle is involved, but because we are aware that the one is more under our control than the other. It was on this ground that Kant expressed the practical law of duty in the form 'seek to make yourself good and other people happy'. He was so persuaded of the internality of virtue that he regarded any attempt by one person to produce virtue in another as bound to produce, at most, only a counterfeit of virtue, the doing of externally right acts not from the true principle of virtuous action but out of regard to another person. It must be admitted that one man cannot compel another to be virtuous; compulsory virtue would just not be virtue. But experience clearly shows that Kant overshoots the mark when he contends that one man cannot do anything to *promote* virtue in another, to bring such influences to bear upon him that his own response to them is more likely to be virtuous than his response to other influences would have been. And our duty to do this is not different in kind from our duty to improve our own characters.

It is equally clear, and clear at an earlier stage of moral development, that if there are things that are bad in themselves we ought, *prima facie*, not to bring them upon others; and on this fact rests the duty of non-maleficence.

The duty of justice is particularly complicated, and the word is used to cover things which are really very different – things such as the payment of debts, the reparation of injuries done by oneself to another, and the bringing about of a distribution of happiness between other people in proportion to merit. I use the word to denote only the last of these three. In the fifth chapter I shall try to show that besides the three (comparatively) simple goods, virtue, knowledge, and pleasure, there is a more complex good, not reducible to these, consisting in the proportionment of happiness to virtue. The bringing of this about is a duty which we owe to all men alike, though it may be reinforced by special responsibilities that we have undertaken to particular men. This, therefore, with beneficence and self-improvement, comes under the general principle that we should produce as much good as possible, though the good here involved is different in kind from any other.

But besides this general obligation, there are special obligations. These may arise, in the first place, incidentally, from acts which were not essentially meant to create such an obligation, but which nevertheless create it. From the nature of the case such acts may be of two kinds – the infliction of injuries on others, and the acceptance of benefits from them. It seems clear that these put us under a special obligation to other men, and that only these acts can do so incidentally. From these arise the twin duties of reparation and gratitude.

And finally there are special obligations arising from acts the very intention of which, when they were done, was to put us under such an obligation. The name for such acts is 'promises'; the name is wide enough if we are willing to include under it implicit promises, i.e. modes of behaviour in which without explicit verbal promise we intentionally create an expectation that we can be counted on to behave in a certain way in the interest of another person.

These seem to be, in principle, all the ways in which *prima facie* duties arise. In actual experience they are compounded together in highly complex ways. Thus, for example, the duty of obeying the laws of one's country arises partly (as Socrates contends in the *Crito*) from the duty of gratitude for the benefits one has received from it; partly from the implicit promise to obey which seems to be involved in permanent residence in a country whose laws we know we are *expected* to obey, and still more clearly involved when we ourselves invoke the protection of its laws (this is the truth underlying the doctrine of the social contract); and partly (if we are fortunate in our country) from the fact that its laws are potent instruments for the general good.

Or again, the sense of a general obligation to bring about (so far as we can) a just apportionment of happiness to merit is often greatly reinforced by the fact that many of the existing injustices are due to a social and economic system which we have, not indeed created, but taken part in and assented to; the duty of justice is then reinforced by the duty of reparation.

It is necessary to say something by way of clearing up the relation between *prima facie* duties and the actual or absolute duty to do one particular act in particular circumstances. If, as almost all moralists except Kant are agreed, and as most plain men think, it is sometimes right to tell a lie or to break a promise, it must be maintained that there is a difference between *prima facie* duty and actual or absolute duty. When we think ourselves justified in breaking, and indeed morally obliged to break, a promise in order to relieve some one's distress, we do not for a moment cease to recognize a *prima facie* duty to keep our promise, and this leads us to feel, not indeed shame or repentance, but certainly compunction, for behaving as we do; we recognize, further, that it is our duty to make up somehow to the promisee for the breaking of the promise. We have to distinguish from the characteristic of being our duty that of tending to be our duty. Any act that we do contains various elements in virtue of which it falls under various categories. In virtue of being the breaking of a promise, for instance, it tends to be wrong; in virtue of being an instance of relieving distress it tends to be right. Tendency to be one's duty may be called a parti-resultant attribute, i.e. one which belongs to an act in virtue of some one component in its nature. *Being* one's duty is a toti-resultant attribute, one which belongs to an act in virtue of its whole nature and of nothing less than this. This distinction between parti-resultant and toti-resultant attributes is one which we shall meet in another context also.

Another instance of the same distinction may be found in the operation of natural laws. *Qua* subject to the force of gravitation towards some other body, each body tends to move in a particular direction with a particular velocity; but its actual movement depends on *all* the forces to which it is subject. It is only by recognizing this distinction that we can preserve the absoluteness of laws of nature, and only by recognizing a corresponding distinction that we can preserve the absoluteness of the general principles of morality. But an important difference between the two cases must be pointed out. When we say that in virtue of gravitation a body tends to move in a certain way, we are referring to a causal influence actually exercised on it by another body or other bodies. When we say that in virtue of being deliberately untrue a certain remark tends to be wrong, we are referring to no causal relation, to no relation that involves succession in time, but to such a relation as connects the various attributes of a mathematical figure. And if the word 'tendency' is thought to suggest too much a causal relation, it is better to talk of certain types of act as being *prima facie* right or wrong (or of different persons as having different and possibly conflicting claims upon us), than of their tending to be right or wrong.

Something should be said of the relation between our apprehension of the *prima facie* rightness of certain types of act and our mental attitude towards particular acts. It is proper to use the word 'apprehension' in the former case and not in the latter. That an act, *qua* fulfilling a promise, or *qua* effecting a just distribution of good, or *qua* returning services rendered, or *qua* promoting the good of others, or *qua* promoting the virtue or insight of the agent, is *prima facie* right, is self-evident; not in the sense that it is evident from the beginning of our lives, or as soon as we attend to the proposition for the first time, but in the sense that when we have reached sufficient mental maturity and have given sufficient attention to the proposition it is evident without any need of proof, or of evidence beyond itself. It is self-evident just as a mathematical axiom, or the validity of a form of inference, is evident. The moral order expressed in these propositions is just as much part of the fundamental nature of the universe (and, we may add, of any possible universe in which there were moral agents at all) as is the spatial or numerical structure expressed in the axioms of geometry or arithmetic. In our confidence that these propositions are true there is involved the same trust in our reason that is involved in our confidence in mathematics; and we should have no justification for trusting it in the latter sphere and distrusting it in the former. In both cases we are dealing with propositions that cannot be proved, but that just as certainly need no proof.

Some of these general principles of *prima facie* duty may appear to be open to criticism. It may be thought, for example, that the principle of returning good for good is a falling off from the Christian principle, generally and rightly recognized as expressing the highest morality, of returning good for evil. To this it may be replied that I do not suggest that there is a principle commanding us to return good for good and forbidding us to return good for evil, and that I do suggest that there is a positive duty to seek the good of all men. What I maintain is that an act in which good is returned for good is recognized as *specially* binding on us just because it is of that character, and that *ceteris paribus* any one would think it his duty to help his benefactors rather than his enemies, if he could not do both; just as it is generally recognized that *ceteris paribus* we should pay our debts rather than give our money in charity, when we cannot do both. A benefactor is not only a man, calling for our effort on his behalf on that ground, but also our benefactor, calling for our *special* effort on *that* ground.

Our judgements about our actual duty in concrete situations have none of the certainty that attaches to our recognition of the general principles of duty. A statement is certain, i.e. is an expression of knowledge, only in one or other of two cases: when it is either self-evident, or a valid conclusion from self-evident premises. And our judgements about our particular duties have neither of these characters, (1) They are not self-evident. Where a possible act is seen to have two characteristics, in virtue of one of which it is *prima facie* right, and in virtue of the other *prima facie* wrong, we are (I think) well aware that we are not certain whether we ought or ought not to do it; that whether we do it or not, we are taking a moral risk. We come in the long run, after consideration, to think one duty more pressing than the other, but we do not feel certain that it is so. And though we do not always recognize that a possible act has two such characteristics, and though there *may* be cases in which it has not, we are never certain that any particular possible act has not, and therefore never certain that it is right, nor certain that it is wrong. For, to go no further in the analysis, it is enough to point out that any particular act will in all probability in the course of time contribute to the bringing about of good or of evil for many human beings, and thus have a *prima facie* rightness or wrongness of which we know nothing. (2) Again, our judgements about our particular duties are not logical conclusions from self-evident premises. The only possible premises would be the general principles stating their *prima facie* rightness or wrongness *qua* having the different characteristics they do have; and even if we could (as we cannot) apprehend the extent to which an act will tend on the one hand, for example, to bring about advantages for our benefactors, and on the other hand to bring about disadvantages for fellow men who are not our benefactors, there is no principle by which we can draw the conclusion that it is on the whole right or on the whole wrong. In this respect the judgement as to the rightness of a particular act is just like the judgement as to the beauty of a particular natural object or work of art. A poem is, for instance, in respect of certain qualities beautiful and in respect of certain others not beautiful; and our judgement as to the degree of beauty it possesses on the whole is never reached by logical reasoning from the apprehension of its particular beauties or particular defects. Both in this and in the moral case we have more or less probable opinions which are not logically justified conclusions from the general principles that are recognized as self-evident.

There is therefore much truth in the description of the right act as a fortunate act. If we cannot be certain that it is right, it is our good fortune if the act we do is the right act. This consideration does not, however, make the doing of our duty a mere matter of chance. There is a parallel here between the doing of duty and the doing of what will be to our personal advantage. We never *know* what act will in the long run be to our advantage. Yet it is certain that we are more likely in general to secure our advantage if we estimate to the best of our ability the probable tendencies of our actions in this respect, than if we act on caprice. And similarly we are more likely to do our duty if we reflect to the best of our ability on the *prima facie* rightness or wrongness of various possible acts in virtue of the characteristics we perceive them to have, than if we act without reflection. With this greater likelihood we must be content.

Many people would be inclined to say that the right act for me is not that whose general nature I have been describing, viz. that which if I were omniscient I should see to be my duty, but that which on all the evidence available to me I should think to be my duty. But suppose that from the state of partial knowledge in which I think act *A* to be my duty, I could pass to a state of perfect knowledge in which I saw act *B* to be my duty, should I not say 'act *B* was the right act for me to do'? I should no doubt add 'though I am not to be blamed for doing act *A*'. But in adding this, am I not passing from the question 'what is right' to the question 'what is morally good'? At the same time I am not making the *full* passage from the one notion to the other; for in order that the act should be morally good, or an act I am not to be blamed for doing, it must not merely be the act which it is reasonable for me to think my duty; it must also be done for that reason, or from some other morally good motive. Thus the conception of the right act as the act which it is reasonable for me to think my duty is an unsatisfactory compromise between the true notion of the right act and the notion of the morally good action.

The general principles of duty are obviously not self-evident from the beginning of our lives. How do they come to be so? The answer is, that they come to be self-evident to us just as mathematical axioms do. We find by experience that this couple of matches and that couple make four matches, that this couple of balls on a wire and that couple make four balls: and by reflection on these and similar discoveries we come to see that it is of the nature of two and two to make four. In a precisely similar way, we see the *prima facie* rightness of an act which would be the fulfilment of a particular promise, and of another which would be the fulfilment of another promise, and when we have reached sufficient maturity to think in general terms, we apprehend *prima facie* rightness to belong to the nature of any fulfilment of promise. What comes first in time is the apprehension of the self-evident *prima facie* rightness of an individual act of a particular type. From this we come by reflection to apprehend the self-evident general principle of *prima facie* duty. From this, too, perhaps along with the apprehension of the self-evident *prima facie* rightness of the same act in virtue of its having another characteristic as well, and perhaps in spite of the apprehension of its *prima facie* wrongness in virtue of its having some third characteristic, we come to believe something not self-evident at all, but an object of probable opinion, viz. that this particular act is (not *prima facie* but) actually right.

In this respect there is an important difference between rightness and mathematical properties. A triangle which is isosceles necessarily has two of its angles equal, whatever other characteristics the triangle may have – whatever, for instance, be its area, or the size of its third angle. The equality of the two angles is a parti-resultant attribute. And the same is true of all mathematical attributes. It is true, I may add, of *prima facie* rightness. But no act is ever, in virtue of falling under some general description, necessarily actually right; its rightness depends on its whole nature[5] and not on any element in it. The reason is that no mathematical object (no figure, for instance, or angle) ever has two characteristics that tend to give it opposite resultant characteristics, while moral acts often (as every one knows) and indeed always (as on reflection we must admit) have different characteristics that tend to make them at the same time *prima facie* right and *prima facie* wrong; there is probably no act, for instance, which does good to any one without doing harm to some one else, and *vice versa*.

Supposing it to be agreed, as I think on reflection it must, that no one *means* by 'right' just 'productive of the best possible consequences', or 'optimific', the attributes 'right' and 'optimific' might stand in either of two kinds of relation to each other, (1) They might be so related that we could apprehend a priori, either immediately or deductively, that any act that is optimific is right and any act that is right is optimific, as we can apprehend that any triangle that is equilateral is equiangular and *vice versa*. Professor Moore's view is, I think, that the coextensiveness of 'right' and 'optimific' is apprehended immediately.[6] He rejects the possibility of any proof of it. Or (2) the two attributes might be such that the question whether they are invariably connected had to be answered by means of an inductive inquiry. Now at first sight it might seem as if the constant connexion of the two attributes could be immediately apprehended. It might seem absurd to suggest that it could be right for any one to do an act which would produce consequences less good than those which would be produced by some other act in his power. Yet a little thought will convince us that this is not absurd. The type of case in which it is easiest to see that this is so is, perhaps, that in which one has made a promise. In such a case we all think that *prima facie* it is our duty to fulfil the promise irrespective of the precise goodness of the total consequences. And though we do not think it is necessarily our actual or absolute duty to do so, we are far from thinking that any, even the slightest, gain in the value of the total consequences will necessarily justify us in doing something else instead. Suppose, to simplify the case by abstraction, that the fulfilment of a promise to A would produce 1,000 units of good[7] for him, but that by doing some other act I could produce 1,001 units of good for B, to whom I have made no promise, the other consequences of the two acts being of equal value; should we really think it self-evident that it was our duty to do the second act and not the first? I think not. We should, I fancy, hold that only a much greater disparity of value between the total consequences would justify us in failing to discharge our *prima facie* duty to A. After all, a promise is a promise, and is not to be treated so lightly as the theory we are examining would imply. What, exactly, a promise is, is not so easy to determine, but we are surely agreed that it constitutes a serious moral limitation to our freedom of action. To produce the 1,001 units of good for B rather than fulfil our promise to A would be to take, not perhaps our duty as philanthropists too seriously, but certainly our duty as makers of promises too lightly.

Or consider another phase of the same problem. If I have promised to confer on A a particular benefit containing 1,000 units of good, is it self-evident that if by doing some different act I could produce 1,001 units of good for A himself (the other consequences of the two acts being supposed equal in value), it would be right for me to do so? Again, I think not. Apart from my general *prima facie* duty to do A what good I can, I have another *prima facie* duty to do him the particular service I have promised to do him, and this is not to be set aside in consequence of a disparity of good of the order of 1,001 to 1,000, though a much greater disparity might justify me in so doing.

[5] To avoid complicating unduly the statement of the general view I am putting forward, I have here rather overstated it. Any act is the origination of a great variety of things many of which make no difference to its rightness or wrongness. But there are always many elements in its nature (i.e. in what it is the origination of) that make a difference to its rightness or wrongness, and no element in its nature can be dismissed without consideration as indifferent.

[6] *Ethics*, 181.

[7] I am assuming that good is objectively quantitative but not that we can accurately assign an exact quantitative measure to it. Since it is of a definite amount, we can make the *supposition* that its amount is so-and-so, though we cannot with any confidence *assert* that it is.

[...]

Such instances – and they might easily be added to – make it clear that there is no self-evident connexion between the attributes 'right' and 'optimific'. The theory we are examining has a certain attractiveness when applied to our decision that a particular act is our duty (though I have tried to show that it does not agree with our actual moral judgements even here). But it is not even plausible when applied to our recognition of *prima facie* duty. For if it were self-evident that the right coincides with the optimific, it should be self-evident that what is *prima facie* right is *prima facie* optimific. But whereas we are certain that keeping a promise is *prima facie* right, we are not certain that it is *prima facie* optimific (though we are perhaps certain that it is *prima facie* bonific). Our certainty that it is *prima facie* right depends not on its consequences but on its being the fulfilment of a promise. The *theory* we are examining involves too much difference between the evident ground of our conviction about *prima facie* duty and the alleged ground of our conviction about actual duty.

The coextensiveness of the right and the optimific is, then, not self-evident. And I can see no way of proving it deductively; nor, so far as I know, has any one tried to do so. There remains the question whether it can be established inductively. Such an inquiry, to be conclusive, would have to be very thorough and extensive. We should have to take a large variety of the acts which we, to the best of our ability, judge to be right. We should have to trace as far as possible their consequences, not only for the persons directly affected but also for those indirectly affected, and to these no limit can be set. To make our inquiry thoroughly conclusive, we should have to do what we cannot do, viz. trace these consequences into an unending future. And even to make it reasonably conclusive, we should have to trace them far into the future. It is clear that the most we could possibly say is that a large variety of typical acts that are judged right appear, so far as we can trace their consequences, to produce more good than any other acts possible to the agents in the circumstances. And such a result falls far short of proving the constant connexion of the two attributes. But it is surely clear that no inductive inquiry justifying even this result has ever been carried through. The advocates of utilitarian systems have been so much persuaded either of the identity or of the self-evident connexion of the attributes 'right' and 'optimific' (or 'felicific') that they have not attempted even such an inductive inquiry as is possible. And in view of the enormous complexity of the task and the inevitable inconclusiveness of the result, it is worth no one's while to make the attempt. What, after all, would be gained by it? If, as I have tried to show, for an act to be right and to be optimific are not the same thing, and an act's being optimific is not even the ground of its being right, then if we could ask ourselves (though the question is really unmeaning) which we ought to do, right acts because they are right or optimific acts because they are optimific, our answer must be 'the former'. If they are optimific as well as right, that is interesting but not morally important; if not, we still ought to do them (which is only another way of saying that they *are* the right acts), and the question whether they are optimific has no importance for moral theory.

There is one direction in which a fairly serious attempt has been made to show the connexion of the attributes 'right' and 'optimific'. One of the most evident facts of our moral consciousness is the sense which we have of the sanctity of promises, a sense which does not, on the face of it, involve the thought that one will be bringing more good into existence by fulfilling the promise than by breaking it. It is plain, I think, that in our normal thought we consider that the fact that we have made a promise is in itself sufficient to create a duty of keeping it, the sense of duty resting on remembrance of the past promise and not on thoughts of the future consequences of its fulfilment. Utilitarianism tries to show that this is not so, that the sanctity of promises rests on the good consequences of the fulfilment of them and the bad consequences of their non-fulfilment. It does so in this way: it points out that when you break a promise you not only fail to confer a certain advantage on your promisee but you diminish his confidence, and indirectly the confidence of others, in the fulfilment of promises. You thus strike a blow at one of the devices that have been found most useful in the relations between man and man – the device on which, for example, the whole system of commercial credit rests – and you tend to bring about a state of things wherein each man, being entirely unable to rely on the keeping of promises by others, will have to do everything for himself, to the enormous impoverishment of human well-being.

To put the matter otherwise, utilitarians say that when a promise ought to be kept it is because the total good to be produced by keeping it is greater than the total good to be produced by breaking it, the former including as its main element the maintenance and strengthening of general mutual confidence, and the latter being greatly diminished by a weakening of this confidence. They say, in fact, that the case I put some pages back never arises – the case in which by fulfilling a promise I shall bring into being 1,000 units of good for my promisee, and by breaking it 1,001 units of good for some one else, the other effects of the two acts being of equal value. The other effects, they say, never are of equal value. By keeping my promise I am helping to strengthen the system of mutual confidence; by breaking it I am helping to weaken this; so that really the first act produces $1,000 + x$ units of good, and the second $1,001 - y$ units, and the difference between $+x$ and $-y$ is enough to outweigh the slight superiority in the *immediate* effects of the second act. In answer to this it may be pointed out that there must be *some* amount of good that exceeds the difference between $+x$ and $-y$ (i.e. exceeds $x + y$); say, $x + y + z$. Let us suppose the *immediate* good effects of the second act to be assessed not at 1,001 but at $1,000 + x + y + z$. Then its *net* good effects are $1,000 + x + z$, i.e. greater than those of the fulfilment of the promise; and the utilitarian is bound to say forthwith that the promise should be broken. Now, we may ask whether that is really the way we think about promises? Do we really think that the production of the slightest balance of good, no matter who will enjoy it, by the breach of a promise frees us from the obligation to keep our promise? We need not doubt that a system by which promises are made and kept is one that has great advantages for the general well-being. But that is not the whole truth. To make a promise is not merely to adapt an ingenious device for promoting the general well-being; it is to put oneself in a new relation to one person in particular, a relation which creates a specifically new *prima facie* duty to him, not reducible to the duty of promoting the general well-being of society. By all means let us try to foresee the net good effects of keeping one's promise and the net good effects of breaking it, but even if we assess the first at $1,000 + x$ and the second at $1,000 + x + z$, the question still remains whether it is not our duty to fulfil the promise. It may be suspected, too, that the effect of a single keeping or breaking of a promise in strengthening or weakening the fabric of mutual confidence is greatly exaggerated by the theory we are examining. And if we suppose two men dying together alone, do we think that the duty of one to fulfil before he dies a promise he has made to the other would be extinguished by the fact that neither act would have any effect on the general confidence? Any one who holds this may be suspected of not having reflected on what a promise is.

I conclude that the attributes 'right' and 'optimific' are not identical, and that we do not know either by intuition, by deduction, or by induction that they coincide in their application, still less that the latter is the foundation of the former. It must be added, however, that if we are ever under no special obligation such as that of fidelity to a promisee or of gratitude to a benefactor, we ought to do what will produce most good; and that even when we are under a special obligation the tendency of acts to promote general good is one of the main factors in determining whether they are right.

In what has preceded, a good deal of use has been made of 'what we really think' about moral questions; a certain theory has been rejected because it does not agree with what we really think. It might be said that this is in principle wrong; that we should not be content to expound what our present moral consciousness tells us but should aim at a criticism of our existing moral consciousness in the light of theory. Now I do not doubt that the moral consciousness of men has in detail undergone a good deal of modification as regards the things we think right, at the hands of moral theory. But if we are told, for instance, that we should give up our view that there is a special obligatoriness attaching to the keeping of promises because it is self-evident that the only duty is to produce as much good as possible, we have to ask ourselves whether we really, when we reflect, *are* convinced that this is self-evident, and whether we really *can* get rid of our view that promise-keeping has a bindingness independent of productiveness of maximum good. In my own experience I find that I cannot, in spite of a very genuine attempt to do so; and I venture to think that most people will find the same, and that just because they cannot lose the sense of special obligation, they cannot accept as self-evident, or even as true, the theory which would require them to do so. In fact it seems, on reflection, self-evident that a promise, simply as such, is something that *prima facie* ought to be kept, and it does *not*, on reflection, seem self-evident that production of maximum good is the only thing that makes an act obligatory. And to ask us to give up at the bidding of a theory our actual apprehension of what is right and what is wrong seems like asking people to repudiate their actual experience of beauty, at the bidding of a theory which says 'only that which satisfies such and such conditions can be beautiful'. If what I have called our actual apprehension is (as I would maintain that it is) truly an apprehension, i.e. an instance of knowledge, the request is nothing less than absurd.

I would maintain, in fact, that what we are apt to describe as 'what we think' about moral questions contains a considerable amount that we do not think but know, and that this forms the standard by reference to which the truth of any moral theory has to be tested, instead of having itself to be tested by reference to any theory. I hope that I have in what precedes indicated what in my view these elements of knowledge are that are involved in our ordinary moral consciousness.

It would be a mistake to found a natural science on 'what we really think', i.e. on what reasonably thoughtful and well-educated people think about the subjects of the science before they have studied them scientifically. For such opinions are interpretations, and often misinterpretations, of sense-experience; and the man of science must appeal from these to sense-experience itself, which furnishes his real data. In ethics no such appeal is possible. We have no more direct way of access to the facts about rightness and goodness and about what things are right or good, than by thinking about them; the moral convictions of thoughtful and well-educated people are the data of ethics just as sense-perceptions are the data of a natural science. Just as some of the latter have to be rejected as illusory, so have some of the former; but as the latter are rejected only when they are in conflict with other more accurate sense-perceptions, the former are rejected only when they are in conflict with other convictions which stand better the test of reflection. The existing body of moral convictions of the best people is the cumulative product of the moral reflection of many generations, which has developed an extremely delicate power of appreciation of moral distinctions; and this the theorist cannot afford to treat with anything other than the greatest respect. The verdicts of the moral consciousness of the best people are the foundation on which he must build; though he must first compare them with one another and eliminate any contradictions they may contain.

It is worth while to try to state more definitely the nature of the acts that are right. We may try to state first what (if anything) is the universal nature of *all* acts that are right. It is obvious that any of the acts that we do has countless effects, directly or indirectly, on countless people, and the probability is that any act, however right it be, will have adverse effects (though these may be very trivial) on some innocent people. Similarly, any wrong act will probably have beneficial effects on some deserving people. Every act therefore, viewed in some aspects, will be *prima facie* right, and viewed in others, *prima facie* wrong, and right acts can be distinguished from wrong acts only as being those which, of all those possible for the agent in the circumstances, have the greatest balance of *prima facie* rightness, in those respects in which they are *prima facie* right, over their *prima facie* wrongness, in those respects in which they are *prima facie* wrong – *prima facie* rightness and wrongness being understood in the sense previously explained. For the estimation of the comparative stringency of these *prima facie* obligations no general rules can, so far as I can see, be laid down. We can only say that a great deal of stringency belongs to the duties of 'perfect obligation' – the duties of keeping our promises, of repairing wrongs we have done, and of returning the equivalent of services we have received. For the rest, ἐν τῇ αἰσθήσει ἡ κρίσις.[8] This sense of our particular duty in particular circumstances, preceded and informed by the fullest reflection we can bestow on the act in all its bearings, is highly fallible, but it is the only guide we have to our duty.

When we turn to consider the nature of individual right acts, the first point to which attention should be called is that any act may be correctly described in an indefinite, and in principle infinite, number of ways. An act is the production of a change in the state of affairs (if we ignore, for simplicity's sake, the comparatively few cases in which it is the maintenance of an existing state of affairs; cases which, I think, raise no special difficulty). Now the only changes we can *directly* produce are changes in our own bodies or in our own minds. But these are not, as such, what as a rule we think it our duty to produce. Consider some comparatively simple act, such as telling the truth or fulfilling a promise. In the first case what I produce directly is movements of my vocal organs. But what I think it my duty to produce is a true view in some one else's mind about some fact, and between my movement of my vocal organs and this result there intervenes a series of physical events and events in his mind. Again, in the second case, I may have promised, for instance, to return a book to a friend. I may be able, by a series of movements of my legs and hands, to place it in his hands. But what I am just as likely to do, and to think I have done my duty in doing, is to send it by a messenger or to hand it to his servant or to send it by post; and in each of these cases what I *do* directly is worthless in itself and is connected by a series of intermediate links with what I do think it is my duty to bring about, viz. his receiving what I have promised to return to him. This being so, it *seems* as if what I *do* has no obligatoriness in itself and as if one or other of three accounts should be given of the matter, each of which makes rightness not belong to what I do, considered in its own nature.

(1)   One of them would be that what is obligatory is not *doing* anything in the natural sense of producing any change in the state of affairs, but *aiming at* something – at, for instance, my friend's reception of the book. But this account will not do. For (*a*) to aim at something is to act from a motive consisting of the wish to bring that thing about. But we have seen that motive never forms part of the content of our duty; if anything is certain about morals, that, I think, is certain. And (*b*) if I have promised to return the book to my friend, I obviously do not fulfil my promise and do my duty merely by aiming at his receiving the book; I must see that he actually receives it. (2) A more plausible account is that which says I must do that which is likely to produce the result.

---

[8] 'The decision rests with perception'. Arist. *Nic. Eth.* 1109 b 23, 1116 b 4.

But this account is open to the second of these objections, and probably also to the first. For in the first place, however likely my act may seem, even on careful consideration, and even however likely it may in fact be, to produce the result, if it does not produce it I have not done what I promised to do, i.e. have not done my duty. And secondly, when it is said that I ought to do what is likely to produce the result, what is *probably* meant is that I ought to do a certain thing as a result of the wish to produce a certain result, and of the thought that my act is likely to produce it; and this again introduces motive into the content of duty. (3) Much the most plausible of the three accounts is that which says, 'I ought to do that which will actually produce a certain result.' This escapes objection (*b*). Whether it escapes objection (*a*) or not depends on what exactly is meant. If it is meant that I ought to do a certain thing from the wish to produce a certain result and the thought that it will do so, the account is still open to objection (*a*). But if it is meant simply that I ought to do a certain thing, and that the reason why I ought to do it is that it will produce a certain result, objection (*a*) is avoided. Now this account in its second form is that which utilitarianism gives. It says what is right is certain acts, not certain acts motivated in a certain way; and it says that acts are never right by their own nature but by virtue of the goodness of their actual results. And this account is, I think, clearly nearer the truth than one which makes the rightness of an act depend on the goodness of either the *intended* or the *likely* results.

Nevertheless, this account appears not to be the true one. For it implies that what we consider right or our duty is what we do *directly*. It is this, e.g. the packing up and posting of the book, that derives its moral significance not from its own nature but from its consequences. But this is *not* what we should describe, strictly, as our duty; our duty is to fulfil our promise, i.e. to put the book into our friend's possession. This we consider obligatory in its own nature, just because it is a fulfilment of promise, and not because of *its* consequences. But, it might be replied by the utilitarian, I do not do this; I only do something that leads up to this, and what I do has no moral significance in itself but only because of its consequences. In answer to this, however, we may point out that a cause produces not only its immediate, but also its remote consequences, and the latter no less than the former. I, therefore, not only produce the immediate movements of parts of my body but also my friend's reception of the book, which results from these. Or, if this be objected to on the grounds that I can hardly be said to have produced my friend's reception of the book when I have packed and posted it, owing to the time that has still to elapse before he receives it, and that to say I have produced the result hardly does justice to the part played by the Post Office, we may at least say that I have *secured* my friend's reception of the book. What I do is as truly describable in this way as by saying that it is the packing and posting of a book. (It is equally truly describable in many other ways; e.g. I have provided a few moments' employment for Post Office officials. But this is irrelevant to the argument.) And if we ask ourselves whether it is *qua* the packing and posting of a book, or *qua* the securing of my friend's getting what I have promised to return to him, that my action is right, it is clear that it is in the second capacity that it is right; and in this capacity, the only capacity in which it is right, it is right by its own nature and not because of its consequences.

[...]

If the book had been destroyed in a railway accident or stolen by a dishonest postman, that would prove that my immediate act was not sufficient to produce the desired result. We get the curious consequence that however carelessly I pack or dispatch the book, if it comes to hand I have done my duty, and however carefully I have acted, if the book does not come to hand I have not done my duty. Success and failure are the only test, and a sufficient test, of the performance of duty. Of course, I should deserve more praise in the second case than in the first; but that is an entirely different question; we must not mix up the question of right and wrong with that of the morally good and the morally bad. And that our conclusion is not as strange as at first sight it might seem is shown by the fact that if the carelessly dispatched book comes to hand, it is not my duty to send another copy, while if the carefully dispatched book does not come to hand I must send another copy to replace it. In the first case I have not my duty still to do, which shows that I have done it; in the second I have it still to do, which shows that I have not done it.

We have reached the result that my act is right *qua* being an ensuring of one of the particular states of affairs of which it is an ensuring, viz., in the case we have taken, of my friend's receiving the book I have promised to return to him. But this answer requires some correction; for it refers only to the *prima facie* rightness of my act. If to be a fulfilment of promise were a sufficient ground of the rightness of an act, all fulfilments of promises would be right, whereas it seems clear that there are cases in which some other *prima facie* duty overrides the *prima facie* duty of fulfilling a promise. The more correct answer would be that the ground of the actual rightness of the act is that, of all acts possible for the agent in the circumstances, it is that whose *prima facie* rightness in the respects in which it is *prima facie* right most outweighs its *prima facie* wrongness in any respects in which it is *prima facie* wrong. But since its *prima facie* rightness is mainly due to its being a fulfilment of promise, we may call its being so the salient element in the ground of its rightness.

Subject to this qualification, then, it is as being the production (or if we prefer the word, the securing or ensuring) of the reception by my friend of what I have promised him (or in other words as the fulfilment of my promise) that my act is right. It is not right as a packing and posting of a book. The packing and posting of the book is only incidentally right, right only because it is a fulfilment of promise, which is what is directly or essentially right.

Our duty, then, is not to do certain things which will produce certain results. Our acts, at any rate our acts of special obligation, are not right because they will produce certain results – which is the view common to all forms of utilitarianism. To say that is to say that in the case in question what is essentially right is to pack and post a book, whereas what is essentially right is to secure the possession by my friend of what I have promised to return to him. An act is not right because it, being one thing, produces good results different from itself; it is right because it is itself the production of a certain state of affairs. Such production is right in itself, apart from any consequence.

But, it might be said, this analysis applies only to acts of special obligation; the utilitarian account still holds good for the acts in which we are not under a special obligation to any person or set of persons but only under that of augmenting the general good. Now merely to have established that there *are* special obligations to do certain things irrespective of their consequences would be already to have made a considerable breach in the utilitarian walls; for according to utilitarianism there is no such thing, there is only the single obligation to promote the general good. But, further, on reflection it is clear that just as (in the case we have taken) my act is not only the packing and posting of a book but the fulfilling of a promise, and just as it is in the latter capacity and not in the former that it is my duty, so an act whereby I augment the general good is not only, let us say, the writing of a begging letter on behalf of a hospital, but the producing (or ensuring) of whatever good ensues therefrom, and it is in the latter capacity and not in the former that it is right, if it *is* right. That which is right is right not because it is an act, one thing, which will produce another thing, an increase of the general welfare, but because it is itself the producing of an increase in the general welfare. Or, to qualify this in the necessary way, its being the production of an increase in the general welfare is the salient element in the ground of its rightness. Just as before we were led to recognize the *prima facie* rightness of the fulfilment of promises, we are now led to recognize the *prima facie* rightness of promoting the general welfare. In both cases we have to recognize the *intrinsic* rightness of a certain type of act, not depending on its consequences but on its own nature.

3

Language, Truth and Logic

Alfred Jules Ayer

Under the influence of a group of philosophers and scientists known as the Vienna Circle, the British philosopher A.J. Ayer wrote *Language, Truth and Logic* with the explicit goal of defending a particular version of verificationism. To put it roughly, *verificationism* is the view that only linguistic statements that are capable of being empirically demonstrated to be true or false can be said to be meaningful. The only exceptions are analytic truths or tautologies, where truth is guaranteed in virtue of the meaning of words (e.g. if 'bachelor' is simply definable as 'an unmarried man', then 'bachelors are unmarried men' is necessarily true). Ayer claimed that legitimate philosophical claims are all, with one important exception, analytic truths; he admits the doctrine of verificationism itself is not analytic, but he thinks it is a doctrine that experience can tell us is probably true.

Verificationism, even of the somewhat weakened form that Ayer endorsed, was short-lived. Few contemporary philosophers hold to verificationism. However, non-cognitivism – a form of which Ayer defended under the name of 'emotivism' in the short section of his book reproduced here – continues to be a popular view about the moral enterprise. Non-cognitivism is the view that our moral thought and talk is not *about* anything – at a fundamental level, it is not at all about representing the moral properties or facts that moral realists or objectivists suppose it is about representing – but is rather in the business of *motivating* us to act in various ways.

Ayer contends that core ethical statements are 'simply expressions of emotions which can be neither true nor false', and it is this view that he labels 'emotivism'. It is easily confused with one of the two forms of 'subjectivism' he explicitly rejects, according to which moral statements *report* the feelings of approval or disapproval that individuals experience. If a person stands on my foot, I might manage to calmly report, 'I am in pain', but I might instead simply scream out in pain; only the second counts as expressing that I am in pain (in the sense of 'express' that Ayer has in mind). If I scream, 'I am in pain!' I may count as both reporting and expressing my feeling; but crying, 'Ouch!' does not count as a way of reporting that I am in pain, as 'Ouch!' is not something that can be true or false.

Emotivism is sometimes called the Boo/Hurrah theory of moral language, because it would have us interpret sincerely uttered sentences that make direct use of moral terms as either taking the form Boo! (descriptive claim or property) when a negative attitude is evinced, or the positive form Hurrah! (descriptive claim or property) when a positive attitude is evinced. Take Ayer's own example: if I say 'You acted wrongly in stealing that money', the only thing I can be said to be asserting is, 'You stole the money'; however, says Ayer, it is as though I had said this shorter sentence with a 'peculiar tone of horror', or had added 'some special exclamation marks'. And, Ayer claims, if I say 'Stealing money is wrong', I am not asserting any proposition at all, but simply expressing moral disapproval of the property of stealing, which some acts possess. Moral concepts, on this view, are mere 'pseudo-concepts' because, unlike genuine concepts, they

History of Ethics – Essential Readings with Commentary, First Edition. Edited by Daniel Star and Roger Crisp.
© 2020 John Wiley & Sons Ltd. Published 2020 by John Wiley & Sons Ltd.

are incapable of enabling us to represent to ourselves any properties in the world (even the concept 'unicorn' has a definition provided to us through fiction, so presumably it is not a pseudo-concept).

One challenge that emotivism, and non-cognitivism more generally, faces is explaining the many significant differences between the wide range of moral terms in our language and the sentence structures in which they appear (if we take the sentence 'virtue is its own reward', for instance, it is not clear how one would break this down into descriptive and emotive components). Ayer does not attempt to distinguish between many moral terms. He at one point provides a dubious suggestion regarding how 'good' might differ from 'ought', but, more significantly, he supplements his original claim about the function of ethical terms as serving to express feelings, with the further claim that they may also be used to arouse feelings in others, and to encourage others to act in various ways (C.L. Stevenson's defense of emotivism makes more of these other functions of moral language).

When criticizing utilitarianism and subjectivism, Ayer utilizes the open question argument ('It is not self-contradictory to say that some pleasant things are not good', etc.). The reader may wonder why these particular views are discussed. It helps to bear in mind that the target here is really any form of naturalist descriptivism regarding ethical properties. Ayer thoroughly agrees with Moore's critique of naturalist (descriptive) ethics, yet thoroughly rejects Moore's non-naturalist intuitionism, arguing that it makes ethical statements unverifiable. Even readers unsympathetic to verificationism in general may find themselves sympathetic to his claim that 'unless it is possible to provide some criterion by which one may decide between conflicting intuitions, a mere appeal to intuition is worthless as a test of a proposition's validity.' Whatever one thinks of the weakness of Ayer's defense of emotivism, and the challenges it would need to overcome for us to find it satisfactory, there is something quite attractive about the idea that one can accept the guiding thought behind the open question argument (no analysis of fundamental ethical terms is possible), yet not be forced to give up on, or supplement, a naturalistic stance regarding the contents of reality.

An interesting consequence of Ayer's emotivism that he is only too happy to accept is that normative ethics is not really a part of philosophy. This is a consequence of his view that all talk of truth and falsity, with respect to normative ethical statements, is a mistake. A key way in which subsequent non-cognitivist approaches to the moral enterprise have differed from Ayer's is by purposely becoming more hospitable to talk of truth and falsity: rather than claiming such talk is wholly inappropriate, latter day non-cognitivists argue that a 'deflationary' account can be given of such talk. Such non-cognitivists endorse a 'quasi-realism' that hopes to capture the most crucial features of moral objectivity that traditional realists defend, and does not accept the strong conclusion Ayer ends up endorsing at the end of the text reproduced here regarding the supposed non-existence of genuine moral disagreement. This has effectively freed up normative ethicists to get back to searching for true ethical principles; they may, if they wish, remain neutral as to whether quasi-realism, robust realism, or some other non-revisionary metaethical theory is correct (non-revisionary with respect to ethical truth claims, that is).

THERE IS STILL one objection to be met before we can claim to have justified our view that all synthetic propositions are empirical hypotheses. This objection is based on the common supposition that our speculative knowledge is of two distinct kinds – that which relates to questions of empirical fact, and that which relates to questions of value. It will be said that "statements of value" are genuine synthetic propositions, but that they cannot with any show of justice be represented as hypotheses, which are used to predict the course of our sensations; and, accordingly, that the existence of ethics and æsthetics as branches of speculative knowledge presents an insuperable objection to our radical empiricist thesis.

In face of this objection, it is our business to give an account of "judgements of value" which is both satisfactory in itself and consistent with our general empiricist principles. We shall set ourselves to show that in so far as statements of value are significant, they are ordinary "scientific" statements; and that in so far as they are not scientific, they are not in the literal sense significant, but are simply expressions of emotion which can be neither true nor false. In maintaining this view, we may confine ourselves for the present to the case of ethical statements. What is said about them will be found to apply, *mutatis mutandis*, to the case of æsthetic statements also.

The ordinary system of ethics, as elaborated in the works of ethical philosophers, is very far from being a homogeneous whole. Not only is it apt to contain pieces of metaphysics, and analyses of non-ethical concepts: its actual ethical contents are themselves of very different kinds. We may divide them, indeed, into four main classes. There are, first of all, propositions which express definitions of ethical terms, or judgements about the legitimacy or possibility of certain definitions. Secondly, there are propositions describing the phenomena of moral experience, and their causes. Thirdly, there are exhortations to moral virtue. And, lastly, there are actual ethical judgements. It is unfortunately the case that the distinction between these four classes, plain as it is, is commonly ignored by ethical philosophers; with the result that it is often very difficult to tell from their works what it is that they are seeking to discover or prove.

In fact, it is easy to see that only the first of our four classes, namely that which comprises the propositions relating to the definitions of ethical terms, can be said to constitute ethical philosophy. The propositions which describe the phenomena of moral experience, and their causes, must be assigned to the science of psychology, or sociology. The exhortations to moral virtue are not propositions at all, but ejaculations or commands which are designed to provoke the reader to action of a certain sort. Accordingly, they do not belong to any branch of philosophy or science. As for the expressions of ethical judgements, we have not yet determined how they should be classified. But inasmuch as they are certainly neither definitions nor comments upon definitions, nor quotations, we may say decisively that they do not belong to ethical philosophy. A strictly philosophical treatise on ethics should therefore make no ethical pronouncements. But it should, by giving an analysis of ethical terms, show what is the category to which all such pronouncements belong. And this is what we are now about to do.

A question which is often discussed by ethical philosophers is whether it is possible to find definitions which would reduce all ethical terms to one or two fundamental terms. But this question, though it undeniably belongs to ethical philosophy, is not relevant to our present enquiry. We are not now concerned to discover which term, within the sphere of ethical terms, is to be taken as fundamental; whether, for example, "good" can be defined in terms of "right" or "right" in terms of "good," or both in terms of "value." What we are interested in is the possibility of reducing the whole sphere of ethical terms to non-ethical terms. We are enquiring whether statements of ethical value can be translated into statements of empirical fact.

That they can be so translated is the contention of those ethical philosophers who are commonly called subjectivists, and of those who are known as utilitarians. For the utilitarian defines the rightness of actions, and the goodness of ends, in terms of the pleasure, or happiness, or satisfaction, to which they give rise; the subjectivist, in terms of the feelings of approval which a certain person, or group of people, has towards them. Each of these types of definition makes moral judgements into a sub-class of psychological or sociological judgements; and for this reason they are very attractive to us. For, if either was correct, it would follow that ethical assertions were not generically different from the factual assertions which are ordinarily contrasted with them; and the account which we have already given of empirical hypotheses would apply to them also.

Nevertheless we shall not adopt either a subjectivist or a utilitarian analysis of ethical terms. We reject the subjectivist view that to call an action right, or a thing good, is to say that it is generally approved of, because it is not self-contradictory to assert that some actions which are generally approved of are not right, or that some things which are generally approved of are not good. And we reject the alternative subjectivist view that a man who asserts that a certain action is right, or that a certain thing is good, is saying that he himself approves of it, on the ground that a man who confessed that he sometimes approved of what was bad or wrong would not be contradicting himself. And a similar argument is fatal to utilitarianism. We cannot agree that to call an action right is to say that of all the actions possible in the circumstances it would cause, or be likely to cause, the greatest happiness, or the greatest balance of pleasure over pain, or the greatest balance of satisfied over unsatisfied desire, because we find that it is not self-contradictory to say that it is sometimes wrong to perform the action which would actually or probably cause the greatest happiness, or the greatest balance of pleasure over pain, or of satisfied over unsatisfied desire. And since it is not self-contradictory to say that some pleasant things are not good, or that some bad things are desired, it cannot be the case that the sentence "x is good" is equivalent to "x is pleasant," or to "x is desired." And to every other variant of utilitarianism with which I am acquainted the same objection can be made. And therefore we should, I think, conclude that the validity of ethical judgements is not determined by the felicific tendencies of actions, any more than by the nature of people's feelings; but that it must be regarded as "absolute" or "intrinsic," and not empirically calculable.

If we say this, we are not, of course, denying that it is possible to invent a language in which all ethical symbols are definable in non-ethical terms, or even that it is desirable to invent such a language and adopt it in place of our own; what we are denying is that the suggested reduction of ethical to non-ethical statements is consistent with the conventions of our actual language. That is, we reject utilitarianism and subjectivism, not as proposals to replace our existing ethical notions by new ones, but as analyses of our existing ethical notions. Our contention is simply that, in our language, sentences which contain normative ethical symbols are not equivalent to sentences which express psychological propositions, or indeed empirical propositions of any kind.

It is advisable here to make it plain that it is only normative ethical symbols, and not descriptive ethical symbols, that are held by us to be indefinable in factual terms. There is a danger of confusing these two types of symbols, because they are commonly constituted by signs of the same sensible form. Thus a complex sign of the form "x is wrong" may constitute a sentence which expresses a moral judgement concerning a certain type of conduct, or it may constitute a sentence which states that a certain type of conduct is repugnant to the moral sense of a particular society. In the latter case, the symbol "wrong" is a descriptive ethical symbol, and the sentence in which it occurs expresses an ordinary sociological proposition; in the former case, the symbol "wrong" is a normative ethical symbol, and the sentence in which it occurs does not, we maintain, express an empirical proposition at all. It is only with normative ethics that we are at present concerned; so that whenever ethical symbols are used in the course of this argument without qualification, they are always to be interpreted as symbols of the normative type.

In admitting that normative ethical concepts are irreducible to empirical concepts, we seem to be leaving the way clear for the "absolutist" view of ethics – that is, the view that statements of value are not controlled by observation, as ordinary empirical propositions are, but only by a mysterious "intellectual intuition." A feature of this theory, which is seldom recognized by its advocates, is that it makes statements of value unverifiable. For it is notorious that what seems intuitively certain to one person may seem doubtful, or even false, to another. So that unless it is possible to provide some criterion by which one may decide between conflicting intuitions, a mere appeal to intuition is worthless as a test of a proposition's validity. But in the case of moral judgements, no such criterion can be given. Some moralists claim to settle the matter by saying that they "know" that their own moral judgements are correct. But such an assertion is of purely psychological interest, and has not the slightest tendency to prove the validity of any moral judgement. For dissentient moralists may equally well "know" that their ethical views are correct. And, as far as subjective certainty goes, there will be nothing to choose between them. When such differences of opinion arise in connection with an ordinary empirical proposition, one may attempt to resolve them by referring to, or actually carrying out, some relevant empirical test. But with regard to ethical statements, there is, on the "absolutist" or "intuitionist" theory, no relevant empirical test. We are therefore justified in saying that on this theory ethical statements are held to be unverifiable. They are, of course, also held to be genuine synthetic propositions.

Considering the use which we have made of the principle that a synthetic proposition is significant only if it is empirically verifiable, it is clear that the acceptance of an "absolutist" theory of ethics would undermine the whole of our main argument. And as we have already rejected the "naturalistic" theories which are commonly supposed to provide the only alternative to "absolutism" in ethics, we seem to have reached a difficult position. We shall meet the difficulty by showing that the correct treatment of ethical statements is afforded by a third theory, which is wholly compatible with our radical empiricism.

We begin by admitting that the fundamental ethical concepts are unanalysable, inasmuch as there is no criterion by which one can test the validity of the judgements in which they occur. So far we are in agreement with the absolutists. But, unlike the absolutists, we are able to give an explanation of this fact about ethical concepts. We say that the reason why they are unanalysable is that they are mere pseudo-concepts. The presence of an ethical symbol in a proposition adds nothing to its factual content. Thus if I say to someone, "You acted wrongly in stealing that money," I am not stating anything more than if I had simply said, "You stole that money." In adding that this action is wrong I am not making any further statement about it. I am simply evincing my moral disapproval of it. It is as if I had said, "You stole that money," in a peculiar tone of horror, or written it with the addition of some special exclamation marks. The tone, or the exclamation marks, adds nothing to the literal meaning of the sentence. It merely serves to show that the expression of it is attended by certain feelings in the speaker.

If now I generalise my previous statement and say, "Stealing money is wrong," I produce a sentence which has no factual meaning – that is, expresses no proposition which can be either true or false. It is as if I had written "Stealing money!!" – where the shape and thickness of the exclamation marks show, by a suitable convention, that a special sort of moral disapproval is the feeling which is being expressed. It is clear that there is nothing said here which can be true or false. Another man may disagree with me about the wrongness of stealing, in the sense that he may not have the same feelings about stealing as I have, and he may quarrel with me on account of my moral sentiments. But he cannot, strictly speaking, contradict me. For in saying that a certain type of action is right or wrong, I am not making any factual statement, not even a statement about my own state of mind. I am merely expressing certain moral sentiments. And the man who is ostensibly contradicting me is merely expressing his moral sentiments. So that there is plainly no sense in asking which of us is in the right. For neither of us is asserting a genuine proposition.

What we have just been saying about the symbol "wrong" applies to all normative ethical symbols. Sometimes they occur in sentences which record ordinary empirical facts besides expressing ethical feeling about those facts: sometimes they occur in sentences which simply express ethical feeling about a certain type of action, or situation, without making any statement of fact. But in every case in which one would commonly be said to be making an ethical judgement, the function of the relevant ethical word is purely "emotive." It is used to express feeling about certain objects, but not to make any assertion about them.

It is worth mentioning that ethical terms do not serve only to express feeling. They are calculated also to arouse feeling, and so to stimulate action. Indeed some of them are used in such a way as to give the sentences in which they occur the effect of commands. Thus the sentence "It is your duty to tell the truth" may be regarded both as the expression of a certain sort of ethical feeling about truthfulness and as the expression of the command "Tell the truth." The sentence "You ought to tell the truth" also involves the command "Tell the truth," but here the tone of the command is less emphatic. In the sentence "It is good to tell the truth" the command has become little more than a suggestion. And thus the "meaning" of the word "good," in its ethical usage, is differentiated from that of the word "duty" or the word "ought." In fact we may define the meaning of the various ethical words in terms both of the different feelings they are ordinarily taken to express, and also the different responses which they are calculated to provoke.

We can now see why it is impossible to find a criterion for determining the validity of ethical judgements. It is not because they have an "absolute" validity which is mysteriously independent of ordinary sense-experience, but because they have no objective validity whatsoever. If a sentence makes no statement at all, there is obviously no sense in asking whether what it says is true or false. And we have seen that sentences which simply express moral judgements do not say anything. They are pure expressions of feeling and as such do not come under the category of truth and falsehood. They are unverifiable for the same reason as a cry of pain or a word of command is unverifiable – because they do not express genuine propositions.

Thus, although our theory of ethics might fairly be said to be radically subjectivist, it differs in a very important respect from the orthodox subjectivist theory. For the orthodox subjectivist does not deny, as we do, that the sentences of a moralizer express genuine propositions. All he denies is that they express propositions of a unique non-empirical character. His own view is that they express propositions about the speaker's feelings. If this were so, ethical judgements clearly would be capable of being true or false. They would be true if the speaker had the relevant feelings, and false if he had not. And this is a matter which is, in principle, empirically verifiable. Furthermore they could be significantly contradicted. For if I say, "Tolerance is a virtue," and someone answers, "You don't approve of it," he would, on the ordinary subjectivist theory, be contradicting me. On our theory, he would not be contradicting me, because, in saying that tolerance was a virtue, I should not be making any statement about my own feelings or about anything else. I should simply be evincing my feelings, which is not at all the same thing as saying that I have them.

The distinction between the expression of feeling and the assertion of feeling is complicated by the fact that the assertion that one has a certain feeling often accompanies the expression of that feeling, and is then, indeed, a factor in the expression of that feeling. Thus I may simultaneously express boredom and say that I am bored, and in that case my utterance of the words, "I am bored," is one of the circumstances which make it true to say that I am expressing or evincing boredom. But I can express boredom without actually saying that I am bored. I can express it by my tone and gestures, while making a statement about something wholly unconnected with it, or by an ejaculation, or without uttering any words at all. So that even if the assertion that one has a certain feeling always involves the expression of that feeling, the expression of a feeling assuredly does not always involve the assertion that one has it. And this is the important point to grasp in considering the distinction between our theory and the ordinary subjectivist theory. For whereas the subjectivist holds that ethical statements actually assert the existence of certain feelings, we hold that ethical statements are expressions and excitants of feeling which do not necessarily involve any assertions.

We have already remarked that the main objection to the ordinary subjectivist theory is that the validity of ethical judgements is not determined by the nature of their author's feelings. And this is an objection which our theory escapes. For it does not imply that the existence of any feelings is a necessary and sufficient condition of the validity of an ethical judgement. It implies, on the contrary, that ethical judgements have no validity.

There is, however, a celebrated argument against subjectivist theories which our theory does not escape. It has been pointed out by Moore that if ethical statements were simply statements about the speaker's feelings, it would be impossible to argue about questions of value. To take a typical example: if a man said that thrift was a virtue, and another replied that it was a vice, they would not, on this theory, be disputing with one another. One would be saying that he approved of thrift, and the other that *he* didn't; and there is no reason why both these statements should not be true. Now Moore held it to be obvious that we do dispute about questions of value, and accordingly concluded that the particular form of subjectivism which he was discussing was false.

It is plain that the conclusion that it is impossible to dispute about questions of value follows from our theory also. For as we hold that such sentences as "Thrift is a virtue" and "Thrift is a vice" do not express propositions at all, we clearly cannot hold that they express incompatible propositions. We must therefore admit that if Moore's argument really refutes the ordinary subjectivist theory, it also refutes ours. But, in fact, we deny that it does refute even the ordinary subjectivist theory. For we hold that one really never does dispute about questions of value.

This may seem, at first sight, to be a very paradoxical assertion. For we certainly do engage in disputes which are ordinarily regarded as disputes about questions of value. But, in all such cases, we find, if we consider the matter closely, that the dispute is not really about a question of value, but about a question of fact. When someone disagrees with us about the moral value of a certain action or type of action, we do admittedly resort to argument in order to win him over to our way of thinking. But we do not attempt to show by our arguments that he has the "wrong" ethical feeling towards a situation whose nature he has correctly apprehended. What we attempt to show is that he is mistaken about the facts of the case. We argue that he has misconceived the agent's motive: or that he has misjudged the effects of the action, or its probable effects in view of the agent's knowledge; or that he has failed to take into account the special circumstances in which the agent was placed. Or else we employ more general arguments about the effects which actions of a certain type tend to produce, or the qualities which are usually manifested in their performance. We do this in the hope that we have only to get our opponent to agree with us about the nature of the empirical facts for him to adopt the same moral attitude towards them as we do. And as the people with whom we argue have generally received the same moral education as ourselves, and live in the same social order, our expectation is usually justified. But if our opponent happens to have undergone a different process of moral "conditioning" from ourselves, so that, even when he acknowledges all the facts, he still disagrees with us about the moral value of the actions under discussion, then we abandon the attempt to convince him by argument. We say that it is impossible to argue with him because he has a distorted or undeveloped moral sense; which signifies merely that he employs a different set of values from our own. We feel that our own system of values is superior, and therefore speak in such derogatory terms of his. But we cannot bring forward any arguments to show that our system is superior. For our judgement that it is so is itself a judgement of value, and accordingly outside the scope of argument. It is because argument fails us when we come to deal with pure questions of value, as distinct from questions of fact, that we finally resort to mere abuse.

In short, we find that argument is possible on moral questions only if some system of values is presupposed. If our opponent concurs with us in expressing moral disapproval of all actions of a given type *t*, then we may get him to condemn a particular action A, by bringing forward arguments to show that A is of type *t*. For the question whether A does or does not belong to that type is a plain question of fact. Given that a man has certain moral principles, we argue that he must, in order to be consistent, react morally to certain things in a certain way. What we do not and cannot argue about is the validity of these moral principles. We merely praise or condemn them in the light of our own feelings.

If anyone doubts the accuracy of this account of moral disputes, let him try to construct even an imaginary argument on a question of value which does not reduce itself to an argument about a question of logic or about an empirical matter of fact. I am confident that he will not succeed in producing a single example. And if that is the case, he must allow that its involving the impossibility of purely ethical arguments is not, as Moore thought, a ground of objection to our theory, but rather a point in favour of it.

Having upheld our theory against the only criticism which appeared to threaten it, we may now use it to define the nature of all ethical enquiries. We find that ethical philosophy consists simply in saying that ethical concepts are pseudo-concepts and therefore unanalysable. The further task of describing the different feelings that the different ethical terms are used to express, and the different reactions that they customarily provoke, is a task for the psychologist. There cannot be such a thing as ethical science, if by ethical science one means the elaboration of a "true" system of morals. For we have seen that, as ethical judgements are mere expressions of feeling, there can be no way of determining the validity of any ethical system, and, indeed, no sense in asking whether any such system is true. All that one may legitimately enquire in this connection is, What are the moral habits of a given person or group of people, and what causes them to have precisely those habits and feelings? And this enquiry falls wholly within the scope of the existing social sciences.

It appears, then, that ethics, as a branch of knowledge, is nothing more than a department of psychology and sociology. And in case anyone thinks that we are overlooking the existence of casuistry, we may remark that casuistry is not a science, but is a purely analytical investigation of the structure of a given moral system. In other words, it is an exercise in formal logic.

When one comes to pursue the psychological enquiries which constitute ethical science, one is immediately enabled to account for the Kantian and hedonistic theories of morals. For one finds that one of the chief causes of moral behaviour is fear, both conscious and unconscious, of a god's displeasure, and fear of the enmity of society. And this, indeed, is the reason why moral precepts present themselves to some people as "categorical" commands. And one finds, also, that the moral code of a society is partly determined by the beliefs of that society concerning the conditions of its own happiness – or, in other words, that a society tends to encourage or discourage a given type of conduct by the use of moral sanctions according as it appears to promote or detract from the contentment of the society as a whole. And this is the reason why altruism is recommended in most moral codes and egotism condemned. It is from the observation of this connection between morality and happiness that hedonistic or eudæmonistic theories of morals ultimately spring, just as the moral theory of Kant is based on the fact, previously explained, that moral precepts have for some people the force of inexorable commands. As each of these theories ignores the fact which lies at the root of the other, both may be criticized as being one-sided; but this is not the main objection to either of them. Their essential defect is that they treat propositions which refer to the causes and attributes of our ethical feelings as if they were definitions of ethical concepts. And thus they fail to recognise that ethical concepts are pseudo-concepts and consequently indefinable.

4

The Naturalistic Fallacy

W. K. Frankena

In the article reproduced here, Frankena forcefully objects to naming the mistake Moore purports to have identified in *Principia Ethica* 'the naturalistic fallacy'. It may seem at first that he is merely concerned with terminology: since we should reserve 'fallacy' for mistakes in reasoning, especially mistakes that consist in making use of invalid arguments, and since the mistake that Moore purports to identify is not really of this kind, 'fallacy' is the wrong term for it. Terminological disputes are rather uninteresting: if this were all Frankena was claiming, Moore could reply that it does not really matter to him whether the word 'fallacy' is used, as long as we agree with him that a mistake of the kind he is interested in is being made by ethical naturalists.

Frankena appears to think Moore is unfairly attempting to gain some dialectical mileage out of using the term 'fallacy' that he simply is not entitled to. Although terminological disputes should not be confused with substantive disputes, choice of terminology can matter if one term happens to carry more rhetorical force than another: perhaps it is unfair of Moore to attempt to bludgeon his opponents with this term, in particular. Still, there are two deeper points that Frankena also intends to make.

First, whenever we offer a definition of anything whatsoever, an uncharitable interpreter might wrongly take us to be failing to recognize the truth of the statement from Butler that Moore placed at the beginning of his book, 'Everything is what it is, and not another thing.' If someone says 'goodness is pleasantness', we should not, observes Frankena, take this to mean that they are seeing one thing and saying that this thing is the same as a second, different thing they also happen to be seeing. After all, they might just as easily have said, 'The word "good" and the word "pleasant" mean the same thing' (this is what Frankena says, but the point might have been better made by saying, 'The word "good" and the word "pleasant" *refer to* the same thing', since meaning is not exhausted by reference). Consider an example of a kind that Frankena does not mention: a scientist who asserts that water *is* H_2O is clearly not claiming that there is one thing, water, and another thing, H_2O, and that these two separate things are one. Rather, when we discovered that water is H_2O, we discovered something about water (as well as something about hydrogen and oxygen) that we did not previously know. Frankena quips, 'Everything is what it is, and not another thing, unless it is another thing, and even then, it is what it is.'

Second, Frankena contends that since definitions are often useful and not illegitimate, the essential claim that Moore is making must be that moral properties and natural properties are of two very different metaphysical *kinds*, such that no definition of one in terms of the other is possible. Naturalists, on this view, are guilty of a kind of moral blindness, since in claiming that some natural properties are identical to moral properties, they are effectively failing to keep in view the moral properties (although they do not themselves realize this). If non-naturalism is true, then in attempting to define goodness as pleasantness the naturalist must, in fact, be moving his or her attention away from goodness. That being said, it would be question begging for the non-naturalist to *argue* for non-naturalism by starting with the claim that

History of Ethics – Essential Readings with Commentary, First Edition. Edited by Daniel Star and Roger Crisp.
© 2020 John Wiley & Sons Ltd. Published 2020 by John Wiley & Sons Ltd.

naturalists are morally blind, for such a claim can only be the result of having established that moral properties and natural properties are of two different metaphysical kinds. If the non-naturalist fails to present an argument for this claim, the naturalist may well assert that the non-naturalist is effectively hallucinating properties (that is, seeing moral properties where they do not exist) and will be in no worse a dialectical position than the non-naturalist in saying this.

Might not Moore's open question argument be the argument that the non-naturalist can rely on at this point? Frankena thinks that asking ourselves whether it is an open question that one property is identical to another will simply lead to a clash of intuitions: the naturalist will judge that it is not an open question, and the non-naturalist will judge that it is. Subsequent developments in the philosophy of language suggest that things may be even worse than this for the non-naturalist: in brief, it is now generally thought to be the case that reflections on our intuitions about the meaning of linguistic terms can be very unreliable, or incomplete. To return to the example mentioned earlier: reflection on the term 'water' may yield some reliable beliefs (e.g. water is the stuff that flows in our rivers and lakes, and out of our taps in our homes), but it cannot rule either in or out the claim that water just is H_2O. This means the naturalist can even afford to admit that it does not feel like an open question whether goodness is identical to some natural property (even to him or herself) while asserting, with some warrant, that our judgements about such matters can be unreliable.

Frankena's article is an early part of the move in metaethics away from being concerned primarily with language, at the expense of metaphysics. We saw a concentration on moral language in Moore and Ayer, but we might think debates about moral realism of naturalist and non-naturalist varieties are best construed as primarily metaphysical debates. Developments in philosophy more generally appear to have borne out that Frankena was right to want to shift metaethics in this direction, although metaphysics is now done, both inside ethics and outside of it, in a manner that is more conscious of the need also to keep considering the complex ways in which language and reality are related (and so the linguistic turn continues to influence philosophy, arguably for the better).

THE future historian of "thought and expression" in the twentieth century will no doubt record with some amusement the ingenious trick, which some of the philosophical controversialists of the first quarter of our century had, of labelling their opponents' views "fallacies". He may even list some of these alleged fallacies for a certain sonority which their inventors embodied in their titles: the fallacy of initial predication, the fallacy of simple location, the fallacy of misplaced concreteness, the naturalistic fallacy.

Of these fallacies, real or supposed, perhaps the most famous is the naturalistic fallacy. For the practitioners of a certain kind of ethical theory, which is dominant in England and capably represented in America, and which is variously called objectivism, non-naturalism, or intuitionism, have frequently charged their opponents with committing the naturalistic fallacy. Some of these opponents have strongly repudiated the charge of fallacy, others have at least commented on it in passing, and altogether the notion of a naturalistic fallacy has had a considerable currency in ethical literature. Yet, in spite of its repute, the naturalistic fallacy has never been discussed at any length, and, for this reason, I have elected to make a study of it in this paper. I hope incidentally to clarify certain confusions which have been made in connexion with the naturalistic fallacy, but my main interest is to free the controversy between the intuitionists and their opponents of the notion of a logical or quasi-logical fallacy, and to indicate where the issue really lies.

The prominence of the concept of a naturalistic fallacy in recent moral philosophy is another testimony to the great influence of the Cambridge philosopher, Mr G. E. Moore, and his book, *Principia Ethica*. Thus Mr Taylor speaks of the "vulgar mistake" which Mr Moore has taught us to call "the naturalistic fallacy",[1] and Mr G. S. Jury, as if to illustrate how well we have learned this lesson, says, with reference to naturalistic definitions of value, "All such definitions stand charged with Dr Moore's 'naturalistic fallacy'."[2] Now, Mr Moore coined the notion of the naturalistic fallacy in his polemic against naturalistic and metaphysical systems of ethics. "The naturalistic fallacy is a fallacy," he writes, and it "must not be committed." All naturalistic and metaphysical theories of ethics, however, "are *based* on the naturalistic fallacy, in the sense that the commission of this fallacy has been the main cause of their wide acceptance".[3] The best way to dispose of them, then, is to expose this fallacy. Yet it is not entirely clear just what is the status of the naturalistic fallacy in the polemics of the intuitionists against other theories. Sometimes it is used as a weapon, as when Miss Clarke says that if we call a thing good simply because it is liked we are guilty of the naturalistic fallacy.[4] Indeed, it presents this aspect to the reader in many parts of *Principia Ethica* itself. Now, in taking it as a weapon, the intuitionists use the naturalistic fallacy as if it were a logical fallacy on all fours with the fallacy of composition, the revelation of which disposes of naturalistic and metaphysical ethics and leaves intuitionism standing triumphant. That is, it is taken as a fallacy in advance, for use in controversy. But there are signs in *Principia Ethica* which indicate that the naturalistic fallacy has a rather different place in the intuitionist scheme, and should not be used as a weapon at all. In this aspect, the naturalistic fallacy must be proved to be a fallacy. It cannot be used to settle the controversy, but can only be asserted to be a fallacy when the smoke of battle has cleared. Consider the following passages: (*a*) "the naturalistic fallacy consists in the contention that good *means* nothing but some simple or complex notion, that can be defined in terms of natural qualities"; (*b*) "the point that good is indefinable and that to deny this involves a fallacy, is a point capable of strict proof".[5] These passages seem to imply that the fallaciousness of the naturalistic fallacy is just what is at issue in the controversy between the intuitionists and their opponents, and cannot be wielded as a weapon in that controversy. One of the points I wish to make in this paper is that the charge of committing the naturalistic fallacy can be made, if at all, only as a conclusion from the discussion and not as an instrument of deciding it.

The notion of a naturalistic fallacy has been connected with the notion of a bifurcation between the 'ought' and the 'is', between value and fact, between the normative and the descriptive. Thus Mr D. C. Williams says that some moralists have thought it appropriate to chastise as the naturalistic fallacy the attempt to derive the Ought from the Is.[6] We may begin, then, by considering this bifurcation, emphasis on which, by Sidgwick, Sorley, and others,

---

[1] A. E. Taylor, *The Faith of a Moralist*, vol. I, p. 104 n.

[2] *Value and Ethical Objectivity*, p. 58.

[3] *Principia Ethica*, pp. 38, 64.

[4] M. E. Clarke, "Cognition and Affection in the Experience of Value", *Journal of Philosophy*, 1938.

[5] *Principia Ethica*, pp. 73, 77. See also p. xix.

[6] "Ethics as Pure Postulate", *Philosophical Review*, 1933. See also T. Whittaker, *The Theory of Abstract Ethics*, pp. 19 f.

came largely as a reaction to the procedures of Mill and Spencer. Hume affirms the bifurcation in his *Treatise*: "I cannot forbear adding to these reasonings an observation, which may, perhaps, be found of some importance. In every system of morality which I have hitherto met with, I have always remarked, that the author proceeds for some time in the ordinary way of reasoning, and establishes the being of a God, or makes observations concerning human affairs; when of a sudden I am surprised to find, that instead of the usual copulations of propositions, *is* and *is not*, I meet with no proposition that is not connected with an *ought*, or an *ought not*. This change is imperceptible; but is, however, of the last consequence. For as this *ought*, or *ought not*, expresses some new relation or affirmation, it is necessary that it should be observed and explained; and at the same time that a reason should be given, for what seems altogether inconceivable, how this new relation can be a deduction from others, which are entirely different from it. But as authors do not commonly use this precaution, I shall presume to recommend it to the readers; and am persuaded, that this small attention would subvert all the vulgar systems of morality, and let us see that the distinction of vice and virtue is not founded merely on the relations of objects, nor is perceived by reason."[7]

Needless to say, the intuitionists *have* found this observation of some importance.[8] They agree with Hume that it subverts all the vulgar systems of morality, though, of course, they deny that it lets us see that the distinction of virtue and vice is not founded on the relations of objects, nor is perceived by reason. In fact, they hold that a small attention to it subverts Hume's own system also, since this gives naturalistic definitions of virtue and vice and of good and evil.[9]

Hume's point is that ethical conclusions cannot be drawn validly from premises which are non-ethical. But when the intuitionists affirm the bifurcation of the 'ought' and the 'is', they mean more than that ethical propositions cannot be deduced from non-ethical ones. For this difficulty in the vulgar systems of morality could be remedied, as we shall see, by the introduction of definitions of ethical notions in non-ethical terms. They mean, further, that such definitions of ethical notions in non-ethical terms are impossible. "The essential point", says Mr Laird, "is the irreducibility of values to non-values."[10] But they mean still more. Yellow and pleasantness are, according to Mr Moore, indefinable in non-ethical terms, but they are natural qualities and belong on the 'is' side of the fence. Ethical properties, however, are not, for him, mere indefinable natural qualities, descriptive or expository. They are properties of a different *kind*—non-descriptive or non-natural.[11] The intuitionist bifurcation consists of three statements:—

1. Ethical propositions are not deducible from non-ethical ones.[12]
2. Ethical characteristics are not definable in terms of non-ethical ones.
3. Ethical characteristics are different in kind from non-ethical ones.

Really it consists of but one statement, namely, (3), since (3) entails (2) and (2) entails (1). It does not involve saying that any ethical characteristics are absolutely indefinable. That is another question, although this is not always noticed.

What, now, has the naturalistic fallacy to do with the bifurcation of the 'ought' and the 'is'? To begin with, the connexion is this: many naturalistic and metaphysical moralists proceed as if ethical conclusions can be deduced from premises all of which are non-ethical, the classical examples being Mill and Spencer. That is, they violate (1). This procedure has lately been referred to as the "factualist fallacy" by Mr Wheel-wright and as the "valuational fallacy" by Mr Wood.[13] Mr Moore sometimes seems to identify it with the naturalistic fallacy, but in the main he holds only that it involves, implies, or rests upon this fallacy.[14] We may now consider the charge that the procedure in question is or involves a fallacy.

It may be noted at once that, even if the deduction of ethical conclusions from non-ethical premises is in no way a fallacy, Mill certainly did commit a fallacy in drawing an analogy between visibility and desirability in his argument for hedonism; and perhaps his committing *this* fallacy, which, as Mr Broad has said, we all learn about at our mothers' knees, is chiefly responsible for the notion of a naturalistic *fallacy*. But is it a fallacy to deduce ethical

---

[7] Book III, part ii, section i.
[8] See J. Laird, *A Study in Moral Theory*, pp. 16 f.; Whittaker, *op. cit.*, p. 19.
[9] See C. D. Broad, *Five Types of Ethical Theory*, ch. iv.
[10] *A Study in Moral Theory*, p. 94 n.
[11] See *Philosophical Studies*, pp. 259, 273 f.
[12] [3] See J. Laird, *op. cit.*, p. 318. Also pp. 12 ff.
[13] P. E. Wheelwright, *A Critical Introduction to Ethics*, pp. 40–51, 91 f.; L. Wood, "Cognition and Moral Value," *Journal of Philosophy*, 1937, p. 237.
[14] See *Principia Ethica*, pp. 114, 57, 43, 49. Whittaker identifies it with the naturalistic fallacy and regards it as a "logical" fallacy, *op. cit.*, pp. 19 f.

conclusions from non-ethical premises? Consider the Epicurean argument for hedonism which Mill so unwisely sought to embellish: pleasure is good, since it is sought by all men. Here an ethical conclusion is being derived from a non-ethical premise. And, indeed, the argument, taken strictly as it stands, *is* fallacious. But it is not fallacious because an *ethical* term occurs in the conclusion which does not occur in the premise. It is fallacious because any argument of the form "A is B, therefore A is C" is invalid, if taken strictly as it stands. For example, it is invalid to argue that Crœsus is rich because he is wealthy. Such arguments are, however, not intended to be taken strictly as they stand. They are enthymemes and contain a suppressed premise. And, when this suppressed premise is made explicit, they are valid and involve no logical fallacy.[15] Thus the Epicurean inference from psychological to ethical hedonism is valid when the suppressed premise is added to the effect that what is sought by all men is good. Then the only question left is whether the premises are true.

It is clear, then, that the naturalistic fallacy is not a logical fallacy, since it may be involved even when the argument is valid. How does the naturalistic fallacy enter such "mixed ethical arguments"[16] as that of the Epicureans? Whether it does or not depends on the nature of the suppressed premise. This may be either an induction, an intuition, a deduction from a "pure ethical argument," a definition, or a proposition which is true by definition. If it is one of the first three, then the naturalistic fallacy does not enter at all. In fact, the argument does not then involve violating (1), since one of its premises will be ethical. But if the premise to be supplied is a definition or a proposition which, is true by definition, as it probably was for the Epicureans, then the argument, while still valid, involves the naturalistic fallacy, and will run as follows: –

a.   Pleasure is sought by all men.
b.   What is sought by all men is good (by definition).
c.   Therefore, pleasure is good.

Now I am not greatly interested in deciding whether the argument as here set up violates (1). If it does not, then no 'mixed ethical argument' actually commits any factualist or valuational fallacy, except when it is unfairly taken as complete in its enthymematic form. If it does, then a valid argument may involve the deduction of an ethical conclusion from non-ethical premises and the factualist or valuational fallacy is not really a fallacy. The question depends on whether or not (b) and (c) are to be regarded as ethical propositions. Mr Moore refuses so to regard them, contending that, by hypothesis, (b) is analytic or tautologous, and that (c) is psychological, since it really says only that pleasure is sought by all men.[17] But to say that (b) is analytic and not ethical and that (c) is not ethical but psychological is to prejudge the question whether 'good' can be defined; for the Epicureans would contend precisely that if their definition is correct then (b) is ethical but analytic and (c) ethical though psychological. Thus, unless the question of the definability of goodness is to be begged, (b) and (c) must be regarded as ethical, in which case our argument does not violate (1). However, suppose, if it be not nonsense, that (b) is non-ethical and (c) ethical, then the argument will violate (1), but it will still obey all of the canons of logic, and it is only confusing to talk of a 'valuational logic' whose basic rule is that an evaluative conclusion cannot be deduced from non-evaluative premises.[18]

For the only way in which either the intuitionists or postulationists like Mr Wood can cast doubt upon the conclusion of the argument of the Epicureans (or upon the conclusion of any parallel argument) is to attack the premises, in particular (b). Now, according to Mr Moore, it is due to the presence of (b) that the argument involves the naturalistic fallacy. (b) involves the identification of goodness with 'being sought by all men', and to make this or any other such identification is to commit the naturalistic fallacy. The naturalistic fallacy is not the procedure of violating (1). It is the procedure, implied in many mixed ethical arguments and explicitly carried out apart from such arguments by many moralists, of defining such characteristics as goodness or of substituting some other characteristic for them. To quote some passages from *Principia Ethica*: –

a.   "... far too many philosophers have thought that when they named those other properties [belonging to all things which are good] they were actually defining good; that these properties, in fact, were simply not 'other', but absolutely and entirely the same with goodness. This view I propose to call the 'naturalistic fallacy'...."[19]

[15] See *ibid.*, pp. 50, 139; Wheelwright, *loc. cit.*
[16] See C. D. Broad, *The Mind and its Place in Nature*, pp. 488 f.; Laird, *loc. cit.*
[17] See *op. cit.*, pp. 11 f.; 19, 38, 73, 139.
[18] See L. Wood, *loc. cit.*
[19] p. 10.

b. "I have thus appropriated the name Naturalism to a particular method of approaching Ethics....This method consists in substituting for 'good' some one property of a natural object or of a collection of natural objects...."[20]

c. "... the naturalistic fallacy [is] the fallacy which consists in identifying the simple notion which we mean by 'good' with some other notion."[21]

Thus, to identify 'better' and 'more evolved', 'good' and 'desired', etc., is to commit the naturalistic fallacy.[22] But just why is such a procedure fallacious or erroneous? And is it a fallacy only when applied to good? We must now study Section 12 of *Principia Ethica*. Here Mr Moore makes some interesting statements: –

"... if anybody tried to define pleasure for us as being any other natural object; if anybody were to say, for instance, that pleasure *means* the sensation of red....Well, that would be the same fallacy which I have called the naturalistic fallacy.... I should not indeed call that a naturalistic fallacy, although it is the same fallacy as I have called naturalistic with reference to Ethics.... When a man confuses two natural objects with one another, defining the one by the other ... then there is no reason to call the fallacy naturalistic. But if he confuses 'good', which is not ... a natural object, with any natural object whatever, then there is a reason for calling that a naturalistic fallacy...."[23]

Here Mr Moore should have added that, when one confuses 'good', which is not a metaphysical object or quality, with any metaphysical object or quality, as metaphysical moralists do, according to him, then the fallacy should be called the metaphysical fallacy. Instead he calls it a naturalistic fallacy in this case too, though he recognises that the case is different since metaphysical properties are non-natural[24] – a procedure which, has misled many readers of *Principia Ethica*. For example, it has led Mr Broad to speak of "theological naturalism".[25]

To resume: "Even if [goodness] were a natural object, that would not alter the nature of the fallacy nor diminish its importance one whit".[26]

From these passages it is clear that the fallaciousness of the procedure which Mr Moore calls the naturalistic fallacy is not due to the fact that it is applied to good or to an ethical or non-natural characteristic. When Mr R. B. Perry defines 'good' as 'being an object of interest' the trouble is not merely that he is defining *good*. Nor is the trouble that he is defining an *ethical* characteristic in terms of *non-ethical* ones. Nor is the trouble that he is regarding a *non-natural* characteristic as a *natural* one. The trouble is more generic than that. For clarity's sake I shall speak of the definist fallacy as the generic fallacy which underlies the naturalistic fallacy. The naturalistic fallacy will then, by the above passages, be a species or form of the definist fallacy, as would the metaphysical fallacy if Mr Moore had given that a separate name.[27] That is, the naturalistic fallacy, as illustrated by Mr Perry's procedure, is a fallacy, not because it is naturalistic or confuses a non-natural quality with a natural one, but solely because it involves the definist fallacy. We may, then, confine our attention entirely to an understanding and evaluation of the definist fallacy.

To judge by the passages I have just quoted, the definist fallacy is the process of confusing or identifying two properties, of defining one property by another, or of substituting one property for another. Furthermore, the fallacy is always simply that two properties are being treated as one, and it is irrelevant, if it be the case, that one of them is natural or non-ethical and the other non-natural or ethical. One may commit the definist fallacy without infringing on the bifurcation of the ethical and the non-ethical, as when one identifies pleasantness and redness or rightness and goodness. But even when one infringes on that bifurcation in committing the definist fallacy, as when one identifies goodness and pleasantness or goodness and satisfaction, then the *mistake* is still not that the bifurcation is being infringed on, but only that two properties are being treated as one. Hence, on the present interpretation, the definist *fallacy* does not, in any of its forms, consist in violating (3), and has no essential connexion with the bifurcation of the 'ought' and the 'is'.

This formulation of the definist fallacy explains or reflects the motto of *Principia Ethica*, borrowed from Bishop Butler: "Everything is what it is, and not another thing". It follows from this motto that goodness is what it is and not another thing. It follows that views which try to identify it with something else are making a mistake of an

[20] p. 40.
[21] p. 58, *cf.* pp. xiii, 73.
[22] *Cf.* pp. 49, 53, 108, 139.
[23] p. 13.
[24] See pp. 38–40, 110–112.
[25] *Five Types of Ethical Theory*, p. 259.
[26] p. 14.
[27] As Whittaker has, *loc. cit.*

elementary sort. For it *is* a mistake to confuse or identify two properties. If the properties really are two, then they simply are not identical. But do those who define ethical notions in non-ethical terms make this mistake? They will reply to Mr Moore that they are not identifying two properties; what they are saying is that two words or sets of words stand for or mean one and the same property. Mr Moore was being, in part, misled by the material mode of speech, as Mr Carnap calls it, in such sentences as "Goodness is pleasantness", "Knowledge is true belief", etc. When one says instead, "The word 'good' and the word 'pleasant' mean the same thing", etc., it is clear that one is not identifying two things. But Mr Moore kept himself from seeing this by his disclaimer that he was interested in any statement about the use of words.[28]

The definist fallacy, then, as we have stated it, does not rule out any naturalistic or metaphysical definitions of ethical terms. Goodness is not identifiable with any 'other' characteristic (if it is a characteristic at all). But the question is: *which* characteristics are other than goodness, which names stand for characteristics other than goodness? And it is begging the question of the definability of goodness to say out of hand that Mr Perry, for instance, is identifying goodness with something else. The point is that goodness is what it is, even if it is definable. That is why Mr Perry can take as the motto of his naturalistic *Moral Economy* another sentence from Bishop Butler: "Things and actions are what they are, and the consequences of them will be what they will be; why then should we desire to be deceived?" The motto of *Principia Ethica* is a tautology, and should be expanded as follows: Everything is what it is, and not another thing, unless it is another thing, and even then it is what it is.

On the other hand, if Mr Moore's motto (or the definist fallacy) rules out any definitions, for example of 'good', then it rules out all definitions of any term whatever. To be effective at all, it must be understood to mean, "Every term means what it means, and not what is meant by any other term". Mr Moore seems implicitly to understand his motto in this way in Section 13, for he proceeds as if 'good' has no meaning, if it has no unique meaning. If the motto be taken in this way, it will follow that 'good' is an indefinable term, since no synonyms can be found. But it will also follow that no term is definable. And then the method of analysis is as useless as an English butcher in a world without sheep.

Perhaps we have misinterpreted the definist fallacy. And, indeed, some of the passages which I quoted earlier in this paper seem to imply that the definist fallacy is just the error of defining an indefinable characteristic. On this interpretation, again, the definist fallacy has, in all of its forms, no essential connexion with the bifurcation of the ethical and the non-ethical. Again, one may commit the definist fallacy without violating that bifurcation, as when one defines pleasantness in terms of redness or goodness in terms of rightness (granted Mr Moore's belief that pleasantness and goodness are indefinable). But even when one infringes on that bifurcation and defines goodness in terms of desire, the *mistake* is not that one is infringing on the bifurcation by violating (3), but only that one is defining an indefinable characteristic. This is possible because the proposition that goodness is indefinable is logically independent of the proposition that goodness is non-natural: as is shown by the fact that a characteristic may be indefinable and yet natural, as yellowness is; or non-natural and yet definable, as rightness is (granted Mr Moore's views about yellowness and rightness).

Consider the definist fallacy as we have just stated it. It is, of course, an error to define an indefinable quality. But the question, again, is: which qualities are indefinable? It is begging the question in favour of intuitionism to say in advance that the quality goodness is indefinable and that, therefore, all naturalists commit the definist fallacy. One must know that goodness is indefinable before one can argue that the definist fallacy *is* a fallacy. Then, however, the definist fallacy can enter only at the end of the controversy between intuitionism and definism, and cannot be used as a weapon in the controversy.

The definist fallacy may be stated in such a way as to involve the bifurcation between the 'ought' and the 'is'.[29] It would then be committed by anyone who offered a definition of any ethical characteristic in terms of non-ethical ones. The trouble with such a definition, on this interpretation, would be that an *ethical* characteristic is being reduced to a *non-ethical* one, a *non-natural* one to a *natural* one. That is, the definition would be ruled out by the fact that the characteristic being defined is ethical or non-natural and therefore cannot be defined in non-ethical or natural terms. But on this interpretation, too, there is danger of a *petitio* in the intuitionist argumentation. To assume that the ethical characteristic is exclusively ethical is to beg precisely the question which is at issue when the definition is offered. Thus, again, one must know that the characteristic is non-natural and indefinable in natural terms before one can say that the definists are making a mistake.

---

[28] See *op. cit.*, pp. 6, 8, 12.
[29] See J. Wisdom, MIND, 1931, p. 213, note 1.

Mr Moore, McTaggart, and others formulate the naturalistic fallacy sometimes in a way somewhat different from any of those yet discussed. They say that the definists are confusing a universal synthetic proposition about *the good* with a definition of *goodness*.[30] Mr Abraham calls this the "fallacy of misconstrued proposition".[31] Here again the difficulty is that, while it is true that it is an error to construe a universal synthetic proposition as a definition, it is a *petitio* for the intuitionists to say that what the definist is taking for a definition is really a universal synthetic proposition.[32]

At last, however, the issue between the intuitionists and the definists (naturalistic or metaphysical) is becoming clearer. The definists are all holding that certain propositions involving ethical terms are analytic, tautologous, or true by definition, *e.g.*, Mr Perry so regards the statement, "All objects of desire are good". The intuitionists hold that such statements are synthetic. What underlies this difference of opinion is that the intuitionists claim to have at least a dim awareness of a simple unique quality or relation of goodness or rightness which appears in the region which our ethical terms roughly indicate, whereas the definists claim to have no awareness of any such quality or relation in that region, which is different from all other qualities and relations which belong to the same context but are designated by words other than 'good' and 'right' and their obvious synonyms.[33] The definists are in all honesty claiming to find but one characteristic where the intuitionists claim to find two, as Mr Perry claims to find only the property of being desired where Mr Moore claims to find both it and the property of being good. The issue, then, is one of inspection or intuition, and concerns the awareness or discernment of qualities and relations.[34] That is why it cannot be decided by the use of the notion of a fallacy.

If the definists may be taken at their word, then they are not actually confusing two characteristics with each other, nor defining an indefinable characteristic, nor confusing definitions and universal synthetic propositions – in short they are not committing the naturalistic or definist fallacy in any of the interpretations given above. Then the only fallacy which they commit – the real naturalistic or definist fallacy – is the failure to descry the qualities and relations which are central to morality. But this is neither a logical fallacy nor a logical confusion. It is not even, properly speaking, an error. It is rather a kind of blindness, analogous to colour-blindness. Even this moral blindness can be ascribed to the definists only if they are correct in their claim to have no awareness of any unique ethical characteristics and if the intuitionists are correct in affirming the existence of such characteristics, but certainly to call it a 'fallacy', even in a loose sense, is both unamiable and profitless.

On the other hand, of course, if there are no such characteristics in the objects to which we attach ethical predicates, then the intuitionists, if we may take them at their word, are suffering from a corresponding moral hallucination. Definists might then call this the intuitionistic or moralistic fallacy, except that it is no more a 'fallacy' than is the blindness just described. Anyway, they do not believe the claim of the intuitionists to be aware of unique ethical characteristics, and consequently do not attribute to them this hallucination. Instead, they simply deny that the intuitionists really do find such unique qualities or relations, and then they try to find some plausible way of accounting for the fact that very respectable and trustworthy people think they find them.[35] Thus they charge the intuitionists with verbalism, hypostatisation, and the like. But this half of the story does not concern us now.

What concerns us more is the fact that the intuitionists do not credit the claim of the definists either. They would be much disturbed, if they really thought that their opponents were morally blind, for they do not hold that we must be regenerated by grace before we can have moral insight, and they share the common feeling that morality is something democratic even though not all men are good. Thus they hold that "we are all aware" of certain unique characteristics when we use the terms 'good', 'right', etc., only due to a lack of analytic clearness of mind, abetted perhaps by a philosophical prejudice, we may not be aware at all that they are different from other characteristics of which we are also aware.[36] Now, I have been arguing that the intuitionists cannot charge the definists with committing any fallacy unless and until they have shown that we are all, the definists included, aware of the disputed unique characteristics. If, however, they were to show this, then, at least at the end of the controversy, they could accuse the definists of the error of confusing two characteristics, or of the error of defining an indefinable one, and these errors might, since the term is somewhat loose in its habits, be called 'fallacies', though they are not logical

[30] See *Principia Ethica*, pp. 10, 16, 38; *The Nature of Existence*, vol. ii, p. 398.

[31] Leo Abraham, "The Logic of Intuitionism", *International Journal of Ethics*, 1933.

[32] As Mr Abraham points out, *loc. cit.*

[33] See R. B. Perry, *General Theory of Value*, p. 30; cf. *Journal of Philosophy*, 1931, p. 520.

[34] See H. Osborne, *Foundations of the Philosophy of Value*, pp. 15, 19, 70.

[35] Cf. R. B. Perry, *Journal of Philosophy*, 1931, pp. 520 ff.

[36] *Principia Ethica*, pp. 17, 38, 59, 61.

fallacies in the sense in which an invalid argument is. The fallacy of misconstrued proposition depends on the error of confusing two characteristics, and hence could also on our present supposition, be ascribed to the definists, but it is not really a *logical* confusion,[37] since it does not actually involve being confused about the difference between a proposition and a definition.

Only it is difficult to see how the intuitionists can prove that the definists are at least vaguely aware of the requisite unique characteristics.[38] The question must surely be left to the inspection or intuition of the definists themselves, aided by whatever suggestions the intuitionists may have to make. If so, we must credit the verdict of their inspection, especially of those among them who have read the writings of the intuitionists reflectively, and, then, as we have seen, the most they can be charged with is moral blindness.

Besides trying to discover just what is meant by the naturalistic fallacy, I have tried to show that the notion that a logical or quasi-logical fallacy is committed by the definists only confuses the issue between the intuitionists and the definists (and the issue between the latter and the emotists or postulationists), and misrepresents the way in which the issue is to be settled. No logical fallacy need appear anywhere in the procedure of the definists. Even fallacies in any less accurate sense cannot be implemented to decide the case against the definists; at best they can be ascribed to the definists only after the issue has been decided against them on independent grounds. But the only defect which can be attributed to the definists, *if* the intuitionists are right in affirming the existence of unique indefinable ethical characteristics, is a peculiar moral blindness, which is not a fallacy even in the looser sense. The issue in question must be decided by whatever method we may find satisfactory for determining whether or not a word stands for a characteristic at all, and, if it does, whether or not it stands for a unique characteristic. What method is to be employed is, perhaps, in one form or another, the basic problem of contemporary philosophy, but no generally satisfactory solution of the problem has yet been reached. I shall venture to say only this: it does seem to me that the issue is not to be decided against the intuitionists by the application *ab extra* to ethical judgments of any empirical or ontological meaning dictum.[39]

---

[37] But see H. Osborne, *op. cit.*, pp. 18 f.

[38] For a brief discussion of their arguments, see *ibid*, p. 67; L. Abraham, *op. cit.* I think they are all inconclusive, but cannot show this here.

[39] See *Principia Ethica*, pp. 124 f., 140.

5

Modern Moral Philosophy[1]

G. E. M. Anscombe

Anscombe's paper makes several significant claims in an unusually forthright style. It has proved influential particularly in encouraging a focus on virtue, which led to the rise of so-called 'virtue ethics' in the writings of her colleague Philippa Foot and others.

Anscombe begins by summarizing her three main claims: (i) the *unprofitability claim*: moral philosophy should be replaced by philosophy of psychology; (ii) the *anti-morality claim*: concepts of 'obligation', 'duty', and so on are anachronistic and should be avoided; and (iii) the *lack-of-difference claim*: there is little difference between the main English moral philosophers from Sidgwick until the present. One might think (ii) less significant than (i), since if we set moral philosophy aside we shall also of course stop using concepts of moral obligation. But Anscombe believes there is hope for an Aristotelian moral philosophy based on a proper understanding of psychology, and particularly of action and virtue.

Anscombe is not a careful historian of philosophy, and her condemnations of Butler, Kant, and others, although entertaining, are too swift to be taken especially seriously (4–9). But she does raise some important questions about the moral concepts, and the contrast she draws between ancient and modern ethics has been widely accepted since at least the time of Hobbes. Anscombe claims that the very notion of the 'moral' is absent from Aristotle (2), partly because he has no conception of peculiarly moral blame. Whether she is right depends on whether one takes Aristotle in his discussion of the doctrine of the mean to be speaking of moral obligations, such as an obligation not to feel inappropriate fear and to stand one's ground for the sake of what is noble (see the third selection from Aristotle in this volume, as well as *Nicomachean Ethics* 3.7, which is not included here).

Anscombe has more respect for Hume: although he is a 'sophist', he opens up some new and significant issues (9–14, 38–41). One of these is the relation between 'facts' and moral judgements (Anscombe has in mind Hume's famous criticism of those who try to infer 'ought-statements' from 'is-statements'). Consider a case in which a person known to be innocent is punished. According to Anscombe, 'there can be absolutely no argument about the description of this as unjust' (39). Further, Anscombe believes that such actions should never even be considered, and that anyone who doubts this 'shows a corrupt mind' (41). And it is the readiness of English philosophers since Sidgwick not only to consider such actions, but to consider them justifiable, that Anscombe claims puts them in a category of their own (27–32). Again, her history is doubtful. The question whether morality consisted only in impartial benevolence and could justify actions such as punishing the innocent was standard not only before Sidgwick but in ancient ethics (book 3 of Cicero's *De Officiis*, for example, written in 44 BCE, is on this very topic). Further, Anscombe's own view – that justice should be done whatever the consequences – was far from the standard view before Sidgwick. But her strong deontological position is certainly worth consideration.

---

[1] This paper was originally read to the Voltaire Society in Oxford.

History of Ethics – Essential Readings with Commentary, First Edition. Edited by Daniel Star and Roger Crisp.

Anscombe's position on the contrast between ancient and modern ethics is based not just on her reading of Aristotle, but on a general theory of the history and nature of the moral concepts (15–26). She claims that our notion of obligation arose from the Christian divine law conception of ethics and has no sense outside of that conception. The word 'ought', she suggests, has become a word of 'mere mesmeric force' (24). As noted earlier, one might claim to find our notion of 'ought' in Aristotle (the impersonal verb he uses in the doctrine of the mean – *dei* – has standardly been translated as 'one ought'). Further, modern moral philosophers such as Sidgwick or Ross might claim that, regardless of the origin of the notion of 'ought', all they meant by the claim that one ought to φ is that one has strongest or overall reason to φ. But Anscombe's attempt to understand the history of our moral concepts and the relation of that history to their current sense is both significant and welcome.

Anscombe does not recommend entirely eschewing ethics in favour of psychology. We can make judgements using what Bernard Williams has called the 'thick' concepts, such as 'justice' or 'courage', rather than thin concepts such as 'ought' (26). It is important to note that adopting that recommendation will leave questions about justice, punishing the innocent, and so on, entirely open. Some might argue, for example, that benevolence can conflict with justice, and in extreme circumstances override it.

One of Anscombe's most important contributions to philosophy was her theory of intention. This essay raises some deep questions about the role of intention in ethics, and in particular the distinction between intending and foreseeing (30–32; see also the selection from Foot in this volume). Anscombe focuses in particular on the view that one is responsible for all the foreseen consequences of one's actions, whether one intended them or not. She offers the following example. A man is responsible for supporting a child. He is then offered a choice between being sent to prison or doing something disgraceful. If it makes no moral difference that withdrawing support from the child as a consequence of going to prison is a side-effect rather than something he intends, then he may well decide to do the disgraceful thing. Anscombe's own view is that one is responsible only for what one intends, and not the foreseen but unintended consequences of what one does. This is the so-called 'doctrine of double effect', and it is easy to see how it lines up with her theory of justice. If I am given a choice between intentionally punishing some innocent person (even if the punishment is not all that severe) or refraining from doing so with the foreseen consequence that millions of people will die slowly and in agony, Anscombe believes it is clear – if these really are my only options – that I should choose the second.

I will begin by stating three theses which I present in this paper. The first is that it is not profitable for us at present to do moral philosophy; that should be laid aside at any rate until we have an adequate philosophy of psychology, in which we are conspicuously lacking. The second is that the concepts of obligation, and duty – *moral* obligation and *moral* duty, that is to say – and of what is *morally* right and wrong, and of the *moral* sense of "ought," ought to be jettisoned if this is psychologically possible; because they are survivals, or derivatives from survivals, from an earlier conception of ethics which no longer generally survives, and are only harmful without it. My third thesis is that the differences between the well-known English writers on moral philosophy from Sidgwick to the present day are of little importance.

Anyone who has read Aristotle's *Ethics* and has also read modern moral philosophy must have been struck by the great contrasts between them. The concepts which are prominent among the moderns seem to be lacking, or at any rate buried or far in the background, in Aristotle. Most noticeably, the term "moral" itself, which we have by direct inheritance from Aristotle, just doesn't seem to fit, in its modern sense, into an account of Aristotelian ethics. Aristotle distinguishes virtues as moral and intellectual. Have some of what he calls "intellectual" virtues what *we* should call a "moral" aspect? It would seem so; the criterion is presumably that a failure in an "intellectual" virtue – like that of having good judgment in calculating how to bring about something useful, say in municipal government – may be *blameworthy*. But – it may reasonably be asked – cannot *any* failure be made a matter of blame or reproach? Any derogatory criticism, say of the workmanship of a product or the design of a machine, can be called blame or reproach. So we want to put in the word "morally" again: sometimes such a failure may be *morally* blameworthy, sometimes not. Now has Aristotle got this idea of *moral* blame, as opposed to any other? If he has, why isn't it more central? There are some mistakes, he says, which are causes, not of involuntariness in actions, but of scoundrelism, and for which a man is blamed. Does this mean that there is a *moral* obligation not to make certain intellectual mistakes? Why doesn't he discuss obligation in general, and this obligation in particular? If someone professes to be expounding Aristotle and talks in a modern fashion about "moral" such-and-such, he must be very imperceptive if he does not constantly feel like someone whose jaws have somehow got out of alignment: the teeth don't come together in a proper bite.

We cannot, then, look to Aristotle for any elucidation of the modern way of talking about "moral" goodness, obligation, etc. And all the best-known writers on ethics in modern times, from Butler to Mill, appear to me to have faults as thinkers on the subject which make it impossible to hope for any direct light on it from them. I will state these objections with the brevity which their character makes possible.

Butler exalts conscience, but appears ignorant that a man's conscience may tell him to do the vilest things.

Hume defines "truth" in such a way as to exclude ethical judgments from it, and professes that he has proved that they are so excluded. He also implicitly defines "passion" in such a way that aiming at anything is having a passion. His objection to passing from "is" to "ought" would apply equally to passing from "is" to "owes" or from "is" to "needs." (However, because of the historical situation, he has a point here, which I shall return to.)

Kant introduces the idea of "legislating for oneself," which is as absurd as if in these days, when majority votes command great respect, one were to call each reflective decision a man made a *vote* resulting in a majority, which as a matter of proportion is overwhelming, for it is always 1–0. The concept of legislation requires superior power in the legislator. His own rigoristic convictions on the subject of lying were so intense that it never occurred to him that a lie could be relevantly described as anything but just a lie (e.g. as "a lie in such-and-such circumstances"). His rule about universalizable maxims is useless without stipulations as to what shall count as a relevant description of an action with a view to constructing a maxim about it.

Bentham and Mill do not notice the difficulty of the concept "pleasure." They are often said to have gone wrong through committing the "naturalistic fallacy"; but this charge does not impress me, because I do not find accounts of it coherent. But the other point – about pleasure – seems to me a fatal objection from the very outset. The ancients found this concept pretty baffling. It reduced Aristotle to sheer babble about "the bloom on the cheek of youth" because, for good reasons, he wanted to make it out both identical with and different from the pleasurable activity. Generations of modern philosophers found this concept quite unperplexing, and it reappeared in the literature as a problematic one only a year or two ago when Ryle wrote about it. The reason is simple: since Locke, pleasure was taken to be some sort of internal impression. But it was superficial, if that was the right account of it, to make it the point of actions. One might adapt something Wittgenstein said about "meaning" and say "Pleasure cannot be an internal impression, for no internal impression could have the consequences of pleasure."

Mill also, like Kant, fails to realize the necessity for stipulation as to relevant descriptions, if his theory is to have content. It did not occur to him that acts of murder and theft could be otherwise described. He holds that where a proposed action is of such a kind as to fall under some one principle established on grounds of utility, one must go by that; where it falls under none or several, the several suggesting contrary views of the action, the thing to do is to calculate particular consequences. But pretty well any action can be so described as to make it fall under a variety of principles of utility (as I shall say for short) if it falls under any.

I will now return to Hume. The features of Hume's philosophy which I have mentioned, like many other features of it, would incline me to think that Hume was a mere – brilliant – sophist; and his procedures are certainly sophistical. But I am forced, not to reverse, but to add to, this judgment by a peculiarity of Hume's philosophizing: namely that although he reaches his conclusions – with which he is in love – by sophistical methods, his considerations constantly open up very deep and important problems. It is often the case that in the act of exhibiting the sophistry one finds oneself noticing matters which deserve a lot of exploring: the obvious stands in need of investigation as a result of the points that Hume pretends to have made. In this, he is unlike, say, Butler. It was already well known that conscience could dictate vile actions; for Butler to have written disregarding this does not open up any new topics for us. But with Hume it is otherwise: hence he is a very profound and great philosopher, in spite of his sophistry. For example:

Suppose that I say to my grocer "Truth consists in *either* relations of ideas, as that 20s. = £1, *or* matters of fact, as that I ordered potatoes, you supplied them, and you sent me a bill. So it doesn't apply to such a proposition as that I *owe* you such-and-such a sum."

Now if one makes this comparison, it comes to light that the relation of the facts mentioned to the description "X owes Y so much money" is an interesting one, which I will call that of being "brute relative to" that description. Further, the "brute" facts mentioned here themselves have descriptions relatively to which *other* facts are "brute" – as, e.g., *he had potatoes carted to my house* and *they were left there* are brute facts relative to "he supplied me with potatoes." And the fact *X owes Y money* is in turn "brute" relative to other descriptions – e.g. "X is solvent." Now the relation of "relative bruteness" is a complicated one. To mention a few points: if xyz is a set of facts brute relative to a description A, then xyz is a set out of a range some set among which holds if A holds; but the holding of some set among these does not necessarily entail A, because exceptional circumstances can always make a difference; and what are exceptional circumstances relatively to A can generally only be explained by giving a few diverse examples, and *no* theoretically adequate provision can be made for exceptional circumstances, since a further special context can theoretically always be imagined that would reinterpret any special context. Further, though in normal circumstances, xyz would be a justification for A, that is not to say that A just comes to the same as "xyz"; and also there is apt to be an institutional context which gives its point to the description A, of which institution A is of course not itself a description. (E.g. the statement that I give someone a shilling is not a description of the institution of money or of the currency of this country.) Thus, though it would be ludicrous to pretend that there can be no such thing as a transition from, e.g., "is" to "owes," the character of the transition is in fact rather interesting and comes to light as a result of reflecting on Hume's arguments.[1]

That I owe the grocer such-and-such a sum would be one of a set of facts which would be "brute" in relation to the description "I am a bilker." "Bilking" is of course a species of "dishonesty" or "injustice." (Naturally the consideration will not have any effect on my actions unless I want to commit or avoid acts of injustice.)

So far, in spite of their strong associations, I conceive "bilking," "injustice" and "dishonesty" in a merely "factual" way. That I can do this for "bilking" is obvious enough; "justice" I have no idea how to define, except that its sphere is that of actions which relate to someone else, but "injustice," its defect, can for the moment be offered as a generic name covering various species. E.g.: "bilking," "theft" (which is relative to whatever property institutions exist), "slander," "adultery," "punishment of the innocent."

In present-day philosophy an explanation is required how an unjust man is a bad man, or an unjust action a bad one; to give such an explanation belongs to ethics; but it cannot even be begun until we are equipped with a sound philosophy of psychology. For the proof that an unjust man is a bad man would require a positive account of justice as a "virtue." This part of the subject-matter of ethics is, however, completely closed to us until we have an account of what *type of characteristic* a virtue is – a problem, not of ethics, but of conceptual analysis – and how it relates to the actions in which it is instanced: a matter which I think Aristotle did not succeed in really making clear. For this we certainly need an account at least of what a human action is at all, and how its description as "doing such-and-such" is affected by its motive and by the intention or intentions in it; and for this an account of such concepts is required.

---

[1] The above two paragraphs are an abstract of a paper "On Brute Facts": *Analysis* 18: 69–72 (1958).

The terms "should" or "ought" or "needs" relate to good and bad: e.g. machinery needs oil, or should or ought to be oiled, in that running without oil is bad for it, or it runs badly without oil. According to this conception, of course, "should" and "ought" are not used in a special "moral" sense when one says that a man should not bilk. (In Aristotle's sense of the term "moral" (ἠθικός), they are being used in connection with a *moral* subject-matter: namely that of human passions and (non-technical) actions.) But they have now acquired a special so-called "moral" sense – i.e. a sense in which they imply some absolute verdict (like one of guilty / not guilty on a man) on what is described in the "ought" sentences used in certain types of context: not merely the contexts that *Aristotle* would call "moral" – passions and actions – but also some of the contexts that he would call "intellectual."

The ordinary (and quite indispensable) terms "should," "needs," "ought," "must" – acquired this special sense by being equated in the relevant contexts with "is obliged," or "is bound," or "is required to," in the sense in which one can be obliged or bound by law, or something can be required by law.

How did this come about? The answer is in history: between Aristotle and us came Christianity, with its *law* conception of ethics. For Christianity derived its ethical notions from the Torah. (One might be inclined to think that a law conception of ethics could arise only among people who accepted an allegedly divine positive law; that this is not so is shown by the example of the Stoics, who also thought that whatever was involved in conformity to human virtues was required by divine law.)

In consequence of the dominance of Christianity for many centuries, the concepts of being bound, permitted, or excused became deeply embedded in our language and thought. The Greek word "ἁμαρτάνειν," the aptest to be turned to that use, acquired the sense "sin," from having meant "mistake," "missing the mark," "going wrong." The Latin *peccatum* which roughly corresponded to ἁμάρτημα was even apter for the sense "sin," because it was already associated with "culpa" – "guilt" – a juridical notion. The blanket term "illicit," "unlawful," meaning much the same as our blanket term "wrong," explains itself. It is interesting that Aristotle did not have such a blanket term. He has blanket terms for wickedness – "villain," "scoundrel"; but of course a man is not a villain or a scoundrel by the performance of one bad action, or a few bad actions. And he has terms like "disgraceful," "impious"; and specific terms signifying defect of the relevant virtue, like "unjust"; but no term corresponding to "illicit." The extension of this term (i.e. the range of its application) could be indicated in his terminology only by a quite lengthy sentence: that is "illicit" which, whether it is a thought or a consented-to passion or an action or an omission in thought or action, is something contrary to one of the virtues the lack of which shows a man to be bad *qua* man. That formulation would yield a concept co-extensive with the concept "illicit."

To have a *law* conception of ethics is to hold that what is needed for conformity with the virtues failure in which is the mark of being bad *qua* man (and not merely, say, *qua* craftsman or logician) – that what is needed for *this*, is required by divine law. Naturally it is not possible to have such a conception unless you believe in God as a law-giver; like Jews, Stoics, and Christians. But if such a conception is dominant for many centuries, and then is given up, it is a natural result that the concepts of "obligation," of being bound or required as by a law, should remain though they had lost their root; and if the word "ought" has become invested in certain contexts with the sense of "obligation," it too will remain to be spoken with a special emphasis and a special feeling in these contexts.

It is as if the notion "criminal" were to remain when criminal law and criminal courts had been abolished and forgotten. A Hume discovering this situation might conclude that there was a special sentiment, expressed by "criminal," which alone gave the word its sense. So Hume discovered the situation in which the notion "obligation" survived, and the notion "ought" was invested with that peculiar force having which it is said to be used in a "moral" sense, but in which the belief in divine law had long since been abandoned: for it was substantially given up among Protestants at the time of the Reformation.[2] The situation, if I am right, was the interesting one of the survival of a concept outside the framework of thought that made it a really intelligible one.

When Hume produced his famous remarks about the transition from "is" to "ought," he was, then, bringing together several quite different points. One I have tried to bring out by my remarks on the transition from "is" to "owes" and on the relative "bruteness" of facts. It would be possible to bring out a different point by enquiring about the transition from "is" to "needs"; from the characteristics of an organism to the environment that it needs, for example. To say that it needs that environment is not to say, e.g., that you want it to have that environment,

---

[2] They did not deny the existence of divine law; but their most characteristic doctrine was that it was given, not to be obeyed, but to show man's incapacity to obey it, even by grace; and this applied not merely to the ramified prescriptions of the Torah, but to the requirements of "natural divine law." Cf. in this connection the decree of Trent against the teaching that Christ was only to be trusted in as mediator, not obeyed as legislator.

but that it won't flourish unless it has it. Certainly, it all depends whether you *want* it to flourish! as Hume would say. But what "all depends" on whether you want it to flourish is whether the fact that it needs that environment, or won't flourish without it, has the slightest influence on your actions, Now *that* such-and-such "ought" to be or "is needed" is supposed to have an influence on your actions: from which it seemed natural to infer that to judge that it "ought to be" was in fact to grant what you judged "ought to be" influence on your actions. And no amount of truth as to what *is* the case could possibly have a logical claim to have influence on your actions. (It is not judgment as such that sets us in motion; but our judgment on how to get or do something we *want*.) Hence it *must* be impossible to infer "needs" or "ought to be" from "is." But in the case of a plant, let us say, the inference from "is" to "needs" is certainly not in the least dubious. It is interesting and worth examining; but not at all fishy. Its interest is similar to the interest of the relation between brute and less brute facts: these relations have been very little considered. And while you can contrast "what it needs" with "what it's got" – like contrasting *de facto* and *de jure* – that does not make its needing this environment less of a "truth."

Certainly in the case of what the plant needs, the thought of a need will only affect action if you want the plant to flourish. Here, then, there is no necessary connection between what you can judge the plant "needs" and what you want. But there is some sort of necessary connection between what you think *you* need, and what you want. The connection is a complicated one; it is possible *not* to want something that you judge you need. But, e.g., it is not possible never to want *anything* that you judge you need. This, however, is not a fact about the meaning of the word "to need," but about the phenomenon of *wanting*. Hume's reasoning, we might say, in effect, leads one to think it must be about the word "to need," or "to be good for."

Thus we find two problems already wrapped up in the remark about a transition from "is" to "ought"; now supposing that we had clarified the "relative bruteness" of facts on the one hand, and the notions involved in "needing," and "flourishing" on the other – there would *still* remain a third point. For, following Hume, someone might say: Perhaps you have made out your point about a transition from "is" to "owes" and from "is" to "needs": but only at the cost of showing "owes" and "needs" sentences to express a *kind* of truths, a *kind* of facts. And it remains impossible to infer "*morally ought*" from "is" sentences.

This comment, it seems to me, would be correct. This word "ought," having become a word of mere mesmeric force, could not, in the character of having that force, be inferred from anything whatever. It may be objected that it could be inferred from other "morally ought" sentences: but that cannot be true. The appearance that this is so is produced by the fact that we say "All men are ϕ" and "Socrates is a man" implies "Socrates is ϕ." But here "ϕ" is a dummy predicate. We mean that if you substitute a real predicate for "ϕ" the implication is valid. A real predicate is required; not just a word containing no intelligible thought: a word retaining the suggestion of force, and apt to have a strong psychological effect, but which no longer signifies a real concept at all.

For its suggestion is one of a *verdict* on my action, according as it agrees or disagrees with the description in the "ought" sentence. And where one does not think there is a judge or a law, the notion of a verdict may retain its psychological effect, but not its meaning. Now imagine that just this word "verdict" *were* so used – with a characteristically solemn emphasis – as to retain its atmosphere but not its meaning, and someone were to say: "For a *verdict*, after all, you need a law and a judge." The reply might be made: "Not at all, for if there were a law and a judge who gave a verdict, the question for us would be whether accepting that verdict is something that there is a *Verdict* on." This is an analogue of an argument which is so frequently referred to as decisive: If someone does have a divine law conception of ethics, all the same, he has to agree that he has to have a judgment that he *ought* (morally ought) to obey the divine law; so his ethic is in exactly the same position as any other: he merely has a "practical major premise"[3]: "Divine law ought to be obeyed" where someone else has, e.g., "The greatest happiness principle ought to be employed in all decisions."

I should judge that Hume and our present-day ethicists had done a considerable service by showing that no content could be found in the notion "morally ought"; if it were not that the latter philosophers try to find an alternative (very fishy) content and to retain the psychological force of the term. It would be most reasonable to drop it. It has no reasonable sense outside a law conception of ethics; they are not going to maintain such a conception; and you can do ethics without it, as is shown by the example of Aristotle. It would be a great improvement if, instead of "morally wrong," one always named a genus such as "untruthful," "unchaste," "unjust." We should no longer ask whether doing something was "wrong," passing directly from some description of an action to this notion; we should ask whether, e.g., it was unjust; and the answer would sometimes be clear at once.

---

[3] As it is absurdly called. Since major premise = premise containing the term which is predicate in the conclusion, it is a solecism to speak of it in the connection with practical reasoning.

I now come to the epoch in modern English moral philosophy marked by Sidgwick. There is a startling change that seems to have taken place between Mill and Moore. Mill assumes, as we saw, that there is no question of calculating the particular consequences of an action such as murder or theft; and we saw too that his position was stupid, because it is not at all clear how an action *can* fall under just one principle of utility. In Moore and in subsequent academic moralists of England we find it taken to be pretty obvious that "the right action" is the action which produces the best possible consequences (reckoning among consequences the intrinsic values ascribed to certain kinds of act by some "Objectivists"[4]). Now it follows from this that a man does well, subjectively speaking, if he acts for the best in the particular circumstances according to his judgment of the total consequences of this particular action. I say that this follows, not that any philosopher has said precisely that. For discussion of these questions can of course get extremely complicated: e.g. it can be doubted whether "such-and-such is the right action" is a satisfactory formulation, on the grounds that things have to exist to have predicates – so perhaps the best formulation is "I am obliged"; or again, a philosopher may deny that "right" is a "descriptive" term, and then take a roundabout route through linguistic analysis to reach a view which comes to the same thing as "the right action is the one productive of the best consequences" (e.g. the view that you frame your "principles" to effect the end you choose to pursue, the connexion between "choice" and "best" being supposedly such that choosing reflectively means that you choose how to act so as to produce the best consequences); further, the roles of what are called "moral principles" and of the "motive of duty" have to be described; the differences between "good" and "morally good" and "right" need to be explored, the special characteristics of "ought" sentences investigated. Such discussions generate an appearance of significant diversity of views where what is really significant is an overall similarity. The overall similarity is made clear if you consider that every one of the best known English academic moral philosophers has put out a philosophy according to which, e.g., it is not possible to hold that it cannot be right to kill the innocent as a means to any end whatsoever and that someone who thinks otherwise is in error. (I have to mention both points; because Mr. Hare, for example, while teaching a philosophy which would encourage a person to judge that killing the innocent would be what he "ought" to choose for over-riding purposes, would also teach, I think, that if a man chooses to make avoiding killing the innocent for any purpose his "supreme practical principle," he cannot be impugned for error: that just is his "principle." But with that qualification, I think it can be seen that the point I have mentioned holds good of every single English academic moral philosopher since Sidgwick.) Now this is a significant thing: for it means that all these philosophies are quite incompatible with the Hebrew-Christian ethic. For it has been characteristic of that ethic to teach that there are certain things forbidden whatever *consequences* threaten, such as: choosing to kill the innocent for any purpose, however good; vicarious punishment; treachery (by which I mean obtaining a man's confidence in a grave matter by promises of trustworthy friendship and then betraying him to his enemies); idolatry; sodomy; adultery; making a false profession of faith. The prohibition of certain things simply in virtue of their description as such-and-such identifiable kinds of action, regardless of any further consequences, is certainly not the whole of the Hebrew-Christian ethic; but it is a noteworthy feature of it; and if every academic philosopher since Sidgwick has written in such a way as to exclude this ethic, it would argue a certain provinciality of mind not to see this incompatibility as the most important fact about these philosophers, and the differences between them as somewhat trifling by comparison.

It is noticeable that none of these philosophers displays any consciousness that there is such an ethic, which he is contradicting: it is pretty well taken for obvious among them all that a prohibition such as that on murder does not operate in face of some consequences. But of course the strictness of the prohibition has as its point *that you are not to be tempted by fear or hope of consequences.*

If you notice the transition from Mill to Moore, you will suspect that it was made somewhere by someone; Sidgwick will come to mind as a likely name; and you will in fact find it going on, almost casually, in him. He is rather a dull author; and the important things in him occur in asides and footnotes and small bits of argument which are not concerned with his grand classification of the "methods of ethics." A divine law theory of ethics is reduced to an insignificant variety by a footnote telling us that "the best theologians" (God knows whom he meant) tell us that God is to be obeyed in his capacity of a *moral* being, ἢ φορτικός ὁ ἔπαινος; one seems to hear Aristotle saying: "Isn't the praise vulgar?"[5] – But Sidgwick *is* vulgar in that kind of way: he thinks, for example, that humility consists in underestimating your own merits – i.e. in a species of untruthfulness; and

[4] Oxford Objectivists of course distinguish between "consequences" and "intrinsic values" and so produce a misleading appearance of not being "consequentialists." But they do not hold – and Ross explicitly denies – that the gravity of, e.g., procuring the condemnation of the innocent is such that it cannot be outweighed by, e.g., national interest. Hence their distinction is of no importance.

[5] E.N. 1178b16.

that the ground for having laws against blasphemy was that it was offensive to believers; and that to go accurately into the virtue of purity is to offend against its canons, a thing he reproves "medieval theologians" for not realizing.

From the point of view of the present enquiry, the most important thing about Sidgwick was his definition of intention. He defines intention in such a way that one must be said to intend any foreseen consequences of one's voluntary action. This definition is obviously incorrect, and I dare say that no one would be found to defend it now. He uses it to put forward an ethical thesis which would now be accepted by many people: the thesis that it does not make any difference to a man's responsibility for something that he foresaw, that he felt no desire for it, either as an end or as a means to an end. Using the language of intention more correctly, and avoiding Sidgwick's faulty conception, we may state the thesis thus: it does not make any difference to a man's responsibility for an effect of his action which he can foresee, that he does not intend it. Now this sounds rather edifying; it is I think quite characteristic of very bad degenerations of thought on such questions that they sound edifying. We can see what it amounts to by considering an example. Let us suppose that a man has a responsibility for the maintenance of some child. Therefore deliberately to withdraw support from it is a bad sort of thing for him to do. It would be bad for him to withdraw its maintenance because he didn't want to maintain it any longer; *and* also bad for him to withdraw it because by doing so he would, let us say, compel someone else to do something. (We may suppose for the sake of argument that compelling that person to do that thing is in itself quite admirable.) But now he has to choose between doing something disgraceful and going to prison; if he goes to prison, it will follow that he withdraws support from the child. By Sidgwick's doctrine, there is no difference in his responsibility for ceasing to maintain the child, between the case where he does it for its own sake or as a means to some other purpose, and when it happens as a foreseen and unavoidable consequence of his going to prison rather than do something disgraceful. It follows that he must weigh up the relative badness of withdrawing support from the child and of doing the disgraceful thing; and it may easily be that the disgraceful thing is in fact a less vicious action than intentionally withdrawing support from the child would be; if then the fact that withdrawing support from the child is a side effect of his going to prison does not make any difference to his responsibility, this consideration will incline him to do the disgraceful thing; which can still be pretty bad. And of course, once he has started to look at the matter in this light, the only reasonable thing for him to consider will be the consequences and not the intrinsic badness of this or that action. So that, given that he judges reasonably that no *great* harm will come of it, he can do a much more disgraceful thing than deliberately withdrawing support from the child. And if his calculations turn out in fact wrong, it will appear that he was not responsible for the consequences, because he did not foresee them. For in fact Sidgwick's thesis leads to its being quite impossible to estimate the badness of an action except in the light of *expected* consequences. But if so, then *you* must estimate the badness in the light of the consequences *you* expect; and so it will follow that you can exculpate yourself from the *actual* consequences of the most disgraceful actions, so long as you can make out a case for not having foreseen them. Whereas I should contend that a man is responsible for the bad consequences of his bad actions, but gets no credit for the good ones; and contrariwise is not responsible for the bad consequences of good actions.

The denial of *any* distinction between foreseen and intended consequences, as far as responsibility is concerned, was not made by Sidgwick in developing any one "method of ethics"; he made this important move on behalf of everybody and just on its own account; and I think it plausible to suggest that *this* move on the part of Sidgwick explains the difference between old-fashioned Utilitarianism and that *consequentialism*, as I name it, which marks him and every English academic moral philosopher since him. By it, the kind of consideration which would formerly have been regarded as a temptation, the kind of consideration urged upon men by wives and flattering friends, was given a status by moral philosophers in their theories.

It is a necessary feature of consequentialism that it is a shallow philosophy. For there are always borderline cases in ethics. Now if you are either an Aristotelian, or a believer in divine law, you will deal with a borderline case by considering whether doing such-and-such in such-and-such circumstances is, say, murder, or is an act of injustice; and according as you decide it is or it isn't, you judge it to be a thing to do or not. This would be the method of casuistry; and while it may lead you to stretch a point on the circumference, it will not permit you to destroy the centre. But if you are a consequentialist, the question "What is it right to do in such-and-such circumstances?" is a stupid one to raise. The casuist raises such a question only to ask "Would it be *permissible* to do so-and-so?" or "Would it be permissible *not* to do so-and-so?" Only if it would *not* be permissible *not* to do so-and-so could he say

"*This* would be *the* thing to do."[6] Otherwise, though he may speak *against* some action, he cannot prescribe any – for in an *actual* case, the circumstances (beyond the ones imagined) might suggest all sorts of possibilities, and you can't know in advance what the possibilities are going to be. Now the consequentialist has no footing on which to say "This would be permissible, this not"; because by his own hypothesis, it is the consequences that are to decide, and he has no business to pretend that he can lay it down what possible twists a man could give doing this or that; the most he can say is: a man must not *bring about* this or that; he has no right to say he will, in an actual case, bring about such-and-such unless he does so-and-so. Further, the consequentialist, in order to be imagining borderline cases at all, has of course to assume some sort of law or standard according to which this is a borderline case. Where then does he get the standard from? In practice the answer invariably is: from the standards current in his society or his circle. And it has in fact been the mark of all these philosophers that they have been extremely conventional; they have nothing in them by which to revolt against the conventional standards of their sort of people; it is impossible that they should be profound. But the chance that a whole range of conventional standards will be decent is small. – Finally, the point of considering hypothetical situations, perhaps very improbable ones, *seems* to be to elicit from yourself or someone else a hypothetical decision to do something of a bad kind. I don't doubt this has the effect of predisposing people – who will never get into the situations for which they have made hypothetical choices – to consent to similar bad actions, or to praise and flatter those who do them, so long as their crowd does so too, when the desperate circumstances imagined don't hold at all.

Those who recognize the origins of the notions of "obligation" and of the emphatic, "moral," *ought*, in the divine law conception of ethics, but who reject the notion of a divine legislator, sometimes look about for the possibility of retaining a law conception without a divine legislator. This search, I think, has some interest in it. Perhaps the first thing that suggests itself is the "norms" of a society. But just as one cannot be impressed by Butler when one reflects what conscience can tell people to do, so, I think, one cannot be impressed by this idea if one reflects what the "norms" of a society can be like. That legislation can be "for oneself" I reject as absurd; whatever you do "for yourself" may be admirable; but is not legislating. Once one sees this, one may say: I have to frame my own rules, and these are the best I can frame, and I shall go by them until I know something better: as a man might say "I shall go by the customs of my ancestors." Whether this leads to good or evil will depend on the *content* of the rules or of the customs of one's ancestors. If one is lucky it will lead to good. Such an attitude would be hopeful in this at any rate: it seems to have in it some Socratic doubt where, from having to fall back on such expedients, it should be clear that Socratic doubt is good; in fact rather generally it must be good for anyone to think "Perhaps in some way I can't see, I may be on a bad path, perhaps I am hopelessly wrong in some essential way". – The search for "norms" might lead someone to look for laws of nature, as if the universe were a legislator; but in the present day this is not likely to lead to good results: it might lead one to eat the weaker according to the laws of nature, but would hardly lead anyone nowadays to notions of justice; the pre-Socratic feeling about justice as comparable to the balance or harmony which kept things going is very remote to us.

There is another possibility here: "obligation" may be contractual. Just as we look at the law to find out what a man subject to it is required by it to do, so we look at a contract to find out what the man who has made it is required by it to do. Thinkers, admittedly remote from us, might have the idea of a *foedus rerum*, of the universe not as a legislator but as the embodiment of a contract. Then if you could find out what the contract was, you would learn your obligations under it. Now, you cannot be under a law unless it has been promulgated to you; and the thinkers who believed in "natural divine law" held that it was promulgated to every grown man in his knowledge of good and evil. Similarly you cannot be in a contract without having contracted, i.e. given signs of entering upon the contract. Just possibly, it might be argued that the use of language which one makes in the ordinary conduct of life amounts in some sense to giving the signs of entering into various contracts. If anyone had this theory, we should want to see it worked out. I suspect that it would be largely formal; it might be possible to construct a system embodying the law (whose status might be compared to that of "laws" of logic): "what's sauce for the goose is sauce for the gander," but hardly one descending to such particularities as the prohibition on murder or sodomy. Also, while it is clear that you can be subject to a law that you do not acknowledge and have not thought of as law, it does not seem reasonable to say that you can enter upon a contract without knowing that you are doing so; such ignorance is usually held to be destructive of the nature of a contract.

---

[6] Necessarily a rare case: for the positive precepts, e.g. "Honour your parents," hardly ever prescribe, and seldom even necessitate, any particular action.

It might remain to look for "norms" in human virtues: just as *man* has so many teeth, which is certainly not the average number of teeth men have, but is the number of teeth for the species, so perhaps the species *man*, regarded not just biologically, but from the point of view of the activity of thought and choice in regard to the various departments of life – powers and faculties and use of things needed – "has" such-and-such virtues: and this "man" with the complete set of virtues is the "norm," as "man" with, e.g., a complete set of teeth is a norm. But in *this* sense "norm" has ceased to be roughly equivalent to "law." In *this* sense the notion of a "norm" brings us nearer to an Aristotelian than a law conception of ethics. There is, I think, no harm in that; but if someone looked in this direction to give "norm" a sense, then he ought to recognize what has happened to the notion "norm," which he wanted to mean "law – without bringing God in" – it has ceased to mean "law" at all; and *so* the notions of "moral obligation," "the moral ought," and "duty" are best put on the Index, if he can manage it.

But meanwhile – is it not clear that there are several concepts that need investigating simply as part of the philosophy of psychology and, – as I should recommend – *banishing ethics totally* from our minds? Namely – to begin with: "action," "intention," "pleasure," "wanting." More will probably turn up if we start with these. Eventually it might be possible to advance to considering the concept "virtue"; with which, I suppose, we should be beginning some sort of a study of ethics.

I will end by describing the advantages of using the word "ought" in a non-emphatic fashion, and not in a special "moral" sense; of discarding the term "wrong" in a "moral" sense, and using such notions as "unjust."

It is possible, if one is allowed to proceed just by giving examples, to distinguish between the intrinsically unjust, and what is unjust given the circumstances. To arrange to get a man judicially punished for something which it can be clearly seen he has not done is intrinsically unjust. This might be done, of course, and often has been done, in all sorts of ways; by suborning false witnesses, by a rule of law by which something is "deemed" to be the case which is admittedly not the case as a matter of fact, and by open insolence on the part of the judges and powerful people when they more or less openly say: "A fig for the fact that you did not do it; we mean to sentence you for it all the same." What is unjust given, e.g., normal circumstances is to deprive people of their ostensible property without legal procedure, not to pay debts, not to keep contracts, and a host of other things of the kind. Now, the circumstances can clearly make a great deal of difference in estimating the justice or injustice of such procedures as these; and these circumstances may *sometimes* include expected consequences; for example, a man's claim to a bit of property can become a nullity when its seizure and use can avert some obvious disaster: as, e.g., if you could use a machine of his to produce an explosion in which it would be destroyed, but by means of which you could divert a flood or make a gap which a fire could not jump. Now this certainly does not mean that what would ordinarily be an act of injustice, but is not intrinsically unjust, can always be rendered just by a reasonable calculation of better consequences; far from it; but the problems that would be raised in an attempt to draw a boundary line (or boundary area) here are obviously complicated. And while there are certainly some general remarks which ought to be made here, and some boundaries that can be drawn, the decision on particular cases would for the most part be determined κατὰ τὸν ὀρθὸν λόγον "according to what's reasonable." – E.g. that *such-and-such* a delay of payment of a *such-and-such* debt to a person *so* circumstanced, on the part of a person *so* circumstanced, would or would not be unjust, is really only to be decided "according to what's reasonable"; and for this there can *in principle* be no canon other than giving a few examples. That is to say, while it is because of a big gap in philosophy that we can give no general account of the concept of virtue and of the concept of justice, but have to proceed, using the concepts, only by giving examples; still there is an area where it is not because of any gap, but is in principle the case, that there is no account except by way of examples: and that is where the canon is "what's reasonable": which of course is *not* a canon.

That is all I wish to say about what is just in some circumstances, unjust in others; and about the way in which expected consequences can play a part in determining what is just. Returning to my example of the intrinsically unjust: if a procedure *is* one of judicially punishing a man for what he is clearly understood not to have done, there can be absolutely no argument about the description of this as unjust. No circumstances, and no expected consequences, which do *not* modify the description of the procedure as one of judicially punishing a man for what he is known not to have done can modify the description of it as unjust. Someone who attempted to dispute this would only be pretending not to know what "unjust" means: for this is a paradigm case of injustice.

And here we see the superiority of the term "unjust" over the terms "morally right" and "morally wrong." For in the context of English moral philosophy since Sidgwick it appears legitimate to discuss whether it *might* be "morally right" in some circumstances to adopt that procedure; but it cannot be argued that the procedure would in any circumstances be just.

Now I am not able to do the philosophy involved – and I think that no one in the present situation of English philosophy *can* do the philosophy involved – but it is clear that a good man is a just man; and a just man is a man who habitually refuses to commit or participate in any unjust actions for fear of any consequences, or to obtain any advantage, for himself or anyone else. Perhaps no one will disagree. But, it will be said, what *is* unjust is sometimes determined by expected consequences; and certainly that is true. But there are cases where it is not: now if someone says, "I agree, but all this wants a lot of explaining," then he is right, and, what is more, the situation at present is that we can't do the explaining; we lack the philosophic equipment. But if someone really thinks, *in advance*,[7] that it is open to question whether such an action as procuring the judicial execution of the innocent should be quite excluded from consideration – I do not want to argue with him; he shows a corrupt mind.

In such cases our moral philosophers seek to impose a dilemma upon us. "If we have a case where the term 'unjust' applies purely in virtue of a factual description, can't one raise the question whether one sometimes conceivably ought to do injustice? If 'what is unjust' is determined by consideration of whether it is *right* to do so-and-so in such-and-such circumstances, then the question whether it is 'right' to commit injustice can't arise, just because 'wrong' has been built into the definition of injustice. But if we have a case where the description 'unjust' applies purely in virtue of the facts, without bringing 'wrong' in, then the question can arise whether one 'ought' perhaps to commit an injustice, whether it might not be 'right' to? And of course 'ought' and 'right' are being used in their *moral* senses here. Now either you must decide what is 'morally right' in the light of certain *other* 'principles,' or you make a 'principle' about *this* and decide that an injustice is never 'right'; but even if you do the latter you are going beyond the facts; you are making a decision that you will not, or that it is wrong to, commit injustice. But in either case, *if* the term 'unjust' is determined simply by the facts, it is not the term 'unjust' that determines that the term 'wrong' applies, but a decision that injustice is *wrong*, together with the diagnosis of the 'factual' description as entailing injustice. But the man who makes an absolute decision that injustice is 'wrong' has no footing on which to criticize someone who does *not* make that decision as judging falsely."

In this argument "wrong" of course is explained as meaning "morally wrong," and all the atmosphere of the term is retained while its substance is guaranteed quite null. Now let us remember that "morally wrong" is the term which is the heir of the notion "illicit," or "what there is an obligation *not* to do"; which belongs in a divine law theory or ethics. Here it really does add something to the description "unjust" to say there is an obligation not to do it; for what obliges is the divine law – as rules oblige in a game. So if the divine law obliges not to commit injustice by forbidding injustice, it really does add something to the description "unjust" to say there is an obligation not to do it. And it is because "morally wrong" is the heir of this concept, but an heir that is cut off from the family of concepts from which it sprang, that "morally wrong" *both* goes beyond the mere factual description "unjust" *and* seems to have no discernible content except a certain compelling force, which I should call purely psychological. And such is the force of the term that philosophers actually suppose that the divine law notion can be dismissed as making no essential difference even if it is held – *because* they think that a "practical principle" running "I *ought* (i.e. am morally obliged) to obey divine laws" is required for the man who believes in divine laws. But actually this notion of obligation is a notion which only operates in the context of law. And I should be inclined to congratulate the present-day moral philosophers on depriving "morally ought" of its now delusive appearance of content, if only they did not manifest a detestable desire to retain the atmosphere of the term.

It may be possible, if we are resolute, to discard the notion "morally ought," and simply return to the ordinary "ought", which, we ought to notice, is such an extremely frequent term of human language that it is difficult to imagine getting on without it. Now if we do return to it, can't it reasonably be asked whether one might ever need to commit injustice, or whether it won't be the best thing to do? Of course it can. And the answers will be various. One man – a philosopher – may say that since justice is a virtue, and injustice a vice, and virtues and vices are built up by the performances of the action in which they are instanced, an act of injustice will tend to make a man bad; and essentially the flourishing of a man *qua* man consists in his being good (e.g. in virtues); but for any X to which such terms apply, X needs what makes it flourish, so a man needs, or ought to perform, only virtuous actions; and

---

[7] If he thinks it in the concrete situation, he is of course merely a normally tempted human being. In discussion when this paper was read, as was perhaps to be expected, this case was produced: a government is required to have an innocent man tried, sentenced and executed under threat of a "hydrogen bomb war," It would seem strange to me to have much hope of so averting a war threatened by such men as made this demand. But the most important thing about the way in which cases like this are invented in discussions, is the assumption that only two courses are open: here, compliance and open defiance. No one can say in advance of such a situation what the possibilities are going to be – e.g. that there is none of stalling by a feigned willingness to comply, accompanied by a skillfully arranged "escape" of the victim.

even if, as it must be admitted may happen, he flourishes less, or not at all, in inessentials, by avoiding injustice, his life is spoiled in essentials by not avoiding injustice – so he still needs to perform only just actions. That is roughly how Plato and Aristotle talk; but it can be seen that philosophically there is a huge gap, at present unfillable as far as we are concerned, which needs to be filled by an account of human nature, human action, the type of characteristic a virtue is, and above all of human "flourishing." And it is the last concept that appears the most doubtful. For it is a bit much to swallow that a man in pain and hunger and poor and friendless is "flourishing," as Aristotle himself admitted. Further, someone might say that one at least needed to stay alive to "flourish." Another man unimpressed by all that will say in a hard case "What we need is such-and-such, which we won't get without doing this (which is unjust) – so this is what we ought to do." Another man, who does not follow the rather elaborate reasoning of the philosophers, simply says "I know it is in any case a disgraceful thing to say that one had better commit this unjust action." The man who believes in divine laws will say perhaps "It is forbidden, and however it looks, it cannot be to anyone's profit to commit injustice"; he like the Greek philosophers can think in terms of "flourishing." If he is a Stoic, he is apt to have a decidedly strained notion of what "flourishing consists" in; if he is a Jew or Christian, he need not have any very distinct notion: the way it will profit him to abstain from injustice is something that he leaves it to God to determine, himself only saying "It can't do me any good to go against his law." (But he also hopes for a great reward in a new life later on, e.g. at the coming of Messiah; but in this he is relying on special promises.)

It is left to modern moral philosophy – the moral philosophy of all the well-known English ethicists since Sidgwick – to construct systems according to which the man who says "We need such-and-such, and will only get it this way" *may* be a virtuous character: that is to say, it is left open to debate whether such a procedure as the judicial punishment of the innocent may not in some circumstances be the "right" one to adopt; and though the present Oxford moral philosophers would accord a man *permission* to "make it his principle" not to do such a thing, they teach a philosophy according to which the particular consequences of such an action *could* "morally" be taken into account by a man who was debating what to do; and if they were such as to conflict with his "ends," it might be a step in his moral education to frame a moral principle under which he "managed" (to use Mr. Nowell-Smith's phrase[8]) to bring the action; or it might be a new "decision of principle," making which was an advance in the formation of his moral thinking (to adopt Mr. Hare's conception), to decide: in such-and-such circumstances one ought to procure the judicial condemnation of the innocent. And that is my complaint.

[8] *Ethics*, p. 308.

6

The Problem of Abortion and the Doctrine of the Double Effect[1]

Philippa Foot

This article by Philippa Foot provides a particularly excellent and influential example of a type of philosophical exercise that became popular in normative ethics in the second half of the twentieth century. The method put to work here is, broadly speaking, the method of seeking 'reflective equilibrium' between ethical principles we find ourselves attracted to and a range of individual moral judgments or intuitions concerning cases (Rawls is responsible for the popularity of the term 'reflective equilibrium', but he is hardly the first to use the method he recommends). The cases in question are often fanciful, but the virtue of using such artificial cases is that they enable us to focus on particular features of situations that, in real-life cases, are often just part of a messy tableau of morally relevant features. Foot reminds us at certain junctures that the fanciful cases she is considering share crucial features with important real-life cases. Fictional cases of the kind she describes and reflects on have come to be known as 'thought experiments'. Foot says things that suggest that some of the thought experiments she discusses were already in circulation in Oxford, but she is rightly credited by later deontologists like Judith Jarvis Thomson and Frances Kamm for her discussion of what has come to be known as 'the trolley case' (some of Foot's other cases, such as the cases of the fat man in the cave and the life-saving serum, have also been much discussed).

At the beginning of her article, it appears as though Foot wishes to locate a defensible version of the doctrine of double effect, which, as we saw earlier in this volume, can be traced back to Aquinas. In fact, she ends up transforming this doctrine into a doctrine concerning how we might best compare benefits to people with harms to people, after also considering the importance in our ordinary moral thought of the distinction between doing and allowing. The topic of abortion is less relevant to the arguments of the article than the title suggests; its relevance is mainly just that the doctrine of double effect has, in the past, been put to use by Catholic thinkers in a way that Foot considers "sophistical" (she likely also found it repugnant, as many people do): according to this tradition, abortion in cases where it might be used to save the life of a woman carrying a fetus, is impermissible, even though it is permissible, in other cases, to make use of a medical procedure that aims to save a woman's life where this will foreseeably put an end to the life of her fetus (as a side effect). Foot believes there is something right about the doctrine, despite its (mis)application with respect to cases such as these, and she is determined to work out what it is.

We need the doctrine of double effect, or something similar to it, Foot says, in order to vindicate the different reactions we have to two cases that look similar. Intuitively, a judge may not frame an innocent person and order his execution in order to save five hostages that will be killed by a mob if he does not find this person guilty. Yet a driver of a trolley (or tram) may steer it away from the track it is on, where it is bound to kill five people, onto a separate track, in order that it might kill only one person (in another

[1] 'The Problem of Abortion and the Doctrine of the Double Effect' originally appeared in the *Oxford Review*, Number 5, 1967.

version of the trolley case, much discussed in the subsequent literature, we are to imagine that a bystander has a lever that can move the trolley from the first to the second track). The doctrine of double effect offers to explain the grounds of the moral difference here: in the first case, one person must be directly killed in order to bring about the end of saving five lives, whereas, in the second case, the one person who will lose his or her life will do so only as a side effect. If you are unsure what to make of the appeal to common-sense intuitions Foot and many others normative ethicists rely on with respect to pairs of cases such as these – intuitions that utilitarians, for instance, do not share, or, in any case, do not heed – you might find it interesting to consider whether you would rather have your own death be instrumental in the saving of five lives, or have it simply occur as a side effect, after five lives have already been saved (to rule out irrel-evant considerations, imagine that you are unconscious in both scenarios). Doing so suggests that our intuitions can shift depending on the perspective we take up.

In any case, Foot is interested in providing a principled vindication of the commonsense intuitions that she relies on. She first points out that the distinction between *doing* a certain act and *allowing* a certain outcome to be brought about is similar, but not identical to the distinction between direct and oblique intention (or, if you prefer, intentions proper, and foreseen side effects) that the doctrine of double effect relies on. Foot next notes that allowing a bad thing to occur, in the sense of not preventing it from occur-ring, sometimes strikes us as morally much preferable to purposely doing a bad thing. However, she takes it to be important to recognize that this is not always the case (an example from a different philosopher: if one allows a relative to drown in order to inherit money when one could easily save his or her life, this is clearly no more permissible than actively holding the relative underwater). This leads her to suggest that there is no getting around reliance on a ground-level appeal to duties here: in particular, we must distin-guish between 'positive' duties to *benefit* other people and 'negative' duties not to *harm* other people. To return to the earlier examples, the driver of the trolley is said to be weighing a negative duty (not to kill one innocent person) against a negative duty (not to kill five innocent people), while the judge is weighing a positive duty (to bring aid to people who might be killed by a mob) against a negative duty (not to kill an innocent person). No formula is provided for exactly how much weight we are to give to each kind of duty, and it might be too much to hope for one, but Foot takes there to be a crucial difference between positive and negative duties when it comes to how they may be weighed against each other. In sum, our duties not to harm are ('in general') much stronger than our duties to benefit.

One of the reasons why most of us feel puzzled about the problem of abortion is that we want, and do not want, to allow to the unborn child the rights that belong to adults and children. When we think of a baby about to be born it seems absurd to think that the next few minutes or even hours could make so radical a difference to its status; yet as we go back in the life of the foetus we are more and more reluctant to say that this is a human being and must be treated as such. No doubt this is the deepest source of our dilemma, but it is not the only one. For we are also confused about the general question of what we may and may not do where the interests of human beings conflict. We have strong intuitions about certain cases; saying, for instance, that it is all right to raise the level of education in our country, though statistics allow us to predict that a rise in the suicide rate will follow, while it is not all right to kill the feeble-minded to aid cancer research. It is not easy, however, to see the principles involved, and one way of throwing light on the abortion issue will be by setting up parallels involving adults or children once born. So we will be able to isolate the 'equal rights' issue and should be able to make some advance.

I shall not, of course, discuss all the principles that may be used in deciding how to act where the interests or rights of human beings conflict. What I want to do is to look at one particular theory, known as the 'doctrine of the double effect' which is invoked by Catholics in support of their views on abortion but supposed by them to apply elsewhere. As used in the abortion argument this doctrine has often seemed to non-Catholics to be a piece of complete sophistry. In the last number of the *Oxford Review* it was given short shrift by Professor Hart.[2] And yet this principle has seemed to some non-Catholics as well as to Catholics to stand as the only defence against decisions on other issues that are quite unacceptable. It will help us in our difficulty about abortion if this conflict can be resolved.

The doctrine of the double effect is based on a distinction between what a man foresees as a result of his voluntary action and what, in the strict sense, he intends. He intends in the strictest sense both those things that he aims at as ends and those that he aims at as means to his ends. The latter may be regretted in themselves but nevertheless desired for the sake of the end, as we may intend to keep dangerous lunatics confined for the sake of our safety. By contrast a man is said not strictly, or directly, to intend the foreseen consequences of his voluntary actions where these are neither the end at which he is aiming nor the means to this end. Whether the word 'intention' should be applied in both cases is not of course what matters: Bentham spoke of 'oblique intention', contrasting it with the 'direct intention' of ends and means, and we may as well follow his terminology. Everyone must recognise that some such distinction can be made, though it may be made in a number of different ways, and it is the distinction that is crucial to the doctrine of the double effect. The words 'double effect' refer to the two effects that an action may produce: the one aimed at, and the one foreseen but in no way desired. By 'the doctrine of the double effect' I mean the thesis that it is sometimes permissible to bring about by oblique intention what one may not directly intend. Thus the distinction is held to be relevant to moral decision in certain difficult cases. It is said for instance that the operation of hysterectomy involves the death of the foetus as the foreseen but not strictly or directly intended consequence of the surgeon's act, while other operations kill the child and count as the direct intention of taking an innocent life, a distinction that has evoked particularly bitter reactions on the part of non-Catholics. If you are permitted to bring about the death of the child, what does it matter how it is done? The doctrine of the double effect is also used to show why in another case, where a woman in labour will die unless a craniotomy operation is performed, the intervention is not to be condoned. There, it is said, we may not operate but must let the mother die. We foresee her death but do not directly intend it, whereas to crush the skull of the child would count as direct intention of its death.[3]

This last application of the doctrine has been queried by Professor Hart on the ground that the child's death is not strictly a means to saving the mother's life and should logically be treated as an unwanted but foreseen consequence by those who make use of the distinction between direct and oblique intention. To interpret the doctrine in this way is perfectly reasonable given the language that has been used; it would, however, make nonsense of it from the beginning. A certain event may be desired under one of its descriptions, unwanted under another, but we cannot treat these as two different events, one of which is aimed at and the other not. And even if it be argued that there are here two different events – the crushing of the child's skull and its death – the two are obviously much too close for an application of the doctrine of the double effect. To see how odd it would be to apply the principle like this we may consider the story, well known to philosophers, of the fat man stuck in the mouth of the cave.

[2] H. L. A. Hart, 'Intention and Punishment', *Oxford Review*, Number 4, Hilary 1967. Reprinted in Hart, *Punishment and Responsibility* (Oxford, 1968). I owe much to this article and to a conversation with Professor Hart, though I do not know whether he will approve of what follows.
[3] For discussions of the Catholic doctrine on abortion see Glanville Williams, *The Sanctity of Life and the Criminal Law* (New York, 1957); also N. St. John Stevas, *The Right to Life* (London, 1963).

A party of potholers have imprudently allowed the fat man to lead them as they make their way out of the cave, and he gets stuck, trapping the others behind him. Obviously the right thing to do is to sit down and wait until the fat man grows thin; but philosophers have arranged that flood waters should be rising within the cave. Luckily (luckily?) the trapped party have with them a stick of dynamite with which they can blast the fat man out of the mouth of the cave. Either they use the dynamite or they drown. In one version the fat man, whose head is *in* the cave, will drown with them; in the other he will be rescued in due course.[4] Problem: may they use the dynamite or not? Later we shall find parallels to this example. Here it is introduced for light relief and because it will serve to show how ridiculous one version of the doctrine of the double effect would be. For suppose that the trapped explorers were to argue that the death of the fat man might be taken as a merely foreseen consequence of the act of blowing him up. ('We didn't want to kill him…only to blow him into small pieces' or even '… only to blast him out of the cave.') I believe that those who use the doctrine of the double effect would rightly reject such a suggestion, though they will, of course, have considerable difficulty in explaining where the line is to be drawn. What is to be the criterion of 'closeness' if we say that anything very close to what we are literally aiming at counts as if part of our aim?

Let us leave this difficulty aside and return to the arguments for and against the doctrine, supposing it to be formulated in the way considered most effective by its supporters, and ourselves bypassing the trouble by taking what must on any reasonable definition be clear cases of 'direct' or 'oblique' intention.

The first point that should be made clear, in fairness to the theory, is that no one is suggesting that it does not matter what you bring about as long as you merely foresee and do not strictly intend the evil that follows. We might think, for instance, of the (actual) case of wicked merchants selling, for cooking, oil they knew to be poisonous and thereby killing a number of innocent people, comparing and contrasting it with that of some unemployed gravediggers, desperate for custom, who got hold of this same oil and sold it (or perhaps *they* secretly gave it away) in order to create orders for graves. They strictly (directly) intend the deaths they cause, while the merchants could say that it was not part of their *plan* that anyone should die. In morality, as in law, the merchants, like the gravediggers, would be considered as murderers; nor are the supporters of the doctrine of the double effect bound to say that there is the least difference between them in respect of moral turpitude. What they are committed to is the thesis that *sometimes* it makes a difference to the permissibility of an action involving harm to others that this harm, although foreseen, is not part of the agent's direct intention. An end such as earning one's living is clearly not such as to justify *either* the direct or oblique intention of the death of innocent people, but in certain cases one is justified in bringing about knowingly what one could not directly intend.

It is now time to say why this doctrine should be taken seriously in spite of the fact that it sounds rather odd, that there are difficulties about the distinction on which it depends, and that it seemed to yield one sophistical conclusion when applied to the problem of abortion. The reason for its appeal is that its opponents have often *seemed* to be committed to quite indefensible views. Thus the controversy has raged around examples such as the following. Suppose that a judge or magistrate is faced with rioters demanding that a culprit be found for a certain crime and threatening otherwise to take their own bloody revenge on a particular section of the community. The real culprit being unknown, the judge sees himself as able to prevent the bloodshed only by framing some innocent person and having him executed. Beside this example is placed another in which a pilot whose aeroplane is about to crash is deciding whether to steer from a more to a less inhabited area. To make the parallel as close as possible it may rather be supposed that he is the driver of a runaway tram which he can only steer from one narrow track on to another; five men are working on one track and one man on the other; anyone on the track he enters is bound to be killed. In the case of the riots the mob have five hostages, so that in both the exchange is supposed to be one man's life for the lives of five. The question is why we should say, without hesitation, that the driver should steer for the less occupied track, while most of us would be appalled at the idea that the innocent man could be framed. It may be suggested that the special feature of the latter case is that it involves the corruption of justice, and this is, of course, very important indeed. But if we remove that special feature, supposing that some private individual is to kill an innocent person and pass him off as the criminal we still find ourselves horrified by the idea. The doctrine of double effect offers us a way out of the difficulty, insisting that it is one thing to steer towards someone foreseeing that you will kill him and another to aim at his death as part of your plan. Moreover there is one very important element of good in what is here insisted. In real life it would hardly ever be certain that the

---

[4] It was Professor Hart who drew my attention to this distinction.

THE PROBLEM OF ABORTION AND THE DOCTRINE OF DOUBLE EFFECT

man on the narrow track would be killed. Perhaps he might find a foothold on the side of the tunnel and cling on as the vehicle hurtled by. The driver of the tram does *not* then leap off and brain him with a crowbar. The judge, however, needs the death of the innocent man for his (good) purposes. If the victim proves hard to hang he must see to it that he dies another way. To choose to execute him is to choose that this evil *shall come about*, and this must therefore count as a *certainty* in weighing up the good and evil involved. The distinction between direct and oblique intention is crucial here, and is of great importance in an uncertain world. Nevertheless this is no way to defend the doctrine of double effect. For the question is whether the difference between aiming at something and obliquely intending it is *in itself* relevant to moral decisions; not whether it is important when correlated with a difference of certainty in the balance of good and evil. Moreover we are particularly interested in the application of the doctrine of the double effect to the question of abortion, and no one can deny that in medicine there are sometimes certainties so complete that it would be a mere quibble to speak of the 'probable outcome' of this course of action or that. It is not, therefore, with a merely philosophical interest that we should put aside the uncertainty and scrutinise the examples to test the doctrine of the double effect. Why can we not argue from the case of the steering driver to that of the judge?

Another pair of examples poses a similar problem. We are about to give a patient who needs it to save his life a massive dose of a certain drug in short supply. There arrive, however, five other patients each of whom could be saved by one-fifth of that dose. We say with regret that we cannot spare our whole supply of the drug for a single patient, just as we should say that we could not spare the whole resources of a ward for one dangerously ill individual when ambulances arrive bringing in victims of a multiple crash. We feel bound to let one man die rather than many if that is our only choice. Why then do we not feel justified in killing people in the interests of cancer research or to obtain, let us say, spare parts for grafting on to those who need them? We can suppose, similarly, that several dangerously ill people can be saved only if we kill a certain individual and make a serum from his dead body. (These examples are not over-fanciful considering present controversies about prolonging the life of mortally ill patients whose eyes or kidneys are to be used for others.) Why cannot we argue from the case of the scarce drug to that of the body needed for medical purposes? Once again the doctrine of the double effect comes up with an explanation. In one kind of case but not the other we aim at the death of an innocent man.

A further argument suggests that if the doctrine of the double effect is rejected this has the consequences of putting us hopelessly in the power of bad men. Suppose for example that some tyrant should threaten to torture five men if we ourselves would not torture one. Would it be our duty to do so, supposing we believed him, because this would be no different from choosing to rescue five men from his torturers rather than one? If so, anyone who wants us to do something we think wrong has only to threaten that otherwise he himself will do something we think worse. A mad murderer, known to keep his promises, could thus make it our duty to kill some innocent citizen to prevent him from killing two. From this conclusion we are again rescued by the doctrine of the double effect. If we refuse, we foresee that the greater number will be killed but we do not intend it: it is he who intends (that is strictly or directly intends) the death of innocent persons; we do not.

At one time I thought that these arguments in favour of the doctrine of the double effect were conclusive, but I now believe that the conflict should be solved in another way. The clue that we should follow is that the strength of the doctrine seems to lie in the distinction it makes between what we *do* (equated with direct intention) and what we allow (thought of as obliquely intended). Indeed it is interesting that the disputants tend to argue about whether we are to be held responsible for what we allow as we are for what we do.[5] Yet it is not obvious that this is what they should be discussing, since the distinction between what one does and what one allows to happen is not the same as that between direct and oblique intention. To see this one has only to consider that it is possible *deliberately* to allow something to happen, aiming at it either for its own sake or as part of one's plan for obtaining something else. So one person might want another person dead and deliberately allow him to die. And again one may be said to *do* things that one does not aim at, as the steering driver would kill the man on the track. Moreover there is a large class of things said to be brought about rather than either done or allowed where either kind of intention is possible. So it is possible to *bring about* a man's death by getting him to sea in a leaky boat, and the intention of his death may be either direct or oblique.

Whatever it may, or may not, have to do with the doctrine of the double effect, the idea of *allowing* is worth looking into in this context. I shall leave aside the special case of giving permission, which involves the idea of

---

[5] See, e.g., J. Bennett, 'Whatever the Consequences', *Analysis*, January 1966, and G. E. M. Anscombe's reply in *Analysis*, June 1966. See also Miss Anscombe's 'Modern Moral Philosophy' in *Philosophy*, January 1958.

authority, and consider the two main divisions into which cases of allowing seem to fall. There is firstly the allowing which is forbearing to prevent. For this we need a sequence thought of as somehow already in train, and something that an agent could do to intervene. (The agent must be able to intervene, but does not do so.) So, for instance, he could warn someone, but *allows* him to walk into a trap. He could feed an animal but *allows* it to die tor lack of food. He could stop a leaking tap but *allows* the water to go on flowing. This is the case of allowing with which we shall be concerned, but the other should be mentioned. It is the kind of allowing which is roughly equivalent to *enabling*; the root idea being the removal of some obstacle which is, as it were, holding back a train of events. So someone may remove a plug and *allow* water to flow; open a door and *allow* an animal to get out; or give someone money and *allow* him to get back on his feet.

The first kind of allowing requires an omission, but there is no other general correlation between omission and allowing, commission and bringing about or doing. An actor who fails to turn up for a performance will generally spoil it rather than allow it to be spoiled. I mention the distinction between omission and commission only to set it aside.

Thinking of the first kind of allowing (forbearing to prevent), we should ask whether there is any difference, from the moral point of view, between what one does or causes and what one merely allows. It seems clear that on occasions one is just as bad as the other, as is recognised in both morality and law. A man may murder his child or his aged relatives by allowing them to die of starvation as by giving poison; he may also be convicted of murder on either account. In another case we would, however, make a distinction. Most of us allow people to die of starvation in India and Africa, and there is surely something wrong with us that we do; it would be nonsense, however, to pretend that it is only in law that we make the distinction between allowing people in the underdeveloped countries to die of starvation and sending them poisoned food. There is worked into our moral system a distinction between what we owe people in the form of aid and what we owe them in the way of non-interference. Salmond, in his *Jurisprudence*, expressed as follows the distinction between the two.

A positive right corresponds to a positive duty, and is a right that he on whom the duty lies shall do some positive act on behalf of the person entitled. A negative right corresponds to a negative duty, and is a right that the person bound shall refrain from some act which would operate to the prejudice of the person entitled. The former is a right to be positively benefited; the latter is merely a right not to be harmed.[6]

As a general account of rights and duties this is defective, since not all are so closely connected with benefit and harm. Nevertheless for our purposes it will do well. Let us speak of negative duties when thinking of the obligation to refrain from such things as killing or robbing, and of the positive duty, e.g., to look after children or aged parents. It will be useful, however, to extend the notion of positive duty beyond the range of things that are strictly called duties, bringing acts of charity under this heading. These are owed only in a rather loose sense, and some acts of charity could hardly be said to be *owed* at all, so I am not following ordinary usage at this point.

Let us now see whether the distinction of negative and positive duties explains why we see differently the action of the steering driver and that of the judge, of the doctors who withhold the scarce drug and those who obtain a body for medical purposes, of those who choose to rescue five men rather than one man from torture and those who are ready to torture the one man themselves in order to save five. In each case we have a conflict of duties, but what kind of duties are they? Are we, in each case, weighing positive duties against positive, negative against negative, or one against the other? Is the duty to refrain from injury, or rather to bring aid?

The steering driver faces a conflict of negative duties, since it is his duty to avoid injuring five men and also his duty to avoid injuring one. In the circumstances he is not able to avoid both, and it seems clear that he should do the least injury he can. The judge, however, is weighing the duty of not inflicting injury against the duty of bringing aid. He wants to rescue the innocent people threatened with death but can do so only by inflicting injury himself. Since one does not *in general* have the same duty to help people as to refrain from injuring them, it is not possible to argue to a conclusion about what he should do from the steering driver case. It is interesting that, even where the strictest duty of positive aid exists, this still does not weigh as if a negative duty were involved. It is not, for instance, permissible to commit a murder to bring one's starving children food. If the choice is between inflicting injury on one or many there seems only one rational course of action; if the choice is between aid to some at the cost of injury to others, and refusing to inflict the injury to bring the aid, the whole matter is open to dispute. So it is not inconsistent of us to think that the driver must steer for the road on which only one man stands while

---

[6] J. Salmond, *Jurisprudence*, 11th edition, p. 283.

the judge (or his equivalent) may not kill the innocent person in order to stop the riots. Let us now consider the second pair of examples, which concern the scarce drug on the one hand and on the other the body needed to save lives. Once again we find a difference based on the distinction between the duty to avoid injury and the duty to provide aid. Where one man needs a massive dose of the drug and we withhold it from him in order to save five men, we are weighing aid against aid. But if we consider killing a man in order to use his body to save others, we are thinking of doing him an injury to bring others aid. In an interesting variant of the model, we may suppose that instead of killing someone we deliberately let him die. (Perhaps he is a beggar to whom we are thinking of giving food, but then we say 'No, they need bodies for medical research.') Here it does seem relevant that in allowing him to die we are aiming at his death, but presumably we are inclined to see this as a violation of negative rather than positive duty. If this is right, we see why we are unable in either case to argue to a conclusion from the case of the scarce drug.

In the examples involving the torturing of one man or five men, the principle seems to be the same as for the last pair. If we are bringing aid (rescuing people about to be tortured by the tyrant), we must obviously rescue the larger rather than the smaller group. It does not follow, however, that we would be justified in inflicting the injury, or getting a third person to do so, in order to save the five. We may therefore refuse to be forced into acting by the threats of bad men. To refrain from inflicting injury ourselves is a stricter duty than to prevent other people from inflicting injury, which is not to say that the other is not a very strict duty indeed.

So far the conclusions are the same as those at which we might arrive following the doctrine of the double effect, but in others they will be different, and the advantage seems to be all on the side of the alternative. Suppose, for instance, that there are five patients in a hospital whose lives could be saved by the manufacture of a certain gas, but that this inevitably releases lethal fumes into the room of another patient whom for some reason we are unable to move. His death, being of no use to us, is clearly a side effect, and not directly intended. Why then is the case different from that of the scarce drug, if the point about that is that we foresaw but did not strictly intend the death of the single patient? Yet it surely is different. The relatives of the gassed patient would presumably be successful if they sued the hospital and the whole story came out. We may find it particularly revolting that someone should be *used* as in the case where he is killed or allowed to die in the interest of medical research, and the fact of *using* may even determine what we would decide to do in some cases, but the principle seems unimportant compared with our reluctance to bring such injury for the sake of giving aid.

My conclusion is that the distinction between direct and oblique intention plays only a quite subsidiary role in determining what we say in these cases, while the distinction between avoiding injury and bringing aid is very important indeed. I have not, of course, argued that there are no other principles. For instance it clearly makes a difference whether our positive duty is a strict duty or rather an act of charity: feeding our own children or feeding those in faraway countries. It may also make a difference whether the person about to suffer is one thought of as uninvolved in the threatened disaster, and whether it is his presence that constitutes the threat to the others. In many cases we find it very hard to know what to say, and I have not been arguing for any general conclusion such as that we may never, whatever the balance of good and evil, bring injury to one for the sake of aid to others, even when this injury amounts to death. I have only tried to show that even if we reject the doctrine of the double effect we are not forced to the conclusion that the size of the evil must always be our guide.

Let us now return to the problem of abortion, carrying out our plan of finding parallels involving adults or children rather than the unborn. We must say something about the different cases in which abortion might be considered on medical grounds.

First of all there is the situation in which nothing that can be done will save the life of child and mother, but where the life of the mother can be saved by killing the child. This is parallel to the case of the fat man in the mouth of the cave who is bound to be drowned with the others if nothing is done. Given the certainty of the outcome, as it was postulated, there is no serious conflict of interests here, since the fat man will perish in either case, and it is reasonable that the action that will save someone should be done. It is a great objection to those who argue that the direct intention of the death of an innocent person is never justifiable that the edict will apply even in this case. The Catholic doctrine on abortion must here conflict with that of most reasonable men. Moreover we would be justified in performing the operation whatever the method used, and it is neither a necessary nor a good justification of the special case of hysterectomy that the child's death is not directly intended, being rather a foreseen consequence of what is done. What difference could it make as to how the death is brought about?

Secondly we have the case in which it is possible to perform an operation which will save the mother and kill the child or kill the mother and save the child. This is parallel to the famous case of shipwrecked mariners who believed that they must throw someone overboard if their boat was not to founder in a storm, and to the other famous case of the two sailors, Dudley and Stephens, who killed and ate the cabin boy when adrift on the sea without food. Here again there is no conflict of interests so far as the decision to act is concerned; only in deciding whom to save. Once again it would be reasonable to act, though one would respect someone who held back from the appalling action either because he preferred to perish rather than do such a thing or because he held on past the limits of reasonable hope. In real life the certainties postulated by philosophers hardly ever exist, and Dudley and Stephens were rescued not long after their ghastly meal. Nevertheless if the certainty were absolute, as it might be in the abortion case, it would seem better to save one than none. Probably we should decide in favour of the mother when weighing her life against that of the unborn child, but it is interesting that, a few years later, we might easily decide it the other way.

The worst dilemma comes in the third kind of example where to save the mother we must kill the child, say by crushing its skull, while if nothing is done the mother will perish but the child can be safely delivered after her death. Here the doctrine of the double effect has been invoked to show that we may not intervene, since the child's death would be directly intended while the mother's would not. On a strict parallel with cases not involving the unborn we might find the conclusion correct though the reason given was wrong. Suppose, for instance, that in later life the presence of a child was certain to bring death to the mother. We would surely not think ourselves justified in ridding her of it by a process that involved its death. For in general we do not think that we can kill one innocent person to rescue another, quite apart from the special care that we feel is due to children once they have prudently got themselves born. What we would be prepared to do when a great many people were involved is another matter, and this is probably the key to one quite common view of abortion on the part of those who take quite seriously the rights of the unborn child. They probably feel that if *enough* people were involved one must be sacrificed, and they think of the mother's life against the unborn child's life as if it were many against one. But of course many people do not view it like this at all, having no inclination to accord to the foetus or unborn child anything like ordinary human status in the matter of rights. I have not been arguing for or against these points of view but only trying to discern some of the currents that are pulling us back and forth. The levity of the examples is not meant to offend.

7

Ethics: Inventing Right and Wrong

J. L. Mackie

Although Mackie's *Ethics* was published in 1977, the important contribution to metaethics made by Chapter 1 of the book has its origins in earlier work of his (especially 'A Refutation of Morals', published in 1946). Like Ayer, Mackie defends an anti-realist view of moral claims, but it is of a very different kind. Mackie, unlike Ayer, takes moral language at face value: in his view, it is clear that such language purports to describe some part of reality. The basic mistake of the realist is not that he or she is confused about what moral language is up to; rather, the mistake is to think that the moral facts and properties denoted when we make direct use of moral terms actually exist.

To understand this view, it can be helpful to think of examples of types of things that do not exist, but that people elsewhere or at other times have believed to exist. Witches, for instance, do not really exist (of course, the people who are incorrectly thought to be witches exist, but at least some of the properties that are taken to be essential to being a witch, e.g. being able to cast spells, are not genuine properties). People who believe in witches may take very seriously various methods for determining who is and who is not a witch, and such methods may trace natural patterns (e.g. an ability to float when forced into water). Still, such committed discussion of witches suffers from a presupposition failure, as there simply are no witches. Nonetheless, people who believe in witches are guided in their actions and conversations by such always-untrue beliefs, often in very significant ways. Similarly, in Mackie's view, the moral claim that we have categorical reason to treat all rational beings with respect, for instance, simply cannot be true, since there are no categorical moral reasons of any kind. And this is so even though people might succeed in using an untrue belief in propositions such as this one to guide their behavior.

The example just provided of a categorical reason is particularly to the point, since Mackie spends a good part of this chapter providing the reader with grounds for thinking that it is a central presupposition of our moral thought and talk, both historically and in present-day society, that reality contains categorical moral reasons: reasons that are prescriptive for all of us, regardless of what we happen to desire (see, especially, sections 5 through 7). It is precisely this presupposition that Mackie takes to be an error. In passing, he interestingly observes that not all talk of reasons and values must rely on such an error: in many domains ('the classing of wool, the grading of apples, the awarding of prizes at sheepdog trials …'), we agree on evaluative standards that have a restricted scope, and there can be true or false evaluative statements in such domains, as well as genuine hypothetical reasons that rest on the contingent desires that communities of people share (he even suggests talk of justice and injustice can be truthful when restricted to such a domain).

Having established to his satisfaction that we are committed to the existence of objective and prescriptive values (that is, values that provide us with categorical reasons), Mackie provides two main arguments for his 'error theory': the *argument from relativity* (sometimes called the argument from disagreement) and the *argument from queerness* (this second argument is sometimes divided into two arguments by

History of Ethics – Essential Readings with Commentary, First Edition. Edited by Daniel Star and Roger Crisp.
© 2020 John Wiley & Sons Ltd. Published 2020 by John Wiley & Sons Ltd.

commentators, but Mackie himself describes it as one argument with two parts). The argument from relativity takes off from the observation that moral codes across the world, and across time, vary enormously (although Mackie does not seem to worry that this great variation might extend to the very presuppositions of morality that he earlier claims to have isolated). A common error when people report this argument is to leave out a separate premise that Mackie takes to be crucial. To establish that there is no truth in some domain, it is not enough to point out that there is widespread disagreement in claims made concerning that domain; if it were, we would not be entitled to objectivism about the workings of the natural world (or, at least, nobody would have been entitled to be an objectivist regarding the workings of nature prior to the large degree of consensus produced by the modern scientific revolution). The essential separate premise is that the hypothesis that the variations in moral codes are to be explained by underlying differences in ways of life is significantly more likely to be true than the hypothesis that the variation is due to inadequacies and distortions in varying perceptions of objective values.

The ontological argument from queerness is said to have two parts: a metaphysical part and an epistemological part. If we take Mackie at his word that there is just one argument here, it is a little unclear how these two parts are to be related. Here is a plausible interpretation. One part of the argument is supposed to establish that it is highly improbable that moral properties exist, given how weird they would have to be, and the other part of the argument is supposed to establish that it is highly improbable that moral properties exist, given how weird our faculty for knowing them would have to be; the conclusion then consists of the conjunction of the first probability claim with the second probability claim, which is equivalent to the proposition that it is *extremely* improbable that moral properties exist. The epistemological part of the argument is discussed first, and it is worth comparing with Ayer's earlier comments about intuitionism. The metaphysical part of the argument makes use of an interesting observation regarding the supervenience of moral properties on natural properties: for any act that is wrong, it will seem true to say that it is wrong *because* of some underlying natural features; 'But', Mackie asks, 'what *in the world* is signified by this "because"?'

An important difference between Ayer and Mackie, distinct from the one we began with, is that Mackie is not merely happy for philosophers to continue to discuss normative ethical issues, but the remainder of his book consists of such discussion. He outlines a substantive account of morality that takes it to be something that we are in a position to purposely construct (see Chapter 5 of *Ethics*, in particular). Some contemporary philosophers influenced by Mackie sometimes refer to the type of error theory that allows one to go on with the moral enterprise as *fictionalism*. If morality is a fiction, it is clearly very different than other fictions (e.g. unlike most fictions, it has no single author, there appear to be more stringent constraints on how we might go about further constructing the fiction, and one will not stop acting as if it is true when one discovers it is a fiction). In any case, it is clear from the very first section of the first chapter that Mackie wishes to insist that acceptance of his 'second order' error theory should not be confused with the adoption of a 'first order' view that we ought not be moral (or that we are permitted to not be moral).

Chapter 1: The Subjectivity of Values

1. Moral Scepticism

There are no objective values. This is a bald statement of the thesis of this chapter, but before arguing for it I shall try to clarify and restrict it in ways that may meet some objections and prevent some misunderstanding.

The statement of this thesis is liable to provoke one of three very different reactions. Some will think it not merely false but pernicious; they will see it as a threat to morality and to everything else that is worthwhile, and they will find the presenting of such a thesis in what purports to be a book on ethics paradoxical or even outrageous. Others will regard it as a trivial truth, almost too obvious to be worth mentioning, and certainly too plain to be worth much argument. Others again will say that it is meaningless or empty, that no real issue is raised by the question whether values are or are not part of the fabric of the world. But, precisely because there can be these three different reactions, much more needs to be said.

The claim that values are not objective, are not part of the fabric of the world, is meant to include not only moral goodness, which might be most naturally equated with moral value, but also other things that could be more loosely called moral values or disvalues – rightness and wrongness, duty, obligation, an action's being rotten and contemptible, and so on. It also includes non-moral values, notably aesthetic ones, beauty and various kinds of artistic merit. I shall not discuss these explicitly, but clearly much the same considerations apply to aesthetic and to moral values, and there would be at least some initial implausibility in a view that gave the one a different status from the other.

Since it is with moral values that I am primarily concerned, the view I am adopting may be called moral scepticism. But this name is likely to be misunderstood: 'moral scepticism' might also be used as a name for either of two first order views, or perhaps for an incoherent mixture of the two. A moral sceptic might be the sort of person who says 'All this talk of morality is tripe,' who rejects morality and will take no notice of it. Such a person may be literally rejecting all moral judgements; he is more likely to be making moral judgements of his own, expressing a positive moral condemnation of all that conventionally passes for morality; or he may be confusing these two logically incompatible views, and saying that he rejects all morality, while he is in fact rejecting only a particular morality that is current in the society in which he has grown up. But I am not at present concerned with the merits or faults of such a position. These are first order moral views, positive or negative: the person who adopts either of them is taking a certain practical, normative, stand. By contrast, what I am discussing is a second order view, a view about the status of moral values and the nature of moral valuing, about where and how they fit into the world. These first and second order views are not merely distinct but completely independent: one could be a second order moral sceptic without being a first order one, or again the other way round. A man could hold strong moral views, and indeed ones whose content was thoroughly conventional, while believing that they were simply attitudes and policies with regard to conduct that he and other people held. Conversely, a man could reject all established morality while believing it to be an objective truth that it was evil or corrupt.

With another sort of misunderstanding moral scepticism would seem not so much pernicious as absurd. How could anyone deny that there is a difference between a kind action and a cruel one, or that a coward and a brave man behave differently in the face of danger? Of course, this is undeniable; but it is not to the point. The kinds of behaviour to which moral values and disvalues are ascribed are indeed part of the furniture of the world, and so are the natural, descriptive, differences between them; but not, perhaps, their differences in value. It is a hard fact that cruel actions differ from kind ones, and hence that we can learn, as in fact we all do, to distinguish them fairly well in practice, and to use the words 'cruel' and 'kind' with fairly clear descriptive meanings; but is it an equally hard fact that actions which are cruel in such a descriptive sense are to be condemned? The present issue is with regard to the objectivity specifically of value, not with regard to the objectivity of those natural, factual, differences on the basis of which differing values are assigned.

2. Subjectivism

Another name often used, as an alternative to 'moral scepticism', for the view I am discussing is 'subjectivism'. But this too has more than one meaning. Moral subjectivism too could be a first order, normative, view, namely that everyone really ought to do whatever he thinks he should. This plainly is a (systematic) first order view; on examination it soon ceases to be plausible, but that is beside the point, for it is quite independent of the second order thesis at present under consideration. What is more confusing is that different second order views compete for the name 'subjectivism'. Several of these are doctrines about the meaning of moral terms and moral statements. What is often called moral subjectivism is the doctrine that, for example, 'This action is right' *means* 'I approve of this action', or more generally that moral judgements are equivalent to reports of the speaker's own feelings or attitudes. But the view I am now discussing is to be distinguished in two vital respects from any such doctrine as this. First, what I have called moral scepticism is a negative doctrine, not a positive one: it says what there isn't, not what there is. It says that there do not exist entities or relations of a certain kind, objective values or requirements, which many people have believed to exist. Of course, the moral sceptic cannot leave it at that. If his position is to be at all plausible, he must give some account of how other people have fallen into what he regards as an error, and this account will have to include some positive suggestions about how values fail to be objective, about what has been mistaken for, or has led to false beliefs about, objective values. But this will be a development of his theory, not its core: its core is the negation. Secondly, what I have called moral scepticism is an ontological thesis, not a linguistic or conceptual one. It is not, like the other doctrine often called moral subjectivism, a view about the meanings of moral statements. Again, no doubt, if it is to be at all plausible, it will have to give some account of their meanings, and I shall say something about this in Section 7 […]. But this too will be a development of the theory, not its core.

It is true that those who have accepted the moral subjectivism which is the doctrine that moral judgements are equivalent to reports of the speaker's own feelings or attitudes have usually presupposed what I am calling moral scepticism. It is because they have assumed that there are no objective values that they have looked elsewhere for an analysis of what moral statements might mean, and have settled upon subjective reports. Indeed, if all our moral statements were such subjective reports, it would follow that, at least so far as we are aware, there are no objective moral values. If we were aware of them, we would say something about them. In this sense this sort of subjectivism entails moral scepticism. But the converse entailment does not hold. The denial that there are objective values does not commit one to any particular view about what moral statements mean, and certainly not to the view that they are equivalent to subjective reports. No doubt if moral values are not objective they are in some very broad sense subjective, and for this reason I would accept 'moral subjectivism' as an alternative name to 'moral scepticism'. But subjectivism in this broad sense must be distinguished from the specific doctrine about meaning referred to above. Neither name is altogether satisfactory: we simply have to guard against the (different) misinterpretations which each may suggest.

[…]

4. Is Objectivity a Real Issue?

[…]

R.M. Hare has said that he does not understand what is meant by 'the objectivity of values', and that he has not met anyone who does. We all know how to recognize the activity called 'saying, thinking it to be so, that some act is wrong', and he thinks that it is to this activity that the subjectivist and the objectivist are both alluding, though one calls it 'an attitude of disapproval' and the other 'a moral intuition': these are only different names for the same thing. […] He sums up his case thus: 'Think of one world into whose fabric values are objectively built; and think of another in which those values have been annihilated. And remember that in both worlds the people in them go on being concerned about the same things – there is no difference in the "subjective" concern which people have for things, only in their "objective" value. Now I ask, "What is the difference between the states of affairs in these two worlds?" Can any answer be given except "None whatever"?'

Now it is quite true that it is logically possible that the subjective concern, the activity of valuing or of thinking things wrong, should go on in just the same way whether there are objective values or not. But to say this is only to reiterate that there is a logical distinction between first and second order ethics: first order judgements are not necessarily affected by the truth or falsity of a second order view. But it does not follow, and it is not true, that there is no difference whatever between these two worlds. In the one there is something that backs up and validates some of the subjective concern which people have for things, in the other there is not. Hare's argument is similar to the positivist claim that there is no difference between a phenomenalist or Berkeleian world in which there are only minds and their ideas and the commonsense realist one in which there are also material things, because it is logically possible that people should have the same experiences in both. If we reject the positivism that would make the dispute between realists and phenomenalists a pseudo-question, we can reject Hare's similarly supported dismissal of the issue of the objectivity of values.

In any case, Hare has minimized the difference between his two worlds by considering only the situation where people already have just such subjective concern; further differences come to light if we consider how subjective concern is acquired or changed. If there were something in the fabric of the world that validated certain kinds of concern, then it would be possible to acquire these merely by finding something out, by letting one's thinking be controlled by how things were. But in the world in which objective values have been annihilated the acquiring of some new subjective concern means the development of something new on the emotive side by the person who acquires it, something that eighteenth-century writers would put under the head of passion or sentiment.

The issue of the objectivity of values needs, however, to be distinguished from others with which it might be confused. To say that there are objective values would not be to say merely that there are some things which are valued by everyone, nor does it entail this. There could be agreement in valuing even if valuing is just something that people do, even if this activity is not further validated. Subjective agreement would give inter-subjective values, but intersubjectivity is not objectivity. Nor is objectivity simply universalizability: someone might well be prepared to universalize his prescriptive judgements or approvals – that is, to prescribe and approve in just the same ways in all relevantly similar cases, even ones in which he was involved differently or not at all – and yet he could recognize that such prescribing and approving were his activities, nothing more. Of course if there were objective values they would presumably belong to *kinds* of things or actions or states of affairs, so that the judgements that reported them would be universalizable; but the converse does not hold.

A more subtle distinction needs to be made between objectivism and descriptivism. Descriptivism is again a doctrine about the meanings of ethical terms and statements, namely that their meanings are purely descriptive rather than even partly prescriptive or emotive or evaluative, or that it is not an essential feature of the conventional meaning of moral statements that they have some special illocutionary force, say of commending rather than asserting. It contrasts with the view that commendation is in principle distinguishable from description (however difficult they may be to separate in practice) and that moral statements have it as at least part of their meaning that they are commendatory and hence in some uses intrinsically action-guiding. But descriptive meaning neither entails nor is entailed by objectivity. Berkeley's subjective idealism about material objects would be quite compatible with the admission that material object statements have purely descriptive meaning. Conversely, the main tradition of European moral philosophy from Plato onwards has combined the view that moral values are objective with the recognition that moral judgements are partly prescriptive or directive or action-guiding. Values themselves have been seen as at once prescriptive and objective. In Plato's theory the Forms, and in particular the Form of the Good, are eternal, extra-mental, realities. They are a very central structural element in the fabric of the world. But it is held also that just knowing them or 'seeing' them will not merely tell men what to do but will ensure that they do it, overruling any contrary inclinations. The philosopher-kings in the *Republic* can, Plato thinks, be trusted with unchecked power because their education will have given them knowledge of the Forms. Being acquainted with the Forms of the Good and Justice and Beauty and the rest they will, by this knowledge alone, without any further motivation, be impelled to pursue and promote these ideals. Similarly, Kant believes that pure reason can by itself be practical, though he does not pretend to be able to explain how it can be so. Again, Sidgwick argues that if there is to be a science of ethics – and he assumes that there can be, indeed he defines ethics as 'the science of conduct' – what ought to be 'must in another sense have objective existence: it must be an object of knowledge and as such the same for all minds'; but he says that the affirmations of this science 'are also precepts', and he speaks of happiness as 'an end *absolutely* prescribed by reason'. Since many philosophers have thus held that values are objectively prescriptive, it is clear that the ontological doctrine of objectivism must be distinguished from descriptivism, a theory about meaning.

But perhaps when Hare says that he does not understand what is meant by 'the objectivity of values' he means that he cannot understand how values could be objective, he cannot frame for himself any clear, detailed, picture of what it would be like for values to be part of the fabric of the world. This would be a much more plausible claim; as we have seen, even Kant hints at a similar difficulty. Indeed, even Plato warns us that it is only through difficult studies spread over many years that one can approach the knowledge of the Forms. The difficulty of seeing how values could be objective is a fairly strong reason for thinking that they are not so; this point will be taken up in Section 9 but it is not a good reason for saying that this is not a real issue.

I believe that as well as being a real issue it is an important one. It clearly matters for general philosophy. It would make a radical difference to our metaphysics if we had to find room for objective values – perhaps something like Plato's Forms – somewhere in our picture of the world. It would similarly make a difference to our epistemology if it had to explain how such objective values are or can be known, and to our philosophical psychology if we had to allow such knowledge, or Kant's pure practical reason, to direct choices and actions. Less obviously, how this issue is settled will affect the possibility of certain kinds of moral argument. For example, Sidgwick considers a discussion between an egoist and a utilitarian, and points out that if the egoist claims that his happiness or pleasure is objectively desirable or good, the utilitarian can argue that the egoist's happiness 'cannot be more objectively desirable or more a good than the similar happiness of any other person: the mere fact … that *he is he* can have nothing to do with its objective desirability or goodness'. In other words, if ethics is built on the concept of objective goodness, then egoism as a first order system or method of ethics can be refuted, whereas if it is assumed that goodness is only subjective it cannot. But Sidgwick correctly stresses what a number of other philosophers have missed, that this argument against egoism would require the objectivity specifically of goodness: the objectivity of what ought to be or of what it is rational to do would not be enough. If the egoist claimed that it was objectively rational, or obligatory upon him, to seek his own happiness, a similar argument about the irrelevance of the fact that he is he would lead only to the conclusion that it was objectively rational or obligatory for each other person to seek *his* own happiness, that is, to a universalized form of egoism, not to the refutation of egoism. And of course insisting on the universalizability of moral judgements, as opposed to the objectivity of goodness, would yield only the same result.

5. Standards of Evaluation

One way of stating the thesis that there are no objective values is to say that value statements cannot be either true or false. But this formulation, too, lends itself to misinterpretation. For there are certain kinds of value statements which undoubtedly can be true or false, even if, in the sense I intend, there are no objective values. Evaluations of many sorts are commonly made in relation to agreed and assumed standards. The classing of wool, the grading of apples, the awarding of prizes at sheepdog trials, flower shows, skating and diving championships, and even the marking of examination papers are carried out in relation to standards of quality or merit which are peculiar to each particular subject-matter or type of contest, which may be explicitly laid down but which, even if they are nowhere explicitly stated, are fairly well understood and agreed by those who are recognized as judges or experts in each particular field. Given any sufficiently determinate standards, it will be an objective issue, a matter of truth and falsehood, how well any particular specimen measures up to those standards. Comparative judgements in particular will be capable of truth and falsehood: it will be a factual question whether this sheepdog has performed better than that one.

The subjectivist about values, then, is not denying that there can be objective evaluations relative to standards, and these are as possible in the aesthetic and moral fields as in any of those just mentioned. More than this, there is an objective distinction which applies in many such fields, and yet would itself be regarded as a peculiarly moral one: the distinction between justice and injustice. In one important sense of the word it is a paradigm case of injustice if a court declares someone to be guilty of an offence of which it knows him to be innocent. More generally, a finding is unjust if it is at variance with what the relevant law and the facts together require, and particularly if it is known by the court to be so. More generally still, any award of marks, prizes, or the like is unjust if it is at variance with the agreed standards for the contest in question: if one diver's performance in fact measures up better to the accepted standards for diving than another's, it will be unjust if the latter is awarded higher marks or the prize. In this way the justice or injustice of decisions relative to standards can be a thoroughly objective matter, though there may still be a subjective element in the interpretation or application of standards. But the statement that a certain decision is thus just or unjust will not be objectively prescriptive: in so far as it can be simply true it leaves open the question whether there is any objective requirement to do what is just and to refrain from what is unjust, and equally leaves open the practical decision to act in either way.

Recognizing the objectivity of justice in relation to standards, and of evaluative judgements relative to standards, then, merely shifts the question of the objectivity of values back to the standards themselves. The subjectivist may try to make his point by insisting that there is no objective validity about the choice of standards. Yet he would clearly be wrong if he said that the choice of even the most basic standards in any field was completely arbitrary. The standards used in sheepdog trials clearly bear some relation to the work that sheepdogs are kept to do, the standards for grading apples bear some relation to what people generally want in or like about apples, and so on.

On the other hand, standards are not as a rule strictly validated by such purposes. The appropriateness of standards is neither fully determinate nor totally indeterminate in relation to independently specifiable aims or desires. But however determinate it is, the objective appropriateness of standards in relation to aims or desires is no more of a threat to the denial of objective values than is the objectivity of evaluation relative to standards. In fact it is logically no different from the objectivity of goodness relative to desires. Something may be called good simply in so far as it satisfies or is such as to satisfy a certain desire; but the objectivity of such relations of satisfaction does not constitute in our sense an objective value.

6. Hypothetical and Categorical Imperatives

We may make this issue clearer by referring to Kant's distinction between hypothetical and categorical imperatives, though what he called imperatives are more naturally expressed as 'ought'-statements than in the imperative mood. 'If you want X, do Y' (or 'You ought to do Y') will be a hypothetical imperative if it is based on the supposed fact that Y is, in the circumstances, the only (or the best) available means to X, that is, on a causal relation between Y and X. The reason for doing Y lies in its causal connection with the desired end, X; the oughtness is contingent upon the desire. But 'You ought to do Y' will be a categorical imperative if you ought to do Y irrespective of any such desire for any end to which Y would contribute, if the oughtness is not thus contingent upon any desire. But this distinction needs to be handled with some care. An 'ought'-statement is not in this sense hypothetical merely because it incorporates a conditional clause. 'If you promised to do Y, you ought to do Y' is not a hypothetical imperative merely on account of the stated if-clause; what is meant may be either a hypothetical or a categorical imperative, depending upon the implied reason for keeping the supposed promise. If this rests upon some such further unstated conditional as 'If you want to be trusted another time', then it is a hypothetical imperative; if not, it is categorical.

[...]

A categorical imperative, then, would express a reason for acting which was unconditional in the sense of not being contingent upon any present desire of the agent to whose satisfaction the recommended action would contribute as a means – or more directly: 'You ought to dance', if the implied reason is just that you want to dance or like dancing, is still a hypothetical imperative. Now Kant himself held that moral judgements are categorical imperatives, or perhaps are all applications of one categorical imperative, and it can plausibly be maintained at least that many moral judgements contain a categorically imperative element. So far as ethics is concerned, my thesis that there are no objective values is specifically the denial that any such categorically imperative element is objectively valid. The objective values which I am denying would be action-directing absolutely, not contingently (in the way indicated) upon the agent's desires and inclinations.

[...]

7. The Claim to Objectivity

If I have succeeded in specifying precisely enough the moral values whose objectivity I am denying, my thesis may now seem to be trivially true. Of course, some will say, valuing, preferring, choosing, recommending, rejecting, condemning, and so on, are human activities, and there is no need to look for values that are prior to and logically independent of all such activities. There may be widespread agreement in valuing, and particular value-judgements are not in general arbitrary or isolated: they typically cohere with others, or can be criticized if they do not, reasons can be given for them, and so on: but if all that the subjectivist is maintaining is that desires, ends, purposes, and the like figure somewhere in the system of reasons, and that no ends or purposes are objective as opposed to being merely inter-subjective, then this may be conceded without much fuss.

But I do not think that this should be conceded so easily. As I have said, the main tradition of European moral philosophy includes the contrary claim, that there are objective values of just the sort I have denied. I have referred already to Plato, Kant, and Sidgwick. Kant in particular holds that the categorical imperative is not only categorical and imperative but objectively so: though a rational being gives the moral law to himself, the law that he thus makes is determinate and necessary. Aristotle begins the *Nicomachean Ethics* by saying that the good is that at which all things aim, and that ethics is part of a science which he calls 'politics', whose goal is not knowledge but practice; yet he does not doubt that there can be *knowledge* of what is the good for man, nor, once he has identified this as well-being or happiness, *eudaimonia*, that it can be known, rationally determined, in what happiness consists; and it is plain that he thinks that this happiness is intrinsically desirable, not good simply because it is desired. The rationalist Samuel Clarke holds that

> these eternal and necessary differences of things make it *fit and reasonable* for creatures so to act ... even separate from the consideration of these rules being the *positive will* or *command of God*; and also antecedent to any respect or regard, expectation or apprehension, of any *particular private and personal advantage or disadvantage, reward or punishment*, either present or future ...

Even the sentimentalist Hutcheson defines moral goodness as 'some quality apprehended in actions, which procures approbation ...', while saying that the moral sense by which we perceive virtue and vice has been given to us (by the Author of nature) to direct our actions. Hume indeed was on the other side, but he is still a witness to the dominance of the objectivist tradition, since he claims that when we 'see that the distinction of vice and virtue is not founded merely on the relations of objects, nor is perceiv'd by reason', this 'wou'd subvert all the vulgar systems of morality'. And Richard Price insists that right and wrong are 'real characters of actions', not 'qualities of our minds', and are perceived by the understanding; he criticizes the notion of moral sense on the ground that it would make virtue an affair of taste, and moral right and wrong 'nothing in the objects themselves'; he rejects Hutcheson's view because (perhaps mistakenly) he sees it as collapsing into Hume's.

But this objectivism about values is not only a feature of the philosophical tradition. It has also a firm basis in ordinary thought, and even in the meanings of moral terms. No doubt it was an extravagance for Moore to say that 'good' is the name of a non-natural quality, but it would not be so far wrong to say that in moral contexts it is used as if it were the name of a supposed non-natural quality, where the description 'non-natural' leaves room for the peculiar evaluative, prescriptive, intrinsically action-guiding aspects of this supposed quality. This point can be illustrated by reflection on the conflicts and swings of opinion in recent years between non-cognitivist and naturalist views about the central, basic, meanings of ethical terms. If we reject the view that it is the function of such terms to introduce objective values into discourse about conduct and choices of action, there seem to be two main alternative types of account. One (which has importantly different subdivisions) is that they conventionally express either attitudes which the speaker purports to adopt towards whatever it is that he characterizes morally, or prescriptions or recommendations, subject perhaps to the logical constraint of universalizability. Different views of this type share the central thesis that ethical terms have, at least partly and primarily, some sort of non-cognitive, non-descriptive, meaning. Views of the other type hold that they are descriptive in meaning, but descriptive of natural features, partly of such features as everyone, even the non-cognitivist, would recognize as distinguishing kind actions from cruel ones, courage from cowardice, politeness from rudeness, and so on, and partly (though these two overlap) of relations between the actions and some human wants, satisfactions, and the like. I believe that views of both these types capture part of the truth. Each approach can account for the fact that moral judgements are action-guiding or practical. Yet each gains much of its plausibility from the felt inadequacy of the other. It is a very natural reaction to any non-cognitive analysis of ethical terms to protest that there is more to ethics than this, something more external to the maker of moral judgements, more authoritative over both him and those of or to whom he speaks, and this reaction is likely to persist even when full allowance has been made for the logical, formal, constraints of full-blooded prescriptivity and universalizability. Ethics, we are inclined to believe, is more a matter of knowledge and less a matter of decision than any non-cognitive analysis allows. And of course naturalism satisfies this demand. It will not be a matter of choice or decision whether an action is cruel or unjust or imprudent or whether it is likely to produce more distress than pleasure. But in satisfying this demand, it introduces a converse deficiency. On a naturalist analysis, moral judgements can be practical, but their practicality is wholly relative to desires or possible satisfactions of the person or persons whose actions are to be guided; but moral judgements seem to say more than this. This view leaves out the categorical quality of moral requirements. In fact both naturalist and non-cognitive analyses leave out the apparent authority of ethics, the one by excluding the categorically imperative aspect, the other the claim to objective validity or truth. The ordinary user of moral language means to say something about whatever it is that he characterizes morally, for example a possible action, as it is in itself, or would be if it were realized, and not about, or even simply expressive of, his, or anyone else's, attitude or relation to it. But the something he wants to say is not purely descriptive, certainly not inert, but something that involves a call for action or for the refraining from action, and one that is absolute, not contingent upon any desire or preference or policy or choice, his own or anyone else's. Someone in a state of moral perplexity, wondering whether it would be wrong for him to engage, say, in research related to bacteriological warfare, wants to arrive at some judgement about this concrete case, his doing this work at this time in these actual circumstances; his relevant characteristics will be part of the subject of the judgement, but no relation between him and the proposed action will be part of the predicate. The question is not, for example, whether he really wants to do this work, whether it will satisfy or dissatisfy him, whether he will in the long run have a pro-attitude towards it, or even whether this is an action of a sort that he can happily and sincerely recommend in all relevantly similar cases. Nor is he even wondering just whether to recommend such action in all relevantly similar cases. He wants to know whether this course of action would be wrong in itself. Something like this is the everyday objectivist concept of which talk about non-natural qualities is a philosopher's reconstruction.

The prevalence of this tendency to objectify values – and not only moral ones – is confirmed by a pattern of thinking that we find in existentialists and those influenced by them. The denial of objective values can carry with it an extreme emotional reaction, a feeling that nothing matters at all, that life has lost its purpose. Of course this does not follow; the lack of objective values is not a good reason for abandoning subjective concern or for ceasing to want anything. But the abandonment of a belief in objective values can cause, at least temporarily, a decay of subjective concern and sense of purpose. That it does so is evidence that the people in whom this reaction occurs have been tending to objectify their concerns and purposes, have been giving them a fictitious external authority. A claim to objectivity has been so strongly associated with their subjective concerns and purposes that the collapse of the former seems to undermine the latter as well.

This view, that conceptual analysis would reveal a claim to objectivity, is sometimes dramatically confirmed by philosophers who are officially on the other side. Bertrand Russell, for example, says that 'ethical propositions should be expressed in the optative mood, not in the indicative'; he defends himself effectively against the charge of inconsistency in both holding ultimate ethical valuations to be subjective and expressing emphatic opinions on ethical questions. Yet at the end he admits:

Certainly there *seems* to be something more. Suppose, for example, that some one were to advocate the introduction of bull-fighting in this country. In opposing the proposal, I should *feel*, not only that I was expressing my desires, but that my desires in the matter are *right*, whatever that may mean. As a matter of argument, I can, I think, show that I am not guilty of any logical inconsistency in holding to the above interpretation of ethics and at the same time expressing strong ethical preferences. But in feeling I am not satisfied.

But he concludes, reasonably enough, with the remark: 'I can only say that, while my own opinions as to ethics do not satisfy me, other people's satisfy me still less.'

I conclude, then, that ordinary moral judgements include a claim to objectivity, an assumption that there are objective values in just the sense in which I am concerned to deny this. And I do not think it is going too far to say that this assumption has been incorporated in the basic, conventional, meanings of moral terms. Any analysis of the meanings of moral terms which omits this claim to objective, intrinsic, prescriptivity is to that extent incomplete; and this is true of any non-cognitive analysis, any naturalist one, and any combination of the two.

If second order ethics were confined, then, to linguistic and conceptual analysis, it ought to conclude that moral values at least are objective: that they are so is part of what our ordinary moral statements mean: the traditional moral concepts of the ordinary man as well as of the main line of western philosophers are concepts of objective value. But it is precisely for this reason that linguistic and conceptual analysis is not enough. The claim to objectivity, however ingrained in our language and thought, is not self-validating. It can and should be questioned. But the denial of objective values will have to be put forward not as the result of an analytic approach, but as an 'error theory', a theory that although most people in making moral judgements implicitly claim, among other things, to be pointing to something objectively prescriptive, these claims are all false. It is this that makes the name 'moral scepticism' appropriate.

But since this is an error theory, since it goes against assumptions ingrained in our thought and built into some of the ways in which language is used, since it conflicts with what is sometimes called common sense, it needs very solid support. It is not something we can accept lightly or casually and then quietly pass on. If we are to adopt this view, we must argue explicitly for it. Traditionally it has been supported by arguments of two main kinds, which I shall call the argument from relativity and the argument from queerness, but these can, as I shall show, be supplemented in several ways.

8. The Argument from Relativity

The argument from relativity has as its premiss the well-known variation in moral codes from one society to another and from one period to another, and also the differences in moral beliefs between different groups and classes within a complex community. Such variation is in itself merely a truth of descriptive morality, a fact of anthropology which entails neither first order nor second order ethical views. Yet it may indirectly support second order subjectivism: radical differences between first order moral judgements make it difficult to treat those judgements as apprehensions of objective truths. But it is not the mere occurrence of disagreements that tells against the objectivity of values. Disagreement on questions in history or biology or cosmology does not show that there are no objective issues in these fields for investigators to disagree about. But such scientific disagreement results from speculative inferences or explanatory hypotheses based on inadequate evidence, and it is hardly plausible to interpret moral disagreement in the same way. Disagreement about moral codes seems to reflect people's adherence to and participation in different ways of life. The causal connection seems to be mainly that way round: it is that people approve of monogamy because they participate in a monogamous way of life rather than that they participate in a monogamous way of life because they approve of monogamy. Of course, the standards may be an idealization of the way of life from which they arise: the monogamy in which people participate may be less complete, less rigid, than that of which it leads them to approve. This is not to say that moral judgements are purely conventional. Of course there have been and are moral heretics and moral reformers, people who have turned against the established rules and practices of their own communities for moral reasons, and often for moral reasons that we would endorse. But this can usually be understood as the extension, in ways which, though new and unconventional, seemed to them to be required for consistency, of rules to which they already adhered as arising out of an existing way of life. In short, the argument from relativity has some force simply because the actual variations in the moral codes are more readily explained by the hypothesis that they reflect ways of life than by the hypothesis that they express perceptions, most of them seriously inadequate and badly distorted, of objective values.

But there is a well-known counter to this argument from relativity, namely to say that the items for which objective validity is in the first place to be claimed are not specific moral rules or codes but very general basic principles which are recognized at least implicitly to some extent in all society – such principles as provide the foundations of what Sidgwick has called different methods of ethics: the principle of universalizability, perhaps, or the rule that one ought to conform to the specific rules of any way of life in which one takes part, from which one profits, and on which one relies, or some utilitarian principle of doing what tends, or seems likely, to promote the general happiness. It is easy to show that such general principles, married with differing concrete circumstances, different existing social patterns or different preferences, will beget different specific moral rules; and there is some plausibility in the claim that the specific rules thus generated will vary from community to community or from group to group in close agreement with the actual variations in accepted codes.

The argument from relativity can be only partly countered in this way. To take this line the moral objectivist has to say that it is only in these principles that the objective moral character attaches immediately to its descriptively specified ground or subject: other moral judgements are objectively valid or true, but only derivatively and contingently – if things had been otherwise, quite different sorts of actions would have been right. And despite the prominence in recent philosophical ethics of universalization, utilitarian principles, and the like, these are very far from constituting the whole of what is actually affirmed as basic in ordinary moral thought. Much of this is concerned rather with what Hare calls 'ideals' or, less kindly, 'fanaticism'. That is, people judge that some things are good or right, and others are bad or wrong, not because – or at any rate not only because – they exemplify some general principle for which widespread implicit acceptance could be claimed, but because something about those things arouses certain responses immediately in them, though they would arouse radically and irresolvably different responses in others. 'Moral sense' or 'intuition' is an initially more plausible description of what supplies many of our basic moral judgements than 'reason'. With regard to all these starting points of moral thinking the argument from relativity remains in full force.

9. The Argument from Queerness

Even more important, however, and certainly more generally applicable, is the argument from queerness. This has two parts, one metaphysical, the other epistemological. If there were objective values, then they would be entities or qualities or relations of a very strange sort, utterly different from anything else in the universe. Correspondingly, if we were aware of them, it would have to be by some special faculty of moral perception or intuition, utterly different from our ordinary ways of knowing everything else. These points were recognized by Moore when he spoke of non-natural qualities, and by the intuitionists in their talk about a 'faculty of moral intuition'. Intuitionism has long been out of favour, and it is indeed easy to point out its implausibilities. What is not so often stressed, but is more important, is that the central thesis of intuitionism is one to which any objectivist view of values is in the end committed: intuitionism merely makes unpalatably plain what other forms of objectivism wrap up. Of course the suggestion that moral judgements are made or moral problems solved by just sitting down and having an ethical intuition is a travesty of actual moral thinking. But, however complex the real process, it will require (if it is to yield authoritatively prescriptive conclusions) some input of this distinctive sort, either premises or forms of argument or both. When we ask the awkward question, how we can be aware of this authoritative prescriptivity, of the truth of these distinctively ethical premises or of the cogency of this distinctively ethical pattern of reasoning, none of our ordinary accounts of sensory perception or introspection or the framing and confirming of explanatory hypotheses or inference or logical construction or conceptual analysis, or any combination of these, will provide a satisfactory answer; 'a special sort of intuition' is a lame answer, but it is the one to which the clear-headed objectivist is compelled to resort.

Indeed, the best move for the moral objectivist is not to evade this issue, but to look for companions in guilt. For example, Richard Price argues that it is not moral knowledge alone that such an empiricism as those of Locke and Hume is unable to account for, but also our knowledge and even our ideas of essence, number, identity, diversity, solidity, inertia, substance, the necessary existence and infinite extension of time and space, necessity and possibility in general, power, and causation. If the understanding, which Price defines as the faculty within us that discerns truth, is also a source of new simple ideas of so many other sorts, may it not also be a power of immediately perceiving right and wrong, which yet are real characters of actions?

This is an important counter to the argument from queerness. The only adequate reply to it would be to show how, on empiricist foundations, we can construct an account of the ideas and beliefs and knowledge that we have of all these matters. I cannot even begin to do that here, though I have undertaken some parts of the task elsewhere. I can only state my belief that satisfactory accounts of most of these can be given in empirical terms. If some supposed metaphysical necessities or essences resist such treatment, then they too should be included, along with objective values, among the targets of the argument from queerness.

This queerness does not consist simply in the fact that ethical statements are 'unverifiable'. Although logical positivism with its verifiability theory of descriptive meaning gave an impetus to non-cognitive accounts of ethics, it is not only logical positivists but also empiricists of a much more liberal sort who should find objective values hard to accommodate. Indeed, I would not only reject the verifiability principle but also deny the conclusion commonly drawn from it, that moral judgements lack descriptive meaning. The assertion that there are objective values or intrinsically prescriptive entities or features of some kind, which ordinary moral judgements presuppose, is, I hold, not meaningless but false.

Plato's Forms give a dramatic picture of what objective values would have to be. The Form of the Good is such that knowledge of it provides the knower with both a direction and an overriding motive; something's being good both tells the person who knows this to pursue it and makes him pursue it. An objective good would be sought by anyone who was acquainted with it, not because of any contingent fact that this person, or every person, is so constituted that he desires this end, but just because the end has to-be-pursuedness somehow built into it. Similarly, if there were objective principles of right and wrong, any wrong (possible) course of action would have not-to-be-doneness somehow built into it. Or we should have something like Clarke's necessary relations of fitness between situations and actions, so that a situation would have a demand for such-and-such an action somehow built into it.

The need for an argument of this sort can be brought out by reflection on Hume's argument that 'reason' – in which at this stage he includes all sorts of knowing as well as reasoning – can never be an 'influencing motive of the will'. Someone might object that Hume has argued unfairly from the lack of influencing power (not contingent upon desires) in ordinary objects of knowledge and ordinary reasoning, and might maintain that values differ from natural objects precisely in their power, when known, automatically to influence the will. To this Hume could, and would need to, reply that this objection involves the postulating of value-entities or value-features of quite a different order from anything else with which we are acquainted, and of a corresponding faculty with which to detect them. That is, he would have to supplement his explicit argument with what I have called the argument from queerness.

Another way of bringing out this queerness is to ask, about anything that is supposed to have some objective moral quality, how this is linked with its natural features. What is the connection between the natural fact that an action is a piece of deliberate cruelty – say, causing pain just for fun – and the moral fact that it is wrong? It cannot be an entailment, a logical or semantic necessity. Yet it is not merely that the two features occur together. The wrongness must somehow be 'consequential' or 'supervenient'; it is wrong because it is a piece of deliberate cruelty. But just what *in the world* is signified by this 'because'? And how do we know the relation that it signifies, if this is something more than such actions being socially condemned, and condemned by us too, perhaps through our having absorbed attitudes from our social environment? It is not even sufficient to postulate a faculty which 'sees' the wrongness: something must be postulated which can see at once the natural features that constitute the cruelty, and the wrongness, and the mysterious consequential link between the two. Alternatively, the intuition required might be the perception that wrongness is a higher order property belonging to certain natural properties; but what is this belonging of properties to other properties, and how can we discern it? How much simpler and more comprehensible the situation would be if we could replace the moral quality with some sort of subjective response which could be causally related to the detection of the natural features on which the supposed quality is said to be consequential.

It may be thought that the argument from queerness is given an unfair start if we thus relate it to what are admittedly among the wilder products of philosophical fancy – Platonic Forms, non-natural qualities, self-evident relations of fitness, faculties of intuition, and the like. Is it equally forceful if applied to the terms in which everyday moral judgements are more likely to be expressed – though still, as has been argued in Section 7, with a claim to objectivity – 'you must do this', 'you can't do that', 'obligation', 'unjust', 'rotten', 'disgraceful', 'mean', or talk about good reasons for or against possible actions? Admittedly not; but that is because the objective prescriptivity, the element a claim for whose authoritativeness is embedded in ordinary moral thought and language, is not yet isolated in these forms of speech, but is presented along with relations to desires and feelings, reasoning about the means to desired ends, interpersonal demands, the injustice which consists in the violation of what are in the context the accepted standards of merit, the psychological constituents of meanness, and so on. There is nothing queer about any of these, and under cover of them the claim for moral authority may pass unnoticed. But if I am right in arguing that it is ordinarily there, and is therefore very likely to be incorporated almost automatically in philosophical accounts of ethics which systematize our ordinary thought even in such apparently innocent terms as these, it needs to be examined, and for this purpose it needs to be isolated and exposed as it is by the less cautious philosophical reconstructions.

10. Patterns of Objectification

Considerations of these kinds suggest that it is in the end less paradoxical to reject than to retain the common-sense belief in the objectivity of moral values, provided that we can explain how this belief, if it is false, has become established and is so resistant to criticisms. This proviso is not difficult to satisfy.

On a subjectivist view, the supposedly objective values will be based in fact upon attitudes which the person has who takes himself to be recognizing and responding to those values. If we admit what Hume calls the mind's 'propensity to spread itself on external objects', we can understand the supposed objectivity of moral qualities as arising from what we can call the projection or objectification of moral attitudes. This would be analogous to what is called the 'pathetic fallacy', the tendency to read our feelings into their objects. If a fungus, say, fills us with disgust, we may be inclined to ascribe to the fungus itself a non-natural quality of foulness. But in moral contexts there is more than this propensity at work. Moral attitudes themselves are at least partly social in origin: socially established – and socially necessary – patterns of behaviour put pressure on individuals, and each individual tends to internalize these pressures and to join in requiring these patterns of behaviour of himself and of others. The attitudes that are objectified into moral values have indeed an external source, though not the one assigned to them by the belief in their absolute authority. Moreover, there are motives that would support objectification. We need morality to regulate interpersonal relations, to control some of the ways in which people behave towards one another, often in opposition to contrary inclinations. We therefore want our moral judgements to be authoritative for other agents as well as for ourselves: objective validity would give them the authority required. Aesthetic values are logically in the same position as moral ones; much the same metaphysical and epistemological considerations apply to them. But aesthetic values are less strongly objectified than moral ones; their subjective status, and an 'error theory' with regard to such claims to objectivity as are incorporated in aesthetic judgements, will be more readily accepted, just because the motives for their objectification are less compelling.

But it would be misleading to think of the objectification of moral values as primarily the projection of feelings, as in the pathetic fallacy. More important are wants and demands. As Hobbes says, 'whatsoever is the object of any man's Appetite or Desire, that is it, which he for his part calleth *Good*'; and certainly both the adjective 'good' and the noun 'goods' are used in non-moral contexts of things because they are such as to satisfy desires. We get the notion of something's being objectively good, or having intrinsic value, by reversing the direction of dependence here, by making the desire depend upon the goodness, instead of the goodness on the desire. And this is aided by the fact that the desired thing will indeed have features that make it desired, that enable it to arouse a desire or that make it such as to satisfy some desire that is already there. It is fairly easy to confuse the way in which a thing's desirability is indeed objective with its having in our sense objective value. The fact that the word 'good' serves as one of our main moral terms is a trace of this pattern of objectification.

Similarly related uses of words are covered by the distinction between hypothetical and categorical imperatives. The statement that someone 'ought to' or, more strongly, 'must' do such-and-such may be backed up explicitly or implicitly by reference to what he wants or to what his purposes and objects are. Again, there may be a reference to the purposes of someone else, perhaps the speaker: 'You must do this' – 'Why?' – 'Because I want such-and-such'. The moral categorical imperative which could be expressed in the same words can be seen as resulting from the suppression of the conditional clause in a hypothetical imperative without its being replaced by any such reference to the speaker's wants. The action in question is still required in something like the way in which it would be if it were appropriately related to a want, but it is no longer admitted that there is any contingent want upon which its being required depends. Again this move can be understood when we remember that at least our central and basic moral judgements represent social demands, where the source of the demand is indeterminate and diffuse. Whose demands or wants are in question, the agent's, or the speaker's, or those of an indefinite multitude of other people? All of these in a way, but there are advantages in not specifying them precisely. The speaker is expressing demands which he makes as a member of a community, which he has developed in and by participation in a joint way of life; also, what is required of this particular agent would be required of any other in a relevantly similar situation; but the agent too is expected to have internalized the relevant demands, to act as if the ends for which the action is required were his own. By suppressing any explicit reference to demands and making the imperatives categorical we facilitate conceptual moves from one such demand relation to another. The moral uses of such words as 'must' and 'ought' and 'should', all of which are used also to express hypothetical imperatives, are traces of this pattern of objectification.

It may be objected that this explanation links normative ethics too closely with descriptive morality, with the mores or socially enforced patterns of behaviour that anthropologists record. But it can hardly be denied that moral thinking starts from the enforcement of social codes. Of course it is not confined to that. But even when moral judgements are detached from the mores of any actual society they are liable to be framed with reference to an ideal community of moral agents, such as Kant's kingdom of ends, which but for the need to give God a special place in it would have been better called a commonwealth of ends.

Another way of explaining the objectification of moral values is to say that ethics is a system of law from which the legislator has been removed. This might have been derived either from the positive law of a state or from a supposed system of divine law. There can be no doubt that some features of modern European moral concepts are traceable to the theological ethics of Christianity. The stress on quasi-imperative notions, on what ought to be done or on what is wrong in a sense that is close to that of 'forbidden', are surely relics of divine commands. Admittedly, the central ethical concepts for Plato and Aristotle also are in a broad sense prescriptive or intrinsically action-guiding, but in concentrating rather on 'good' than on 'ought' they show that their moral thought is an objectification of the desired and the satisfying rather than of the commanded. Elizabeth Anscombe has argued that modern, non-Aristotelian, concepts of *moral* obligation, *moral* duty, of what is *morally* right and wrong, and of the *moral* sense of 'ought' are survivals outside the framework of thought that made them really intelligible, namely the belief in divine law. She infers that 'ought' has 'become a word of mere mesmeric force', with only a 'delusive appearance of content', and that we would do better to discard such terms and concepts altogether, and go back to Aristotelian ones.

There is much to be said for this view. But while we can explain some distinctive features of modern moral philosophy in this way, it would be a mistake to see the whole problem of the claim to objective prescriptivity as merely local and unnecessary, as a post-operative complication of a society from which a dominant system of theistic belief has recently been rather hastily excised. As Cudworth and Clarke and Price, for example, show, even those who still admit divine commands, or the positive law of God, may believe moral values to have an independent objective but still action-guiding authority. Responding to Plato's *Euthyphro* dilemma, they believe that God commands what he commands because it is in itself good or right, not that it is good or right merely because and in that he commands it. Otherwise God himself could not be called good. Price asks, 'What can be more preposterous, than to make the Deity nothing but will; and to exalt this on the ruins of all his attributes?' The apparent objectivity of moral value is a widespread phenomenon which has more than one source: the persistence of a belief in something like divine law when the belief in the divine legislator has faded out is only one factor among others. There are several different patterns of objectification, all of which have left characteristic traces in our actual moral concepts and moral language.

11. The General Goal of Human Life

[…]

If it is claimed that something is objectively the right or proper goal of human life, then this is tantamount to the assertion of something that is objectively categorically imperative, and comes fairly within the scope of our previous arguments carriage return. […] The objectivist may have recourse to the purpose of God: the true purpose of human life is fixed by what God intended (or, intends) men to do and to be. Actual human strivings and satisfactions have some relation to this true end because God made men for this end and made them such as to pursue it – but only *some* relation, because of the inevitable imperfection of created beings.

I concede that if the requisite theological doctrine could be defended, a kind of objective ethical prescriptivity could be thus introduced. Since I think that theism cannot be defended, I do not regard this as any threat to my argument.

[…]

12. Conclusion

I have maintained that there is a real issue about the status of values, including moral values. Moral scepticism, the denial of objective moral values, is not to be confused with any one of several first order normative views, or with any linguistic or conceptual analysis. Indeed, ordinary moral judgements involve a claim to objectivity which both non-cognitive and naturalist analyses fail to capture. Moral scepticism must, therefore, take the form of an error theory, admitting that a belief in objective values is built into ordinary moral thought and language, but holding that this ingrained belief is false. As such, it needs arguments to support it against 'common sense'. But solid arguments can be found. The considerations that favour moral scepticism are: first, the relativity or variability of some important starting points of moral thinking and their apparent dependence on actual ways of life; secondly, the metaphysical peculiarity of the supposed objective values, in that they would have to be intrinsically action-guiding and motivating; thirdly, the problem of how such values could be consequential or supervenient upon natural features; fourthly, the corresponding epistemological difficulty of accounting for our knowledge of value entities or features and of their links with the features on which they would be consequential; fifthly, the possibility of explaining, in terms of several different patterns of objectification, traces of which remain in moral language and moral concepts, how even if there were no such objective values people not only might have come to suppose that there are but also might persist firmly in that belief. These five points sum up the case for moral scepticism; but of almost equal importance are the preliminary removal of misunderstandings that often prevent this thesis from being considered fairly and explicitly, and the isolation of those items about which the moral sceptic is sceptical from many associated qualities and relations whose objective status is not in dispute.

8

A Theory of Justice

John Rawls

The publication of *A Theory of Justice* in 1971 led to a major revitalization of the field of political philosophy. It offers sophisticated arguments against utilitarianism (as applied to decisions concerning the distribution of goods within society at large) and a broadly Kantian approach to social contract theory as an alternative to the approach associated with Hobbes. Its subject matter is 'justice [as] the first virtue of social institutions' (section 1), rather than the whole of morality, and the particular theory of justice defended in the book is a theory that Rawls calls 'justice as fairness', since a guiding idea of this theory is that principles of justice should be determined in a way that is fair to everyone who will be affected by them.

A fair procedure for determining the principles of justice needs to neutralize the significant differences in bargaining power that are present in all actual societies, and not take account of advantages that some of us have over others that are not credit-worthy but are simply the result of luck – that is, the 'natural lottery'. To this end, Rawls asks us to imagine a special scenario he calls the 'original position': we are to imagine people standing behind a 'veil of ignorance' that prevents them from having any access to facts about their own particular positions in the world, working together to formulate and agree upon principles of justice that will govern the basic structure of society (that is, all basic social institutions). The full version of the theory requires that the agents in the original position be thought of as representatives of citizens, but much of the time, as in the excerpts reproduced here, Rawls simplifies things by speaking simply of individual agents concerned to craft principles of justice for a society of which they will be members.

Rawls argues that two principles would be selected from behind the veil of ignorance (hence these two principles are the correct principle of justice): (i) a principle concerning the equal rights of all people when it comes to basic liberties; and (ii) the 'difference principle', which states that social and economic inequalities must be arranged so that they are to everyone's advantage and attached to offices open to all. The difference principle is then further interpreted as saying that only inequalities that can be justified to the worst off in a society are justifiable – some inequalities make things better for the worse off than they would otherwise be, and it is these inequalities alone that are justifiable (for instance: too little disparity in wages, and there may be too little incentive for people to work hard; hence the poor may end up worse off than they would in a system with more disparity in wages).

The difference principle is just one part of Rawls's theory, and it is important not to overlook the fact that the other principle is said to have 'lexical priority' over it (that is, basic rights claims cannot be overridden to favor particular distributions of goods, even where such distributions benefit the worst off). Still, it is not surprising that this principle has received so much attention in commentary on *A Theory of Justice*. It is an appealing principle that, in practice, would probably have us tread a path between egalitarian and unconstrained market capitalist ideologies. However, the justification for this principle is not that it represents some type of compromise between these ideologies, as Rawls takes it to be a contestable empirical matter which political and economic system will best conform with the difference principle. Rather, we are to

History of Ethics – Essential Readings with Commentary, First Edition. Edited by Daniel Star and Roger Crisp.

understand it, along with the less novel first principle, as a principle that the deliberators in the original position would arrive at, given their shared interest in locating a principle that is rationally justifiable to every agent, no matter where they are located in the social world (for, once the veil is removed, as it were, they may turn out to be any of these agents).

An argument for the claim that agents in the original position would opt for the difference principle is presented in section 26. It is complex, but the basic idea here is that, in conditions of uncertainty of the kind that we find present in the original position, the rational decision procedure to adopt when choosing a means to one's end of living a good life is the procedure that focuses on avoiding the worst outcomes (this is the 'maximin' solution) rather than simply maximizing expected utility. Rawls emphasizes the importance of the risk avoidance involved here when he says that his two principles are those 'a person would choose for the design of a society in which his enemy is to assign him a place.' It should be noted that Rawls later came to think that the third of the three conditions he mentions here for determining when the maximin decision procedure is appropriate is not actually met in the original position when complex 'mixed' theories of justice are considered (rather than when a simple alternative theory, utilitarianism, is considered) and proffered an alternative argument for the difference principle. This alternative argument appeals to the ideal of establishing and maintaining mutual trust between people of different social classes (even in *A Theory of Justice*, Rawls is concerned to discuss envy and resentment, as he takes these to be phenomena that may undermine stability in many societies but are particularly unlikely to do so in societies that conform to his principles). In any case, his commitment to providing a rational alternative to utilitarianism, a theory which, he claims here, 'does not take seriously the distinction between persons', never wavered.

Although it is not essential to the main, original arguments of his book, Rawls provides a Kantian interpretation of his theory (see the last section reproduced here). The element in Kant that he viewed himself as defending within the political realm is the emphasis on the ideal of people in the kingdom of ends autonomously deciding on fundamental principles. As commentators have pointed out, Rawls here fails to note that he earlier told us that the rationality in question behind the veil of ignorance is purely instrumental and does not involve the selection of ends that Kant took to be essential to acting autonomously (acting on hypothetical imperatives in no way guarantees autonomy). Nonetheless, the perspectives that *we*, actual rational agents, adopt when we consider agents behind the veil of ignorance and the principles they would adopt may be thought of as perspectives that aim to meet the Kantian ideal. It is up to us to pursue 'reflective equilibrium' by testing whether or not 'justice as fairness' best makes sense of, and helps improve on, our fundamental commitments concerning the basic structure of the just society.

3. The Main Idea of the Theory of Justice

My aim is to present a conception of justice which generalizes and carries to a higher level of abstraction the familiar theory of the social contract as found, say, in Locke. Rousseau, and Kant.[1] In order to do this we are not to think of the original contract as one to enter a particular society or to set up a particular form of government. Rather, the guiding idea is that the principles of justice for the basic structure of society are the object of the original agreement. They are the principles that free and rational persons concerned to further their own interests would accept in an initial position of equality as defining the fundamental terms of their association. These principles are to regulate all further agreements; they specify the kinds of social cooperation that can be entered into and the forms of government that can be established. This way of regarding the principles of justice I shall call justice as fairness.

Thus we are to imagine that those who engage in social cooperation choose together, in one joint act, the principles which are to assign basic rights and duties and to determine the division of social benefits. Men are to decide in advance how they are to regulate their claims against one another and what is to be the foundation charter of their society. Just as each person must decide by rational reflection what constitutes his good, that is, the system of ends which it is rational for him to pursue, so a group of persons must decide once and for all what is to count among them as just and unjust. The choice which rational men would make in this hypothetical situation of equal liberty, assuming for the present that this choice problem has a solution, determines the principles of justice.

In justice as fairness the original position of equality corresponds to the state of nature in the traditional theory of the social contract. This original position is not, of course, thought of as an actual historical state of affairs, much less as a primitive condition of culture. It is understood as a purely hypothetical situation characterized so as to lead to a certain conception of justice.[2] Among the essential features of this situation is that no one knows his place in society, his class position or social status, nor does any one know his fortune in the distribution of natural assets and abilities, his intelligence, strength, and the like. I shall even assume that the parties do not know their conceptions of the good or their special psychological propensities. The principles of justice are chosen behind a veil of ignorance. This ensures that no one is advantaged or disadvantaged in the choice of principles by the outcome of natural chance or the contingency of social circumstances. Since all are similarly situated and no one is able to design principles to favor his particular condition, the principles of justice are the result of a fair agreement or bargain. For given the circumstances of the original position, the symmetry of everyone's relations to each other, this initial situation is fair between individuals as moral persons, that is, as rational beings with their own ends and capable, I shall assume, of a sense of justice. The original position is, one might say, the appropriate initial status quo, and thus the fundamental agreements reached in it are fair. This explains the propriety of the name "justice as fairness": it conveys the idea that the principles of justice are agreed to in an initial situation that is fair. The name does not mean that the concepts of justice and fairness are the same, any more than the phrase "poetry as metaphor" means that the concepts of poetry and metaphor are the same.

Justice as fairness begins, as I have said, with one of the most general of all choices which persons might make together, namely, with the choice of the first principles of a conception of justice which is to regulate all subsequent criticism and reform of institutions. Then, having chosen a conception of justice, we can suppose that they are to choose a constitution and a legislature to enact laws, and so on, all in accordance with the principles of justice initially agreed upon. Our social situation is just if it is such that by this sequence of hypothetical agreements

---

[1] As the text suggests. I shall regard Locke's *Second Treatise of Government*, Rousseau's *The Social Contract*, and Kant's ethical works beginning with *The Foundations of the Metaphysics of Morals* as definitive of the contract tradition. For all of its greatness. Hobbes's *Leviathan* raises special problems. A general historical survey is provided by J.W. Gough, *The Social Contract*, 2nd ed. (Oxford, The Clarendon Press, 1957), and Otto Gierke, *Natural Law and the Theory of Society*, trans, with an introduction by Ernest Barker (Cambridge, The University Press, 1934). A presentation of the contract view as primarily an ethical theory is to be found in G. R. Grice, *The Grounds of Moral Judgment* (Cambridge, The University Press, 1967).

[2] Kant is clear that the original agreement is hypothetical. See *The Metaphysics of Morals*, pt. I *(Rechtslehre)*, especially §§47, 52; and pt. II of the essay "Concerning the Common Saying: This May Be True in Theory but It Does Not Apply in Practice," in *Kant's Political Writings*, ed. Hans Reiss and trans, by H. B. Nisbet (Cambridge, The University Press, 1970), pp. 73–87. See Georges Vlachos, *La Pensée politique de Kant* (Paris, Presses Universitaires de France, 1962), pp. 326–335; and J. G. Murphy. *Kant: The Philosophy of Right* (London, Macmillan, 1970), pp. 109–112, 133–136, for a further discussion.

we would have contracted into the general system of rules which defines it. Moreover, assuming that the original position does determine a set of principles (that is, that a particular conception of justice would be chosen), it will then be true that whenever social institutions satisfy these principles those engaged in them can say to one another that they are cooperating on terms to which they would agree if they were free and equal persons whose relations with respect to one another were fair. They could all view their arrangements as meeting the stipulations which they would acknowledge in an initial situation that embodies widely accepted and reasonable constraints on the choice of principles. The general recognition of this fact would provide the basis for a public acceptance of the corresponding principles of justice. No society can, of course, be a scheme of cooperation which men enter voluntarily in a literal sense; each person finds himself placed at birth in some particular position in some particular society, and the nature of this position materially affects his life prospects. Yet a society satisfying the principles of justice as fairness comes as close as a society can to being a voluntary scheme, for it meets the principles which free and equal persons would assent to under circumstances that are fair. In this sense its members are autonomous and the obligations they recognize self-imposed.

One feature of justice as fairness is to think of the parties in the initial situation as rational and mutually disinterested. This does not mean that the parties are egoists, that is, individuals with only certain kinds of interests, say in wealth, prestige, and domination. But they are conceived as not taking an interest in one another's interests. They are to presume that even their spiritual aims may be opposed, in the way that the aims of those of different religions may be opposed. Moreover, the concept of rationality must be interpreted as far as possible in the narrow sense, standard in economic theory, of taking the most effective means to given ends. I shall modify this concept to some extent, as explained later, but one must try to avoid introducing into it any controversial ethical elements. The initial situation must be characterized by stipulations that are widely accepted.

In working out the conception of justice as fairness one main task clearly is to determine which principles of justice would be chosen in the original position. To do this we must describe this situation in some detail and formulate with care the problem of choice which it presents. These matters I shall take up in the immediately succeeding chapters. It may be observed, however, that once the principles of justice are thought of as arising from an original agreement in a situation of equality, it is an open question whether the principle of utility would be acknowledged. Off-hand it hardly seems likely that persons who view themselves as equals, entitled to press their claims upon one another, would agree to a principle which may require lesser life prospects for some simply for the sake of a greater sum of advantages enjoyed by others. Since each desires to protect his interests, his capacity to advance his conception of the good, no one has a reason to acquiesce in an enduring loss for himself in order to bring about a greater net balance of satisfaction. In the absence of strong and lasting benevolent impulses, a rational man would not accept a basic structure merely because it maximized the algebraic sum of advantages irrespective of its permanent effects on his own basic rights and interests. Thus it seems that the principle of utility is incompatible with the conception of social cooperation among equals for mutual advantage. It appears to be inconsistent with the idea of reciprocity implicit in the notion of a well-ordered society. Or, at any rate, so I shall argue.

I shall maintain instead that the persons in the initial situation would choose two rather different principles: the first requires equality in the assignment of basic rights and duties, while the second holds that social and economic inequalities, for example inequalities of wealth and authority, are just only if they result in compensating benefits for everyone, and in particular for the least advantaged members of society. These principles rule out justifying institutions on the grounds that the hardships of some are offset by a greater good in the aggregate. It may be expedient but it is not just that some should have less in order that others may prosper. But there is no injustice in the greater benefits earned by a few provided that the situation of persons not so fortunate is thereby improved. The intuitive idea is that since everyone's well-being depends upon a scheme of cooperation without which no one could have a satisfactory life, the division of advantages should be such as to draw forth the willing cooperation of everyone taking part in it, including those less well situated. The two principles mentioned seem to be a fair basis on which those better endowed, or more fortunate in their social position, neither of which we can be said to deserve, could expect the willing cooperation of others when some workable scheme is a necessary condition of the welfare of all.[3] Once we decide to look for a conception of justice that prevents the use of the accidents of natural endowment and the contingencies of social circumstance as counters in a quest for political and economic

---

[3] For the formulation of this intuitive idea I am indebted to Allan Gibbard.

advantage, we are led to these principles. They express the result of leaving aside those aspects of the social world that seem arbitrary from a moral point of view.

The problem of the choice of principles, however, is extremely difficult. I do not expect the answer I shall suggest to be convincing to everyone. It is, therefore, worth noting from the outset that justice as fairness, like other contract views, consists of two parts: (1) an interpretation of the initial situation and of the problem of choice posed there, and (2) a set of principles which, it is argued, would be agreed to. One may accept the first part of the theory (or some variant thereof), but not the other, and conversely. The concept of the initial contractual situation may seem reasonable although the particular principles proposed are rejected. To be sure, I want to maintain that the most appropriate conception of this situation does lead to principles of justice contrary to utilitarianism and perfectionism, and therefore that the contract doctrine provides an alternative to these views. Still, one may dispute this contention even though one grants that the contractarian method is a useful way of studying ethical theories and of setting forth their underlying assumptions.

Justice as fairness is an example of what I have called a contract theory. Now there may be an objection to the term "contract" and related expressions, but I think it will serve reasonably well. Many words have misleading connotations which at first are likely to confuse. The terms "utility" and "utilitarianism" are surely no exception. They too have unfortunate suggestions which hostile critics have been willing to exploit; yet they are clear enough for those prepared to study utilitarian doctrine. The same should be true of the term "contract" applied to moral theories. As I have mentioned, to understand it one has to keep in mind that it implies a certain level of abstraction. In particular, the content of the relevant agreement is not to enter a given society or to adopt a given form of government, but to accept certain moral principles. Moreover, the undertakings referred to are purely hypothetical: a contract view holds that certain principles would be accepted in a well-defined initial situation.

The merit of the contract terminology is that it conveys the idea that principles of justice may be conceived as principles that would be chosen by rational persons, and that in this way conceptions of justice may be explained and justified. The theory of justice is a part, perhaps the most significant part, of the theory of rational choice. Furthermore, principles of justice deal with conflicting claims upon the advantages won by social cooperation; they apply to the relations among several persons or groups. The word "contract" suggests this plurality as well as the condition that the appropriate division of advantages must be in accordance with principles acceptable to all parties. The condition of publicity for principles of justice is also connoted by the contract phraseology. Thus, if these principles are the outcome of an agreement, citizens have a knowledge of the principles that others follow. It is characteristic of contract theories to stress the public nature of political principles. Finally there is the long tradition of the contract doctrine. Expressing the tie with this line of thought helps to define ideas and accords with natural piety. There are then several advantages in the use of the term "contract." With due precautions taken, it should not be misleading.

A final remark. Justice as fairness is not a complete contract theory. For it is clear that the contractarian idea can be extended to the choice of more or less an entire ethical system, that is, to a system including principles for all the virtues and not only for justice. Now for the most part I shall consider only principles of justice and others closely related to them; I make no attempt to discuss the virtues in a systematic way. Obviously if justice as fairness succeeds reasonably well, a next step would be to study the more general view suggested by the name "rightness as fairness." But even this wider theory fails to embrace all moral relationships, since it would seem to include only our relations with other persons and to leave out of account how we are to conduct ourselves toward animals and the rest of nature. I do not contend that the contract notion offers a way to approach these questions which are certainly of the first importance; and I shall have to put them aside. We must recognize the limited scope of justice as fairness and of the general type of view that it exemplifies. How far its conclusions must be revised once these other matters are understood cannot be decided in advance.

4. The Original Position and Justification

I have said that the original position is the appropriate initial status quo which insures that the fundamental agreements reached in it are fair. This fact yields the name "justice as fairness." It is clear, then, that I want to say that one conception of justice is more reasonable than another, or justifiable with respect to it, if rational persons in the initial situation would choose its principles over those of the other for the role of justice. Conceptions of justice are to be ranked by their acceptability to persons so circumstanced. Understood in this way the question of justification is settled by working out a problem of deliberation: we have to ascertain which principles it would be rational to adopt given the contractual situation. This connects the theory of justice with the theory of rational choice.

If this view of the problem of justification is to succeed, we must, of course, describe in some detail the nature of this choice problem. A problem of rational decision has a definite answer only if we know the beliefs and interests of the parties, their relations with respect to one another, the alternatives between which they are to choose, the procedure whereby they make up their minds, and so on. As the circumstances are presented in different ways, correspondingly different principles are accepted. The concept of the original position, as I shall refer to it, is that of the most philosophically favored interpretation of this initial choice situation for the purposes of a theory of justice.

But how are we to decide what is the most favored interpretation? I assume, for one thing, that there is a broad measure of agreement that principles of justice should be chosen under certain conditions. To justify a particular description of the initial situation one shows that it incorporates these commonly shared presumptions. One argues from widely accepted but weak premises to more specific conclusions. Each of the presumptions should by itself be natural and plausible; some of them may seem innocuous or even trivial. The aim of the contract approach is to establish that taken together they impose significant bounds on acceptable principles of justice. The ideal outcome would be that these conditions determine a unique set of principles; but I shall be satisfied if they suffice to rank the main traditional conceptions of social justice.

One should not be misled, then, by the somewhat unusual conditions which characterize the original position. The idea here is simply to make vivid to ourselves the restrictions that it seems reasonable to impose on arguments for principles of justice, and therefore on these principles themselves. Thus it seems reasonable and generally accept-able that no one should be advantaged or disadvantaged by natural fortune or social circumstances in the choice of principles. It also seems widely agreed that it should be impossible to tailor principles to the circumstances of one's own case. We should insure further that particular inclinations and aspirations, and persons' conceptions of their good do not affect the principles adopted. The aim is to rule out those principles that it would be rational to propose for acceptance, however little the chance of success, only if one knew certain things that are irrelevant from the standpoint of justice. For example, if a man knew that he was wealthy, he might find it rational to advance the principle that various taxes for welfare measures be counted unjust; if he knew that he was poor, he would most likely propose the contrary principle. To represent the desired restrictions one imagines a situation in which every-one is deprived of this sort of information. One excludes the knowledge of those contingencies which sets men at odds and allows them to be guided by their prejudices. In this manner the veil of ignorance is arrived at in a natural way. This concept should cause no difficulty if we keep in mind the constraints on arguments that it is meant to express. At any time we can enter the original position, so to speak, simply by following a certain procedure, namely, by arguing for principles of justice in accordance with these restrictions.

It seems reasonable to suppose that the parties in the original position are equal. That is, all have the same rights in the procedure for choosing principles; each can make proposals, submit reasons for their acceptance, and so on. Obviously the purpose of these conditions is to represent equality between human beings as moral persons, as crea-tures having a conception of their good and capable of a sense of justice. The basis of equality is taken to be similarity in these two respects. Systems of ends are not ranked in value; and each man is presumed to have the requisite ability to understand and to act upon whatever principles are adopted. Together with the veil of ignorance, these conditions define the principles of justice as those which rational persons concerned to advance their interests would consent to as equals when none are known to be advantaged or disadvantaged by social and natural contingencies.

There is, however, another side to justifying a particular description of the original position. This is to see if the principles which would be chosen match our considered convictions of justice or extend them in an acceptable way. We can note whether applying these principles would lead us to make the same judgments about the basic structure of society which we now make intuitively and in which we have the greatest confidence; or whether, in cases where our present judgments are in doubt and given with hesitation, these principles offer a resolution which we can affirm on reflection. There are questions which we feel sure must be answered in a certain way. For example, we are confident that religious intolerance and racial discrimination are unjust. We think that we have examined these things with care and have reached what we believe is an impartial judgment not likely to be distorted by an excessive attention to our own interests. These convictions are provisional fixed points which we presume any conception of justice must fit. But we have much less assurance as to what is the correct distribution of wealth and authority. Here we may be looking for a way to remove our doubts. We can check an interpretation of the initial situation, then, by the capacity of its principles to accommodate our firmest convictions and to provide guidance where guidance is needed.

In searching for the most favored description of this situation we work from both ends. We begin by describing it so that it represents generally shared and preferably weak conditions. We then see if these conditions are strong enough to yield a significant set of principles. If not, we look for further premises equally reasonable. But if so, and these principles match our considered convictions of justice, then so far well and good. But presumably there will be discrepancies. In this case we have a choice. We can either modify the account of the initial situation or we can revise our existing judgments, for even the judgments we take provisionally as fixed points are liable to revision. By going back and forth, sometimes altering the conditions of the contractual circumstances, at others withdrawing our judgments and conforming them to principle, I assume that eventually we shall find a description of the initial situation that both expresses reasonable conditions and yields principles which match our considered judgments duly pruned and adjusted. This state of affairs I refer to as reflective equilibrium.[4] It is an equilibrium because at last our principles and judgments coincide; and it is reflective since we know to what principles our judgments conform and the premises of their derivation. At the moment everything is in order. But this equilibrium is not necessarily stable. It is liable to be upset by further examination of the conditions which should be imposed on the contractual situation and by particular cases which may lead us to revise our judgments. Yet for the time being we have done what we can to render coherent and to justify our convictions of social justice. We have reached a conception of the original position.

I shall not, of course, actually work through this process. Still, we may think of the interpretation of the original position that I shall present as the result of such a hypothetical course of reflection. It represents the attempt to accommodate within one scheme both reasonable philosophical conditions on principles as well as our considered judgments of justice. In arriving at the favored interpretation of the initial situation there is no point at which an appeal is made to self-evidence in the traditional sense either of general conceptions or particular convictions. I do not claim for the principles of justice proposed that they are necessary truths or derivable from such truths. A conception of justice cannot be deduced from self-evident premises or conditions on principles; instead, its justification is a matter of the mutual support of many considerations, of everything fitting together into one coherent view.

A final comment. We shall want to say that certain principles of justice are justified because they would be agreed to in an initial situation of equality. I have emphasized that this original position is purely hypothetical. It is natural to ask why, if this agreement is never actually entered into, we should take any interest in these principles, moral or otherwise. The answer is that the conditions embodied in the description of the original position are ones that we do in fact accept. Or if we do not, then perhaps we can be persuaded to do so by philosophical reflection. Each aspect of the contractual situation can be given supporting grounds. Thus what we shall do is to collect together into one conception a number of conditions on principles that we are ready upon due consideration to recognize as reasonable. These constraints express what we are prepared to regard as limits on fair terms of social cooperation. One way to look at the idea of the original position, therefore, is to see it as an expository device which sums up the meaning of these conditions and helps us to extract their consequences. On the other hand, this conception is also an intuitive notion that suggests its own elaboration, so that led on by it we are drawn to define more clearly the standpoint from which we can best interpret moral relationships. We need a conception that enables us to envision our objective from afar: the intuitive notion of the original position is to do this for us.[5]

5. Classical Utilitarianism

There are many forms of utilitarianism, and the development of the theory has continued in recent years. I shall not survey these forms here, nor take account of the numerous refinements found in contemporary discussions. My aim is to work out a theory of justice that represents an alternative to utilitarian thought generally and so to all of these different versions of it. I believe that the contrast between the contract view and utilitarianism remains essentially the same in all these cases. Therefore I shall compare justice as fairness with familiar variants of intuitionism, perfectionism, and utilitarianism in order to bring out the underlying differences in the simplest way. With this end

---

[4] The process of mutual adjustment of principles and considered judgments is not peculiar to moral philosophy. See Nelson Goodman, *Fact, Fiction, and Forecast* (Cambridge, Mass., Harvard University Press, 1955), pp. 65–68, for parallel remarks concerning the justification of the principles of deductive and inductive inference.

[5] Henri Poincaré remarks: "Il nous faut une faculté qui nous fasse voir le but de loin, et, cette faculté, c'est l'intuition." *La Valeur de la science* (Paris, Flammarion, 1909), p. 27.

in mind, the kind of utilitarianism I shall describe here is the strict classical doctrine which receives perhaps its clearest and most accessible formulation in Sidgwick. The main idea is that society is rightly ordered, and therefore just, when its major institutions are arranged so as to achieve the greatest net balance of satisfaction summed over all the individuals belonging to it.[6]

We may note first that there is, indeed, a way of thinking of society which makes it easy to suppose that the most rational conception of justice is utilitarian. For consider: each man in realizing his own interests is certainly free to balance his own losses against his own gains. We may impose a sacrifice on ourselves now for the sake of a greater advantage later. A person quite properly acts, at least when others are not affected, to achieve his own greatest good, to advance his rational ends as far as possible. Now why should not a society act on precisely the same principle applied to the group and therefore regard that which is rational for one man as right for an association of men? Just as the well-being of a person is constructed from the series of satisfactions that are experienced at different moments in the course of his life, so in very much the same way the well-being of society is to be constructed from the fulfill-ment of the systems of desires of the many individuals who belong to it. Since the principle for an individual is to advance as far as possible his own welfare, his own system of desires, the principle for society is to advance as far as possible the welfare of the group, to realize to the greatest extent the comprehensive system of desire arrived at from the desires of its members. Just as an individual balances present and future gains against present and future losses, so a society may balance satisfactions and dissatisfactions between different individuals. And so by these reflections one reaches the principle of utility in a natural way: a society is properly arranged when its institutions maximize the net balance of satisfaction. The principle of choice for an association of men is interpreted as an extension of the principle of choice for one man. Social justice is the principle of rational prudence applied to an aggregative conception of the welfare of the group.[7]

This idea is made all the more attractive by a further consideration. The two main concepts of ethics are those of the right and the good; the concept of a morally worthy person is, I believe, derived from them. The structure of an ethical theory is, then, largely determined by how it defines and connects these two basic notions. Now it seems that the simplest way of relating them is taken by teleological theories: the good is defined independently from the right, and then the right is defined as that which maximizes the good.[8] More precisely, those institutions and acts are right which of the available alternatives produce the most good, or at least as much good as any of the other

---

[6] I shall take Henry Sidgwick's The Methods of Ethics, 7th ed. (London, 1907), as summarizing the development of utilitarian moral theory. Book III of his Principles of Political Economy (London, 1883) applies this doctrine to questions of economic and social justice, and is a precursor of A. C. Pigou. The Economics of Welfare (London, Macmillan, 1920). Sidgwick's Outlines of the History of Ethics, 5th ed. (London, 1902), contains a brief history of the utilitarian tradition. We may follow him in assuming, somewhat arbitrarily, that it begins with Shaftesbury's An Inquiry Concerning Virtue and Merit (1711) and Hutcheson's An Inquiry Concerning Moral Good and Evil (1725). Hutcheson seems to have been the first to state clearly the principle of utility. He says in Inquiry, sec. 111, §8, that "that action is best, which procures the greatest happiness for the greatest numbers; and that, worst, which, in like manner, occasions misery." Other major eighteenth century works are Hume's A Treatise of Human Nature (1739), and An Enquiry Concerning the Principles of Morals (1751); Adam Smith's A Theory of the Moral Sentiments (1759); and Bentham's The Principles of Morals and Legislation (1789). To these we must add the writings of J. S. Mill represented by Utilitarianism (1863) and F.Y. Edgeworth's Mathematical Psychics (London, 1888).

The discussion of utilitarianism has taken a different turn in recent years by focusing on what we may call the coordination problem and related questions of publicity. This development stems from the essays of R. F. Harrod, "Utilitarianism Revised," Mind, vol. 45 (1936); J. D. Mabbott, "Punishment," Mind, vol. 48 (1939); Jonathan Harrison, "Utilitarianism, Universalisation, and Our Duty to Be Just," Proceedings of the Aristotelian Society, vol. 53 (1952–53); and J. O. Urmson, "The Interpretation of the Philosophy of J. S. Mill," Philosophical Quarterly, vol. 3 (1953). See also J. J. C. Smart, "Extreme and Restricted Utilitarianism," Philosophical Quarterly, vol. 6 (1956), and his An Outline of a System of Utilitarian Ethics (Cambridge, The University Press, 1961). For an account of these matters, see David Lyons, Forms and Limits of Utilitarianism (Oxford, The Clarendon Press, 1965); and Allan Gibbard, "Utilitarianisms and Coordination" (dissertation, Harvard University, 1971). The prob-lems raised by these works, as important as they are, I shall leave aside as not bearing directly on the more elementary question of distribution which I wish to discuss.

Finally, we should note here the essays of J. C. Harsanyi, in particular, "Cardinal Utility in Welfare Economics and in the Theory of Risk-Taking." Journal of Political Economy, 1953, and "Cardinal Welfare, Individualistic Ethics, and Interpersonal Comparisons of Utility," Journal of Political Economy, 1955; and R. B. Brandt, "Some Merits of One Form of Rule-Utilitarianism," University of Colorado Studies (Boulder, Colorado, 1967).

[7] On this point see also D. P. Gauthier, Practical Reasoning (Oxford, Clarendon Press, 1963), pp. 126 f. The text elaborates the suggestion found in "Constitutional Liberty and the Concept of Justice," Nomos VI: Justice, ed. C. J. Friedrich and J. W. Chapman (New York, Atherton Press, 1963), pp. 124f, which in turn is related to the idea of justice as a higher-order administrative decision. See "Justice as Fairness," Philosophical Review, 1958, pp. 185–187. That the principle of social integration is distinct from the principle of personal integration is stated by R. B. Perry, General Theory of Value (New York, Longmans, Green, and Company, 1926), pp. 674–677. He attributes the error of overlooking this fact to Emile Durkheim and others with similar views. Perry's conception of social integration is that brought about by a shared and dominant benevolent purpose.

[8] Here I adopt W. K. Frankena's definition of teleological theories in Ethics (Englewood Cliffs, N.J., Prentice Hall, Inc., 1963), p. 13.

institutions and acts open as real possibilities (a rider needed when the maximal class is not a singleton). Teleological theories have a deep intuitive appeal since they seem to embody the idea of rationality. It is natural to think that rationality is maximizing something and that in morals it must be maximizing the good. Indeed, it is tempting to suppose that it is self-evident that things should be arranged so as to lead to the most good.

It is essential to keep in mind that in a teleological theory the good is defined independently from the right. This means two things. First, the theory accounts for our considered judgments as to which things are good (our judgments of value) as a separate class of judgments intuitively distinguishable by common sense, and then proposes the hypothesis that the right is maximizing the good as already specified. Second, the theory enables one to judge the goodness of things without referring to what is right. For example, if pleasure is said to be the sole good, then presumably pleasures can be recognized and ranked in value by criteria that do not presuppose any standards of right, or what we would normally think of as such. Whereas if the distribution of goods is also counted as a good, perhaps a higher order one, and the theory directs us to produce the most good (including the good of distribution among others), we no longer have a teleological view in the classical sense. The problem of distribution falls under the concept of right as one intuitively understands it, and so the theory lacks an independent definition of the good. The clarity and simplicity of classical teleological theories derives largely from the fact that they factor our moral judgments into two classes, the one being characterized separately while the other is then connected with it by a maximizing principle.

Teleological doctrines differ, pretty clearly, according to how the conception of the good is specified. If it is taken as the realization of human excellence in the various forms of culture, we have what may be called perfectionism. This notion is found in Aristotle and Nietzsche, among others. If the good is defined as pleasure, we have hedonism; if as happiness, eudaimonism, and so on. I shall understand the principle of utility in its classical form as defining the good as the satisfaction of desire, or perhaps better, as the satisfaction of rational desire. This accords with the view in all essentials and provides, I believe, a fair interpretation of it. The appropriate terms of social cooperation are settled by whatever in the circumstances will achieve the greatest sum of satisfaction of the rational desires of individuals. It is impossible to deny the initial plausibility and attractiveness of this conception.

The striking feature of the utilitarian view of justice is that it does not matter, except indirectly, how this sum of satisfactions is distributed among individuals any more than it matters, except indirectly, how one man distributes his satisfactions over time. The correct distribution in either case is that which yields the maximum fulfillment. Society must allocate its means of satisfaction whatever these are, rights and duties, opportunities and privileges, and various forms of wealth, so as to achieve this maximum if it can. But in itself no distribution of satisfaction is better than another except that the more equal distribution is to be preferred to break ties.[9] It is true that certain common sense precepts of justice, particularly those which concern the protection of liberties and rights, or which express the claims of desert, seem to contradict this contention. But from a utilitarian standpoint the explanation of these precepts and of their seemingly stringent character is that they are those precepts which experience shows should be strictly respected and departed from only under exceptional circumstances if the sum of advantages is to be maximized.[10] Yet, as with all other precepts, those of justice are derivative from the one end of attaining the greatest balance of satisfaction. Thus there is no reason in principle why the greater gains of some should not compensate for the lesser losses of others; or more importantly, why the violation of the liberty of a few might not be made right by the greater good shared by many. It simply happens that under most conditions, at least in a reasonably advanced stage of civilization, the greatest sum of advantages is not attained in this way. No doubt the strictness of common sense precepts of justice has a certain usefulness in limiting men's propensities to injustice and to socially injurious actions, but the utilitarian believes that to affirm this strictness as a first principle of morals is a mistake. For just as it is rational for one man to maximize the fulfillment of his system of desires, it is right for a society to maximize the net balance of satisfaction taken over all of its members.

The most natural way, then, of arriving at utilitarianism (although not, of course, the only way of doing so) is to adopt for society as a whole the principle of rational choice for one man. Once this is recognized, the place of the impartial spectator and the emphasis on sympathy in the history of utilitarian thought is readily understood. For it is by the conception of the impartial spectator and the use of sympathetic identification in guiding our imagination that the principle for one man is applied to society. It is this spectator who is conceived as carrying out the required organization of the desires of all persons into one coherent system of desire; it is by this construction that many

[9] On this point see Sidgwick, *The Methods of Ethics*, pp. 416 f.
[10] See J. S. Mill, *Utilitarianism*, ch. V, last two parts.

persons are fused into one. Endowed with ideal powers of sympathy and imagination, the impartial spectator is the perfectly rational individual who identifies with and experiences the desires of others as if these desires were his own. In this way he ascertains the intensity of these desires and assigns them their appropriate weight in the one system of desire the satisfaction of which the ideal legislator then tries to maximize by adjusting the rules of the social system. On this conception of society separate individuals are thought of as so many different lines along which rights and duties are to be assigned and scarce means of satisfaction allocated in accordance with rules so as to give the greatest fulfillment of wants. The nature of the decision made by the ideal legislator is not, therefore, materially different from that of an entrepreneur deciding how to maximize his profit by producing this or that commodity, or that of a consumer deciding how to maximize his satisfaction by the purchase of this or that collection of goods. In each case there is a single person whose system of desires determines the best allocation of limited means. The correct decision is essentially a question of efficient administration. This view of social cooperation is the consequence of extending to society the principle of choice for one man, and then, to make this extension work, conflating all persons into one through the imaginative acts of the impartial sympathetic spectator. Utilitarianism does not take seriously the distinction between persons.

[…]

11. Two Principles of Justice

I shall now state in a provisional form the two principles of justice that I believe would be agreed to in the original position. The first formulation of these principles is tentative. As we go on I shall consider several formulations and approximate step by step the final statement to be given much later. I believe that doing this allows the exposition to proceed in a natural way.

The first statement of the two principles reads as follows.

First: each person is to have an equal right to the most extensive scheme of equal basic liberties compatible with a similar scheme of liberties for others.

Second: social and economic inequalities are to be arranged so that they are both (a) reasonably expected to be to everyone's advantage, and (b) attached to positions and offices open to all.

[…]

These principles primarily apply, as I have said, to the basic structure of society and govern the assignment of rights and duties and regulate the distribution of social and economic advantages. Their formulation presupposes that, for the purposes of a theory of justice, the social structure may be viewed as having two more or less distinct parts, the first principle applying to the one, the second principle to the other. Thus we distinguish between the aspects of the social system that define and secure the equal basic liberties and the aspects that specify and establish social and economic inequalities. Now it is essential to observe that the basic liberties are given by a list of such liberties. Important among these are political liberty (the right to vote and to hold public office) and freedom of speech and assembly; liberty of conscience and freedom of thought; freedom of the person, which includes freedom from psychological oppression and physical assault and dismemberment (integrity of the person); the right to hold personal property and freedom from arbitrary arrest and seizure as defined by the concept of the rule of law. These liberties are to be equal by the first principle.

The second principle applies, in the first approximation, to the distribution of income and wealth and to the design of organizations that make use of differences in authority and responsibility. While the distribution of wealth and income need not be equal, it must be to everyone's advantage, and at the same time, positions of authority and responsibility must be accessible to all. One applies the second principle by holding positions open, and then, subject to this constraint, arranges social and economic inequalities so that everyone benefits.

These principles are to be arranged in a serial order with the first principle prior to the second. This ordering means that infringements of the basic equal liberties protected by the first principle cannot be justified, or compensated for, by greater social and economic advantages. These liberties have a central range of application within which they can be limited and compromised only when they conflict with other basic liberties. Since they may be limited when they clash with one another, none of these liberties is absolute; but however they are adjusted to form one system, this system is to be the same for all. It is difficult, and perhaps impossible, to give a complete specification of these liberties independently from the particular circumstances – social, economic, and technological – of a given society. The hypothesis is that the general form of such a list could be devised with sufficient exactness to sustain this conception of justice. Of course, liberties not on the list, for example, the right to own certain kinds of property (e.g., means of production) and freedom of contract as understood by the doctrine of laissez-faire are not basic; and so they are not protected by the priority of the first principle. Finally, in regard to the second principle, the distribution of wealth and income, and positions of authority and responsibility, are to be consistent with both the basic liberties and equality of opportunity.

The two principles are rather specific in their content, and their acceptance rests on certain assumptions that I must eventually try to explain and justify. For the present, it should be observed that these principles are a special case of a more general conception of justice that can be expressed as follows.

All social values – liberty and opportunity, income and wealth, and the social bases of self-respect – are to be distributed equally unless an unequal distribution of any or all, of these values is to everyone's advantage.

Injustice, then, is simply inequalities that are not to the benefit of all. Of course, this conception is extremely vague and requires interpretation.

As a first step, suppose that the basic structure of society distributes certain primary goods, that is, things that every rational man is presumed to want. These goods normally have a use whatever a person's rational plan of life. For simplicity, assume that the chief primary goods at the disposition of society are rights, liberties, and opportunities, and income and wealth. (Later on in Part Three the primary good of self-respect has a central place.) These are the social primary goods. Other primary goods such as health and vigor, intelligence and imagination, are natural goods; although their possession is influenced by the basic structure, they are not so directly under its control. Imagine, then, a hypothetical initial arrangement in which all the social primary goods are equally distributed: everyone has similar rights and duties, and income and wealth are evenly shared. This state of affairs provides a benchmark for judging improvements. If certain inequalities of wealth and differences in authority would make everyone better off than in this hypothetical starting situation, then they accord with the general conception.

Now it is possible, at least theoretically, that by giving up some of their fundamental liberties men are sufficiently compensated by the resulting social and economic gains. The general conception of justice imposes no restrictions on what sort of inequalities are permissible; it only requires that everyone's position be improved. We need not suppose anything so drastic as consenting to a condition of slavery. Imagine instead that people seem willing to forego certain political rights when the economic returns are significant. It is this kind of exchange which the two principles rule out; being arranged in serial order they do not permit exchanges between basic liberties and economic and social gains except under extenuating circumstances.

[…]

The fact that the two principles apply to institutions has certain consequences. First of all, the rights and basic liberties referred to by these principles are those which are defined by the public rules of the basic structure. Whether men are free is determined by the rights and duties established by the major institutions of society. Liberty is a certain pattern of social forms. The first principle simply requires that certain sorts of rules, those defining basic liberties, apply to everyone equally and that they allow the most extensive liberty compatible with a like liberty for all. The only reason for circumscribing basic liberties and making them less extensive is that otherwise they would interfere with one another.

Further, when principles mention persons, or require that everyone gain from an inequality, the reference is to representative persons holding the various social positions, or offices established by the basic structure. Thus in applying the second principle I assume that it is possible to assign an expectation of well-being to representative individuals holding these positions. This expectation indicates their life prospects as viewed from their social station. In general, the expectations of representative persons depend upon the distribution of rights and duties throughout the basic structure. Expectations are connected: by raising the prospects of the representative man in one position we presumably increase or decrease the prospects of representative men in other positions. Since it applies to institutional forms, the second principle (or rather the first part of it) refers to the expectations of representative individuals. As I shall discuss below, neither principle applies to distributions of particular goods to particular individuals who may be identified by their proper, names. The situation where someone is considering how to allocate certain commodities to needy persons who are known to him is not within the scope of the principles. They are meant to regulate basic institutional arrangements. We must not assume that there is much similarity from the standpoint of justice between an administrative allotment of goods to specific persons and the appropriate design of society. Our common sense intuitions for the former may be a poor guide to the latter.

Now the second principle insists that each person benefit from permissible inequalities in the basic structure. This means that it must be reasonable for each relevant representative man defined by this structure, when he views it as a going concern, to prefer his prospects with the inequality to his prospects without it. One is not allowed to justify differences in income or in positions of authority and responsibility on the ground that the disadvantages of those in one position are outweighed by the greater advantages of those in another. Much less can infringements of liberty be counterbalanced in this way. It is obvious, however, that there are indefinitely many ways in which all may be advantaged when the initial arrangement of equality is taken as a benchmark. How then are we to choose among these possibilities? The principles must be specified so that they yield a determinate conclusion.

[…]

24. The Veil of Ignorance

The idea of the original position is to set up a fair procedure so that any principles agreed to will be just. The aim is to use the notion of pure procedural justice as a basis of theory. Somehow we must nullify the effects of specific contingencies which put men at odds and tempt them to exploit social and natural circumstances to their own advantage. Now in order to do this I assume that the parties are situated behind a veil of ignorance. They do not know how the various alternatives will affect their own particular case and they are obliged to evaluate principles solely on the basis of general considerations.[11]

It is assumed, then, that the parties do not know certain kinds of particular facts. First of all, no one knows his place in society, his class position or social status; nor does he know his fortune in the distribution of natural assets and abilities, his intelligence and strength, and the like. Nor, again, does anyone know his conception of the good, the particulars of his rational plan of life, or even the special features of his psychology such as his aversion to risk or liability to optimism or pessimism. More than this, I assume that the parties do not know the particular circumstances of their own society. That is, they do not know its economic or political situation, or the level of civilization and culture it has been able to achieve. The persons in the original position have no information as to which generation they belong. These broader restrictions on knowledge are appropriate in part because questions of social justice arise between generations as well as within them, for example, the question of the appropriate rate of capital saving and of the conservation of natural resources and the environment of nature. There is also, theoretically anyway, the question of a reasonable genetic policy. In these cases too, in order to carry through the idea of the original position, the parties must not know the contingencies that set them in opposition. They must choose principles the consequences of which they are prepared to live with whatever generation they turn out to belong to.

As far as possible, then, the only particular facts which the parties know is that their society is subject to the circumstances of justice and whatever this implies. It is taken for granted, however, that they know the general facts about human society. They understand political affairs and the principles of economic theory; they know the basis of social organization and the laws of human psychology. Indeed, the parties are presumed to know whatever general facts affect the choice of the principles of justice. There are no limitations on general information, that is, on general laws and theories, since conceptions of justice must be adjusted to the characteristics of the systems of social cooperation which they are to regulate, and there is no reason to rule out these facts. It is, for example, a consideration against a conception of justice that, in view of the laws of moral psychology, men would not acquire a desire to act upon it even when the institutions of their society satisfied it. For in this case there would be difficulty in securing the stability of social cooperation. An important feature of a conception of justice is that it should generate its own support. Its principles should be such that when they are embodied in the basic structure of society men tend to acquire the corresponding sense of justice and develop a desire to act in accordance with its principles. In this case a conception of justice is stable. This kind of general information is admissible in the original position.

---

[11] The veil of ignorance is so natural a condition that something like it must have occurred to many. The formulation in the text is implicit. I believe, in Kant's doctrine of the categorical imperative, both in the way this procedural criterion is defined and the use Kant makes of it. Thus when Kant tells us to test our maxim by considering what would be the case were it a universal law of nature, he must suppose that we do not know our place within this imagined system of nature. See. for example, his discussion of the topic of practical judgment in The Critique of Practical Reason, Academy Edition, vol. 5, pp. 68–72. A similar restriction on information is found in J. C. Harsanyi. "Cardinal Utility in Welfare Economics and in the Theory of Risk-taking," Journal of Political Economy, vol. 61 (1953). However, other aspects of Harsanyi's view are quite different, and he uses the restriction to develop a utilitarian theory. See the last paragraph of §27.

The notion of the veil of ignorance raises several difficulties. Some may object that the exclusion of nearly all particular information makes it difficult to grasp what is meant by the original position. Thus it may be helpful to observe that one or more persons can at any time enter this position, or perhaps better, simulate the deliberations of this hypothetical situation, simply by reasoning in accordance with the appropriate restrictions. In arguing for a conception of justice we must be sure that it is among the permitted alternatives and satisfies the stipulated formal constraints. No considerations can be advanced in its favor unless they would be rational ones for us to urge were we to lack the kind of knowledge that is excluded. The evaluation of principles must proceed in terms of the general consequences of their public recognition and universal application, it being assumed that they will be complied with by everyone. To say that a certain conception of justice would be chosen in the original position is equivalent to saying that rational deliberation satisfying certain conditions and restrictions would reach a certain conclusion. If necessary the argument to this result could be set out more formally. I shall, however, speak throughout in terms of the notion of the original position. It is more economical and suggestive, and brings out certain essential features that otherwise one might easily overlook.

These remarks show that the original position is not to be thought of as a general assembly which includes at one moment everyone who will live at some time; or, much less, as an assembly of everyone who could live at some time. It is not a gathering of all actual or possible persons. If we conceived of the original position in either of these ways, the conception would cease to be a natural, guide to intuition and would lack a clear sense. In any case, the original position must be interpreted so that one can at any time adopt its perspective. It must make no difference when one takes up this viewpoint, or who does so: the restrictions must be such that the same principles are always chosen. The veil of ignorance is a key condition in meeting this requirement. It insures not only that the information available is relevant, but that it is at all times the same.

It may be protested that the condition of the veil of ignorance is irrational. Surely, some may object, principles should be chosen in the light of all the knowledge available. There are various replies to this contention. Here I shall sketch those which emphasize the simplifications that need to be made if one is to have any theory at all. [...] To begin with, it is clear that since the differences among the parties are unknown to them, and everyone is equally rational and similarly situated, each is convinced by the same arguments. Therefore, we can view the agreement in the original position from the standpoint of one person selected at random. If anyone after due reflection prefers a conception of justice to another, then they all do, and a unanimous agreement can be reached. We can, to make the circumstances more vivid, imagine that the parties are required to communicate with each other through a referee as intermediary, and that he is to announce which alternatives have been suggested and the reasons offered in their support. He forbids the attempt to form coalitions, and he informs the parties when they have come to an understanding. But such a referee is actually superfluous, assuming that the deliberations of the parties must be similar.

Thus there follows the very important consequence that the parties have no basis for bargaining in the usual sense. No one knows his situation in society nor his natural assets, and therefore no one is in a position to tailor principles to his advantage. We might imagine that one of the contractees threatens to hold out unless the others agree to principles favorable to him. But how does he know which principles are especially in his interests? The same holds for the formation of coalitions: if a group were to decide to band together to the disadvantage of the others, they would not know how to favor themselves in the choice of principles. Even if they could get everyone to agree to their proposal, they would have no assurance that it was to their advantage, since they cannot identify themselves either by name or description. The one case where this conclusion fails is that of saving. Since the persons in the original position know that they are contemporaries (taking the present time of entry interpretation), they can favor their generation by refusing to make any sacrifices at all for their successors; they simply acknowledge the principle that no one has a duty to save for posterity. Previous generations have saved or they have not; there is nothing the parties can now do to affect that. So in this instance the veil of ignorance fails to secure the desired result. Therefore, to handle the question of justice between generations, I modify the motivation assumption and add a further constraint. With these adjustments, no generation is able to formulate principles especially designed to advance its own cause and some significant limits on savings principles can be derived. Whatever a person's temporal position, each is forced to choose for all.[12]

---

[12] Rousseau, *The Social Contract*, bk. II. ch. IV, par. 5.

The restrictions on particular information in the original position are, then, of fundamental importance. Without them we would not be able to work out any definite theory of justice at all. We would have to be content with a vague formula stating that justice is what would be agreed to without being able to say much, if anything, about the substance of the agreement itself. The formal constraints of the concept of right, those applying to principles directly, are not sufficient for our purpose. The veil of ignorance makes possible a unanimous choice of a particular conception of justice. Without these limitations on knowledge the bargaining problem of the original position would be hopelessly complicated. Even if theoretically a solution were to exist, we would not, at present anyway, be able to determine it.

The notion of the veil of ignorance is implicit, I think, in Kant's ethics. Nevertheless the problem of defining the knowledge of the parties and of characterizing the alternatives open to them has often been passed over, even by contract theories. Sometimes the situation definitive of moral deliberation is presented in such an indeterminate way that one cannot ascertain how it will turn out.

[…]

26. The Reasoning Leading to the Two Principles of Justice

[…]

Now consider the point of view of anyone in the original position. There is no way for him to win special advantages for himself. Nor, on the other hand, are there grounds for his acquiescing in special disadvantages. Since it is not reasonable for him to expect more than an equal share in the division of social primary goods, and since it is not rational for him to agree to less, the sensible thing is to acknowledge as the first step a principle of justice requiring an equal distribution. Indeed, this principle is so obvious given the symmetry of the parties that it would occur to everyone immediately. Thus the parties start with a principle requiring equal basic liberties for all, as well as fair equality of opportunity and equal division of income and wealth.

But even holding firm to the priority of the basic liberties and fair equality of opportunity, there is no reason why this initial acknowledgment should be final. Society should take into account economic efficiency and the requirements of organization and technology. If there are inequalities in income and wealth, and differences in authority and degrees of responsibility, that work to make everyone better off in comparison with the benchmark of equality, why not permit them? One might think that ideally individuals should want to serve one another. But since the parties are assumed to be mutually disinterested, their acceptance of these economic and institutional inequalities is only the recognition of the relations of opposition in which men stand in the circumstances of justice. They have no grounds for complaining of one another's motives. Thus the parties would agree to these differences only if they would be dejected by the bare knowledge or perception that others are better situated; but I suppose that they decide as if they are not moved by envy. Thus the basic structure should allow these inequalities so long as these improve everyone's situation, including that of the least advantaged, provided that they are consistent with equal liberty and fair opportunity. Because the parties start from an equal division of all social primary goods, those who benefit least have, so to speak, a veto. Thus we arrive at the difference principle. Taking equality as the basis of comparison, those who have gained more must do so on terms that are justifiable to those who have gained the least.

[…]

It seems from these remarks that the two principles are at least a plausible conception of justice. The question, though, is how one is to argue for them more systematically. Now there are several things to do. One can work out their consequences for institutions and note their implications for fundamental social policy. In this way they are tested by a comparison with our considered judgments of justice. […] But one can also try to find arguments in their favor that are decisive from the standpoint of the original position. In order to see how this might be done, it is useful as a heuristic device to think of the two principles as the maximin solution to the problem of social justice. There is a relation between the two principles and the maximin rule for choice under uncertainty.[13] This is evident

[13] An accessible discussion of this and other rules of choice under uncertainty can be found in W. J. Baumol, *Economic Theory and Operations Analysis*, 2nd ed. (Englewood Cliffs, N.J., Prentice Hall Inc., 1965), ch. 24. Baumol gives a geometric interpretation of these rules, including the diagram used in §13 to illustrate the difference principle. See pp. 558–562. See also R. D. Luce and Howard Raiffa, *Games and Decisions* (New York, John Wiley and Sons, Inc., 1957), ch. XIII, for a fuller account.

from the fact that the two principles are those a person would choose for the design of a society in which his enemy is to assign him his place. The maximin rule tells us to rank alternatives by their worst possible outcomes: we are to adopt the alternative the worst outcome of which is superior to the worst outcomes of the others.[14] The persons in the original position do not, of course, assume that their initial place in society is decided by a malevolent opponent. As I note below, they should not reason from false premises. The veil of ignorance does not violate this idea, since an absence of information is not misinformation. But that the two principles of justice would be chosen if the parties were forced to protect themselves against such a contingency explains the sense in which this conception is the maximin solution. And this analogy suggests that if the original position has been described so that it is rational for the parties to adopt the conservative attitude expressed by this rule, a conclusive argument can indeed be constructed for these principles. Clearly the maximin rule is not, in general, a suitable guide for choices under uncertainty. But it holds only in situations marked by certain special features. My aim, then, is to show that a good case can be made for the two principles based on the fact that the original position has these features to a very high degree.

Now there appear to be three chief features of situations that give plausibility to this unusual rule.[15] First, since the rule takes no account of the likelihoods of the possible circumstances, there must be some reason for sharply discounting estimates of these probabilities. Offhand, the most natural rule of choice would seem to be to compute the expectation of monetary gain for each decision and then to adopt the course of action with the highest prospect. [...] Thus it must be, for example, that the situation is one in which a knowledge of likelihoods is impossible, or at best extremely insecure. In this case it is unreasonable not to be skeptical of probabilistic calculations unless there is no other way out, particularly if the decision is a fundamental one that needs to be justified to others.

The second feature that suggests the maximin rule is the following: the person choosing has a conception of the good such that he cares very little, if anything, for what he might gain above the minimum stipend that he can, in fact, be sure of by following the maximin rule. It is not worthwhile for him to take a chance for the sake of a further advantage, especially when it may turn out that he loses much that is important to him. This last provision brings in the third feature, namely, that the rejected alternatives have outcomes that one can hardly accept. The situation involves grave risks. Of course these features work most effectively in combination. The paradigm situation for following the maximin rule is when all three features are realized to the highest degree.

Let us review briefly the nature of the original position with these three special features in mind. To begin with, the veil of ignorance excludes all knowledge of likelihoods. The parties have no basis for determining the probable nature of their society, or their place in it. Thus they have no basis for probability calculations. They must also take into account the fact that their choice of principles should seem reasonable to others, in particular their descendants, whose rights will be deeply affected by it. These considerations are strengthened by the fact that the parties know very little about the possible states of society. Not only are they unable to conjecture the likelihoods of the various possible circumstances, they cannot say much about what the possible circumstances are, much less

[14] Consider the gain-and-loss table below. It represents the gains and losses for a situation which is not a game of strategy. There is no one playing against the person making the decision; instead he is faced with several possible circumstances which may or may not obtain. Which circumstances happen to exist does not depend upon what the person choosing decides or whether he announces his moves in advance. The numbers in the table are monetary values (in hundreds of dollars) in comparison with some initial situation. The gain (g) depends upon the individual's decision (d) and the circumstances (c). Thus $g = f(d, c)$. Assuming that there are three possible decisions and three possible circumstances, we might have this gain-and-loss table.

Decisions	Circumstances		
	c1	c2	c3
d1	−7	8	12
d2	−8	7	14
d3	5	6	8

The maximin rule requires that we make the third decision. For in this case the worst that can happen is that one gains five hundred dollars, which is better than the worst for the other actions. If we adopt one of these we may lose either eight or seven hundred dollars. Thus, the choice of d3 maximizes $f(d,c)$ for that value of c, which for a given d, minimizes f. The term "maximin" means the *maximum minimorum;* and the rule directs our attention to the worst that can happen under any proposed course of action, and to decide in the light of that.
[15] Here I borrow from William Fellner, *Probability and Profit* (Homewood, Ill., R. D. Irwin, Inc 1965), pp. 140–142, where these features are noted.

enumerate them and foresee the outcome of each alternative available. Those deciding are much more in the dark than illustrations by numerical tables suggest. It is for this reason that I have spoken only of a relation to the maximin rule.

Several kinds of arguments for the two principles of justice illustrate the second feature. Thus, if we can maintain that these principles provide a workable theory of social justice, and that they are compatible with reasonable demands of efficiency, then this conception guarantees a satisfactory minimum. There may be, on reflection, little reason for trying to do better. Thus much of the argument, especially in Part Two, is to show, by their application to some main questions of social justice, that the two principles are a satisfactory conception. These details have a philosophical purpose. Moreover, this line of thought is practically decisive if we can establish the priority of liberty. For this priority implies that the persons in the original position have no desire to try for greater gains at the expense of the basic equal liberties. The minimum assured by the two principles in lexical order is not one that the parties wish to jeopardize for the sake of greater economic and social advantages.

Finally, the third feature holds if we can assume that other conceptions of justice may lead to institutions that the parties would find intolerable. For example, it has sometimes been held that under some conditions the utility principle (in either form) justifies, if not slavery or serfdom, at any rate serious infractions of liberty for the sake of greater social benefits. We need not consider here the truth of this claim. For the moment, this contention is only to illustrate the way in which conceptions of justice may allow for outcomes which the parties may not be able to accept. And having the ready alternative of the two principles of justice which secure a satisfactory minimum, it seems unwise, if not irrational, for them to take a chance that these conditions are not realized.

[…]

40. The Kantian Interpretation of Justice as Fairness

For the most part I have considered the content of the principle of equal liberty and the meaning of the priority of the rights that it defines. It seems appropriate at this point to note that there is a Kantian interpretation of the conception of justice from which this principle derives. This interpretation is based upon Kant's notion of autonomy. It is a mistake, I believe, to emphasize the place of generality and universality in Kant's ethics. That moral principles are general and universal is hardly new with him; and as we have seen these conditions do not in any case take us very far. It is impossible to construct a moral theory on so slender a basis, and therefore to limit the discussion of Kant's doctrine to these notions is to reduce it to triviality. The real force of his view lies elsewhere.[16]

For one thing, he begins with the idea that moral principles are the object of rational choice. They define the moral law that men can rationally will to govern their conduct in an ethical commonwealth. Moral philosophy becomes the study of the conception and outcome of a suitably defined rational decision. This idea has immediate consequences. For once we think of moral principles as legislation for a kingdom of ends, it is clear that these principles must not only be acceptable to all but public as well. Finally Kant supposes that this moral legislation is to be agreed to under conditions that characterize men as free and equal rational beings. The description of the original position is an attempt to interpret this conception. I do not wish to argue here for this interpretation on the basis of Kant's text. Certainly some will want to read him differently. Perhaps the remarks to follow are best taken as suggestions for relating justice as fairness to the high point of the contractarian tradition in Kant and Rousseau.

Kant held, I believe, that a person is acting autonomously when the principles of his action are chosen by him as the most adequate possible expression of his nature as a free and equal rational being. The principles he acts upon

---

[16] Especially to be avoided is the idea that Kant's doctrine provides at best only the general, or formal, elements for a utilitarian or indeed for any other moral conception. This idea is found in Sidgwick, *The Methods of Ethics*, 7th ed. (London, Macmillan, 1907), pp. xvii and xx of the preface; and in F. H. Bradley, *Ethical Studies*, 2nd ed. (Oxford, Clarendon Press, 1927), Essay IV; and goes back at least to Hegel. One must not lose sight of the full scope of his view and take the later works into consideration. Unfortunately, there is no commentary on Kant's moral theory as a whole; perhaps it would prove impossible to write. But the standard works of H. J. Paton, *The Categorical Imperative* (Chicago, University of Chicago Press, 1948), and L. W. Beck, *A Commentary on Kant's Critique of Practical Reason* (Chicago, University of Chicago Press, 1960), and others need to be further complemented by studies of the other writings. See here M. J. Gregor's *Laws of Freedom* (Oxford, Basil Blackwell, 1963), an account of *The Metaphysics of Morals*, and J. G. Murphy's brief *Kant: The Philosophy of Right* (London, Macmillan, 1970). Beyond this, *The Critique of Judgment, Religion within the Limits of Reason*, and the political writings cannot be neglected without distorting his doctrine. For the last, see *Kant's Political Writings*, ed. Hans Reiss and trans. H. B. Nisbet (Cambridge, The University Press, 1970).

are not adopted because of his social position or natural endowments, or in view of the particular kind of society in which he lives or the specific things that he happens to want. To act on such principles is to act heteronomously. Now the veil of ignorance deprives the persons in the original position of the knowledge that would enable them to choose heteronomous principles. The parties arrive at their choice together as free and equal rational persons knowing only that those circumstances obtain which give rise to the need for principles of justice.

To be sure, the argument for these principles does add in various ways to Kant's conception. For example, it adds the feature that the principles chosen are to apply to the basic structure of society; and premises characterizing this structure are used in deriving the principles of justice. But I believe that this and other additions are natural enough and remain fairly close to Kant's doctrine, at least when all of his ethical writings are viewed together. Assuming, then, that the reasoning in favor of the principles of justice is correct, we can say that when persons act on these principles they are acting in accordance with principles that they would choose as rational and independent persons in an original position of equality. The principles of their actions do not depend upon social or natural contingencies, nor do they reflect the bias of the particulars of their plan of life or the aspirations that motivate them. By acting from these principles persons express their nature as free and equal rational beings subject to the general conditions of human life. For to express one's nature as a being of a particular kind is to act on the principles that would be chosen if this nature were the decisive determining element. Of course, the choice of the parties in the original position is subject to the restrictions of that situation. But when we knowingly act on the principles of justice in the ordinary course of events, we deliberately assume the limitations of the original position. One reason for doing this, for persons who can do so and want to, is to give expression to one's nature.

The principles of justice are also analogous to categorical imperatives. For by a categorical imperative Kant understands a principle of conduct that applies to a person in virtue of his nature as a free and equal rational being. The validity of the principle does not presuppose that one has a particular desire or aim. Whereas a hypothetical imperative by contrast does assume this: it directs us to take certain steps as effective means to achieve a specific end. Whether the desire is for a particular thing, or whether it is for something more general, such as certain kinds of agreeable feelings or pleasures, the corresponding imperative is hypothetical. Its applicability depends upon one's having an aim which one need not have as a condition of being a rational human individual. The argument for the two principles of justice does not assume that the parties have particular ends, but only that they desire certain primary goods. These are things that it is rational to want whatever else one wants. Thus given human nature, wanting them is part of being rational; and while each is presumed to have some conception of the good, nothing is known about his final ends. The preference for primary goods is derived, then, from only the most general assumptions about rationality and the conditions of human life. To act from the principles of justice is to act from categorical imperatives in the sense that they apply to us whatever in particular our aims are. This simply reflects the fact that no such contingencies appear as premises in their derivation.

We may note also that the motivational assumption of mutual disinterest parallels Kant's notion of autonomy, and gives another reason for this condition. So far this assumption has been used to characterize the circumstances of justice and to provide a clear conception to guide the reasoning of the parties. We have also seen that the concept of benevolence, being a second-order notion, would not work out well. Now we can add that the assumption of mutual disinterest is to allow for freedom in the choice of a system of final ends.[17] Liberty in adopting a conception of the good is limited only by principles that are deduced from a doctrine which imposes no prior constraints on these conceptions. Presuming mutual disinterest in the original position carries out this idea. We postulate that the parties have opposing claims in a suitably general sense. If their ends were restricted in some specific way, this would appear at the outset as an arbitrary restriction on freedom. Moreover, if the parties were conceived as altruists, or as pursuing certain kinds of pleasures, then the principles chosen would apply, as far as the argument would have shown, only to persons whose freedom was restricted to choices compatible with altruism or hedonism. As the argument now runs, the principles of justice cover all persons with rational plans of life, whatever their content, and these principles represent the appropriate restrictions on freedom. Thus it is possible to say that the constraints on conceptions of the good are the result of an interpretation of the contractual situation that puts no prior limitations on what men may desire. There are a variety of reasons, then, for the motivational premise of mutual disinterest. This premise is not only a matter of realism about the circumstances of justice or a way to make the theory manageable. It also connects up with the Kantian idea of autonomy.

---

[17] For this point I am indebted to Charles Fried.

There is, however, a difficulty that should be clarified. It is well expressed by Sidgwick.[18] He remarks that nothing in Kant's ethics is more striking than the idea that a man realizes his true self when he acts from the moral law, whereas if he permits his actions to be determined by sensuous desires or contingent aims, he becomes subject to the law of nature. Yet in Sidgwick's opinion this idea comes to naught. It seems to him that on Kant's view the lives of the saint and the scoundrel are equally the outcome of a free choice (on the part of the noumenal self) and equally the subject of causal laws (as a phenomenal self). Kant never explains why the scoundrel does not express in a bad life his characteristic and freely chosen selfhood in the same way that a saint expresses his characteristic and freely chosen selfhood in a good one. Sidgwick's objection is decisive, I think, as long as one assumes, as Kant's exposition may seem to allow, both that the noumenal self can choose any consistent set of principles and that acting from such principles, whatever they are, is sufficient to express one's choice as that of a free and equal rational being. Kant's reply must be that though acting on any consistent set of principles could be the outcome of a decision on the part of the noumenal self, not all such action by the phenomenal self expresses this decision as that of a free and equal rational being. Thus if a person realizes his true self by expressing it in his actions, and if he desires above all else to realize this self, then he will choose to act from principles that manifest his nature as a free and equal rational being. The missing part of the argument concerns the concept of expression. Kant did not show that acting from the moral law expresses our nature in identifiable ways that acting from contrary principles does not.

This defect is made good, I believe, by the conception of the original position. The essential point is that we need an argument showing which principles, if any, free and equal rational persons would choose and these principles must be applicable in practice. A definite answer to this question is required to meet Sidgwick's objection. My suggestion is that we think of the original position as in important ways similar to the point of view from which noumenal selves see the world. The parties qua noumenal selves have complete freedom to choose whatever principles they wish; but they also have a desire to express their nature as rational and equal members of the intelligible realm with precisely this liberty to choose, that is, as beings who can look at the world in this way and express this perspective in their life as members of society. They must decide, then, which principles when consciously followed and acted upon in everyday life will best manifest this freedom in their community, most fully reveal their independence from natural contingencies and social accident. Now if the argument of the contract doctrine is correct, these principles are indeed those defining the moral law, or more exactly, the principles of justice for institutions and individuals. The description of the original position resembles the point of view of noumenal selves, of what it means to be a free and equal rational being. Our nature as such beings is displayed when we act from the principles we would choose when this nature is reflected in the conditions determining the choice. Thus men exhibit their freedom, their independence from the contingencies of nature and society, by acting in ways they would acknowledge in the original position.

Properly understood, then, the desire to act justly derives in part from the desire to express most fully what we are or can be, namely free and equal rational beings with a liberty to choose. It is for this reason, I believe, that Kant speaks of the failure to act on the moral law as giving rise to shame and not to feelings of guilt. And this is appropriate, since for him acting unjustly is acting in a manner that fails to express our nature as a free and equal rational being. Such actions therefore strike at our self-respect, our sense of our own worth, and the experience of this loss is shame). We have acted as though we belonged to a lower order, as though we were a creature whose first principles are decided by natural contingencies. Those who think of Kant's moral doctrine as one of law and guilt badly misunderstand him. Kant's main aim is to deepen and to justify Rousseau's idea that liberty is acting in accordance with a law that we give to ourselves. And this leads not to a morality of austere command but to an ethic of mutual respect and self-esteem.[19]

The original position may be viewed, then, as a procedural interpretation of Kant's conception of autonomy and the categorical imperative within the framework of an empirical theory. The principles regulative of the kingdom of ends are those that would be chosen in this position, and the description of this situation enables us to explain the sense in which acting from these principles expresses our nature as free and equal rational persons. No longer are these notions purely transcendent and lacking explicable connections with human conduct, for the procedural conception of the original position allows us to make these ties. Of course, I have departed from Kant's views in

---

[18] See *The Methods of Ethics*, Appendix, "The Kantian Conception of Free Will" (reprinted from *Mind*, vol. 13, 1888), pp. 511–516. esp. p. 516.

[19] See B. A. O. Williams, "The Idea of Equality," in *Philosophy, Politics and Society*, Second Series, ed. Peter Laslett and W. G. Runciman (Oxford, Basil Blackwell, 1962), pp. 115 f. For confirmation of this interpretation, see Kant's remarks on moral education in *The Critique of Practical Reason*, pt. II. See also Beck, *A Commentary on Kant's Critique of Practical Reason*, pp. 233–236.

several respects. I cannot discuss these matters here; but two points should be noted. The person's choice as a noumenal self I have assumed to be a collective one. The force of the self's being equal is that the principles chosen must be acceptable to other selves. Since all are similarly free and rational, each must have an equal say in adopting the public principles of the ethical commonwealth. This means that as noumenal selves, everyone is to consent to these principles. Unless the scoundrel's principles would be agreed to, they cannot express this free choice, however much a single self might be of a mind to adopt them. Later I shall try to define a clear sense in which this unanimous agreement is best expressive of the nature of even a single self. It in no way overrides a person's interests as the collective nature of the choice might seem to imply. But I leave this aside for the present.

Secondly, I have assumed all along that the parties know that they are subject to the conditions of human life. Being in the circumstances of justice, they are situated in the world with other men who likewise face limitations of moderate scarcity and competing claims. Human freedom is to be regulated by principles chosen in the light of these natural restrictions. Thus justice as fairness is a theory of human justice and among its premises are the elementary facts about persons and their place in nature. The freedom of pure intelligences not subject to these constraints (God and the angels) are outside the range of the theory. Kant may have meant his doctrine to apply to all rational beings as such and therefore that men's social situation in the world is to have no role in determining the first principles of justice. If so, this is another difference between justice as fairness and Kant's theory.

But the Kantian interpretation is not intended as an interpretation of Kant's actual doctrine but rather of justice as fairness. Kant's view is marked by a number of deep dualisms, in particular, the dualism between the necessary and the contingent, form and content, reason and desire, and noumena and phenomena. To abandon these dualisms as he understood them is, for many, to abandon what is distinctive in his theory. I believe otherwise. His moral conception has a characteristic structure that is more clearly discernible when these dualisms are not taken in the sense he gave them but recast and their moral force reformulated within the scope of an empirical theory. What I have called the Kantian interpretation indicates how this can be done.

9

Ethical Theory and Utilitarianism

R. M. Hare

In the 1970s, there was a turn from analytical metaethics (the study of the nature of moral judgements) to specific topics in practical ethics. Hare welcomes this, but suggests that those engaging in practical ethics have not learned enough from the earlier analytic work (1–2). Hare's own view of ethics (3–9) developed after the rise of emotivism (see the selection from Ayer in this volume), according to which, in its most simple form, a statement such as 'Lying is wrong' is equivalent to 'Boo to lying!' One problem many found with emotivism was its irrationalism: it seemed to make ethics a matter of taste (so a hardened fraud might say, 'Hurray for lying!'). Hare saw this problem but was attracted to the metaphysics behind emotivism, disagreeing with so-called 'descriptivists' who believed that moral predicates describe the world. His view of moral judgements, he calls *prescriptivism*. A statement is prescriptive if it entails an imperative. One form of prescriptive statement is self-referential: I might say, 'Let me through!' This is not a moral judgement, because it lacks the other property Hare saw as essential to such judgements: *universalizability*. Here we see the influence of Kant's conception of categorical imperatives on Hare. If I make a moral judgement, I have sincerely to accept that this imperative applies to all relevantly similar situations, including those, for example, in which roles are reversed. If I say, 'You ought to pay me back what I lent you', I have to accept that, were you instead the lender and I the borrower, and if there were no relevant differences between the two cases, I would be morally required to pay you back.

When I am deciding how much weight to attach to the interests of people in the various situations covered by a moral judgement, I have to take into account their desires or preferences, asking myself what I would prefer were I in the other individual's position *with the preferences they have*. Further, all these preferences must be 'rational' – that is, properly informed (11–12). This takes Hare all the way from an account of the meaning of a word – 'ought' – to substantive moral judgements that are, in effect, utilitarian. That is, if I understand the logic of 'ought' properly, I will recognize that what I ought to do is to maximize preference-satisfaction impartially.

One important criticism of Hare's account is similar to certain objections made to Kant by Hegel and others. The central idea here is that substantive conclusions cannot come from mere logic or the analysis of meaning. So, despite Hare's doubts about 'intuitions', there must be some intuitions hidden in his account – for example, in his views about what prudence consists in, or what properly constitutes putting oneself in the position of others. As Rawls might suggest, there is no way of entirely escaping one's 'intuitions', but there may be intellectual exercises, such as imagining oneself behind a veil of ignorance, which increase their overall justificatory weight.

Over the centuries, many objections to utilitarianism have been raised, and a good deal of Hare's essay is an attempt to respond to these objections. He claims that there is no reason to see justice as at odds with utility, since the principle that one should treat equal interests equally is itself a plausible account of

History of Ethics – Essential Readings with Commentary, First Edition. Edited by Daniel Star and Roger Crisp.
© 2020 John Wiley & Sons Ltd. Published 2020 by John Wiley & Sons Ltd.

distribution (10). But it will of course be open to an opponent to claim that equality has weight independently of utility, and then the debate will have to return to Hare's linguistic analysis.

Another common objection to utilitarianism is that it gives equal weight to 'bad' desires and 'good' desires (17). Hare responds that in real life, allowing sadists to satisfy their desires is unlikely to maximize utility. However, what about some very unusual case, in which it would? At this point Hare introduces his 'two-level' account of utilitarianism (18–19), a development of earlier views in Mill and others (see the selections from Mill and Sidgwick in this volume). Utilitarianism is a 'level-2', purely philosophical principle, which tells us which actions are right and wrong. Because of various contingent facts about human beings – such as our limited knowledge and impartiality – utility would not in fact be maximized were we to try in real life always to act on this principle. So utilitarianism recommends that we live by various 'level-1' principles, such as 'Don't lie' and 'Don't harm others'. So it is no surprise, Hare suggests, that many people react with horror at the idea that a sadist could be justified, or even required, to torture others, in some bizarre imaginary case in which her action would maximize utility. Once one recognizes the role of such level-1 principles in a utilitarian moral education, and properly understands some details of the two-level position (24–30), one will see that many of the objections to utilitarianism based on counter-examples fail (20–23, 31–3).

The likely response to Hare at this point will be similar to that mentioned earlier on equality. First, it may be objected that some desires are, say, evil, and just shouldn't be given any weight at all. Hare will reply that this is inconsistent with an adequate understanding of moral concepts. The objector then has at least two further rejoinders. She might grant Hare's account of the moral concepts, but suggest replacing them with some other concepts that allow for non-utilitarian judgements. Or she might insist that, since Hare himself appeals to basic intuitions at various points, he cannot object to her doing the same in making judgements about imaginary examples.

Some have argued that views such as Hare's result in what Michael Stocker has called 'moral schizophrenia'. When I am outside the philosophical study, I should think that lying is wrong, that I should give special weight to the interests of those I love, that I should be loyal to my friends, and so on. But in the study, I believe that all these judgements are, strictly speaking, mistaken. Hare might respond, perhaps with reference to Aristotle, that living by level-1 principles is a matter of having been brought up with the right dispositions to act without one's having to make individual decisions. But questions remain about the nature of these dispositions and their stability in the light of philosophical reflection.

Contemporary moral philosophy (and the British is no exception) is in a phase which must seem curious to anybody who has observed its course since, say, the 1940s. During all that time moral philosophers of the analytic tradition have devoted most of their work to fundamental questions about the analysis or the meaning of the moral words and the types of reasoning that are valid on moral questions. It may be that some of them were attracted by the intrinsic theoretical interest of this branch of philosophical logic; and indeed it is interesting. But it may surely be said that the greater part, like myself, studied these questions with an ulterior motive: they saw this study as the philosopher's main contribution to the solution of practical moral problems such as trouble most of us. For if we do not understand the very terms in which the problems are posed, how shall we ever get to the root of them? I, at least, gave evidence of this motive in my writings and am publishing many papers on practical questions.[1] But, now that philosophers in greater numbers have woken up to the need for such a contribution, and whole new journals are devoted to the practical applications of philosophy, what do we find the philosophers doing? In the main they proceed as if nothing had been learnt in the course of all that analytical enquiry – as if we had become no clearer now than in, say, 1936, or even 1903, how good moral arguments are to be distinguished from bad.

I cannot believe that we need be so pessimistic; nor that I am alone in thinking that logic can help with moral argument. But surprisingly many philosophers, as soon as they turn their hands to a practical question, forget all about their peculiar art, and think that the questions of the market place can be solved only by the methods of the market place – i.e. by a combination of prejudice (called intuition) and rhetoric. The philosopher's special contribution to such discussions lies in the ability that he ought to possess to clarify the concepts that are being employed (above all the moral concepts themselves) and thus, by revealing their logical properties, to expose fallacies and put valid arguments in their stead. This he cannot do unless he has an understanding (dare I say a theory?) of the moral concepts; and that is what we have been looking for all these years. And yet we find philosophers writing in such a way that it is entirely unclear what understanding they have of the moral concepts or of the rules of moral reasoning.[2] It is often hard to tell whether they are naturalists, relying on supposed equivalences between moral and non-moral concepts, or intuitionists, whose only appeal is to whatever moral sentiments they can get their readers to share with them. Most of them seem to be some sort of descriptivists; but as they retreat through an ever vaguer naturalism into a hardly avowed intuitionism, it becomes more and more obscure what, in their view, moral statements say, and therefore how we could decide whether to accept them or not. Philosophy, as a rational discipline, has been left behind.

It is the object of this paper to show how a theory about the meanings of the moral words can be the foundation for a theory of normative moral reasoning. The conceptual theory is of a non-descriptivist but nevertheless rationalist sort.[3] That this sort of theory could claim to provide the basis of an account of moral reasoning will seem paradoxical only to the prejudiced and to those who have not read Kant. It is precisely that sort of prejudice which has led to the troubles I have been complaining of: the belief that only a descriptivist theory can provide a rational basis for morality, and that therefore it is better to explore any blind alley than expose oneself to the imputation of irrationalism and subjectivism by becoming a non-descriptivist.

The normative theory that I shall advocate has close analogies with utilitarianism, and I should not hesitate to call it utilitarian, were it not that this name covers a wide variety of views, all of which have been the victims of prejudices rightly excited by the cruder among them. In calling my own normative theory utilitarian, I beg the reader to look at the theory itself, and ask whether it cannot avoid the objections that have been made against other kinds of utilitarianism. I hope to show in this paper that it can avoid at least some of them. But if I escape calumny while remaining both a non-descriptivist and a utilitarian, it will be a marvel.

---

[1] See, for example, my *Freedom and Reason* (FR) (Oxford, 1963), ch. 11; *Applications of Moral Philosophy* (London, 1972); 'Rules of War and Moral Reasoning', *Ph. and Public Affairs*, 1 (1972); 'Language and Moral Education', *New Essays in the Philosophy of Education*, G. Langford and D. J. O'Connor (eds) (London, 1973); 'Abortion and the Golden Rule', *Ph. and Public Affairs*, 4 (1975); 'Political Obligation', *Social Ends and Political Means*, T. Honderich (ed.); and 'Contrasting Methods of Environmental Planning', *Nature and Conduct*, R. S. Peters (ed.) (London, 1975).

[2] See the beginning of my paper 'Abortion and the Golden Rule', cited in note 1.

[3] It is substantially that set out in FR. For the distinction between non-descriptivism and subjectivism, see my 'Some Confusions about Subjectivity', Lindley Lecture, 1974, University of Kansas.

In my review of Professor Rawls's book[4] I said that there were close formal similarities between rational contractor theories such as Rawls's, ideal observer theories such as have been advocated by many writers[5] and my own universal prescriptivist theory. I also said that theories of this form can be made to lead very naturally to a kind of utilitarianism, and that Rawls avoided this outcome only by a very liberal use of intuitions to make his rational contractors come to a non-utilitarian contract. Rawls advocates his theory as an alternative to utilitarianism. Whether the system which I shall sketch is to be regarded as utilitarian or not is largely a matter of terminology. The form of argument which it employs is, as I have already said, formally extremely similar to Rawls's; the substantive conclusions are, however, markedly different. I should like to think of my view as, in Professor Brandt's expression, 'a credible form of utilitarianism';[6] no doubt Rawls would classify it as an incredible form of utilitarianism; others might say that it is a compromise between his views and more ordinary kinds of utilitarianism. This does not much matter.

I try to base myself, unlike Rawls, entirely on the formal properties of the moral concepts as revealed by the logical study of moral language; and in particular on the features of prescriptivity and universalisability which I think moral judgements, in the central uses which we shall be considering, all have. These two features provide a framework for moral reasoning which is formally similar to Rawls's own more dramatic machinery. But, rather than put the argument in his way, I will do overtly what he does covertly – that is to say, I do not speculate about what some fictitious rational contractors *would* judge if they were put in a certain position subject to certain restrictions; rather, I subject myself to certain (formally analogous) restrictions and put myself (imaginatively) in this position, as Rawls in effect does,[7] and *do* some judging. Since the position and the restrictions are formally analogous, this ought to make no difference.

In this position, I am prescribing universally for all situations just like the one I am considering; and thus for all such situations, *whatever* role, among those in the situations, I might myself occupy. I shall therefore give equal weight to the equal interests of the occupants of all the roles in the situation; and, since any of these occupants might be myself, this weight will be positive. Thus the impartiality which is the purpose of Rawls's 'veil of ignorance' is achieved by purely formal means; and so is the purpose of his insistence that his contractors be rational, i.e. prudent. We have therefore, by consideration of the logic of the moral concepts alone, put ourselves in as strong a position as Rawls hopes to put himself by his more elaborate, but at the same time, as I have claimed, less firmly based apparatus.

Let us now use these tools. Rawls himself says that an ideal observer theory leads to utilitarianism; and the same ought to be true of the formal apparatus which I have just sketched. How does giving equal weight to the equal interests of all the parties lead to utilitarianism? And to what kind of utilitarianism does it lead? If I am trying to give equal weight to the equal interests of all the parties in a situation, I must, it seems, regard a benefit or harm done to one party as of equal value or disvalue to an equal benefit or harm done to any other party. This seems to mean that I shall promote the interests of the parties most, while giving equal weight to them all, if I maximise the total benefits over the entire population; and this is the classical principle of utility. For fixed populations it is practically equivalent to the average utility principle which bids us maximise not total but average utility; when the size of the population is itself affected by a decision, the two principles diverge, and I have given reasons in my review of Rawls's book for preferring the classical or total utility principle. In these calculations, benefits are to be taken to include the reduction of harms.

I am not, however, going to put my theory in terms of benefits and the reduction of harms, because this leads to difficulties that I wish to avoid. Let us say, rather, that what the principle of utility requires of me is to do for each man affected by my actions what I wish were done for me in the hypothetical circumstances that I were in precisely his situation; and, if my actions affect more than one man (as they nearly always will) to do what I wish, all in all, to be done for me in the hypothetical circumstances that I occupied all their situations (not of course at the same time but, shall we say?, in random order). This way of putting the matter, which is due to C. I. Lewis,[8] emphasises that I have to give the same weight to everybody's equal interests; and we must remember that, in so far as I am one of

[4] *Ph.Q.*, 23 (1973); cf. my paper 'Rules of War and Moral Reasoning', cited in note 1, and B. Barry, *The Liberal Theory of Justice* (Oxford, 1973), pp. 12–13.
[5] See, for example, the discussion between R. Firth and R. B. Brandt in *Ph. and Phen. Res.*, 12 (1952) and 15 (1955); also D. Haslett, *Moral Rightness* (The Hague, 1974).
[6] R. B. Brandt, 'Towards a Credible Form of Utilitarianism', *Morality and the Language of Conduct*, H.-N. Castaneda and G. Nakhnikian (eds) (Detroit, 1963).
[7] See my review of Rawls, *Ph.Q.*, 23 (1973), p. 249.
[8] *An Analysis of Knowledge and Valuation* (La Salle, 1946), p. 547; see also Haslett, op. cit., ch. 3.

the people affected (as in nearly all cases I am) my own interests have to be given the same, and no more, weight – that is to say, my own actual situation is one of those that I have to suppose myself occupying in this random order.

Some further notes on this suggestion will be in place here. First, it is sometimes alleged that justice has to be at odds with utility. But if we ask how we are to be just between the competing interests of different people, it seems hard to give any other answer than that it is by giving equal weight, impartially, to the equal interests of everybody. And this is precisely what yields the utility principle. It does not necessarily yield equality in the resulting distribution. There are, certainly, very good utilitarian reasons for seeking equality in distribution too; but justice is something distinct. The utilitarian is sometimes said to be indifferent between equal and unequal distributions, provided that total utility is equal. This is so; but it conceals two important utilitarian grounds for a fairly high degree of equality of actual goods (tempered, of course, as in most systems including Rawls's, by various advantages that are secured by moderate inequalities). The first is the diminishing marginal utility of all commodities and of money, which means that approaches towards equality will tend to increase total utility. The second is that inequalities tend to produce, at any rate in educated societies, envy, hatred and malice, whose disutility needs no emphasising. I am convinced that when these two factors are taken into account, utilitarians have no need to fear the accusation that they could favour extreme inequalities of distribution in actual modern societies. Fantastic hypothetical cases can no doubt be invented in which they would have to favour them; but, as we shall see, this is an illegitimate form of argument.

Secondly, the transition from a formulation in terms of interests to one in terms of desires or prescriptions, or vice versa, is far from plain sailing. Both formulations raise problems which are beyond the scope of this paper. If we formulate utilitarianism in terms of interests, we have the problem of determining what are someone's true interests. Even if we do not confuse the issue, as some do, by introducing moral considerations into this prudential question (i.e. by alleging that becoming morally better, or worse, in itself affects a man's interests),[9] we still have to find a way of cashing statements about interests in terms of such states of mind as likings, desires, etc., both actual and hypothetical. For this reason a formulation directly in terms of these states of mind ought to be more perspicuous. But two difficult problems remain: the first is that of how present desires and likings are to be balanced against future, and actual desires and likings against those which would be experienced if certain alternative actions were taken; the second is whether desires need to be mentioned at all in a formulation of utilitarianism, or whether likings by themselves will do. It would seem that if we arrive at utilitarianism via universal prescriptivism, as I am trying to do, we shall favour the former of the last pair of alternatives; for desires, in the required sense, are assents to prescriptions. All these are questions within the theory of prudence, with which, although it is an essential adjunct to normative moral theory, I do not hope to deal in this paper.[10]

I must mention, however, that when I said above that I have to do for each man affected by my actions what I wish were done for me, etc., I was speaking inaccurately. When I do the judging referred to on page 116, I have to do it as rationally as possible. This, if I am making a moral judgement, involves prescribing universally; but in prescribing (albeit universally) I cannot, if rational, ignore prudence altogether, but have to universalise this prudence. Put more clearly, this means that, whether I am prescribing in my own interest or in someone else's (see the next paragraph), I must ask, not what I or he does actually at present wish, but what, prudentially speaking, we should wish. It is from this rational point of view (in the prudential sense of 'rational') that I have to give my universal prescriptions. In other words, it is *qua* rational that I have to judge; and this involves at least judging with a clear and unconfused idea of what I am saying and what the actual consequences of the prescription that I am issuing would be, for myself and others. It also involves, when I am considering the desires of others, considering what they would be if those others were perfectly prudent – i.e. desired what they would desire if they were fully informed and unconfused. Thus morality, at least for the utilitarian, can only be founded on prudence, which has then to be universalised. All this we shall have to leave undiscussed, remembering, however, that when, in what follows, I say 'desire', 'prescribe', etc., I mean 'desire, prescribe, etc., from the point of view of one who is prudent so far as his own interest goes'. It is important always to supply this qualification whether I am speaking of our own desires or those of others; but I shall omit it from now on because it would make my sentences intolerably cumbrous, and signalise the omission, in the next paragraph only, by adding the subscript '$_p$' to the words 'desire', etc., as required, omitting even this subscript thereafter. I hope that one paragraph will suffice to familiarise the reader with this point.

---

[9] Cf. Plato, *Republic*, 335.

[10] The theory of prudence is ably handled in D. A. J. Richards, *A Theory of Reasons for Action* (Oxford, 1971); Haslett, op. cit.; and R. B. Brandt, John Locke Lectures (Oxford).

Thirdly, when we speak of the 'situations' of the various parties, we have to include in the situations all the desires$_p$, likings$_p$, etc., that the people have in them – that is to say, I am to do for the others what I wish$_p$ to be done for me were I to have their likings$_p$, etc., and not those which I now have. And, similarly, I am not to take into account (when I ask what I wish$_p$ should be done to me in a certain situation) my own present desires$_p$, likings$_p$, etc. There is one exception to this: I have said that one of the situations that I have to consider is my own present situation; I have to love$_p$ my neighbour *as*, but *no more than* and *no less than*, myself, and likewise to do to others *as* I wish$_p$ them to do to me. Therefore just as, when I am considering what I wish$_p$ to be done to me were I in *X*'s situation, where *X* is somebody else, I have to think of the situation as including *his* desires$_p$, likings$_p$, etc., and discount my own, so, in the single case where *X* is myself, I have to take into account *my* desires$_p$, likings$_p$, etc. In other words, *qua* author of the moral decision I have to discount my own desires$_p$, etc., and consider only the desires$_p$, etc., of the affected party; but where (as normally) I am one of the affected parties, I have to consider my own desires$_p$, etc., *qua* affected party, on equal terms with those of all the other affected parties.[11]

It will be asked: if we strip me, *qua* author of the moral decision, of all desires and likings, how is it determined what decision I shall come to? The answer is that it is determined by the desires and likings of those whom I take into account as affected parties (including, as I said, myself, but only *qua* affected party and not *qua* author). I am to ask, indeed, what I do wish should be done for me, were I in their situations; but were I in their situations, I should have their desires, etc., so I must forget about my own present desires (with the exception just made) and consider only the desires which *they* have; and if I do this, what I *do* wish for will be the satisfaction of *those* desires; that, therefore, is what I shall prescribe, so far as is possible.

I wish to point out that my present formulation enables me to deal in an agreeably clear way with the problem of the fanatic, who has given me so much trouble in the past.[12] In so far as, in order to prescribe universally, I have to strip away (*qua* author of the moral decision) all my present desires, etc., I shall have to strip away, among them, all the ideals that I have; for an ideal is a kind of desire or liking (in the generic sense in which I am using those terms); it is, to use Aristotle's word, an *orexis*.[13] This does not mean that I have to give up having ideals, nor even that I must stop giving any consideration to my ideals when I make my moral decisions; it means only that I am not allowed to take them into account *qua* author of the moral decision. I am, however, allowed to take them into account, along with the ideals of all the other parties affected, when I consider my own position, among others, as an affected party. This means that for the purposes of the moral decision it makes no difference *who has* the ideal. It means that we have to give impartial consideration to the ideals of ourselves and others. In cases, however, where the pursuit of our own ideals does not affect the ideals or the interests of others, we are allowed and indeed encouraged to pursue them.

All this being so, the only sort of fanatic that is going to bother us is the person whose ideals are so intensely pursued that the weight that has to be given to them, considered impartially, out-balances the combined weights of all the ideals, desires, likings, etc., that have to be frustrated in order to achieve them. For example, if the Nazi's desire not to have Jews around is intense enough to outweigh all the sufferings caused to Jews by arranging not to have them around, then, on this version of utilitarianism, as on any theory with the same formal structure, it ought to be satisfied. The problem is to be overcome by, first, pointing out that fanatics of this heroic stature are never likely to be encountered (that no *actual* Nazis had such intense desires is, I think, obvious); secondly, by remembering that, as I shall be showing in a moment, cases that are never likely to be actually encountered do not have to be squared with the thinking of the ordinary man, whose principles are not designed to cope with such cases. It is therefore illegitimate to attack such a theory as I have sketched by saying 'You can't ask us to believe that it would be right to give this fantastic fanatical Nazi what he wanted'; this argument depends on appealing to the ordinary man's judgement about a case with which, as we shall see, his intuitions were not designed to deal.

A similar move enables us to deal with another alleged difficulty (even if we do not, as we legitimately might, make use of the fact that all desires that come into our reasoning are desires$_p$, i.e. desires that a man will have after

[11] Professor Bernard Williams says, 'It is absurd to demand of such a man, when the sums come in from the utility network which the projects of others have in part determined, that he should just step aside from his own project and decision and acknowledge the decision which utilitarian calculation requires.' (J. J. C. Smart and B. A. O. Williams, *Utilitarianism: For and Against* (Cambridge, 1973), p. 116, and cf. p. 117n.) Christian humility and *agape* and their humanist counterparts are, then, according to Williams's standards, an absurd demand (which is hardly remarkable). What is more remarkable is the boldness of the persuasive definition by which he labels the self-centred pursuit of one's own projects 'integrity' and accounts it a fault in utilitarianism that it could conflict with this.

[12] *FR*, ch. 9; 'Wrongness and Harm', in my *Essays on the Moral Concepts* (London, 1972).

[13] *De Anima*, 433a 9 ff.

he has become perfectly prudent). It is sometimes said to be a fault in utilitarianism that it makes us give weight to bad desires (such as the desire of a sadist to torture his victim) solely in proportion to their intensity; received opinion, it is claimed, gives no weight at all, or even a negative weight, to such desires. But received opinion has grown up to deal with cases likely to be encountered; and we are most *unlikely*, even if we give sadistic desires weight in accordance with their intensity, to encounter a case in which utility will be maximised by letting the sadist have his way. For first, the suffering of the victim will normally be more intense than the pleasure of the sadist. And, secondly, sadists can often be given substitute pleasures or even actually cured. And, thirdly, the side-effects of allowing the sadist to have what he wants are enormous. So it will be clear, when I have explained in more detail why fantastic cases in which these disutilities do not occur cannot legitimately be used in this kind of argument, why it is perfectly all right to allow weight to bad desires.

We have now, therefore, to make an important distinction between two kinds or 'levels' of moral thinking. It has some affinities with a distinction made by Rawls in his article 'Two Concepts of Rules'[14] (in which he was by way of defending utilitarianism), though it is not the same; it also owes something to Sir David Ross,[15] and indeed to others. I call it the difference between level-1 and level-2 thinking, or between the principles employed at these two levels.[16] Level-1 principles are for use in practical moral thinking, especially under conditions of stress. They have to be general enough to be impartable by education (including self-education), and to be 'of ready application in the emergency',[17] but are not to be confused with rules of thumb (whose breach excites no compunction). Level-2 principles are what would be arrived at by leisured moral thought in completely adequate knowledge of the facts, as the right answer in a specific case. They are universal but can be as specific (the opposite of 'general', not of 'universal'[18]) as needs be. Level-1 principles are inculcated in moral education; but the selection of the level-1 principles for this purpose should be guided by leisured thought, resulting in level-2 principles for specific considered situations, the object being to have those level-1 principles whose general acceptance will lead to actions in accord with the best level-2 principles in most situations that are actually encountered. Fantastic and highly unusual situations, therefore, need not be considered for this purpose.

I have set out this distinction in detail elsewhere;[19] here we only need to go into some particular points which are relevant. The thinking that I have been talking about so far in this paper, until the preceding paragraph, and indeed in most of my philosophical writings until recently, is level-2. It results in a kind of act-utilitarianism which, because of the universalisability of moral judgements, is practically equivalent to a rule-utilitarianism whose rules are allowed to be of any required degree of specificity. Such thinking is appropriate only to 'a cool hour', in which there is time for unlimited investigation of the facts, and there is no temptation to special pleading. It can use hypothetical cases, even fantastic ones. In principle it can, given superhuman knowledge of the facts, yield answers as to what should be done in any cases one cares to describe.

The commonest trick of the opponents of utilitarianism is to take examples of such thinking, usually addressed to fantastic cases, and confront them with what the ordinary man would think. It makes the utilitarian look like a moral monster. The anti-utilitarians have usually confined their own thought about moral reasoning (with fairly infrequent lapses which often go unnoticed) to what I am calling level 1, the level of everyday moral thinking on ordinary, often stressful, occasions in which information is sparse. So they find it natural to take the side of the ordinary man in a supposed fight with the utilitarian whose views lead him to say, if put at the disconcertingly unfamiliar standpoint of the archangel Gabriel, such extraordinary things about these carefully contrived examples.

To argue in this way is entirely to neglect the importance for moral philosophy of a study of moral education. Let us suppose that a fully-informed archangelic act-utilitarian is thinking about how to bring up his children. He will obviously not bring them up to practise on every occasion on which they are confronted with a moral question the kind of archangelic thinking that he himself is capable of; if they are ordinary children, he knows that they will get it wrong. They will not have the time, or the information, or the self-mastery to avoid self-deception prompted by self-interest; this is the real, as opposed to the imagined, veil of ignorance which determines our moral principles.

[14] *Ph. Rev.*, 64 (1955).
[15] *The Right and the Good* (Oxford, 1930), pp. 19 ff.
[16] See my review of Rawls, cited in note 4, p. 153; 'Principles', *Proc. Arist. Soc.*, 72 (1972–3); 'Rules of War and Moral Reasoning', cited in note 1; *FR*, pp. 43–5.
[17] Burke; see *FR*, p. 45.
[18] See 'Principles', cited in note 16.
[19] See note 16.

So he will do two things. First, he will try to implant in them a set of good general principles. I advisedly use the word 'implant'; these are not rules of thumb, but principles which they will not be able to break without the greatest repugnance, and whose breach by others will arouse in them the highest indignation. These will be the principles they will use in their ordinary level-1 moral thinking, especially in situations of stress. Secondly, since he is not always going to be with them, and since they will have to educate *their* children, and indeed continue to educate themselves, he will teach them, as far as they are able, to do the kind of thinking that he has been doing himself. This thinking will have three functions. First of all, it will be used when the good general principles conflict in particular cases. If the principles have been well chosen, this will happen rarely; but it will happen. Secondly, there will be cases (even rarer) in which, though there is no conflict between general principles, there is something highly unusual about the case which prompts the question whether the general principles are really fitted to deal with it. But thirdly, and much the most important, this level-2 thinking will be used to *select* the general principles to be taught both to this and to succeeding generations. The general principles may change, and should change (because the environment changes). And note that, if the educator were not (as we have supposed him to be) archangelic, we could not even assume that the best level-1 principles were imparted in the first place; perhaps they might be improved.

How will the selection be done? By using level-2 thinking to consider cases, both actual and hypothetical, which crucially illustrate, and help to adjudicate, disputes between rival general principles. But, because the general principles are being selected for use in actual situations, there will have to be a careful proportioning of the weight to be put upon a particular case to the probability of its actually occurring in the lives of the people who are to use the principles. So the fantastic cases that are so beloved of anti-utilitarians will have very little employment in this kind of thinking (except as a diversion for philosophers or to illustrate purely logical points, which is sometimes necessary). Fantastic unlikely cases will never be used to turn the scales as between rival general principles for practical use. The result will be a set of general principles, constantly evolving, but on the whole stable, such that their use in moral education, including self-education, and their consequent acceptance by the society at large, will lead to the nearest possible approximation to the prescriptions of archangelic thinking. They will be the set of principles with the highest acceptance-utility. They are likely to include principles of justice.

It is now necessary to introduce some further distinctions, all of which, fortunately, have already been made elsewhere, and can therefore be merely summarised. The first, alluded to already, is that between specific rule-utilitarianism (which is practically equivalent to universalistic act-utilitarianism) and general rule-utilitarianism.[20] Both are compatible with act-utilitarianism if their roles are carefully distinguished. Specific rule-utilitarianism is appropriate to level-2 thinking, general rule-utilitarianism to level-1 thinking; and therefore the rules of specific rule-utilitarianism can be of unlimited specificity, but those of general rule-utilitarianism have to be general enough for their role. The thinking of our archangel will thus be of a specific rule-utilitarian sort; and the thinking of the ordinary people whom he has educated will be for the most part of a general rule-utilitarian sort, though they will supplement this, when they have to and when they dare, with such archangelic thinking as they are capable of.

The second distinction is that between what Professor Smart[21] calls (morally) 'right' actions and (morally) 'rational' actions. Although Smart's way of putting the distinction is not quite adequate, as he himself recognises, I shall, as he does, adopt it for the sake of brevity. Both here, and in connexion with the 'acceptance-utility' mentioned above, somewhat more sophisticated calculations of probability are required than might at first be thought. But for simplicity let us say that an action is rational if it is the action most likely to be right, even if, when all the facts are known, as they were not when it was done, it turns out not to have been right. In such a society as we have described, the (morally) rational action will nearly always be that in accordance with the good general principles of level 1, because they have been selected precisely in order to make this the case. Such actions may not always turn out to have been (morally) right in Smart's sense when the cards are turned face upwards; but the agent is not to be blamed for this.

It is a difficult question, just how simple and general these level-1 principles ought to be. If we are speaking of the principles to be inculcated throughout the society, the answer will obviously vary with the extent to which the members of it are sophisticated and morally self-disciplined enough to grasp and apply relatively complex principles without running into the dangers we have mentioned. We might distinguish sub-groups within the society, and individuals within these sub-groups, and even the same individual at different stages, according to their ability to handle complex principles. Most people's level-1 principles become somewhat more complex as they gain experi-

---

[20] See 'Principles', cited in note 16.
[21] Smart and Williams, op. cit., pp. 46 f.

ence of handling different situations, and they may well become so complex as to defy verbal formulation; but the value of the old simple maxims may also come to be appreciated. In any case, level-1 principles can never, because of the exigencies of their role, become as complex as level-2 principles are allowed to be.

A third distinction is that between good actions and the right action.[22] The latter is the action in accordance with level-2 principles arrived at by exhaustive, fully-informed and clear thinking about specific cases. A good action is what a good man would do, even if not right. In general this is the same as the morally rational action, but there may be complications, in that the motivation of the man has to be taken into account. The good (i.e. the morally well-educated) man, while he is sometimes able and willing to question and even to amend the principles he has been taught, will have acquired in his upbringing a set of motives and dispositions such that breaking these principles goes very much against the grain for him. The very goodness of his character will make him sometimes do actions which do not conform to archangelic prescriptions. This may be for one of at least two reasons. The first is that when he did them he was not fully informed and perhaps knew it, and knew also his own moral and intellectual weaknesses, and therefore (humbly and correctly) thought it morally rational to abide by his level-1 principles, and thus did something which turned out in the event not to be morally right. The second is that, although he could have known that the morally rational action was on this unusual occasion one in breach of his ingrained principles (it required him, say, to let down his closest friend), he found it so much against the grain that he just could not bring himself to do it. In the first case what he did was both rational and a morally good action. In the second case it was morally good but misguided – a wrong and indeed irrational act done from the best of motives. And no doubt there are other possibilities.

The situation I have been describing is a somewhat stylised model of our own, except that we had no archangel to educate us, but rely on the deliverances, not even of philosopher kings, but of Aristotelian *phronimoi* of very varying degrees of excellence. What will happen if a lot of moral philosophers are let loose on this situation? Level-1 thinking forms the greater part of the moral thinking of good men, and perhaps the whole of the moral thinking of good men who have nothing of the philosopher in them, including some of our philosophical colleagues. Such are the intuitionists, to whom their good ingrained principles seem to be sources of unquestionable knowledge. Others of a more enquiring bent will ask why they should accept these intuitions, and, getting no satisfactory answer, will come to the conclusion that the received principles have no ground at all and that the only way to decide what you ought to do is to reason it out on each occasion. Such people will at best become a crude kind of act-utilitarians. Between these two sets of philosophers there will be the sort of ludicrous battles that we have been witnessing so much of. The philosopher who understands the situation better will see that both are right about a great deal and that they really ought to make up their quarrel. They are talking about different levels of thought, both of which are necessary on appropriate occasions.

What kind of philosopher will this understanding person be? Will he be any kind of utilitarian? I see no reason why he should not be. For, first of all, level-2 thinking, which is necessary, is not only utilitarian but act-utilitarian (for, as we have seen, the specific rule-utilitarian thinking of this level and universalistic act-utilitarianism are practically equivalent). And there are excellent act-utilitarian reasons for an educator to bring up his charges to follow, on most occasions, level-1 thinking on the basis of a set of principles selected by high-quality level-2 thinking. This applies equally to self-education. So at any rate all acts that could be called educative or self-educative can have a solid act-utilitarian foundation. To educate oneself and other men in level-1 principles *is* for the best, and only the crudest of act-utilitarians fails to see this. There will also be good act-utilitarian reasons for *following* the good general principles in nearly all cases; for to do so will be rational, or most likely to be right; and even an act-utilitarian, when he comes to tell us how we should proceed when choosing what to do, can only tell us to do what is *most probably* right, because we do not know, when choosing, what *is* right.

There will be occasions, as I have said, when a man brought up (on good general principles) by a consistent act-utilitarian will do a rational act which turns out not to be right; and there will even be occasions on which he will do a good action which is neither rational nor right, because, although he could have known that it would be right on this unusual occasion to do an act contrary to the good general principles, he could not bring himself to contemplate it, because it went so much against the grain. And since one cannot pre-tune human nature all that finely, it may well be that the act-utilitarian educator will have to put up with the possibility of such cases, in the assurance that, if his principles are well chosen, they will be rare. For if he attempted to educate people so that they would do the rational thing in these cases, it could only be by incorporating into their principles clauses which

---

[22] See my *The Language of Morals*, p. 186.

might lead them, in other more numerous cases, to do acts most likely to be wrong. Moral upbringing is a compromise imposed by the coarseness of the pupil's discrimination and the inability of his human educators to predict with any accuracy the scrapes he will get into.

The exclusion from the argument of highly unusual cases, which I hope I have now achieved, is the main move in my defence of this sort of utilitarianism. There are also some subsidiary moves, some of which I have already mentioned, and all of which will be familiar. It is no argument against act-utilitarianism that in some unusual cases it would take a bad man to do what according to the utilitarian is the morally right or even the morally rational thing; good men are those who are firmly wedded to the principles which *on nearly all actual occasions* will lead them to do the right thing, and it is inescapable that on unusual occasions moderately good men will do the wrong thing. The nearer they approach archangelic status, the more, on unusual occasions, they will be able to chance their arm and do what they think will be the right act in defiance of their principles; but most of us ordinary mortals will be wise to be fairly cautious. As Aristotle said, we have to incline towards the vice which is the lesser danger for *us*, and away from that extreme which is to *us* the greater temptation.[23] For some, in the present context, the greater danger may be too much rigidity in the application of level-1 principles; but perhaps for more (and I think that I am one of them) it is a too great readiness to let them slip. It is a matter of temperament; we have to know ourselves (empirically); the philosopher cannot tell each of us which is the greater danger for him.

The moves that I have already made will, I think, deal with some other cases which are well known from the literature. Such are the case of the man who is tempted, on utilitarian grounds, to use electricity during a power crisis, contrary to the government's instructions; and the case of the voter who abstains in the belief that enough others will vote. In both these cases it is alleged that some utility would be gained, and none lost, by these dastardly actions. These are not, on the face of it, fantastic or unusual cases, although the degree of knowledge stipulated as to what others will do is perhaps unusual. Yet it would be impolitic, in moral education, to bring up people to behave like this, if we were seeking level-1 principles with the highest acceptance-utility; if we tried, the result would be that nearly everyone would consume electricity under those conditions, and hardly anybody would vote. However, the chief answer to these cases is that which I have used elsewhere[24] to deal with the car-pushing and death-bed promise cases which are also well canvassed. It is best approached by going back to the logical beginning and asking whether I am prepared to prescribe, or even permit, that others should (*a*) use electricity, thus taking advantage of my law-abidingness, when I am going without it; (*b*) abstain from voting when I do so at inconvenience to myself, thereby taking advantage of my public spirit; (*c*) only pretend to push the car when I am rupturing myself in the effort to get it started; (*d*) make death-bed promises to me (for example to look after my children) and then treat them as of no weight. I unhesitatingly answer 'No' to all these questions; and I think that I should give the same answer even if I were perfectly prudent and were universalising my prescriptions to cover other perfectly prudent affected parties (see above, page 119). For it is not imprudent, but prudent rather, to seek the satisfaction of desires which are important to me, even if I am not going to know whether they have been satisfied or not. There is nothing in principle to prevent a fully informed and clear-headed person wanting above all that his children should not starve after his death; and if that is what he wants above all, it is prudent for him to seek what will achieve it, and therefore prescribe this.

Since the logical machinery on which my brand of utilitarianism is based yields these answers, so should the utilitarianism that is based on it; and it is worth while to ask, How? The clue lies in the observation that to frustrate a desire of mine is against my interest even if I do not know that it is being frustrated, or if I am dead. If anybody does not agree, I ask him to apply the logical apparatus direct and forget about interests. Here is a point at which, perhaps, some people will want to say that my Kantian or Christian variety of utilitarianism, based on giving equal weight to the prudent prescriptions or desires of all, diverges from the usual varieties so much that it does not deserve to be called a kind of utilitarianism at all. I am not much interested in that terminological question; but for what it is worth I will record my opinion that the dying man's interests *are* harmed if promises are made to him and then broken, and even more that mine are harmed if people are cheating me without my knowing it. In the latter case, they are harmed because I very much want this not to happen; and my desire that it should not happen is boosted by my level-1 sense of justice, which the utilitarian educators who brought me up wisely inculcated in me.

Whichever way we put it, whether in terms of what I am prepared to prescribe or permit universally (and therefore also for when I am the victim) or in terms of how to be fair as between the interests of all the affected

---

[23] *Nicomachean Ethics*, 1109 b 1.

[24] See my paper 'The Argument from Received Opinion' in my *Essays on Philosophical Method* (London, 1971), pp. 128 ff.; *FR*, pp. 132 ff.

parties, I conclude that the acts I have listed will come out wrong on the act–utilitarian calculation, because of the harms done to the interests of those who are cheated, or the non-fulfilment of prescriptions to which, we may assume, they attach high importance. If we add to this move the preceding one which rules out fantastic cases, and are clear about the distinction between judgements about the character of the agent, judgements about the moral rationality of the action, and judgements about its moral rightness as shown by the outcome, I think that this form of utilitarianism can answer the objections I have mentioned. Much more needs to be said; the present paper is only a beginning, and is not very original.[25] I publish it only to give some indication of the way in which ethical theory can help with normative moral questions, and to try to get the discussion of utilitarianism centred round credible forms of it, rather than forms which we all know will not do.

---

[25] Among many others from whose ideas I have learnt, I should like in particular to mention Dr Lynda Sharp (Mrs Lynda Paine), in whose thesis *Forms and Criticisms of Utilitarianism* (deposited in the Bodleian Library at Oxford) some of the above topics are discussed in greater detail.

Index

abortion, 389 *see also* double effect, doctrine of
Abraham, L., 374–5n
absolutist, 361
acts
  in accord with nature, 102, 105, 107–8, 110
  contemplated acts, 311
  intended acts, 121–2, 135
  as involuntary, 77, 79–80, 171, 215 (*see also* ignorance)
  irrational acts, 306–7
  as mixed, 77, 79
  as non-voluntary, 77, 79–80
  unintended acts, 121–2
  as voluntary, 77, 79–80, 83–4, 143, 305–6, 311, 391
Adeimantus, 23–4
adultery, 38, 73, 118–19, 162
Aegisthus, 298
Aeolus, 101
Aeschylus, 21–2, 80
affections, 147, 149, 152, 154–6, 168, 170–1, 178, 185, 201, 206, 329
  and the good, 158 (*see also* Butler, J.)
  and poetry, 196
Africa, 394
Agamemnon, 61n
Aglaion, 36
agony, 99
Agrarian, 188
Alcibiades, 197
Alcmaeon, 79
Alexander, 212
altruism, 365
ambiguity, 189, 194, 226
ambition, 156, 186
America, 139, 142, 369
Amphion, 6
Anacharsis, 63
analogy, 57
Anaxagoras, 65

Andron, 7
Androtion, 7
anger, 25, 37, 67–8, 70, 72–4, 80, 106, 144, 204, 293
anguish, 204
animals, 2, 5–6, 26, 37, 47–8, 59, 61, 65, 71, 80, 88, 125, 128–9, 133, 182, 210, 255
  and the absence of moral laws, 174
  as brute, 130
  as complex objects, 335
  instincts of, 268
  as irrational, 132
    desire of, 273
      as impulse accompanied with sensation, 322
  lower animals, 258
  as non–human, 99, 147
  similarity with humans, 131, 132, 272, 282, 284, 297
    as endowed with spirit (*see* spirit)
    and the possession of reason, 187
  welfare of, 140
Anscombe, G.E.M., x, xiii, 377–8, 393n, 409
  and anti-morality claim, 377, 379
  and claim of unprofitability, 377–9
  and justice, 380, 386
    and intention, 380, 384
      and doctrine of double effect, 378
  and the lack-of-difference claim, 377, 379, 383
anthropology, 234
antipathy
  principle of, 252
anxiety, 139, 155, 178, 195–6, 204, 215, 237
  and detrimental results, 224
apathy, 230
Aphidnae, 7
appetite, 126–8, 147, 149–50, 154–5, 158, 182, 185
  as bad, 65, 71
  sensual appetites, 150, 152, 156–7, 311
  towards good, 124–4, 168

History of Ethics – Essential Readings with Commentary, First Edition. Edited by Daniel Star and Roger Crisp.
© 2020 John Wiley & Sons Ltd. Published 2020 by John Wiley & Sons Ltd.

approbation, 205–7, 209, 249n–52, 266, 312
  of self, 217
Aquinas, St., ix, xi–xii, 121–2
  and pursuit of the good, 124–6, 130–2
    by intellect, 123–5, 128, 130
      eternal law, 126–30, 133–4
        human law
          and 'cardinal' virtues, 121, 130–5
    by nature, 123–5
    by will, 127–30
aristocratic, 285
Ariston, 23, 28
Aristotelian, xi, 377, 379, 384, 386, 439
Aristotle, ix–xi, 41, 53, 77–8, 114, 123n–4n, 126n–7,
          129–30n, 132, 299, 301, 304–5, 321–2,
          329, 355n, 377–83, 388, 403, 409, 419,
          432, 436, 440
  good, 57, 76
    the highest good, 53, 121
      and cleverness, 77, 88
      as instrumental, 53–4, 57, 62–5, 71
      and political science, 55–6, 61, 64, 69, 71, 85
      in relation to happiness, 53, 56, 58–9, 62–3, 88
        as activity of the soul in accordance with virtue,
              54, 59, 60–1, 63, 69, 72, 85
        and contemplation, 57, 62–5, 69–70, 77, 80–2,
              85–9 (see also acts, as voluntary)
        as the exercise of moral virtue (ēthos), 53,
              69–74, 78
          in relation to pleasure and pain, 71
            as the mean, 73–6, 77–8, 84
        as God-given, 60, 63–4
        as noble, 61, 63
        as universal, 58, 64
arrogance, 221
art, 12–14, 35, 50, 124, 126, 133, 142, 153, 167, 188, 317
  love of, 157
  as practical, 126
  in relation to the good, 14
  as science, 48, 141
  as speculative, 126
  as system, 148
  as utility, 186, 188
  works of, 150, 178
ascetic, 282
assimilation, 126
Assyria, 56n
atheism, 296
Athenian, 7, 61n, 196
Athens, 77, 194
Augustine, St., xi, 114, 121
  pure goodness, 113, 115–16, 119
    and virtue
      as belief in the existence of God, 120 (see also evil, as
        the absence of good)
authority, 13
autonomy, 99, 412 see also freedom
  Kant's notion of, 426–9 (see also Kant, I.)

avarice, 186
aversion, 156
Ayer, A. J., x, xii, 359–60, 368, 397–8, 431 see also
          subjectivism
  ethical concepts, 362–3, 365 (see also moral concepts)

Bacon, F., 194, 318
barbarism, 261
barbarity, 177, 187, 196
Barker, E., 413n
Baumol, W. J., 424n
Mons. Bayle, 190
beatitude, 127–8
beauty, 47, 115, 129, 159, 181, 194, 257, 295
  absolute beauty, 45
  as author of truth (see Plato, and the Good)
  degree of, 351
  experience of, 354
  and falsity, 165
  non-moral value of, 399
  perfect beauty, 43–4
Beck, L. W., 426n, 428n
beliefs, 86–7
  as conventional, 41
  as false or delusional, 113–4, 117, 397 (see also lying,
          as evil)
  as precondition of ethical reflection, 53 (see also Aristotle,
          and contemplation)
  as true, 80, 110
Bendidea, 19
benevolence, x, 192, 195, 211, 262, 345, 377–8
  divine benevolence, 216
  maxim of, 324 (see also Sidgwick, H.)
  as natural, 166, 185, 198 (see also Butler, J.)
Bennett, J., 393n
Bentham, J., x, xiii, 247–8, 257, 275, 339–40, 379, 418n
  and happiness, 249
    and the principle of utility, 247, 249–52
      and the diminishing of pain, 249
      and the promotion of pleasure, 249
        and measurement of, 248, 253–4
          in relation to the community, 249–50, 253
          in relation to the self, 249, 254
Berkeleian, 400
Berkeley, 401
Berlin, 220
blame, 77, 83, 94, 99, 101, 107, 110, 160, 171, 173n–5,
          178–80, 190–1, 197, 206, 209, 213, 316,
          379 see also disapprobation
  moral blame, 199, 377
    and moral luck, 201–2, 214
blasphemy, 384
Bradley, F. H., 426
Brandt, R. B., 418n, 434–5n
brave, 102
British, 433
Broad, C. D., 370–1n
Buddhism, 283, 297

Butler, J., x–xi, 147–8, 184, 299, 302, 304–5, 306–8n, 315, 321–2, 329, 367, 373, 377, 379–80, 385
  virtue
    and conscience, 160, 162
      as absolute authority, 151
    and happiness, 151–2, 154, 161
      as acting in conformity with human nature, 150
        and benevolence, 147–8, 150, 152–5, 157, 162–3
          as compatible with love of self, 156, 158
        and self-love, 147, 150, 152–5, 158–9
          in contradistinction to selfishness, 156

Caesar, 105, 110, 212
Callicles, 3, 6–8
Calypso, 75
Caria, 65
Carnap, R., 373
Cartesian, 318
casuistry, 313, 364, 384
Catholic, xiii, 389, 391
  and doctrine of double effect (see double effect, doctrine of)
Cerinthians, 131
Chapman, J. W., 418n
charity, 157, 350, 394
Charybdis, 322
children, 6, 28, 31–2, 37, 43, 45, 58, 61, 63, 79–80, 83, 88, 102–3, 108, 110, 141–2, 256
  begetting of, 130
  kindness towards, 168
  noble children, 60
  ordinary children, 437–8
  possessing spirit (see spirit)
  rights of, 188, 391
China, 180
Chinese, 289, 291
choice, 93–4, 152, 165, 172n
  and good ends, 220
    as free, 227, 290
      and moral laws (see Kant, I.)
  of nature, 221
  rational choice, 77, 80–1, 309, 413
    and justice, 416 (see also justice, as fairness)
    and virtue, 88, 91 (see also Aristotle)
      as voluntary, 82
  relation to desire, 227
  and the social contract, 139 (see also Hobbes, T.)
    and regard for others, 184, 197
Cholarges, 7
Christ, 118–19, 131, 381
Christian, 258, 289–90, 296, 306, 313, 315n, 350, 381, 383, 388
  Europe, 276
  morality, 282
  revelation, 264
Christianity, xi–xii, 113, 270, 284, 298, 381
Chrysippus, 103, 111–12
Cicero, 337

citizens, 13, 28–31, 38–9, 51, 64, 69–70, 97, 105, 110, 142, 411
  ordinary, 122
  Roman citizens, 109
  of the universe, 103
Clarke, M. E., 369
Clarke, S., 189, 304, 404, 407, 409
Cleitophon, 11
cleverness, 78 see also Aristotle
cognitive, 41
Coke, E., 146
Communists, 270
compassion, 150, 160–2, 184, 187, 195–6, 201 see also sympathy
  instinct of, 283
conscience, 160, 162, 171, 302, 313, 316, 327, 345
  liberty of, 420
  and personal responsibility, 282 (see also Nietzsche, F.)
  as reason applied to practice, 322
  rules of, 322
  and vile intent, 380
  voice of, 201, 213
consequentialism, 334
  as shallow, 384
  utilitarian version of, 148
consequentialist, 385
contempt, 288
contentment, 102
contractualism, 92, 140
convention, 55
corruption, 115–16, 125, 154
courage, 101, 212, 221, 326, 404 (see also Aristotle; Plato)
  of life, 283 (see also Nietzsche, F.)
  as thick moral concept, 378
covetousness, 158
cowardice, 22, 30, 39, 404
Cretans, 69
criminal, 171–2, 174, 186, 190, 293, 381, 392
  action, 213
  intent, 213
Croesus, 21
Croton, 73n
cruel, 175
cruelty, 153, 157, 161, 187
  naturalistic account of, 282
Cudworth, R., 189, 409
custom, 5, 7–8, 191, 194, 317, 319, 323–4
  and definitions of the good, 335
  morality of, 291
Cyrenaic, 329

danger, 141–2, 162, 194, 204, 213
Davies, J. L., 262
death, 100, 103, 107–8, 119, 122, 135, 142, 144, 146–8, 150, 157, 174, 201, 210, 213, 390
  dread of, 205
  as nothing (see Epicurus)
  voluntarily embraced, 247
    at the call of duty, 329
  wish for, 222

definists, 373–5 *see also* Frankena, W. K.
deformity, 15
delight, 127–9, 154, 157
Delos, 60
delusion, 103
Demosthenes, 194
deontological, 334
deontologists, 389
deontology, 334, 377
depravity, 175
Descartes, R., 318
descriptivism, 401, 431, 433
desire, 25, 31, 36–7, 55–6, 69, 107–8, 110, 129, 428
    as basis of moral action, 165 (*see also* Hume, D.)
    and deliberation, 77, 82
    evil desires, 432
    faculty of, 227, 235, 241
    as insatiable, 42
    as natural or vain, 93, 95–6
    non-rational desire, 311
    universal object of, 35
        and ends, 126, 128–9
            and God, 127
despair, 158
despotism, 296
dignity, 62, 110, 234, 258
    of human beings, 232
    and the possible kingdom of ends, 244
        as a kingdom of nature, 245 (*see also* nature)
dikaiosunê, 3
Diogenes, 108
Dionysius, 125
disapprobation, 205, 209, 211–12, 250–2, 266, 268, 271, 307,
            312 *see also* blame
disgrace, 5, 13–14, 79, 110, 150, 157
dishonour, 38, 61, 74, 109
divine, 22–3, 39, 63, 108, 125–6, 133, 139
    commands, 409
    dispensation, 60
    governance, 102–3
    light, 134
    origin, 167
    providence, 134
    right, 265
    spectators, 294
    will, 235
divinity, 101
    spark of, 99
dogmatic, 301
dogmatism, 183
dominant
    theorists
        with respect to Aristotle, 54
Donatists, 117
double effect
    doctrine of (*see* Anscombe, G. E. M.; *see* Foot, P.)
Durkheim, E., 418n

duty, 27, 51, 57, 119, 163, 172n, 174
    actual duty, 350, 352–3
    and common agreement, 143 (*see also* Hobbes, T.)
        as social cooperation, 413, 421 (*see also* Rawls, J.)
    deviation from, 224
    of the good, 104
    imperatives of
        as universal a priori (*see* Kant, I.)
    moral duty, 399
        as anachronistic, 377 (*see also* Anscombe, G. E. M.)
        as negative, 390, 394
        as positive, 390, 394–5
    prima facie duty, 343, 346–50, 353–4
        and *prima facie* rightness, 350–3, 355–7

economic, 414, 422
    advantages, 420–1
    systems, 411
Edgeworth, F. Y., 418n
education, 30, 50, 102, 107, 190, 391, 432
    and human instinct, 191, 193
    liberal education, 6
    moral education, x, 364, 437
egalitarian, 281, 411 *see also* equality
egoism, 91, 184, 260, 303, 315, 345
    psychological egoism, 299
        psychological hedonistic egoism, 247, 299 (*see also*
            hedonism)
    rational egoism, x, 147, 300, 343
        and harmony with utilitarianism (*see* Sidgwick, H.)
    suppression of, 301
egoistic, 201, 285, 326 *see also* unegoistic
egoists, 344, 402, 414
egotism, 365
Egyptian(s), 34, 102, 104, 190
emotivism
    defense of, 359
    and irrationalism, 431
    metaphysics of, 431
empiricist, 165
Endymion, 65
England, 180, 188, 369
English, 216, 250n, 257, 286, 325, 336, 373
    ethicists, 377, 383–4, 386–8
    psychologists, 281, 284–5 (*see also* Nietzsche, F.)
Entsagen, 259
envy, 49, 68, 72–3, 75, 106, 108, 197, 212, 222, 258, 412
    disutility of, 435
Epictetus, x, 99–101
    as freedom, 102, 107–8, 110
    and happiness
        and action, 105, 108–9, 111
        and judgement, 105, 107–8, 111
        and the will, 99–100, 102–3, 105, 107–9
Epicurean, 303, 329, 371
    theory of life, 258
Epicureanism, 309

Epicureans, 131, 152–3, 257–8
Epicurus, x, 91–2, 257
  and happiness, 93
    and belief in god, 93–4
    as compact between people, 92
      as justice, 96
    and death, 94, 97
      as nothing, 91–3, 95
    and necessary natural desire, 93–4
      and pleasure, 94–5
    and prudence, 94–5
equality, 5, 141, 187
  and Communism (*see* Communism)
  and egalitarian justice, 7, 183 (*see also* justice)
    and original agreement, 413 (*see* justice, as fairness)
  and nature, 188
  right to, 275
    and the sexes, 256 (*see also* Mill, J. S.)
equity, 186
Eschines, 194
eternal, 57
ethics *see also* moral
  practical ethics, 431, 433
  as science, 364, 401
    as systematic, 335
etymology, 270
eudaemonistic
  theories of morals, 365 (*see also* hedonism)
eudaimonism, 419
Euripides, 5–6, 79, 85
Europe, 281, 326
European, 283, 289
  as superior, 187
evil, 14, 22, 27, 50, 62, 78, 82, 105, 125, 131, 134, 143, 153,
      211, 234, 237
  as the absence of good, 113, 115–16, 119
    and the good will, 221 (*see also* Kant, I.)
  aversion to, 168
  causes of, 298
  and deliberation, 86
  as dependent on customs, 385
  doers, 17–18, 111, 265, 293
  ends, 220
  existence of, 320
    and actual evil, 215
  genealogy of (*see* Nietzsche, F.)
  immunity from, 273
  and legal order, 269
  and lying (*see* lying)
  moral evil, 170–2, 176, 182, 193, 197
    as opposed to natural evil, 161
      and non-natural evil, 109
  positive evils, 261
  prevention of, 249
  and *prima facie* wrongness, 351
  problem of, 113
  and sensual pleasure, 91, 93–5

temperament, 221
  and tendency towards, 254
  as tolerable, 186
existence, 32
  lower grade of, 258
  original existence
    and passion, 168 (*see also* Hume, D.)
  real existence, 49, 175, 181
    as actual existence, 320–1

fairness *see* justice, as fairness
fanaticism, 327, 406
fear, 25, 27, 70, 72–4, 78, 92–3, 95, 108, 134, 168, 177, 196, 222
  of a common power, 141–2 (*see also* sovereign)
Fellner, W., 425n
fictionalism, 398 *see also* Mackie, J. L.
folly, 162
Foot, P., xii, 121, 377–8, 389–90 *see also* duty, as either
                    negative or positive
  and doctrine of double effect, 378, 389, 391–3
    resolution of, 393–6
force, 77, 78, 80
  and involuntary acts (*see* acts, as involuntary)
fortune, 75, 94, 132, 158, 181
  bad fortune, 61, 105
  disfavour of, 221
  gifts of, 221
  good fortune, 60, 62, 68, 172n, 261, 351
  natural fortune, 416
  vicissitudes of, 261
France, 26
Frankena, W. K., 334, 367–8, 418n
  and the naturalistic fallacy, 369, 372–5
    and bifurcation of ought and is, 370–1, 373
fraud, 13, 142, 161–2
freedom, 6–7, 13, 94, 99, 102, 107, 110, 157, 230, 274, 420, 428
  of action, 352
  in contradistinction to morality, 291
  from external disturbance, 133, 139
  as ground of the dignity of human nature, 244
  inner freedom, 228
  from pain, 257 (*see also* utilitarianism)
  from passion, 108
  from social constraint, 289
  of the soul, 93
  as weakness, 290
  of the will, 292, 294, 295
freeman, 32
free-will, 22
French, 257, 270, 336
Fried, C., 427
Friedrich, C. J., 418n
friendship, 17, 92, 96, 150, 153, 155–6, 162, 185, 192, 233,
                    247, 255, 289, 383

Galt, J., 257
Gauthier, D. P., 418n

genealogy *see* Nietzsche, F.
generosity, 179, 185, 272, 326
German(s), 257, 286, 291, 293, 336
Geryon, 5
Gibbard, A., 414n, 418n
Gierke, O., 413n
Glaucon
    Gorgias, 3, 4
    Republic, 9–10, 14–15, 20, 22–3, 26, 29, 32, 42, 45, 47, 50–1
God(s), 175, 201, 202
    in ancient Greece, 18, 21–3, 28, 40, 46, 50, 57, 60, 65, 89,
            94, 99, 101–3, 107–8, 110, 297
    fear of, 365
    origin of, 296
        and monotheism, 296–7, 370
            and Christian belief, 113–18, 123, 125–7, 129, 131–3,
                    148, 157, 290, 296
                as 'always actually understanding', 121, 126
                as archetype of the good, 215, 234
                ennobling of, 296
                as father of evil, 283
                fear of, 145
                knowledge of, 125–6, 131
                as lawgiver, 381
                self-crucifixion of, 287
                as a utilitarian, 255, 264
von Goethe, J. W., 285
good *see also* happiness
    absolute good, 45
        and God, 113 (*see also* Augustine, St.)
    common good, 122, 136
    in contradistinction to happiness, 314
    customary use of, 335, 385
        as simple, 338
        as the sole object of particular laws of justice, 188
    future good, 325n
    as indefinable, 333, 336, 338–40
        and the naturalistic fallacy, 337–9
    moral good, 171–2, 176, 182, 193, 197 (*see also* moral)
    in relation to honour, 47
    in relation to the mind, 41
    as perfect (*see* Plato)
        as imperfect, 115
    as pleasure (*see* pleasure)
    as system of ends defined by reason, 413 (*see also* Kant, I.)
    as wisdom, 17
Goodman, N., 417n
goods
    distribution of, 411 (*see also* Rawls, J.)
    natural goods, 321
    non-hedonic goods, 299–300, 330
good-will, 6–7
Gorgias, 6
Gospel, 143
government, 10, 14, 51, 142, 162, 189, 212, 222, 413, 415
    protection of, 186
    rights of, 144
    of society, 276, 279

gratitude, 160, 162, 201, 203, 209–12, 215
    as transitory, 214
Greece, 180, 196, 270, 304, 321
Greek(s), 54, 188, 216, 278, 281, 298, 381, 388
    nobility, 288
    philosophy, 329
Grice, G. R., 413n
grief, 92, 141, 168, 177, 201, 204–6, 208, 213, 223
    hopeless grief, 222
Guicciardin, 196
guilt, 118, 160, 171–2n, 174, 213
    as bad conscience, 282 (*see also* conscience)
Gyges, 21

von Haller, A., 229
happiness, 13, 51 (*see also* good)
    and action, 105 (*see also* Epictetus)
    as activity of the soul, 54
        and the good, 53 (*see also* Aristotle)
    as advantage, 249
        and the principle of utility (*see* Bentham, J.)
            as hedonist
                Greatest Happiness Principle (*see* Mill, J.S.)
    as artificial (*see* Nietzsche, F.)
    as civil order, 186
        as compact between people, 96 (*see also* Epicurus)
    as contingent
        on a good will (*see* Kant, I.)
    and death, 94 (*see also* Epicurus)
    as the exercise of moral virtue (*ēthos*), 53 (*see also*
            Aristotle)
    false happiness, 128
    as furtherance of the ends of others (*see* Kant, I.)
    and God
        belief in, 93 (*see also* Epicurus)
        given by, 60 (*see also* Aristotle)
        knowledge of, 117 (*see also* Augustine, St.)
        understanding of (beatitude), 125 (*see also* Aquinas, St.)
    and honour, 56, 63
    and intellect, 57, 123 (*see also* Aquinas, St.; Aristotle)
    and the intuition of rational benevolence (*see* Sidgwick, H.)
    and judgement, 105 (*see also* Epictetus)
    as luck, 53
    and nature, 123 (*see also* Aquinas, St.)
        acting in conformity with, 150 (*see also* Butler, J.)
        and necessary natural desire, 93 (*see also* Epicurus)
            and instinct, 221
    as noble, 61 (*see also* Aristotle)
        and a nobler aristocratic form of valuation (*see*
                Nietzsche, F.)
    as satisfaction, 221
    as unattainable, 255
    and the will, 99, 127 (*see also* Aquinas, St.; Epictetus)
Hare, R. M., xii–xiii, 383, 388, 400–1, 431
harm, 22, 28, 33, 55, 96, 100, 103, 110–11, 118, 140, 152,
            156–7, 160–1, 172n, 347, 384
    in contradistinction to use, 71
    as corruption of the good, 116

as disagreeable, 166
reduction of, 434
harmful, 221
harmony, x, 17, 38, 60, 69, 102, 112, 159, 199, 385
of emotion
and outward expression, 208
perfect harmony, 207
state of, 156
in relation to the psyche, 42
society, 208
and the good life, 26
as temperance, 25 (see also Plato)
Harrison, J., 418n
Harrod, R. F., 418n
Harsanyi, J. C., 418n, 422n
Hart, H. L. A., 391–2n
Haslett, D., 434n–5n
hate, 110, 175
hatred, 18, 153, 155, 176, 178, 181, 192
disutility of, 435
global hatred, 290
health, 20, 182, 221, 237, 259, 266
bodily health, 307
and the expectation of happiness, 223
and a tranquil mind, 230
heaven, 146, 213, 240
Hebrew, 383
hedonism, 314, 343, 345, 348, 370–1, 419
denial of, 255
egoistic hedonism, 247, 309, 316, 339 (see also Bentham, J.)
common-sense aversion to, 329
ethical hedonism, 302, 371
explanatory and substantive accounts, 91 (see also
Epicurus)
psychological hedonism, 302, 339, 371
universalistic hedonism, 301, 309, 316
and intuitionism (see Sidgwick, H.)
hedonist, 255
hedonistic, 317, 323
method, 302, 305
theories of morals, 365
utilitarianism, 299, 345
Hegel, G. W. F., 426n, 431–2
Helen of Troy, 76
Heracles, 5
Heraclitus, 71, 108, 294
Hesiod, 56
Hobbes, T., ix–x, 92, 139, 152, 160, 201, 303, 377, 409,
411, 413n
and morality, 139, 140
and justice, 139, 142, 144–6
as social compact, 142–3
either express or by inference, 144
as voluntary, 143
and some good, 143
and the Sovereign (see Sovereign)
holy, 190, 235
Homer, 37, 49, 75, 82, 111

homicide, 73, 135
Honderich, T., 433n
honesty, 222
honour(s), 9, 14, 21–3, 28–9, 43, 47, 49, 51–3, 56–8, 61,
63–5, 74, 79, 94–5, 108–10, 152, 156–7,
199, 205, 208, 216, 221, 223, 261
and the good, 47 (see also Plato)
as happiness, 56, 63
justice (see justice)
as restraint, 179
rules of, 319
and the ultimate good, 53
hope, 93, 128, 141, 168, 177
Horace, 195–6
horror, 188, 190, 203, 213, 217, 432
humanity, 57, 159, 185–6, 192–3, 195, 197, 202, 204, 206,
208, 213, 228, 262, 276
danger to, 284
as end in itself, 242 (see also Kant, I.)
laws of, 187
natural constitution of, 240
Hume, D., xii–xiii, 165, 183, 201
morality, 165–6, 170, 175
and conscience, 171
and ideas, 170
and reason, 165–8, 171–5, 180, 182
and perception, 170, 175
and passion, 165, 169–70, 175, 187
and combat with reason, 167–8, 171
and pain, 166–7, 171, 182
and vice, 175–8
and pleasure, 166–7, 171, 175, 182
and virtue, 175–81, 197
and justice, 183–9, 192–6, 198
humility, 176–8, 326, 382
Christian humility, 436n
as contrary to the laws of justice, 179
hunger, 35, 37
Hutcheson, F., 418n

ignorance, 7, 15–16, 77, 79–80, 112–13, 117, 152, 187, 190
acting in and acting through, 77, 83, 88 (see also acts, as
involuntary; acts, as non-voluntary)
duty to diminish, 228
as injustice, 17
veil of, 411, 431, 434, 437
as irrational, 423
and original position of equality, 413 (see also Rawls, J.)
imagination, 124, 153, 177, 179, 181, 185, 194, 196, 210,
252n, 260, 419–21
connections of, 189, 191
immoral, 190
immorality, 171
impartial
benevolent spectator, 262
rational spectator, 221
spectator, 201, 202, 211–13, 217, 349, 419
impiety, 29

imprudence, 288 *see also* Nietzsche, F.
inclusivists
    with respect to Aristotle, 53
India, 394
Indian(s), 168, 187
inequality, 188
    as justified (*see* Rawls, J., and the 'difference principle')
ingratitude, 174
inheritance, 191, 195
inhumanity, 210
injustice, 3, 5, 7, 15–20, 29, 51, 73, 96, 161–2, 201
    acts of, 380
        as contrary to nature, 150 (*see also* Butler, J.)
        and voluntarily breaking an agreement, 143
            as violation of faith, 144
    as defect of the soul, 19
    as gainful, 13, 15, 21
    as gross negligence, 214
    impossibility of, 142, 145 (*see also* Hobbes, T.)
    and inequalities, 421
    as intemperance, 39
    and opinion, 170
    as strife, 39
    and variance with law, 402
innocence, 160
intention
    either direct or oblique, 391–3, 395
intuition 423, 431, 434
    and common-sense, 390–1, 421
    as prejudice, 433
intuitionism, xii, 344, 369, 407, 417, 433 (*see also* moral
                    language, anti-realist accounts)
    dogmatic intuitionism, 300
    perceptional intuitionism, 300
intuitionists, 302, 369, 370, 374, 433, 439
    as descriptivists, 433
inutility, 216
irony, 9
irrationalism, 433
Isabella, 216
Israel, 287

jealousy, 108, 185
Jesuits, 190
Jesus of Nazareth, 262, 287, 291
Jew(s), 102, 131, 286, 290, 381, 388, 436
Jewish, 281
Jocasta, 216
joy, 168, 177
Judea, 290, 291
Judeo-Christian, 281 (*see also* genealogy)
judgement, 181
    false judgement, 165, 171
    moral judgements, 183 (*see also* moral)
Juno, 241
Jupiter, 146
Jury, G. S., 369

just, 10–11, 13, 15–21, 29, 37–8, 55, 70–1, 83, 413
    acts, 88
    commands, 51
        and practical wisdom, 87
    distinction between seeming and being, 21, 23
    as human nature, 88
    as noble, 102
    in relation to the good, 45
justice, 6, 21–2, 29, 37, 44, 60, 110, 135, 139, 160, 166, 179
    as absolute, 50 (*see also* Plato, allegory of the Cave)
    indefeasibility of, 275
    as advantage, 9, 15, 18
    and common-sense, 256
    as compact between people, 92 (*see also* Epicurus)
        as the keeping of valid covenants (*see* Hobbes, T.)
            impossibility of, 142 (*see also* Hobbes, T.)
        and voluntary conventions, 179
    and conformity with utility, 431 (*see also* utilitarianism,
                    two-level account of)
        public utility, 185, 191
        and safety of all, 189 (*see also* Hume, D.)
    and duty, 9, 11 (*see also* duty)
        and obligation of, 191 (*see also* obligation)
    as equality, 7
        as actions between equals, 145 (*see also* Aquinas, St.)
        and distributive justice, 275
        and opinion of the many, 7, 10
    as excellence of the soul, 19
    as fairness, 411–12
    and hypothetical reasons, 397
    and impartiality, 323 (*see also* Sedgwick, H.)
    natural justice, 3, 5, 7, 142, 270
    sentiment of, 272–3
    suspension of, 186
    as virtue, 15, 17, 19, 31–2, 75, 134 (*see also* Aquinas, St.;
                    Aristotle)
        as first virtue of social institutions (*see* Rawls, J.)
    as wisdom, 8, 17–19

Kamm, F., 389
Kant, I., ix–xii, 219, 272–3, 283, 303–5, 307–9n, 319n, 345,
            349–50, 365, 377, 379, 401–3, 412–13,
            422n, 424, 426, 431, 433
    and the will, 235, 243
    and duty, 220, 222, 228, 233
        as categorical, 229, 235, 238, 240 (*see also* reason)
            maxims of, 219, 231–2
                acts that conform with, 219, 222, 233
                acts done from, 219, 222–4, 233, 242
                as universal a priori motives, 219, 223–5, 233–5,
                    238–9, 241, 246
            as hypothetical, 235, 238, 240 (*see also* reason)
                and a posteriori incentives, 220–3, 225–6, 241
        and reason, 221–2, 226–7
            and the good will, 219–21, 224–5, 235, 240, 245–6
            and virtue, 220, 228–9
                as unattainable, 230, 244

Kantian, 290, 411–12
Kidlington, 165
knowledge, 16, 20, 22, 25, 29–30, 39, 41, 43, 47, 50, 86, 103, 142
  and action, 55
  and the beautiful, 46
  and belief, 86
  forms of, 88
  and good judgment, 86
  highest objects of, 63 (*see also* Aristotle, and happiness)
  intellectual and sensitive knowledge, 131
  love of, 34
  and opinion, 103
  scientific knowledge, 78, 84–7
Kos, 77

Laird, J., 370n
Langford, G., 433n
language, 31, 153, 180–1, 381, 385, 387
  ambiguities of, 310
  ordinary language, 271, 341, 346
    as common language, 160, 198, 266
    conventions of, 361
    seduction of, 290
  philosophy of, 368
    and moral language (*see* moral language)
  and private-public distinction, 5
Laslett, P., 428
Lateranus, 101
Latin, 270, 381
law, 21, 30, 69, 112, 140, 142, 215, 233, 270, 279, 293
  eternal law, 121, 134, 139, 174
    as Christian divine law, 378, 381–2, 384–5, 387–8
      as positive law of God, 409–10
  human law, 121, 160, 319
    constitutional law, 250n, 413
    courts of, 50, 313
    of the many, 7, 10, 96
    as modification of natural justice, 189
    and practical reason, 121 (*see also* Aquinas, St.)
  and moral interest, 160, 224, 227 (*see also* Kant, I.)
  of nature, 385
  pre-moral laws, 139
  primitive form of, 270
Leontius, 26, 36
Lewis, C. I., 434
liberty, 21, 139, 141–4, 156, 161, 172n, 185, 413, 427
  love of, 258
  as natural to humankind, 269
Locke, J., 379, 407, 413, 435n
love, 166, 168, 175–8, 180–1, 205–6, 222, 224
  of humankind, 233
  distinction between pathological and practical, 223
Luce, R. D., 424n
luck, 53, 411
  moral luck, 201–2, 214
Lucullus, 212

lust, 172
lying, 99, 117, 166, 337, 379
  as evil, 113–14, 118–19, 238
  with respect to moral duty, 224, 232 (*see also* duty)
  as wrong, 112, 165, 255, 432
Lyons, D., 418n

Mabbott, J. D., 418n
Mackie, J. L., x, xii, 397–8 *see also* moral value
  and argument from queerness (*see* moral language)
  and argument from relativity (*see* moral language)
McTaggart, J. M. E., 374
Malebranche, N., 189
malevolent, 209, 211, 214, 216
malice, 186, 196
malicious, 284
Manichean(s), 113, 197
mankind, 5, 13, 150–1, 154, 163
Marcus Brutus, 180
Maro, 117
Matthew, St., 127
Battle of Megara, 23
Merope, 80
Messiah, 388
metaethics, xi, 247, 333, 368, 397
  as analytical, 431, 433
  and non-revisionary theory, 360
metaphysical, 167, 191, 268, 301, 367
metaphysicians, 169
metaphysics, 193, 235, 360, 368
  of morals, 234, 241
Mill, J. S., x, 248, 255, 299, 302–5, 325, 340, 370–1, 379, 383, 418n–19n
  and happiness, 255–9, 266, 275
    and theory of utility, 255, 257–8, 265, 273–4
      distribution of, 255, 259–63, 266, 272
        and justice, 256, 268
          as correlative to the moral considerations, 271–2
        and obligation, 268–74
          and equality, 256, 275, 277
            and the subjection of women, 276–9
          and impartiality, 275
      and self-sacrifice, 261
Milo, 73
Mirabeau, 288
misery, 142, 150, 155–6, 158, 160–3, 186, 194, 203–5, 237, 294
  avoidance of, 182
misfortune, 56, 61–3, 75, 93, 107, 204–7, 213, 216
misology, 222
modesty, 7, 179
Mohammedans, 131
Monimia, 216
Monoeceus, 91
Moore, G. E., xii, 299, 333–4, 345, 352, 360, 363–4, 367–74, 404, 407

moral, 4, 26, 42, 99–100, 165, 173–4, 184, 360, 437
    activities, 131–2, 135, 165
        as either natural or unnatural, 166
        and the social contract, 139 (*see also* Hobbes, T.)
    cognition, 221, 248
    concepts
        as lacking objective validity, 363, 365
        as thick, 378
        as unanalysable pseudo-concepts, 359, 362, 365
    judgements, 148, 166, 219, 335, 341, 360–1, 434
        non-utilitarian judgements, 432
        as rational, 148
    language, xii, 99, 321, 360, 368, 404, 434
        and anti-realist accounts
            and argument from queerness, 397–8, 405–8
            and argument from relativity, 397, 405–6
        and prescriptivism, 431, 434–5
        and universalizability, 431, 434–5, 437
        and realism, 359, 368
        and symbols, 361–2 (*see also* descriptivism)
    luck, 201–2, 214
    obligation (*see* obligation)
    prejudice, 283
    properties, 333, 398
        in contradiction to natural properties, 367 (*see also* naturalistic fallacy)
    reason, 140
        categorical moral reason, 397 (*see also* Kant, I.)
        as correct, 339
    risk, 351
    sanctions, 365
    scepticism (*see* skepticism)
    schizophrenia (*see* Stocker, M.)
    sentiments, 258, 268, 276, 305, 312, 316, 362, 437
    subjectivism (*see* subjectivism)
    value (*see* value)
moralists, 170, 234, 263, 271, 275, 301, 306–7, 310–11, 313, 322, 350, 361, 369, 383
    orthodox moralists, 308, 316, 330
morality, 4, 54, 91, 411
    as conventional, 42
    as mere phantom of imagination, 233
    as radically externalized, 42
    as radically internalized, 42
    as science, 173, 321
    supreme principle of, 219
mortality, 204
murder, 163, 264, 379, 383–5
Murphy, J. G., 426n
music, 101, 176, 185

naturalism, 333, 340, 372, 433
    and ethical properties, 360 (*see also* descriptivism)
    with respect to vice, 147
naturalist, xii, 404, 433
naturalistic, 139
    ethics, 367–8
        fallacy of, xii, 337–9, 369, 379

nature, 5, 21, 28, 30–1, 33, 36, 55, 59, 72, 81, 95, 99, 105, 111–15, 133, 188
    Author of, 210, 215
    as God's will, 101
    human nature, 7–8, 15–16, 21, 25, 32, 34, 37–9, 58, 75, 79, 87, 141, 439
        and animal instincts, 268
        as anti-egoistic, 315
        bad propensities of, 279
            frailty and impurity of, 233
            infirmities of, 265
        as benevolent, 166
            and equality of the sexes (*see* Mill, J. S.)
        as contrary to religion, 176
        as enlightened or unenlightened, 48, 92
        excellence of, 308
        as finite, 121
        as good, 116
        higher ruling in relation to lower, 285, 291 (*see also* Nietzsche, F.)
        as opposed to artificial, 176–7
        superiority over reason, 221
        and intellect, 123–4, 126
        passions of, 203
        sympathy, 201 (*see also* sympathy)
    kingdom of, 245
        as possible kingdom of ends (*see* Kant, I.)
    laws of, 189
    order of, 128, 130
    state of, 139
        as state of war, 142, 145, 187 (*see also* Hobbes, T.)
    wisdom of, 216, 222
Nausicydes, 7
Nazi, 436
Neoplatonist, 113
Nero, 101, 196, 198
Newtwon, I., 192, 284n
Nietzsche, F., x–xi, 3, 419
    and genealogy of morals, 281, 283, 285, 295
        and moral scepticism, 282–3
            and compassion, 283
            and bad, 285, 288–9
            and the good, 285, 287–8, 290
            and herd instinct, 285–7
               and priestly manner, 290
               and ressentiment, 281
                  and good, 289
                  and evil, 289–90
                  as revolt in morality, 281, 287–9
            and conscience, 291
               and bad-conscience, 291, 293–8
nihilism, 283, 289, 297
nihilist, 281
Nisbet, H. B., 413n, 426n
noble, 55–6, 71, 79–80, 82–3, 102
    acts, 88, 128, 175
        in accordance with virtue, 60 (*see also* Aristotle)

of soul, 286
substance, 126
non-cognitivist, 359, 404–5, 407
and deflationary account, 360
non-consequentialism, 148
non-descriptivist, 433
non-naturalism, 369
non-naturalist, 368
normative
ethics, 247, 360, 361, 389, 398, 433
Novalis, 260
Nowell-Smith, P., 388

obedience, 103
objectivism, 369
Objectivists, 383
obligation, 143, 145, 148, 151, 170, 172n–3, 185, 190,
271, 274
cases of conflicting obligation, 265
juridical obligation, 295
moral obligation, xiii, 100, 139, 186–7, 229, 258, 265,
377–9, 385, 399
as absolute, 325
as anachronistic 377 (*see also* Anscombe, G. E. M.)
general forms of, 349–50
as imperfect, 220, 231–2, 239, 271, 345
as negative (*see* duty, as negative)
as perfect, 231, 239, 271, 345, 355 (*see also*
promises)
as positive (*see* duty, as positive)
as self-imposed, 414
special obligation, 349, 354, 357
towards others, 228
as contractual, 385
sentimental obligation, 295
O'Connor, D. J., 433n
Oedipus, 216
Olympian, 298
Olympic, 60, 112
opinion, 45–8, 50, 94–5, 142, 168, 194
as distinct from knowledge, 103–4
of the many, 110
as right, 109–10
as subject to calm passions, 181 (*see also* passion)
as wrong, 111
Osborne, H., 374n–5n
Oxford, 389
moral philosophers of, 388 (*see also* Objectivists)
Ovid, 196

pain, 68, 71–2, 95, 108, 150, 203, 210, 213 *see also*
Hume, D.
as bad, 91
as empty, 93
as evil, 94
measurement of (*see* Bentham, J.)
against pleasure, 255
Paris, 26

passion, 36, 38, 108, 121, 135, 147–50, 152, 154–5, 157–8,
190, 204, 206, 213
calm passions, 165, 168, 181
and strength of mind, 169 (*see also* Hume, D.)
as inert, 165
as private 136, 147
reflected passion, 208 (*see also* Smith, A.)
and spirit (*see* spirit)
Paton, H. J., 426n
patriotism, 43
peace, 99, 101–2, 107, 131, 145–6, 157, 170, 188,
191, 199
articles of, 142
of mind, 213
penalty, 14
perfection, 228
perfectionism, 414, 417, 419
Pericles, 85
permissibility, xiii, 334
Perry, R. B., 372, 374, 418n
Peters, R. S., 433n
phenomenalist, 400
Phoenician(s), 28, 34
piety, 110
Pigou, A. C., 418n
Pindar, 5, 7
Piraeus, 36
Pisa, 196
pity, 80, 161, 178, 203
Plato, ix–xi, 3, 25–6, 53, 56, 71, 114, 187, 283–4, 315, 321–2,
329, 345, 388, 401, 403, 407, 409–10
and the Good, 45–7
allegory of the Cave, 41–2, 46–51
and justice, 3, 29, 31, 33, 37, 39, 43, 45
as morality, 4
and the ideal community, 4, 25–7, 31, 37, 51
in individual persons, 4, 26–7, 33–4, 37
ethical properties of, 25, 31
courage, 28–30, 32–3, 37, 43
and the auxiliary class, 29, 33, 37
temperance, 31–3, 38, 43, 45
and the class of workers, 25
wisdom, 25
and the guardians, 27–30, 33, 43–4, 52
as perfect, 29
playful, 126
pleasure, 27, 56–8, 76, 110, 141, 153–4, 162, 168, 195, 210,
213, 437 *see also* hedonism
of the animal kingdom, 128
distinction between bad and good pleasures, 44
excesses of, 157
as gracious and pure, 63 (*see also* Aristotle)
higher and lower forms of, 255
impure pleasures, 328
the instrument of, 182
intellectual pleasure, 227
sensual pleasure, 50, 62–3, 71, 93–4, 111, 130–1, 248
(*see also* evil)

pleasure (*cont'd*)
    as the ultimate end of conduct (*see* utilitarianism)
    as unreliable, 99, 104
        susceptibility to, 227
Plutarch, 198
poetry, 185, 196, 260, 413
Poincaré, H., 417n
Polemarchus, 9, 11, 29
political, 70, 188–9, 270, 422
    advantage, 414–15
    economy, 279
    philosophy, 411
    relations, 312
    science, 89, 193
    systems, 186, 411
politics, 5, 51–3, 56, 64, 251, 309
    and the highest good 61 (*see also* Aristotle)
    of revenge, 287
Polus, 5–6
Polybius, 193
Polydamas, 10
Pompey, 212
positivism, 400, 407
postulationists, 375
poverty, 6, 150, 157, 162
praise, 174, 176, 178, 180, 193, 201, 209, 213, 263, 316
                see also approbation
    worthy of, 219
prejudice, 190
Priam, 61–2
Price, R., 404, 407, 409–10
pride, 114, 176–8, 258, 285, 289
prisoners, 48–9, 51, 101, 145
profane, 13
promises, 190, 343
    as binding, 317–18
    and duty, 345–6, 352–5
    implicit promises, 347, 349
propriety, 205
    as fittingness, 201 (*see also* Smith, A.)
Protestants, 381
prudence, 141, 161, 215, 236, 271, 285, 418, 431, 435
    imperatives of, 237
    as a primary condition of existence, 288
        of the lowest order, 290 (*see also* Nietzsche, F.)
    as virtue (*see* Aquinas, St.; Epicurus)
psychogonical, 325
psychological, 301, 337, 361
    oppression, 420
    propensities, 413
psychology
    philosophy of, 377, 380, 385
punishment, 14, 102, 139, 148, 152, 160–1, 168, 175, 190, 206, 212, 247, 269, 274, 297
    divine punishment, 152
    in a future life, 315
    judicial punishment, 378, 388
    measuring of, 252

and moral luck, 201–2
    as retribution, 292–3
Pythagoreans, 57, 73

Quintilian, M. F., 196

Raiffa, H., 424n
rationalism, 147, 165
rationalist, 165, 433
Rawls, J., xii, 411–12, 431, 434, 437
    and justice, 411
        and fairness, 413, 415
            as first virtue of social institutions, 411
                and equality, 416, 421–5
                    and the 'difference principle', 411, 414–15, 420–22
                as hypothetical, 413–15, 421
                    as rational and mutual disinterest, 414, 426
                    as reflective equilibrium, 417–18, 420
realism, 360, 427
realists, 400
reason, 25, 31, 36–7, 48, 50, 59, 69, 71, 76, 88, 99, 112, 114, 126, 132
    autonomous reason, 220
    basic errors of, 290
    categorical moral reason, 397, 403–4, 409–10, 431 (*see also* Kant, I.)
    common reason, 192, 224
        and moral cognition, 225–6
    and conscience (*see* conscience)
    deduction of, 170
    descriptive, 165 (*see also* Hume, D.)
    and the discovery of natural laws, 139, 142
    faculty of, 101
    hypothetical reason, 403, 409, 412
    as impractical, 221
    loss of, 204
    and the most important matters, 95 (*see also* Epictetus)
        eternal reason, 134 (*see also* Aquinas, St.)
            and the Divine, 160
            and God, 120
    practical reason, 121
    right reason, 70, 89
        as correct (*see* Aristotle, and contemplation)
    speculative reason, 160
    as supreme, 322
    true vocation of (*see* Kant, I.)
rebellion, 146
Reiss, H., 426n
religion, 118, 162, 264, 414
    as founded on miracles, 176
    heathen religion, 216
    and obligation
        to benevolence, 159 (*see also* Butler, J.)
religious, xiii, 105, 114, 153, 189
    contemplation, 330
    duties, 38
    fanatics, 188

fears, 277
passion, 190
resentment, 168, 204–6, 208, 210, 213, 252, 412
    animal resentment, 215
    as transitory, 214
ressentiment, 281 *see also* Nietzsche, F.
revenge, 156, 210–11
Richards, D. A. J., 435n
right(s), 45, 119, 172, 250
    of citizenship, 6
    as natural, 5, 7, 143 (*see also* justice)
    popular and vulgar notions of, 5, 110
    as power, 21
    of society, 187
    as utility-maximizing, 248 (*see also* utilitarianism)
Romans, 102, 109, 270, 281, 290
    Empire of, 261
Book of Romans, 154
Rome, 101, 290–1
Ross, W. D., xii, 343, 378, 383, 437 *see also* duty, *prima facie*
                        duty
    good
        acts, 343, 345
            authentic forms of, 347, 349, 354
        and knowledge, 348, 354
        and pleasure, 348–9
        and virtue, 348–9
Rousseau, J. J., 413, 423n, 426, 428
ruin, 158
Runciman, W. G., 428n
Russell, B., 405
Ryle, G., 379

sacred, 13, 190–1, 264, 270, 274, 297
    duty, 57
    and the right of human beings, 229
    texts, 313
sacrifice, 153, 233, 279, 284
sacrilege, 38
sadists, 431–2, 437
Salmond, J., 395
salvation, 30
Sannazarius, 196
Sardanapallus, 56
satisfaction, 155, 157, 162, 167, 175–6, 178, 223
    as happiness, 221
    of needs, 222
    as the performance of duty, 315
Saturn, 146, 186
scepticism, xiii, 281, 283
    about the status of moral claims, 3, 151–2, 193, 199,
            398–9
Schopenhauer, A., 283
science, 47–8, 58, 61, 73, 81, 84, 133, 207, 317
    divine science, 126
    ethical science, 301, 335, 401
    and evil and goodness, 36
    of the *Forms* (*see* 'Theory of the Forms')

and knowledge, 35, 46, 55
natural science, 86, 95, 286, 355
objects of, 175
and politics, 193
practical sciences, 126, 236
as silent
    with respect to virtue, 225
    with respect to what is good, 225
speculative sciences, 126, 175
truth, 47
Scotland, 213–14
Scottish, 201
Scylla, 322
Scythians, 34, 81
secular, 139
sedition, 18
Selene, 65
self
    deception, 265, 290, 437
    denial, 233, 283, 295
    dislike, 151
    forgetfulness of, 279
    interest, ix–x, 139–40, 217, 222–3, 345, 437
        as defence, 122, 135–6, 272
        as preservation, 186
        as reasonable 302 (*see also* Sidgwick, H.)
        as self-love, 147, 151, 193–4, 211, 233, 239, 241 (*see also*
                Butler, J.)
    maltreatment, 282, 295, 297
    mastery, 437
    observation, 267
    respect, 421
    sacrifice, 247, 261, 283, 295, 302, 304, 309, 316
        as the highest virtue, 261
selfishness, 180, 186–7, 193, 197, 259, 272, 277, 279
Seneca, 198
sensualism, 91
sentiments, 201 (*see also* Smith, A.)
    of approbation, 249n
    of justice, 272
    and moral obligation, 271–2 (*see also* moral)
Lord Shaftesbury, 151, 418n
Shakespeare, W., 255
shame, 74, 109, 350
    as form of restraint, 179
Sharp, L., 441n
sickness, 107, 157, 182
Sidgwick, H., ix–xiii, 184, 299–300, 333, 339–40, 369,
            377–9, 383–4, 386, 388, 401–3, 418–19n,
            426n, 428
    and ethical judgements, 306
        and common-sense, 299, 301, 304–5, 311–12, 314, 322
            and happiness, 300, 302, 308
                and conscience, 302, 313, 316, 322, 327
                    and duty, 304, 316, 320
                    and practical reason, 302
                    and rational self-love 304, 314–16, 323, 329
                        and harmony with rational benevolence, 329

Sidgwick, H. (*cont'd*)
    and rational egoism, 300, 302–4, 309, 315–16,
        320, 325
      and utilitarianism, 300, 302–5, 308–9, 314, 325
    and intuitionism, 300–3, 305–6, 313–14, 319, 320, 325
     and universal happiness, 300, 304–5, 308, 316–7, 323,
        325–6, 330
      and harmony with rational self-love, 329
Simonides, 62n
sin, 114, 117–19, 136, 142, 190, 281, 323, 381
  original sin, 297
slave, 5, 8, 13, 18, 30, 32, 41, 63, 94, 101, 108–10, 270,
    275, 281
  of the passions, xii, 165 (*see also* Hume, D.)
  races, 278
  revolt (*see* ressentiment)
slavery, 6, 103, 232, 276, 426
  and the female sex, 187 (*see also* Mill, J. S.)
Smart, J. J. C., 418n, 436n, 438
Smith, A., xi–xii, 201–2, 418n
  and demerit, 209, 211–13, 215
  and human nature
    and sentiments, 205–7, 210, 212, 214–15
      propriety of, 203, 205–6, 208
      and sympathy, 203–8, 213–14
        as compassion, 201, 203–4
        and imagination, 201–6
        as pity, 201, 203
  and merit, 209, 211–16
  and the voice of conscience, 201, 213
sociological, 361
Socrates, 53, 88, 100, 102, 107, 110–12, 225, 228, 258, 321,
    349, 381
  Gorgias, 3, 4–6, 8
  Republic, 9–11, 13–14, 19–20, 22, 26, 34, 39–40, 45
Socratic, 99, 304, 385
solicitude, 155
Solomon, 131
Solon, 61, 65
sophist, 377, 380
sophistry, 380
Soranus, 196
Sorley, W. R., 369
sorrow, 203–6, 208, 214, 216
soul, 6, 20, 30–1, 35, 40, 46–8, 57, 93, 105, 123, 131
  activity of, 54
    as good
      and happiness, 53 (*see also* Aristotle)
  animal soul, 294
  ascent of, 50 (*see also* Plato, allegory of the Cave)
  as compliant-conflicted, 295
  cultivation of, 6
  defect of
    and injustice, 19 (*see also* Plato)
  disorder of, 168
  the ends of, 88
    as excellence, 19
  and error, 117

faculties of, 48
  in relation to the community, 37 (*see also* Plato, and the
    Good)
firmness of, 216
freedom of, 93, 298 (*see also* Epicurus)
health of, 115
and pleasure, 60
and vice, 83
sovereign, 244
  as common power or commonwealth, 139, 144–6 (*see also*
    Hobbes, T.)
Sparta, 188
Spartans, 69
Spencer, H., 285
Speusippus, 57
Spinoza, B., 283
spirit, 25, 38, 51, 71, 80, 102, 295
  in animals, 25
  in children, 25, 37
  disturbance of, 94 (*see also* Epicurus)
  of history, 285
  as noble, 103 (*see also* Epictetus)
  and passion, 34, 36–7
  public spirit, 440
State, 23, 40, 43 *see also* sovereign
Stevenson, C. L., 360
Stocker, M., 432
Stoical, 326
Stoicism, 322
Stoics, 99, 258, 261, 263, 381
subjectivism
  moral subjectivism, 360–1, 399–400, 402, 406, 410
    and non-descriptivism, 433
    and orthodox theory, 363
Suetonius, 196
suffering, 5, 26, 37, 56, 63, 79, 140, 144, 258, 274, 282, 295, 437
superior, 7–8, 12, 14, 17, 22, 32, 63, 69, 71, 89, 111, 151, 212
  desire, 168
  and divine element, 64–5
  human intellect as, 126, 131
  justness, 207
  reason, 174
  virtues, 56, 212
superstition, 190
suspicion, 156
sympathy, 166, 178–81, 184, 187, 230, 280, 419–20
  and compassion, 201, 315n
  feeling of, 272
  intellectual sympathy, 304
  loss of, 223
  natural sympathy, 219
  principle of, 252
  as unavoidable, 196, 198
Syrian, 102, 104, 190

Taylor, A. E., 369
temper, 176–7, 207, 217
  happy temper, 208

temperance, 25
  as virtue (*see* Aquinas, St.; Aristotle; Plato)
terror, 178, 196
theft, 38, 119, 264
theism, 410
theocracy, 188
theologians, 384
theological, 283
'Theory of the Forms', xi, 41, 401, 407–8
  science of, 57 (*see also* Plato, and the Good)
thirst, 35, 36
Thomson, J. J., 389
Thracians, 34
Thrasea, 196
Thrasymachus, 3, 9–20, 22–3, 53
Thucydides, 196
Tiberius, 196
Tigellinus, 198
Tigranes, 214
Tolkien, J. R. R., 4
Torah, 381
torture, 77, 147–8, 150, 294, 394, 432, 437
tranquillity, 99, 157, 168, 196, 208, 260–1
Transcendentalist, 261
treachery, 38, 161–2
treason, 146, 212–13
Trojan, 61
truth, 3, 5–6, 9–10, 14, 22, 27, 46–8, 50–1, 57, 59, 63, 74, 118
  and the arts, 12
  as beautiful, 46
  contemplation of (*see* Aquinas, St., and the good)
  and moral principles (*see* moral)
  nature of, 117
  perfect truth, 7, 44
  practical truths, 78
  and reason, 168, 171, 172 (*see also* reason)
Turks, 278
tyranny, 13, 187–8, 195, 216, 230, 275, 291
tyrants, 63, 393

undutifulness, 193
unegoistic, 283, 285
  actions
    as habit, 285 (*see also* genealogy)
  value of, 295
unjust, 10, 13, 15, 17–18, 20–1, 70, 80, 83, 109, 413
  acts, 21, 39
    distinction between seeming and being, 21
  given the circumstances, 386–7
  intrinsically unjust, 386
Urmson, J. O., 418n
utilitarian, 353–7, 361, 402, 406
  doctrine, 415
  principle, 258
  and substantive moral judgment, 431
utilitarianism, 255–6, 299, 302–4, 308, 315n, 320, 340, 343–5, 353–7, 360, 384, 434, 437 *see also* Mill, J. S.
  Christian variety of, 440

ideal utilitarianism, 345, 347–8
Kantian variety of, 440
opponents of, 232, 257, 259, 261–2, 264–5
  rational alternative to, 411–12 (*see also* Rawls, J.)
and rational benevolence (*see* Sidgwick, H.)
two-level account of, 431–2, 438–40
  and act-utilitarianism, 437, 439–41
  and rule-utilitarianism, 437–9
and version of consequentialism, 148
utilitarians, 390
utility, 201, 207, 215, 255, 299, 380, 383, 412
  as happiness, 255
  as inappropriate, 285
  principle of 414 (*see also* Bentham, J.)
    as dangerous, 250n–1n
    as godless, 264
    and naturalistic fallacy (*see* naturalistic fallacy)
utopia, 317

value, 399
  moral value
    objective value, 397, 399–405, 408 (*see also* scepticism)
    prescriptive value, 397, 401, 405, 410
vanity, 223
Venice, 196
verificationism, 359–60
vice, 15, 17, 39–40, 71, 77, 81–3, 85, 102
  as absence of virtuous principles, 161
  as contrary to human nature, 147
    and want of benevolence, 162 (*see also* Butler, J.)
  as deficiency, 73 (*see also* Aristotle)
  as detestable, 194
  as excess, 73 (*see also* Aristotle)
  and human misery, 151
  and immorality, 172n
  and indolence, 260
  and injustice (*see* injustice)
  as mistake, 108
  as unease (*see* Hume, D.)
vicious, 148, 151, 160, 171, 173–6, 179
  actions, 91, 161
  and falsehood, 172n
victim, 13, 111
Vienna Circle, 359
villain, 18
violence, 36, 141, 144, 157, 162, 186–7, 195, 204, 208
  of emotion, 168, 206–7
  and the kingdom of God, 145
  and legitimate self-defence, 135
Virgil, 117
virtue, 3, 15, 17, 19, 23, 25, 39, 44, 51, 54, 77, 102
  as agreeable (*see* Hume, D.)
  and belief in the existence of God (*see* Aquinas, St.)
  and calm passions (*see* passion)
  'cardinal' virtues, x, 321 (*see also* Aquinas, St.)
  and excellence of conduct (*see* Aristotle)
  as fairness (*see* justice, as fairness)
  as fittingness, 201 (*see also* Smith, A.)

virtue (*cont'd*)
  and happiness (*see* happiness)
  and heroic virtue, 177
  and justice (*see* justice)
  as natural to human beings, 166, 176–7 (*see also* Butler, J.)
    as promoting the good of others, 157 (*see also* Sidgwick, H.)
      as the multiplication of human happiness (*see* utilitarianism)
  as perfection (*see* Plato)
  and prudence, 94–5, 300, 308, 316, 323
  and the soul (*see* soul)
  in a state of war, 142
  as superior (*see* superior)
  and truth, 172n
  as unnatural, 166, 176–8
    and sympathy, 179
  and wilfully fulfilling one's duty (*see* Kant, I.)
  and wisdom 326
virtuous, 53, 153, 175
Vlachos, G., 413n
voluntary, 77

war, 139, 141–3, 145–6, 186
weakness, 99, 126
wealth, 99
Wedderburn, A., 250n–1n
Wheelwright, P. E., 370n
Whewell, W., 302–4

Whittaker, T., 369n–70n, 372n
Williams, B., 378, 428, 436n, 438n
Williams, D. C., 369
Williams, G., 391n
wisdom, 3, 6, 13, 30, 32, 49, 51, 78, 87, 96, 141
  in conduct as against knowledge, 225
  and divine things, 133
  as good, 17
  and justice (*see* justice)
  as practical, 56–7, 59, 64, 69, 78, 84, 86–8
  of society, 261
  and virtue, 50 (*see also* Aristotle; Plato)
Wisdom, J., 373n
Wittgenstein, L., 379
women, 25, 31–2, 43, 187
  subjection of (*see* Mill, J.S.)
Wood, L., 370n–1
worship, 118
wrong, 99, 114, 117–18, 122, 172, 186
  actions, 6, 73, 79, 83, 110, 114, 250
  claims, 50, 96
  systems, 205
wrongdoing, 83

Xerxes, 5

Zeno, 110
Zethus, 6, 8
Zeus, 101, 294, 298

CPSIA information can be obtained
at www.ICGtesting.com
Printed in the USA
LVHW060155110123
736925LV00011B/585